BEETHOVEN
A Life

BEETHOVEN
A Life

JAN CAEYERS

Translated by Brent Annable

UNIVERSITY OF CALIFORNIA PRESS

BTHVN 2020   BEETHOVEN-HAUS BONN

University of California Press
Oakland, California

© 2020 The Regents of the University of California

Originally published as *Beethoven: Een Biografie* by De Bezige Bij,
Amsterdam, © 2009 by Jan Caeyers.

This book was published with the support of Flanders Literature
(www.flandersliterature.be).

**FLANDERS
LITERATURE**

The music examples were prepared by Bryce Cannell.

Library of Congress Cataloging-in-Publication Data

Names: Caeyers, Jan, 1953– author. | Annable, Brent, translator.
Title: Beethoven : a life / Jan Caeyers ; translated by Brent Annable. Other
    titles: Beethoven. English
Description: Oakland, California : University of California Press, [2020] |
    Originally published as: Beethoven : een Biografie by De Bezige Bij,
    Amsterdam, ©2009 by Jan Caeyers. | Includes bibliographical references
    and index.
Identifiers: LCCN 2020010304 | ISBN 9780520343542 (cloth) |
    ISBN 9780520975026 (epub)
Subjects: LCSH: Beethoven, Ludwig van, 1770–1827. | Composers—Austria—
    Biography.
Classification: LCC ML410.B4 C2313 2020 | DDC 780.92 [B]—dc23
LC record available at https://lccn.loc.gov/2020010304

Manufactured in the United States of America

28 27 26 25 24 23 22 21 20
10 9 8 7 6 5 4 3 2

For

Armand Caeyers (1924–1995)

Karl Heinz Füssl (1924–1992)

Frans Verleyen (1941–1997)

Geniuses are the most absurd of all creatures. Absurd, because of their normality. They are as everybody ought to be: a perfect synthesis of means and end, of challenge and capacity. Paradoxically, this means they do what others cannot—they fulfill their purpose.

EGON FRIEDELL

CONTENTS

Plates follow pages 22, 214, and 406

FOREWORD

The music of Ludwig van Beethoven has always been very much an integral part of my life, in my school days, as a member of the Beaux Arts Trio, and as a soloist. How often have I plunged into this cosmos, which is simply inexhaustible for my instrument? I was able time and time again to feel all the freedom, the conflict, and the optimism that emanates from this unique music. Nevertheless it continues to challenge me. I have never felt that I have grasped it completely. On the contrary, I am forever discovering new aspects to it. This is the fascination of Beethoven's music. It never fails to thrill me.

The jubilee year BTHVN2020 offers us a wonderful opportunity to celebrate Beethoven's magnificent music. But at the same time it invites us to make a closer study of the man behind the music. To this end we are promised a very special journey through time by way of this biography by the Belgian conductor and musicologist Jan Caeyers, which as a result of close cooperation with the Beethoven-Haus is published here for the first time in a revised edition in English. Rarely has Beethoven been portrayed in such a knowledgeable, enthralling, and entertaining fashion. Caeyers places Beethoven in the context of a time of transition, that was sparked by the French Revolution and that was fundamentally challenging the established courtly society. In the light of this period of transition, Caeyers describes how Beethoven matures not only musically and culturally but also politically into a figurehead of the new and emancipated bourgeois era. By paying attention to the family members, friends, and patrons who accompanied and supported Beethoven throughout his life, the biography presents a particularly vivid character portrait. The composer is not glorified as a genius, but instead is experienced in all his inconsistency.

I hope that this biography will provide you with stimulating reading and that your fascination with Beethoven's life and work will increase with each page of the book!

Daniel Hope
President, Beethoven-Haus, Bonn

PROLOGUE

Mechelen (Belgium), Saturday, March 29, 1727. Michiel van Beethoven sits at his windowsill, reflecting on life. Having turned forty-three the previous month, he now feels he is getting old, and he yearns for new challenges. For twenty long years he has been rising early to run the bakery that once belonged to his father-in-law, and that novelty has well and truly worn off. In fact, he has derived far more enjoyment in recent years from the purchase of property in Mechelen, the city where his father had come to settle fifty years before. In addition to his own home on Jodenstraat, he has managed to acquire two others on the same street (albeit with the aid of a hefty mortgage). He inherited an additional two houses from his father's side— Meersman and the Appolonia Guild—and will soon take possession of a third (Molenkarre). His penchant for real estate has put him in the footsteps of his great-grandfather Hendrik, who had done exactly the same a century before, only on a more modest scale, as he had made it as a major landowner in Boortmeerbeek, a small village nestled between Mechelen and Leuven.

Most of Michiel van Beethoven's fortune, however, came from his (only slightly shady) dealings in antique furniture and artworks. This is the one area where he now wishes to expand, although he also has his sights set on the lucrative market for Mechelen lace. The risks, he knows, are substantial; earning real money in the lace sector would mean importing cheaper lace from Brussels and Courtray (Kortrijk), which in turn would require sizeable investments and the use of tenuous promissory notes. But he is determined to take the plunge, to satisfy his desire to enter high society and to secure a place among the city's wealthiest.

Michiel's motivation is also fueled by a score that he has to settle with history. Over a century earlier, his great-great-grandmother Josyne van

Beethoven was burned at the stake after having been accused of witchcraft by her neighbors. Josyne was a unique woman: emancipated, self-assured, and idealistic. She also had a lively and independent spirit, which hardly worked in her favor at a time when the lines between faith, naïveté, and superstition were very fine indeed. Paradoxically, this characteristic was precisely what prompted the suspicion that she had concluded a pact with the devil. A small, targeted campaign by several jealous villagers was all that was needed to gather the necessary evidence, and the deadly cocktail of intrigue, slander, and gossip worked its own magic. Josyne van Beethoven was arrested, and after initially refusing to confess (further proof of her diabolical collusion) and subsequently being subjected to horrendous torture, she finally submitted and was publicly executed. For a while it also seemed that all the property belonging to her bewildered husband would be seized, but that fiasco was staved off by a combination of dexterous diplomacy and Beethovenian tenacity.

This traumatic experience was deeply etched into the memories of the Van Beethovens, who went on to nurture a deep-seated and healthy distrust of society in general. At the same time, it also became a source of strength, as all the Van Beethovens possessed an unshakable conviction in their own beliefs and ideals, a quality that they owed to their ancestral mother and martyr, Josyne.

Michiel van Beethoven passed on this ethos to his two children. The eldest son, Cornelius, showed great promise. With his level head, sense of duty, and innate knack for business, he was certain to make a surefooted way through life and the world. The younger son, Louis, was the black sheep of the family. He had a fine voice and as a six-year-old was accepted into Het Koralen Huis, the choirboys' school attached to St. Rombout's Cathedral in Mechelen. Once his son's voice had broken, Michiel drew up a private teaching contract with cathedral organist Antoine Colfs, who was to instruct Louis further on the organ and teach him basso continuo. For make no mistake: Michiel might let his son pursue music, but not without ambition. A mere organist's post at some far-flung parish church was out of the question.

Vienna, Thursday, March 29, 1827. Ludwig van Beethoven died three days ago. Today is his funeral. Because of the many guests expected to attend—townsfolk and visitors from outside the city—the ceremony has been rescheduled for the afternoon. But the turnout far exceeds all expectations; despite the cold (and even the odd remaining patch of snow), an estimated twenty thousand people from all levels of society flock to the House of the Black-Robed Spaniards (the Schwarzspanierhaus) near the city wall, close to Schottentor Tower in Alservorstadt. Beethoven's coffin lies prepared in the inner courtyard, and police have been called in to hold back the pressing crowds at the entry gate. Four trombonists and sixteen singers perform a special arrangement of the Equali for Four Trombones (WoO 30), which Beethoven had composed for All Souls' Day in 1812 in Linz. Another arrangement follows, of the funeral march from the Piano Sonata in A-flat Major (op. 26). The music, with its Beethovenian darkness and chilling penetration, stirs the emotional crowds to the very core.

The majestic cortège sets off at three-thirty that afternoon. Led by a bevy of priests, the richly decorated coffin is borne by eight singers from the opera, surrounded by as many Kapellmeisters wearing white stoles, and joined by about forty other friends and fellow artists—poets, actors, composers, and musicians including Schubert, Czerny, Schuppanzigh, and Franz Grillparzer. All are dressed entirely in black (right down to the gloves), with a white lily in their left hand and a decorated floral torch in the right. Next comes a delegation of conservatory students (the schools are closed as a sign of mourning), and the procession concludes with an impressive assembly of dignitaries.

The entourage presses its way through the undulating crowds with great difficulty, taking an hour and a half to travel five hundred meters and reach the Minorite Church of the Holy Trinity on Alsergasse. After the funeral service, Beethoven's body is placed in a beautifully ornate hearse carriage led by four horses, and driven to Währing Cemetery, escorted by an impressive caravan of around two hundred coaches. At the gates of the cemetery, in a solemn, stirring voice, actor Heinrich Anschütz reads the funeral oration composed by Grillparzer. Graceful and elegant, and with the perfect blend of grandiloquence and pathos, Grillparzer speaks on behalf of the nation and of German-speaking peoples everywhere. He talks of Beethoven, who "is now among the greatest men of all time" and who "inherited and surpassed the immortal fame of Handel and Bach, of Haydn and Mozart." He foretells that all those succeeding Beethoven can go no further, since their predecessor "ended where art itself ends," and concludes with words of consolation to all those present: "Look back to this moment and remember: we were there when he was buried; and when he died, we wept!"[1]

The crowd listens with bated breath, and tears are shed. Once the coffin, bedecked with three laurel wreaths, has been lowered into the ground, several hundred copies of memorial poems by Castelli and Schlechta, printed specially for the occasion, are distributed. As the last of the crowds trickle out of the cemetery, the sun sets.

Leuven, Thursday, March 29, 2007. With a sense of wonder, I picture the spectacle that took place exactly one hundred and eighty years ago around the Schottentor in Vienna. Even if the estimated crowd of twenty thousand is a little dubious, the massive turnout and all the pomp and circumstance must have lent an exceptional allure to the occasion. In Vienna such a funeral is what people would call a *scheene Leich*—literally, a "pretty corpse." There can be no doubt that nowadays such a funeral would be televised live, to the great satisfaction of the Viennese, who have always held a fascination for both death and the theater.

Another sign of Beethoven's importance was the sheer level of hypocrisy demonstrated that chilly afternoon. The surging crowds and emotions were, after all, directly at odds with the marginalized existence that Beethoven had led toward the end of his career. For nearly fifteen years before Beethoven's death, the Viennese cultural scene had been dominated by the common tastes of the Biedermeiers, who wallowed comfortably in their cocoons of simple, pedestrian, nonthreatening art. They were captivated by the brilliant, effortless, and effervescent music of the next generation: Joseph Lanner and Johann Strauss senior, in particular. It was music that titillated the senses but placed no demands on the mind.

Beethoven stood for the opposite of Biedermeier values and had long ceased to be a man of his time. His later works were the very antithesis of agreeableness and elegance. It was willful music, requiring much effort to write, to perform, and to hear—very different from the works he had written for performance at the Congress of Vienna more than ten years before, which *were* pleasing to the ear and had earned him the greatest fame and fortune he had ever known.

Eyebrows might also be raised at the Italian opera singers who literally bore Beethoven to his grave, since not a single note of the late master's music had crossed their lips for over fifteen years. Vienna was under Rossini's spell and had fallen head over heels for his light and bubbly "champagne music." Beethoven and Rossini were musical antipoles, living in different times and writing for different audiences. Rossini's remarks during their only meeting in April 1822 most likely fell—both literally and figuratively—on deaf ears.

And what of the eight Kapellmeisters who with great humility (and possibly even greater relief) accompanied Beethoven to his final banishment outside the city walls? Among them, only the Bohemian composer Johann Nepomuk Hummel could boast enough talent, personality, and success to be justified in his effulgent words and estimation of Beethoven.

And yet there are reasons why so many Viennese felt the need to bid farewell to a man with whom they fundamentally shared little, and whom for years they had treated almost exclusively as a local curiosity. They must have known that Beethoven's principal works were being performed in Europe's major capitals. The *Missa solemnis* had premiered in St. Petersburg, and by 1827 the Ninth Symphony had already been aired in London, Frankfurt, Aachen, Leipzig, and Berlin. They might also have already caught wind of the fact that Beethoven had declined a potential commission from Boston, in far-off America. They knew that Beethoven—born as a common citizen in an age that was extremely sensitive to the subtlest shifts in social hierarchy—had succeeded in penetrating the uppermost echelons of society. The list of emperors who knew and appreciated his music and who commissioned or even played his works was long indeed: Emperor of Russia Alexander I, Kings Frederick William II and III of Prussia, King Frederick Augustus I of Saxony, King Jérôme Bonaparte of Westphalia, and King Charles XIV John of Sweden—not to mention the Hapsburgs, among whom the Archduke Rudolf stood out as an excellent pianist and Beethoven interpreter. And although by then the noblest aristocrats had already withdrawn into their complacent bubbles of seclusion and social irrelevance, Beethoven's status as an icon of their elite cultural identity must still have appealed to the common people.

I too am fascinated by the sheer dimensions assumed by Beethoven's fame within the space of only a few decades. Nowadays the notion of a "meteoric rise to fame" is all too familiar: stories of children making it from paperboy to media tycoon or escaping abject poverty and neglect to become a head of state. But such tales were unimaginable in the eighteenth century, when society was far more static and lines of communication infinitely slower. In this context, the legend of how the great-grandchild of a provincial Belgian baker came to be one of the most illustrious residents of the Viennese musical metropolis, as well as a pivotal figure in European cultural history, captures our imagination—even today.

It is this exceptional tale that I wish to tell: of the journey made by the little boy from Bonn; of the abundance of improvised ideas cascading from his piano and captivating the minds of those around him; of the subsequent struggle to channel his creativity effectively as a piano virtuoso in Vienna; of a tragic auditory condition that forced him to give up his career as a performer and seek renewed and deeper meaning as an artist by devoting himself exclusively to composition; and finally, at the end of his life, of Beethoven the *Tonkünstler* (or the "tonal artist," as he wished to be known), who had obtained such a mastery of his craft that—in complete liberation, utter detachment, and full self-assurance—he could once again give free rein to his imagination despite, or perhaps because of, his deafness.

I also wish to describe the perilous nature of his journey: the many obstacles and setbacks that Beethoven was forced to overcome, as well as the bouts of uncertainty, desperation, and crippling doubt to which he fell victim more than once. I will occasionally even suggest that things might have turned out differently, as Beethoven's fate was not always in his own hands. Several weeks after Beethoven's death, Georg August von Griesinger (a Saxon diplomat in Vienna, friend to Beethoven, and Haydn's first biographer) had the right notion when he claimed that the principal driving force in Beethoven's life was his profound genius.[2] Genius is hardly a guarantee of world fame, however. The same can be said of a genius as of a child prodigy: no gifted child ever becomes a wunderkind through sheer force of will alone. The child's surroundings, support base, upbringing, and circumstances—even marketing—are all factors that help exceptional talent achieve exceptional status. I therefore wish to unravel the networks that influenced Beethoven's career, to paint portraits of those who supported him, and to outline the many interests (both direct and indirect) that were at play.

Of course, no Beethoven biography would be complete without an examination of how the nineteenth-century music scene—and indeed music itself—was radically altered by his influence. After Beethoven, nothing was the same. Composers were no longer the default performers of their own music; musical scores became straightjackets, granting fewer liberties to performers; the onus of creativity had shifted from improvisation to interpretation; composition had become a separate discipline, subject to loftier abstract and aesthetic ideals; music was infused with greater complexity and gravitas, forcing audiences to take a different approach to listening; the gap between connoisseurs and ordinary music lovers widened; and composers enjoyed a new social status, accompanied by the associated economic perils and prospects (we need only recall Beethoven's rocky dealings with the increasingly influential publishing world). In short, composers had evolved from craftsmen into artists, a fact of which they were themselves only too aware. In Beethoven's case, one sign of this mindset was the fact that he rarely threw away a single score, draft, or sketch—he was cognizant of his own "oeuvre" from the very beginning. It is an intriguing realization that this metamorphosis took place within the span of one man's career, a man who fought constantly and mercilessly against the limitations of his time. Of course, these shifts in society were already brewing to some extent. But is genius not characterized by the ability to grasp latent and nebulous trends and bring them to expression with brevity and clarity? Any Beethoven biographer, therefore, cannot sidestep the analysis of what Egon Friedell dubbed the "complicated and inscrutable reconciliation between a genius and his time."[3]

Beethoven biographers are also expected to pepper his life story with other commentaries on that very story. Biographers are, of course, at the mercy of the arbitrary manner in which history covers its tracks, and the portrait one paints is largely determined by whatever information still happens to be available. (One can only imagine how different this account would be if, for example, we still had access to the ten thousand or so letters that specialists believe were sent to or by Beethoven, of which only slightly more than two thousand remain.) In Beethoven's case, the view afforded us is especially blurry due to the egregious treatment suffered by many of the source materials immediately following his death, supposedly with the aim of protecting his image.

The perpetrator of these acts was a man named Anton Felix Schindler. He was a prototypical sycophant, obsessed with infiltrating the famous composer's intimate circle of friends in the hopes of somehow—if not during Beethoven's lifetime, then at the very least afterward—deploying his status as a "Beethoven watcher" to catapult himself out of his own mediocrity. (The fact that Schindler warrants extensive discussion in this very prologue is a testament to his unwavering dedication in this respect.) Schindler claimed to have worked as Beethoven's personal secretary from 1816 until the composer's death and to have done so unpaid, thus earning him the rare and privileged title of *ami de Beethoven*.[4] That he did perform secretarial duties for Beethoven cannot be denied (although it should be noted that matters of genuine import were attended to by others). Beethoven's supposed regard for him as a true friend, however, is a barefaced lie. In reality Schindler was a source of irritation, and Beethoven was usually cold and abrupt with him. In their mutual correspondence, Schindler was one of the rare figures on whom Beethoven never wasted a term of address or even a friendly greeting, and his tone barely rose above a snarl. Schindler was also seldom tolerated at the table. And the more Beethoven rejected Schindler's attentions, the more Schindler longed to be a meaningful presence in his life.

Along with Beethoven's trusted friend from Bonn, Stephan von Breuning, Schindler eventually succeeded in spending the final few weeks of the ailing composer's life at his bedside and thus became a privileged witness to the grim battle with death waged by one of the most important figures of the day. What is more (according to Schindler), several days before Beethoven's passing, he and Breuning had been charged with the solemn responsibility of preserving his creative legacy and reputation. They were asked to see that the right person was appointed to write his biography so that Beethoven could be certain that his name and body of work would not be tarnished by his many enemies who stood to benefit. To this end, Breuning and Schindler were permitted to leave with important documents in hand: Breuning took the papers of a more commercial nature, and Schindler took the rest. Two months later, however, Breuning himself passed away, and his death marked the disappearance of the only eyewitness who could testify to Beethoven's (extremely profitable) bequest to Schindler. The suspicion that Schindler did not receive but rather appropriated his biographical remit and the accompanying documents would shadow him forever.

In September 1827, Schindler asked German music critic Friedrich Rochlitz to do the final editing for the first Beethoven biography. Schindler claimed it had been Beethoven's express wish; it was more likely Schindler's own confection. Rochlitz refused, citing health reasons. Franz Wegeler, a doctor from Koblenz and a childhood friend of Beethoven's, was also asked to supply the material for part 1 of the biography, but ceased collaboration once he saw that Schindler was making little headway with the publication. Wegeler suspected that Schindler had a hidden agenda, and in 1834 he began work on his own biography project. Almost immediately he was joined by Ferdinand Ries, a former pupil of Beethoven's whom Schindler had asked not long before to write about Beethoven's early years in Vienna (to replace the deceased Breuning). But Ries felt it was also important for readers to learn about the great artist's less congenial qualities, and on that score he had several juicy anecdotes of his own to tell. This met with a veto by Schindler, who was determined to keep his deathbed vow to Beethoven; the book was to be a hagiography, plain and simple. As a result, Schindler was ultimately isolated. The circumstance was not entirely to his disadvantage, as he thus retained the exclusive rights to an official biography supposedly authorized by the composer himself, although this can never have been Beethoven's real intention.[5]

The truth is that Schindler was not in a position to bring the project to a successful end. He had only known Beethoven for a short while, after all, and most of the accounts at his disposal were secondhand at best. He also knew too little about music to write effectively on Beethoven's works, and all evidence suggests that his claim of having taken lessons from Beethoven was a further concoction. When his *Biographie von Ludwig van Beethoven* appeared in 1840, the reviews were scathing. Schindler's authority in general was called into question, which troubled him deeply given his primary aim of putting himself in the spotlight. He defended himself by appealing to the unique source materials in his possession, which he called his "magic books"—the nearly two hundred conversation notebooks that he had scavenged from Beethoven's lodgings after his death.[6] Beethoven had been almost completely deaf since 1818, with no choice but to communicate with others in writing, especially in public spaces where for reasons of discretion or to avoid embarrassment he wished to avoid having people bellow into his ears. Occasionally he would use a slate, which was periodically wiped clean. But generally he would resort to small notebooks, in which mainly his interlocutors but sometimes he himself jotted down words and phrases. Like his musical scores and sketches, Beethoven held on to these notebooks, clinging to artifacts from the past as though they could compensate for a lack of human contact. The notebooks are a rich source of information, although they usually contain only half of the "conversation," and it is sometimes impossible to guess what Beethoven himself might have said. (The notebooks can probably best be compared to cassette tapes used to record only one half of a telephone call.)

Schindler had access to this unique body of material, and in the second edition of his biography he included an appendix with key citations from the notebooks, in an attempt to show how implicitly Beethoven trusted him (Schindler even compared their friendship to that between the mythical heroes Orestes and Pylades[7]), and also to demonstrate the elevated caliber of their discourse.

Scholars worked out early on that Schindler—in his well-intentioned attempt to keep Beethoven's image intact—had destroyed many of the conversation books and ripped pages out of others that he believed contained compromising material. But it was not until the 1970s that a far more serious offense was unearthed: the addition of fictitious exchanges between Beethoven and Schindler himself. It was then that researchers from the criminology department of Berlin's Humboldt University made one of the most important discoveries in all of Beethoven research. Using techniques that were originally developed to decipher terrorist communications and letter bombs, they not only demonstrated that many of the notebook entries had been added later by Schindler, but through meticulous analysis of the ink they could also date the forgeries to the precise period between 1840 and 1845. Their forensic expertise also revealed that the culprit's personality had changed in the meantime; whereas Schindler had previously been a timid and subservient party to the conversation, by 1840 his handwriting had changed to that of a scared, threatened, and even neurotic man who, with his back against the wall, doctored the facts to suit his fiction.

The discovery sent shockwaves through Beethoven scholarship, as it proved that much of the information used to sculpt his likeness over the previous 150 years had been falsified and could be relegated to the scrapheap. Even certain seemingly incontrovertible theoretical insights about Beethoven's music—which had provided the basis for an entire tradition of Beethoven interpretation—could no longer be maintained.

But possibly even more distressing is the fact that all of the events reported faithfully by Schindler in his biography are now enveloped in a shroud of uncertainty and are the subject of endless and futile debate between believers and nonbelievers. Conscientious Beethoven biographers will often—and far more often than they would like—face agonizing choices, and the temptation is great to perpetuate fabricated or embellished anecdotes for the sheer pleasure they give in the telling. The stories about Beethoven are, after all, as much a part of the Beethoven story as the story itself.

PART ONE

_____

The Artist as a Young Man

(1770–1792)

Louis van Beethoven

A GRANDFATHER FIGURE

LOUIS VAN BEETHOVEN'S STUDENT CONTRACT with Antoine Colfs in Mechelen expired in the spring of 1727. What he did immediately afterward is unknown, but we do know that in November 1731 he took a job as a "tenorist" at St. Peter's church in Leuven. Several positions had become vacant there following an enormous clearing-out of staff, when all those suspected of Jansenist sympathies were shown the door.[1] This purge had been championed by Rombout van Kiel (himself originally from Mechelen), who in his capacity as university rector always carried out the archbishop's directives to the letter. As thanks for his diligent service, van Kiel had been promoted to canon at St. Peter's church in June 1731. He was a former classmate of Michiel van Beethoven's, and we can assume that it was he who facilitated the relocation of Michiel's son Louis to Leuven. Music at St. Peter's was also led by another former Mechelen resident, Louis Colfs, who helped his cousin Antoine's ex-pupil settle into his new position quickly. And successfully: several weeks after his arrival in Leuven, Louis was asked to step in for the choir conductor, who had taken ill.

Louis van Beethoven did not stay in Leuven for long. Following a successful audition in August 1732, on September 2 he was appointed as a singer at St. Lambert's Cathedral in Liège. The transfer from Leuven to Liège was facilitated by the close ties that had existed between the two cities for centuries. Many professors in Leuven were originally from Liège, and vice versa; the university in Leuven enjoyed appointment privileges for religious posts in the Prince-Bishopric of Liège, and many of the appointments there were arranged in Leuven. A key figure in these transactions was theology professor Jean-François Stoupy, director of the College of Liège in Leuven and a colleague, friend, and neoconservative comrade of Rombout van Kiel's. It was likely he who put Louis van Beethoven forward for the position in Liège.

Louis van Beethoven's time in Liège would likewise only last several months: in March 1733 he was transferred to Bonn, the residential city of the archbishop-elector of Cologne. The elector himself had probably been charmed by the warmth of Louis's voice during one of his many visits to the Prince-Bishopric (which had been under Cologne rule for several centuries). Clemens August of Bavaria was a connoisseur and had a nose for musical talent. In accordance with proper aristocratic tradition, he had received a thorough grounding in music and was a passionate player of the viola da gamba. During his many travels, he had also become well acquainted with music from both Italy and France, and when expanding his own musical forces he always strove to engage the best musicians from these two countries—a fact that would be of no small consequence for the musical development of the young Ludwig van Beethoven several decades later.

By attracting and supporting elite musicians, Clemens August perpetuated a long family tradition. In the second half of the sixteenth century, his two forebears the dukes of Bavaria Albert V and William V had amassed the most prestigious musical ensemble in Europe by importing the best Dutch and Italian musicians to Munich. In the late eighteenth century, Elector Charles Theodore (of the same house, Wittelbach, albeit from the Palatinate branch) followed suit in Mannheim. His orchestra, which recruited musicians from far and wide, was considered the finest in Europe and set a new standard for ensemble discipline. The group was also instrumental in the life of the young Mozart, who was invited to compose his opera *Idomeneo* for the star troupe (and equally stellar vocal ensemble) in 1780, several years after Charles Theodore had also become Elector of Bavaria and had moved the orchestra to the capital in Munich. Perhaps the most striking example of such musical idolatry was provided by King Ludwig II, whose adulation of Wagner in the second half of the nineteenth century prompted him to build his own private Odeon in Bayreuth, centered entirely around the composer's unique talents.

The Wittelbachs had a reputation for being ingenious, megalomaniacal, and occasionally slightly mad. They were also fully aware that they could not compete politically with other ruling houses (the neighboring Hapsburgs, in particular), which drove them to develop fertile, niche ambitions in the less treacherous domains of representational art and music, where their efforts were unconditionally productive and inspired.

When Clemens August of Bavaria was appointed archbishop-elector of Cologne in 1723, his position seemed hardly enviable. Consisting as it did of five separate miniature states—none of which even shared a border, and whose secular and religious groupings did not coincide—the archdiocese and electorate of Cologne was difficult to govern. To make matters worse, electoral Cologne was situated in very sensitive European territory. Not only did part of it occupy the area known as the Left Bank of the Rhine (making it a constant bone of contention in French-German border conflicts); it was also a buffer zone and a thoroughfare for attacking troops during times of war. The elector of Cologne's chief political duty was therefore to adopt as neutral a position as possible in the strategic game of diplomacy being played by the powers that be, which in practice boiled down to constantly raising the price of the neutrality on offer. Here Clemens August was in his element: he took the electorate's structural weaknesses and turned them to his maximum financial advantage. It was no surprise that he developed a rather unflattering reputation as a *Wetterfahne,* or "weathervane."

In addition to the copious winnings landed from this diplomatic game of poker, Elector Clemens August had yet another, centuries-old source of funds: the Teutonic Order, or the Order of Brothers of the German House of Saint Mary in Jerusalem. Over the centuries this knightly order, originally founded on lofty, Christian-inspired ideals, had degenerated into a kind of spectral, extragovernmental framework that existed alongside the various duchies, principalities, dioceses, and districts. It also acted as a lobbying group advocating the interests of rulers and major landowners. Although the order's once-palpable political and ideological significance had since dwindled to almost nothing, the Teutonic Order still maintained a real estate portfolio that generated considerable rental income. This alternative flow of funds worked like a magnet on the German aristocracy, as it provided a means for their second-born sons and daughters to maintain a lifestyle befitting their status. And just as in the military and the church, the Teutonic Order was also subject to another age-old aristocratic principle: the higher up one was in the pecking order, the more flexible the appointment and promotion criteria became. It was thus that Clemens August was appointed grand master (a kind of secretary-general) of the Teutonic Order in 1732. And so, roughly ten years after his installation as elector of Cologne, he also stood at the head of one of the most influential networks in central Europe, furnishing him with plenty of additional funds to divert into his mini-Versailles by the Rhine.

Clemens August made no attempt to hide the fact that he was primarily interested in the more ceremonial aspects of his post. The story goes that while studying in Rome, he was once plagued by doubts regarding his spiritual calling. It was only following a personal intervention by the pope himself, who made him the dual promise that he would be permitted to (a) concentrate mainly on the secular aspects of his position, and (b) take a fairly liberal view of his vows of poverty and chastity, that he finally accepted his promotion to archbishop.[2] It is believed that he thus obtained a kind of papal sanction to thenceforth adorn and conduct his life as though it were a piece of French theater. Amid the sumptuous decor of brand-new and lavishly appointed castles, churches, theaters, and parks, Clemens August orchestrated life at court in such a way that the boundaries between actual theater and theatrical representation, between fiction and feigned reality, became increasingly indistinct. The day would commence with an extravagant mass, the archbishop occupying center stage. Next the horses were saddled for a hawking party—the archbishop's true specialty. Dinner followed in a specially appointed palace restaurant, fitted with bespoke theatrical machinery that raised the bountifully laden tables up out of the floor. The day concluded with theater or dance performances, with or without the participation of the aristocrats themselves. A typical example was the so-called country wedding (a bucolic cousin to the traditional masked ball), in which the aristocrats drew lots for the roles of bride, groom, parents, pastor, village notary, and local peasantry—on the express understanding that the central role of the innkeeper was, of course, reserved for the elector.

This was the weird and wonderful world to which Louis van Beethoven, a baker's son from Mechelen, was introduced in 1733. His life had clearly taken a turn for the better, as had his earnings (especially after a promotion in 1746), enabling him to live comfortably and with some prestige. But he was ambitious and hoped someday to become Kapellmeister, the musical director at court. His disillusionment was therefore profound when not he but the Frenchman Joseph Touchemoulin was appointed as the new Kapellmeister in 1760. Louis van Beethoven boasted a longer period of service, true; but Touchemoulin really was the obvious choice. A brilliant violinist, he had been the elector's favorite for many years. Besides having studied with Tartini in Italy, he had also earned some distinction as a composer in Paris. Louis van Beethoven's references paled somewhat by comparison. He also had a double handicap, so to speak, being "merely" a singer and probably never having composed a single note in his life. Of course, there were examples in the eighteenth-century musical landscape of Kapellmeisters who were themselves not instrumentalists (Hasse in Dresden, and Graun in Berlin), yet these were composers of outstanding international repute. In any case, Louis could not resign himself to this state of affairs. He lodged an official appeal in the form of a long letter, which was summarily dismissed by the elector.[3]

Just when it seemed that Louis van Beethoven's career had plateaued, Elector Clemens August unexpectedly passed away on February 6, 1761, sending Louis's life in a new direction. The archbishop-elector of Cologne died as he had lived, collapsing and perishing in the arms of Baroness von Waldendorf, one of his many mistresses, during a ball at Ehrenbreitstein.[4] The appointment of his successor, Maximilian Friedrich von Königsegg-Rothenfels, represented a break with tradition in Bonn. Like his predecessor, the new elector was no great proponent of asceticism and took equally few pains to suppress his interest in members of the opposite sex. Nevertheless, he understood fully that perpetuating the flamboyant lifestyle of Clemens August would undoubtedly put the electorate on the road to bankruptcy, the more so since the changing political landscape (the Seven Years' War, which raged from 1756 to 1763) had dried up all international sources of funding.

Maximilian Friedrich economized where he could, and one of the first casualties was Kapellmeister Touchemoulin, whose princely income was reduced by two-thirds. Naturally this was unacceptable to Touchemoulin, especially since he was well aware of other available options. He promptly resigned and left for Regensburg. Louis van Beethoven saw his opportunity and gladly accepted the proposition to combine the roles of singer and Kapellmeister for more or less the same salary (his raise was a mere 30 percent). But the rationale of those in charge—the belief they could fill two vacancies for the price of one—was rather naïve and shortsighted. It ignored the simple truth that a tutti violinist who becomes concertmaster will always remain a tutti player in the eyes of his colleagues, and a concertmaster-turned-conductor will never be deemed a *real* conductor. For a choral singer, any such attempt to rise through the ranks was positively death-defying. But there could have been no doubting Louis van Beethoven's dedication. Lacking the natural authority of raw talent, in an attempt to survive he resorted to the qualities traditionally instilled in middle-class children: diligence, discipline, and organization. By all accounts, however, these were not enough. Although there are indications that Louis van Beethoven lobbied earnestly for the interests of the instrumentalists and singers, there were also reports of repeated incidents where the authority of the new Kapellmeister was so severely called into question that the elector himself was forced to intervene.

The wine-trading business that Louis van Beethoven had been running for some time was not affected in the slightest by his new social status. He primarily supplied to Dutch clients and kept a generously stocked cellar. Consequently, private consumption in the Beethoven household increased markedly, allowing alcoholism to take a fatal hold on the family. The first victim was Louis's own wife, who spent her final days in an insane asylum. His only son, Jean, was later stripped of his paternal rights due to excessive drinking, and when Louis's grandson (the composer Ludwig van Beethoven) died in 1827, his liver was all but destroyed.

Exactly how much Louis van Beethoven earned from his wine business is unknown. We do know that after his death in 1773, his son Jean was left in the difficult position of negotiating both the settlement of outstanding debts (for which he was even called to court in 1774) and the collection of moneys owed, not all of which had been properly recorded. The final balance was most likely a profit, however; recent research has shown that Jean van Beethoven inherited quite a sum of money, which allowed him to live in relative comfort for some years. The traditional belief that Ludwig van Beethoven grew up in poverty is therefore romanticized and inaccurate.[5]

The Beethoven family's general inability to handle money seems to have been hereditary. Louis's parents were prosecuted for conducting illicit trade for the first time in 1732, and in an attempt to multiply their assets they subsequently dived ever deeper into a maelstrom of loans, mortgages, and bills of exchange, finally hitting bankruptcy in 1740. Their court conviction in 1744 occurred by default, for in 1739 they had fled Mechelen for Kleve, settling afterward in Bonn where they both passed away in 1749.

Incredible tales of the Van Beethovens' creative entrepreneurship can also be found later in history, of how they nimbly walked the thin line between the possible and the permissible. The late-nineteenth-century business career of a certain Ludwig van Beethoven represents a spectacular low in this family tradition. Ludwig, the only son of Beethoven's nephew Karl and thus the famous composer's great-nephew, was sentenced to four years in prison on major fraud charges. He fled to America, where he initially worked for some time in the railway industry. He then ran a messenger service in New York, Chicago, and Philadelphia and finally embarked on a futuristic, original, and lucrative venture: a wheelchair service for retirees and the disabled at the World's Columbian Exposition in Chicago (1893). Some years later, Ludwig hung up a sign outside his Fourth Avenue offices in New York, bearing the proclamation "New York Commissionaire Company—Louis von Hoven, Managing Director." He ultimately returned to Europe (presumably to Paris, but he may have also visited Brussels) and died penniless and destitute early in the twentieth century. The misery was compounded for his only son, Karl Julius van Beethoven, who wasted away in a Viennese military hospital in 1917. As he was the only remaining scion of the family, his demise also spelled the sad end to the Mechelen branch of the Van Beethoven name.

Since grandparents are usually exempt from childrearing responsibilities, to children they generally appear more likeable than their parents. This was certainly the case with Beethoven, who nurtured boundless admiration and affection for his grandfather, despite hardly having known him at all (Beethoven was barely three years old when Louis van Beethoven died on Christmas Eve in 1773). Beethoven cherished his idealized memories, and he dutifully transported his grandfather's official portrait like a relic from one house to the next, all his life. For a long time, Beethoven's greatest ambition was to follow in his grandfather's footsteps and become Kapellmeister (preferably in Bonn or, failing that, at some prestigious court or other). But although things would ultimately take a different course, nothing could change the fact that the virtual presence of Beethoven's grandfather served as beacon and buoy to him throughout his life.

2

Jean van Beethoven

THE ABSENT FATHER?

BEETHOVEN'S GRANDFATHER LOUIS generally receives gracious treatment by most Beethoven biographers and is portrayed as a respectable citizen: competent, dedicated, moral, kind wherever possible, and firm when necessary. Jean van Beethoven[1]—the only surviving son of Louis, and Ludwig's father—fares very differently. He is invariably portrayed as an outright failure: a frustrated, career-less, and debauched musician patently incapable of caring for his family, and the source of all of Beethoven's childhood traumas. The stories are legion of the brutal, even tyrannical first music lessons given to Ludwig, of the way Jean supposedly projected his own failed musical ambitions onto his obviously gifted son. Nevertheless, a little perspective is in order. Leaving aside the obvious difficulties we face in relating to any eighteenth-century childrearing methods, it must be kept in mind that extreme forms of child discipline will always come across as objectionable, especially if administered by a parent. The fact that Beethoven, at five, received his first piano lessons standing on a footstool may have been unpleasant but was probably unavoidable. Forbidding Beethoven to play without a score or to improvise freely may have been cruel, but it was understandable in view of a training method that valued reproduction over production. Jean also quickly relinquished responsibility for young Ludwig's musical education, much to his credit.

Jean van Beethoven's negative image is primarily the result of the destruction wrought on his character toward the end of his career—particularly following his wife's death in 1787—and the tendency among musicologists to extrapolate this tragic decline across his entire life. In reality, at least the first half of Jean van Beethoven's career was completely normal. After primary school and a failed preparatory year at the Jesuit college, he was accepted into

0

the electoral Kapelle as a soprano at the age of twelve. His father had given him a thorough grounding in singing, keyboard, and violin, and he was adequately equipped for a life as a professional musician. After his voice broke, he was appointed court musician in 1756 (at the age of sixteen). The position entitled him to a salary, but it would be 1764 before he earned enough to make ends meet. While it was common at the time for children to follow in their fathers' footsteps, under the circumstances it is a fairly safe assumption that the adolescent Jean van Beethoven had a difficult time escaping the clutches of his ever-present and domineering father, who controlled his life both at home and at work. The release offered by his late-night jaunts in his father's absence are therefore more a sign of a healthy mind rather than of depravity. The fact that these juvenile escapades had no effect on his work and reputation at the time is evinced by the private lessons he gave for many years, not only to the daughters of court officials and members of the aristocratic elite but also to the children of discerning colleagues. By all accounts he acquitted himself of his teaching duties most adequately.

Around the year 1770, two events took place that would leave a lasting impact on the rest of his life. In 1767, when he was twenty-seven and still unmarried (a rarity for the time), he met Maria Magdalena Keverich. A twenty-one-year-old from Ehrenbreitstein (Koblenz), she had already suffered many a misfortune. She lost her father and four of her five siblings at an early age, then married at sixteen, only to be bereaved of both her husband and her only son several years later. Louis van Beethoven initially objected to the match and even refused to attend the celebrations at Fort Ehrenbreitstein—clearly he considered the bride to be beneath the station of the Van Beethovens. Such was not the case, however; her deceased father had been head chef at the court in Trier and therefore enjoyed the same social status as a Kapellmeister in Bonn. Louis's objections were more likely fueled by fears that the arrival of a young woman on the scene might undermine his authority within the family.

The second key event occurred in the spring of 1770, when Jean van Beethoven was offered a lucrative opportunity to join the Kapelle at St. Lambert's Cathedral in Liège—further evidence that he was still functioning well at the time. He was eager to accept the invitation, perhaps in order to finally lead a life of his own (his father had already moved out, but lived on the same street and was still Jean's immediate superior at court). Why Jean remained in Bonn is unknown; what we do know is that the elector objected to the transfer, and since there were no employment tribunals in the eighteenth century to represent workers' fundamental rights and freedoms, Jean van Beethoven was forced to spend the rest of his career in Bonn.

This turn of events gives rise to a rather haunting prospect. If the transfer had gone ahead and Jean van Beethoven and his wife had moved to Liège in 1770, Ludwig van Beethoven would not have been born and raised in Bonn but would instead have been exposed to an entirely different set of experiences, influences, and career opportunities. He would have undoubtedly become a very different composer, if he had become a composer at all . . .

Some sources claim that in 1774 Jean van Beethoven submitted an application to succeed his deceased father as Kapellmeister.[2] This seems unlikely, as his curriculum vitae paled in comparison to those of Cajetan Mattioli and Andrea Lucchesi, who that year were appointed director of music and Kapellmeister, respectively. These brilliant Italians succeeded in breathing new life into music at the court in Bonn, in part by securing several prominent musicians for the ensemble who would later play a key role in the musical development of the young Ludwig. Such a feat would have been genuinely beyond Jean van Beethoven, and those responsible for the appointments undoubtedly knew it.

From that point on, Jean van Beethoven's career fell into gradual decline. His rising alcohol consumption compromised the quality of his voice, and it was only his friendly relationship with Cologne's first minister Kaspar Anton von Belderbusch that spared him any immediate repercussions. Like the Van Beethovens, Belderbusch had Flemish roots, and was also a family friend and even godfather to one of the children. We will delve more deeply into this intriguing individual's extraordinary career later on, but suffice it to say that the questionable protection he offered to Jean van Beethoven was one of the few generous abuses of power that he exhibited during his many years in the electorate.

Jean van Beethoven collapsed utterly in 1787 when both his wife, Maria Magdalena, and his only daughter, Maria Margaretha, died within the span of several months. As a result, the family responsibilities landed squarely on the shoulders of the eldest son, Ludwig van Beethoven. This arrangement was later formalized by an electoral decree of November 20, 1789, which forced Jean van Beethoven not only to retire early (he was not yet fifty years old) but also to surrender half of his family support payments to his eldest son. This uncommonly drastic measure came at the request of Ludwig van Beethoven himself, who had been urged to take this step by several of his closest friends—Count Ferdinand von Waldstein and the von Breuning family—

following several interventions on his own part to save his inebriated father from arrest. The traumatic effects of this measure, which essentially removed Beethoven's negligent father from the family equation, cannot be underestimated. It would leave a lasting mark on Beethoven's psyche and was without a doubt one of the causes of a permanent sense of melancholy in his heart.

Jean van Beethoven died, marginalized and dejected, on December 18, 1792. Rumors say that on hearing of his death, the elector lamented that the city's alcohol taxes would undoubtedly see a substantial decline, a remark that would stain poor Jean's reputation forever.[3] And yet Beethoven never wrote a bad word about his father or his failure as head of the family. On the contrary, Beethoven's friends attested to him exploding with rage at anyone who dared to speak ill of his name. A copy of C. P. E. Bach's *Morgengesang am Schöpfungstage* bears the touching inscription, "Transcribed by my dear father."[4]

Quite a few commentators are of the opinion that the origin of Jean van Beethoven's later psychological problems lay in the contempt (and even rejection) shown to him by his overbearing father Louis. Rumors even attempt to establish a link between this harsh treatment and the vague circumstances surrounding Jean van Beethoven's birth. They suggest that Louis was the legal but not the biological father of Jean, and that Louis never truly accepted his adopted son. The main source of these rumors is the absence of any available record—either in Bonn or in the surrounding villages—legitimizing Jean van Beethoven's birth. It is also suspicious that Jean had no middle name, which was highly exceptional for the time. (Louis van Beethoven's two eldest children, who died in infancy, each had two Christian names: Maria Bernardina and Markus Joseph.) Some therefore conclude that before his birth, Jean van Beethoven's mother traveled far from the city where, in complete anonymity, she bore an illegitimate child. Beethoven biographer Claus Canisius even posited that this traumatic experience was what drove her to drink and was responsible for her demise in a mental institution.[5]

This fantastical theory leads us conveniently to another baseless anecdote that circulated during Beethoven's lifetime. In 1810/11, a curious passage was published in an article about Beethoven in the (otherwise well-researched and -documented) *Dictionnaire historique des Musiciens* by historians Alexandre-Étienne Choron and François Fayolle. According to the editors,

Beethoven was rumored to be the biological child of the Prussian king William II, implying that his exceptional talent could be attributed to exceptional breeding. The story quickly spread throughout Europe. For five editions (until 1830), the notorious *Brockhaus Lexikon* managed to list both hypothetical fathers alongside one another—the commoner from Bonn, and the king from Berlin—leaving the choice up to the reader's imagination. Opinion was nudged in a certain direction, however; Ludwig's original surname was first changed from "Van Beethoven" to "v. Beethoven," and in the new edition (from around 1820) it officially became "von Beethoven," leaving no doubt as to his aristocratic heritage.[6]

Several friends informed Beethoven of this persistent attack on his mother's honor and tactfully suggested that he take action to put the rumors to rest. Beethoven's friend Franz Wegeler was especially insistent and wrote him several letters on the matter. But for whatever reason, Beethoven always put off his response. Did the prospect of blue blood perhaps tap into some deeply cherished desire of Beethoven's to belong to the aristocracy? In a letter dated December 7, 1826, he writes: "You wrote to me that I have been proclaimed the natural son of the erstwhile King of Prussia. I have heard similar reports before. But my policy is never to write anything about myself, nor to respond to anything written about me. I am therefore happy to leave it to you to inform the rest of the world of the virtue of my parents, and of my mother in particular."[7]

Beethoven "forgot" to post this letter, and it was only in response to a second letter from Wegeler dated February 17, 1827—roughly one month before his death—that he consented to issuing an official denial.

3

The Early Years

JEAN VAN BEETHOVEN AND HIS WIFE, Maria Magdalena, had a total of seven children, only three of whom survived to adulthood: Ludwig (1770), Kaspar Anton Karl (1774), and Nikolaus Johann (1776). The eldest son's given name bore a heavy legacy. By naming him after his highly respected grandfather Louis (or Ludwig, in German), his parents not only gave Beethoven the unspoken duty to follow in his footsteps, but also expressed the secret hope that a child from the third generation might succeed where the second had failed, and perhaps even surpass the first.[1]

Ludwig van Beethoven was probably born on Sunday, December 16, 1770, in Bonn. Because civil birth registries were not introduced until the Napoleonic era, there is no extant document that can verify his birth date with any certainty. We do know that Beethoven was baptized on December 17, and because the custom at that time was to baptize children one or two days after their birth, December 16 is generally taken as Beethoven's birth date.[2]

Beethoven's own indecision concerned not the day but the year of his birth. On various occasions he is known to have claimed to be one or two years younger, and even after receiving an official copy of his baptismal certificate in 1810, he steadfastly continued to deny his real age. Of course, less importance was attached to one's precise age in that era, for unlike contemporary practice, eighteenth- and nineteenth-century citizens were not required to identify themselves at every turn or to constantly supply proof of their address, date of birth, and marital status. Beethoven's desire to be a few years younger may simply be typical of high achievers, many of whom have difficulty accepting the rapid passage of time.

The Beethovens' address in 1770 was Bonngasse 515.[3] Several years later they moved to Rheingasse 934—where grandfather Louis had lived for many years beforehand—into a stylish and spacious apartment occupying the second floor of a house belonging to the Fischer family. The Fischers ran a bakery, and their business had unavoidable ramifications for the biorhythms of all who lived in the building, including the Beethoven youngsters. No music making was allowed in the afternoons, for example, to allow Mr. Fischer to sleep. The Fischers and the Beethovens were good friends, and their warm relationship is extensively documented in the memoir written between 1837 and 1857 by Mr. Fischer's son Gottfried and his elder sister Cecilia: the *Aufzeichnungen über Beethovens Jugend* (Notes on Beethoven's youth), which constitutes the primary scholarly source of information on Beethoven's childhood. There is a need to tread carefully with this "Fischer Manuscript"; it was compiled roughly sixty years after the events it describes, and it is safe to assume that it bears the influence of the many clichés about Beethoven's character that had emerged in the meantime (including those regarding his paranoid tendencies, for example). What remains sincere is the touching nature of the day-to-day scenes it recounts, such as the youngsters' childhood antics, the jolly mood of the family festivities, and Beethoven's early fondness for the outdoors. It quickly becomes apparent just how important nature was to the young Beethoven, as it offered an oasis, refuge, and escape from the stress of the city and the pressures of "ordinary" life. An anecdote about Beethoven's use of a telescope while out walking, allowing him to see "seven hours into the distance,"[4] is a telling metaphor. It would seem that Beethoven began cultivating his visionary capacities at an early age. The Fischer Manuscript also gives the first eyewitness accounts of Beethoven's complex psyche and his tendency to withdraw into himself, a behavior that other contemporaries even labeled as "misanthropic."[5] We read that he suffered a case of smallpox, which would leave his face scarred for life, and there are discreet references to bedwetting. The account is punctuated by some spectacular events that undoubtedly left a lasting impression on the young Beethoven: the fire in the electoral palace in 1777, and the massive flood of 1784 in Bonn.

The Fischer Manuscript reveals little about the two youngest children, Kaspar Anton Karl and Nikolaus Johann (confirming the biased perspective from which it was written), or their relationship to their elder brother. The parents, on the other hand, are portrayed in greater detail. Beethoven's mother is depicted as a hardworking woman who unquestionably ruled the roost (as the story goes, it was she who coordinated the household evacuation during the flood of 1784, while her paralyzed husband looked on helplessly), and who raised her children in a sensible and businesslike manner. The sad consequence of her frugal approach was that the Beethoven children often appeared rather unkempt and neglected (which in that particular stratum of society was more often the rule than the exception). She was well liked and respected, however, and "answered to all, both high and low, in a refined, adept and intelligent manner."[6] And yet she seemed to experience little joy in life. Cecilia Fischer even stated that she could not remember ever having seen Maria Magdalena laugh. Beethoven's mother most likely inherited this downcast tendency from her own mother, whose strict, morbid lifestyle of penance following the death of her husband eventually became so ascetic that the family saw no option other than to have her committed. Beethoven thus had two grandmothers who spent their final days in an asylum.

Beethoven's mother seems to have held a rather pessimistic view of marriage. Cecilia Fischer claims to have been advised by her never to marry; that marital bliss is extremely short-lived and can only ever end in misery. On another occasion Maria Magdalena is reported to have said that many young people marry in a frivolous, indifferent, or careless fashion, and that they would never even consider it if they knew what trials lay ahead of them. Cecilia concludes that the mother's cynical attitude to marriage is the reason Beethoven himself never took a wife; she suspected that his mother's lamentations had been drummed into him throughout his youth, and that he bore her advice in mind.[7]

The references to Jean van Beethoven in the Fischer Manuscript (his excessive drinking aside) generally concern young Ludwig's musical education. We read that the Beethovens owned two keyboard instruments: a harpsichord in the living room facing the street, and a quieter clavichord that was probably in the children's bedroom. We also learn that Beethoven was so short when receiving his first lessons that he needed a footstool to reach the keys. There are also accounts of a heavy-handed and tyrannical approach on the part of his father. Beethoven often stood in tears at the keyboard; his father regularly boxed his ears, mercilessly rapped his wayward fingers, and showed no hesitation in locking the poor stammering child up in the basement. Later, when Jean van Beethoven had handed over the teacher's baton to his colleague Tobias Pfeiffer, there were multiple tales of the two men arriving home drunk around midnight, dragging the wailing child out of bed, and forcing him to play new pieces for hours. In general, however, Beethoven enjoyed playing the piano very much—free improvisation most of all, to his father's considerable chagrin—and practiced diligently.[8] His enthusiastic participation years later in the many drunken musical reunions that took place in the van Beethoven household is therefore not surprising.

The general lack of empathy exhibited by Beethoven's father in the pedagogical approach to his son's education gives rise to several psychological considerations. One noteworthy proposition comes from Maynard Solomon, who claims it was no coincidence that these rather grim scenes played out almost immediately after the death of Beethoven's grandfather Louis. According to Solomon, Jean van Beethoven may have taken advantage of this opportunity to establish his supremacy within the family home.[9]

If we learn one thing from the Fischer Manuscript, it is that Ludwig van Beethoven grew up in circumstances that were more or less typical for a late-eighteenth-century family of musicians. The Beethovens knew their place in society, harbored no illusions of grandeur, and calibrated their ambitions accordingly. They knew that their career opportunities were limited, and that the most direct path to a stable life lay in the perpetuation of the craft from grandfather, to father, to son. Study of a more advanced nature was therefore not only unrealistic but also quite unnecessary. Ludwig's general education went no further than primary school (the *Tirocinium*), where pupils were instructed in the basic principles of mathematics, literacy, religion, and Latin. With the exception of those who would proceed to the *Gymnasium* preparatory college and then to university—and such cases were exceptional indeed—no further education was necessary. But even the brief time Beethoven spent at school was far from a resounding success, and there is no evidence to suggest that he even completed it. We do know that in 1780 he was tutored privately in Latin, French, and Italian by a *Gymnasium* student—Beethoven was therefore willing to learn, but not on command. Later in life he was primarily an autodidact. One detrimental consequence of his brief formal education was that he grew up lacking several fundamental literacy and numeracy skills. It is known, for example, that his arithmetical ability was limited to addition and subtraction—any multiplication problem therefore became a tedious (and comical) set of additions. Such a patent lack of abstract mathematical ability did nothing to stop him from taking a firm stance in financial discussions, however. Beethoven may have been unable to compute, but he could count all the better for it.

Writing also remained a problem. Thomas Mann once described Beethoven's handwriting as follows: "I gazed long at them, those jagged, scrawled lines, the desperate orthography, the utterly half-crazed lack of articulation."[10] Beethoven allowed himself a great many liberties when it came to spelling, applied copious and often incorrect punctuation, and his word order was often convoluted. He would leave out parts of sentences, replacing them with dashes of varying lengths, underlining words and occasionally entire sentences. He also constantly flouted the German convention to capitalize all nouns; his uppercase letters functioned more as an alternative to underscoring, serving to highlight a particular word's emotional import (whether it happened to be a noun, adjective, or adverb). This made Beethoven's writing "affected" in the true sense of the word—that is, artistically expressive rather than contrived. His written communications can therefore only be properly understood by analyzing their visual appearance as well as their semantic meaning. (In Beethoven's defense, it should be noted that there were no established spelling standards in the eighteenth century, and regional differences could be considerable.)

For a long time it was believed that Beethoven's lack of penmanship was attributable to his being left-handed and having been forced to write with his right hand. The reality was that Beethoven simply had too little patience—his hands were too slow for his mind—and he was too much of a nonconformist to capitulate to the conventions of neat writing. He also had a deepseated aversion to expressing himself in writing at all. Although he occasionally did demonstrate an ability to compose letters in accordance with proper etiquette—in obsequious missives to dignitaries, for example—Beethoven detested letter writing his entire life. He would employ any excuse to avoid the chore, and exaggerated about his health many a time to confect an alibi for his procrastination. Countless of his letters begin thus: "I trust that you will forgive me my tardy response. I had taken extremely poorly for some time, as well as being incredibly overburdened by work. I am also far from an avid letter-writer, let that fact also speak in my defense."[11]

Beethoven was predestined to earn a place in society through musical rather than academic achievements, the more so since his above-average abilities were quick to manifest. Ludwig's progress at the keyboard was so rapid, in fact, that his father arranged his first public appearance in Cologne at a very young age. On March 26, 1778, the following advertisement was distributed:

On this day, the 26th of March 1778,
at the University Concert Hall in Sternengasse,
Cologne court tenor Messr. BEETHOVEN

shall have the honour of presenting two of his pupils,
court alto Mlle. Averdonc and his own six-year-old son,
the former presenting various beautiful arias
and the latter performing diverse piano concertos and trios.
Messr. BEETHOVEN flatters himself to thus offer the nobility
such entertainments, particularly since both artists
have already had the opportunity to play before the entire court,
to the full enjoyment of those present.

The concert shall commence at 5 p.m.

Ladies and gentlemen without a subscription will pay one guilder.
Tickets are available from the above-mentioned University Concert Hall,
and also from Messr. Claren auf der Bach in Mühlenstein.[12]

Unfortunately, most Beethoven biographers present this concert in a negative light, condemning it as a sign of Jean van Beethoven's ambition to raise Ludwig as a second Mozart. The fact that, in 1778, he dared to bill his son as a six-year-old is cited as proof of his selfish intentions. In reality, Ludwig, who was born in December 1770, had turned seven only several months before. His father-manager had therefore doctored his age by a "mere" four months, which—at least in marketing terms—is a negligible distortion of the truth.

The 1778 concert was not the sole opportunity afforded the young Beethoven to demonstrate his musical talents. The Fischer Manuscript, for example, talks of "large concerts" that were often organized in the van Beethoven household, and the young Ludwig performed regularly at private concerts hosted by music lovers in Bonn and surrounds. These successes must have had a large impact on the psyche of such a shy and introverted little boy. In any case, it became clear that music offered Beethoven the ideal medium with which to shape his own identity, first within the family circle and later beyond. His father, too, became aware of the immense possibilities and is once purported to have firmly proclaimed: "My Ludwig, my Ludwig. I can see it now, in time he will grow to be a great man in the world."[13] At the same time, Jean van Beethoven quickly realized, much to his credit, that he could not be the one to lead his son down the path to greatness. As a singer he was of course familiar with the fundamental principles of music making (competent singers always respond naturally to questions of melodic shape and take an intrinsic approach to musical storytelling); however, he lacked the technical background necessary to transfer these basic principles to the keyboard or the violin. Moreover, he must have sensed that it is in a student's best interests for the teacher to listen and observe in calmness and objectivity, a role that is difficult for a father to adopt. These insights, too, speak in his favor.

The main problem with Beethoven's musical training was the lack of structured education programs in eighteenth-century Germany. Teachers were selected from the limited pool of professional musicians who happened to be in the area, and lesson content was chosen according to an intuitive sense of the student's needs. Between the ages of eight and ten—a crucial time in the development of musical talent—Beethoven thus became the guinea pig in a somewhat random musicopedagogical experiment. At an age when Mozart had toured Europe, visited royal courts in London, Paris, and Vienna, and was being introduced to the greatest composers of his day, Beethoven's educational fate was entrusted to a delightful assortment of colorful characters from the Bonn musical potpourri. We know of at least six such figures, who with the best of intentions all did their part to help mold young Beethoven's musical destiny. The first was the eighty-year-old Gilles van den Eeden, an old friend and colleague of grandfather Louis's, who gave the young Beethoven lessons in organ and continuo. After his death, the task fell to organists from the various local churches, who also happened to be clergymen: the reverends Koch, Hanzmann, and Zensen. Not only did they familiarize Beethoven with valuable methods and techniques for day-to-day organ practice, but they also introduced him to the less enjoyable aspects of the profession, such as playing for mass at six in the morning. These gentlemen were succeeded by violinist Franz Rovantini, a cousin of Beethoven's mother, who had come to live with them as a newly hired member of the Kapelle in Bonn. By all accounts he was an excellent and well-respected musician, and he gave Beethoven violin and viola lessons. This training ceased abruptly upon Rovantini's untimely death in 1781.

The last (but certainly not the least) to arrive on the scene was the theatrical jack-of-all-trades Tobias Pfeiffer. He was a bona fide performing machine: young, tall, stylish, versatile, imaginative, and ever-so-slightly mad. He was a singer, a gifted comic actor, an excellent oboist and pianist, and even had some experience with composition. In 1779 he joined the theatrical troupe that was resident in Bonn, from which he was expunged one year later due to reports of "poor conduct."[14] Like Rovantini, Pfeiffer lodged with the Beethovens throughout this period, and shared the father's fondness for the occasional tipple. In exchange for room, board, and alcohol, he thus became teacher to the young Ludwig. But it was not the lessons as such that left their mark on Beethoven: Pfeiffer and Rovantini could play and improvise together for hours on end (in modern terms, this might be called jamming), and the young Beethoven was regularly permitted to join in. It was here that he developed a skill that would be of inestimable value later on, and where he learned that imagination is an essential ingredient in compelling artistry.

This realization may very well have been the key influence of this chaotic period on the composer's later development. By escaping the tutelage of dedicated but mediocre teachers, Beethoven learned the fundamentals of the profession without being subjected to the crippling confines of a formal system. Instead, at a crucial time in his life, the young Beethoven learned to trust in the power of his imagination—a quality that would later be attributed to his "willful" character.

Beethoven in 1802

Mechelen town center, mid-nineteenth century

The Electoral Palace in Bonn

Coadjutor Maximilian Francis's visit to Bonn, 1780

View of the Rhein and Siebengebirge Mountains, Bonn

Garden view of Beethoven's birthplace in Bonn

Beethoven at age fifteen

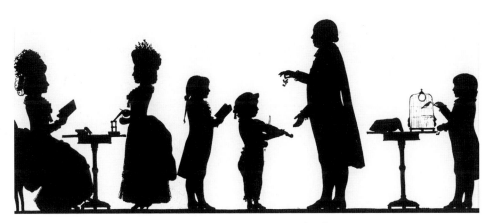

Silhouette of the von Breuning family

Grandfather Louis van Beethoven

Helene von Breuning

Franz Anton Ries

Franz Gerhard Wegeler

Promenade at the Vienna city limits

Kohlmarkt Square, Vienna

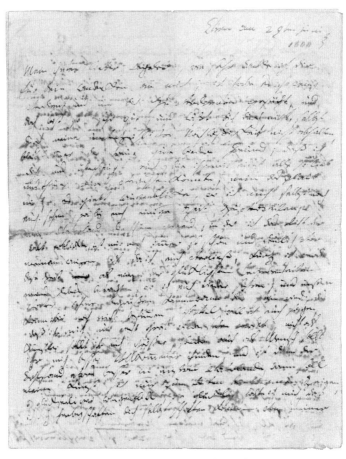

Letter from Beethoven to Franz Gerhard Wegeler, June 29, 1801

Heiligenstadt in the early nineteenth century

4

Christian Gottlob Neefe

THE MENTOR

DESPITE THE LIVELY CAVALCADE OF AVAILABLE TEACHERS, Beethoven was still in need of a long-term coach, a mentor who could hone the young man's skills and help raise his intellect and performance to new heights. This need was met in the person of Christian Gottlob Neefe, who is generally considered to have been Beethoven's first real teacher. It is difficult to glean precisely how much the young pupil actually learned from him, however, as Neefe's own musical achievements (in composition and in other areas) were rather limited. He was a self-taught musician, and one with a strong theoretical bent. Nevertheless, his intellectual and ideological background allowed him to exert a major influence on Beethoven's artistic temperament, and his commitment to the cultivation of social relationships and networks was of particular benefit in launching Beethoven's professional career.

Neefe was born in 1748 in Chemnitz and studied law in Leipzig. He then became a lawyer, graduating with the virtually autobiographical dissertation "Whether a father may be permitted to disown his son for dedicating his life to the theatre." His conclusion was in the negative. Neefe put this theoretical proof into practice by embarking on a rather successful musical career, thanks in part to the support of Johann Adam Hiller, one of the most powerful figures on the Leipzig musical scene at the time. Hiller had earned a reputation as the spiritual father of the singspiel, a new form of half-sung, half-spoken musical theater that gained rapid popularity due to the need in Germany for a homegrown brand of entertainment. Neefe thus entered the theater world, and via several intermediate posts became, in 1779, musical director of the Grossmann Troupe, a private theater company that operated first in Frankfurt and later in Bonn. In 1782 he was appointed court organist in the latter city, and some time later, as Kapellmeister, became responsible for all musical matters in church and at court. He was a busy man and earned a reasonable living, which was accompanied by no small measure of power.

As one of Germany's most cosmopolitan cities, Leipzig had a major influence on Neefe's own development. Its many trade fairs worked like a magnet, attracting bankers and rich merchants from all over Europe and lending the city a dynamic allure. The old aristocratic customs and traditions in this "miniature Paris" had long since made way for a new lifestyle. People dressed in the modern "galant" style and were extremely sensitive to the latest trends and fashions. Leisure time was also freed from the shackles of old. Citizens went to the theater or to concerts out of a genuine desire to do so, not to satisfy imposed and outdated social and hierarchical structures. For their entry fee audiences felt justly entitled to material that they could at least understand. In this light the singspiel was a perfect fit, as it presented real-life stories featuring everyday, vulnerable characters of flesh and blood, who spoke and sang in the vernacular.

So, unlike Dresden—where the tone was still set by the court, and day-to-day life was dominated by stale, aristocratic etiquette—in Leipzig the winds of change were blowing. Adam Friedrich Oeser, the director of the art academy, had emerged as the guru of an entire generation of artists, composers, and writers (including Winckelmann and the young Goethe) who were searching for what they had dubbed a "gospel of beauty," a creed dedicated to good taste and pleasing aesthetics. A movement was born that is now commonly defined as Weimar Classicism, based on a specific interpretation of art forms from classical antiquity and derived from the axiom of "noble simplicity and silent greatness." Here was a new conceptualization of perfect beauty in response to the core inquiry into the meaning and ultimate purpose of modern art. All adherents of Oeser were steeped in these ideas, and Neefe too referred back to his own spiritual mentor throughout his life. Beethoven's early sensibility to the artist's lofty, utopian purpose can therefore perhaps be traced back to his teacher's ideological roots in Leipzig.

But Leipzig was first and foremost the city of the Bach family. Of course, Neefe cannot have known the "old Bach," Johann Sebastian, personally, and it is even doubtful whether he ever met his son, Carl Philipp Emanuel. Neefe knew and appreciated the music of both and had thoroughly studied C. P. E. Bach's *Essay on the True Art of Playing Keyboard Instruments* (Versuch über die wahre Art das Clavier zu spielen), in its day the best-selling standard work on both music in general, and on keyboard playing in particular.

In the latter half of the eighteenth century, Carl Philipp Emanuel Bach was known as the "great Bach" and enjoyed more popularity than his father. His music was modern, not only due to its unrivaled blend of various styles (learned, galant, and sentimental), but also because its fleeting melodic phrases, interplay of light and shadow, daring harmonies, and brusque changes of mood all served as an effective vehicle for individual expression. Carl Philipp Emanuel Bach was thus deemed to be an *Originalgenie,* or "original genius." According to contemporaries, his improvisations at the clavichord were known to bring about moments of trance, a sense of the infinite, and loss of awareness. In essence, they represented a departure from the rational.

Although Neefe lacked both the talent and the inventiveness for composing music to match the imaginative likes of Carl Philipp Emanuel Bach, he nonetheless subscribed fully to the latter's aesthetic doctrine and based his later teachings on the principles of the *Essay.* This approach was crucial to the development of the young Beethoven, who learned at an early age that all musical performance relies on clear and expressive execution, and that all good musicians must think like singers and sing like actors. It is no coincidence that the categories later used to describe Beethoven as an "original genius" can be traced back to the musical philosophy that he inherited, via Neefe, from Carl Philipp Emanuel Bach. Beethoven, too, was regarded as a musical polyglot; his playing flirted with the irrational, and his compositions exhibited bizarre, daring, and unconventional traits. Thanks to Neefe, it was impressed on Beethoven from the outset that good music constitutes the infinite expression of the "hyperindividual."[1]

Beethoven remained true to this doctrine and continued to study the music of C. P. E. Bach throughout his life. He carried a copy of the *Essay* wherever he went, and advised his pupils to do the same. Carl Czerny writes, for example, that after being accepted as Beethoven's pupil in 1801, Beethoven insisted that he obtain a copy of the *Essay* and bring it with him to every lesson.[2]

In addition to the music of the "great Bach," in Leipzig Neefe of course also became acquainted with the music of the "old Bach," whom he held in high academic and pedagogical esteem. Neefe believed it was essential for all music students to make a thorough study of Bach's *Well-Tempered Clavier.* Beethoven too was confronted early on with this collection of preludes and fugues, and in March 1783 Neefe published an article in Cramer's *Magazin der Musik* (a Hamburg-based journal that published reports on musical life in the various German cities), stating that his pupil had learned almost all of the great master's magnum opus:

> Louis [Ludwig] Van Beethoven, son of the aforementioned tenor, is a boy of 11 years and of very promising talent. He plays the keyboard with great skill and power, reads fluently at sight, and in a nutshell: he plays almost the entire Well-Tempered Clavier by Johann Sebastian Bach, to which he was introduced by Messr. Neefe. All those familiar with this collection of preludes and fugues in all keys (which might easily be considered the *non plus ultra* of our art) will understand the significance of this fact. Messr. Neefe has also given him some instruction in figured bass, as much as his other activities would allow. He now teaches him composition, and as a means of encouragement, has had his set of *Nine Variations on a March* for the keyboard published in Mannheim. This young genius deserves support, so that he might travel. He will undoubtedly become a second Wolfgang Amadeus Mozart, if he continues as he has begun.[3]

This article (the focus of which was naturally more on the teacher than the student) was of great visionary significance due to its Mozart reference and the subtle insinuation that Bonn as a city was too small for Beethoven. (In both 1787 and 1792, Neefe would be instrumental in convincing the elector to allow Beethoven to travel to Vienna.) Most of all, the article highlighted the importance attached by Neefe to the study of early compositional techniques. In addition to the *Well-Tempered Clavier,* Neefe also brought other Bach works with him from Leipzig, and we can assume that Beethoven played and studied these too, the fruits of which were borne out toward the end of his career.

Neefe was asked to take charge of Beethoven's education on his arrival in Bonn, a task that he undertook with conviction for several years.[4] He can be credited with broadening Beethoven's intellectual, musical, and cultural horizons, as well as laying the groundwork for Beethoven's strong professional work ethic. Neefe's dedication, however, was motivated to no small degree by a spiritual mandate of primarily Masonic origin. Neefe had been a devoted Freemason since his student years in Leipzig. It was through this avenue that he had secured the friendship and protection of Johann Adam Hiller, one of the leading figures in the Leipzig Masonic world, and been introduced to Frankfurt theater director Grossmann, who hired him and took him to Bonn. There Neefe continued his twofold career as a Freemason;

he joined a traditional lodge in Neuwied—a prestigious chapter with connections to the lodge in Vienna, where Joseph Haydn was a member—and also joined the Illuminati, who were based in Bonn itself.

The Illuminati were a secret society with their own structures and rituals. Unlike the ordinary Freemasons, they also had a clearly defined political agenda. Driven by a humanist worldview, their aim was to overturn the old social and political order and (quoting the founder Adam Weishaupt) to transform "humankind into one big family, and the world into a home for the wise."[5] Their objective was to reorganize the state from the inside out, and they therefore attempted to infiltrate key government and religious positions. Because of their lofty principles (the fight against evil and injustice, and the restoration of virtues considered lost), fostering the moral qualities of their members had become a core aspect of their program, which involved a rigorous and systematic approach to personality development. It is for this reason that the Illuminati introduced a rigorous system of psychological self-analysis, and members were obliged to draw up personal "psychograms" based on questionnaires that asked them to confess their innermost feelings. They were also forced to accept that their conduct would be constantly monitored by their colleagues, which ultimately led to institutionalized mutual espionage.

The Illuminati society (which in view of the above was essentially a fundamentalist branch of the Freemasons) quickly amassed a relatively large following in Germany and Austria. In the early 1780s, the society counted at least two and a half thousand highly placed officials, university professors, lawyers, and artists. The confidential member lists included the likes of Goethe, Herder, and Viennese first minister Kaunitz. In Bonn, too, most personalities were both Freemasons and Illuminati, including several musicians who would later figure notably in Beethoven's career: violinist Franz Ries, and horn player and music publisher Nikolaus Simrock.

Neefe, who had already cultivated a reasonable Masonic résumé, rose rapidly through the ranks of the Bonn Illuminati, known locally as the Minervalkirche Stagira. His exemplary efforts, diligence, and maturity meant that he quickly completed his trial period, and in 1781 he became an official member. Two years later he was appointed to the rank of prince (*Princeps*), thereby becoming de facto director of the Bonn chapter. But he also made many enemies and was accused of both opportunism and a lack of inner conviction very early on. It was said (perhaps not entirely without justification) that his entire musical career had been propelled using Masonic resources, and he was criticized for his conceit, pride, and lack of discretion. These recriminations would prove to be irrelevant, however, as the parent Grand Lodge in Munich was forced to close in 1786, and the Bonn Illuminati order disbanded one year later. For most members, establishing a *Lesegesellschaft*, or "literary society," was the only remaining option for continuing their (still clandestine) activities.

The Illuminati attached great importance to the efficient recruitment of young (i.e., malleable) adherents. All members were instructed to act as the spiritual guide for one young candidate, who in the greatest obeisance and psychological dependency was to be subsequently brainwashed. These young men were essentially told what they could and could not read, how to behave, and what they were permitted to think. According to Beethoven biographer Hans-Josef Irmen, this is the context in which Neefe's relationship with Beethoven should be understood. While Neefe deemed it his noble duty to help launch his young pupil's career, Beethoven was also the chosen target for Neefe's Illuminist conversion efforts. It was to be expected that Beethoven's personality would ultimately resist such treatment, and in 1785 the relationship between teacher and the adolescent pupil turned sour. Given that the Illuminati order also disbanded shortly afterward, Beethoven was never formally initiated. Yet we can still assume that this period left its mark on him, to some extent stimulating his spiritual potential and sharpening his ethical awareness. He emerged with several musical contacts (the Masonic network would benefit him in later years), while the process also bolstered his skepticism toward people in general. Lastly, according to Irmen, the possibility cannot be excluded that the movement's underlying misogynistic leanings served to considerably complicate his relationship with the opposite sex.[6]

5

The Young Professional

NEEFE THREW THE YOUNG BEETHOVEN to the proverbial musical
wolves early on, regularly passing on odd jobs in the conviction that experience is the best teacher. This strategy also served Neefe's own interests. Neefe
was a busy man and did what many musicians do: they bite off more than
they can chew and outsource the less pleasant engagements to their most
talented pupils, who in turn develop an early taste for earning a living. This
is one way teachers discourage their students from seeking instruction elsewhere while simultaneously quashing potential frustrations arising from any
pedagogical nonchalance.

The rising public demand for music and theater had given Neefe a full
schedule. The sweeping austerity measures from the early years of Maximilian
Friedrich had abated, and the orchestra had plenty of work performing
Italian operas, symphonies, and religious music. From 1779 on, its repertoire
was further supplemented by the inclusion of the latest German works. In
Vienna, Joseph II had given the singspiel an upgrade, redubbing it officially
as the Teusches Nationalsingspiel (German National Musical Theater) and
sparking a desire in many other German-speaking cities to follow suit. The
switch was made possible in Bonn through one of the earliest known examples of public-private partnership: the court engaged a private theater company (the Frankfurt troupe run by the Grossmanns) and supplied its own
orchestra. The various powers and interests quickly intermingled, which led
to Neefe—who had come to Bonn as a member of the Grossmann company—not only being appointed court organist but also becoming involved
as both conductor and director of the regular Italian opera productions. In
addition, the contract between Gustav Friedrich Grossmann and the court
also permitted the theater group to perform elsewhere, further lowering the

overhead for the court in Bonn. All of this meant that Neefe was frequently on tour and needed a replacement back home.

This was Beethoven's big opportunity. He was first asked to stand in for Neefe when he was only ten, and in June 1782—at around eleven and a half—he was appointed Neefe's official deputy.[1] He was not paid to do so, a practice that was fully in keeping with the conventions of the day. Young musicians (called "accessists") were always required to complete a trial period before being offered paid employment, which usually only happened when an older musician passed away. In such cases, the candidate would submit a servile letter of application to the elector and await his gracious reply. Beethoven had to wait until the spring of 1784 to submit his initial application. The prospects seemed favorable, but the elector's unexpected death on April 15, 1784, and the resulting administrative vacuum delayed the response until June. From that point on, Beethoven was the official deputy court organist and received an annual salary of 150 guilders, raising the basic income of the entire Beethoven family by 50 percent.

Beethoven gradually eased into full-time work. In the morning he would play the organ for masses and other religious ceremonies; before noon he rehearsed with singers; and in the afternoons and evenings he was employed as a continuo player in operatic and orchestral productions. His work as a *repetiteur* at the piano was particularly grueling, as he was required to reduce and play entire opera scores at sight. Taxing though it was, it was also a valuable learning experience, as it allowed Beethoven not only to train his reading ability but also to consolidate his understanding of the language of music. When asked later where he got his capacity to sight-read the most fiendishly difficult piano scores, and how on earth he could play faster than he could read, Beethoven replied that reading all the notes simply wasn't necessary—fast readers, he claimed, are not distracted by the many typographical errors in the score. Skimming the music like this is only possible, however, if one is already familiar with the language at hand.

Beethoven must have possessed incredible self-assurance to shoulder such a level of musical responsibility at such a young age. There is a telling anecdote how, as a fourteen-year-old, he managed to utterly derail the bass Ferdinand Heller (who was well known for his unwavering ear) by improvising an extremely complex piano accompaniment entirely on the spot. After that, the elector warned him to keep things simple.[2] Pulling off such antics requires not only considerable musical skill but also a great deal of nerve.

The fact that his first published compositions appeared around this time is further evidence for Beethoven's early musical self-awareness, although it is clear that Neefe was the one who encouraged the eleven-year-old Beethoven to compose the Nine Variations on a March by Dressler (WoO 63) and the three early *Electoral* Sonatas (WoO 47) dedicated to Elector Maximilian Friedrich. Neefe—in suitably high-blown style, in accordance with the prevailing etiquette—wrote the dedication to the elector, and it was certainly also he who decided that Beethoven's debut work should be a set of variations. It was common eighteenth-century teaching practice to have composition students write new melodies to a given bass line, in the belief that the variation was simply the most indispensable of all compositional techniques. We know, for example, that Mozart's father had young Wolfgang improvise on minuets whose melodies had been omitted, and that C. P. E. Bach, Neefe's guru when it came to the keyboard, had published a set of sonatas "with varied reprises." Beethoven also felt very much at home in the genre, as composing variations was merely an extension of improvisation, a skill that he had developed very early on (we need only recall the "jam sessions" with Pfeiffer and Rovantini at his family home). It is therefore no coincidence that in his younger years, Beethoven produced more sets of variations than sonatas. Beethoven the Composer would need time to emerge from the shadow of Beethoven the Pianist.

Neefe was also undoubtedly the one who suggested Dressler's somewhat inane march theme for Beethoven's first set of variations. It met all the necessary criteria: clear structure, unambiguous harmonic and tonal progression, several distinctive rhythmic patterns, and—most importantly—very little in the way of substance. Neefe therefore must have been the one to teach Beethoven one of the cardinal and seemingly paradoxical laws of composition: it is better to write good variations on poor themes than the other way around, since good themes are less accommodating of alterations or additions.

Neefe thus sent Beethoven off well prepared, with a thorough practical grounding in many facets of the profession. Unlike Mozart—whose extensive travels and numerous contacts from the uppermost echelons of society had given him an idealized sense of the musical world—the young Beethoven had no choice but to slave away and survive in the harsh musical ecosystem of a provincial orchestra. He did have one lucky star to thank, namely the fact that day-to-day music making in Bonn was of a very high caliber. Under the leadership of the Italians Lucchesi and Mattioli, the ensemble in Bonn had evolved into one of the best in Germany. They played in the "modern" style, which included great attention to articulation and declamation, large contrasts, and a more flexible approach to bowing. Despite the orchestra's extreme discipline (which was itself quite uncommon for that era), its performances were renowned for their vitality and spontaneity. In a report on the Bonn orchestra published in 1783 in Cramer's *Magazin der Musik,* Neefe even ventured a comparison to the Mannheim orchestra, undoubtedly one of the finest in Europe at the time. At this early stage, Beethoven's ear thus became preprogrammed with a high degree of musical sensitivity to orchestral color.[3]

The young professional Beethoven led the life of a court musician. He enjoyed wearing the electoral uniform: a set of sea-green tails, a vest with golden buttons, white knee-length trousers, and white silk stockings. On his left side he carried a dagger on a silver sword-belt. Beethoven was not exceedingly tall, but he was slender and powerfully built. He had a florid, pockmarked complexion, black hair, thick eyebrows, and piercing eyes, earning him the nickname "The Spaniard."[4] He was a proud adolescent and marched through the streets in elegant, fashionable attire. His status as a young professional in service of the state had boosted his confidence, and music had become his road to self-actualization.

In the autumn of 1783, Beethoven left his familiar Bonn surroundings for the first time and accompanied his mother on a trip to the Netherlands.[5] The excursion began as a personal affair, as mother and son wished to visit relatives in Rotterdam. Still, the Beethovens made good use of the opportunity to have young Ludwig give several concerts, not least—according to the Fischer Manuscript—because of the attractive financial opportunities. One of their Rotterdam acquaintances would later reveal that Beethoven performed in many houses of note, astonishing listeners and receiving valuable gifts wherever he went. The Beethovens, however—unlike the Mozarts several decades earlier—relayed no news of their triumphs to the home front, and so no further details are known about these performances. We know only of a single important concert given by Beethoven on November 23, 1783, in the stadtholder's quarter of the Binnenhof in The Hague. A recovered copy of a receipt provides evidence that Beethoven performed a piano concerto on that day, accompanied by the orchestra of Prince William V of Orange-Nassau, under the baton of the famous contemporary Kapellmeister

Christian Ernst Graaf. For his performance he was to receive the sum of sixty-three guilders—nearly half his annual salary in Bonn—plus several nonmonetary gifts. And yet on his return he was heard to complain about the Dutch mentality: "Those Dutchmen are such cheese-parers, all they care about is money. I will never set foot there again."[6]

6

Bonn Turns to Vienna

ON AUGUST 5, 1784, BEETHOVEN GOT A NEW BOSS. It was on that day that Archduke Maximilian Francis of Austria, the youngest brother of Emperor Joseph II, was inaugurated as archbishop-elector of Cologne. Since Maximilian Francis, now twenty-seven, had already been waiting in the wings for four years as "coadjutor," the appointment came as a surprise to nobody, but for electoral Cologne it did mean severing historic ties with France in favor of a new alliance with the Hapsburgs. The political ramifications of this diplomatic change of course were far-reaching, and the effects on the cultural scene were palpable. In a broader sense, it is impossible to imagine what would have become of Beethoven's life and work had Bonn maintained its connections with Paris.

This about-face was but the tip of a historical iceberg, whose crystallization began with the unexpected death of Clemens August in 1761. The Bavarian house that had supplied an unbroken chain of claimants to the throne for one hundred years suddenly had no suitable candidate available, so an alternative was necessary. Europe was in the midst of the Seven Years' War, struggling for stability amid the rapid rise of Prussia, and was therefore in no position to find a successor to Clemens August who could simultaneously serve as both grand master of the Teutonic Order and elector of Cologne. Given the circumstances, it was only barely feasible that the Austrians might orchestrate the appointment of Charles Alexander of Lorraine (Maria Theresa's brother-in-law) as grand master. But the position of the archbishop-elector of Cologne was of a separate order entirely and could only be negotiated within a broader context; fundamental discussions on the future of the religious principalities were inevitable and would necessitate a major exchange of territories involving the Austrian Netherlands and

Poland. Eventually a provisional course of action was chosen, and the Swabian Maximilian Friedrich von Königsegg-Rothenfels was appointed. He ticked all the boxes: he was fairly neutral and low-profile, which would limit the extent of any potential damage, and because he was advancing in years and was not expected to live much longer, his appointment would buy precious time during which a more permanent solution could be arranged. The decision proved to be a case of best-laid plans: the placeholder elector reached the age of seventy-seven and ruled for over twenty years, and so— contrary to all expectations—the interregnum period was strongly marked by his own brand of politics after all. But because Maximilian Friedrich's personal ambitions were rather modest (like his predecessor, his chief concern was the maintenance of hormonal rather than political balances), they left all the more room for those of his immediate subordinate, Count Kaspar Anton von Belderbusch. Belderbusch, a powerful background figure and a political force to be reckoned with, executed silent but ruthless machinations in the game of behind-the-scenes macropolitics.

For twenty-five years it was Belderbusch who wielded real power in electoral Cologne. He was a particularly colorful personage: charming yet cold-blooded, visionary yet pragmatic, generous yet calculating, and most of all, corrupt to the very core. He was a family friend of the Beethovens' and god-father to Beethoven's youngest brother, whose namesake he shared (the god-motherhood had gone to Belderbusch's mistress, abbess Caroline von Satzenhofen). When Belderbusch died, however, and all who had known him wished to deny any and all previous association, Kaspar Anton Karl van Beethoven felt the need to bury his compromising connection to the former First Minister by thenceforth being known solely by his third name, Karl.

Belderbusch came from a region close to Verviers, a small city in the Prince-Bishopric of Liège, and had studied law in Leuven. His parents, of modest extraction, saw a career with the Teutonic Order as the only means of climbing the ranks of society. This path led him first to Aachen and later to Bonn, where he entered the service of Clemens August and gradually won his trust. His sharp mind, enormous efficiency, cunning, flair, and sense of diplomatic timing meant that by the 1750s he had worked his way to the very top of the political establishment. It is noteworthy that when Maximilian Friedrich took the helm in 1761, Belderbusch was the only member of the old guard who was permitted to remain. He ensured continuity, and his thorough knowledge of state finances made him both the brains and the driving force behind the new elector's plans to overhaul the administration.

Belderbusch also chalked up some diplomatic successes of his own, earning him the title of first minister (a position that he himself often misinterpreted as "Sole Minister"). He was a control freak and interfered wherever he could, even appointing himself theater manager and taking charge of the austerity measures in the Kapelle. He was therefore directly responsible for the ousting of Touchemoulin and the appointment of Louis van Beethoven as new Kapellmeister; he had a hand in both the ups and the downs of Jean van Beethoven's career and provided ample support to aid the rise of the young Ludwig van Beethoven.[1]

Where Belderbusch truly excelled, however, was in the manipulation of the major European powers. Like Clemens August, Maximilian Friedrich was dependent on foreign sources of funding. Since most countries had been all but bankrupted by the astronomical costs of the coalition war, Belderbusch turned to the only two countries who were still prepared to buy influence in the Rhineland outright: the Republic of the United Netherlands, and England (whose king, incidentally, was from Hannover). The Austrians would not take this lying down and made attempts to banish Belderbusch— who meanwhile had further ascended in the ranks of the Teutonic Order—to the Commandery of Alden Biezen in Belgian Limburg. Their efforts were in vain. Ultimately, external factors drove Bonn into the hands of the Viennese regardless, a development for which Austrian diplomats could take no credit whatsoever. The unrest in America and the eventual Declaration of Independence in 1776 forced England to withdraw from the European stage, in turn prompting Belderbusch to open the doors to Austria after all (France had become far too unstable by that time). In 1775 Belderbusch gave the first signal to Vienna that he was prepared to consider Archduke Maximilian Francis, the youngest son of Maria Theresa, as a candidate for the next elector of Cologne.

The offer came at a convenient time for Maria Theresa. Not only did she have certain territorial interests to protect, but she was also in need of dynastic solutions for her ample progeny—two historical birds that were often killed with one stone, under the old Austrian adage, *Bella gerant alii, tu felix Austria nube*.[2] She had managed to pawn off most of her daughters to the various dukes of Bourbon in Italy, and her crowning achievement was the fatal marriage of Marie Antoinette to French crown prince Louis XIV in 1770. No solution had yet been found for her youngest son, however. Although Maria Theresa had been successful in making him coadjutor and official successor to the grand master of the Teutonic Order in 1769 (the fact that Maximilian Francis came to stand at the head of this immense organization, without having completed even the most basic initiation, was a formality to be rectified later), so far she had been unable to find him a suitable appanage. She and her prince regent Emperor Joseph II therefore jumped at Belderbusch's offer and paid handsomely for the privilege. This circumstance led to one of the greatest bribery and corruption scandals in all of Austro-German history: to have Maximilian Francis "elected" as the successor to the throne in Cologne, Vienna paid around one million guilders (roughly equivalent to thirty million euros[3]), around one third of which disappeared straight into Belderbusch's pockets. One undeniable consequence was the shift in Bonn's attentions to Vienna as of 1776, manifested by the rise in prominence of German-language theater productions (among other developments). The associated intellectual, cultural, and musical ramifications were considerable and would serve to benefit Beethoven in the long term.

Maximilian Francis established himself as coadjutor in Bonn in 1780 but did not take on full responsibility until the death of his predecessor Maximilian Friedrich on April 15, 1784. Belderbusch had also died several months previously, giving the elector a clean slate to start afresh. He first needed to pick up both the physical and the proverbial pieces, as the city had suffered greatly from the February floods of that year and was still in a sorry state. The economy also needed an overhaul, and following the example of his eldest brother, Maximilian Francis set to work in a pragmatic fashion. He imposed strict austerity measures, slimmed down the government apparatus, cut privileges, and slashed the ever-excessive ceremonial and entertainment budget. His vision for rebuilding the state was what today might be described as liberal left-wing. The elector was devoted to the belief that his duty was to rule in the interests of his subjects in an unprejudiced manner, regardless of rank or standing. He also made a conscious choice to dress in ordinary, inconspicuous, and even provocatively unkempt clothing. His wig was symbolically cast off, and he traded in the electoral palace for a more modest civilian address on the banks of the Rhine.[4] Maximilian Francis also upheld the conviction that the key to a higher standard of living lay in improvements to basic education. In other words, he believed that the maximum height attainable at the top of an education pyramid—namely, the quality of higher education—was determined by the breadth of its base. He therefore launched a major education reform that left behind the formalism of traditional Jesuit programs, concentrating more on teachers' academic training and fundamental improvements to their working conditions.

Only once these ground-level reforms were in place did Maximilian Francis direct his attention to the formation of an intellectual elite. In 1786 he founded a new university that immediately became known for its distinctly progressive character. The body of professors included several "enlightened" philosophers, to whom Maximilian Francis had given carte blanche to disseminate the latest ideas and theories under the banner of intellectual independence. The elector even demanded the secularization of certain professors, forcing them to leave their respective religious institutions in the interests of free speech and thought. This of course quickly led to conflicts with the sister university in Cologne, which was a bastion of Catholic reactionaries. On multiple occasions, the Cologne chapter and curia put pressure on Maximilian Francis to take action against the unorthodox teachings of the university in Bonn, pressure which he steadfastly resisted. He may have been an archbishop, but his lack of a traditional religious upbringing (he had grown up in nonclerical milieus) meant that his mental programming was strongly antidogmatic. He was more a proponent of practical Christianity based on personal confession, and eschewed the tyranny of Roman doctrine. It is therefore no surprise that Maximilian Francis consistently supported his professors, virtually never forcing them to leave the university or to modify the content of their teachings.

Maximilian Francis adopted a similar attitude of tolerance—and even encouragement—toward the *Lesegesellschaft,* or "literary society," that was founded in 1787. The society originally served as a haven for the ex-Illuminati but quickly evolved into a club where intellectuals and artists could engage with the latest books and journals (including French writings) and discuss the most recent political and ideological developments. The members included virtually all prominent figures in Bonn, among them many of Beethoven's friends and colleagues, including Neefe, Antonin Reicha, Ries, Simrock, and recent Bonn import Count Ferdinand von Waldstein (who even served as society president for some time). Elector Maximilian Francis adopted a moderately positive attitude to the *Lesegesellschaft.* He was a regular visitor and even provided venues for the group to meet. His benevolent interest had several possible origins. Unlike his brother, Maximilian Francis was firmly against secret societies of any kind. He condemned Freemasonry, dismissing it as a waste of time for bored intellectuals, labeling their rituals as comical, ceremonial theater, and was skeptical of all forms of overorganized contemplation.[5] He was more inclined toward the literary society, on the other hand, because of the absence of ethereal rituals and the higher degree of intellectual honesty and transparency. The latter would have been of especial importance, because—just like his brother in Vienna—Maximilian walked a tightrope between the need for enlightened politics on the one hand, and fears of the political and social system being undermined on the other.

Under these conditions, by the late 1780s Bonn had developed into a bulwark for progressive intellectuals. Ideological debates (including those in response to certain condemnations from Cologne) were by no means confined to the academic sphere; new philosophical beliefs, such as Kant's idealism, were eagerly assimilated; and artists were encouraged to express themselves freely. Moreover, because Maximilian Francis's character was less imposing than that of his brother or his spiritual father in Vienna, his interventions were less drastic, met with less resistance, and paradoxically enough achieved greater impact.

Like all the Hapsburgs, Maximilian Francis was an excellent amateur musician. He was an outstanding singer, played a range of instruments, and also curated an extensive and carefully catalogued library of opera scores. According to Neefe, the elector even took pleasure in leafing through them after fulfilling his government duties of an afternoon.[6] We can therefore surmise that his grasp of composition was sufficient for him to make an informed judgment on the subject. Further evidence of his commitment to music was the fact that, rather than using the austerity measures (which unavoidably affected the music sector) to whittle away the Kapelle, he saw them as a vehicle for elevating both the standard and the image of the ensemble. The reorganization efforts therefore focused not on downsizing, but instead on improving quality and the return on investment. To this end the elector had the entire Kapelle audited by a human resources manager avant la lettre, Count Salm-Reifferscheid. A comprehensive evaluation was compiled of each and every musician, listing their strengths and weaknesses and family circumstances alongside a detailed character analysis. Some, for example, were described as a little skittish or given to drink. Beethoven's evaluation said that he was young, talented, showed exemplary conduct, and was quite poor.[7] On the basis of these reports, Maximilian Francis drew up a new strategy for the orchestra. A number of privileges and abuses were done away with, particularly those pertaining to "paid leave." Following the example set by his colleague in Salzburg (who several years earlier had fought a legendary battle with the Mozarts, both junior and senior, on precisely this matter), he withdrew all permissions enabling musicians to moonlight by taking on additional engagements elsewhere. Directors Mattioli and Lucchesi were summarily recalled from their sojourns abroad; the former was fired on the spot, while the latter took a substantial pay cut and was obligated to play during all services from then on.

Mattioli's dismissal presented an ideal opportunity for Maximilian Francis to hire Wolfgang Amadeus Mozart as the new musical director. The two of them had been friends since childhood. The Mozarts' first trip to Vienna and their visit to the imperial court was the scene of the well-known anecdote of the young Wolfgang sitting on Maria Theresa's lap, and running riot in the castle with the young prince Maximilian Francis. Their mutual amity had remained (which included a shared aversion to court rituals and etiquette), and they never lost contact with one another. A gala performance of Mozart's *Il re pastore* was organized in the prince's honor in Salzburg in 1775, for example, and after Mozart settled in Vienna in late 1781 they met many times in a warm and cordial atmosphere. On one such occasion, Maximilian Francis is believed to have expressed the wish to take Mozart with him to his new residence in Bonn.[8] But it was not to be; on June 28, 1785, the Bohemian cellist Joseph Reicha was appointed as the new musical director.

We can only guess as to why Mozart's transfer to Bonn never eventuated. Perhaps it was a question of money, and Maximilian Francis's austerity policy could not accommodate the expense of such a high-profile celebrity from Vienna. The most likely explanation, however, is that when Maximilian Francis acceded to the elector's throne, Mozart was on such a winning streak that a transfer to the provinces was simply out of the question. His piano concertos and string quartets had become exceedingly popular, and he had just begun work on *The Marriage of Figaro,* the first of the three great Da Ponte operas. He thus had good reason to entertain hopes of soon succeeding the aging Bonno as Kapellmeister at the court in Vienna.

At this juncture we are once again forced to consider a turning point in Beethoven's career and ruminate on what might have occurred if Mozart had moved to Bonn in 1785. Leaving aside the fact that musical history would most likely have taken a turn for the worse if Mozart had left Vienna (and Beethoven had likewise never traveled to the Austrian capital), we can say with almost complete surety that in this case, fate was kind to Beethoven. Of course, the alternative scenario fulfills the fantasy of Beethoven having taken lessons from the most gifted musician of the age, placing him in close proximity to the very source of the cutting edge in composition. On the other hand, we can assume that Beethoven, as a fourteen-year-old pupil, would simply not have withstood the avalanche of Mozart's talent.

7

Beethoven's First Crisis

BEETHOVEN WAS CONFRONTED with the harsher aspects of a musical career early on. After an initial flying start, events in 1784 triggered a series of setbacks and disappointments that effectively stalled his compositional activities for about five years, from 1785 until around 1790.[1] The first of these events was the death of Belderbusch in January 1784, and of Elector Maximilian Friedrich several months later. For a brief period the electorate of Cologne was without governance (the new elector would not be appointed until August), during which time several courtiers and musicians seized the opportunity to spin webs of deception and intrigue in order to gain a personal advantage. In a veritable climate of postwar oppression, the court was divided into two camps, and lists exposing the so-called sleuthhounds and spies from the former regime were put into circulation. Owing to his close ties with Belderbusch, Jean van Beethoven was named on one such list of collaborators.[2]

In climates of uncertainty it is the leader who must take the fall. Beethoven's teacher Neefe had made himself unpopular by the means he had employed to rise up through the ranks, and could only look sadly on as various colleagues attempted to orchestrate his downfall. A sore point for the young Beethoven was the fact that the rebels were advocating him as the new candidate for principal organist, thrusting him into direct competition with his own teacher. The newly appointed elector eventually intervened and insisted on retaining Neefe as principal organist, on the painful condition that he surrender part of his salary to the deputy organist, Beethoven. Neefe briefly considered trying his luck elsewhere but ultimately accepted the proposal, remaining with the ensemble in Bonn until it was disbanded in 1794.

Matters were compounded by the ever-widening psychological rift between Beethoven and Neefe. As Beethoven's temperament revolted ever more strongly against Neefe's oppressive attempts to groom him for the Illuminati, the authoritarian and somewhat narrow-minded Neefe struggled with Beethoven's headstrong and passionate disposition. Beethoven was also vexed by his teacher's critical assessment of his newest compositions.

Some time would pass before Beethoven saw the events of 1784 and 1785 from a clearer perspective. Nearly ten years later he wrote a letter to Neefe from Vienna, expressing gratitude for his dedication as a teacher: "I thank you for the wealth of advice that you often issued to me in the pursuance of my divine art. If ever I should make something of myself, it will be due in part to you."[3]

Other factors also contributed to Beethoven's compositional hiatus. At a time when he was already confounded by the fuss surrounding Neefe and the other court intrigues, Beethoven received a scathing review in Johann Nikolaus Forkel's *Musikalischer Almanach,* which dismissed his compositions as the paltry attempts of a novice and compared them to essays written by third- or fourth-grade pupils.[4] This devastating commentary must have dealt him quite a blow, and the fact that his newly composed Piano Quartets (WoO 36) were refused for publication (unlike the *Dressler* Variations and the *Electoral* Sonatas) must have been equally discouraging. It is a peculiar paradox that the most headstrong personalities generally have the greatest difficulty accepting negative criticism.

Beethoven's limited output during these few years does not mean that he was entirely inactive.[5] Despite the strict ordinance preventing any more leave requests, in the spring of 1787 he was given permission to travel to Vienna. It is generally surmised that the principal aim of this trip was to meet Mozart and to take composition lessons from him if possible.[6] We can also assume that Beethoven wished to network with other composers active within the establishment of the institutionalized Viennese court, such as Gluck and Salieri—a move that could have done no harm to his career prospects in Bonn (or elsewhere).

We are poorly informed of Beethoven's trip to Vienna, not least because Beethoven himself (according to Schindler) was "generally unforthcoming and often uncertain or confused about events that had taken place in the distant past, if he spoke about them at all."[7] All evidence seems to suggest that Beethoven left Bonn before the new year in 1787, taking the traditional post-chaise route via Frankfurt am Main, Würzburg, Nuremberg, Regensburg, Passau, and Linz, and arriving in Vienna after a journey of nearly one thousand kilometers on or around January 14.[8]

Beethoven's time in Vienna is shrouded in the mists of theory and speculation, particularly as regards his encounters with Mozart, which was presumably the main purpose of the whole undertaking. Whatever can be said of their meetings, it is certain that none could have taken place until mid-February, when Mozart returned from conducting several performances of *The Marriage of Figaro* in Prague. For a description of the meetings themselves we are primarily reliant on the accounts by Schindler and Jahn, which were not committed to paper until many years after Beethoven's death and should therefore be treated with extreme caution. In accordance with proper eighteenth-century tradition, Beethoven is said to have improvised during their initial introduction, first on an original theme and later on a fugal subject chosen by Mozart—quite a tour de force, and one which Beethoven is said to have mastered "supremely." Mozart supposedly gave a succinct response, saying that Beethoven would make his mark on the world someday.[9] Equally fascinating is the impression that Mozart reportedly left on Beethoven. Czerny writes that Beethoven did indeed hear Mozart play on several occasions.[10] We might imagine, for example, that Beethoven was present at the Kärntnertortheater on February 23, 1787, when Mozart performed during the farewell concert for famous soprano Nancy Storace. Czerny notes that Beethoven disdainfully characterized Mozart's playing as "choppy" and not sufficiently adapted to the capabilities of the modern fortepiano.[11]

Indeed, all evidence points to the existence of an enormous pianistic gulf between Beethoven and Mozart. Mozart would undoubtedly have furrowed his brow at the tempestuous, unpolished, rough-hewn, and even sloppy way Beethoven let loose at the keyboard. His playing may have been expressive and brilliant, but its powerful impact came at the expense of subtlety and nuance. Beethoven, who originally trained as an organist, also had a preference for a more fully sustained tone. All who heard him play were struck by his ability to play legato, even when playing sequences of chords. And his generous use of the knee lever (the forerunner to the modern sustain pedal) is evidence of an acoustic aesthetic that clearly differed markedly from Mozart's own.[12]

We shall probably never know whether (and if so, to what extent) Beethoven took lessons from Mozart. For this reason, some Beethoven biographers tend to downplay the significance of this first trip to Vienna.[13] Nor can we disregard the fact that at the time, Mozart was working on *Don Giovanni* and grappling with problems of a personal nature, and may not have been especially disposed to investing much time in a young musician from Bonn, however talented he may have been.

On March 28 at the latest, after staying for over two months, Beethoven left Vienna. Sources suggest that for whatever reason, he made the return journey via Munich, making an additional detour via Regensburg—again, for reasons unknown. It is tempting to speculate that he applied for a position at the House of Thurn and Taxis, whose court orchestra was among the most renowned in southern Germany. An even more seductive supposition is that Regensburg Kapellmeister Joseph Touchemoulin—the predecessor of Beethoven's grandfather in Bonn—had a hand in matters.

On his homeward journey Beethoven also called in at Augsburg, where he met organ and keyboard builder Johann Andreas Stein. The encounter must have left a deep impression on Beethoven, since Stein had a reputation as a builder of high-quality pianofortes. He earned eternal fame for perfecting the *Prellzungenmechanik,* or "flipping action," a new mechanism that allowed the hammer to strike the string quickly and with great sensitivity. German pianos (and later their Viennese counterparts) owed their reputation as light, responsive, flexible, and expressive instruments to this new mechanism, which is what set them apart from the heavier, louder pianos from England and France. Like Mozart, Beethoven was a great proponent of Stein's instruments. We can only imagine Beethoven's giddiness at walking around in Stein's studio—the very epicenter of modern piano development.

It was there that Beethoven also met Stein's daughter, Anna Maria (Nannette). She was herself an outstanding pianist—Mozart praised her playing greatly—and had inherited her father's affinity for piano construction. In the early 1790s she married pianist Johann Andreas Streicher and moved to Vienna, where her own piano factory grew into one of the biggest in Europe, under the Streicher name. She would later come to play an important role in Beethoven's life.

Augsburg was also where Beethoven took his leave of government official Joseph Freiherr von Schaden, who is thought to have provided logistical and diplomatic support for Beethoven's journey both to and from Vienna. Schaden was the ideal foothold between Bonn and the Austrian capital. Not only had he married into the Austrian aristocracy, but he also had like-minded Masonic friends in both cities; plans to set up a local chapter of the Illuminati in Augsburg were initially what had put him in touch with Neefe. Schaden also lent the young musician a sum of money to help finance the final leg of his return journey—a debt that Beethoven almost certainly never repaid. On September 15, 1787, Beethoven sent Schaden a long and impassioned letter, begging for more time to settle his debt. He explains in minute detail how a report of his mother's ailing health left him no choice but to hasten back to Bonn, and how her death on July 17 affected him both emotionally and physically: "She was such a kind and loving mother to me, she was my best friend [. . .] Since my return I have been arrested by shortness of breath, and I fear that consumption may not be far away. Melancholy also weighs down heavily upon me, and is almost as oppressive as my physical ailments."[14]

From the viewpoint of a biographer familiar with Beethoven's entire body of correspondence, this letter—the earliest from his own hand that has survived—foreshadows many hundreds to follow in which Beethoven is forced to explain his precarious financial situation and provide excuses as to why he cannot meet his obligations. The possibility can therefore not be excluded that this letter, too, is imbued with feigned melodrama intended to move the reader to a certain measure of sympathy, and should therefore be interpreted with due caution.

Nevertheless, virtually all biographers have accepted Beethoven's dramatic version of events and attribute his hasty departure from Vienna to alarming reports of his mother's health. Ignoring for a moment that it would be highly uncommon in the eighteenth century to undertake a hazardous ten-day journey on hearing of the illness or death of a close family member, the newly reconstructed itinerary of his return trip proves that Beethoven was in no rush to reach the city where his mother was ailing.

The eventual death of Beethoven's mother remained a heavy blow, however, not least because it marked the moment when he was forced to shoulder full responsibility of his entire family, his father included. The adolescent Beethoven thus lost his innocence, leaving him not only in a sad state of mind but also obsessed with the Novalisian thought that death is never far away. Twenty years later he wrote: "It is a fool who is not prepared for death! This I knew as a boy of fifteen."[15]

One week after his wife's death, Jean van Beethoven applied to the elector for an advance on his salary. When he was refused, his financial need became so great that he saw no option but to sell his late wife's clothing via an intermediary on the secondhand market. He even briefly pawned the cherished portrait of his father, Louis, and to cap off his misfortunes, his only daughter, Maria Margaretha, died in November at the age of one and a half, thus robbing the Beethoven household of its last female member.

8

A Second Home, and New Horizons

BEETHOVEN WEATHERED THESE HARD TIMES with the support of a few trusted friends who in their own ways helped prevent him from sinking into the depths of despondency. His greatest source of support was Franz Anton Ries, one of the more accomplished players in the Bonn orchestra. The Ries family had maintained close ties with the Beethovens for decades. The father, Johann, played trumpet and violin in the Kapelle, initially as a colleague of Louis van Beethoven's and later under his direction. His children—Anna, who was a singer, and Franz Anton, a violinist—were appointed later by Louis and were thus colleagues of Beethoven's father, Jean. Both families also lived on the same street, which provided a strong sense of community since their daily lives were closely intertwined.

Franz Anton Ries was a gifted violinist, and nothing would have stopped him from making a career as an international soloist. But despite a successful visit to Vienna in 1779, he chose to return home and contribute to the growth of the ensemble in Bonn, much to the joy of the elector. Ries was also a member of the Illuminati, and after it was disbanded he joined the newly founded literary society (*Lesegesellschaft*). After the death of Beethoven's mother and the many problems with his father, Ries saw it as his proper duty to use his court contacts to help the struggling family in any way he could. Later, during Beethoven's initial years in Vienna, Ries also took care of Beethoven's brothers, Karl and Johann, who had remained in Bonn. Beethoven was eternally grateful to Ries for doing so and in turn took Ries's son Ferdinand under his wing.

The support provided by Ries was thus chiefly of a practical nature. For genuine warmth and affection, Beethoven's first port of call was always the Breuning family. The mother, Helene von Breuning, had been widowed in

January 1777 when her husband, court adviser Emanuel Josef von Breuning, perished during a conscientious and overzealous attempt to rescue as many archives as he could from the blazing electoral palace. She was only twenty-seven and survived him with three young children: the five-year-old Eleonore and her two younger brothers, Christoph and Stephan. Not only that, but she was pregnant with her fourth child, Lorenz, who was to be born in August of that same year. In her attempts to make the best of a bad situation, she effectively transformed her home into a kind of cultural salon, where guests made music, painted, wrote poetry, gave recitations, and engaged in genial and intelligent conversation. The young Beethoven was hired as a piano teacher, first for Eleonore and later also for the young Lorenz. When Beethoven's mother died, Helene embraced him as an adopted son. He became part of the family, spent time there during the day (occasionally also spending the night), and was invited along on summer outings, some of which lasted several days. It was here that the orphaned Beethoven found a second home and enjoyed a sense of freedom, liberated from the troubles of his own family. It is important to realize that the Breunings' world was entirely new to Beethoven: they were relatively well-off, daily life ran smoothly, and family members always had time for one another—notions that were altogether foreign to Beethoven in his own home. We might also imagine that he rather enjoyed the role assigned to him within the Breuning familial tapestry. He was the "odd one out," the splash of color that brightened up the superficial, somewhat beige conviviality of upper-middle-class family life. Franz Wegeler later reported how Beethoven diverted the assemblage with his inspiring piano playing, and was "often asked to impersonate some character or other."[1]

Beethoven would later tell Schindler that his ersatz-mother, Helene Breuning, also tried to offer him pedagogical and psychological guidance. She regularly corrected his behavior and succeeded in keeping him away from certain acquaintances—"like an insect from flowers"—who awakened his vanity with excessive praise and posed a threat to the natural development of his talent.[2] At the same time, however, she responded tenderly to his notorious eruptions of pent-up frustration and perceived injustice, a pattern of behavior that we will see more of later. Helene Breuning was familiar with such episodes, knew how to read them, and had accepted that living with the darker aspects of Beethoven's character was necessary in order to enjoy his brighter qualities. The main way she defused Beethoven's outbursts was by giving them a name, referring to them as his *raptus*.[3] Beethoven found the designation almost flattering and continued to use the term throughout his life, both ironically and as a means of dulling some of his sharp edges.

Time went on, and very soon the inevitable occurred: for the first time, and certainly not the last, Beethoven developed warm affections for his female pupil, which—more to the point—were reciprocated. And here, too, on the first of many occasions, things ended badly. Eleonore bore little guilt in the matter, except that she was perhaps a little too insistent in expressing her adoration. She regularly wrote little notes in which she teased Beethoven; discreetly at first but gradually making less and less effort to disguise her true feelings (one such occasion being New Year's Day 1791). Beethoven, who seems to have been terrified of commitment, found it all too much; he felt suffocated and fled.[4] Eleonore always retained a special place in his heart, however; he later wrote her several touching letters asking her to try to understand his position, in an attempt to keep her friendship at the very least.[5] He also dedicated several compositions to her[6] and carried her portrait with him his entire life. Further support for their ongoing connection was the fact that many years later she married Beethoven's best friend, Franz Wegeler. Beethoven continued to express his unabated affection for her, concluding a letter to Wegeler in 1810 with "Embrace and kiss your dear wife," and in 1826, "Please give your dear Elly and the children a big hug and a kiss from me." He was prone to expressing his nostalgia for times gone by: "I still keep a silhouette of your Elly, which shows how I continue to cherish all that is good and dear to me from my youth." Eleonore, too, had no hesitation in expressing her fondness for Beethoven: "A visit from you would fulfil one of my deepest longings."[7]

Beethoven also spent many a happy hour at the Zehrgarten—the "Garden of Refreshment"—a restaurant and inn on the Bonn market square. The Zehrgarten was a traditional German tavern, a sparsely furnished venue offering food and drink at democratic prices. A fairly pungent *odeur locale* hung in the air, made up of a mixture of alcohol, tobacco, and greasy comestibles. It was a hub of communal enjoyment, where men ruminated for hours on the meaning of life, solving society's problems one by one as the hours went by.

The Zehrgarten was run by Anna Koch, a good friend to both Helene von Breuning and Beethoven's parents. Originally she worked alongside her husband; when he died, she expanded the business into a literary café-cum-book-store. The Zehrgarten, which also happened to be close to the university, thus became a regular haunt for the city's intellectual elite. All names of repute frequented the establishment, including influential university professors, the more highly placed officials at court, artists, poets, and several of the more culturally minded musicians from the Kapelle. Of course, it was also the place where the members of the literary society met to discuss matters in a more secular setting. But first and foremost, it developed into the meeting place par excellence for fanatical left-wing intellectuals steeped in Enlightenment philosophies, who were eager to discuss new political ideas and ideologies.

At the Zehrgarten, as at many ordinary taverns, the daughter of the house was the belle of the ball. Wegeler described Barbara Koch (Babette) as "a lady who, of all the members of the fairer sex I have met throughout the many years of my eventful life, came closest to the ideal of the perfect woman. All who have ever had the pleasure of her company agree."[8] It therefore goes without saying that she was courted by many men, not least by the elector himself. Beethoven also pursued her, and her lack of response to two letters that he sent to her from Vienna vexed him immeasurably. When the news eventually reached him of her impending marriage to the immensely wealthy Carl von Belderbusch—nephew to the former First Minister, a French collaborator, and the future mayor of Bonn—Beethoven responded in his furiously cynical manner: "The change in Koch does not surprise me. Fortune is fickle, and does not always favour the best or most deserving."[9]

Although Babette Koch's enticing presence at the Zehrgarten should not be underestimated, it was primarily Beethoven's intellectual curiosity and the satisfaction of belonging to a circle of like-minded peers that drove him to the market tavern. These peers were the same friends who suggested he enroll at the university in 1789 to take courses in philosophy and classical literature.[10] This may seem surprising given Beethoven's minimal prior education, and the fact that his intellectual milieu had hitherto been limited more or less to the musicians' canteen. But Beethoven had caught up tremendously at the Breuning household, aided by canon Lorenz Breuning, Helene's brother-in-law, who had moved in with the family to take charge of the children's intellectual upbringing (among other things). He taught Beethoven how to read and interpret the writers from antiquity and was particularly taken with Plutarch's *Parallel Lives*. Like many of his contemporaries, Beethoven viewed the study of history as a form of moral training and as a source of inspiration for his own life. He was especially fascinated by the psychological portrayal of great figures from the past, and by the motivations underlying their actions. Beethoven thus developed a strong awareness of his own ego, and his identification with the Greek and Roman heroes gradually fed the realization that he, too, might one day grow into an exceptional individual with an almost divine purpose in life.[11]

Like most of his Zehrgarten friends, Beethoven was also very much a devotee of Kantian philosophy. The notion of the "categorical imperative" was one that he held close to his heart and which featured in many of his letters. In fairness, we should add that Beethoven's enthusiasm for Kant was rather faddish and superficial, and his contributions on the matter were usually limited to the regurgitation of a few terms and aphorisms gleaned from eighteenth-century philosophical anthologies and quotation collections.

His real icons, however, were the heroes of the theater which—mainly thanks to Grossmann's troupe—had been gaining popularity in Bonn since the turn of the decade. An impressive list of works filled the theater programs: alongside masterpieces by Lessing, Molière, and Carlo Goldoni, new works by the French enfants terribles Voltaire and Beaumarchais were also presented. Even Shakespeare's plays were programmed regularly, including *Richard III, King Lear,* and *Macbeth.* These performances undoubtedly "set the scene" for Beethoven's lifelong fascination with Shakespeare. He owned the *Opera Omnia* in German translation and entertained the notion for some time of writing an opera on *Macbeth.*[12]

Schiller, too, also featured prominently on the stage. At a time when this controversial author had the greatest difficulty even being performed (let alone understood), audiences in Bonn embraced him utterly. Both *The Robbers* and *Fiesco* had already seen productions by 1783, while *Intrigue and Love* was performed in 1784 shortly after Grossmann had returned from directing the world premiere in Frankfurt. It is intriguing that *Fiesco* flopped in many parts of Germany but enjoyed great success in Bonn, most likely due to the republican winds blowing through the city at the time.

It is impossible to overstate the extent of Schiller's influence on Beethoven. It was through Schiller that Beethoven learned much about the grammar of the stage: how dramatic gestures can be systematically codified and channeled, the relationship between rhetoric and architecture, and by extension, the interplay between form and content. As a composer, Beethoven may have learned more about the nature of his calling by analyzing Schiller's work than by performing the symphonies of Danzi, Dittersdorf, Gyrowetz, or Pleyel.

Another crucial influence on Beethoven was Bartholomeus Fischenich, a lawyer who had befriended Schiller during his student years in Jena and maintained contact with him ever since. When he later became a university professor in Bonn, Fischenich cultivated the habit of peppering his lectures on natural and international law with recitations of Schiller's poetry. It was thanks to Fischenich that Beethoven came to know Schiller's "Ode to Joy," the end result of which speaks for itself.

9

Renewed Vigor and the
First Major Works

MAXIMILIAN FRANCIS QUICKLY PUT the state's finances in order, and cultural life at court flourished. After several years of pared-down policy, the elector now had the resources at his disposal to launch new initiatives and to realize his predecessor's dream of establishing a permanent local opera company. Previously, Bonn's only options had been to hire itinerant theater and opera troupes or to embark on joint productions, both of which involved compromises on performance quality. The old theater received a complete overhaul, including the installment of several additional rows of box seats. The grand reopening on January 3, 1789, featured a production of *The Tree of Diana,* the hit opera by famous composer Vincente Martín y Soler.[1] The everpresent Neefe pulled out all the stops during his speech for the occasion, extolling the elector in every way he knew how.

The growth in opera productions and the resulting workload brought with it a much-needed expansion of musical forces. An ensemble of around twenty singers was formed;[2] Joseph Reicha was promoted to the position of opera director; Neefe became general director and continuo player; and Beethoven received an official contract as a violist and *Kammermusicus* ("chamber musician"). No fewer than fifteen additional players were recruited, including several heavyweights on the scene: flautist and violinist Antonin Reicha, violin virtuoso Andreas Romberg, and his cellist cousin Bernhard Romberg. The preponderance of musicians from Bohemia was particularly striking, and their high degree of musical sensitivity and sensuality exerted a major influence on the orchestra's sound. They also had a reputation as consummate melodists and were masters in the production of bittersweet phrases—a talent that Beethoven himself would continue to develop throughout his career.

By around 1790 the Bonn Kapelle employed roughly fifty contracted musicians, making it one of the largest in the German-speaking world; only the court orchestras of a few European metropolises (Paris, Berlin, and Milan) boasted greater numbers. The scope of the orchestral winds in particular was remarkable: all the winds were doubled, including the clarinets, which was more often the exception than the rule in the eighteenth century. The orchestra owed its bountiful winds to the Viennese roots of Maximilian Francis. On his installation in 1784, he immediately followed his brother Joseph's example by establishing an imperial *Harmonie,* an eight-man wind ensemble, which though independent also served to augment the orchestra. Wind octets of this type, consisting of doubled oboes, clarinets, horns, and bassoons, were very popular in Vienna for around two decades and were liberally deployed for a wide variety of purposes (including open-air concerts). They were particularly in vogue among members of the lower aristocracy and the bourgeois nouveau riche. By hiring these miniature private orchestras (sometimes even in a sextet version without oboes), this middle layer of society could effectively attempt a sociocultural upgrade, motivated by aspirations to identify with the more elevated aristocracy. Music for this new market, whether original or arranged, was therefore in high demand. Beethoven himself composed two works for wind octet during his time in Bonn—the well-known Octet in E-flat Major (op. 103) and the lesser-known Rondo in E-flat (WoO 25)—giving him a thorough introduction to the instruments' technical and expressive capabilities. The sense of instrumental balance that he thus developed—the more emancipated role of the clarinet as a solo melodic instrument, for example—was crucial in his later work as an orchestral composer. With a few minor exceptions, all of his symphonies and concertos draw from a fundamental sound ideal that was galvanized by his experiences in Bonn.

Maximilian Francis was extremely proud of his Kapelle and seized every opportunity to put his elite musicians on display. So it was that in the autumn of 1791 the stars of the troupe (including Beethoven) accompanied him on a three-month trip to Mergentheim, to attend the congress of the general chapter of the Teutonic Order. En route to Mergentheim—a journey that was made by boat, where the musicians' boisterous, unruly behavior rivaled that of touring schoolchildren—an encounter took place in Aschaffenburg between Beethoven and pianist Johann Sterkel, a far more renowned pianist who was twenty years Beethoven's senior. Abbé Sterkel was Kapellmeister in Mainz and had earned some regard as a pianist in Germany and Italy with a piano technique typical for its time. Some described it as galant and elegant; others dismissed it as mannered, even "effeminate."[3] Mozart, too, was annoyed by his superficial and indulgent tempi.[4] Following an exchange of the usual courtly platitudes and compliments (sincere or otherwise), Sterkel performed one of his own sonatas in his characteristic style, accompanied on the violin by Andreas Romberg. Afterward, Sterkel rather provocatively proposed that Beethoven regale the company with his set of recently published *Righini* Variations, as he was convinced that the work was unplayable. After some initial hesitation, Beethoven then performed—completely unprepared and entirely from memory—the full set of variations, improvising several additional ones to boot. Much to the amusement of his fellow colleagues Romberg, Ries, and Simrock, Beethoven then proceeded to imitate and caricature Sterkel's playing, mercilessly demonstrating his own pianistic and musical superiority.[5]

Having arrived in Mergentheim, the orchestra gave several concerts, and the woodwinds performed various works for *Harmonie*. Beethoven also made some appearances, albeit only in private circles since the only pianos available for public performance were, in his view, not suitable. Heinrich Philipp Bossler's musical journal, *Musikalische Korrespondenz,* printed an extensive review of Beethoven's playing, in which the reporter claimed not to know of "any shortcomings that might prevent him [Beethoven] from becoming a great artist." The nigh-inexhaustible wealth of his musical ideas, his expressive, unique style of playing, and his virtuosity in works both fast and slow were also praised, and it was casually noted that Beethoven was admired by all of his colleagues, who listened intently whenever he was at the piano. All of this was followed by the prophetic words, "His playing differs so greatly from the traditional approach to the piano, it seems as though his aim has been to break entirely new ground, in order to achieve the goal of perfection before which he currently stands."[6]

This flattering summation was penned by a critical commentator, writer and amateur musician Carl Ludwig Junker. But despite having heard Germany's finest orchestras and soloists on many occasions and having developed a thorough, well-informed understanding of the musical landscape, not even Junker could have suspected just how much Beethoven's unique approach to the piano (and by extension to music in general) would alter the course of musical history. Junker's only real purpose had been to point out that the twenty-year-old Beethoven was already moving up in the world, from which we might conclude that the time was gradually becoming ripe for his departure from Bonn. Beethoven is likely to have sensed as much himself, although he later wrote that Junker's evaluation dated from a time when he was "all innocence, and nothing more."[7]

It is interesting that Junker's appraisal of Beethoven's musicianship was limited to his piano playing. The same had been the case one year earlier in a review of the elector's Kapelle (also in the journal *Musikalische Korrespondenz*[8]), which mentioned Beethoven purely in his capacity as instrumentalist and performer of piano concertos—only Joseph Reicha, the two Rombergs, and a certain Andreas Perner were listed as composers. And understandably so, since in the eighteenth century, "composer" was simply one of the many statuses enjoyed by any ordinary Kapellmeister, not a separate aspiration in itself. Beethoven was also a late bloomer in this respect and went through multiple periods of inactivity, owing often to extramusical circumstances. These "hiatuses," of which there would be several throughout his life, manifested for the first time, as described previously, in 1784; besides a Trio for Piano, Flute, and Bassoon (WoO 37) and several other works of little consequence, Beethoven seems to have written almost nothing during this period.

It is therefore surprising that in the spring of 1790, Beethoven was solicited to write a funerary cantata to commemorate the death of Emperor Joseph II. Joseph had died on February 20, and the members of the literary society decided to hold a memorial service on March 19, the deceased emperor's name day. The initiative was championed by one Eulogius Schneider who was to deliver the eulogy, while a large musical work written specially for the occasion would be performed by three soloists, a choir, and an orchestra. One of Schneider's young acolytes, Severin Anton Averdonk, wrote the text, and the equally young Beethoven was chosen to supply the music. Those organizing the project would come to regret passing over the more experienced composers, such as Neefe, Reicha, or the Rombergs: the minutes of a meeting held on March 17—two days before the scheduled performance—reveal that the cantata could not be performed "for various reasons."[9] Some sources suggest that Beethoven's composition had been conceived on too grand a scale, that it went far beyond its intended purpose (as bookends to Schneider's speech), and that it was too ambitious for the somewhat limited technique of the performers (a mix of professionals from the court and some of the city's more talented amateurs).[10] The reality was most likely far more banal. Since Beethoven had only received the final version of the text on February 28, he was probably simply unable to complete the work he had envisaged within the short span of less than three weeks.

Beethoven's failure to complete the cantata on time was a portent of things to come. The list of major works in his oeuvre whose completion was delayed is long, and myriad were the premieres that flopped due to a lack of adequate rehearsal time for the performers. Beethoven would continue to struggle with deadlines his entire life—the tendency among geniuses to be late comes not from a lack of motivation, after all, but from an excess thereof.

Despite the failed *Joseph* Cantata (WoO 87), several months later Beethoven was commissioned to write another work, this time for the coronation of Emperor Leopold II. It was a fortunate development, as it gave Beethoven the opportunity to write the new cantata as an extension of the previous one (according to tradition), allowing both pieces to be regarded as a single large work.[11] This project was likewise a failure, and plans to perform one of the two cantatas during the congress of the Teutonic Order in Mergentheim in the autumn of 1791 were also canceled. On this occasion, however, the testimonies were unanimous as to the cause: according to horn player Simrock, the musicians had reservations about the degree of difficulty in some sections and found several of the musical twists and turns highly irregular.[12] These objections were shared by Franz Anton Ries, who led the rehearsals. As a friend of the Beethovens' he would—if anything—have been prejudiced in Beethoven's favor and would have done his utmost to make the performance a success. But orchestral musicians are not always in the best position to evaluate the quality of new music; because they are "in the thick of it" and forced to concentrate on smaller details in the present moment, their view of the music lacks perspective, allowing their judgments to align all too quickly with their prejudices. It is therefore easy to imagine, had the cantatas been written not by a novice colleague but instead by a reputable composer such as Haydn, Mozart, Salieri, Dittersdorf, or Paisiello, that the musicians in Bonn would have taken greater pains to ensure its success.

The purported technical difficulty of the cantatas is also questionable. While it is true that the two obbligato parts for flute and cello in the *Leopold* Cantata's long soprano aria place high demands on the players, their technical difficulty does not exceed that of several concertos and chamber works by Romberg and Reicha. One alternative possibility is that some sections came across as so foreign to the performers that they simply gave up due to incomprehension. In his youthful impetuousness, Beethoven certainly took a few risks, and it cannot be denied that both imperial cantatas exhibit some technical flaws in their composition. They suffer from juvenile enthusiasm, employ too many disparate ideas, and the treatment of the material lacks economy—having too much to say is sometimes worse than having too little. The most beautiful sections in particular are somewhat long-winded, and the most inventive material, such as the opening, is dulled through repetition. They are compelling pieces nonetheless, if only because they represent the embryonic forms of the later, greater Beethoven works. In the *Joseph* Cantata, for example, grief at the emperor's death is assuaged through the adoration of his intellectual gifts, which he used to suppress evil (embodied here by the vice of intolerance). In the *Leopold* Cantata, the jubilation at the accession of the new emperor serves as a metaphor for resurrection after death. The young Beethoven thus composed two works on the universal themes of good and evil, joy and sadness, death and salvation. He pulled out all the affective stops, depicting fear, rage, and sorrow on the one hand, and deeply moving, ecstatic joy on the other. Even at this early stage, he reveals himself as a composer able to distill a utopian yearning for love, brotherhood, and transcendence into the gripping music that the world would later come to admire in *Fidelio,* the *Missa solemnis,* and the Ninth Symphony.[13]

The two cantatas were therefore never performed during Beethoven's lifetime, and vanished from the musical stage until they were rediscovered and given their first performances in 1884. When Johannes Brahms heard the *Joseph* Cantata, he wrote that even if Beethoven's name were missing from the title page, there could be no other possible candidate for the work's origin, as it is utterly drenched in Beethovenian sensibilities.[14]

Despite Beethoven's frustrating experience with the cantatas, they served to break his compositional drought, and between 1790 and 1792 he produced a wealth of new music. The more monumental genres—opera, mass, and oratorio—were all still out of reach, of course. Such works required a commission, and Beethoven's fame was still far too modest. He did have plans to start writing a symphony, however, and also wrote several concertos.[15] Beethoven's output at this time included songs (lieder, some with orchestral accompaniment), chamber music, and experiments in a wide range of genres: the string trio, piano trio, and winds in many different combinations. But works for piano—variations, in particular—remained his primary occupation. Not only did Beethoven feel very much at home in the genre, but there was enormous market demand for it. Many female aristocrats were excellent amateur pianists and were in constant need of new works to play; music publishers were mushrooming, and so composers had their work cut out for them. The publishers also wished to capitalize on the latest trends by ordering sets of variations on popular arias, such as "Venni amore" by Vincenzo Righini, "Es war einmal ein alter Mann" from Dittersdorf's *Little Red Riding Hood,* or "Se vuol ballare" from Mozart's *Marriage of Figaro.*

Financial motivations aside, there is another explanation for Beethoven's peculiar love of the variation form. The standard piano sonata had become so fossilized during the eighteenth century that it was ill-suited as a vehicle for a young composer to gain recognition. (Beethoven would need to take lessons from Haydn before embarking on the genre seriously, many years after his initial attempts in the form of the *Electoral* Sonatas.) The theme and variations form, on the other hand, had never left its infancy. Beethoven thus found himself in unexplored territory, with an opportunity to break new ground without the risk of being compared to established masters such as Haydn or Mozart. And break ground he did. In the *Righini* Variations (WoO 65), Beethoven took the former "written-out improvisations" of the variation genre and transformed them into well-structured compositions based on previous original material. Beethoven truly strove to give each new variation its own character, with a unique idea as a starting point. This germinal thought might be a musical one—such as a melodic figure or a fugal exposition—or an aspect of piano technique, such as rapid staccato octaves or parallel thirds. The variations were then ordered and reordered (Beethoven's sketches show just how hard he struggled to find the right sequence), until each one found its place within a cohesive narrative arc, leading to a natural and inevitable conclusion. This approach explains how instead of capping off the *Righini* Variations in the usual fashion (with a brilliant and rapturous finale), Beethoven could allow them to gradually fade away to nothing. Perhaps the expansive ending even offers its own succinct commentary on the "Venni amore" theme, suggesting a love that was gained . . . and lost.

It was partly through the work's sheer scope—twenty-four variations totaling twenty-five minutes of music—that Beethoven transcended the original amateur character of the form and created a work for connoisseurs. Most commentators thus see the *Righini* Variations as Beethoven's first great work for the piano,[16] a view that was shared by the young composer himself.

According to his later pupil Czerny, Beethoven always brought a copy of the work with him whenever introductions were to be made. He used them as reference material, and they were rightly a source of pride to him.

The monolithic dimensions of the *Righini* Variations could not conceal the fact that as a composer Beethoven was still more of a sprinter than a marathon runner. First and foremost, he was a brilliant extemporizer with a unique conceptual sound ideal, bursting with exciting and captivating ideas and in possession of an unbridled imagination. He subscribed firmly to Carl Philipp Emanuel Bach's belief that it is the performer's duty to surprise the listener with originality and changes of mood in rapid succession. The latter was fully commensurate with Beethoven's own temperament. His *rapti,* as they were tenderly dubbed by Helene von Breuning, found their musical equivalent in his sudden and frequent dissonances and runaway modulations. Beethoven's greatest challenge would be to take a more controlled approach—both to music and to his life in general.

Farewell to Bonn

THE STARK CONTRAST BETWEEN the debacle of the two Imperial cantatas on the one hand, and Beethoven's Mergentheim encounter with Sterkel and the gushing review in Bossler's *Musikalische Korrespondenz* on the other, illustrates the degree of disparity among appraisals of the young Beethoven. To a large extent this was due to his lack of any appreciable status in Bonn. Despite Beethoven's obviously exceptional and unique talent, in the eyes of those around him he was still the little boy from next door, the grandson of the dedicated but dull ex-director Louis van Beethoven, and the son of their derelict colleague Jean. It was this view that prevented their amazement from developing into any sort of admiration or respect. While those who followed his progress must have known that he had the necessary qualities to fulfill his ambition and become Kapellmeister in Bonn (like his grandfather before him), they must also have known that doing so would first require him to spend some time abroad and to cut his teeth in a major musical metropolis.

Beethoven had clearly exhausted his opportunities for growth in Bonn. He was desperately in need of new horizons and of opportunities to unleash his musical imagination on more challenging genres such as the piano sonata, the string quartet, the symphony, and the opera. His only option was to go in search of an experienced guide in a new and stimulating environment. Unsurprisingly, his thoughts once again turned to Vienna.

Two people in particular made it possible for Beethoven to return to the Austrian capital in December 1792: Joseph Haydn—who since Mozart's death had become the most venerated composer both in Vienna and far beyond—and the flamboyant Count Ferdinand von Waldstein, whose greatest merit was simply his status as the flamboyant Count Ferdinand von Waldstein.

Joseph Haydn had retired in 1790 after nearly thirty years of dedicated service at Esterháza. His retirement finally allowed him to take up an attractive offer from violinist, conductor, and impresario Johann Salomon. Salomon had invited Haydn to London to conduct a series of concerts featuring his own orchestral works, which were to include six modern and newly composed symphonies. In December 1790, Haydn and Salomon left Vienna for the English capital and—needless to say—sojourned for several days in the Hapsburg outpost of Bonn. For Salomon in particular, the stopover was a return to his roots. His father, Philipp Salomon, had played oboe under Louis van Beethoven; his brother and two sisters had taken singing lessons from Jean van Beethoven and also performed in the electoral choir and orchestra their whole lives.

Haydn was given a royal reception in Bonn. One of his masses was performed, after which the elector arranged a lavish dinner for the celebrated composer and several of his fellow musicians. Being well acquainted with the Beethovens, Salomon arranged for the young Ludwig to be introduced to the master from Vienna.[1] During their second meeting, on Haydn's return from London in July 1792, Beethoven showed Haydn one of his cantatas and arrangements were made for Beethoven to travel to Vienna for lessons (studying with Mozart had ceased to be an option, of course, since his death in 1791).

The man who subsequently facilitated the entire operation was Count Ferdinand Ernst Gabriel von Waldstein und Wartenberg zu Dux, far and away one of the most colorful figures from the Viennese aristocracy. In addition to his support for Beethoven, this eccentric character also made it into the history books for aiding another famous genius, Giacomo Casanova. When Casanova was being hunted down by the Venetian authorities at the end of his life, Waldstein and his brother granted him asylum in their family castle in Bohemia and assisted him with the German translation of his *Histoire de ma vie.*

Waldstein's life was no less adventurous than Casanova's. As a Bohemian aristocrat of the highest pedigree (his mother was a born Liechtenstein, his grandmother a Trauttmansdorff), he was destined for a career in the Teutonic Order. After the obligatory displays of heroism with the Sovereign Military Order of Malta along the Moroccan coast, in the spring of 1788 he was knighted in Mergentheim during a ceremony staged with great pomp and circumstance, including a grand ball and the musical participation of the entire Bonn Kapelle. He was then hired into the electoral diplomatic corps (exempted, of course, from any test of professional competence), where he was chiefly occupied with financial matters. He also revealed his talents as a court *maître de plaisir,* as he was a brilliant event planner, penned his own stage sketches and vaudeville acts, and entertained audiences with unparalleled impersonations in various French dialects—by all accounts, his langue d'oc was flawless. He also staged large-scale, all-encompassing spectacles—genuine *Gesamtkunstwerke*—entirely from his own hand, producing the script, the music (he was an excellent pianist and a composer of some merit), the costumes, and the scenography himself. An example of one such work was the Ritterballet, a major carnival spectacle that premiered in the Redoutensaal ballroom in Bonn on March 6, 1791, in which members of the nobility donned traditional German costume to pay nostalgic homage to the central preoccupations of their forefathers: war, hunting, love, and drink.[2] Afterward it transpired that the music had been composed not by the count but by a ghostwriter in the person of his young protégé, Ludwig van Beethoven (given the historical context, this was a minor and negligible embellishment of the truth). In any case, within a very short time Waldstein emerged as a key figure in Bonn high society. He was a welcome guest at the city's busiest salons, a regular at the Zehrgarten, and a member of the literary society, where he also served as president for some time.

When large parts of the electorate of Cologne fell to French occupation and the elector fled to Vienna in 1794, Waldstein's carefree life in Bonn ground to an abrupt halt—not least since he had racked up debts with virtually everybody, and with the Breuning family in particular. He chose the life of adventure: following a political dispute with his former employer, he defected to the side of the English, first recruiting an army of mercenaries in Germany and Austria and then leading a military expedition in the West Indies. In 1809, at the behest of the English king, he returned to his hometown in Austria to lead a diplomatic mission. In 1812 he completely overturned his life once again, leaving the Teutonic Order and the English army to marry an alarmingly rich Polish widow. His coffers thus replenished, he was once again ready to take on a starring role in high society; he was even one of the principal directors and entertainers during the Congress of Vienna. Thereafter, things quickly went downhill. The combination of his frivolity, pompous lifestyle, penchant for adventure, and heedless financial speculation caught up with him, and he died completely penniless in 1823.

Beethoven was introduced to Waldstein by the Breunings. He immediately won the count's friendship, who went on to support him by financial and other means. We might assume, for example, that Count Waldstein had an important hand in the literary society's decision to approach Beethoven for the Imperial cantatas. In return, Beethoven acted as a kind of musical handyman, first composing the music for the Ritterballet (WoO 1) and later dedicating a set of variations to him (Variations on a Theme by Waldstein, WoO 67). It was also Waldstein who, following Haydn's assent in July 1792, convinced the elector to send Beethoven to Vienna on paid leave, and with some pocket money to boot.

It is generally assumed that Beethoven expressed his gratitude to Waldstein through the dedication of his Sonata in C Major (op. 53). Yet the dedication is surrounded by an air of mystery. Some claim that Waldstein was on the mainland for several months in the autumn of 1802 and took advantage of the opportunity to visit Vienna. However, there is no historical record at all of Waldstein's presence in the capital at that time, nor of any meetings with Beethoven. Another striking fact is that Waldstein's name appears nowhere on the handwritten manuscript of the sonata and is only first sighted on the printed version from 1805. Lastly, we are at a loss to explain why Beethoven never met his ex-benefactor again, despite Waldstein's confirmed presence in Vienna from 1809 on.

Several months would pass before Beethoven could finally leave for Vienna, a circumstance due entirely to the fact that the elector—who was responsible for approving not only the trip itself but also the necessary funding—had more important things on his mind. After spending the summer months in Mergentheim, the elector's autumn was completely overshadowed by the battles taking place in the Rhineland and the accompanying threat that the French might occupy his Cologne principality. Europe's greater powers—Austria and Prussia, in particular—had forged a coalition during the summer and were planning to besiege Paris in order to reinstall the French king and restore the old values and social order. But after a long and arduous march, on September 20, 1792, the allies were held back during the famous cannonade at Valmy (around two hundred kilometers from Paris). Exhausted, intimidated, and without even having engaged in a proper battle, they sounded the retreat. Pursued by a motley crew of French irregulars, the Prussian and Austrian armies retreated to Frankfurt, leaving the northern road to the upper-left bank of the Rhine completely undefended and making the threat of a French invasion of Cologne and Bonn very real indeed. Maximilian Francis chose the better part of valor, collected his most important documents, secured his music library, and fled for Mergentheim.

From then on Bonn was in the throes of war, refugees were streaming in, and the atmosphere was oppressive. Beethoven, whose enthusiasm for the French and their revolution had been severely dampened by the ever-increasing wave of terrorist reports, was only too happy to seize the opportunity and leave his hometown. On November 1, a farewell party was held for him at the Zehrgarten. All of Beethoven's close friends attended, and they presented him with a beautifully illustrated album, or *Stammbuch,* a collection of poetically formulated sentiments and nostalgic reflections on friendship that was to serve as an antidote to the inevitable future moments of loneliness and melancholy. This *album amicorum,* which contained quotes and paraphrases from popular poets of the day, including Schiller, Herder, and Klopstock, was essentially a catalogue of Beethoven's nearest and dearest. In it we find no names of fellow musicians, young or old, but instead those of university professors, a few diplomats, magistrates, doctors, and of course Waldstein, the Breunings, and the Kochs (Babette excepted). Waldstein's was a particularly striking entry:

> Dear Beethoven! Finally, you are to travel to Vienna, in fulfilment of a wish so long denied. Mozart's genius still mourns, lamenting the death of its disciple. It has found refuge with the indefatigable Haydn, but no occupation; through him, it yearns to be reunited with humanity. Through constant diligence, may you now receive: Mozart's spirit through Haydn's hands.
>
> Bonn, 29th of October 1792.
>
> Your true friend, Waldstein.[3]

The entry's final line is usually taken to be quite prophetic. In it, Beethoven is mentioned in a single breath alongside both Haydn and Mozart, making Waldstein the first to conceptualize the triumvirate of the First Viennese School. In reality, he simply wished to express the hope that through Haydn, Beethoven would have an opportunity to absorb the newly emerging style in Vienna, whose former chief exponent had been Mozart. He may have also secretly hoped that Beethoven would fill the void that Mozart's death had left behind. What he cannot have intended (or indeed even have been capable of) was to make some kind of musical macrohistorical proclamation. On the contrary, by reducing Haydn to a mere surrogate for Mozart's ideas, he trivializes both Haydn's contribution to the Viennese style and his influence on Beethoven's development.[4]

Beethoven left Bonn very early on the morning of Friday, November 2. He had a traveling companion, with whom he shared the costs of the coach and lodging, and he carried with him a modicum of personal possessions (which nonetheless included all of his scores, notes, and sketchbooks). He left with an eager but anxious heart; he was not fond of travel, later mastering the art of finding excuses to avoid it as much as possible, despite the opportunities he missed as a result. Clearly, he was more suited to adventures of the musical variety.

The first stretch of their journey passed through the war zone and, given the unstable nature of the route, must have been quite turbulent. The coach driver even had to forge a path through the allied troops, and to avoid further hazards they journeyed all the way to Frankfurt in a single leg, where the company arrived at seven in the morning.[5] In hindsight, the plan proved to be a good decision, as the French troops marched the very next day, which would have stopped the coach in its tracks. Had that been the case, both Beethoven himself and musical history in general would have taken a different turn, especially if the plans being put off had led to them being put away.

From November 3 on, Beethoven followed the traditional route via Nuremberg, Regensburg, Passau, and Linz and completed the final leg to Vienna by public transport. Beethoven arrived there on Saturday, November 10, 1792, a somewhat grayish autumn day. At the time, he still had no inkling that Vienna would become his second home, the place where he would eventually build his entire career, and that he would never see the city of his birth again.

PART TWO

A Time of Proving

(1792–1802)

Vienna in 1792

LIKE BONN, VIENNA WAS A CITY WITH a high natural density. As the capital of the archdukedom of Austria and the epicenter of the Hapsburg monarchy, it was one of the four main powers in the international political arena, alongside London, Paris, and St. Petersburg. It also held absolute sway over the region of central Europe. As competitors, Prague and Munich had already been relegated to secondary status, and Berlin, while powerful and well organized, lacked an aura of tradition. Vienna was also the residential city of the emperor, the head of the "Holy Roman Empire and the German Nation." He was thus the only world leader with a mandate legitimized by God, an influence that had a palpable effect on both the city of Vienna and its population.

The immensity of Vienna's power stood in stark contrast to its physical size. The city center—the modern-day First District—covered less than one and a half square kilometers. The distance from north to south (Rotenturmtor to Kärtnertor), or from east to west (Stubentor to Schottentor), could be traversed on foot in just over fifteen minutes. One English traveler even reported that "the walls of Vienna can be walked round by a party of ladies, chattering all the time, within the hour."[1] But even the area occupied by the city's thirty-four suburbs, encircled by the Linienwall (more or less the current ring road), amounted to no more than around fifty square kilometers. Starting from the city center and traveling via Burgtor and Mariahilferstrasse, the suburban city limits (the Mariahilfer Linie) could therefore be reached within thirty minutes. The current Westbahnhof railway station is where the Weg zum Schönbrunn—or Schönbrunn Palace Road—once began, and after traveling its two and a half kilometers, one could truly say that one had reached the countryside.

In 1792 Vienna had a population of around 250,000, a figure dwarfed by the cities of London (with over one million), Paris (over half a million), and even Naples and Glasgow. But given its limited surface area, Vienna was still one of the most densely populated cities in Europe. In the city center, nigh on sixty thousand inhabitants were crammed into large residential blocks at least four stories high. Driven by necessity, the elevated construction gave Vienna a unique allure and left a majestic impression on foreign visitors. English writer Mary Montagu once remarked that it looked as though several cities had been built one on top of the other.[2] But because the narrowness of the city's medieval streets and squares was disproportionate to its elevation, Vienna also had an oppressive quality. There was a mighty stench, which reached its height during the summer; in winter the overcast skies and lack of light, air, and space, in combination with the tall buildings, weighed heavily on the residents' constitutions. Vienna was also unbelievably hectic—there was always a hideous din—and the tiny streets were quite unable to accommodate the nervous jostling of the dense crowds. The Vienna of 1792 was paralyzed by traffic: carriages came to a standstill, there were myriad reports of traffic jams and gridlocks at intersections, and defenseless pedestrians were constantly at risk of being run down. The city's nightscape, on the other hand, was illuminated by around three thousand streetlights, making nighttime transport easier and increasing the residents' sense of safety and security.

The high concentration of people and industry gave Vienna a metropolitan flair. In many respects it was not only a modern but also a wealthy city, offering a high degree of luxury and comfort. Even at the end of the eighteenth century, the "face" of the city was determined to a large extent by its many exclusive stores and stylish cafés and restaurants—in stark contrast to the suburbs, which were squalid, miserable, and unhygienic. Among other things, a serious problem with the drinking water made suburban living conditions particularly woeful, leading to mortality rates far exceeding those in any other major European city.

The high quality of life in the inner city was due chiefly to its skewed demographic composition. Besides court officials (who along with their families constituted one fifth of the population), the city's makeup was colored by the many public servants and bureaucrats who populated the government institutions. Vienna was, after all, the seat of a great many administrative entities. The centralization policy implemented by Maria Theresa and Joseph II had given rise to administrative bodies that ran not only the Holy Roman Empire but also the archdukedom of Austria, the kingdoms of Bohemia and Hungary, and of course the city of Vienna itself. As a result, within the span of several decades, fully one tenth of the buildings in the Viennese city center had acquired an administrative function and one third of the population belonged to the new class of civil servants. Other denizens included the many lawyers and lobbyists, who gravitated traditionally toward such epicenters of power, along with a new elite of bankers and entrepreneurs drawn to the capital by modern mercantilism. The casualties were the ordinary citizens and practitioners of traditional professions—craftspeople and tradesmen—who were expunged from the center and driven toward the city's outskirts.

The apex of the Viennese social pyramid was, however, still occupied by the imperial court and the old nobility, although the court had lost some prominence, having sought rural refuge in the cocoons of Schönbrunn, Laxenburg, and Favorita (in light of the rather uninspiring natural surroundings of the more central Hofburg). Empress Maria Theresa also led an austere lifestyle, keeping the ceremonial (and thus more culturally oriented) aspects of her office to an absolute minimum. Her successor, the dispassionate Joseph II, pushed this no-nonsense policy to its limits, leaving the doors open for other noble families to rise to social and cultural prominence. There were also clear consequences for the architecture of the city. The eighteenth century saw the construction of no fewer than three hundred noble residences, some of which—Schwarzenberg Palace at Mehlmarkt (the modern-day Neue Markt), Palais Lobkowitz on Spiegelgasse, Liechtenstein Palace at Minoritenplatz, Esterháza on Wallnerstrasse, and Kinsky at Freyung Square—had an allure and furnishings to rival even the most impressive buildings of church and state.

The nobility was thus a powerful force in Vienna despite its limited physical scope. There were twenty "princely" families, seventy "counts," and around sixty "barons" (*Freiherrschaften*). The caste was also very self-contained—not only did they all know one another; they also intermarried. In the case of Beethoven's patrons, this resulted in the following tangle of interfamilial relations: Prince Franz Joseph von Lobkowitz, who married Maria Karolina von Schwarzenberg, was related to the Ulfeldts on his father's side. One of his cousins (Countess Maria Wilhelmine von Ulfeldt) married Count Franz Joseph von Thun and had several daughters, one of whom married Prince Karl von Lichnowsky, and another—Countess Maria Elisabeth von Thun—who married Count Andrey Razumovsky. The other cousin, Countess Elisabeth von Ulfeldt, married Count Georg Christian von Waldstein. His brother, Count Emanuel von Waldstein, was married to Princess Maria Anna von Liechtenstein and was the father of Count

Ferdinand von Waldstein, whose acquaintance we made in the previous chapter. Maria Anna von Liechtenstein's brother, Count Franz Joseph von Liechtenstein, had a daughter, Princess Maria Hermenegild, who was married to Prince Nikolaus Esterházy, and a granddaughter, Princess Maria von Liechtenstein, who married Prince Ferdinand von Lobkowitz—the father of Prince Franz Joseph von Lobkowitz—making the circle complete.[3]

But nature is unforgiving, and while the concentration of genetic material may help to safeguard the integrity of the patrimony and preserve cultural values, such a high degree of inbreeding also permits dangerous genes to be expressed, which can undermine the strength of future generations. Tales of psychological affliction and hereditary illness among the nobility are legion. Both Karl Lichnowsky and his wife, Christiane, would today be diagnosed as neurotic; Archduke Rudolph was epileptic; and Countess Erdődy—one of Beethoven's most faithful followers—was addicted to opium. Their decadent lifestyles (combined with unfavorable economic conditions in the early nineteenth century) also eroded many a family fortune. The virtually bankrupt Lobkowitz was ultimately put under guardianship; Count Moritz von Fries, also bankrupt, committed suicide; and Count Johann Georg von Browne was institutionalized (more about him later). And as we saw previously, Ferdinand von Waldstein tried to escape his perilous situation first by leaving the Teutonic Order and then by marrying into money; he then squandered his wife's family fortune and ultimately wasted away, dejected and alone, in a dismal garret somewhere.

But in 1792, most noble families still seemed to prosper. They sourced their income from the large estates they had acquired over the bygone centuries in exchange for imperial favors. The Esterházys were the wealthiest by far; they owned 400,000 hectares of land (an area slightly larger than Rhode Island) and ruled over 45,000 families, securing them roughly 700,000 guilders—a paltry twenty million euros—in tax-free interest per year. The Schwarzenberg, Kinsky, Lobkowitz, Waldstein, and Lichnowsky families also collected exorbitant incomes. Under such conditions it is hardly surprising that the aristocrats had their own ideas about what constituted a meaningful life. Aristocrats did not "work"; rather, they "spent their day" engaging in activities whose importance was dictated by the conventions of their social status. They attended religious ceremonies, paraded through town, made excursions to the Prater (an amusement park to the north of the city), frequented cafés and restaurants, attended concerts, theater performances, balls, and other gatherings, and put in appearances at events organized by other members of the aristocracy. These might include prestigious concerts by one's own Kapelle, a wind ensemble, or a private pianist—some families (including the Auerspergs and the Lobkowitzes) even staged entire opera productions. Generally the bar was set a little lower, however. When a Viennese nobleman "made a house" (i.e., threw a party), one could be assured of an evening's free entertainment which—in addition to food, drink, and a measure of music, dance, and engaging conversation—also entailed less lofty cultural pursuits, such as cards, gossip, and flirting.

The Viennese nobility lived according to their own biorhythms (one's social status rose the later one could afford to get out of bed and, by extension, have lunch) as well as their own set of values. The time and energy required to ferry oneself from one event to another and to don suitable attire for each occasion—which for noblewomen was already half a day's work—were just as valuable as the time spent at the events themselves. Style therefore clearly ranked above substance. According to Madame de Staël, the Viennese social delights were considered part of one's obligations; diversions exacted the same level of discipline as business affairs, and time was systematically used and abused.[4]

This carefree cheerfulness, a pained superficiality, was all show, however. It camouflaged a fundamental sense of melancholy that was attributable partly to the Viennese character and partly to the prevailing ethos of the age, which would later receive the fitting epithet *Weltschmerz,* or "world-weariness." The Viennese aristocracy were, after all, grappling not only with an undefined turn-of-the-century angst but also with a deep-rooted sense of desperation. Their times were changing: they were losing their grip on society, and their decadent lifestyles were clearly no longer sustainable. The majestic consecration of the present moment was the only remaining escape from this perceived impasse, and constituted a buffer zone between the nostalgic glorification of the past and the dismal prospects for the future.

The social isolation of the aristocrats thus became ever more pronounced; only occasionally did they condescend to mix with the *zweite Gesellschaft,* or those of lesser or no aristocratic heritage. The Hofburg Palace's Redoutensaal ballrooms—one large and one small—were the most suitable arena for this purpose. The pseudoanonymity and promiscuous atmosphere of the masked balls, held mostly during carnival, offered the ideal opportunity to be less discerning in the company one chose to keep. But while there were well-intentioned attempts to open up the concerts in the Augarten, picnics in the Prater, and the many Freemason gatherings to a broader public, whether they served to promote integration or confrontation is still a matter of debate. What is certain is that the new aristocrats and wealthy citizens made little progress with the old guard and came no further than imitating their noble, hedonistic lifestyles.

In 1792 the Viennese had every reason to be concerned for their future. The preceding years had been turbulent indeed. The extravagances of Joseph II had generated much consternation among the old elite and had brought about serious conflicts, while the best-laid plans of his successor Leopold II (to make improvements by charting a course of moderation and reconciliation) were thwarted by his passing on March 1, 1792. His sudden death gave rise to all manner of wild hypotheses—that he was supposedly poisoned by Freemasons, Jesuits, or French spies[5]—none of which are probably true. But the conspiracy theories do serve to illustrate the widely held belief that Austria would have become a very different place had Leopold II succeeded in implementing his reforms.

Leopold II's successor, his eldest son Francis, was cut from different cloth. He was of below-average intelligence and clearly preferred idleness to exhaustion. He was obsessed with maintaining the status quo, was particularly paranoid when it came to revolutions, and many feared that his accession would usher in a dark period in Austria's history (he was coronated, of all days, on July 14—the anniversary of the storming of the Bastille in Paris). The Viennese were quite disdainful toward their new emperor, claiming that while Emperor Francis was not the first of his name, he would most certainly be the last. The first half of his long reign in particular was punctuated by multiple fiascos, the most dramatic of which were the collapse of the Holy Roman Empire in 1806 and his demotion by Napoleon from "Emperor Francis II of the Holy Roman Empire" to "Emperor Francis I of Austria." One year earlier he had failed to defend Vienna from occupation by a foreign power for the first time in 350 years, when Napoleon literally spent the night in Schönbrunn Palace. The crises did not stop there. In May 1809 a strategic blunder by Francis I resulted in a second occupation of Vienna by the French. He suffered the ultimate humiliation one year later, when to prevent further catastrophe he was forced to offer up his eldest daughter, Louise, as a pawn in marriage to his archrival Napoleon. Francis did experience a fleeting moment of glory in 1814 when given the opportunity to organize the Congress of Vienna, although even then his role was more as master of ceremonies than as a diplomat, and he delegated most of the important work to his deputy, Metternich.

The year 1792 therefore represented a turning point in Austrian history. The death of Leopold II had dashed any remaining hopes for a mild and nonconfrontational modernization of the antiquated regime. The repressive and restorative policy pursued by Francis I was both nostalgic and unproductive and did nothing to hide the fact that Austria had reached a period of transition; the old was already out, but the new was not yet in. Beethoven's arrival in the city at this precise moment, while coincidental, was nonetheless of crucial importance. For average citizens, such transition periods are generally cause for concern and even anxiety; for great artists, however, they offer fertile ground for exploration and development.

Beethoven arrived in Vienna on Saturday, November 10, 1792. While not terribly cold, the overcast sky lent the city an unwelcoming, even eerie atmosphere. Viennese autumns and winters can be quite dismal and oppressive, as the days are short and evening usually begins sometime in the afternoon. It is then that people seek out the communal comfort of the cafés; for those who know nobody, melancholy soon becomes a trusted friend.

The initial days were arduous. Beethoven had a laundry list of practical matters to attend to: obtaining new (warm) clothes, wood for heating, and last but not least, a piano. The latter was no insurmountable problem in itself, as late-eighteenth-century Vienna had a large piano rental market. The Viennese moved house often—Beethoven would do the same—which meant that twice a year, on April 23 (St. George's Day) and September 29 (St. Michael's Day), many of the city's denizens changed address. Only the most personal items—clothing, books, paintings, and household necessities—were brought along; basic furnishings were provided by the landlord. Pianos naturally did not fall under this category, and so those wishing for a piano were reliant on the specialized market for rental instruments. It was a flourishing and lucrative one to be sure, since Vienna boasted around six thousand amateur pianists and three hundred or so professional piano teachers (at the time, the city had more piano teachers than doctors). Most pianos available for rent were of rather poor quality, and Beethoven had trouble finding an instrument that met his high standards, for which he paid a relatively large price.[6]

Vienna was an expensive city. According to Viennese chronicler Johann Pezzl, those who "had no family, were not civil servants, and did not gamble or keep a regular mistress" could live reasonably well in 1793 Vienna on an annual salary of 775 guilders.[7] But for a young musician whose income was, in principle, limited to an annual stipend of 300 guilders, this was a considerable sum. Beethoven therefore tried to live economically, keeping a ledger during the first few months to maintain an overview of his expenses.[8] He did permit himself certain luxuries, including coffee, cocoa, sugar, and cosmetics such as pomade and powder. He also purchased beautiful and expensive clothes, silk stockings, and very smart footwear, as he quickly sensed that the Viennese attached great importance to external appearances and attractive attire.[9] To aid in his integration, at one point he even purchased an old-fashioned wig; the same rationale likely prompted his decision to take dancing lessons. He must have heard that the many Viennese balls offered the perfect opportunity to earn oneself a place in society, and being unable to dance in Vienna was a social handicap—a maxim that still applies to this day.[10]

Beethoven therefore needed additional income, which he earned by giving piano lessons and publishing various piano and other works composed in Bonn. Yet these means seemed insufficient, and his financial situation gave him cause for concern on more than one occasion. Panic even arose upon his father's sudden death on December 18, 1792, when it turned out that the imperial decree granting Beethoven half of his father's salary as a maintenance payment for his two brothers—150 guilders—had gone missing. After a politely worded but desperate letter from Vienna, and most likely an intervention on the home front by Franz Ries, the matter was eventually resolved. This period left Beethoven, who was already scarred by the problems of his youth, with an almost existential fear of poverty that would last the rest of his life.

Beethoven's First Patron

KARL VON LICHNOWSKY

BEETHOVEN WAS SPARED AT LEAST ONE major inconvenience on his arrival in Vienna. Thanks to recommendations by Waldstein, he had obtained lodgings in the Alsergasse home of the count's relative, friend, and fellow Freemason Karl von Lichnowsky. Beethoven was initially put up in the attic, but after complaining of feeling miserable he was moved to the ground floor after only a few weeks. Lichnowsky himself lived one floor above, allowing the prevailing social standings to be preserved. Most chic and prestigious first and second floors were occupied by the rich and the nobility; the ground floors were for stores and small workshops, while the uppermost rooms (called *garçonnières*) were reserved for young functionaries and students.

Beethoven thus lived in a small ground-floor room for over eighteen months, until he accepted Lichnowsky's invitation in October 1794 to join him on the first floor. This was a crucial development. By so doing, Lichnowsky not only provided the young pianist with room, board, and even an allowance during the first few years, but he also gave Beethoven a new social standing, which would later be recognized as his first step toward the life of a free artist. In effect, Lichnowsky proclaimed himself Beethoven's patron, introducing a new dependency into their relationship, of which Beethoven was probably well aware but was in no position to refuse.

Lichnowsky's decision to take the young Beethoven under his wing was a perfectly natural one given the personal histories of both himself and his wife. During his law studies in Leipzig and Göttingen, he had concerned himself primarily with matters more musical than legal in nature. He was an excellent pianist and in Leipzig had become intrigued by the music of J. S. Bach. It was also then that he joined the Freemasons and the Illuminati, where rather than blossoming directly into a great ideologist, he was chiefly preoccupied with the maintenance of international relations.[1] He thus built up a network that would be of particular benefit to him later during his charitable musical endeavors. Interestingly, on being initiated into the Illuminati, Lichnowsky chose the very prophetic pseudonym of "Maecenas."[2]

Back in Vienna, Lichnowsky took piano lessons with Mozart, attended the Sunday afternoon soirées at the home of Baron van Swieten (as befitting a proper Bach apologist), and frequented the salon run by Countess Thun, the most popular society address in all of Vienna. It was there that in 1788 he first entered into a relationship with a daughter of the house and his future wife, Maria Christiane, thus anchoring him firmly to the sociocultural epicenter of Viennese life.

Lichnowsky's mother-in-law, Countess Maria Wilhelmine Thun, had cultivated an excellent reputation as the hostess of her splendid salon. Her guests could always be assured of the most select company and were frequently introduced to the latest celebrities in the arts and sciences. Her salon's fine repute was due chiefly to her greatest talent, that of social management. With charm, flair, and a healthy dose of feigned enthusiasm, she moved among her guests like a seasoned director, artfully rescuing a flagging conversation on one side while elegantly defusing a volatile discussion on the other. She seemed to be everywhere at once, introducing two strangers here while at the same time (and virtually unnoticed) shepherding another, somewhat overexcited guest into less dangerous conversational territory elsewhere. She was the beloved matriarch of social ritual, where it was not thoughts but opinions that mattered, and her principal skill lay in keeping a finger on the social pulse—and more importantly, keeping her own under control.

Countess Thun's mastery of the art of sociocultural choreography was matched only by her tragic ineptitude at marrying off her three daughters. Despite being among the most beautiful and desirable debutantes in Vienna (it was not for nothing that they were dubbed "the three Graces") and receiving petitions from many a rich and elegant aristocrat, at least two of them were corralled into marriages that ended in disaster. The eldest daughter, Maria Elisabeth, was driven into the arms of Russian ambassador Andrey Razumovsky, who would later play a pivotal role in Beethoven's career. He had built up such a sordid reputation that the emperor himself felt compelled to warn Countess Thun of the impending danger. At first glance, Razumovsky appeared to be a handsome, intelligent, well-bred, and spiritually inclined gentleman, and a brilliant representative of the Russian aristocracy. Behind this façade, however, lurked a man of highly questionable moral standards; these he may or may not have acquired at the court of St. Petersburg, which at the time warranted comparison to a snake pit, a bordello, or perhaps both.[3] He was appointed ambassador by Catherine II and sent to various European capital cities, where he left a string of astronomical debts, broken hearts, and illegitimate children in his wake. Eventually he settled in Vienna, where he subsequently plunged Maria Elisabeth Thun into a dire marital misadventure.

The other mismarried daughter, Maria Christiane, fared no better with her Lichnowsky. Alarmed by her elder sister's experience (who had suffered a severe *prima nox* trauma), she tried to cancel the wedding at the last minute and fled to a nunnery. To the great amusement of the Viennese newspapers— the historical equivalent of our tabloids—a deluge of reciprocal damage claims followed, accompanied by a legal battle, much of which was conducted in public. The matter was ultimately resolved, albeit far from amicably. The marriage went ahead; however, it was said of the "happy couple" that they had ceased talking to each other even before the wedding took place. Family friend Ludovika (Lulu) von Thürheim wrote in her memoirs that their emotional distance was due in part to their conflicting temperaments. Von Thürheim reports that although highly intelligent, cultivated, and eloquent, the countess also suffered from chronic melancholy, was haughty, stubborn and aloof, and suspicious to the point of paranoia.[4] By contrast, the count was characterized as "a cynical savage and a shameless coward" who almost considered himself to be "above the law."[5] Although her analysis may be slightly biased by a measure of female solidarity, other sources confirm Lichnowsky's promiscuous conduct. It is known that he had at least one illegitimate child (who was subsequently raised by his wife) and that he died from the complications of syphilis. These same sources also state that Lichnowsky had an anxious and insecure personality and that he constantly and compulsively yearned for the love and affection that he never received at home. Neither of these two assessments necessarily excludes the other, of course.

The grating disharmony of their private lives contrasted sharply with the Lichnowskys' shared love of music and the joint efforts they expended on their adopted son Beethoven. Like her mother, Maria Christiane kept a salon, where every Friday morning the city's best musicians would perform. The Schuppanzigh Quartet, which would later specialize in the performance of Beethoven's string quartets, gave their first performances in the Lichnowsky home. Mozart had always been a welcome guest and an old friend of the family. In an attempt to promote him abroad and help him obtain a permanent post, Lichnowsky even organized a grand concert tour for Mozart in the spring of 1789. Traveling via Prague, Dresden, and Leipzig, they ultimately arrived in Berlin, where Mozart (unlike Beethoven seven years later) was given a rather cool reception—political relations between Berlin and Vienna were strained, and diplomatically the Prussian king could not afford to welcome the star of the Viennese music scene with open arms. It was also during this trip that the relationship soured between Mozart and Lichnowsky, and the latter revealed once again just how petty he could be. Despite the enthusiastic response wherever he went, Mozart returned to Vienna with hardly any new prospects and was weighed down by the debts he had incurred to match his companion's standard of living. His situation went from bad to worse: two years later, some weeks before his death, Mozart was ordered to repay a debt of 1,435 guilders to Lichnowsky. The patron had taken his own protégé to court.[6]

Perhaps Lichnowsky's conscience plagued him after Mozart's tragic death, and he attempted to atone for his behavior by providing for Mozart's predestined successor. Whatever the case, his initial motives would still have served his own purposes. All Viennese aristocrats had a fondness for music and a long tradition of organizing private concerts and opera productions. But not all members of the nobility had the financial resources to maintain a private orchestra, especially as rising inflation was causing priorities to shift. They therefore went in search of alternatives, such as the extremely popular wind octets (*Harmoniemusik*) of the 1780s. Some went a step further and limited themselves to a single piano virtuoso, not only thanks to the more attractive price/quality ratio but also because a "house pianist" was far more flexible in terms of time and space than any other ensemble form. A piano soloist also satisfied the increasing demand for the deeply personal, expressive, and even bizarre leanings in the arts, granting even more opportunities for aristocratic sponsors to stand out from their peers.

It took some time for Lichnowsky to realize that Beethoven could fill the void created by Mozart's death and that he had a golden opportunity to distinguish himself both from other aristocratic families and from the increasingly influential "new nobility" and other wealthy citizens. Despite having been thoroughly briefed by Waldstein, he had Beethoven wait for two years in the wings (or rather, in a tiny room on the ground floor) until he was adequately convinced of Ludwig's exceptional talent. But after that there was no stopping him, and Beethoven was asked by Lichnowsky to entertain the nobility at every opportunity with his dazzling, fantastical, and "unprecedented" skill at the piano. Occasionally piano duels were held, where Beethoven was pitted against a fellow pianist to the great enjoyment of the audience-cum-jury. This budding form of the musical "eisteddfod" was extremely popular in Vienna. One famous example was the duel organized in 1781 by Joseph II between Mozart and his rival Clementi, which remained the talk of the town for years afterward. After the start was sounded with a mighty *A vous, allez-y!* (Over to you, gentlemen!), the artists staged a head-to-head battle like seasoned wrestlers, each gradually raising the musical and technical bar with cleverness and cunning. The battle culminated in a stunning combined finale, a magnificent to-and-fro of call and response, of subject and countersubject. Both pianists performed literally and figuratively *con brio* and enjoyed themselves immensely.[7]

Unlike Mozart and Clementi, Beethoven nurtured a profound dislike for this type of competitive spectacle. The greatest threat to Beethoven's ego was Beethoven himself, after all, and *that* battle was already complex enough. What is more, the responses from his contenders (who inevitably lost) ranged unpredictably from humble admiration to vicious envy. Following a masterful victory at the home of Count Kinsky against the house pianist and erstwhile friend of Mozart's, Abbé Joseph Gelinek, the latter—with Christian meekness—graciously acknowledged his superior in Beethoven: "This young man is possessed by the devil. Never before have I heard such playing! And he improvised on a theme of my choosing in a manner that I never heard even from Mozart [...] He draws out the greatest complexities and effects from the piano, the likes of which none of us ever dreamed were possible."[8] In 1800, by contrast, a duel with Berlin pianist Daniel Steibelt ended in great hostility. The protégé of Count Fries first played one of his own piano quintets and then presented a very well prepared "improvisation" on the theme from Beethoven's Trio for Piano, Clarinet, and Cello (op. 11) that he had heard several days before.[9] Steibelt, whom Beethoven considered a charlatan in any case, played in his own somewhat primitive style, with limited melodic refinement and simplistic left-hand parts containing an abundance of tremolos, a trick that always garnered him immediate but superficial success. Beethoven was so incensed at this caricature of his own music that on the way to the piano he snatched up the cello part from Steibelt's quintet, placed it ostentatiously upside-down on the stand, and proceeded to hammer out the (now inverted) cello theme with a single finger, following up with an impressive set of variations. Steibelt stormed out, declared

Beethoven his archrival, and swore that he would never show his face in public alongside Beethoven's again.[10] Five years later, a similar circumstance involving Pleyel would see a more amicable conclusion. After a concert of Pleyel quartets at the Lobkowitz residence, Beethoven was also urged to perform. At the insistence of various female admirers, a grumbling Beethoven made his way to the piano, grabbing the second violin part from the Pleyel quartet as he did so. During his improvisation, he brought out a fragment of the violin part in the inner voices as a kind of cantus firmus, after which an astounded Pleyel could do nothing but kiss Beethoven's hands in admiration.[11]

Occasionally more lofty interests were at stake. The 1798 battle between Beethoven and Joseph Wölfl (who was three years' Beethoven's junior) gave rise to a controversy that received wide press coverage and which some commentators compared to the 1770s battle between the adherents of Gluck and Piccinni in Paris. Their arguments extended beyond the duel's mere athletic nature, crossing into the realms of market positioning and territoriality, as well as musical and social ideologies. At the time of their confrontation, Beethoven and Wölfl both had strong reputations and were vying for the public's favor. Their artistic visions, however, could not have been more different. Wölfl, from the Salzburg school, was technically very gifted—his large hands were capable of conjuring passages from the piano at breakneck speed—but of rather superficial substance.[12] Beethoven's playing, while rough and even sloppy, sacrificed everything in favor of expression, imagination, and compositional complexity. The confrontation was further fueled by the social schism that lay between their respective patrons and supporters. Wölfl had the backing of Baron Raimund von Wetzlar, a new aristocrat from the nouveau riche. He was thus a "meritocrat" and not a "real" aristocrat in the eyes of the traditional nobility. Wölfl's popularity thus resided chiefly among the wider but less cultured public. Beethoven, on the other hand, was the protégé of a genuine prince, who represented the elite among cultural consumers. The former group (the "music lovers") required easily accessible music, while the latter (the "connoisseurs") pretended to a love of greater complexity and an aversion to low-hanging fruit. Beethoven turned these social positions to his advantage; one witness to the battle against Wölfl wrote that Beethoven aimed not to impress through empty virtuosity but instead went in search of the "mysterious" and the "somber." His offerings were described as a kind of "Sanskrit" or "an arcane language, whose hieroglyphs are decipherable only by the initiated."[13] This last remark in particular illustrates the ideological schism cultivated by Beethoven's supporters. The report was written in an elevated, sentimental, quasi-religious tone that aimed to provide a literary counterpart to Beethoven's musical style, and which probably revealed more about the beliefs of the adorers than those of the adored. Beethoven's audience did not merely "listen"; they "took part" in séances of an almost spiritual nature, were transported and moved to tears, and felt privileged and elevated through their communion with the artistic genius.

Strangely enough, the mesmerizing quality of Beethoven's improvisations lay not exclusively in the power of his imagination. It may seem counterintuitive, but Beethoven always went into his improvisations well prepared; he never worked impulsively and generally always had a clear structure in mind. According to Czerny, he usually selected his material very carefully.[14] Of course, Beethoven sometimes incorporated superficial passagework à la Steibelt, or gave "narrations" in recitativo style. But he also amazed with well-conceived, truly operatic melodies and even dashed off a baroque fugue now and then. Some improvisations—again according to Czerny—had a free, rhapsodic structure, and occasionally Beethoven did play a potpourri of sorts, but as a rule he always extemporized within a discernible framework, such as a sonata or rondo form. Beethoven also regularly employed the panoply of tried-and-true techniques, playing to his audience's sensibilities. He generally had a preconceived idea of when he would impress with surprises and unexpected changes of mood, and calculated the moments when he would pit low and high musical culture against one another, which must have charmed those in Lichnowsky's camp very much indeed.

Lichnowsky and Beethoven ended up in their codependent partnership because of their largely overlapping interests. The relationship was complex, partly because both were strident personalities with an affinity for the eccentric, but also since neither could rely on any social norms to provide a model for this rather subtle form of servitude. Lichnowsky's intentions were sincere, but the more he tried to treat Beethoven like an equal, the more Beethoven rebelled against his protection. He refused, for example, to take "lunch" with the Lichnowskys every day at four, and other well-meant initiatives by Lichnowsky also met with some resistance.[15] When the prince instructed his staff always to serve Beethoven first and with the greatest deference, Beethoven hired his own servant. And when Lichnowsky gave him the use of his horses, Beethoven—who was barely able to provide for his own needs—purchased a horse of his own.[16]

Lichnowsky took all of this in his stride and shepherded Beethoven's career like a true manager. He organized informal play-throughs, hiring musicians who would then make suggestions for improving Beethoven's new compositions; he had Beethoven's first works published and distributed in Vienna; and he helped Beethoven acquire concert engagements and commissions, even organizing a major concert tour in 1796. He also gifted Beethoven a marvelous set of quartet instruments to foster the best possible performance of his chamber music,[17] and from 1800 onward—in anticipation of Beethoven finding a suitable post—paid him an annual wage of six hundred guilders. This magnanimous gesture had a flipside, however; the amount, though small change at the time for Lichnowsky, was both too great for Beethoven to refuse and too small to allow him to live and work comfortably. Beethoven therefore needed to supplement his income from other sources but could not escape the shackles imposed by Lichnowsky. With this stipend, the "benefactor" had essentially obtained exclusive rights to the artist at a bargain price, a fact that heightened Beethoven's ambivalence toward his new status. On the one hand, he viewed Christiane as "a second mother" and declared that Lichnowsky, despite some minor "disagreements [. . .] was always, and still is, my closest friend." On the other, he suffered from an almost irrepressible urge to escape their suffocating protection: "The grandmotherly love shown to me went so far, at times it was like I had been covered with a bell-glass, shielding me from the touch or breath of any unworthy figure."[18]

Beethoven tried to escape by living elsewhere, and in the spring of 1795 he moved to a house several streets away on Kreuzgasse. He understood that it was better for him to live apart, but at the same time was sensible enough to remain in the Lichnowskys' vicinity. This arrangement kept their relationship manageable while also keeping the door open to certain opportunities, such as Beethoven's regular visits to the Lichnowsky country estate in Grätz.[19] Furthermore, there are indications that for many years the Lichnowskys remained Beethoven's confidantes when it came to artistic matters. It was the Lichnowskys who urged Beethoven to remain true to his compositional style in the face of ongoing criticism that condemned the extravagance of his music. And although barely credible, the well-known *Leonore* anecdote—in which the Lichnowskys hosted a crisis meeting in December 1805 after the failed premiere of Beethoven's first opera, and when Christiane supposedly convinced Beethoven to make much-needed and fundamental changes to the score—remains a testament to the close bond that existed between Beethoven and his patrons.

Nevertheless, 1806 saw an end to Lichnowsky's patronage and his stipend to Beethoven, a turn of events that is generally attributed to an incident that took place that same year at Lichnowsky's castle in Grätz. After a dinner organized for the French military, Beethoven was summoned to improvise at the piano. He refused, partly due to a provocation by one of the officers (who, unaware of whom he was talking to, asked Beethoven whether he also knew how to play the violin) but also partly because he simply happened to be in a rather Francophobic mood. The more Lichnowsky insisted, the more obstinate Beethoven became; eventually he stormed out of the castle, trudging through wind and weather to reach Troppau (Opava) some distance away. Beethoven was so out of sorts that he did not notice the irreparable damage done to the scores he was carrying, among them the *Appassionata* Sonata. He is then purported to have sent a letter from Troppau with the following famous words: "Prince, what you are, you owe to chance and birth; what I am, I owe only to myself. Princes have and will always exist in their thousands—of Beethoven, there is only one."[20] On his return to Vienna, he took the bust of Lichnowsky that had stood on his piano for years, and dashed it to smithereens.

It is difficult to separate the romanticism in this tale from reality. Beethoven's alleged use of the anarchic slogan—as authentic as it may seem— is secondhand, and in more ways than one. It is actually a variation on a very well known contemporary aphorism by Bonn aesthetics professor Eulogius Schneider, who in a contentious apology for the French Revolution claimed that "true nobility can only be attained through greatness of spirit and goodness of heart."[21] It is also hardly likely that the incident was what prompted Lichnowsky to terminate the contract, as we can safely assume that over the years he had become only too familiar with the workings of Beethoven's *raptus*. Another theory, suggesting that Beethoven had taken umbrage at Lichnowsky's meddling in his private life, is undoubtedly closer to the truth (Lichnowsky had shamelessly colluded to thwart Beethoven's love for Josephine von Brunsvik). However, the real cause most likely lies in Lichnowsky's sorry financial state and the extravagant lifestyle he had led for so many years. Swimming in debt and embroiled in an unpleasant inheritance case, the prince was forced to economize drastically. And while Beethoven's six hundred guilders were but a fraction of Lichnowsky's total debts, it is a universal law that the arts are always the first casualty in times of economic need.

Thus a partnership came to an end that had lasted nearly a decade, and Beethoven was forced to go in search of alternative means of survival. The

Lichnowskys nonetheless earned themselves a place in the music history books, not only through their own initiatives but also because Beethoven dedicated a number of major works to them. The prince's name graced the title pages of the Piano Trios (op. 1), the *Sonate pathétique* (op. 13), the Piano Sonata in A-flat Major (op. 26), and the Second Symphony (op. 36), while the princess was honored with a ballet, *The Creatures of Prometheus* (op. 43).

13

Haydn and Albrechtsberger

BEETHOVEN'S SUCCESSES AS A PIANIST quickly allowed him to find his feet in the fickle city of Vienna. He was not distracted from the primary purpose of his visit, however, which was to take composition lessons from Haydn. Beethoven reached out to the old master almost immediately on his arrival, and Haydn agreed to see him several times a week at his Seilerstätte residence. Haydn first had Beethoven complete exercises in what is known as "strict" or "species counterpoint": a training method that was devised by Viennese church musician and composer Johann Joseph Fux and is elucidated in his treatise *Gradus ad Parnassum* (1725), a volume still used today to familiarize young pupils with the principles of voice leading. It is an abstract discipline in which additional voices (or "counterpoints") are written to accompany a given theme consisting only of long, even notes (the cantus firmus, or "fixed song"). As a rule, each additional voice may consist only of a single note value—minims, crotchets, or syncopated minims—and must obey several strict criteria. Four-part textures are thus created. The example below illustrates just how abstract the discipline is:

The technique is exceptionally contrived. Species counterpoint is to real music as crossword puzzles are to poetry. Still, the seasoned musical pedagogues of the day remained convinced of the benefits of putting students through this musical and intellectual wringer. Haydn, too, subjected Beethoven to exercises of this type, although his approach was a relatively mild one. Beethoven breezed through the entire Fux course within only a few weeks, and Haydn's correction of the three-hundred-odd exercises was rather cursory. Counterpoint aficionados have since pointed out many errors that Haydn himself failed to identify, interpreting Haydn's oversights as a lack of dedication to his young pupil from Bonn. Viennese composer Johann Baptist Schenk even circulated a rumor that Beethoven simultaneously took counterpoint lessons from him, so frustrated was he by Haydn's lax attitude. The claim is a blatant lie, however; Schenk simply harbored an intense dislike for his fellow composer, and the story was a fabrication intended to bring Haydn into discredit.[1]

In reality both teacher and student simply had better things to talk about, namely their ideas on the newest directions and developments in composition. Since Mozart's death, Haydn had indisputably taken his place as the most influential and modern of all composers. His many years spent in relative seclusion at the court at Esterháza, away from the hustle and bustle of the capital, had allowed him to experiment freely with the string quartet and symphonic genres and develop a set of modern and cohesive compositional techniques. His new successes in Paris and London were also proof that he understood the tastes of the growing middle classes, making him the ideal candidate to teach Beethoven how to translate effects and expression into a well-conceived and structured musical framework. Haydn made use of a tried-and-tested pedagogical approach: Beethoven was instructed to transcribe entire works by Haydn himself and Mozart (Bach had done the same with works by Buxtehude) to learn the finer points of composition through imitation. We can assume that Beethoven also showed Haydn his newest efforts, eager to obtain his teacher's feedback and suggestions. Lastly, Beethoven completed a kind of internship in Haydn's own "laboratory"; in the summer of 1793 he accompanied Haydn to Eisenstadt, where he shadowed the composer as he worked on one of his *London* symphonies (no. 99) and two sets of string quartets (opp. 71 and 74).

The significance of this latter period of study cannot be underestimated. In Bonn, Beethoven had already demonstrated his command of the fundamentals of composition. He could write a beautiful and coherent melody, knew the principles of classical structure, had mastered every stock-standard harmonic device, and had a thorough grounding in orchestration. In short, he practiced the profession the way hundreds of his colleagues—from Abel to Zumsteeg—did every day. At the same time, however, he was only too aware that Haydn and Mozart had an edge that set them apart from the rest of their colleagues: more-complex thematic material, richer polyphony, more-adventurous modulations, greater motivic integrity (often spanning multiple movements), and a well-measured but healthy serving of unpredictability. Beethoven also wished to compose this way, and his time with Haydn was a unique opportunity to witness and absorb such creative bounty with his own eyes and ears.

After one year, both teacher and student posted a report to the elector in Bonn. The parcel they sent contained not only two letters (one each from Haydn and Beethoven) but also copies of five "newly composed" works as proof of Beethoven's diligence and progress. In a suitably servile tone, Haydn made a fervent case not only to extend Beethoven's time in Vienna but also to increase his allowance. Haydn professed that his pupil took a frugal and thoughtful approach to spending, and assured the elector that the funds would continue to be put to judicious use. (The plea was also partly motivated by self-interest, as Haydn charged royally for his lessons to Beethoven, and several months prior he had lent him the considerable sum of five hundred guilders.[2]) But the elector would have none of it. He accused Beethoven (and by extension, Haydn) of attempting to swindle him by presenting works that had already been composed *and* performed in Bonn, and suggested that Beethoven might be better off returning home: "For I am in grave doubt as to whether his tastes or compositional skill will have improved significantly, and—just like his first trip to Vienna—I fear that he will bring home nothing but debts."[3]

Beethoven is generally denounced for his purported attempt to pull the wool over the elector's eyes—an attempt that is regarded as an early instance of a recurring tendency by the composer to engage in deception. The reality could not be more different, however. New research (including an analysis of the sketches from 1793) has demonstrated that four of the five works sent to Bonn were either composed or at the very least revised/rewritten in Vienna. The elector's accusation thus held little water and most likely arose from a cursory and superficial assessment by his advisors, who were intent on having Beethoven return to Bonn as soon as possible. The elector issued no ultimatum, however; Beethoven was not summoned back to Bonn, and the payments continued, albeit without Haydn's proposed increase. Beethoven's decision was a simple one.

Haydn continued to support Beethoven, and when invited back to London in 1794 he even contemplated taking Beethoven along with him. When this proved impossible (and we can only guess as to why), Haydn sought out the best alternative for continuing Beethoven's instruction and introduced him to a man who was the very embodiment of both master and schoolmaster: Johann Albrechtsberger.

After their parting, Haydn and Beethoven never lost sight of one another. Haydn was in attendance, for example, at the premiere of Beethoven's Piano Trios (op. 1) at the Lichnowskys' in August 1795. Haydn is reported to have expressed some concerns about the third trio—Beethoven's favorite—in C minor. Some cite this moment as a crucial turning point in the rising tensions between the celebrated veteran and his ex-pupil. But Haydn's comments merely expressed his doubts regarding the popularity of such an unorthodox work. The fact that he never would have published such a trio himself had nothing to do with the quality of the music: the risk was simply too great.

That same year, Beethoven was invited by Haydn to perform as a soloist in a high-profile concert in the Hofburg's main Redoutensaal. The program included three of the old master's *London* symphonies, a selection of concert arias, and Beethoven's own First Piano Concerto (op. 15). The concert was so successful that it was repeated after several weeks. One year later, Beethoven insisted on dedicating his first three published piano sonatas (op. 2) to Haydn—a noteworthy gesture, since apart from the opus 12 Violin Sonatas (which were dedicated to Salieri), Beethoven would never again dedicate a work to a fellow composer. And although we cannot entirely exclude opportunism as a motive (Haydn's name on the title page lent a certain weight to the publication), Beethoven's gesture was nonetheless a fundamentally sincere one. Haydn did once suggest that Beethoven present himself as a "pupil of Haydn"; for Beethoven, this was clearly a bridge too far. According to Ries, Beethoven confided in him that while he had certainly taken lessons from Haydn, he never actually learned anything...[4]

The relationship between Beethoven and his former teacher became somewhat troubled after 1800, when Haydn achieved immense public acclaim with his oratorio *The Creation*. Beethoven, who at the time was poised to become the number-one celebrity on the Viennese music scene, was frustrated by Haydn's popularity and scoffed at the cheap word painting employed in his oratorios.[5] In turn, the elderly and increasingly frustrated

Haydn had difficulty accepting the fact that he was forced to step aside and make way for Beethoven's mighty new brand of music making. It was not for nothing that he referred to Beethoven as a "Telemachus" and a "mogul."[6] Some historians even claim that the reason Haydn never completed the commissions he received from Prince Lobkowitz (for six string quartets) and Count Fries (for six string quintets) was because these gentlemen had placed identical concurrent orders with Beethoven.[7] Haydn's remark at the end of his final unfinished quartet (op. 103)—"All my strength is gone, I am old and weak"[8]—might be interpreted as an admission that he no longer felt able to compete with Beethoven. If this is so, the question remains as to why Haydn should have confessed his inferiority to Beethoven in, of all genres, a string quartet.

The story came to a happy end, however. On March 27, 1808, a gala concert was held in the auditorium of the University of Vienna to celebrate Haydn's seventy-sixth birthday. The city's crème de la crème, with Prince Esterházy's wife as the belle of the ball, gathered for a performance of *The Creation*. Salieri conducted, and the well-known violinist Franz Clement (who one year earlier had premiered Beethoven's violin concerto) led the strings. Haydn was literally carried into the hall to the jubilant eruptions of trumpets and timpani; afterward, the crowd cheered with a standing ovation that lasted minutes. Salieri left the podium and embraced the old master, upon which Beethoven approached and kissed his hands, with tears in his eyes.[9] Viennese high society thus bore witness to the theatrical reconciliation of two great musical masters.

Several weeks before Beethoven's own death, he received a touching gift from Anton Diabelli, a lithograph depicting the house of Joseph Haydn's birth in Rohrau. According to Gerhard von Breuning, Beethoven was moved and said: "Look, look at what I received today. Such a tiny house! And to think that such a great man was born there."[10] Beethoven then made a final symbolic gesture and had the artwork framed.

But back to 1794. Haydn had sent Beethoven to Johann Albrechtsberger. Haydn and Albrechtsberger had long been good friends; they were not only contemporaries but compatriots as well, both hailing from Lower Austria. Albrechtsberger was from Kosterneuburg in the north, and Haydn from Rohrau bei Bruck an der Leitha in the east. One might therefore say that Haydn had more "gypsy blood" in his veins, which occasionally found expression in his music and lifestyle. They both spoke the same German dialect, however, and were kindred spirits from the countryside. Their childhoods were also remarkably similar; as choirboys (Albrechtsberger in Melk, and Haydn in Vienna) they had both received a thorough musical education during their formative years and been instilled with the spirit and morals of the church. This left an especially prominent mark on Albrechtsberger, who not only spent his whole life in choir lofts and organ boxes but also maintained a rather conservative outlook on humanity and the world in general. His views on music, too, were nostalgic and pessimistic. As a zealous proponent of the stile antico, he felt little affinity with contemporary musical culture. He was fond of lamenting the decline of the old values, of denouncing the inferior craftsmanship among the new generation of composers, of complaining about new audiences' lack of decorum, and saw opera buffa as the bête noire of depravity and decadence, laying waste to the art of true music.[11] His own output was limited mainly to religious works, counting over forty masses and several hundred graduals, offertories, antiphons, hymns, motets, and other works for liturgical use. This earned him the favor of Emperor Francis II, who duly appointed him Kapellmeister of St. Stephen's Cathedral in 1793.

Albrechtsberger had thus mastered the techniques of "early" music like no other. He was a bona fide counterpoint machine, of whom it was said that not one of his musical ideas was ever unsuitable for double counterpoint. He also felt a calling to profess and pass on his knowledge, experience, and musical ideology to young musicians who were still open to the old ways. He therefore also wrote two treatises, one of which—the 1790 *Gründliche Anweisung zur Composition* (Fundamentals of composition)—became a best seller, making him the most prominent and successful teacher of composition in Vienna and surrounds.

When Beethoven commenced lessons with Albrechtsberger three times a week in the spring of 1794, he undoubtedly knew whom he was dealing with and what he might expect. But in contrast to his lessons with Haydn, Beethoven now exclusively took instruction in "free" counterpoint. While his studies with Neefe had already given him a thorough grounding in Bach's *Well-Tempered Clavier,* he now learned to construct his own two, three, and four-part fugues, assimilating the principles of imitation (both *rectus* and *inversus*), augmentation and diminution, as well as canonic techniques. Beethoven was not well disposed to the discipline and struggled with the stringency of the imposed limitations. He found Albrechtsberger a "musical pedant,"[12] but was spurred on by the realization that such learning was essential for him to grow into a fully fledged composer. He would later emphasize, on multiple occasions, just how valuable his studies with Albrechtsberger had been. When the English pianist and composer Cipriani Potter asked him to recommend a good teacher in 1817, Beethoven's wistful response was reported as, "I have lost my Albrechtsberger, and have no confidence in anyone else."[13] Previously, Beethoven had sent Ferdinand Ries, the son of his Bonn acquaintance Franz Anton Ries, to Albrechtsberger for the theoretical component of his studies. There is also testimony of Beethoven having recommended Albrechtsberger's treatise as the best available counterpoint textbook in 1825.[14] As a token of gratitude, from 1816 to 1817 (at a time when he was quite preoccupied with other matters) Beethoven gave composition lessons to Albrechtsberger's grandson, Carl Friedrich Hirsch. Aside from Archduke Rudolph himself, no other could claim to have enjoyed this exclusive privilege.

The counterpoint lessons continued for just under eighteen months, after which Beethoven felt adequately equipped to venture out on his own. His training was now complete. Unlike most of his contemporaries, whose horizons remained limited to the new "simplicity" and "ease" of the rococo style, Beethoven's lessons with Neefe, Haydn, and Albrechtsberger, plus the weekly Bach and Handel concerts at the home of Baron van Swieten, had made him very familiar with the handiwork of the great baroque composers. From Carl Philipp Emanuel Bach and Joseph Haydn, he had also learned how to harness his natural sense of freedom and fantasy and channel it into a coherent musical form. In other words, Beethoven's own principles, which would henceforth govern the expressions of his "exalted and free musical spirit" (in the words of Albrechtsberger[15]), had now been embedded within a long tradition, the laws of which he had thoroughly and meticulously made his own.

Meanwhile, the tumult in the Rhineland continued to worsen. Shortly after Beethoven had left Bonn, the French made several major military advances. All signs pointed to an imminent occupation of the Left Bank, which would fulfill the long-cherished French dream of having their national border coincide with the natural divide of the river. Maximilian Francis saw the trouble looming and fled once again, this time to Münster; he would not return until April of the following year, when it was clear that the tables had well and truly turned. The execution of Louis XVI boosted solidarity among the other European nations, giving rise to a major anti-French coalition among virtually all countries. Although originally it appeared as though the coalition might finally take control, in December 1793 the French gained the upper hand once more, forcing the allies to retreat further beyond the Rhine. Until 1794, Cologne had managed to resist total defeat only due to internal problems among the French; this time, their capitulation was complete. On October 9 a French revolutionary tree of liberty was planted in the Cologne market square, complete with a Jacobean cap and tricolor sash. The 1795 Peace of Basel legitimized and legalized the French occupation of the Left Bank; Koblenz became the region's new epicenter, and the court in Bonn was dismantled. The former electoral residence gradually became deserted and bled dry.

Maximilian Francis watched this scene unfold with grim resignation, and from a safe distance. In October 1794 he once again left Bonn—this time for good—and was given responsibility for a smaller, less prestigious but far more agreeable Hapsburg appanage. He spent the rest of his life south of Vienna at Hetzendorf Castle, one of the summer mansions of the late lamented empress, and died there on July 27, 1801. Beethoven, who visited his old master on multiple occasions, very nearly dedicated the First Symphony to him. That he eventually never did so is a historical accident with great symbolic meaning.

Given the circumstances, Beethoven returning to Bonn was out of the question—a fact of which he was only too aware and which filled him with mixed feelings. On the one hand, it conveniently resolved the nagging issue of whether his future lay in Bonn or elsewhere in some more prestigious musical metropolis. On the other, he retained a nostalgic longing for his homeland. In the summer of 1801, he wrote to his best friend Wegeler: "my fatherland, that lovely place where I was brought into the world, is still as clear and as beautiful to me as when I left you [. . .] the moment when I shall be able to see you again and greet old Father Rhein will be one of the happiest of my life."[16] His longing to return to his hometown would become especially keen during his final years. In 1820 he wrote to Bonn publisher Simrock, expressing hopes of visiting his parents' graves the following year; he reiterated the same wish one year later. Likewise, letters from his childhood friend Wegeler and his wife, Eleonore née Breuning, tell of how much they longed to embrace him once more.[17] Alas, they never would.

14

Career Plans

WE CAN ONLY IMAGINE WHAT MIGHT HAVE HAPPENED if Maximilian Francis had remained in Bonn and succeeded in maintaining political control. Would Beethoven, after one or two years of study in Vienna, have returned to his beloved hometown? Or would a headstrong Beethoven— euphoric from his successes in the musical metropolis and spurred on by enthusiastic supporters—have emulated Mozart's infamous exodus from Salzburg and allowed a quarrel with his superiors to escalate beyond resolution? Beethoven always had terrible difficulty making such agonizing choices. Luckily, fate was in his favor this time; in the absence of either an elector to summon him home or a dominating father to influence his decision, he was spared the anguish of that particular thorny dilemma.

Beethoven's greatest ambition was still to become a Kapellmeister. Once Bonn was no longer an option and Beethoven was forced to set his sights on other European courts, his first order of business was to build up a solid reputation, first in Vienna and then elsewhere. But despite its many promenades, Vienna was no "walk in the park"; competition was fierce, and opportunities were relatively scarce compared to London or Paris. His strategy therefore demanded cleverness and caution, and a good measure of determination.

It is unclear who played the role of "PR manager" in Beethoven's first years in Vienna, or who plotted out the career path he was to take. Lichnowsky likely had a strong hand in the matter, although we can assume that Beethoven also had his own ideas on how to win the hearts of the Viennese. Whatever the case, the marketing plan was sound, and within a short time the unknown young provincial pianist from Bonn had become the icon of the Austrian capital's new music scene. Although the public's enchantment with the new virtuoso was attributable both to Beethoven's unique brand of musical charisma and to the void that Mozart's death had left behind, the ingenious approach taken to the various promotional activities also moved things along appreciably.

With forethought and careful timing, Beethoven's circle of followers and admirers was gradually expanded. Beethoven's first two years in Vienna were devoted principally to convincing the core of the network—the discerning aristocracy—of his exceptional talent. Although Waldstein had enthusiastically sounded the propaganda trumpet in advance, it was still vital for Lichnowsky's friends and relations to witness Beethoven's unique musical abilities with their own eyes and, more importantly, their own ears. For this reason, Beethoven initially gave only private concerts, either at the Lichnowsky home or in the salons of other members of the nobility. The programs consisted mainly of long solo improvisations, occasionally interspersed with chamber works, during which Beethoven was accompanied by one or more musical aristocrats. On rarer occasions, Beethoven would present one of his piano-sonatas-in-progress, as a means of gauging its effects on the audience. There is a record, for example, of a performance at the Lichnowskys' of the Piano Sonatas (op. 2) dedicated to his teacher Haydn, with Haydn himself in attendance.[1] The recitals hosted by Gottfried van Swieten from the 1780s onward were somewhat unique and focused exclusively on the music of Bach and Handel. Beethoven, who had acquired a thorough familiarity and appreciation of Bach's music during his studies with Neefe, was a welcome guest and impressed the company with his ability to rapidly master works by Bach and, especially, Handel (who in Beethoven's estimation was the greater of the two). These sessions, which took place in a casual atmosphere, often carried on until after midnight. Because the city gates were already locked by that time and Beethoven could no longer return home, the baron would invite him to spend the night: "I shall expect you here at eight-thirty in the evening, with your nightcap!"[2]

After two years, the time was ripe to go in search of new audiences. This was no easy task, as late-eighteenth-century Vienna offered few opportunities for young virtuosi to present themselves to a wider public. The Viennese cultural scene was dominated by opera and theater. On any given evening, one could choose between performances in the two "state theaters" (the Burgtheater and the Kärntnertortheater) or any of the less prestigious houses in Josefstadt, Leopoldstadt, and Auf der Wieden. Only on *Normatagen,* or the major feast days on which opera and theater performances were prohibited (on Fridays, during Advent after December 15, in the final three days of

Lent, and on official public holidays), were theaters open to ordinary concerts. Other sporadic opportunities arose in the Hofburg's two ballrooms—the large and small Redoutensaal—however, these were subject to the same restrictions as the state theaters. One final option was offered by the prestigious morning concerts given in the Augarten park (usually in the open air) and in Mehrzwecksäle, multipurpose venues in restaurants and private ballrooms that offered an alternative public stage for appearances by orchestras and virtuosi. These included the Trattnerhof (Graben), the Mehlgrube (Neuer Markt), and the Jahnse Saal (Himmelpfortgasse).

The city was thus utterly lacking in both institutionalized concert-giving organizations and purpose-built concert halls (Vienna would not see its first, the Musikverein, until 1831). Musicians turning to one of the city's major theaters to organize an *Akademie* (an independent concert put on for one's own benefit *and* at one's own expense) were generally required to run the entire operation themselves: hall hire, police permits, advertising, ticket sales, even arranging a passable orchestra. These independent events had also been greatly discouraged since Joseph II drastically limited the number of accessible days in these venues to fifty per year, in an attempt to seize control of public and cultural life. Baron Peter von Braun, who had been appointed superintendent of the state theaters in 1794, eagerly supported the new policy and took pleasure in his attempts to thwart any and all private initiatives. Arranging an *Akademie* was therefore tantamount to a kamikaze mission, especially for a young virtuoso who could not yet be assured of a major following.

The benefit concerts run by the Viennese Tonkünstler-Sozietät (Musicians' Society) founded in 1771 were another matter entirely. On two occasions per year, shortly before Easter and Christmas, two concerts were held to benefit the Fund for Widows and Orphans of Court Musicians. All of the city's musical professionals voluntarily lent their talents to the performance of a major oratorio, and during the intermission an international or rising star would perform a concerto. The lack of any financial reward was amply compensated for by the amount of free publicity, and so it made sense for Beethoven to make his first public appearances in this arena. On March 29 and 30, 1795, Antonio Salieri conducted the oratorio *Gioas re di Giuda* by his student Antonio Carellieri. Beethoven performed his Piano Concerto in B-flat Major (op. 19) during the first evening's intermission,[3] substituting it the next evening with a long improvisation.

A critic from the *Wiener Zeitung* reported "a completely new concerto for the pianoforte";[4] in reality, the work was a revised version of a concerto that

Beethoven had composed in Bonn in 1790.[5] Telltale signs lie in the instrumentation (which was quite modest by Viennese standards: only seven winds and no trumpets or timpani) and in the choice of thematic material, which is more reminiscent of Mozart's style. Beethoven had already revised the concerto once before for a private performance given in Vienna in 1793. The new changes were even more drastic, however; he completely overhauled the second movement and composed an entirely new finale with greater rhythmic interest and a more diabolical character.[6] The concerto would not attain its final form for some time: more changes were introduced in 1798 for a concert performance in Prague, and in preparation for final publication by Franz Anton Hoffmeister in 1801, Beethoven revised it yet again. This was the first time the piano part had ever been written out in full, as Beethoven's prior performances had always been from memory and included extemporized passages. To Beethoven, a written-out piano concerto was a contradiction in terms, as it eliminated the all-important element of surprise. It was also the reason he wrote to Breitkopf & Härtel saying that it was always advisable not to publish the best concertos straightaway, but to keep them in reserve.[7]

This protracted compositional process can only be described as typically Beethovenian. Can we name a single work by Haydn or Mozart that saw five different versions over a ten-year period? It also highlights the insecurities and indecision that plagued the young and inexperienced Beethoven. When making revisions, for example, it was not uncommon for him to resurrect an idea that had already been laid to rest during a previous correction.

The concerts on March 29 and 30, 1795, were a success, and the *Wiener Zeitung* reported "unanimous applause" from the audience.[8] As a direct result, the following day Beethoven was invited to perform as the guest soloist in a benefit concert organized by Mozart's widow at the Burgtheater. During the intermission of a concert performance of *La clemenza di Tito*, Beethoven performed one of his favorite concertos, Mozart's Piano Concerto in D Minor (K. 466). He did so with great fervor and captivated the audience with brilliant cadenzas.[9]

The following winter, Beethoven performed twice more in the small Redoutensaal: once on December 18, 1795, during a benefit concert for Haydn, and a second time on January 8, 1796—with the same program but this time organized by opera singer Maria Bolla. These concerts, too, enjoyed widespread acclaim. Haydn had just returned triumphantly from London and was eager to present some of his new symphonies to the Viennese public. With the entire establishment in attendance, Beethoven made use of the opportunity to present a new work of his own, the Piano Concerto in C Major (op. 15). Preparations were hectic. The final movement was finished only just in time, and four copyists were hired to transcribe the orchestral parts from the score while the ink was still wet on the page.[10] The work was so unorthodox that the customary single rehearsal on the morning of the concert was grossly inadequate, necessitating an additional rehearsal at Beethoven's home with the principal members of the orchestra. The rehearsal was almost canceled, however, as Beethoven's piano had been tuned a semitone lower than orchestral pitch. Without batting an eye, Beethoven salvaged the situation by playing the entire concerto a semitone higher, a superhuman feat of musical prowess. Nothing is more difficult than transposing a piece of music up or down by one semitone, not least since any previously learned fingering is rendered utterly useless (for this reason, transposing by a whole tone is much easier). But rather than simply recalling visual scores or executing fingering patterns, Beethoven's musical thought was entirely abstract and could be recalibrated to suit the new key. Even under the given circumstances, however, this was no easy feat: the concerto's musical contours were fundamentally rooted in the C-major tonality of the trumpets and timpani and therefore directly at odds with the character of the new—albeit virtual—key of D-flat major. According to Schindler, Beethoven believed that ignoring the idiosyncrasies of the various tonalities was tantamount to "denying the influence of the sun and moon, or the ebb and flow of the tide,"[11] and constituted a form of musical heresy. During the rehearsal, Beethoven may therefore have even improvised new solo material to some extent.[12]

During his initial years in Vienna, Beethoven's strategy was to build up his image as a pianist and improviser. This was no easy task, for competition was cutthroat and we have it on record that Beethoven saw most of his fellow pianists as sworn enemies.[13] Nevertheless, he quickly reached the top of the pianistic pecking order, and the time was eventually ripe to add composition to his musical portfolio.

Beethoven had hitherto been very selective when publishing his own music—a deliberate choice on his part, as he still did not feel fully fledged and first wanted to complete his studies in counterpoint. He had also planned to make an impressive debut with several large-scale works that had been in the pipeline for some years. In the meantime, while waiting to introduce several of his "more important works"[14] to the world, he made efforts to prevent the unauthorized publication of several less important sets of variations. This was far easier said than done: in a time without copyright law, music piracy was a serious problem. But legal issues aside, Beethoven also wished to retain absolute control over the quality of any publications that did appear. When news reached him that Bonn publisher Simrock had engraved his *Waldstein* Variations (WoO 67) without his permission, Beethoven wrote a furious letter ordering him to print a new version based on the recently revised manuscript. He fulminated that "at the very least, I might expect to see my works appear in their best possible condition."[15]

It was not until the spring of 1795 that the young artist and his patron-manager Lichnowsky felt that the time had come for Beethoven the composer to share the spotlight with Beethoven the pianist. Beethoven had completed his studies with Albrechtsberger and felt adequately equipped to venture into the realm of free composition. Lichnowsky, for his part, was convinced that Beethoven's support network was extensive and responsive enough to warrant the financial risk of a first genuine publication. The consensus was reached for Beethoven to debut with a set of piano trios, which were to bear the all-important designation of "Opus 1." It was a strategic attempt to generate public interest and is what nowadays might be called a "reboot"; a line was drawn below the past, renouncing all previous compositions, as it were, and shifting the focus on to the new works to come. Lichnowsky first organized some informal play-throughs at his home, allowing Beethoven to make some final corrections. On May 3, 13, and 16—several weeks after Beethoven's successes in the Burgtheater—the *Wiener Zeitung* announced the publication of the new piano trios, with instructions on how to reserve a copy. The response must have been swift and sizeable, as the composer had obtained adequate expressions of interest by May 19 to sign a publishing contract. On October 21, 1795, the "Trois trios pour le Pianoforte, Violon et Violoncelle [. . .] par Louis van Beethoven—Oeuvre première" were released.

The contract signed by Beethoven was extremely biased in favor of the publisher, Artaria & Co. All risk was to be borne by the composer, who needed to sell at least thirty-five copies to cover the costs—a figure that was reached without issue thanks to support by Lichnowsky, who rallied the entire Viennese aristocracy to the cause as though championing a communal charity drive. No fewer than 123 members of the nobility put their names down, some even reserving multiple copies (Lichnowsky set a good example by purchasing twenty himself). Ultimately 245 copies were sold and Beethoven made a net profit of seven hundred guilders (the average annual wage of a civil servant). As was still customary in the eighteenth century, Beethoven was obliged to relinquish the rights to the works for some time.

During that same period, Beethoven also completed work on the three Piano Sonatas (op. 2). Their publication was understandably postponed until the spring of 1796—even aristocratic charity has its limits, and stalling for time would also ensure sufficient interest among the nonaristocratic public. As mentioned previously, Beethoven dedicated the second opus to his former teacher, Haydn. The old master's hand is all but invisible, however, and any discernible influence can be traced back to his symphonic style rather than his piano works. Like Haydn's symphonies, Beethoven's new sonatas each contained four movements, with a minuet or scherzo following the slow movement and an energetic finale. Their length (one and a half times that of the average sonata), sonorous intensity, and overall seriousness and grandeur also suggest a more symphonic allure. In particular, it is the highly structured nature of Beethoven's sonatas that sets them vastly apart from Haydn's keyboard music, which tends to be more capricious and unfettered, even disorderly in places. Beethoven's works, on the other hand, display a level of complexity that is irreconcilable with the typical sonata style up until that time. Some themes are more contrapuntal than melodic in nature; modulations are complex and unpredictable; and some movements are consistently asymmetrical in every respect. Nor is there a single superfluous note to be found, and all traces of facile scales and broken chords are gone. Beethoven had developed an early aversion to "passageworkers," a category of pianist to which he had relegated, among others, his younger colleague Ignaz Moscheles. Unlike such players, Beethoven subscribed to a higher level of "pianism": the force, speed, and complex coordination demanded by his writing almost seems to require an extra finger on each hand, and his pupil Czerny would later attest that when it came to the sheer velocity of scales, double trills, and leaps, nobody was a match for Beethoven—not even Hummel.[16]

During his brief period of instruction with Haydn, Beethoven had come to greatly admire his teacher's achievements in the field of symphonic composition. His admiration was a double-edged sword, however: on the one hand, he had witnessed, analyzed, and assimilated Haydn's methods for symphonic writing, and was champing at the bit to incorporate these new insights into his own work. On the other, he was so intimidated by the success of Haydn's *London* symphonies that he felt the time was not yet ripe to challenge the master on his home turf. A more "symphonic" conception of his piano works allowed Beethoven to circumvent this particular impasse and make musical history by definitively breaking down the stylistic divide between the two genres. Beethoven's first opus number therefore marks the beginning not only of a new period in his own compositional development but also of a new stylistic era.[17]

Beethoven's fame had now reached critical mass, and in November 1795 he was granted a special privilege: an invitation to compose two sets of minuets and German dances for the Austrian Gesellschaft der bildenden Künstler, or Visual Arts Society. This renowned association had organized annual and prestigious gala balls in the Hofburg's two ballrooms since 1792 and, as a special attraction, always commissioned two sets of dances from a prominent composer (or composers). Each year the organizing committee's decision was eagerly awaited, not least by the composers themselves. The list of those selected is a veritable *Who's Who* of the Viennese musical elite: Haydn opened the series in 1792, followed by Leopold Kozeluch in 1793. In 1794 Karl Ditters von Dittersdorf was chosen for the dances in the large ballroom, and Joseph von Eybler for the smaller; this same division was maintained in 1795, when Franz Xaver Süssmayr (well known for completing Mozart's Requiem) was assigned the large Redoutensaal while Beethoven was allocated its smaller neighbor. Beethoven, the youngest composer of them all by far, was therefore already keeping good company.

Dance collections of this type were pure *Gebrauchsmusik* ("utility music," pieces written for a specific event or purpose) and as a rule were not subject to any lofty artistic expectations. Beethoven remained true to himself, however, and set the bar high by composing each group of dances—the Twelve Minuets (WoO 7) and the Twelve German Dances (WoO 8)—as a coherent set. To do so, he drew extensively from the rich store of techniques he had cultivated while writing his sets of variations, expertly walking the fine line between unity and diversity. In both sets, all twelve dances share some thematic or motivic connection and—atypically for the genre—are locked into a rigid tonal scheme of descending thirds and fifths:

Minuets: D—B♭—G—E♭—C—A—D—B♭—G—E♭—C—F
German dances: C—A—F—B♭—E♭—G—C—A—F—D—G—C[18]

The galas always enjoyed a heightened and high-spirited atmosphere, with gracious dancing and courtly flirting, ecstatic twirls and elegant turns, dainty skips, wild leaps, and unruly foot stomping, as well as tender kissing and mischievous groping. Kings were imitated when the minuets were danced, and the peasantry impersonated during the *Deutscher* (the German dances). Under the circumstances, it is doubtful whether the revelers paid any heed to Beethoven's compositional efforts. And yet they must have been impressed, since the same dances were announced again two years later in November 1797 (on December 16, 1795, publisher Artaria & Co. had already announced a piano reduction prepared by the composer himself, so that music lovers could enjoy the dances at home[19]). The lion's share of the newspaper advertisement was dedicated to Beethoven; Süssmayr's contribution was not mentioned until the very end.

Beethoven's next career move was to start giving concerts internationally—an important step in generating publicity for any artist, even today. Though international tours may not always be profitable and can entail astronomical costs, they are often a necessary evil for reinforcing one's position in the domestic market. In Beethoven's case, each concert also had the character of an unofficial audition. Beethoven had realized some years before that returning to Bonn was no longer possible, and was now trying to gain a foothold at several important central-European courts in the hopes of obtaining a post as Kapellmeister.

Early in February 1796, Beethoven and Lichnowsky left Vienna on a concert tour that would take them through Prague, Dresden, Leipzig, and Berlin. If this selection and sequence of cities seems familiar, it might well be—an identical journey was made by Lichnowsky and Mozart in 1789. Lichnowsky's chosen route would have been based first and foremost on his personal network of professional, Masonic, and family relations. But we might also imagine that Lichnowsky was plagued by a lingering sense of guilt from the failed tour with Mozart in 1789, lending the second, identical tour an air of atonement.

Information on Beethoven's time in Prague is scarce. We know that he was warmly received by a public with close ties to his aristocratic support base in Vienna. Many members of the Austrian nobility had Bohemian heritage and regularly shuttled back and forth between Vienna and their second residences in Prague. The Thun family—Lichnowsky's in-laws—were extremely well connected and would certainly have helped Beethoven to gain a foothold in the Bohemian capital.[20]

It is unclear how many concerts Beethoven gave in Prague; we know of only two performances held in the prestigious Convict Hall on February 11 and March 11 in 1796. Audiences were enthusiastic, and reviews appeared praising Beethoven as a "genius" and a "god." Only sporadically were dissident voices heard from critics similar to those in Vienna, who were vexed by Beethoven's rough and untidy playing, his obsession with originality, and his overbearing and overblown sense of expression. Wistfully they longed for a return of what they described as the "controlled, refined and transparent" playing by their former idol, Mozart. According to these "nostalgists," Beethoven had only hyperbole to thank for his reputation. They were convinced that there were many amateurs and connoisseurs alike who refused to be misled by prejudice and political connections, and who also acknowledged—alongside Beethoven's masterful playing—the rising star's substantial shortcomings.[21]

Originally Beethoven was to spend only a few weeks in the Bohemian capital; exactly why he remained for nearly three months remains unclear. It is tempting to draw parallels with the suspiciously large number of works he composed for the eighteen-year-old Josephine von Clary, the daughter of one of the city's preeminent aristocrats. Beethoven must have had extramusical purposes in mind when dedicating two sonatinas, an adagio, and an andante con variazioni (WoO 43 and 44) to her, all written for the unspeakable combination of mandolin and harpsichord. Thankfully, Josephine von Clary was not only a dedicated amateur mandolin player but also a talented singer. Beethoven was obviously far more taken with her voice, as it inspired him to write the commanding concert aria "Ah! Perfido" (op. 65).[22] It is unknown whether she ever sang it in public; we know only that the renowned opera star Josepha Duschek presented it during a concert in Leipzig later that year. Duschek was not just any old singer, as ten years earlier Mozart had written "Bella mia fiamma" (K. 528) for her, which also deals with a woman's sorrow and rage at her abandonment. The work was most likely known to Beethoven, and his own aria is occasionally reminiscent of Mozart's, although its melodic contours and vast arsenal of expressive devices hardly bear comparison.

Beethoven left Prague in late April and traveled on to Dresden. Lichnowsky, however, returned to Vienna as their unexpectedly long sojourn in Prague had eaten into his schedule. He of course gave Beethoven the requisite addresses and references to ensure his further success. Beethoven spent one week in Dresden and had the honor of appearing before Frederick Augustus III of

Saxony (later King Frederick Augustus I of Saxony), whom he regaled with improvisations lasting a full hour and a half. Afterward the elector (who by all accounts had a discerning ear) presented him with a golden tobacco box. But a potential post as Kapellmeister was not in the cards.

Nothing is known about how Beethoven spent his time in Leipzig. But it would seem odd if while in the mecca of the publishing world, Beethoven did not make use of the opportunity to establish as many new contacts as possible. Another tempting thought is that he might have played the Bach organ in St. Thomas's Church, as Mozart himself did in 1789. If so, what a unique experience it must have been for him to stroke the keys and bathe in the sonorities of the very organ where the music was conceived that had so dominated his youth.

Berlin was simultaneously the tour's conclusion and its climax. The Prussian capital had a cosmopolitan flair that differed vastly from that of the other cities, and boasted centuries of musical tradition as well as a strong affinity with the newest trends in the world of music. It was therefore the ideal place for Beethoven to truly establish himself as a modern pianist. His first visit was to the Berlin Singakademie, a choral society founded in 1791 that had attained notoriety as the first institution in Germany to include women in performances of religious music. Alongside its lauded role in the enrichment of society and bringing culture to the middle classes, the Singakademie thus also made a major contribution to the emancipation of women. The same progressive mentality was evident in its bold, refreshing programs, culminating in the historical 1829 performance of Bach's *St. Matthew Passion* under the direction of Felix Mendelssohn. This forward-looking mind-set provided the perfect platform for Beethoven to introduce himself to audiences in Berlin. During the interval of a concert of psalm settings (including some by Singakademie director himself, Carl Friedrich Fasch), Beethoven entertained the audience with a long and impressive fugal improvisation on one of the themes presented during the first half, and was promptly asked to duplicate the feat one week later.

Arguably of greater significance were Beethoven's performances at court, where the Prussian kings had a reputation as connoisseurs. As amateur musicians they were more than competent and spared neither expense nor effort in securing the greatest virtuosi as teachers and composers in residence for the courts in Berlin and Potsdam. The flute-playing Frederick the Great engaged the well-known Johann Joachim Quantz, and Frederick William II—himself an excellent cellist—concluded contracts first with the Italian-Spanish virtuoso Luigi Boccherini and later with the French brothers Jean-Pierre and Jean-Louis Duport. During his visits to court in May and June of 1796, Beethoven not only played his way into the king's good graces but also became intrigued and inspired by the modern and superb cello playing by the Duport brothers. The younger, Jean-Louis, was particularly adept; he had a rich and expressive tone, combined supremely subtle bowing with a mastery of the upper positions (due in part to his use of the thumb), and made ample use of other special effects, such as double-stops and harmonics. When Beethoven was asked to write several new cello works for the king, he immediately put some of these newly acquired insights into practice. And as luck would have it, neither Haydn nor Mozart had ever produced any cello sonatas, which also allowed him to compose freely without the stifling pressure of having to measure up to his predecessors. The opus 5 Cello Sonatas are thus possessed of a highly outspoken and individual character, and later on, when composing the cello parts for his chamber and orchestral works, Beethoven would continue to draw extensively from his experiences in Berlin.[23]

The king was impressed. And unlike the political climate during Mozart's visit seven years earlier, the positive diplomatic relations with the Hapsburgs now *did* allow the king to embrace a poster child of the Viennese aristocracy. Reports by Czerny indicate that Frederick William II even considered taking Beethoven into his service.[24] Concrete negotiations never ensued, however, due in part to the Prussian king's unexpected death in the autumn of 1797. Beethoven's reward was therefore limited to a show of admiration and another golden snuffbox containing several valuable louis d'or. In line with proper eighteenth-century etiquette, Frederick William II thus demonstrated his belief that it was perfectly acceptable for artists to be coddled with a little attention, some encouraging remarks, a few vague promises, and a token gift. But despite such obvious condescension, Beethoven still felt honored. Ferdinand Ries recounts Beethoven's gloating over the fact that he received not just any old snuffbox but one customarily reserved for international delegates. Ries does go on to say that Beethoven could still be of two minds when receiving such tributes: "Although he drew no distinction in his own conduct between those of high or low standing, he was not immune to the attentions of the former."[25] Beethoven would later continue to take pride in the distinctions bestowed on him by both foreign heads of state and international cultural and academic institutions.[26]

During his stay in Berlin, Beethoven also made the acquaintance of Prince Frederick Ludwig Christian of Prussia, better known as Louis Ferdinand of

Prussia. Women were positively electrified by this flamboyant and highly intelligent nephew of Frederick the Great. He had an athletic build, long, blond, curly hair, tanned skin, and luminous blue eyes. Reports by contemporaries describe him as Mars, Adonis, and Alcibiades all rolled into one. Although his uncle Frederick II had predestined him for a military career, his favorite preoccupation was music. He was an avid collector of valuable instruments—apparently owning no fewer than thirteen English pianos—and was himself a gifted pianist, a brilliant extemporizer, and a composer of some merit. Beethoven was heard to have said of him, "He plays not like a prince or a king, but instead like a competent pianist," and even rated his playing above that of Kapellmeister Friedrich Heinrich Himmel.[27] Beethoven got along well with Louis Ferdinand and found him to be an engaging conversationalist. Eight years later they would meet again in Vienna during the prince's diplomatic mission to Austria and Bohemia, when Louis Ferdinand would play a pivotal role in the *Eroica* saga.[28]

After nearly four months on the road, Beethoven returned to Vienna in July 1796. Several days after his arrival, he fell seriously ill with a high fever, severe headaches, a rash, constant nausea, and vomiting. One source, known as the "Fischhof Miscellany" in Berlin, states that he arrived home one hot summer's day dripping with sweat and became "dangerously ill" after opening all the doors and windows and catching a chill from the draft.[29] A far more plausible theory, however, is offered by the Innsbruck-born surgeon Dr. Aloys Weissenbach, with whom Beethoven maintained close contact both during and after the Congress of Vienna. According to Weissenbach, Beethoven had contracted "a dreadful case of typhus."[30] All evidence suggests that Beethoven suffered from a form known as "murine typhus," a disease that was typical of the eighteenth century and quite common in the warmer summer months, and which he had acquired in Berlin through flea bites. Though infectious, ordinary typhus was usually not deadly (even in the days before antibiotics, the mortality rate was only 4 percent) and patients generally made a full recovery within a few weeks. Murine typhus, on the other hand, could cause lasting neurological damage that would not manifest for some time (contemporary reports put the prevalence of these cases at around 15 percent). It would later become apparent that Beethoven belonged to the relatively small percentage of typhus survivors to suffer permanent damage to the nervous system, in his case manifesting tragically as irreversible hearing loss. The same Dr. Weissenbach who diagnosed his typhus later also established this causal connection in 1816.

If all of this is true, it represents a paradoxical turning point in Beethoven's career. During a major concert tour aimed at putting him in the international spotlight, Beethoven acquired the seeds of an affliction that would eventually force him to give up his career as a pianist entirely, as well as his dreams of becoming Kapellmeister. It is unimaginable what course history might have taken if Beethoven had belonged to the 85 percent of patients whose experience of murine typhus was nothing more than a few worrying weeks spent in bed, and a moderate fever.

15

Family, Friends, and Loves in Vienna

IN JUST UNDER FOUR YEARS, Beethoven's career had advanced in leaps and bounds. Gone was the rather timid music student from the provincial town of Bonn, and in his place stood a confident celebrity with a reputation extending far beyond the limits of his new hometown. Evidence for his successful rise to the top of the Austrian music scene can be found in the *Musical Almanac of Vienna and Prague* (Jahrbuch der Tonkunst von Wien und Prag) published by the Viennese-Bohemian businessman and author Johann von Schönfeld in 1796. The *Almanac* is a comprehensive survey of contemporary musical figures from Prague and Vienna, and the section on "Viennese Virtuosi and Amateurs" provides an alphabetized commentary on roughly two hundred composers, from Adamberger to Zois, including Albrechtsberger, Hummel, Kozeluch, Salieri, and Süssmayr (Mozart is sadly missing, since only living musicians were eligible for inclusion). The longest entries are on Haydn and Beethoven, about whom was said: "*Bethofen,* a musical genius who two years ago chose Vienna as his place of residence and is admired far and wide for the speed and effortlessness with which he executes the greatest feats of technical difficulty. Some time ago he appears to have uncovered the art's innermost secrets, the hallmarks of which are precision, sensitivity and refined taste, increasing his fame all the more [...] He has already produced several beautiful sonatas, the most recent of which are particularly striking."[1]

Beethoven therefore had reason to expect a bright future, and one that most likely lay in the Austrian capital. He felt comfortable, had found his feet in more ways than one, and enjoyed the support of several key players in the establishment. Even more important than his dealings with the aristocracy, however, was the comfort he derived from being close to his brothers and the many friends who had since joined him in Vienna. Bonn had been occupied since 1794, and for many of Beethoven's friends and family, seeking refuge in the elector's hometown (temporarily or otherwise) was the obvious choice. As is often the case with immigrant populations, the Rhinelanders formed a contingent, a cocoon-like enclave where they could speak their native dialect, share some home cooking, and enjoy a warm feeling of togetherness. Although Beethoven acknowledged that the Viennese aristocracy was indispensable in his efforts to move up in the world of music—making integration a priority—he remained a fish out of water in aristocratic circles. The Bonn colony acted as a counterbalance, where Beethoven felt at home politically, ideologically, and emotionally.

Although Beethoven's two brothers moved to Vienna chiefly for practical reasons (it was impossible for Beethoven to watch over them while they were in Bonn), their close presence also gave him a deeper sense of security. The elder brother, who now only went by the name of Karl (having dropped Kaspar Anton to avoid associations with Count Belderbusch), arrived in Vienna in mid-1794. Like Ludwig, he had trained as a musician but was clearly far less gifted and had difficulty earning an adequate living. Beethoven even made an attempt to launch him into the world of "light music" as a producer of dances and arrangements (among other things). But these efforts, too, were in vain, and Kaspar Karl ultimately found employment as a civil servant at the Ministry of Finance.[2]

In 1802, Kaspar Karl also became his older brother's private secretary. He wrote letters, negotiated with publishers (sometimes on his own terms), and tried to widen somewhat Beethoven's profit margin. He acted as any devoted manager should, taking a bold, occasionally merciless approach and not always ensuring full transparency. Beethoven regularly received complaints, and his brother's representation frequently did him more harm than good. Still, Beethoven chose to remain sheltered behind his brother's protective screen, and when Kaspar Karl married in May 1806 and could no longer be his secretary, Beethoven was grieved to have to find a replacement.

One year after Kaspar Karl moved to Vienna, Beethoven's youngest brother, Nikolaus Johann, followed his example. Like Kaspar Karl, he also felt the need to change his first name, simply going by "Johann." Beethoven obliged depending on his mood, occasionally even addressing his brother as *"fratello,"* "chemist," "Cain," or sometimes even *"assassino."* Johann had trained as a pharmacist and started working near Kärntnertor gate. He purchased his own pharmacy in Linz in 1808 (the Apotheke zur Krone), his business went well, and he eventually became the wealthiest of the three Beethoven brothers.

The bond shared by Ludwig, Karl, and Johann was strong and was evident in the way they came to each other's aid in times of need. However, their relationship was also complex, made the more so by the tendency of the eldest to interfere in the lives of the other two—particularly when sisters-in-law entered the scene. Much ink has already been spilled on the possible root causes underlying Beethoven's conduct toward his brothers and their wives. It is striking that the critical turning points in his familial relationships always came on the heels of disasters in his own love life, suggesting that his obsessive meddling in his family's private affairs may have been a projection of his own frustrated desires. In his defense, Beethoven was saddled with familial responsibilities at far too young an age, and his judgment may have been so clouded that he was not always able to respect his brothers' rights to manage their own lives.

Some months after Kaspar Karl had settled in Vienna, Franz Gerhard Wegeler also made the journey to the Austrian capital. Wegeler was Beethoven's soul mate, a fast friend and confidant with whom Beethoven could share his innermost feelings. It should be noted that the stability of their relationship benefited in part from the physical distance between them. By 1796, Wegeler had already returned to Bonn, after which their written exchanges remained sporadic and they never met in person again. Still, whenever Beethoven turned to Wegeler it was always in the most heartfelt terms, and Wegeler enjoyed the exclusive privilege of being addressed by Beethoven as "my dearest old friend."

Wegeler was an exceptional man. Born the lowly son of a shoemaker, he quickly rose to prominence as a doctor, a university professor, and—at the ripe old age of twenty-eight—rector of the university in Bonn. He was thus a brilliant exponent of the middle classes, as his career advancement was due in no small part to the democratic policies of Elector Maximilian Francis. In 1782 (when Wegeler was seventeen) he met Helene von Breuning, who welcomed him warmly and, like Beethoven some years later, introduced him to the world of culture and aristocratic etiquette. At around that same time, Wegeler also joined the Freemasons, the Illuminati, and the literary society.[3]

Although it is unclear when Beethoven and Wegeler first met (it may have been in 1784), there is no doubt that despite their five-year age difference they shared an immediate bond and feelings of mutual respect. It is generally assumed that Wegeler was the one who introduced Beethoven to the Breunings, recommending him as piano teacher to Eleonore and Lorenz.

The turbulence of the 1790s made Wegeler's position as university rector very tenuous. His exodus to Vienna in 1794 elegantly circumvented his internal dilemma between loyalty to the old elite, to whom he owed his social advancement, and his revolutionary sympathies, which had been cultivated in the literary society and elsewhere. In 1796 he returned to Bonn, and after the Left Bank was annexed by the French and the university closed in 1798, he became a general practitioner and later the director of the nearby midwifery training institute. In 1807 he moved to Koblenz, the then headquarters of the Rhin-et-Moselle department of the First French Empire. There he embarked on a new career in fundamental healthcare education, launched a crusade against child labor, and performed groundbreaking work in psychiatry, pharmacy, midwifery, and other fields that today would be classified under "alternative medicine."

Beethoven and Wegeler were kindred spirits in many ways. They each viewed their professions as a higher calling, were utterly convinced that they should devote their talents to making the world a better and fairer place, and struggled against the limitations forced on them by tradition. Their friendship was further strengthened in 1802 by Wegeler's marriage to Beethoven's former sweetheart, Eleonore Breuning.

As is not uncommon among the best of friends, Beethoven and Wegeler corresponded relatively little. After 1801, for example, there followed an extended period of unbroken silence until 1810, when Beethoven needed Wegeler's assistance with a banal, practical matter (the acquisition of a birth certificate from Bonn). Such was typical of Beethoven the egocentric: he seldom put pen to paper as a spontaneous expression of kindness and sympathy, but when he needed something, the ink could not flow fast enough. Wegeler never held this against him; on the contrary, he later regretted not having cherished Beethoven's letters more—most had been either destroyed or given away. The few that remain are among the most moving examples of Beethoven's writing still in existence, as Wegeler was the only person with whom Beethoven was always completely honest about his physical and emotional state.

Beethoven's lasting influence on the lives of the Wegelers is evinced by a letter that he received from Eleonore in 1825: "He [Wegeler] greatly enjoys playing the themes of your variations, the old ones are always his favourites, yet still sometimes—with incredible patience—he learns a new one [...] never does he enter the living room without touching the piano—that fact alone, dear Beethoven, shows how you are ever and always in our memory."[4] The Wegelers implored Beethoven to visit them late in 1825; in February 1827, Eleonore once again impressed on him that a reunion would mean the fulfillment of her greatest wish. Beethoven was sadly too ill to brave the long and arduous journey to his hometown and died several weeks later.

Just as there was never a reunion in Bonn, Beethoven never dedicated a single composition to his closest friend (although in May 1810 he did clearly suggest that one of his more recent works was intended for Wegeler). Like he did with his letter writing, Beethoven took a utilitarian approach to the dedication of his works, and his friends always drew the short straw. In the end, Wegeler never took it to heart: "My lot was the same as that of his student Ries: the dedications were only ever in his letters. But does that not merely mean that they are worth even more?"[5]

Wegeler himself helped influence how Beethoven was perceived after his death. He was closely involved in Schindler's biographical plans from the outset and had plenty of material to offer. But once Wegeler suspected Schindler's hidden agenda, he withdrew his support, collaborating instead with Ferdinand Ries on the *Biographical Notes on Ludwig van Beethoven* (Biographische Notizen über Ludwig van Beethoven), which was published in Koblenz in 1838. A supplement to the *Biographical Notes* followed in 1845, coinciding with the unveiling of the Beethoven Monument in Bonn.

Wegeler and Ries by no means intended to write a comprehensive biography, and they wished to relay only firsthand anecdotes. In so doing, they hoped not only to supply useful material for future biographies but also to neutralize the many apocryphal stories that circulated even then: "As regards the content of the ensuing pages, I feel obliged to note that I report only that of which I am absolutely certain. This may go some way to explaining the perhaps somewhat exaggerated compulsion to offer substantiation for every fact. The same applies to my colleague Ries. This approach also gives us the right, however, to suppose that our contributions might serve to dispel various misapprehensions, falsehoods and other distorted reports that have since appeared in writing about Beethoven."[6] In a certain sense their approach was regrettable, as these key figures thus missed a unique opportunity to comment on the more subjective and emotional aspects of Beethoven's life. Wegeler, the doctor and academic, remained particularly superficial in this respect. It is understandable, however, that he was hesitant to embark on a character analysis of his respected and beloved friend and to explore the darker and less personable aspects of Beethoven's psyche.

The Breuning family brothers also followed their adoptive sibling to Vienna. The youngest, Lorenz, accompanied his mentor Wegeler to Vienna as a medical student in October 1794. He visited Beethoven almost daily, in part to continue his formal instruction but certainly also to enjoy making music with his teacher. Both were extremely fond of each other's company, and when Lorenz returned to Bonn in 1797 Beethoven wrote a touching farewell letter: "Never shall I forget the time I have spent with you here or in Bonn. Preserve our friendship, and you shall ever find it with me also."[7] News of Lorenz's sudden death only months later must have grieved Beethoven deeply.

In December 1795, the two elder Breunings—Christoph and Stephan, both lawyers—came to Vienna. The journey, taken in the company of Beethoven's brother Johann, was eventful. A problem with their papers led to their spending five days in police custody in Linz, and they were even at risk of being sent back to Bonn. Their time with Beethoven would be brief, however. In February Beethoven left for Prague on his concert tour; Christoph returned to Bonn six months later, and after only three months Stephan left the city to take up a post in Mergentheim at the headquarters of the Teutonic Order. He returned to Vienna for good in June 1801 to pursue a career in government service. In 1803 he was appointed *Konzipist*—a kind of junior minister—and by 1805 he had been promoted to secretary in the defense department, where high-stakes decisions were made in the field of international relations.

Around that time, Beethoven shared Stephan von Breuning's lodgings in the Rothes Haus, and their cohabitation was both intense and complicated. Although Breuning tried to be as accommodating as possible to his friend in good times and bad, grievances piled up on both sides, culminating in a heated quarrel in July 1804. Beethoven fled to Baden, and wrote a strongly worded letter to Ferdinand Ries, venting his spleen about their mutual friend: "I have nothing more whatsoever to say to Breuning—his attitude and conduct towards me are proof that we never should have become friends, nor shall we ever be so [...] I aim to show him unequivocally that I am in no respect as petty as he is."[8] Beethoven then maintained silence for several months, only to return—as was so often the case—with his tail between his legs, contrite and racked with guilt. As a gesture of reconciliation, he gifted Breuning the lovely miniature made of him by Danish painter

Christian Horneman in 1802, accompanied by a typically Beethovenian, heartrending cry for love and affection:

> My dear Stephan, may this portrait forever <u>bury</u> that which has <u>passed between us</u> of late—I know, I have crippled <u>your heart,</u> and my own feelings—which you cannot but have noticed—have already been punishment enough, it was not <u>anger</u> that rose up in me, no, for then would I no longer be deserving of your friendship […] forgive me if I caused you pain, I suffered as much myself, and it took your long absence from my life to show me just how dear you are to <u>my</u> heart, and ever will be.
>
> Your [Beethoven]
>
> I hope and trust that you will still welcome my embrace as <u>warmly</u> as ever.[9]

Thus mended, their friendship remained intact for another ten years. Stephan Breuning was also closely involved with the *Leonore* rescue attempts in 1806, and that same year he wrote the lyrics for the song "Als die Geliebte sich trennen wollte" (When my beloved wished to leave me, WoO 132). Beethoven expressed his sense of fellowship by dedicating the Violin Concerto to him; the arrangement for piano and orchestra went to Breuning's first wife, Julie von Vering, at whose side Beethoven had spent many a fond evening at the piano.

Their relationship ran thoroughly aground once more in 1815, when Stephan Breuning dared to question Beethoven's guardianship of his nephew Karl. On this occasion, the cuts ran deep and a rapid reconciliation was out of the question, not least because Beethoven's psychological tunnel vision had increasingly narrowed over the course of the "Karl affair." Contact was not reestablished for another ten years, when Beethoven moved to Schwarzspanierstrasse near Stephan Breuning's Rothes Haus, after which he saw his friend almost daily. When Beethoven fell terminally ill, Stephan and his son Gerhard were among the last faithful visitors to his bedside. Stephan himself passed away several months later.

Beethoven had difficulty making new friends, and his chief source of emotional comfort was the small circle of loyal companions from his hometown. The theologist and violinist Karl Amenda from Courland (Latvia) formed the principal exception to this rule, a fact that Beethoven expressly pointed out to him: "You are no mere <u>Vienna friend</u>, no, you are of the sort that are generally to be found in my home town of Bonn."[10]

Amenda spent only a short time in Vienna. In 1798–99 he worked as a private teacher in the Lobkowitz household and for Mozart's widow, and we can assume that it was one of these two who introduced Beethoven to him. They became close friends, and Beethoven (who was feeling particularly desolate after the departure of both Wegeler and the Breunings) stuck fast to his new friend. They were often out and about together, so much so that people often wondered, on seeing one alone, where the other was. Alas, Amenda was forced to return to his homeland in the autumn of 1799 to assume guardianship of his brother's children after their father had suffered a fatal accident. As a farewell gift, Beethoven presented him with the score of the newly composed String Quartet no. 1 in F Major (op. 18, no. 1), which very likely premiered at Amenda's home. On that occasion, Amenda is said to have remarked that the second movement reminded him of a farewell between two friends, which Beethoven confirmed in part: a note left in the margin of a sketchbook reveals his intention to depict the tomb scene from *Romeo and Juliet*. Soon afterward, Beethoven implored his friend never to show the F-major quartet to anybody; it had been so extensively revised that the first version was to be declared null and void. Amenda received the new score, but could never bring himself to destroy the old one.

Although Beethoven and Amenda would never meet again, they corresponded regularly. The tenor of their exchanges was rich with exalted romanticism à la Werther, and lyrical outpourings were more often the rule than the exception: "O my Beethoven! I beg you, do never forget your friend who, though possibly forever distant, shall do his utmost to be more worthy of your affection. As ever, you fill my heart completely, in a manner that other friendships seemingly cannot. I long for you, dearest friend, wherever you may be!"[11] To which Beethoven responded: "Dear, dear Amenda, my precious friend! I was deeply moved to receive your last letter, which I read with simultaneous pangs of joy and sorrow. How can I ever hope to return the loyalty and devotion you have shown to me? How wonderful it is that you still regard me with such favour."[12] In another letter, Beethoven gushes: "Verily, alongside the two people on earth who have ever received my full affections, only one of whom is still living, you are the third. Never shall my memory of you fade away."[13] This remark is broadly taken as declaration by Beethoven that his affection for Amenda was on equal footing with his feelings for Wegeler and (the then already deceased) Lorenz Breuning. These three friends were all possessed of a high degree of empathy, which lubricated their dealings with Beethoven somewhat. Wegeler and Breuning were doctors, after all, and Amenda a theologist. They also knew enough about music to properly appreciate Beethoven's exceptional talents, but because they were not strictly "colleagues" (competitors), they could still look up to him with sufficient adoration. Lastly, it is worth noting that the time spent by Wegeler, Breuning, and Amenda in Beethoven's company was limited, keeping the risk of conflict to a minimum and giving their relationship with Beethoven a "virtual" character. Their exclusively written communication became sporadic and was limited to lyrical expressions of nostalgia. In the words of American Beethoven expert Maynard Solomon, these friends were thus transmuted into "idealised brother figures" and used by Beethoven as surrogates to compensate for the many conflicts he endured with his real brothers.[14]

As he had himself declared to Amenda, Beethoven could not obtain such emotional warmth from his "Vienna friends." These were more like amenable by-standers, whose value to Beethoven was directly proportional to their manipulability and utility. Beethoven did little to hide this fact: "I see him [Zmeskall] and S. [Schuppanzigh] as nothing more than instruments that I play upon now and again as it pleases me, but they shall never become the noble vehicles of my inward or outward purpose, nor ever know me truly. I appraise them entirely in terms of their service to me."[15] Beethoven himself thus proclaimed Nikolaus Zmeskall and Ignaz Schuppanzigh as the primary objects of his cynical and egotistical opportunism. The latter, Schuppanzigh, at least maintained a healthy degree of give-and-take. He had premiered many of Beethoven's string quartets and did more than any other to ensure the success of Beethoven's music throughout Vienna. In return, he earned a place in both Viennese musical life and music history. The Hungarian lawyer Zmeskall (in full, Nikolaus von Zmeskall von Domanovecz und Lestine) sought and found in Vienna a semblance of the former glory of his noble predecessors. He pursued a career as a senior civil servant, and thanks to his musical abilities—he was an excellent cellist and composed around fifteen string quartets—he could actively take part in social musical events at the Liechtenstein, Lobkowitz, and Razumovsky palaces. This is also where he met the greatest artists, including Mozart, Haydn, and Beethoven, and he relished every opportunity to rub shoulders with the musical elite. He derived immense gratification, for example, from dining with Beethoven at The White Swan (Zum weissen Schwan) near Kärtnerstrasse. No inconvenience was too great, not even if Beethoven's whims meant throwing his schedule into disarray at the last minute. Beethoven constantly called on him to arrange all manner of practicalities, large and small, effectively turning him into a glorified minion, a general factotum, and dubbing him "the astounding *plenipotentiarius Regnis Beethovensis*."[16] Zmeskall saw to the hiring of servants and the resolution of any related problems, the search for accommodations, the purchase of sundry items (such as mirrors and glasses), and the procurement of funding. And because of his assiduity in the tedious production of quill pens, he became Beethoven's regular supplier.

Overall the correspondence between Zmeskall and Beethoven (or what remains of it—Zmeskall diligently preserved every letter and note, while Beethoven threw everything away) is polite, brief, and businesslike, and for Beethoven's part drenched in a species of humor verging on the sarcastic. He addressed Zmeskall with cordial but often almost insulting salutations, such as "my dear old count of music" or "Venerable Baron Muck-hauler,"[17] reinforcing the impression that Beethoven held little respect for his crony. Zmeskall must have realized it, but he took it on the chin nonetheless. In April 1809, two days before he was to help premiere one of the opus 70 Piano Trios in his own home, he received a note from Beethoven coolly informing him that he was to be replaced by professional cellist Anton Kraft. He offered not the slightest objection.

Unlike Beethoven's "real" friends Wegeler and Amenda, in return for his faithful service Zmeskall *was* honored with the dedication of one of Beethoven's most significant works, the String Quartet in F Minor (op. 95), demonstrating yet again how Beethoven extended greater generosity to his pseudofriends than to his real ones.

There are few remaining accounts of Beethoven's amorous escapades during his first years in Vienna, owing to the fact that in the late eighteenth and early nineteenth centuries such matters were rarely discussed and virtually never put into writing. Strictly speaking, we have evidence of only one serious affair prior to 1799; in 1795 (or at the very latest the spring of 1796), Beethoven is said to have made a proposal of marriage to singer Magdalena Willmann, also originally from Bonn. Despite the odds appearing to be in his favor, he was turned down. The Willmanns and the Beethovens were old acquaintances. The father, Ignaz Willmann, had been a violinist in the Bonn Kapelle since 1767 and had therefore worked under grandfather Louis and alongside father Jean van Beethoven. In the 1780s he toured Europe with his brood of talented children. The family also resided in Vienna for some time, where they befriended Mozart, and it is even plausible that they took the young Beethoven in during his first trip to Vienna in 1787. But by 1788, the Willmanns had returned to Bonn, where—going by the newspaper reports—Magdalena became a hit with "her elegant and expressive voice" and "her lively and charming performances."[18] Like the court's top musicians, she took part in the infamous Mergentheim concert tour in 1791, where we might suspect that she shared many fond moments with Beethoven. The Willmanns left Bonn in 1793, and father Ignaz became Kapellmeister in Kassel. Some (possibly spurious) sources even posit that he lobbied for Beethoven to be transferred to the Westphalian capital.[19] After various travels through Italy, Austria, and Germany, Magdalena herself arrived in Vienna in the spring of 1795, where her fame also spread rapidly.

It makes sense that Magdalena would have sought contact with the Bonn contingent immediately on her arrival in Vienna, and one might also expect that Beethoven's feelings for her went beyond mere friendship (singers seemed to have that effect on him). Circumstances thus seemed favorable for a marriage proposal, but Magdalena Willmann refused him, instead marrying a wealthy merchant from Trieste in the summer of 1796. The pair stayed in touch, and on one occasion—on January 30, 1801—they even gave a concert together in the Redoutensaal. Magdalena Willmann died unexpectedly several months later.

It is, of course, difficult to ascertain why Magdalena declined Beethoven's offer. A niece of hers later wrote that her aunt thought Beethoven ugly and not a little crazy, although we might question the authenticity of a claim that remained undocumented until 1860.[20] The real explanation may have been that both families simply knew each other too well, and that Magdalena—who was undoubtedly all too aware of the Beethovens' domestic situation and of his father's depraved conduct—was disinclined toward any sort of escapade with the young Ludwig (who had not yet risen to stardom) and, erring on the side of caution, decided instead to marry her Italian merchant.

Her purported opinion that Beethoven was "ugly" and "not a little crazy" is at odds with the many accounts by Beethoven's friends of his popularity among women. Without putting too fine a point on it, Wegeler reported that the young pianist was an attractive force to be reckoned with. Sources state that Beethoven was "never without a love interest, with whom he was generally extremely smitten."[21] In addition to his delight in the charms of Babette

Koch, with whom we are already familiar, Wegeler also mentions affairs with a certain Jeanette d'Honrath, a blonde beauty whom Beethoven had met at the Breuning household, and the purportedly stunning Marie Westerholt, "along with the rest of the et ceteras."[22] Wegeler continues, "For at least as long as I was living in Vienna, Beethoven was always involved with someone or other, and had made conquests that, while not impossible, had certainly vexed many an Adonis."[23] Ries confirmed this assessment: "Beethoven was fond of women, and of young, beautiful faces in particular," although he qualified this statement immediately by adding: "He was frequently love-struck, but usually only briefly. Once, when I pestered him about having won over some beauty or other, he confessed that she had indeed presented a long and intense preoccupation for him—a full seven months." Ries also reported that "whenever we sauntered past a comely maiden, he would make an about-face, appraise her thoroughly once more through his eyeglass, and laugh or grin upon finding his attentions reciprocated."[24]

Beethoven often felt attracted to the young women of the nobility to whom he gave piano lessons or to the singers he accompanied, without explic-itly pursuing any greater intimacy (this was, incidentally, the entire reason Beethoven maintained a long list of private female pupils, despite his aversion to teaching in general). However, given the social barriers that eliminated any prospect of a serious relationship between an aristocratic pupil and a middle-class teacher, it behooved Beethoven to exercise caution in how far he ventured out on the limb of seduction and flirtation. Whatever the case, the singers Josephine von Clary and Christine von Gerhardi, along with pianist Barbara (Babette) von Keglevics, were certainly the objects of Beethoven's augmented sympathies and could count on him as a supremely patient and dedicated mentor. Babette Keglevics (known after her marriage as Princess Odescalchi) was the recipient of a generous many dedications, including the Sonata in E-flat Major (op. 7), the First Piano Concerto (op. 15), the Variations on a Theme by Salieri (WoO 73), and the Six Variations in F (op. 34). According to Czerny, the Sonata in E-flat was written during a "most impas-sioned mood."[25] In Vienna, the sonata was later nicknamed "Die Verliebte" (The beloved), though this does not necessarily prove anything.

Leaving aside the fact that Beethoven's efforts were consistently frustrated by his lower social standing, there are other potential reasons why he never entered into a committed relationship. Maynard Solomon and Barry Cooper subscribe to the idealized and romantic notion that marriage was inherently incompatible with Beethoven's higher artistic calling and that the "high priest of music" had imposed on himself a vow of celibacy.[26] A less lofty appraisal suggests that—analogous to the way his true friends could maintain their status provided they played no major part in Beethoven's daily life—any woman who was fully devoted to him could never reach the level of perfection that he would later idolize in *Leonore/Fidelio*. This skepticism toward marriage, according to Solomon, was fueled by the events of Beethoven's childhood and the negative attitudes associated with his mother.[27] The stifled sexual morals of the Illuminati that colored Beethoven's youth may also have saddled him with some inhibitions.[28] Beethoven may even have derived some comfort from the notion that the perfect marriage to the ideal woman was also the only possible marriage. The more highly qualified the women who won Beethoven's affections, the less available they were and the less pressure he was therefore under to confront his true feelings.

There is a rumor that Beethoven lost his virginity to a prostitute. Schuppanzigh is said to have pushed him into it after some rowdy festivities, after which Beethoven felt so ashamed that he went into hiding for several weeks.[29]

There is a tendency in the Beethoven literature to sweep this fact under the carpet, since it is clearly at odds with his idealistic notions of love and sexuality. It is true that Beethoven, on several occasions, vehemently denounced all forms of promiscuity and prostitution. In a letter from Prague to his youngest brother in 1796, for example, he warns Johann to "be on guard against the league of unchaste women,"[30] and he later called his own sister-in-law a "whore."[31] But in a city where Stefan Zweig declared that it was more difficult to avoid a prostitute than to locate one, the claim that Beethoven never once entered a bordello or a "private chamber"—even purely out of curiosity—cannot be refuted with any certainty.

16

In Anticipation of Greater Things

BEETHOVEN SEEMED TO RECOVER QUICKLY from the malady that had stricken him in 1796, and after a good month of convalescence was able to resume his normal activities. But despite his growing reputation, the time was not yet ripe for his own *Akademie* concert, and he needed to content himself with guest appearances at concerts given by fellow musicians. We know, for example, that he performed the First Piano Concerto (op. 15) in Pressburg on November 11, 1796 (and quite probably several days later again in Pest), and that he was the support act for a concert given in Vienna on December 30, 1796, by the cellist brothers Andreas and Bernhard Romberg, two of Beethoven's former colleagues and Zehrgarten companions from Bonn. Although it was Beethoven's custom to impress audiences with long improvisations, he did sometimes perform works of his own that were already well known, and of course presented new material on occasion. During a concert given by his friend Schuppanzigh on April 6, 1797, he premiered his Quintet for Piano and Winds (op. 16), and on March 29, 1798—also with Schuppanzigh—debuted one of the opus 12 Violin Sonatas.

Opportunities for high-profile international appearances remained elusive, however. Only in October 1798 did Beethoven return to Prague once more to give three public concerts. These would be his final performances abroad, as his hearing difficulties would bring a premature end to his promising career as a concert pianist. He did later make plans to travel as a composer to both Paris and London, and his letters make sporadic mention of intentions to visit Italy, Poland, and Russia. For various reasons, his plans never came to fruition.

In the meantime, Beethoven kept composing fervently, although most of his new works (especially when viewed within the context of his entire oeuvre) were more "occasional" in nature, such as the Serenade for String Trio (op. 8), the Wind Sextet (op. 71), the Three String Trios (op. 9), the two Piano Sonatas (op. 49), and the Trio for Piano, Clarinet, and Cello (op. 11). A prime example of such occasional pieces are the Variations on a Theme by Wranitzky (WoO 71). Anton Wranitzky was a successful and influential colleague of Beethoven's. In 1797, he had become Kapellmeister of Prince Lobkowitz's new orchestra, and his own opera *Das Waldmädchen* (The forest maiden) became a particular favorite among Viennese audiences. Beethoven, who despite his eccentricities never lost his practical business sense, capitalized eagerly on the work's popularity by composing an accessible set of variations on one of the opera's Russian themes, dedicating it to the wife of Count Johann Georg von Browne, one of the city's wealthiest denizens.[1] As a token of her gratitude, the countess gifted Beethoven a horse. What became of the animal we shall never know.

Alongside these many occasional pieces, Beethoven still continued to write works of a more profound nature, which consciously or subconsciously served to expand his musical horizons. The Sonata in E-flat Major (op. 7), composed for his favorite pupil at the time, Babette Keglevics, achieves a level of technical pianism far exceeding any of his previous works in the genre. The opening movement, a sweeping and brilliant Allegro molto e con brio, places new athletic demands on the player, with large leaps, smooth legato and rippling broken octaves, and written-out tremolos. The tone of the piano takes on a depth that was unprecedented for the time—in the third and fourth movements especially, the sonata's predominantly introverted character is disrupted by sudden and diabolical explosions of sound. And because Beethoven was only too aware that expanding his tonal palette had consequences for the overarching musical narrative—in the same way that brush thickness affects canvas size—the dimensions of the sonata expanded accordingly. The second movement, Largo con grande espressione, advances in long, languid strides, generating slow-paced but intense momentum. All of these features make the sonata one of the most monumental that Beethoven ever composed, and consequently one that could not tolerate the close proximity of any other. Beethoven was of the opinion that he could not include the sonata in a traditional set of three and published it separately as the *Grande Sonate* in E-flat Major.

Another groundbreaking work was the song "Adelaide" (op. 46), which although begun much earlier was not published until February 1797. It bears no resemblance whatsoever to the simplistic, strophic ditties for keyboard and voice that enjoyed widespread popularity in eighteenth-century Germany, and to which Beethoven had been introduced by Neefe many years earlier. "Adelaide" is a long, through-composed work, and despite the pervasive symmetry in the poem by Friedrich von Matthisson, the variety in Beethoven's treatment and its ever-increasing scope and complexity blend the song's four verses into a single, elongated eruption of gripping musical expression, itself simultaneously coherent and divergent. Even the refrain—a single cry, "Adelaide!"—is never set the same way twice, as though the composer cannot conceive of enough ways to declare his mounting rapture. In this sense, it loses its function as a refrain and instead takes on the character of a bridging passage, guiding the listener into each successive wave of emotions. Here we discover a new side to Beethoven, who is no longer reasoning deductively but responding associatively, relying on the uniformity of the piano accompaniment and his intuitive mastery of musical rhetoric to lend overall cohesion to the work.[2] Instead of a mere *Lied,* or "song," "Adelaide" has all the hallmarks of an "aria" and was therefore published initially as a *Kantate.* It would be twenty years before Schubert dared to replicate such a feat.

"Adelaide" became immensely popular. It was republished many times during Beethoven's life—a rarity in itself—and was crowned with the greatest possible honor one could hope for in Vienna: it became the immediate subject of parody. It also went down in history as one of the first *Lieder* ever to be performed in public, a privilege ordinarily reserved for opera arias and stage songs. "Adelaide" was aired during a prestigious concert held in the Hofburg's Great Hall (Rittersaal) in honor of the visit by the Russian tsar on December 23, 1814; sources say that the emperor himself authorized the work's inclusion on the program.[3]

Some years prior, in 1811, Matthisson wrote the following about Beethoven's setting of "Adelaide": "Several composers have graced this little lyric fantasy of mine with their music; it is my deepest conviction, however, that the Viennese genius Ludwig van Beethoven succeeded like no other in placing the text so utterly in the shadow of the melody."[4] Such a humble admission is to his credit.

Despite these successes, the two years following his 1796 concert tour constituted a transitional period, leaving Beethoven at somewhat of an impasse. Later he would confess that he was already suffering from the first symptoms of his deafness—his first inkling that the "dreadful typhus" had left lasting damage. However, the main problem was a lack of stimulating projects, such as commissions for string quartets or symphonies. Beethoven felt ready and was waiting for the opportunity to venture out into this more challenging terrain. His chance would come in the autumn of 1798, when he was asked by none other than Prince Lobkowitz himself—the preeminent musical patron of the day—to compose a set of six string quartets. For two and a half years Beethoven would slave over the commission, pouring his heart and soul into his first works in the genre, with a determination that would usher in a new phase in his compositional development.

This turning point was marked by a fundamental change in Beethoven's working methods. In the summer of 1798, he began making systematic use of sketchbooks as the primary means of organizing his musical thoughts. In the past, Beethoven had used reams of loose manuscript paper to document and develop certain ideas (recall that he left Bonn in 1792 carrying not only finished scores but also bundles of sketches). Now, however, these sketchbooks became an essential vehicle in the production of new compositions. Beethoven would spend hours at the piano, playing and replaying certain fragments until he had found just the right solution, then notating them in a book lying on a table beside the piano specifically for that purpose. The process of writing down the sketch introduced an important moment of reflection between the impulsive act of improvisation and the more deliberate act of composition. The time required to direct his thoughts through his hands via pen and paper often afforded a greater clarity, forcing him to modify or let go of certain ideas. Of course, Beethoven's hands never could keep up with his mind, which is why he only ever scribbled out the essence of an idea, leaving formalities such as clefs, time signatures, key signatures, and accidentals for later. The many smaller details, such as ornaments and articulations, which were essential to the expression of the musical material, remained absent at this initial stage of the creation process. Beethoven sketched in the very literal sense of the word, outlining the mere skeleton of an idea that was to be "fleshed out" later.

The sketchbooks are also a frightful mess, serving as both compositional diaries and repositories for new ideas that had no immediate application. At times they give the impression of embryonic databases for as-yet uncomposed works. Beethoven's impulsive character caused him to switch rapidly and without warning from one composition to another and also to include all manner of information in between, such as addresses and expenses. All of this took place within such cramped margins (Beethoven was frugal with paper and used every available inch of space) that his sketches evolved into miniature visual works of art, reminiscent of the rhythmic landscapes of Paul Klee or certain art brut works by Dubuffet.

The sketchbooks, which are emblematic of Beethoven's metamorphosis from a composing pianist to a piano-playing composer, embody a crucial paradox. Despite the chaotic impression they make, they provided the structural impetus necessary to harness and channel the ever-increasing complexity of Beethoven's musical thought. Later, when he began filling entire pages with drafts and ideas for a single work, the sketchbooks would only gain in importance. After some time, Beethoven went one step further: when he began composing more and more during his long walks, he would use much smaller notebooks to jot down musical ideas and subsequently work them out in greater detail in the main sketchbooks at home. This shift in compositional strategy was concurrent with the advent of a more cerebral phase in his music.

The love and care with which Beethoven cherished his sketchbooks contrasts sadly with the nonchalant treatment they received after his death. On November 9, 1827, several months after his passing, they were sold for a pittance at auction. The publisher Artaria obtained the lion's share and tore them literally to pieces, selling the pages to collectors or simply giving them away. The books were thus scattered far and wide,[5] causing irreparable damage to what was not only the most significant but also one of the most fascinating relics of Beethoven's creative process.

Conductor Ignaz von Seyfried, who worked closely with Beethoven, believed that the mixture of order and chaos in the sketchbooks had its origins in a typically Beethovenian dichotomy. On the one hand, Beethoven "would always stress, with the eloquence of Cicero, just how much value he placed on precision and orderliness." Seyfried also noted, however, that Beethoven's lodgings resembled a pigsty:

> There were books and scores everywhere one looked, here the cold remains of a repast, there a pile of full or half-empty wine bottles. A music stand held the hasty sketches for a new quartet, not far from the remains of breakfast . . . The piano harboured the dormant, embryonic scrawlings of a new and majestic symphony, while elsewhere lay the long-suffering proofs from some publisher or other. The floor was bestrewn with correspondence—both business and personal—and the window-sill boasted a sizeable lump of stracchino cheese alongside the bountiful debris of a genuine Verona salami [. . .] Sometimes, after hours, days, or even weeks of fruitless searching for some necessary item,

he would finally fly into a rage, leaving other poor innocents to resolve the matter. But the servants knew their gentle curmudgeon well enough, let him repine to his heart's content, and several minutes later all was forgotten—until a similar circumstance would cause the scene to play out anew.[6]

French general Baron de Trémont painted a similar picture, with a description so vivid that it later became a classic in the compendium of popular Beethoven anecdotes:

> Imagine the filthiest and most disorderly scene possible; I tell you, there were pools of water on the floor. Piles of handwritten and printed scores competed with the dust for space atop a rather old grand piano, beneath which sheltered—and this is no exaggeration—an unemptied chamber-pot. Beside it was a small table made of walnut, accustomed to being swamped with the overturned contents of the writing-case it supported, and a mass of quills encrusted in ink made the proverbial quills provided by taverns seem excellent by comparison. The chairs, almost all with straw seats, were buried beneath items of clothing and plates of leftover food from the day before. Balzac and Dickens would expend another two pages on this description, and would require as many again to depict the illustrious composer's outward appearance and clothing.[7]

Lobkowitz's "Center of Excellence"

ON JANUARY 19, 1797, Franz Joseph Maximilian von Lobkowitz officially came of age. It was on this day that the twenty-five-year-old Bohemian prince became the sole proprietor of one of the largest family-run real estate portfolios of the day, consisting of several hundred thousand hectares of land, three prestigious palaces in Vienna (including the central Palais Althan on Augustinerplatz), three immense castles near Prague, and a sizeable cash inheritance. Despite his riches, the young Lobkowitz succeeded in frittering away his entire family fortune within a mere fifteen years, owing to a fatal combination of mismanagement, a lavish lifestyle, and good-old-fashioned bad luck.

Lobkowitz had inherited not only his father's wealth but also his penchant for extravagance and a desire to cultivate a prominent image in the world of science, art, and music. His father had successfully joined the Prussian Academy of Sciences and was a great admirer and generous sponsor of Gluck, one of the most influential composers of the day. Because Lobkowitz's father traveled extensively throughout Europe practicing his hobby, his son suffered a terrible sense of neglect (Lobkowitz met him for the first time at the age of seven), and it is telling that Lobkowitz did not shed the feeling until his father's untimely death. In addition to his psychological traumas, Lobkowitz also had a serious physical disability: as a child he had suffered a complex hip fracture as the result of a serious fall. The subsequent sloppy medical treatment he received had left him crippled, and he was doomed to walk on crutches for the rest of his life (which incidentally did nothing to stop him giving several dazzling theatrical performances). He thenceforth compensated for his limited capacity for physical expression by concentrating on intellectual and artistic pursuits. Lobkowitz became a linguistic genius and a consummate musician, excelling greatly on both the violin and cello as well as through song.

On January 19, 1797, Lobkowitz gained access to enough financial and other resources to satisfy his yearning for love and affection, which he achieved principally by roping half of the Viennese musical population into his own private, all-encompassing, and costly cultural initiative. Lobkowitz became Vienna's proverbial musical godfather for a full fifteen years, acting simultaneously as minister for culture, theater manager, impresario, senior librarian, conservatory director, and chief lobbyist. His adherence (or not) to a clear plan was of little relevance; what mattered was that he was driven by a single creed: the best is never good enough, and nothing is ever good enough for the best. Lobkowitz had the brains to realize that benefactors or patrons cannot trigger qualitative or substantive innovation themselves; their role must be limited to the facilitation of the modalities.

Lobkowitz initially took the road well traveled, first joining the Society of the Associated Cavaliers (Gesellschaft der associerten Kavaliere) and organizing performances of orchestral and chamber music in his own home at the Schwarzenberg family palace (the Schwarzenbergs were his in-laws). He also belonged to a group of patrons who worked to promote the new oratorios by Joseph Haydn, and even had the texts translated into Czech for performances in Bohemia (where, it should be noted, he himself sang the bass parts). But his aspirations soon deviated, and when it became clear that his own palaces offered no venues suitable for large-scale concert projects, he commissioned a number of ambitious infrastructural works. One such example was the conversion of an entire wing of the Palais Lobkowitz into a concert hall, including separate, delineated areas for the performers and the audience. The former were to occupy a slightly raised dais, clearly illustrating his conceptualization of a new musical hierarchy in which the audience came for the performers, and not the other way around.[1] He then proceeded to construct theaters in his Bohemian castles in Raudnitz (Roudnice nad Labem) and Eisenberg (Jezeří), and his children were gifted their own state-of-the-art puppet theater.

Lobkowitz also wanted his own orchestra. In this sense he was somewhat of a contrarian, as most of his aristocratic contemporaries had decided that running one's own ensemble was no longer de rigueur, and far too expensive besides. But Lobkowitz would not be dissuaded and in 1797 introduced a brand-new orchestral formula that might today be described as "modular"; he installed a permanent core of ten elite musicians, around whom he enlisted freelancers as necessary, allowing for the construction of a range of instrumental ensembles. This approach gave Kapellmeister Anton Wranitzky a broad spectrum of possibilities, from intimate chamber groups to a thirty-piece orchestra for major symphonic, oratorio, or opera productions. The inner circle thus formed the beating heart of the ensemble and set the musical standard, making it crucial for Lobkowitz to attract the very best from Vienna and surrounds. The key determinant in this respect was money, and Lobkowitz needed to pay higher wages than the emperor himself—if only to compensate for the lack of job security in private enterprise. He also dispensed facilities and privileges with prodigal affluence, acquiring and lending out valuable instruments free of charge and even assisting his musicians with more practical day-to-day matters, such as accommodations. The strategy bore fruit: Viennese musicians swarmed around the Lobkowitz honeypot, and Wranitzky was free to select the very best.

Good musicians seek not only financial rewards, however; they are just as sensitive to the caliber of the works they perform and the culture of the organization in which they operate. Here too they were in good hands. Lobkowitz attached great importance to "works in progress" and kept sizeable sums in reserve for rehearsals and run-throughs. In June 1804—with a pared-down orchestra, a limited audience, and almost a full year before its first public performance—Beethoven conducted several studio rehearsals of the *Eroica* Symphony in order to establish a proof-of-concept and incorporate some final corrections. Other composers, too, could take advantage of these opportunities, and certain chamber ensembles (such as the Schuppanzigh Quartet) gained access to invaluable rehearsal facilities. German composer and musicographer Johann Friedrich Reichardt professed that Lobkowitz was only ever too happy to provide the very best rehearsal spaces and that multiple rehearsals were often scheduled simultaneously in different parts of the building. Reichardt called the institution "a genuine musical residence and academy."[2]

And it was true. Lobkowitz had converted his palace into what might indeed be dubbed a "research center for music," a site dedicated entirely to musical experimentation and study. He also built a library to accommodate new scores and books, offered scholarships to talented young musicians, and enabled "apprenticeships" with members of his musical elite. It is therefore no exaggeration to say that new and powerful winds of change were blowing through this "center of excellence." Whereas previous musical developments had been largely dependent on random, unpredictable interactions between composer and audience, Lobkowitz was the first to implement a deliberate strategy that allocated top priority to quality and substance, regardless of the needs or expectations of any audience. On the eve of a new century, Lobkowitz thus created an environment in which composition became an "end in itself."

In Lobkowitz's world, alas, it was a fine line that separated fantasy from folly. Although it was clear from the outset that his extravagant lifestyle was unsustainable (even with his sizeable fortune), and despite the fact that he was forced to take out loans to continue to pay his army of staff (which at one time was nearly two hundred strong), Lobkowitz wished to continue to expand his musical territory. Initial efforts in this direction seemed harmless enough, as he sponsored certain *Akademie* concerts in the city and, true to his background as a Catholic aristocrat, lent his support to the production of symphonic music in the churches of St. Michael and St. Augustine. But when Baron Peter von Braun stepped down as manager of the Viennese court theaters, he felt a hero's calling to charge in and save the opera. Initially he joined forces with several other members of the nobility, including Schwarzenberg, Ferdinand von Pálffy, Stephan Zichy, and Esterházy, but by 1811 he was the last remaining member of this aristocratic alliance. The amounts he flushed down this metaphorical drain were colossal—at one time he was even paying the wages of the entire opera staff, including the pensions of the retirees—and in 1811 he was driven to the very brink of financial ruin, aided by the general economic downturn and the plummeting of the financial markets due to the imperial *Finanzpatent* decree (about which more later). It is unclear precisely what motivated him at this juncture—pride, naive optimism, or perhaps a subliminal form of denial—but whatever the case, his response was to forge bravely on. That very same year, he organized a three-week wedding celebration for his eldest daughter. Here too the sky was the limit, as the list of cultural events was astounding and included opera performances and concerts by the most commanding and highly paid soloists of the day. The precise costs of this insane enterprise remain difficult to estimate (the accounts for the event were destroyed, for obvious reasons), but the solitary fact that nearly twenty thousand banquet meals were served is reason to suspect the worst. To top it all off, Lobkowitz—driven by both genuine charity and pure embarrassment—also distributed thousands of gifts among the Bohemian population.

Most of those in attendance must have known that the *Titanic* was sinking; Lobkowitz was already severely in debt with many of the wedding guests, and his personnel had not been paid in weeks. Still, the band played on. And not only that, but the musicians demanded compensation for loss of income in light of the economic crisis. The elite crew in particular sought recompense in the form of additional allowances, using any excuse—moving house, a set of new strings, or instrumental repair—to submit a claim. Lobkowitz tried to economize here and there. Fewer events were held, and retired musicians were replaced by freelancers. But the situation was dire, and Lobkowitz slowly but surely withdrew from society life. He left letters unopened for years and eventually stopped responding to them altogether.

But Lobkowitz could not play the innocent forever, and in 1813 external parties decided to take action. A textbook scenario ensued: mild initial attempts were made to remove Lobkowitz from the equation by setting up a familial supervisory committee led by Schwarzenberg. When these measures proved inadequate after one year, Lobkowitz was placed under guardianship and declared bankrupt. He was subsequently bombarded with claims for compensation and was forced to hire a league of the very best lawyers to avoid a prison sentence. Eventually he retreated to an estate in Bohemia, where he died in 1816.

Lobkowitz most probably met Beethoven via Kapellmeister Wranitzky, who like Beethoven was a graduate from the Haydn-Albrechtsberger school of composition. On March 2, 1795, Lobkowitz invited the young pianist from Bonn to give a private concert. Several weeks later, he attended Beethoven's major Hofburg debut and signed up for a copy of his Piano Trios (op. 1). However, Beethoven would have to wait until 1798 for his first concrete commission: a set of six string quartets.

In 1795, Beethoven had already received a request from Count Anton Georg Apponyi to compose a string quartet, a proposal that most likely came with too many consequences and challenges at the time. Apponyi, a Masonic friend to both Haydn and Mozart, had ordered two sets of quartets from Haydn in 1793 (opp. 71 and 74). During that time, Beethoven enjoyed the privilege of a front-row seat to observe the master at work, and we might imagine that he was hesitant to venture into what was still very much Haydn's home turf. By 1798, however, the sands had shifted. Although the project was still overshadowed by Haydn's influence (Lobkowitz had commissioned six quartets from Haydn at roughly the same time), Beethoven now felt more fully equipped to take on the challenge. He had gained both compositional experience and self-confidence, as well as a more in-depth understanding of the genre through the transcription and study of Mozart's quartets (K. 387 and 464). The prospect of having the pieces workshopped in Lobkowitz's laboratory by the accomplished Schuppanzigh Quartet—giving him additional opportunities to make corrections and revisions—must also have offered some reassurance.

The composition of these string quartets became a mammoth challenge and one that dominated Beethoven's life for over two years (although during the second of these years he was distracted by his First Symphony and by a new piano concerto). An initial set of three quartets was complete within the year; in June 1799, the scores were copied, one of which (the String Quartet in F Major) Beethoven gifted to his friend Amenda on his departure for Courland.[3] These three quartets were submitted to Lobkowitz in October, and some weeks later Beethoven was awarded a quittance of two hundred guilders. There followed a brief, two-week hiatus, after which he gradually set to work on the second set. But by the time these were completed in the summer of 1800, Beethoven was no longer satisfied with the first three. Because he had refined both his technique and his artistic vision in the meantime, he now believed his first fruits to be flawed. Beethoven felt the need to rewrite them and would proceed to do so, despite the unavoidable few months of additional work. In October, Beethoven was finally able to deliver the full set to Lobkowitz, including the new versions of the first three quartets, and was rewarded almost immediately with a second consideration of two hundred guilders.

It would be over a year before the quartets would be released by publisher T. Mollo & Co. This was partly due to the fact that as patron, Lobkowitz owned the exclusive rights for a period of six months. But Beethoven would have undoubtedly made use of the opportunity to rework and refine his quartets in the meantime. Various performances had already been held at the Lichnowskys' and other venues, and Beethoven could never resist making small improvements to the score. To him, the art of quartet writing itself would forever remain a "work in progress."

Beethoven wrote to Amenda on July 1, 1801, imploring him never to show the previously gifted version of the Quartet in F Major to anyone. He made no bones about it: "Show the quartet to nobody, for I have altered it considerably; only now do I understand how to write quartets, as you will see, no doubt, when you receive them."[4] By writing these words, Beethoven effectively declared his initial version of the quartet null and void.

Unlike Lobkowitz, who promptly disposed of the original versions, Amenda faithfully held on to both copies of the Quartet in F Major. We therefore have a unique opportunity to make a thorough comparison between versions[5]—a happy twist of fate that affords a deeper insight into what Beethoven considered to be the essence of quartet writing.

Curiously, the changes made by Beethoven have no bearing whatsoever on the overall architecture of the work. The structure and character, themes, harmonies, tonal progression, and modulations all remain virtually unaltered. Only extremely rarely were bars added or removed, giving the impression that the new version is largely congruent with the old. But just as it is possible to create an entirely new painting by shading in the original sketch differently, so too has Beethoven created a new, more coherent and robust musical narrative through the introduction of myriad, seemingly minor corrections. In the first movement alone around a hundred small changes were made that all contribute to a clearer realization of his artistic vision: long notes were replaced by repeated short notes to ensure rhythmic continuity (and vice versa); rests were removed to reinforce transitions from previous material (or the opposite); dissonant grace notes were included to emphasize motivic climaxes; ornaments and playful melodic embellishments were added or removed to increase or decrease momentum; accompaniments and counterpoints were simplified or eliminated to lend clarity to the principal voice, and so on.

Beethoven also made changes to the voice leading and texture. On multiple occasions the part entries were reordered to optimize their spatial distribution, as the register of an entry (high, middle, or low) inevitably impacts the narrative as a whole: the effect of a long pause or abrupt dynamic shift can easily be destroyed by an awkward succession of entries. Beethoven also modified the textural density at certain points to match the drama of the moment, heightening intensity through sparser instrumentation or, contrariwise, imparting greater weight by broadening the sonority of his musical palette.

The subtlest and most effective changes were those made to the dynamics. Beethoven had become far more sparing in his application of fortes and fortissimos; crescendos were shifted and delayed; and accents—in the form of sforzati and fortepiano markings—were put to more judicious use in service of the musical discourse. As a result, the listener is better able to sense where the music is headed, since the climaxes, rests, and caesuras are more clearly delineated. The dramatic interplay between tension and release, obscurity and clarity, is thus far more effective, and the improved timing compels listening that is more in accordance with Beethoven's wishes.[6]

The differences between the two versions are simultaneously large and small, and illustrate the hypersensitivity and extreme fastidiousness with which Beethoven agonized over every detail. This minute level of compositional calibration is evidence of a new and elevated work ethic, reinforced by the unique institutional culture engendered by the work's commissioner, Lobkowitz. Beethoven had the good fortune to be able to test and workshop his revisions in practice with experienced quartet players, to learn from his mistakes, and to perfect his quartet writing through trial and error. In this manner he—and, indirectly, also Lobkowitz—accelerated the process of emancipating the string quartet from its light, superficial eighteenth-century amateur context.

18

The Immortal Beloved

EPISODE ONE

EARLY IN MAY 1799, Countess Anna von Brunsvik and her two daughters—the twenty-four-year-old Therese and Josephine, her younger sister by five years—climbed the narrow spiral staircase to Beethoven's apartment on Petersplatz. Beethoven received them with warmth and charm, and after the obligatory exchange of courtly niceties Therese performed one of his piano trios.[1] She knew the work flawlessly by heart, and sang to fill in the missing violin and cello parts. Beethoven was impressed, showed enthusiasm, and promised to call on the Brunsviks to give lessons every day.[2]

Introducing her daughters to Beethoven was one of the main items on the countess's Viennese social agenda. She had been widowed seven years earlier and was determined to provide security for her children's future. Franz, her only son and heir, would manage the family assets, while fitting matches would have to be found for her three daughters. Anna had the benefit of experience. Her own marriage to a civil servant, Anton von Brunsvik de Korompa, had been arranged by Empress Maria Theresa herself, transforming Anna from a humble lady-in-waiting to a countess overnight. The Brunsviks boasted a long aristocratic background and had recently made further advancements in the hierarchy of the nobility (again with the support of Maria Theresa). Their abode was an enormous castle in Martonvásár, a kind of mini-Schönbrunn nestled among sweeping parks and tranquil lakes on the steppes of Hungary. All of this had fallen, as it were, into Anna von Brunsvik's lap. She was cool and calculating (as would be proven time and again), enjoyed her hard-won social status, and was not prepared to let it all slip away.

Securing piano lessons for Therese and Josephine from the most celebrated pianist in Vienna was a key element in her chosen strategy for increasing her daughters' market value and was also very much in line with the pedagogical framework prescribed by their late father. As a professed humanist and fellow devotee of English and American liberalism, he had raised his children in freedom and with an open, cosmopolitan spirit. The Brunsviks were polyglots—they spoke and wrote both French and English—read the latest and most influential books, and were excellent pianists. Josephine was the star of the family. She was not only comely and graceful but also intelligent, with an infectious charm. She coupled noble allure with a certain nonchalance, and elegant flamboyance with a playful and even mischievous ease, lending her a slightly aloof and inaccessible air. Her skills at the piano were astonishing: insiders professed that her renditions of Beethoven's *Sonate pathétique* were the best in Vienna, and she performed alongside the city's most renowned professionals.

Josephine's charms were not lost on Beethoven. Normally one who detested teaching, he called on the Brunsviks every afternoon and devoted many hours to improving their playing. And rather than hastening home after the lessons—despite the great demands placed on his time by his new string quartets—he instead took walks with the sisters in the outdoors, went with them to the theater and balls, and promenaded through Graben and Kärntnerstrasse. Summer was on the horizon and the evenings were long and sultry, setting the perfect scene for laughter and playful flirting.

These halcyon days were cut short after only a few weeks, when Countess Brunsvik found what she considered to be a suitable match for Josephine: forty-seven-year-old Joseph Müller, the eccentric owner of a purported "art gallery" on the corner of Rotenturmstrasse and Adlergasse. The count's real surname was not Müller but Deym—the consequence of a folly committed in his youth, which, culminating in a duel, forced him to flee the country and start a new life in the west of the Netherlands. With the fortune he made there as a maker of wax sculptures, he later traveled to Naples, where he set up a lucrative business in plaster reproductions of the finest sculptures from the royal collection. Thanks to the support of the Austrian emperor (who appointed him court sculptor), Deym made a fresh start in Vienna under the pseudonym of Müller. He acquired an old copper storehouse in the north of the city and converted it into a multipurpose cultural center, a blend of history museum (with Mozart's death mask as the pièce de résistance), waxworks, hall of wonders, and event space. It quickly grew into a local attraction and a popular meeting spot for aristocrats and middle-class citizens alike.

On precisely the day when they first met Beethoven, the Brunsviks attended a society event at Deym's trendy new establishment. Deym would later attest that upon seeing Josephine, he silently vowed then and there to make her his wife. When he finally took concrete steps to do so, the countess wasted no time. With complete disregard for her daughter's aversion, she arranged and concluded the marriage within a matter of weeks, putting an abrupt end to Josephine's carefree life. Naturally, Beethoven could only look on with a heavy heart and accept that the frequency and intensity of their piano lessons would drop appreciably. He wrote a parting gift that subtly but unmistakably expressed his warm affection for Josephine: a song with six variations on Goethe's "Ich denke dein" (I think of thee). Following custom and to avoid any possibility of scandal, the work was dedicated to both Josephine and Therese, in that order. It would later come to light in her diaries that Therese—who was highly idealistic and very charitable and was thus mockingly referred to by her family as "Sister Therese"—had quickly resigned herself to a lower position within the family hierarchy.[3]

One year later, it transpired that Josephine's groom was rather less well-off than the world had been led to believe. Not only that, but he had been forced to reveal his true identity as Count Joseph Deym von Stritetz in order to legally marry Josephine, an act that cost him considerable social and financial credit. The final straw was the sudden appearance of three "adopted" daughters whom Deym had hitherto kept successfully hidden away in his enormous mansion. Though the girls officially bore the surname of Wieder, there seemed to be no doubt that they were shameful souvenirs from Deym's former lascivious life. Countess Brunsvik was furious and, driven by the same determination with which she had forced her daughter into marriage, she now rallied for a divorce. But Josephine would not be moved, and refused to reject the father of her firstborn child. The newlyweds had rapidly formed a close bond after their marriage, and around one hundred recently discovered erotic letters provide evidence that relations between the old Deym and his young bride were, without putting too fine a point on it, very passionate indeed.[4]

Josephine now assumed some of the financial responsibility, and one of her initiatives was to rent out the eighty rooms and apartments in their building complex on Rotenturmstrasse. At the same time, she refused to be downtrodden by her problems. She continued to move among the beau monde with elegance and poise and frequented the many balls in Vienna dressed in opulent evening gowns. She resumed her lessons with Beethoven twice a week, although they were of shorter duration and of course minus any *après-leçon*. Beethoven, who in the meantime had become friends with Josephine's only brother, Franz (and had even spent the summer of 1800 at the Brunsviks' castle in Martonvásár), thus retained a satellite presence in Josephine's life. But despite his ancillary role, Beethoven remained the focal point of the many musical soirées held at the Deym residence, even when sharing the stage with well-known colleagues. When the English-Polish violinist George Bridgetower visited Vienna in the spring of 1803, causing a stir through his exotic appearance (he was of mixed race) and his unparalleled virtuosity, Beethoven dragged him along to the Deyms' to perform his newly composed violin sonatas. It is generally assumed that they then also performed the Violin Sonata in A Major (op. 47), which later famously became known as the *Kreutzer* Sonata.[5]

Today, over two centuries later, it is tempting to fantasize about what may have taken place at casa Deym. On December 9, 1800, for example, a concert was held in honor of the Duchess of Giovane; Josephine first accompanied Schuppanzigh in a rendition of the Violin Sonata in E-flat (op. 12), which was followed by several of the opus 18 string quartets. Let us speculate on the latter for a moment. Could Josephine have deciphered the secret messages that according to Beethoven biographer Ernst Pichler were hidden inside them?[6] Did she deduce that the Adagio affetuoso ed appassionato from the first quartet—an evocation of the tomb scene from *Romeo and Juliet*—employed the melody from "Ich denke dein" as its main subject? Or that the fourth quartet commenced with a paraphrase of the same, in the *pathétique* tonality of C minor? And might the set's concluding Malinconia—a fleet-footed, almost ecstatic dance interspersed with reflective and melancholic adagio passages—have stirred her fantasy?

The chances are remote that Joseph Deym noticed any of this; his knowledge of music was too scant to decipher such subtly embedded, coded messages. Unlike his young wife, whose musical knowledge was an important means of communication with Beethoven, Deym had rather limited musical horizons. But Beethoven showed him some generosity nonetheless, and composed for him a set of five pieces for *Flötenuhr* (WoO 33)—trifling ditties for a musical clock on display in his museum.

Neither Josephine nor Beethoven cherished any desire to give their secret mutual attraction a more "manifest" character through a clandestine extra-marital affair. While certainly dependent on the mores of late-eighteenth-century etiquette, their resolve was also due in no small measure to the moral values upheld by Beethoven in particular when it came to marriage. Following an incident with his married pupil Marie Bigot in 1807, Beethoven wrote that he was firmly principled against anything but purely platonic relations with other men's wives.[7] And in 1805 he would confess to Josephine, "When I came to you, I was fiercely determined not to let even the tiniest spark of love to grow within me."[8] The very fact that he committed such a sentiment to paper is proof enough of his profound frustration, and all the evidence suggests that Josephine did not make things any easier for him.

Life went on. Josephine bore a total of four children to Joseph Deym, and Beethoven met other women. In 1800, for example, he made the acquaintance of one of Josephine's younger cousins, Giulietta ("Julie") Guicciardi. Beethoven gave her piano lessons, and fell in love.

Like Josephine, Giulietta was a beautiful and talented young lady. She had also lived in Italy for many years and had cultivated a distinctly southern flair, with a bold temperament and playful provocativeness. The Brunsviks quite clearly disapproved of their cousin's behavior, finding it coquettish, melodramatic, even a little vacuous. Beethoven seemed to share no such concerns, and in a letter to his bosom friend Wegeler, he wrote of how happy Giulietta made him: "Life has improved of late, I have been getting out a lot more [...] This change was brought about by a dear, enchanting young creature, who loves me and whom I love. It has been two years since I last glimpsed such moments of happiness, and for the first time I feel as though marriage might make me happy." In the very same letter, however, Beethoven added that marriage was not an option: "Sadly she is not of my station, and I could not marry now anyway—I must continue to struggle bravely on."[9] In 1803, Giulietta married Count Wenzel Robert von Gallenberg, a ballet composer who would later achieve some renown by supplying the festival music for the accession of Joseph Bonaparte in Naples. Thereafter, the pinnacle of his achievements amounted to a position as librarian in the Kärntnertor theater in Vienna. He thus dwarfed in comparison to Beethoven but had the advantage of blue blood in his veins. Beethoven later admitted that letting Giulietta's hand slip away had not been such a bad thing after all. Toward the end of his life he told Schindler that Giulietta even tried to seduce him after her marriage, making advances that he claims to have rebuffed. Relieved, he then followed up with, "If I had chosen to devote my energies to that kind of life—what had remained for the nobler, more worthy kind?"[10]

Giulietta Guicciardi's place in history was further assured by the fact that at one time the Brunsvik family put her forward as the so-called immortal beloved, in hopes of removing Josephine from harm's way. Her greatest renown, however, was garnered as the dedicatee of Beethoven's best-known piano sonata, the *Moonlight*. While this is certainly true, we must set the record straight: initially he dedicated the Rondo in G for Piano (op. 51, no. 2) to her, a work whose dimensions are far more commensurate with those of the gesture, but he hastily withdrew it when he was in pressing need of a token for Countess Henriette Lichnowsky, Karl Lichnowsky's sister. Under these circumstances, Beethoven had no choice but to dedicate his very next piano work, the Sonata in C-sharp Minor (op. 27, no. 2), to Giulietta.

And while we are on the subject, the appellation *Moonlight* was neither coined by Beethoven nor is it any reference to the Giulietta affair. It was Berlin-based poet, music critic, and Beethoven admirer Ludwig Rellstab who, in 1824, compared the first movement of the Sonata in C-sharp Minor to "the tranquillity of the ocean in the shimmering moonlight" and the "mournful, yearning tones of a solitary love tumbling mysteriously from an aeolian harp." It was not until 1860, when German musicologist Wilhelm von Lenz made the association with a boat drifting "across a moonlit lake on a still August night," that the title became fixed forever.[11]

Beethoven's contemporaries were therefore unaware of any such associations. And yet the sonata was extremely popular, in part because the designation—quasi una fantasia—was unorthodox. The work's popularity irritated Beethoven, who said of it: "People do go on about the C-sharp minor sonata! Is it not obvious that I have written far better works? The sonata in F-sharp major—now that is something else entirely."[12]

19

The Road to a Broader Public

BEETHOVEN WAS AWARE OF THE "ERUDITE" nature of his first set of string quartets (op. 18). He knew that they would only ever be destined for a small in-crowd of connoisseurs (mostly aristocrats), and that there was an equally important need for him to reach a wider audience. Since the doors to the opera were closed for the time being, the only way to expand his listener base was through the composition of large-scale symphonies. This had not always been an obvious strategy: in aristocratic musical culture, the symphony had been relegated to a marginal "utilitarian" status, making their composition a futile enterprise for composers trying to make a name for themselves. Haydn had clearly succeeded in shifting these goalposts, as the *Paris* and—in particular—the *London* symphonies had forged a grander mold for the genre, and the symphony subsequently began to dominate concert programs, winning enthusiasm among the modern citizenry.

Thereafter, symphonies came to represent the very pinnacle of instrumental music. They became longer and more complex, taking on greater substance and a weightier aesthetic (the common practice of spreading out the four separate movements over the course of an evening did nothing to alter this fact). The psychological barrier to the genre had also been raised, however, and would only grow higher after Beethoven, making it ever more daunting for new composers to enter the field.

Beethoven himself was not immune to these developments. His first plans for a symphony date from as early as 1795, when over the course of several months he completed sketches for a slow introduction and the exposition of a first movement. He resumed work on it during his time in Berlin in the spring of 1796—most likely in the hopes of being able to premiere his first symphony in the Prussian capital—but progress was slow. In total he produced three new versions of the slow introduction and two more of the initial Allegro. He also had drafts of both the second (slow) movement and the Menuetto, but no more than that. The production process stalled at the final movement due to a thorny compositional problem. Beethoven had identified an inherent contradiction between the light-footed quality of a traditional finale (demanding a popular, dancelike, effervescent, and virtuosic character) and his own desire to interpret it as the dramatic counterpole to the first movement while also bringing the entire work to a grandiose conclusion. Beethoven's need to "bookend" the symphony in this way was also driven by his express desire to present all four movements as an uninterrupted whole. He would grapple with the same problem when writing his later symphonies, each of which required a unique and tailored solution (such as the inclusion of a text in the Ninth Symphony). In 1796, no such solutions were forthcoming, and he gave up.

The symphony remained dormant until the winter of 1799, when he resumed work on it once again. He may have been under the assumption that he would soon be ready for his own *Akademie,* and if he wished to launch himself as a composer as well as a pianist, the inclusion of a symphony was paramount. He started afresh on the first three movements, and perhaps for precisely this reason they now flowed from his pen fairly effortlessly. For the final movement he made use of the thematic material that had originally been intended for the opening—a wise decision, as it was already internally consistent enough to provide for the weighty finale Beethoven had in mind. The trickiest hurdle was thus already overcome.

Composing a symphony is one thing, but organizing a performance is quite another—especially in Vienna in 1800, where concert culture still paled in comparison to the scene in London or Paris. Viennese composers, as noted earlier, had only one real way to reach large audiences: organizing an *Akademie* at either the Burgtheater or Kärntnertortheater. But even ignoring the logistical headaches and considerable financial risk, things were made worse by the fact that it was almost impossible to gain access to either venue. The keys to the enterprise lay quite literally in the hands of Baron von Braun, an accidental nobleman and fabric merchant of limited musical gifts who compensated for his bungled artistic ambitions through the shameless abuse of his power as the concessionaire of both theaters. It was his habit, for example, whenever an outsider was granted access to one of his theaters, to sabotage the event by scheduling a guaranteed sellout in the other. Even Haydn needed the support of the empress herself to secure a favorable date for the first public performance of *The Creation*. Johann Friedrich Reichardt described Braun as follows: "Only imperial protection can explain how a man with such a patent lack of sensibility or good taste, in such a city as Vienna—which is known precisely for its passionate love of music and theatre—is able to tyrannise the court, the public and the artists in a manner that would not be tolerated in cities far smaller than she."[1] In a letter to publisher Breitkopf & Härtel, Beethoven's brother Karl described Braun as an "ignorant, boorish lout" who "opened his doors to artists who are mediocre in the extreme."[2] We can assume that Beethoven's estimation of Braun was no different.

Making any headway therefore required putting pressure on Braun via the only two means available: the court, and his wife. Beethoven himself could take care of the latter; he was now quite experienced at currying the favor of older women and won the support of Mrs. Braun by dedicating the opus 14 piano sonatas to her. Matters at court were of course more delicate, but it was here that the Deyms came to the rescue. While Countess Brunsvik still had her fingers in various court pies, Joseph Deym's Neapolitan past had also put him in almost direct contact with Maria Theresa[3] of Naples and Sicily, the second wife of Emperor Francis II. An important role also fell to another old Sicilian acquaintance, the Duchess of Giovane. This chaperone of the young archduchess Marie Louise, later the Lady Napoleon, had boarded for many years with the Deyms on Rotenturmstrasse. When, after New Year's Day in 1800, Beethoven wished to dedicate his freshly minted Septet in E-flat (op. 20) to the empress, permission for him to do so was facilitated through diplomatic interventions by the ladies at court. Dedicating a work to the empress without her express prior consent would have been not only highly inappropriate but counterproductive besides.

The Septet, incidentally, gained enormous popularity and was arranged and released for various ensembles immediately following its premiere. Beethoven had made fast and clever work of it, drawing from a long tradition of leisurely divertimento writing while still imbuing it with his somewhat darker, "trademark" character. It was also rich in modern, sensational effects, giving it great audience appeal. Beethoven would later slight the Septet, claiming that at the time he had had no notion whatsoever of how to compose such a work. Czerny goes so far as to say that Beethoven detested it, resenting the widespread acclaim it received.[4] Both accounts are a testament to the embarrassment often felt by great artists when confronted with the work of their younger years. Beethoven's consternation was compounded by his inability to imagine how compositions whose creation or consumption required little effort could ever be considered great works.[5]

One might also muse that the Septet, with its combination of solemnity and mirth, was made to measure for the lady to whom it was dedicated. Empress Maria Theresa was a passionate music lover as well as an excellent singer and pianist, and frequently organized private concerts in which she herself participated (during one such concert, she even sang the role of Hannah from Haydn's *The Seasons*). She maintained an extensive music library and regularly furnished eminent librettists and composers with ideas for new productions. Her musical tastes ranged from the melodic charm of the Neapolitan school to the harmonic and instrumental richness of the Viennese tradition. At the same time, she saw life itself as one long divertimento and felt an undeniable affinity with its carefree and even trivial aspects.[6]

The dedication to the empress hit its mark, and following an edict from the Hofburg, Braun gave Beethoven permission to organize an *Akademie* for April 2, 1800. Beethoven knew the lay of the land and demonstrated his gratitude by placing the Septet at the center of the program, along with a fitting reference to the graces of the empress.

The concert was announced in the *Wiener Zeitung* on March 26, with the customary note that tickets could be collected from the composer at his own home. It is rather a surreal thought that one of the greatest musicians of all time should spend the days leading up to the most important concert of his life collecting entry fees and allocating seating. The playbill read as follows:

On this day, Wednesday the 2nd of April 1800,
at the Imperial and Royal Court Theatre,
Herr Ludwig van Beethoven
shall have the honour of presenting a
Grand Musical *Akademie*
in his own name.
The following works shall be performed:

1) A grand symphony by the late Herr Kapellmeister Mozart;
2) An aria from *The Creation,* composed by Joseph Haydn, Herr Kapellmeister to Lord Esterházy, and performed by Mlle Saal;
3) A grand concerto for the pianoforte, composed and performed by Herr Ludwig van Beethoven;

4) A *Septet,* most humbly dedicated to Her Imperial Majesty and composed by Herr Ludwig van Beethoven for 4 strings and 3 winds, performed by Messrs. Schuppanzigh, Schreiber, Schindlecker, Bär, Nickel, Matauscheck and Dietzel;

5) A duet from Haydn's *Creation,* sung by Herr and Mlle Saal;

6) An improvisation on the piano by Herr Ludwig van Beethoven;

7) A new grand symphony for full orchestra, composed by Herr Ludwig van Beethoven.

Tickets for boxes and other seats may be obtained directly from Herr Beethoven at his home, 241 Im tiefen Graben, 3rd floor, or from the box manager. Ticket prices are as normal. The concert shall commence at 6:30 p.m.[7]

The program was well balanced and carefully considered. Comprising nearly three and a half hours of music, it was quite long, though not uncommonly so for the time. Its main virtues were sufficient variety and a clear structure: a grand symphony at either end, framing a contrasting chamber work as the centerpiece, interposed between two blocks of vocal soloists and the master himself at the piano. In typical Beethovenian fashion, these musical bricks were further cemented together by an overall tonal and harmonic arc.

The decision to include vocalists also reflected a clear strategy, even if it was only to avoid potential complications with other instrumental soloists. Appearances by less talented artists would blemish the concert, while those of equal or greater talent would draw too much attention. Moreover, by programming an aria and duet from Haydn's *Creation,* Beethoven capitalized as much as possible on the work's popularity. Entrusting the solos to Ignaz and Thérèse Saal not only put the names of two first-class singers on the program (who had premiered the work just over a year before), but also conferred the endearing benefit of having a father and daughter appear on stage together.

Of equally salient interest was the fact that Beethoven only tolerated music of great masters—Mozart and Haydn—alongside his own. Going beyond a mere homage, this was a powerful statement from Beethoven regarding his perceived musical and historical heritage and harks back to Waldstein's famous statement from the friendship album of 1792. Although demonstrating some nerve, this implicit judgment most likely made Beethoven a little less popular in the eyes of his colleagues.

Further cause for a loss of esteem stemmed from his insistence to have the opera orchestra led not by principal conductor Giacomo Conti but instead by the—in Beethoven's view—more competent Anton Wranitzky. The orchestra interpreted this musical démarche (in some ways understandably) as a vote of no confidence against the instrumentalists themselves, prompting them to embark on a subtle form of musical sabotage. Their rebellion was especially noticeable during the piano concerto, when the ensemble between soloist and orchestra was largely dependent on the latter's concentration and flexibility. Their stubborn refusal to follow Beethoven's refined rubato playing often meant that they were not together, and the critics noted that some of the orchestral passages were "lacking fire."[8] Beethoven was furious and harbored a paranoia of orchestral musicians for the rest of his life. He did partly have himself to blame, however; his insistence on replacing the conductor is an early example (and certainly not the last) of how his obsession with perfectionism could do him more harm than good.

But any consternation surrounding the piano concerto paled in comparison to the furor generated by the First Symphony. The audience was disoriented at the outset by the dissonant chords in the winds—on a first hearing, one could be forgiven for thinking they were atonal—accompanied by bizarre-sounding pizzicato strings. At the time, such instrumentation was unheard of, in more ways than one. The critics were at a loss to fathom the role of the winds in general, which Beethoven had used consistently to punctuate key climaxes and structural turning points throughout the symphony. An excerpt from the *Allgemeine musikalische Zeitung* reads, "The employment of the winds was excessive in any case, producing a sound more reminiscent of a wind band [*Harmonie*] than an orchestra."[9]

But the listeners had even more surprises in store, such as the new standard set by Beethoven with regard to tempo and speed. Even from a purely objective standpoint (based on the underlying pulse and the velocity of the shortest note values), the First Symphony moves at a pace unprecedented in comparable works by Haydn or Mozart. The tempo indications reinforce this idea; every movement is preceded by either con brio, con moto, or molto e vivace. The Menuetto in particular leaves behind any semblance of the stately aristocratic dance—though not yet in name, in spirit this movement is already a fully fledged scherzo. But pure velocity aside, the music simply *feels* faster and moves with greater impetus. Ideas cascade in quick succession, crescendos are short-lived and impulsive, and as a whole the work embodies an uncommon nervousness born of its many accents and sforzati. At the dawn of a new century and the beginning of the industrial revolution, Beethoven's First Symphony can almost be heard to herald the ever-increasing pace of life and thought from then on.

Somehow or other, the audience must have felt it too. Despite the extravagances of the First Symphony, the reviewer from the *Allgemeine musikalische Zeitung* concluded that Beethoven's *Akademie* had unquestionably been the most interesting in quite some time.[10]

With his *Akademie* out of the way, it was Beethoven's aim to press on with his string quartets. But first he had one more job to finish: he had promised a sonata to the well-known horn player Giovanni Punto (aka Johann Wenzel Stich), which they were to perform together during Punto's own *Akademie* at the Hofburgtheater on April 18, 1800. Punto was a true phenomenon. Of Bohemian extraction, he had completed his musical education in Dresden, the eighteenth-century mecca for horn players, and his subsequent career resembled a picaresque adventure novel. He first fled Bohemia in true Wild West style, thereafter working throughout Europe under a pseudonym (the Italianized form of his real name), then supporting the revolution in Paris while conducting a variety orchestra, and ultimately making his way to Vienna in 1800. Everywhere he went, he caused a sensation with his virtuosic mastery of what is known as the "stopping technique," which requires the player to insert the right hand into the bell of the horn in various ways, to allow for a far more advanced chromaticism. Punto could literally play anything, and Beethoven took great advantage of his technique when writing the Horn Sonata (op. 17). He took the traditional natural horn idiom and imbued it with new musical dimensions, coloring the melodies with chromatic tones and dissonant grace notes, and creating an alternation between "open" and "closed" tones, between "light" and "dark" timbres. In doing so, Beethoven seized a golden opportunity to broaden his horn vocabulary and gained experience that he would gratefully draw from in his later orchestral works, such as the Trio from the *Eroica* Symphony.

Beethoven and Punto bowled audiences over with the Horn Sonata. According to a report by the *Allgemeine musikalische Zeitung,* the audience's enthusiasm was so great that despite a recent edict forbidding encores or uproarious applause at the Hoftheater, the two virtuosi were forced to repeat the sonata in its entirety. A second performance followed in Pest on May 7. There was no third concert due to a dispute between Beethoven and Punto (over women, it would seem). The conflict was later resolved, and the duo appeared together one last time during a benefit concert organized by soprano Christine Gerhardi on January 21, 1801.

The *Akademie* on April 2, 1800, had established Beethoven's reputation as a composer, and it was soon followed by a commission to supply the music for a ballet production, *The Creatures of Prometheus*. The show's premiere was originally scheduled for March 21, 1801, but was postponed by one week. Rumors claim that Beethoven lost precious time due to illness; however, the possibility cannot be excluded that Beethoven once again simply took his mandate far too seriously. This at least was the tenor of a review in the *Zeitung für die elegante Welt,* which declared the music to be "too academic and unfitting for ballet," as well as "far too grandiose for a *divertissement,* which, in the end, is what a ballet ought to be."[11] Elsewhere reports trickled in that the premiere was delayed because the makers were having trouble bringing the production to a satisfactory conclusion—literally. Some critics found the second half to be appreciably less dramatic than the first, putting an enormous dent in the work's reputation. The widely read *Journal des Luxus und der Moden* even declared the final movement to be "mystical allegorical nonsense."[12] Beethoven imputed these shortcomings to the ballet master himself, Salvatore Viganò, claiming that he had "acquitted himself poorly of his duties."[13]

Viganò had not been chosen on the toss of a coin, however. The Italian dancer, choreographer, and ballet composer had made his career first in Madrid and later in Venice, with some help from his uncle Luigi Boccherini. Accompanied by his wife, the stunningly beautiful Spanish dancer Maria Medina, he then traveled to various cities in Europe and enjoyed some success in Vienna. When the imperial theater manager Braun was confronted with dwindling opera audiences in 1799, he attempted to rekindle interest in and around the theater by programming more ballet. To this end, he offered the popular Viganò a lucrative four-year contract.

The Viennese ballet world was divided into two camps. One half of the public was still enamored of ballet performances in the traditional style: technically brilliant, elegant, and virtuosic but lacking in substance or feeling. The other half were fans of the new ballet d'action, the artistic brainchild of Jean-Georges Noverre and Gasparo Angioli. These ballets were sweeping pieces of dramatic storytelling—expressive, impassioned works set against sumptuous decors and in greater symbiosis with the music. Viganò was originally of the latter camp but gradually developed a new and unique style of movement that was bound even more tightly to the musical structures. His ballets thus became more abstract, resembling animated physical constructs, an effect further enhanced by the absence of traditional costumes. Viganò had his ballerinas appear in skin-tight flesh-colored leotards draped with a few airy, transparent veils and illuminated by suggestive lighting, giving the impression of nakedness on stage. The Viennese flocked to these performances en masse to ensure that they could authoritatively express their outrage at this blasphemy against the theater's true proprietor, the emperor. But Francis sprang resolutely to the choreographer's defense, after which he promptly began an affair with Viganò's (recently divorced) wife. This presumably is what cost her the main role in *Prometheus,* following some behind-the-scenes machinations by the empress (according to the Viennese rumor mill). The scandal did raise the production's popularity, however.

Viganò had unorthodox rehearsal practices. Stendhal, who vehemently defended his methods, stated that Viganò rarely worked with a predetermined scenario but instead—like many of today's theater directors and choreographers—started with a nebulous concept which, in dialogue with the dancers and after considerable experimentation, gradually coalesced and solidified into a full production. The obstacles encountered by the makers of *Prometheus* toward the end of the work—and which may have been responsible for delaying the premiere—might therefore just as easily have been the result of Viganò's anarchistic approach. This theory is supported by the scarce extant early scores of the ballet, which suggest that Beethoven, too, started work without any clearly delineated outline or playbook. The import of the trilingual annotations in the score is inconsistent; they are sometimes minutely detailed but just as often cursory and vague.

The absence of a completed libretto makes reconstructing the ballet itself a difficult matter. The only source material available is the brief summary given on the playbill and the section titles in Beethoven's score,[14] both of which reveal that Viganò's ballet reflected very little of either the Prometheus legend from antiquity (shackling the male lead to a rock for eternity would rather seem to defeat the purpose of a ballet), or the Sturm und Drang of Goethe's well-known poem. Instead, Viganò opted to blend the classical Prometheus myth with the tale of "Apollo and the Muses" and the legend of "the power of music and dance over humanity." In this version, to the immense satisfaction of early-nineteenth-century aristocratic audiences,

Prometheus is cast no longer as the rebellious, fire-stealing liberator of humankind (the theft of fire and the rage of the gods is relegated here to the back story), but instead as an artist, creating man and woman from clay and using his stolen fire as the "spark of life." Upon realizing that he is unable to imbue them with emotion and reason, he then ferries them to Parnassus, leaving the Muses to induct them in the ways of the arts and science. The first to appear are Euterpe and Terpsichore, after which Bacchus and his cronies provide the obligatory martial scene (exactly what they were doing at Parnassus remains a mystery, however). Finally, Melpomene, Thalia, and Pan—also a stranger to Parnassus—act out Prometheus's own death and resurrection. Thus Prometheus's creatures are molded into fully fledged humans, capable of developing feelings of love and gratitude for their maker.

This substantial and substantive shift in focus had major consequences for both the title of the work (which now placed the emphasis squarely on the Creatures rather than Prometheus) and the distribution of roles—choreographer and lead dancer Viganò played the newly created man, not the creator. It also affected the conceptualization of the ballet's entire second act. *The Creatures of Prometheus* culminates in an ode to the power of dance and music and therefore gradually metamorphoses from a highly dramatic ballet d'action into an abstract divertissement in Viganò's newest mode.[15] This stylistic compromise is ultimately what also compromised the future of the work itself.

When composing the music, and the opening sections in particular, Beethoven applied every trick in the late-eighteenth-century book of theatrical musical clichés. He also effectively distinguished between moments of deep expression and pure narration—much like the alternation between aria and recitative—and reveled in depicting the drama of certain scenes, such as Prometheus's stormy entrance, his rage at the indifference of his creations, the grandeur of the battle scene, and his murder. The storm itself sounds like a preliminary study of the Sixth Symphony. The roaring winds that first bluster and then subside, the thunder and lightning, and the final return to tranquility with the suggestion of a rainbow in a clear sky: all are painted using the same tonal palette as the *Pastoral*. But since Viganò's interpretation of the legend also addresses the purifying and uplifting power of music, Beethoven was obliged to conjure up some sumptuous moments of lyrical beauty. Euterpe's entrance is heralded by a sweeping cello melody with harp accompaniment, in evocation of Apollo's lyre; and when Prometheus invites his creatures to follow him to Parnassus, Beethoven's music becomes sweet and tender. A wry smile appears now and then: the first steps taken by the new humans are accompanied by a clumsy, wooden staccato motif in the strings—a faithful auditory depiction of the poor wretches' stumbling and staggering.

Alas, the music loses momentum as the end draws nigh, and Beethoven is condemned to write a protracted series of unrelated dances, one for each soloist, for the purposes of paying their tribute to the arts. An interesting note is the political statement made by Beethoven during the finale. For the joyful conclusion, in which all of the protagonists take part (Prometheus included), Beethoven decided on a series of *Kontretänze,* or contredanses, one of which served as a recurring refrain. His choice carries a deeper meaning, as the *Kontretanz* was a Viennese variant on the English "country dance," which at the turn of the century had a reputation as a very democratic dance form. It was the only occasion when etiquette allowed masters and servants to dance together and was therefore symbolic of the new social order looming on the horizon. Beethoven's decision to conclude *Prometheus* with a series of contredanses—which was tantamount to placing gods and humans on an equal footing—is brimming with ideological significance.

Beethoven developed a special fondness for the theme of the refrain and would reuse it thrice more: in the Twelve Contredanses (WoO 14), in the *Eroica* Variations (op. 35), and in the *Eroica* itself (op. 55). The theme's prominence in the finale of the *Eroica* has led some musicologists to view it as an extension of the ballet and infer an association between the presumed hero of the *Eroica* (Napoleon or otherwise) and Prometheus. Unfortunately, despite its elegance, this hypothesis is not supported by any extant sources from the early nineteenth century.

20

A Word from the Critics

THE REMARK IN THE VIENNA *Zeitung für die elegante Welt* labeling Beethoven's *Prometheus* as too "academic" was penned by a non–music expert. Nevertheless, this line of criticism closely reflected the general tone of the reviews appearing in the only available music journal in the German-speaking world, the Leipzig-based *Allgemeine musikalische Zeitung*. In the journal's early years especially, between 1798 and 1801, critics repeatedly insisted that Beethoven's music was extravagant, contrived, overly complex, and even unnatural:

> His plethora of ideas [...] all too often leads him to pile them up and group them in so wild and bizarre a fashion that a dark artificiality, or an artificial darkness, emerges [...] The reviewer [...] can therefore not shake the idea [...] that this extremely original composer would be well-served by a certain measure of economy in his work. [On the Three Piano Sonatas, op. 10][1]

> With his penchant for unorthodox harmony and a love of the serious, the composer would do well [...] to write in a more *natural*, rather than a con-trived fashion. [On the Trio for Piano, Clarinet, and Cello, op. 11][2]

> His sonatas are idiosyncratic and fraught with eccentric difficulties [...] They are all intellectual, academic and scholarly, without any sense of natural ease or lyricism! [...] Were Herr v. Beethoven to set his own self aside and pursue a more natural course, he would surely produce very fine work for the instrument that he seems so profoundly to have mastered. [On the Three Violin Sonatas, op. 12][3]

As expected, his uncommon use of harmony was also on the chopping block:

Herr v. B. should curb the extravagant freedom of his writing, avoiding the entry of unprepared intervals and [...] the frequent harshness of passing notes. [On the Three Piano Sonatas, op. 10][4]

In summary:

Herr van Beethoven's skill as a pianist is undeniable [...] Whether he is as felicitous a composer is a question that, in the face of the present examples, is more difficult to answer in the positive. [On the Twelve Variations for Cello and Piano on "Ein Mädchen oder Weibchen" from Mozart's *Magic Flute*, op. 66][5]

Not all reviews were so scathing, however, and some made note of Beethoven's very special qualities:

It cannot be denied that Herr v. B. is possessed of genius and originality, and forges no path but his own [...] To the reviewer, this [...] collection thus seems extremely praiseworthy. [On the Three Piano Sonatas, op. 10][6]

Viennese music lovers can rejoice in their proximity to such exemplary artists, of which Herr van *Beethoven* is indisputably one, and we hope that he will continue to bestow on us often the fruits of his genius and diligence. [On the *Sonate pathétique* in C Minor, op. 13][7]

[This music] is of note, and particularly useful as study material for already advanced pianists. There are always some, after all, who find enjoyment in extreme—one might even say rebellious—technical difficulties and musical complexities. [On the Sonatas for Piano and Violin, op. 12][8]

But positive remarks were still in the minority and made little headway against the generally unflattering image of Beethoven's compositional efforts promulgated by the *Allgemeine musikalische Zeitung*. Beethoven felt deeply aggrieved by negative criticism, and it always took several days before his fits of rage and indignation gave way to disdain for those who dared attack him:

The critics in Leipzig? Let them talk—there is no way that their prattle will ever confer immortality to anyone, nor remove that immortality for which they are destined by Apollo.[9]

They do not understand [...] it gives me some consolation, however, when I see how some who are of little consequence among their betters, are praised into the heavens—and then disappear again, however industrious they may have been.[10]

Beethoven's frustration was indeed exacerbated by the benevolence shown by the critics to certain of his colleagues. To Beethoven, the praise and glory showered onto works by such dunces as Philip Freund and Heinrich Eppinger must have been downright humiliating, and the advice that he would do well to study Georg Joseph Vogler's analysis of Forkel's variations on "God Save the King" can only have occasioned a cynical grin. Mozart characterized "Abbé" Vogler as "a tedious musical clown," who was "self-absorbed and incompetent."[11] Beethoven can hardly have thought otherwise.

The tide turned, however, when the publishing house Breitkopf & Härtel—the business behind the *Allgemeine musikalische Zeitung*—realized Beethoven's commercial value and in the spring of 1801 showed interest in publishing his latest works. Beethoven was initially cautious; he felt compelled to express his dissatisfaction with the negative criticism emanating from Leipzig, and set out in no uncertain terms the precise conditions under which he was prepared to collaborate. His protests did not go unheard, and although the editorial freedom of the journal was highly prized by the publisher, the tenor of the articles in the *Allgemeine musikalische Zeitung* changed appreciably. Certain hallmarks of Beethoven's style that had previously met with confusion and been characterized as "capricious" or "extravagant" were now lavished with superlative praise:

> [The sonata] is truly grand and original—the first and third movements especially, which tend towards the eccentric and adventurous. [On the Piano Sonata in D Major, op. 28][12]

> It is a source of great joy, after trawling through mounds of "original" piano works and finding mostly the same thing again and again—lightly seasoned, at most, with the odd fleeting new idea—to finally encounter something truly *original,* such as these two sonatas by Beethoven. The reviewer believes them to be among the very best of Beethoven's works to date, and therefore also among the greatest music being written anywhere at the present moment. [On the Sonatas for Violin and Piano in A Minor and F Major, opp. 23 and 24][13]

Beethoven saw the potential benefits of this change in the wind and promptly sold both the String Quintet (op. 29) and two sets of piano variations (opp. 34 and 35) to Breitkopf & Härtel. Still, his temper continued to flare at the slightest barb from the *Allgemeine musikalische Zeitung*. For example, the review of his *Akademie* on April 5, 1803, which included a performance of the oratorio *Christ on the Mount of Olives*, was hardly flattering, and the attention devoted by the critics to what they considered to be exorbitant ticket prices (and Beethoven's associated income) drove him to his writing desk:

> Please pass on my sincere thanks to the editor of the *Musikalische Zeitung*, for the kindness shown in publishing such a <u>flattering report</u> of my oratorio, and for the <u>blatant lies regarding my supposed income,</u> putting me in the most infamous light (in order to demonstrate the journal's lack of bias towards me, no doubt) [. . .] Oh, the noble-mindedness demanded of a true artist these days! And certainly not without good reason, but in return, others deem it acceptable to trample over us in so dreadful and despicable a fashion.[14]

Tensions rose. In the negotiations for the rights to the *Mount of Olives,* the Third Symphony, the Triple Concerto, and the piano sonatas in C Major, F Major, and F Minor (opp. 53, 54, and 57), Beethoven had raised his prices considerably. Breitkopf & Härtel decided to terminate the relationship for various reasons. Although coincidence cannot be ruled out, the reviews of the *Eroica* that appeared in subsequent weeks were overwhelmingly negative:

> In reality, this long and difficult work is a bold, wild and indulgent rhapsody. While not lacking in beautiful or striking moments that undeniably reveal the energetic and talented spirit of its creator, it nonetheless often spirals into seeming chaos [. . .] Although the reviewer is certainly one of Beethoven's most fervent admirers, in this instance I must confess to finding his bizarre fancies excessive. They serve to obscure the overall impression of the work, and almost destroy any sense of unity.
>
> Though this new work of Beethoven's is possessed of ideas both majestic and bold, and—as one has come to expect from the genius of this composer— a high degree of impact, the symphony (which lasts *a full hour*) would benefit infinitely, were Beethoven to abridge it somewhat, incorporating more light, clarity and unity to the whole [. . .] If, on multiple hearings, a sense of cohesion eludes even the most focused concentration, any reasonable music lover must be forced to acknowledge this fact.[15]

Beethoven responded with vitriol: "I have heard of the recent lashings given in the *Musikalischer Zeitung* to the <u>symphony</u> that I submitted last year (and which was subsequently returned to me). <u>I have not read the article myself,</u> but if you consider yourself able to thus damage <u>my</u> reputation, you are sorely mistaken—you succeed only in plunging your own journal into disrepute."[16]

Only through mediation by Saxon diplomat Griesinger—the publisher's Viennese agent—and an intervention by Herr Härtel himself, who visited Beethoven personally in 1808, was Breitkopf & Härtel able to iron out the conflict and restore fruitful collaboration. All of the major works up to 1812 were subsequently published in Leipzig, and Beethoven's international reputation was secured.

A key figure throughout these developments was the editor in chief of the *Allgemeine musikalische Zeitung,* Friedrich Rochlitz. A theologist and amateur musician, Rochlitz had both a prolific literary pen and a number of compositions to his name. When Breitkopf & Härtel launched its own musical periodical in 1798—ostensibly with pedagogical intentions but in reality serving as a de facto marketing tool—Rochlitz was appointed as editor. He fulfilled the role con brio until 1818, although he did have a tendency to overstep the boundaries of his remit from time to time. It just so happened that Rochlitz also wrote opera libretti, which from his powerful position as editor he attempted to foist on various composers. His ploy worked on Carl Maria von Weber and Louis Spohr, but not on Haydn and certainly not on Beethoven. An initial effort to force a libretto on Beethoven in 1802 ended in failure, not least because Rochlitz also wished to claim some of the royalties for himself. When Breitkopf & Härtel got wind of Beethoven's opera plans in 1803, Rochlitz sent Beethoven a new playbook titled *Liebhabereien, oder die neue Zauberflöte* (Vicissitudes of love, or the new *Magic Flute*). Beethoven was uninterested in a remake of Mozart's popular opera and wrote a diplomatic letter arguing that operas on magical themes were no longer in vogue in Vienna, though he did express the sincere hope that his refusal would not affect their business relationship.[17] The message was clear: Beethoven would brook no meddling when it came to artistic matters—not even from as powerful a figure as Rochlitz—but hoped nonetheless to continue to rely on his friendly support.

Their relationship remained problematic for some time, and Beethoven's paranoia would lead him to accuse Rochlitz multiple times of authoring negative critique. At heart, however, Rochlitz was a Beethoven admirer and never abandoned his dream of having Beethoven set one of his own texts. In August 1822 he renewed his efforts, meeting with Beethoven three times during a trip to Vienna. The atmosphere seemed convivial—Rochlitz described Beethoven as "cheerful, occasionally even jovial, and generally very open-hearted"[18]—but a musical collaboration was not to be.

For a time, it appeared as though Rochlitz might become Beethoven's hagiographer. Several months after Beethoven's death, Schindler tried to enlist the critic for the final editing of his Beethoven biography, saying that it would have been what the master wanted. Rochlitz felt honored but turned down the offer nonetheless.

21

The Disciples

CARL CZERNY AND FERDINAND RIES

A FEW DAYS AFTER *THE CREATURES OF PROMETHEUS* was premiered, Beethoven was introduced to ten-year-old wunderkind Carl Czerny. A mutual friend, the Bohemian mandolinist and violinist Wenzel Krumpholz, had organized an audition in Beethoven's apartment with several other well-known musicians in attendance, including Wranitzky, Süssmayr, and Schuppanzigh. Beethoven as usual was unkempt, shabbily dressed, and had not shaved in days, which made his dark eyes seem even more deep-set than usual. The shy and slightly awkward Czerny later confessed that Beethoven had reminded him of Robinson Crusoe.[1]

Czerny first of all played Mozart's Piano Concerto in C Major (K. 503). Beethoven was intrigued. He drew his chair closer to the piano, and occasionally joined in by tapping out the orchestral wind solos with one finger of his left hand. After several encouraging remarks, the young Czerny felt brave enough to perform the *Sonate pathétique*—entirely from memory, a very uncommon practice at the time. To conclude, he accompanied his father, who was quite a competent singer, in a rendition of "Adelaide." Beethoven was impressed, concluded that the boy was very talented, and took him on as a pupil. He was prepared to see him three times per week, and because the Czernys were far from well-off, he charged virtually nothing. A noteworthy detail: Beethoven insisted that Czerny obtain a copy of C. P. E. Bach's *Essay on the True Art of Playing Keyboard Instruments*—the manual that he himself had worked through with Neefe as a young pupil—and ordered him to bring it to every lesson.

Czerny's first lessons were very technical and quite dry. Beethoven had his pupil play nothing but scales, correcting his basic hand position (Beethoven himself let his hands glide across the keys, as it were, while his fingers did all the work) and showing Czerny how to make better use of that forgotten stepchild of classical piano technique, the thumb.[2] Next on the list was legato playing—Beethoven's specialty—and only after that was any attention devoted to broader matters of musicality or interpretation. Czerny studied Beethoven's entire output for the piano, including the concertos and chamber works, progressing through them with the composer one by one. He thus became an authority on Beethoven's music, which several years later led to an engagement with Karl Lichnowsky. The prince would have Czerny visit every morning and, like a kind of human jukebox, satisfy his every musical whim. Lichnowsky would name a Beethoven opus number at random, which Czerny would then proceed to perform, aided only by his prodigious, Mozartian memory. Czerny would later report that Beethoven, who was present on several such occasions, did not approve of this "playing by heart." He believed that even if Czerny were to play everything correctly, he would nonetheless lose both his overview of the work as a whole and his ability to play at sight. The right expression would undoubtedly also slip through the cracks now and then . . .

Despite the young Czerny's precocity, exceptional memory, flawless sight-reading, and extraordinary technique, he had no career as a child prodigy. Beethoven put it down to his parents and their extreme overprotectiveness— Czerny's father never even let his son go into town alone, for example. But although Beethoven had experienced the downsides of a spartan musical education firsthand, he still believed that a rigorous approach was necessary to raise Czerny to the very top. A conflict arose between Beethoven and Czerny's father, and after several years the lessons were discontinued. Beethoven and the young Czerny remained good friends for life, however, and Czerny later even became the teacher of Beethoven's nephew Karl.

Czerny's overprotective parents were only part of the problem. The Napoleonic wars had made extended travels through Europe a hazardous undertaking, and unlike Mozart's father the Czernys had neither the financial means nor the connections to embark on such a journey. Their son, moreover, was just a little too old to be a wunderkind, and the hype surrounding child prodigies was dwindling. But the biggest obstacle of all was Czerny's adherence to the wrong artistic camp. The masses wanted sensational works performed with panache and bravura, music that Czerny characterized as "fast, loud, staccato, even brutal," and dismissed as "ingenious, well-thought-out musical quackery."[3] Beethoven's music, on the other hand (and by extension that of his pupil Czerny), was expressive and profound and by default less appealing to the general public. But while Beethoven's works still offered something of the spectacular, Czerny's compositions were just a little too mannerly and sweet—like bourgeois furniture in musical form.

Following in his father's footsteps, Czerny became a piano teacher, and a good one too. He had dozens of students at a time (the best known was the young Franz Liszt) and achieved excellent results. Interestingly, as a teacher Czerny saw himself as an evangelist of the Beethoven school of music. In support of his mission, he organized frequent Sunday concerts in his own home, dedicated exclusively to Beethoven's music—often in the presence of the master himself, who would then grace the assembly with an improvisation or two—to enable younger pianists to become better acquainted with his oeuvre. Czerny's true legacy, however, was the codification of Beethoven's piano technique, which he condensed into a didactic work titled *The Art of Finger Dexterity* (op. 740). This collection is both a compendium and a progressive training course of fifty piano etudes, each one singling out a specific aspect of modern piano technique. It was an ambitious project, and anybody who successfully battled through it would be well equipped to tackle any work by Beethoven.[4] Czerny also wrote a book on the correct interpretation of Beethoven (*On the Proper Performance of All Beethoven's Works for the Piano*), relaying the precise directions that he himself had received from the composer, including remarks on tempo indications (given as metronome markings) and the character of the music. Although his pronouncements may not all be equally relevant or correct, they do provide a solid point of departure for Beethoven interpretation, even today.[5]

As invaluable as Czerny's input has been for preserving Beethoven's school of thought, his contributions as a star pupil and Beethoven apologist are not without their contradictions. Czerny, who was a typical exponent of early-nineteenth-century middle-class culture, saw diligence as a vital character trait. He was the first to posit that one could only be an excellent pianist by practicing day in and day out (as though some kind of industrial logic were an integral component of artistic development), and he believed that technical mastery constituted the highest of virtues. He was also the first to recommend performing from memory in public, both as proof of the thoroughness of the soloist's preparation as well as a means of increasing the focus on interpretation (a rationale with which Beethoven disagreed). Although not his express intention, Czerny thus created a codex for Beethoven interpretation that shifted the epicenter of imagination from production to reproduction, and from creation to interpretation. One of Czerny's most talented students, Theodor Leschetizky, perpetuated this tradition. He applied the model during his piano classes in Vienna and St. Petersburg, thus shaping an entire generation of elite pianists (including Arthur Schnabel, Ignaz Paderewski, and Paul Wittgenstein) and setting the standard of Beethoven interpretation for decades to come. Whereas Beethoven himself had "played" the piano, his spiritual children, grandchildren, and great-grandchildren "studied" it.

In the spring of 1803, Beethoven took on a second professional student, Ferdinand Ries from Bonn.[6] Here, too, extramusical motives were at play; we recall that Ferdinand's father, Franz Ries, had been a source of considerable support to Beethoven in the trying years following his mother's death, and later provided a foothold for Beethoven's initial years in Vienna. Beethoven was thus indebted to the Ries family, and when the young Ferdinand first called on him in Vienna, Beethoven was heard to remark: "I cannot reply to your father just now, but do write to him that I have not forgotten the circumstances surrounding my mother's death; that should make him happy."[7] Despite being overburdened with work, Beethoven took Ferdinand's musical instruction very seriously. He spent quite a lot of time on the lessons themselves and solicited Albrechtsberger for the theoretical component of Ferdinand's training. The young Ries was overjoyed and wrote to his relatives back home: "Beethoven is taking greater pains than I had thought possible. I have three lessons a week, usually from one o'clock until two-thirty. I will soon be able to play the *Sonata pathétique* in a manner that I am sure will please you." On another occasion, he wrote, "I can only ascribe his friendliness towards me (only occasionally does he forget himself) to his affection for, and gratitude towards, my father."[8]

Like Czerny, Ries left detailed accounts of Beethoven's teaching methods, describing his teacher as both highly demanding and patient: "During lessons, Beethoven was—contrary to his nature, I must say—uncommonly patient [. . .] He had me repeat some sections over ten times." Of note is also the observation that Beethoven only ever criticized Ries's interpretation, and never his technique: "If ever I made an error, or failed to land certain notes or leaps that he wanted brought out, he rarely said anything; only for shortcomings of expression—crescendos, etc.—or in the character of the piece, did he become enraged, since he believed that while the former was an error of chance, the latter came from a lack of understanding, sensitivity or concentration." Occasionally Beethoven would give a demonstration: Ries described how Beethoven would sit beside him at the keyboard and begin playing "the [fugal] theme first with his left hand, then adding the right, and then continue to develop the material for a full half hour without the least interruption. It remains a mystery to me how he could bear playing for so long in such an uncomfortable position. He was so deeply engrossed, his mind was oblivious to all outside influences." Lastly, Ries told of how Beethoven was able to compose while teaching: "Beethoven composed a section of the second march—and still I fail to understand how—while giving me a lesson on a sonata that I was to perform that evening in a small concert."[9]

Ries was a diligent pupil. He followed his master's instructions to the letter, worked hard on his technique, and in so doing succeeded in camouflaging a certain lack of musical personality. Czerny would later note that Ries imitated many of his teacher's idiosyncrasies, that his playing was cold, and that Beethoven was dissatisfied.[10]

Alongside the free lessons, Beethoven gave his young pupil material support whenever and wherever he could. He knew only too well how difficult it was for a young provincial musician to find footing in an unforgiving city like Vienna. At one point he even chided Ries for not informing him of his precarious financial situation: "I must have words with you for not coming to me sooner. Am I not a true friend? Why hide your troubles from me? None of my friends shall suffer hardship while I still have something to give."[11] This motto would be applied consistently by Beethoven throughout his life, and he sent Ries sums of money without ever asking to be repaid. He also recommended Ries for minor posts with Lichnowsky and Browne and charged him with some secretarial and copyist work. Later, too, when Ries was temporarily called back to the Rhineland for a military service examination (or more to the point, an exemption), Beethoven turned a blind eye when he made some additional earnings in Bonn by producing chamber-music arrangements of his master's works. In all other instances, Beethoven vehemently opposed such practices.

Beethoven stood behind his pupil—sometimes even in a literal sense. When Ries made his Vienna debut in the *Augarten* on August 1, 1804, Beethoven not only gave him permission to be the first to perform one of his own concertos (the Third) but also threw his full artistic weight into the ring by conducting the orchestra himself. Ries later reported that Beethoven's attitude during rehearsals and the performance was one of humble dedication, that he played the part of both conductor and page-turner, and that rarely had a concerto been so beautifully and thoughtfully accompanied. Beethoven had also asked his pupil to present some original work, and after Ries successfully pulled off his own cadenza with magnificent flair, Beethoven leapt up with a loud "Bravo!" Ries could hardly contain his happiness: "The entire audience was electrified, I felt I had been granted an immediate place among the great artists."[12] Never before had anyone been thus publicly presented as Beethoven's pupil.

A falling out between Beethoven and Ries was, of course, inevitable. Later we shall examine in greater detail how the misunderstanding surrounding Beethoven's candidacy at the court of Kassel in the spring of 1809 led to an extended period of silence between them, until eventually—in typical Beethovenian fashion—the conflict was set aside.

Several weeks after their reconciliation, Ries left the Austrian capital forever on a major European concert tour. He ultimately settled in London, where as one of the directors of the Philharmonic Society he championed the dissemination of Beethoven's music in England and collaborated on (sadly unsuccessful) attempts to have Beethoven travel to London. When he moved back to the Rhineland to retire in Godesburg in 1824, Ries remained a fervid Beethoven devotee. In 1825 he even conducted several performances of the Ninth Symphony. Beethoven had always promised to dedicate the work to him, and it was only at the last minute that Ries's name was struck out and replaced by that of the Prussian king, Frederick William III.

Czerny and Ries were the last (male) pianists to enjoy regular lessons with Beethoven. Some years later he would take on Archduke Rudolph as a composition student, but that is a different story entirely.

Wegeler informs us that Beethoven always despised teaching. This was only partially true; Beethoven generally had no objection to female pupils if they were possessed of sufficient beauty and charm. But he could also muster some enthusiasm for their male counterparts, provided they had enough talent and were willing to subscribe to his musical philosophy. Teaching also involves a great deal of self-reflection. The act of critically analyzing and commenting on others' interpretations confronted Beethoven directly with his own music, and he can only have learned much about himself as a result.

Various testimonies state that Beethoven intended to write his own treatise on pianism, since he found most books on the subject to be inadequate.[13]

This was understandable, as these didactic tomes were generally not products of the greatest minds, especially not in Beethoven's opinion. The fact that he never surpassed others' efforts in this respect is equally understandable, as he lacked the time, the energy, and—perhaps most importantly—the methodical discipline for such an undertaking.

22

The Heiligenstadt Testament

BEETHOVEN'S WORK ON THE FIRST SYMPHONY, the String Quartets, and *The Creatures of Prometheus* had taxed his strength to the limit. For many months he had been suppressing signs of stress and exhaustion, and when the initial *Prometheus* season ended in June 1801, the pressures finally took their toll and he broke down. In Beethoven's case, symptoms of stress always manifested as severe abdominal pain, which he first experienced in the early 1790s and then again while preparing for his first *Akademie* in 1795. The problem would be ongoing throughout his life, and medical specialists have now deduced that Beethoven suffered from what is called "irritable bowel syndrome," a widespread but essentially harmless gastrointestinal condition that causes stomach cramps and digestive upsets. The complaint seems particularly common in those who have difficulty coping with stress, a cohort to which Beethoven indisputably belonged.[1]

In that same summer of 1801, Beethoven also reached the disturbing conclusion that the hearing problems he had first noticed in 1797 were more serious than he initially supposed. Until that time, he had confided in nobody, not even his closest friends; they were probably aware that he missed fragments of conversation from time to time, but most likely put it down to general absentmindedness and thought nothing further of it. But Beethoven could keep silent no longer. Although he cannot have realized the true nature or severity of his condition, nor had he any accurate notion of the rate at which his auditory capacity would decline, he nonetheless began to fear not only that his future career as a concert pianist was at stake—and by extension his life as a professional musician—but also that he might start having trouble functioning normally in society. Beethoven felt the foundations of his carefully constructed life giving way beneath him, and in utter desperation wrote several highly emotional letters to Wegeler and Amenda begging for help, comfort, and—in Wegeler's case—medical advice. He expressly asked for their utmost discretion, for fear that his position in the music world would quickly be undermined by any reports or rumors of his hearing loss.

In these letters, Beethoven describes in great detail how, a year after his illness in 1796, he noticed an appreciable drop in his hearing. The symptoms initially manifested in the right ear but would soon spread to the left. He suffered chronic earaches, complaining of "fizzling and sizzling"[2] day and night, and had developed an oversensitivity to sudden increases in volume or loud shouting. Physical pain aside, he was also plagued by a drop in the clarity of higher frequencies, so much so that he needed to sit extremely close to the orchestra at the theater if he wished to understand the singers properly.[3] Playing and composing at the piano presented little trouble; the real problem was verbal communication. Again, this is hardly surprising, as vowel sounds are those that suffer most from a decline in the upper frequencies, compromising linguistic clarity and forming a barrier to normal conversation. Beethoven had mastered the art of avoiding social situations that might present him with difficulties, a trying ordeal for one so fond of stimulating company. The emerging scenario did little to improve his chances of finding a suitable marriage partner, moreover.

Beethoven wrote to Wegeler and Amenda of the fear that had gripped him. He also conceded his tendency to be a rather difficult, ungrateful, and "impatient" patient, as he would embark on each new course of therapy brimming with enthusiasm, often quickly exceeding the prescribed dosage of medication, only to switch doctors just as readily and start a new treatment regime in the absence of immediate results. Viennese medical and academic authorities were powerless to help him. A certain Dr. Frank was too academic, whereas Dr. von Vering was too practical, uninformed, and unsympathetic, while a third (unnamed) doctor was denounced as "some ass or other from the medical profession."[4] Only the last in line, Dr. Johann Adam Schmidt, earned Beethoven's unequivocal trust. Beethoven also sought help in alternative medical circles, even venturing several times to see Father Weiss, the proprietor of a pseudomedical practice in the presbytery by St. Stephen's Cathedral. Unfortunately the eardrops of holy water administered during these sessions brought no relief, much to the patient's immense frustration.

The various treatments endured by Beethoven were many and varied: bathing in either cold or lukewarm water from the Danube; applications of almond oil or other unspecified extracts; bandaging the arms in a blistering agent derived from tree bark; rubbing the belly with a herbal concoction; and experiments with galvanism (muscular electrotherapy), which were quickly called off due to Beethoven's mounting anxiety. At most, these treatments elicited a few short-lived moments of placebo-induced euphoria and temporary pain relief, but they did nothing to dispel the underlying ill. Although Beethoven was forced to acknowledge that his hearing problem was worsening despite the treatments, he did not resign himself to the situation. In a stubborn letter to Wegeler, he writes: "I shall take fate by the throat, and will not be brought to my knees. For to lead such a life—a still life—no, it cannot be that I was made for this."[5]

Despite the steady decline in his hearing, Beethoven succeeded in practicing his profession more or less normally for quite some time. In 1805 he ran the *Leonore* rehearsals without issue; in 1808 he gave a stunning first performance of the Fourth Piano Concerto (where the main problem was not his lack of hearing but his lack of practice), and an anecdote from the same year tells of how he picked out the minutest of errors when observing a performance by child prodigy Wilhelm Rust.[6] His pupil Carl Czerny insisted that in the years 1811 and 1812, Beethoven was still able to correct his students' playing with astonishing accuracy. Only later did his condition take a sudden downturn. The total loss of hearing in his right ear meant that Beethoven became completely reliant on the left, which had itself already degenerated. His life as a performer was over, and he is presumed to have made his final public appearance during a chamber music concert on April 11, 1814.[7] Both composition and conversation had also become increasingly difficult, and Beethoven sought solace in all manner of technical aids. He requested louder instruments from piano builder Johann Andreas Streicher, and from Johann Nepomuk Mälzel—who would later market the first metronomes—he ordered a series of "ear trumpets," conical devices inserted into the ear to serve as auditory amplifiers. Mälzel did his best, but despite building a range of models to suit various circumstances—concerts in large or small spaces, playing the piano at home, verbal communication—the benefits to Beethoven were limited. Ultimately, in 1818, he had no choice but to resort to conversation notebooks or a pen and slate in order to carry on a "conversation." Only if people bellowed into a hand cupped around Beethoven's ear could he discern fragments of speech, and even then he still needed to fill in the gaps himself, risking confusion of a different kind.

Even at this late stage, Beethoven reportedly still made efforts to hear live music now and again. There are records of an attempt in 1822, for example, to listen to Cherubini's opera *Medea* using some kind of musical machine. Dating from that same year, however, is the tragic tale of how Beethoven— now almost completely deaf—drove a rehearsal of *Fidelio* utterly into the ground and was reluctantly but sternly removed from the conductor's podium.

In the last two years of his life, Beethoven also lost the use of his left ear, making him utterly reliant on his "mind's ear" when composing. Beethoven— now stone-deaf—did still attend the rehearsals of the late string quartets, making pertinent remarks based on visual observations and picking up the violin now and again to demonstrate how the music should sound. That some of his notes were off by a full semitone—a fact of which he was blissfully unaware—seems not to have mattered all that much.[8]

The tale of Beethoven's deafness is fascinating and has taken on mythical proportions. By now there are nearly 150 publications speculating on the true nature and cause of Beethoven's crippling condition. The list of possible diagnoses is long and can be whittled down to around twenty categories, ranging from acoustic trauma, alcoholism, arteriosclerosis, amyloidosis and other autoimmune disorders, through to sarcoidosis, sensory neuritis, tuberculosis, typhus, and Whipple disease.[9] Of course, establishing a correct diagnosis nearly two hundred years after a patient's death is a task verging on the impossible, even in light of the extremely detailed reports on the autopsy performed by Dr. Johann Wagner immediately on Beethoven's death in 1827, and the exhumations carried out in 1863 and 1888. Beethoven's friend Dr. Weissenbach was probably closest to the truth when he proposed the connection in 1816 between Beethoven's deafness and his bout of typhus from 1796. At that time, typhus was already known to cause neurological complications in around 15 percent of patients, ranging from various mental conditions to hemiparesis (paralysis on one side of the body). But deafness—full or partial, temporary or permanent—was also known to occur, and the historical medical literature does indeed suggest that there were many deaf and hearing-impaired citizens living in the early nineteenth century.[10]

In Beethoven's case, it is clear that the condition was localized in the inner ear, placing it in the category of "perceptual hearing loss." This diagnosis is supported by the meticulous descriptions of symptoms in his letters to Wegeler and Amenda, which specify a loss of the high frequencies, early difficulties in discerning speech, and an oversensitivity to sudden increases in volume. There are also reports that Beethoven began speaking quite loudly as time went on, a behavior that is typical of those who can no longer hear themselves properly due to inner-ear defects.[11]

At the same time, damage to the fragile bones in the middle and outer ear cannot be ruled out, leaving open the possibility that Beethoven also suffered from second-stage "conductive hearing loss." The earplugs used frequently by Beethoven, soaked in all manner of substances, were hotbeds of infection and caused inflammation that almost certainly damaged his auditory apparatus— not to mention the acoustic trauma inflicted by the aggressive insertion of hearing aids, ear trumpets, and funnels into Beethoven's ear canals.

Of all the possible alternative theories (and especially those in the more popular literature), the most tenacious is the speculation that Beethoven's deafness was of venereal origin. This hypothesis, however, can be dismissed on purely medical grounds. While it is true that late-stage syphilis can affect the central nervous system and thus cause hearing and other sensory problems, in such cases the disease strikes hard and fast, resulting not only in a total loss of hearing within several weeks but also in the deterioration of other cognitive abilities such as speech and memory. Beethoven's extraordinary artistic accomplishments in the three decades following his initial symptoms exclude any such scenario, a conclusion that is also supported by the absence of any other associated complications, such as a loss of balance.[12]

Beethoven initially rebelled at the thought of losing what he called the "noblest of the senses," at being robbed of the best years of his life, and at being denied the opportunity to develop his talents and abilities to their fullest extent. He felt—and rightly so—that his career was just starting to take off, and he was scared of losing momentum.[13] In the summer of 1801, he took stock of his life. His financial problems had been resolved, not only because Lichnowsky had pledged him an annual stipend of six hundred guilders, but also thanks to a new and abundant income from selling his compositions to publishers. Beethoven himself attested that he had more offers of work than he could accept, and at times even had six or seven publishers clamoring simultaneously for the rights to a single piece, eliminating the need to negotiate on price. Work on each new commission began before the previous one was finished, and often he composed three or four works at a time. As a result, his fame had begun to spread far beyond the confines of

Vienna, and it was no coincidence that the Artaria publishing house deemed it opportune to have a portrait of Beethoven made and distributed abroad— not unlike the posters of modern-day pop stars. Even in such a fickle city, Beethoven seemed to have it made. He was convinced that Vienna would continue to be his home and that he would organize an annual *Akademie*.

It was at this time, when success seemed within his grasp and Beethoven felt he had reached full personal and artistic maturity, that his health dealt him such a crippling blow. It would be some time before he came to terms with it, and for a while he even considered abandoning his musical career, returning to Bonn, and becoming a farmer. But after some initial hesitation, and later with increasing conviction, Beethoven eventually wound his way toward what he called "bitter sorrowful resignation."[14] Spurred on by his spiritual guide Plutarch, he resolved to defy fate. In a letter to Wegeler he writes, brimming with optimism and determination, of his refusal to give in to defeat: "Without this ill, O how I would take on the world . . . My youth— I can feel it—is only just beginning [. . .] my body is stronger now than ever before, and my mind no less so . . . Each day I am nearer to reaching the goal that I can sense is there, but cannot describe. Only thus can I, your Beethoven, live life—peace and quiet be damned!"[15]

This optimism was short-lived due to its primarily endorphin-based origins: Beethoven had just fallen in love with Giulietta Guicciardi, after all, and was cherishing hopes of soon being able to marry her. The prospect bolstered his mood and permitted him to set his health issues aside—a genuine necessity, since he had important works to complete. These included both commissions and personal projects: a string quartet for Count Fries, a set of violin sonatas, and also several piano sonatas and variations. But his most pressing objective was to organize a second *Akademie*. And like any painter who requires new (and preferably innovative) material for an exhibition, so too was Beethoven intent on dazzling audiences with groundbreaking symphonic and concerto writing: the monumental Symphony in D (op. 36), lasting nearly forty minutes; the atypical Piano Concerto in C Minor (op. 37); and the Triple Concerto in D for the rare combination of piano, cello, violin, and orchestra.[16]

Alas, in the spring of 1802 Beethoven realized that his love for Giulietta Guicciardi was an illusion and that marrying her was impossible, as it had been with Josephine von Brunsvik before her. To make matters worse, shortly afterward theater despot Braun refused to open his doors for a new *Akademie*—possibly under pressure from the orchestral players, who still resented the demeaning treatment they had received during the previous production. For Beethoven, this was nothing short of a catastrophe. His world seemed to collapse around him, and he fell apart.

His physician, Dr. Schmidt, was abundantly clear on the matter: Beethoven had succumbed to a combination of internal and external pressures, to demons both physical and metaphysical. It was therefore important for him not only to come to terms with the inevitability of his encroaching deafness but also to limit the strain on his nervous system by keeping negative influences and stress to a minimum. Dr. Schmidt thus urged his patient to take better emotional care of himself and to make drastic life and lifestyle changes. He also suggested that Beethoven spend at least six months away from the city, to distance himself from the evils of the world and the music scene; only in the country, far from the urban commotion and in communion with nature, would he be able to relax and find inner solace. Beethoven leapt at the opportunity and promptly authorized his brother Kaspar Karl to manage his daily affairs and to continue negotiations with publishers. On April 22, he announced his retreat in a letter to Breitkopf & Härtel: "I write to you myself, Sir, to inform you that of late, my pressing business and various other unfortunate circumstances have rendered me unable to attend to certain matters. In the meantime, please continue dealings with my brother, who will be seeing to all of my affairs."[17]

He left the next day for Heiligenstadt, taking lodgings in a house on Herrengasse (the modern-day Probusgasse). Heiligenstadt was a small and cozy winemaking town at the foot of the Kahlenberg and Leopoldsberg mountains, around five kilometers north of the Vienna city center. Today it is part of the nineteenth district of Döbling, which has a reputation as one of the *Nobelviertel,* or "noble quarters." The more wealthy Viennese maintain a residence there, and it is home to many a consulate and embassy. It also seems perpetually sun-drenched in the summertime, although the heat is less oppressive than in central Vienna due to its proximity to the forests and mountains. Unfortunately it is also a tourist attraction—a fact for which Beethoven is partly to blame—and the evening's peace and tranquility is often interrupted by the vociferous outpourings of boisterous foreigners, who have underestimated the intoxicating effects of the young Heuriger white wine.

In 1802, however, the locale was still picturesque and idyllic, and a classic Viennese getaway during the summer months. As a health retreat it was both cheaper and less snobbish than the more distant town of Baden, and it could be reached easily by private stagecoach. Beethoven loved it there and would happily stroll for hours through the vineyards and along the river toward Krapfenwaldl, Coblenzl, or Kahlenberg. In the beginning he was able to relax a little, but after several weeks, restlessness took hold and he began composing again. He worked fervently on two new sets of piano variations, in F and E-flat (opp. 34 and 35), and also on a commission from Switzerland, the three Piano Sonatas in G Major, D Minor, and E-flat Major (op. 31). But his hopes of avoiding conflict were soon dashed, as Vienna was still too close by to keep all people and problems at bay. Not only that, but Kaspar Karl was not always tactful in his negotiations with publishers, and Beethoven was not wholly spared the burden of unpleasant correspondence. It seemed that a sabbatical in total isolation was not to be.

Beethoven's six months in Heiligenstadt flew by, and in late October he returned to the Austrian capital troubled by conflicting thoughts and feelings. These he documented in a long, two-part letter, which he never mailed to anyone but carried with him the rest of his life.[18] The letter has become known as the "Heiligenstadt Testament,"[19] and has acquired a certain cult status as one of the principal and most authentic sources providing an insight into the psyche of the great master. It is also the subject of myriad interpretations, most of which miss the mark as they fall into the trap of taking Beethoven's missive too literally. Those that do not, believe instead that the testament represents a spiritual rather than a material bequest and was almost certainly only ever intended for his own personal use.[20]

Beethoven opens the Heiligenstadt Testament by lamenting his fate, having been struck the cruelest of all possible blows and without any hope of respite; he attempts to justify his avoidance of society and feels misunderstood by the outside world. He also seems to have briefly considered ending his life but was prevented from doing so by his art. He nevertheless makes provisions for his brothers' inheritance, enjoining them—and with them, all of humanity—to virtuous conduct. Lastly, he takes new courage: while accepting death as a release from suffering, he still hopes to delay it for as long as possible in order to give his talent the greatest opportunity to fully unfold.

The legal validity of the "testament" is, incidentally, nonexistent due to the lack of a clear addressee. The space for a salutation was originally left blank; only later was the name of Beethoven's brother "Carl" (meaning Kaspar Karl) inserted, while the space after the ensuing "and" remained empty. This omission has led to a host of speculations—a deeper conflict with the younger brother, psychological avoidance of his name "Johann" due to the associations with their father, and so on. There are also doubts regarding the true scope of the "bequest" metaphor, leading to the conjecture that Beethoven's physical brothers serve only to represent a more universal "brotherhood," whose members (depending on whom one asks) vary from humanity at large to a more select group of kindred spirits.

Another hallmark of the Heiligenstadt Testament is the constant alternation between layers of meaning, as Beethoven blurs the lines between reality, fiction, and poetry.[21] Paraphrases of Goethe also thwart interpretive efforts; the "wilting, falling autumn leaves" and even the notion of suicide are direct references to the wildly popular *Sorrows of Young Werther* and provide a contrasting backdrop that serves to bring Beethoven's will to survive into greater relief. The letter is a masterpiece of rhetoric and finishes with an uplifting message, intended first and foremost for himself. The testament took on the form of an autodialogue with a therapeutic effect—a solemn creed set out by Beethoven with great stylistic and calligraphic care in order to convince himself that the path he had chosen was the right one. Modern-day psychologists and counselors frequently apply the same technique and would certainly have urged Beethoven to do the same.

The Heiligenstadt Testament marks a tipping point, when Beethoven realized that he could harness a major setback and turn it to his advantage. Several years later, in the margins of the sketches for the Razumovsky quartets, Beethoven left the following remark: "Let thy deafness be secret no longer—not even in art." Later still, he penned in his diary, "Living for your art—however abandoned by your senses—is nonetheless now the <u>only existence</u> for you."[22]

From our perspective, we might conclude that Beethoven's deafness was more of a blessing than a curse. For one thing, fate thus spared him an agonizing decision by forcing him to give up a promising career as a concert pianist and leaving no other option than to concentrate fully on composition. But perhaps of greater import was his ever-deeper introversion and withdrawal from the outside world, with the inevitable consequences for his musical development. Beethoven became progressively less concerned with existing rules and conventions, and his involuntary auditory abstinence allowed him to develop a new musical language, one that he had already codified as "the new way." In this manner, Beethoven's personal, social, and emotional tragedy transformed into a quality that would push him into unexplored, and unsuspected, musical territory.

Like the heroes he idolized, Beethoven thus needed to suffer in order to transcend his own self and achieve greatness for the benefit of humankind. This, and no other, is the ultimate message of the Heiligenstadt Testament.[23]

PART THREE

The Master

(1802–1809)

23

A "New Way" Forward

BEETHOVEN RETURNED FROM HEILIGENSTADT invigorated, with fresh ideas and heightened ambition. Fate had decided for him that he should devote more energy to composing and less to performing. Earning a living as a composer was difficult, however, and Beethoven recalled how much even a genius such as Mozart had struggled to survive in the Viennese musical jungle. He therefore had no time to lose and resolved to concentrate only on what was essential, jettisoning any dead weight. When German publisher Johann Anton André placed an order for several smaller works, Kaspar Karl responded that moving forward his brother wished to dedicate himself exclusively to opera and oratorio. Should the publisher absolutely insist on "trifles" such as piano sonatas, he would need to be patient and make a generous offer.[1]

From this point on, Beethoven's music would be subject to a new and altered set of criteria. According to Carl Czerny, Beethoven once confessed to his friend Krumpholz that he had become unhappy with all of his previous works and was looking for a "new way" forward.[2] But properties such as "new" or "different" are not artistic qualities in themselves and cannot be summoned on command, a fact of which Beethoven was well aware. Hitherto it had been others who told Beethoven that his ideas represented a departure from the norm. But a note to his publisher in Leipzig concerning the piano variations dating from this period (opp. 34 and 35) reveals that on this occasion, Beethoven was fully cognizant that his treatment of the material was utterly unprecedented.[3]

Although the "new way" had forced itself on him in some respects, its appearance at this juncture was not entirely coincidental. As an extemporizing pianist, Beethoven constantly pushed the limits of imagination and expression in search of new musical possibilities. This attitude found its way into his piano compositions, where Beethoven increasingly explored the gray area between sonata and fantasia, the results of which manifested primarily in his choice of formal structures. The Sonata in A-flat (op. 26), for example, begins most unconventionally with a theme and variations, then moves on to a scherzo, followed by a stylized funeral march and concluding with a perpetuum mobile. The two succeeding Piano Sonatas (op. 27)—not coincidentally subtitled "Quasi una fantasia"—commence not with an Allegro, as dictated by classical sonata tradition, but instead with slow movements employing unique structural concepts. The first of these two sonatas opens with a hybrid rondo-variation-song form, leaving the listener bereft of the usual auditory waypoints. The second sonata—the famous *Moonlight* and a more somber counterweight to the first—begins with a perpetual and ethereal lament devoid of any thematic footholds (perhaps serving as a metaphor for humankind, searching for meaning at the dawn of a promising but uncertain new century). In the final movement, all hell breaks loose. Beethoven declares war not only on himself and on music in general but also on the piano: at times the instrument transforms into a steaming cauldron, spewing forth dark and diabolical musical vapors (again, a potential metaphor for what one might unearth when delving deep into one's own soul in the Freudian age).

The Sonata in D Minor (op. 31, no. 2), composed some time later and now referred to enigmatically as *The Tempest*,[4] goes so far as to shake the very foundations of classical musical grammar. It opens as a free rhapsody, cautious and tentative, with material that can scarcely be considered a "theme" due to its inherently unstable and uncertain character. The thematic allure only really comes to the fore once it is no longer expected and the music has already begun the transition to a new tonality. Such bridging passages traditionally consisted of nonthematic, "neutral" material, such as scales and arpeggios. Beethoven breaks with that tradition here, and as listeners we are in a perpetual state of wondering either when the theme will come or where it went—it never clearly presents. This technique is reminiscent of those used by surrealist painters, who replace familiar concepts with similar ones (such as a door with a window). In *The Tempest,* form and function are thus no longer congruent, an effect that was undoubtedly as aggravating as it was groundbreaking, especially in Beethoven's day.

As Beethoven himself had already said, the conceptual framework underlying the opus 34 and 35 sets of variations was "completely new." Each of the variations in the first set has its own key, time signature, and tempo, rendering the link to the original theme very tenuous, relying only on a few notes acting as signposts. The technique of superficially embellishing a familiar, recurring theme has vanished and been replaced by complex transformations of the thematic essence. In the second set, which would later provide the basis for the final movement of the *Eroica* Symphony, Beethoven goes a step further. Here we are denied even an opening presentation of the theme, which is instead constructed stepwise from the bass line up, as though being gradually coaxed out of the subconscious.

These sets of variations—whose significance in Beethoven's oeuvre is underscored by the fact that they are the first of their kind to receive an official opus number[5]—were a far cry from the *Gebrauchsmusik* that had hitherto been marketed to amateur pianists by Viennese publishers. Beethoven's break with tradition by using original themes rather than popular opera or other melodies was yet another hallmark of his new artistic vision. His piano music therefore not only became technically more difficult to play and to understand, but also illustrated the composer's intention to place himself at the center of the creation and reception process, as an emancipated and independent artist.

Beethoven was not the only variable that had changed. In musical Vienna of the early 1800s, the chasm between amateur and professional pianists was steadily widening due to the latter's experimentation with new music. (The same could not be said of London, where professional pianists continued to focus largely on the more learned, "ancient music" of Handel and friends.) Swiss publisher Hans Georg Nägeli took advantage of this new trend, launching two new piano music series in 1802. The first, titled "Musical Art in the Strict Style" (Musikalisches Kunstwerk der strengen Schreibart), presented only "early music" works by Bach and Handel. The second, with the curious French title of "The Pianists' Compendium" (Répertoire des clavecinistes), was dedicated exclusively to new compositions. In an advertisement in the *Allgemeine musikalische Zeitung,* Nägeli explained that the series was his way of encouraging the best pianists of the day to compose groundbreaking music: "My primary interest lies in piano solos of grand style and scope, that are in many ways divergent from the customary sonata form. These works should be marked by comprehensive musical richness and an abundance of ideas, and interweave contrapuntal passages with pianistic idiom."[6]

One of the first composers to be approached was Beethoven (along with Muzio Clementi, Johann Baptist Cramer, Johann Dussek, and Daniel

Steibelt), who was delighted with this opportunity to release his Piano Sonatas in G Major, D Minor, and E-flat Major (op. 31) onto the international market. Beethoven's "new way" was thus paved initially, in part, via Switzerland.

Beethoven's desire to make a fresh start also necessitated changes of a more practical nature. He henceforth wished to minimize all distraction from his higher purpose by eliminating the petty concerns of everyday life. He was not good with practicalities and said ironically of himself, "Perhaps the only sign of my genius is the fact that my affairs are seldom in order."[7] Beethoven detested writing letters and put them off endlessly; negotiations and calculations were further pet hates of his. He also found it difficult to stand up for himself, and although he had always been concerned with money and financial matters (his middle-class upbringing had taken care of that), he found conversations about money to be almost demeaning. But despite all this, Beethoven realized that he could no longer afford to be unprofessional when it came to his administration. And so, on his return from Heiligenstadt, he asked his brother Kaspar Karl to continue managing his affairs.

Kaspar Karl set boldly and efficiently to work, firmly convinced that the "product" of Beethoven's financial potential was far from exhausted. Given the fierce competition among publishers to acquire his brother's works, he took steps to escalate the price, not infrequently overstepping the bounds of decency. His strategy also included releasing old (i.e., outdated) works that Beethoven had composed in Bonn—a practice to which Beethoven generally objected but that he was powerless to prevent. Kaspar Karl also tried to stem the proliferation of third-party musical arrangements by making his own and submitting them for Beethoven's approval. This too irked Beethoven, who believed that his compositions were tied so intrinsically to the original instrument or ensemble that any arrangement would inevitably compromise on quality. Any legitimate "transcription" therefore also needed to be a "transformation," a feat attainable only by the composer himself, or at least by someone with "a comparable level of skill and inventiveness." We can therefore comprehend Beethoven's relief when he heard that Breitkopf & Härtel had respectfully declined to bring Kaspar Karl's "arranged items" to market.[8]

Although dedicated, Kaspar Karl was often awkward, sometimes dishonest, and occasionally a source of embarrassment to his brother. The complaints were many and varied: "Beethoven is an honest and upright man [...] His brother is less trustworthy, however, and I suspect that he even makes publishing deals of which Beethoven has no knowledge."[9] Or, "Charl [*sic*] Beethoven is the greediest of the lot—he will easily take back 50 words for a single ducat, and makes many enemies for his brother. Louis [Ludwig] plays but a single note, and his brother is already calculating—the petty scoundrel."[10]

This criticism of Kaspar Karl should be viewed with some perspective. It is true that he was often undiplomatic, and his overzealousness was undoubtedly fueled by a desire to exert a certain influence over his elder, dominant, more talented, and highly successful brother. It is not unreasonable to suppose, however, that he did nothing but bear the lot of any manager, carrying out the clear directives issued by his sibling-employer, and was condemned to absorb the blows that were intended for Beethoven himself.

Whatever the case, Kaspar Karl worked at his brother's side for four years, organizing virtually all of his personal affairs and shouldering a great deal of the day-to-day burden. Only when Kaspar Karl left to get married in 1806 did their partnership, which was greatly valued by Beethoven, come to an end.

24

The Laboratorium Artificiosum

BEETHOVEN WAS NOTHING IF NOT DISCIPLINED. He rose early every morning and worked continuously until two or three in the afternoon, taking occasional breaks to go "wander and work," as Schindler put it.[1] Next he enjoyed a meal and—come rain or shine—took a long afternoon walk, although his gait tended more toward the stiff and nervous than the leisurely. When out and about, he generally paid little attention to his surroundings, remaining utterly preoccupied with himself and his music. Now and again he would pause to jot down useful ideas that he wished to explore more fully the next day at his desk or piano. In summary, one might say that Beethoven's mornings were for productivity, and the afternoons for creativity. After his walk he headed to his regular café to enjoy a cup of coffee, smoke a pipe, and read the newspapers. Sometimes he played a game of chess, which he had learned from Haydn. Evenings were usually spent at home, but since composing at that hour was generally too taxing for his eyes, he would normally read a book instead. Now and then he joined friends for a drink (or in his case several drinks), and unless things got particularly rowdy, he was in bed by ten.

For Beethoven, composing was hard work, and he toiled away in what he jokingly called his *laboratorium artificiosum*[2]—a label whose denoted space was more virtual and mental than physical (in truth Beethoven was constantly composing, no matter where he was). To Beethoven, composing meant deliberately working through a series of processes, starting from a vague idea, which took shape very slowly and ultimately—after a great deal of effort, and not always following a logical sequence—crystallized into a fully developed and coherent musical work.

Unlike his approach to the practicalities of day-to-day life (which were always a disaster), Beethoven's compositional practices were extremely methodical. He first decided on the genre and instrumentation and rarely deviated from these parameters once they were set (one important exception being the Eighth Symphony, which started life as a piano concerto). Next he set the tonality, taking into account his former compositions, not only within the genre but within his oeuvre as a whole. Once the key—and thus the character—had been decided on, his attention shifted to the broader structural outlines and the proportions of the various sections relative to the whole. This may come as a surprise, as it is usually believed that Beethoven, like Haydn and Mozart, first conceived of an opening theme from which the rest of the work grew organically. Although there are certainly examples of Beethoven working in this manner, more often than not his starting point was a nebulous conceptualization of an idea within the given tonality, rather than a clearly defined melodic subject. Only once the composition had advanced somewhat did the theme take on its final, concrete form. The initial sketches of the Seventh Symphony, for example, are a mishmash of unrelated compound-duple ideas in A major, only one draft of which sports the characteristic rhythm that would come to dominate the symphony's opening movement:

In a subsequent attempt, the head of the theme takes on a recognizable identity, while the ensuing material remains vague and uninspired:

Only after six pages of experimentation does the theme clearly assume its final form:

Early in the process, Beethoven was thus still unconcerned with melodic or rhythmic details. He once said that he "never lost sight of the whole,"[3] evidenced by the fact that he would sometimes literally notate core ideas in their proper place on an empty page; the surrounding blank measures served as a spatial reminder, allowing him to check whether the work's proportions still made musical sense. Especially when deliberately incorporating novel structural variations, a clear overall vision was paramount. We know, for example, that his unorthodox decision to introduce a completely new theme into the development section of the opening movement of the *Eroica* was made very early on in the composition process.[4]

During a subsequent stage, Beethoven concentrated on producing the transitional passages, or the work's "connective tissue." This was technically often a tricky business, particularly when modulations came thick and fast; the more convoluted the road, after all, the greater the risk of losing one's musical bearings. In particular, the way Beethoven prepared for and effected the return of certain themes cost him more trouble than their initial genesis. And matters often got out of hand, with compositions taking on gargantuan proportions due to Beethoven's patent inability to commit to a fixed trajectory. The sketches of the Sixth Symphony, for example, reveal that although the first movement flowed rather effortlessly from his pen—a fact evident in the ease of the music itself—he lost compositional momentum on the return of the main theme. Beethoven labored long over a solution to the core problem of how to quickly dispel the energy accumulated during the development, allowing for a return of the symphony's underlying "pastoral" tranquility.

Once the overall thematic and tonal progression was fixed, the composition could be fleshed out more fully. Up to this point, Beethoven would notate all of his ideas on a single stave, usually in one voice only and in a fairly rudimentary fashion. His own thoughts were of course not devoid of other parameters such as harmony, counterpoint, and orchestration. But these aspects were bound so inextricably to the ideas themselves that Beethoven initially had no need to write them down—only aberrations of an outlandish or bizarre nature were included in the sketches. Once the theme was set, however, these peripheral aspects came to the fore, and just as photographic images gradually materialize and come into focus when placed in developing fluid, so too did Beethoven's music attain its full vibrancy in the magical bath of melodic refinement, textural richness, and orchestral color. Beethoven's extraordinary sensitivity to rhythmic detail played a crucial role here; the longer he worked on a melody, the more irregular, varied, unpredictable— and hence more "original"—it became.

Toward the very end of the composition process, Beethoven applied the finishing touches: the dynamic markings, accents, and articulations (such as staccatos, tenutos, slurs, and phrasing). These too constitute an essential component of the work's physiognomy and testify to the composer's pro- found level of emotional investment. Almost every measure contains some indication or other, and virtually every note was imbued with its own signifi- cance. Halm, a music critic, referred to this as Beethoven's "sforzatomania."[5] No composer before him had been as fastidious, and even those that came after him showed greater reserve in this respect. Publishers were driven to distraction by Beethoven's obsession with detail and were inundated with letters in which he endlessly nitpicked about the precise length of a slur, or the proper placement of a sforzato or accent.

The composition of vocal music was of course subject to an entirely differ- ent set of rules. To Beethoven, a text served simultaneously as both signpost and straitjacket, an immovable reference point around which all other param- eters revolved. (When publisher George Thomson asked him to arrange a set of folksongs from his Scottish homeland in 1809, Beethoven felt that access to the lyrics was indispensable.) The expression Beethoven sought in vocal works was multilayered, being rooted simultaneously in the color and charac- ter of a work's tonality, as well as in the vocabulary of the musical rhetoric. Although Beethoven disliked banal word painting (we recall his strong criti- cism of Haydn in this regard), he did aspire to create melodic lines that bol- stered the expressive power of the text. His primary concern was the metrical congruence between text and music, which often led him to pace about his room at length, chanting aloud, until he hit upon the lyrics' natural rhythm.

Any given metrical framework still offers a multitude of compositional possibilities, however, and Beethoven often conceived of several melodies to fit the same text. He frequently also met with the peculiar paradox that the most beautiful themes were not always the most suitable. One example is provided by the *Gratias agimus tibi* from the Mass in C (op. 86). Beethoven composed several melodies to this text that were all so charming, they could easily have served as the second subject in a symphony or sonata movement. But Beethoven was forced to acknowledge that their lyricism was at odds with the essence of the *Gloria,* which like the *Credo* was bound to the dogmatic proclamations of the Mass and therefore demanded some emotional restraint. It was for this reason that he ultimately decided on a variant that while perhaps less interesting, was more effective.

Beethoven's *laboratorium artificiosum* set a new standard for composition. Unlike "intuitive" composers such as Haydn and Mozart (who either put musical ideas to immediate use or rejected them out of hand), Beethoven was a "constructive" composer who revisited the same idea again and again, chewing and mulling it over until he hit upon a version that he considered ideal. As he himself once said, he carried ideas with him for a long, sometimes very long, time.[6] Richard Strauss later drew the comparison with young wine, which—like the composition of a musical work—needs time to properly ripen and mature.[7]

Publishing Pains and the
"Warehouse of the Arts"

DESPITE HIS BEST INTENTIONS, several days after returning from Heiligenstadt Beethoven was once again swamped with problems. On November 9, 1802, he received word that the publisher Artaria was preparing an edition of the String Quintet (op. 29)—particularly bad timing, as Beethoven had only just sold the publishing rights to Breitkopf & Härtel. The quintet had been commissioned by Count Fries, on the customary understanding that for a certain period (in this case six months) the count would retain exclusive performance rights to the work, after which Beethoven could sell the rights to a publisher. Before this period had elapsed, however, cousins Francesco and Carlo Artaria had somehow contrived to obtain a copy of the score—either the good-natured count unthinkingly handed it over, or it was brazenly stolen by first violinist Conti—and had also made short work of preparing the plates. This "early access" to the score had given Artaria a head start on the printing process, and their version came to market hot on the heels of the official edition by Breitkopf & Härtel. Though not illegal, this act did sin against the few unwritten rules of fair play that were acknowledged in the publishing world. The major players had agreed to tolerate unauthorized publications, provided they did not interfere either with other market segments (Germany, Austria, France, and England were viewed as closed markets) or with other agreements regarding timing, circulation, and price. Artaria had clearly violated the protocol, thus turning their own "private" copy of the quintet into a "pirate" copy.[1]

When Beethoven got wind of the scheme, he was furious. His relationship with Breitkopf & Härtel was already fraught, and he knew for a fact that those in Leipzig would place the blame squarely on his shoulders. Accompanied by his lawyer Joseph von Sonnleithner, he headed straight to Artaria and made an enormous scene. His initial plan was to dissuade them from publication entirely, for which he was prepared to pay a handsome price: the rights to the two sets of piano variations (opp. 34 and 35). On the recommendation of his lawyer—who was not entirely unjustified in his belief that payment of such a high sum was tantamount to an admission of guilt—Beethoven withdrew the offer. He later thought he might salvage the situation by stalling for time. He asked for, and received, a written declaration from Artaria promising a delay of publication by fourteen days.

Beethoven's next move was to write to Breitkopf & Härtel to inform them of the regrettable situation and of the reasonable compromise he thought to have brokered. Using very colorful vocabulary (referring to the cousins by turns as "conmen," "arrant villains," and "scurrilous frauds"[2]), Beethoven brings Carlo and Francesco Artaria into ample discredit—in itself no challenging feat, as the bigwigs in Leipzig, a city steeped in rich commercial tradition, had little regard to start with for Italians operating in Vienna. But it was to no avail: Breitkopf & Härtel sent a prompt response that had obviously been drawn up by a legal expert and was tactically intended to undermine Beethoven's position in future negotiations. Although they expressly denied calling Beethoven's integrity into question (a polite slur, in reality suggesting quite the opposite), those at Breitkopf & Härtel claimed only to be interested in legal liability, which in their view lay indisputably with Beethoven. He had conferred exclusive rights to them in writing, and it was therefore his responsibility to find a way to keep his word. He could redeem himself either by returning the full compensation and paying a token fine, or by supplying new work at a bargain price. At the very least they assumed that Beethoven would take legal action against Artaria—a very convenient outcome for them, for more reasons than one.

Beethoven felt affronted. He promptly sent word via his brother Kaspar Karl, saying that while such a letter might forgivably be sent to a schoolboy, it was in no way appropriate for a great artist, and that their line of action would be deemed insulting even to a laborer, let alone the likes of him.[3] But since both Beethoven and Breitkopf & Härtel had more to lose than to gain from an endless conflict, Saxon diplomat and Breitkopf & Härtel's chargé d'affaires in Vienna, Georg August von Griesinger, was appointed as a mediator. He had experience in such matters and had intervened on several occasions on behalf of his friend Joseph Haydn. Griesinger's first order of business was to subdue Beethoven's flaring temper. He succinctly explained to the publisher that artists are simply a rather sensitive bunch, and advised the management of Breitkopf & Härtel to reiterate their great admiration for Beethoven in writing, which they did.

Griesinger then met with Fries and formulated a range of options. But there was nothing to be done: Artaria released its edition of the String Quintet (op. 29) at roughly the same time as Breitkopf & Härtel, and Beethoven was forced to take sides. On January 22, 1803, he had the following notice published in the *Wiener Zeitung*:

Dear Music Lovers

I hereby inform the public that my Quintet in C, announced some time ago, has now been published in Leipzig by Breitkopf & Härtel. At the same time, I also wish to declare that the recent edition of the same Quintet released in Vienna by Messrs. Artaria and Mollo was prepared entirely without my involvement. I am obliged to declare as such, primarily because this edition is teeming with errors and inaccuracies, rendering it useless for performance purposes. The rightful owners of the Quintet, Messrs. Breitkopf & Härtel, have, however, done their utmost to produce as fair an edition as possible.

Ludwig van Beethoven.[4]

Beethoven also implored Artaria to send him their fifty printed copies, ostensibly so that he might make the necessary corrections. He delegated the task to his new pupil Ries, who had only just arrived in Vienna, with specific instructions to use as blunt a pen and as much ink as was necessary to render the editions no longer saleable. The cat was now well and truly among the pigeons, and Artaria dragged Beethoven to court. The case was a complicated one, made worse not only by Artaria's complex corporate structure but also by the lack of any clear legislation on the matter. (The caliber of the judicial system is perhaps best illustrated by the fact that an orchestral musician from the opera was appointed as an "expert" to judge whether the errors in Artaria's edition compromised the integrity of Beethoven's work.) On September 26, 1803, Beethoven was ordered to publish a retraction of his declaration from January 22, which he initially refused but later conceded to do (on March 31, 1804). The case was finally closed on September 9, 1805, and ended in a falling out. Artaria, who had published nearly every chamber work by Beethoven during his early years in Vienna, received virtually nothing thereafter. No doubt Breitkopf & Härtel had hoped for such an outcome from the very beginning.

Amid the tumult surrounding the String Quintet, Beethoven met with complications of another kind. In the spring of 1803, he received the first copies of his Piano Sonatas in G Major and D Minor (op. 31) from Swiss publisher

Nägeli, and was outraged at the multitude of errors in the score. In many ways he had himself to blame, since he had broken with habit and neglected to provide a carefully edited and clearly legible score. Not that this was ever any guarantee for an error-free edition; even copyists trained in the art of deciphering Beethoven's handwriting were prone to frequent errors.[5] This time, however, the publisher had been saddled with an all but illegible manuscript, and the consequences were predictable. The problem was compounded by the fact that for various reasons Beethoven had had no opportunity to review the proofs. Although not impossible, removing errors from the plates themselves was a time-consuming and costly process that also severely jeopardized printing quality. Moreover, Beethoven's preoccupation with improving the composition itself often blinded him to many of the transcription errors, which he frequently left uncorrected. Publishers were extremely hesitant to send him proofs for this very reason; it would be 1811 before Beethoven succeeded in contractually obliging them to do so, but even this measure usually fell short. Not only did Beethoven claim the right to a second and third round of corrections, but he also demanded the opportunity to make additional changes prior to any reprints.[6] The publishers were at their wits' end, not least because Beethoven often contradicted himself, undoing alterations that he had made on previous occasions.

The first edition of the opus 31 Piano Sonatas was thus prepared without these error filters, making it both inaccurate and unreliable and frustrating Beethoven's perfectionism immensely. He even accused Nägeli of deliberately altering the score himself, adding four additional bars to the end of the Allegro vivace in the Sonata in G Major. Beethoven felt that his artistic integrity had been compromised, but conveniently forgot that he had confounded matters by first composing and later striking out the four bars in question.[7] In any case, Beethoven wrote immediately to the *Allgemeine musikalische Zeitung,* asking them to warn the public of Nägeli's shoddy edition. He also contacted his old friend Nikolaus Simrock, a music publisher from Bonn, offering him the sonatas for free and sending along Nägeli's score accompanied by a list of eighty printing errors. Simrock was thus able to lead the pack with an official "authorized" edition, which he proudly announced as an *"Editiou* [sic] *tres* [sic] *correcte."*

Over the course of his lifetime, Beethoven conducted business with around forty publishing houses. In some cases, dealings were amicable—as with

Simrock and Hoffmeister—however, in others the tone could vary from formal stiffness to aggressive condescension, occasionally venturing into the realm of pure literary vituperation. Beethoven frequently became incensed at the shortcomings in printed editions of his music (a large part of his correspondence was devoted to correcting errors in his scores), although money matters were also a regular source of aggravation. It is easy to forget that financially Beethoven was extremely dependent on the fluctuating sales of his printed works. He therefore tried to extract as much from the enterprise as possible, a practice that was later held against him by many a biographer. To a large extent, his intractability and changeable loyalties when it came to negotiations were also a product of the way the music industry was organized at the turn of the nineteenth century. (The fact that there are similar stories pertaining to Haydn, who was generally respected as a gentleman, confirms the more systemic nature of the problem.) In Germany and Austria (unlike France), music printing remained a relatively insignificant sideline of the book publishing business until 1780. The initial catalogue of Breitkopf in Leipzig, for example, contained only literary and theological works. Publishers had always operated on a well-organized and insular playing field, subject to some elementary rules of engagement. When more of the citizenry began to participate in musical culture, a fast-growing market emerged: the number of publishing businesses grew exponentially, and many adventurous souls felt a calling to try their luck in the blossoming sector. Many musicians too (the best known of whom were Clementi, Diabelli, Hoffmeister, Pleyel, and Simrock) saw the opportunity to make a fast fortune and launched their own firms. The path forged by Nikolaus Simrock offers a typical example: he first obtained a post as a horn player at the court in Bonn, later shouldered the administrative duty of placing the orchestral parts on the stands before rehearsals, and finally became the music librarian. He also ran a music shop across the street (a peculiar conflict of interests that elicited not a shred of objection in that era), and when the Kapelle was disbanded in 1794 he began publishing scores himself. He made a fortune by reprinting many of Beethoven's works, for which he held a monopoly in Western Europe. He also profited from Bonn's ambiguous political status as a German region in the hands of the French. Yet in the eyes of the established players, Simrock remained an interloper—a brazen upstart who flouted the fact that the music publishers' code was not that of musicians. If he insisted on going in against the heavyweights, then the gloves were off.

The market in Vienna was particularly unstable, and publishing houses were often forced to enter into alliances or even mergers. Turnover may have been ample, but the margins were narrow, and a consistent stream of popular hits was needed in order to finance riskier editions that were less audience-friendly. (Beethoven, too, was in the habit of strategically coupling certain works together; his wildly popular piano sonatas and variations, for example, served to finance the publication of his religious works. In such cases, Beethoven struck a balance between his monetary needs and his desire to publish as much serious work as possible.) Composers were generally on the defensive in this respect and were understandably mercenary in pitting publishers against one another, a situation that remained the status quo for some time. On his deathbed, Beethoven even signed a letter drawn up by Johann Nepomuk Hummel addressed to the parliament in Frankfurt, in which he and his colleagues (Czerny, Ries, Spohr, and Spontini) rose up in defense of composers' rights. The publishers had the same idea, and in May 1829 sixteen major music publishers signed a convention in Leipzig, securing their communal rights. Twenty-seven additional businesses would join them a year later, but it was not until 1832 that the German parliament adopted the first laws safeguarding the rights of both publishers and composers.[8]

Beethoven's tenacity in defending his intellectual property, and his shrewdness in navigating the system, were of course products of the business acumen he had inherited from his forebears. But they also exemplified a certain subversive agenda, for Beethoven, who loathed injustice and social exploitation in all its forms and who was thus sympathetic to new political ideologies, believed that artists and the fruits of their creativity ought not to be subject to the laws of a free-market economy. In a letter written in 1801 to his good friend and publisher Hoffmeister, he formulated a collectivist vision for the future, dreaming aloud of what he called the *Magazin der Kunst,* a "Warehouse of the Arts," an institution where artists could submit their work in exchange for their day-to-day living essentials.[9] Beethoven revisited this theme nearly ten years later when he alerted Breitkopf & Härtel to their vested interest in realizing this perfect world for all composers: "It should fall to you, as the more humane and enlightened among the music publishers, not only to pay composers their scant recompense, but also to support them as much as possible on their journey, that they may be unfettered in producing all they have to give, and what society expects of them."[10]

In formulating this manifesto, it is unclear whether Beethoven took inspiration from the Magasin de Musique, a composers' collective founded in Paris in 1793 for the purposes of producing revolutionist music (among other things). In any case, it is fascinating that Beethoven, long before the birth of

Proudhon, Bakunin, or Marx, dreamed of a Utopia in which the free exchange of intellectual and material goods would liberate him from quotidian banalities and enable him to live from what he himself called "divine art" and "the products of [his] spirit." In 1824 he proudly wrote, "I should thank heaven for so blessing me in my works that, although not wealthy, I am nonetheless able to work and to <u>live for my art</u>."[11] But reality was less rosy, and Beethoven was never spared the drudgery of mundane and worldly problems all his life.

The absence of copyright legislation was also what ultimately derailed another of Beethoven's more ambitious projects, an edition of his complete works to be issued in a consistent format by a single publisher. Initial steps in this direction were taken in 1803 by Breitkopf & Härtel. They had already begun in 1799 and 1800 on the *editions complètes* of Haydn and Mozart and wished to continue with a collected edition of Beethoven's piano sonatas, capitalizing on the *opera omnia* trend that had migrated across from the literature world. Their motives were purely commercial, however; while they officially claimed that music lovers were in need of a reliable and uniform edition of Beethoven's piano sonatas, in reality it was a veiled attempt to gain exclusive rights over Beethoven's intellectual property. The plan was unsuccessful, due in part to uncertainty surrounding Beethoven's ownership of rights that he had formerly sold to other publishers, and in part to a lack of clarity on the price for buying them back. In addition, the publisher Zulehner in Mainz had already started work on an unauthorized and fairly slipshod pirated edition of all the piano sonatas, against which Beethoven had lodged an official complaint but was unable to prohibit.[12]

Beethoven revisited the idea himself in 1810, proposing that Breitkopf & Härtel publish his complete works in collaboration with other unspecified Viennese and Parisian publishers. His plan was dependent on the Viennese (and French) authorities issuing him a dispensation of sorts, intended to shield the project against any copyright claims. Breitkopf & Härtel harbored no illusions in this regard, well aware that any such dispensation would not prevent pirated editions from cropping up outside of Austria. Their arguments were chiefly commercial: the *oeuvres complètes* of Mozart, Haydn, and Clementi were profitable ventures thanks to the lack of composers' fees. Haydn and Mozart were no longer alive, and Clementi—irony of ironies— had become so rich through the sale of exclusive Beethoven editions in

England that he could afford to work for Breitkopf & Härtel for free. Beethoven enjoyed no such luxury. But perhaps their greatest fear was the fact that Beethoven demanded the right to "make changes here and there," for which he was also to receive additional compensation.[13] Financially, Breitkopf & Härtel thus had little to gain from the venture; they had secured the exclusive de facto rights to Beethoven's new compositions in 1809, and their principal interest lay in retaining them and maximizing the gains. A complete edition would do little to advance their position.

Renewed attempts followed with other publishers: Simrock in 1817 and 1820, Peters in 1822 and 1823, and Schott in 1825. Even when Beethoven sought ways to make the proposal more attractive—such as his offer to Schott of composing one additional work per genre—the project always ran aground due to a lack of legal security. Only in 1862, when new legislation in Germany and Austria allowed Breitkopf & Härtel to conclude agreements with the many previous publishers of Beethoven's works, did his dream of releasing a complete edition become a posthumous reality.

Composer in Residence

WHEN HIS PLANS FOR A SECOND *Akademie* were thwarted in April 1802, Beethoven became skeptical about his future in Vienna. It was clear that as long as Braun continued to manage the theaters, Beethoven would be denied independent opportunities to present major works such as symphonies, operas, or oratorios. It also became clear that the court, owing to equal parts cowardice and stupidity, was not prepared to support him openly, all but eliminating the likelihood of a permanent post in aristocratic circles.[1] Then, out of the blue, he received the tantalizing offer of a post as "composer in residence" at the recently opened Theater an der Wien.

Theater an der Wien was a brand-new and modern theater located—both physically and culturally—on the fringes of Vienna. It boasted as its director Emanuel Schikaneder, a formidable artistic director with the proven ability to implement fresh ideas and reach large audiences. In 1789, through his wife's connections, Schikaneder had rather accidentally secured the directorship of what was then known as the Theater auf der Wieden im Freihaus, a one-thousand-seat theater tucked away in a miniature, tax-free enclave between the river Wien and the Wiedner Hauptstrasse to the south of the city, where artists resided in a kind of commune. Schikaneder ran a tight ship, where all were expected to follow a number of house rules regarding discipline and tact. These applied both on- and offstage, during rehearsals, performances, and leisure time, both in the theater and at the neighboring cafés and restaurants. But for all the rigid protocols, the enterprise was highly successful—the theater was always sold out (people would sometimes line up for hours to be assured of a good seat), and new productions were always hotly awaited. The fairy tales and operas on magical themes were presented in a hybrid form of High German and Viennese dialect, and wowed spectators with ingenious stage effects. It thus offered an appealing alternative to both the elevated and moralistic theater at the Hofburg and the popular productions in other suburban theaters. Mozart's *Magic Flute* was a chart-topper and received over two hundred performances over the course of several years.

Schikaneder's grand designs thus quickly outgrew the Theater auf der Wieden, and he devised a daring plan to build his own ultramodern Odeon on the opposite bank of the river. He was aided in his mission by Bartholomäus Zitterbarth, an exceedingly wealthy businessman, fellow Freemason, and theater buff who had come to Schikaneder's financial aid once before and who was now prepared to bankroll his personal Utopia. Long before he was suspected of his ambitious plans, Schikaneder had successfully extracted both a dispensation and a building permit for a new theater from Emperor Joseph II. Both permits were later extended by Joseph's successors, no doubt under the apprehension that Schikaneder would undoubtedly fail to amass the necessary resources for such a harebrained idea. The court now rued their condescending attitude, not least because Schikaneder's plans enjoyed widespread support: both the Freemasons (for whom the project was particularly symbolic[2]) and a large cohort of influential aristocrats were eager to see the project succeed. Under such circumstances, Braun's efforts to derail the process were limited to a few legal and bureaucratic rearguard actions—futile quibbles concerning the location, obligatory fire-safety concerns, and as a final, desperate attempt at sabotage, complaining to some department or other that the new building reeked too strongly of fresh paint. But Braun could not thwart the construction of Theater an der Wien, which rose into one of the largest and finest theaters in all of Germany and Austria, capable of seating 2,200 guests and a mere stone's throw from his own Kärntnertortheater. The stage machinery—the product of Schikaneder's own technical and theatrical imagination—offered limitless possibilities, due in part to the addition of a flytower that enabled backdrops and scenery to be raised and lowered for the first time. The lighting capacity had also increased tremendously (the house lights in particular; their use would not be tempered until 1850, when more attention was focused on the stage). Only the heating left much to be desired, which would cause Beethoven some problems later.

The festive opening was held on July 15, 1801, and was a high-society gala event. The emperor's diplomatic absence was palpable, but as a half-hearted gesture of sympathy he sent his aunt and mother-in-law Queen Maria Carolina of Naples and Sicily in his stead, accompanied by her three daughters and his uncle Albert, the Duke of Saxony. On the program was the premiere of the heroic opera *Alexander,* with music by organist and Kapellmeister Franz Teyber. The libretto and stage direction were by Schikaneder, who also played the main role, thus putting himself—more so than the king of Macedonia—in the limelight.

The euphoria of the opening was short-lived, however, due to a simmering conflict between Schikaneder and his sponsor, who regarded the new theater as his own personal plaything. Schikaneder could not abide Zitterbarth's arrogant meddling and tried to resist it, but less than a year after the opening, Schikaneder was paid out and summarily shown the door. Zitterbarth thus obtained carte blanche to realize his lifelong dream of becoming a theater director. He was quickly disillusioned, however, on discovering that running a successful artistic enterprise involves more than simply turning up at performances and making small talk in the lobby. He quickly admitted defeat and had no choice but to recall Schikaneder, who—armed with a small fortune and his newfound authority—set about realizing his own outlandish plans. But by then the public had lost interest in him; business was foundering; and Zitterbarth (himself at risk of financial ruin) was forced to sell Theater an der Wien in February 1804 to none other than royal theater manager Herr Braun, who thus obtained a monopoly on the full Viennese theater and music scene. As Braun's first act of policy, Schikaneder was ejected from the theater a second time.

The sale of Theater an der Wien in 1803 brought an end to a theater war that had been raging for two years. The imperial Burgtheater had hitherto afforded itself a complacent existence of routinely trotting out Italian operas; the new Theater an der Wien beyond the city limits, by contrast, was astounding audiences not only with young voices and a new generation of stage performers but also with attractive programming and the latest operas from France. This trend began on March 23, 1802, with the premiere of *Lodoiska,* a "heroic comedy" by composer Luigi Cherubini, who had achieved great renown in Paris. Viennese audiences responded with tremendous enthusiasm and were enchanted by the unique character and dramatic intensity of Cherubini's music, and perhaps more so by the political relevance of this genre of "rescue opera," in which an innocent prisoner is freed by an act of love from the clutches of a despicable tyrant, who is then served his just desserts. *Lodoiska*'s success triggered a race between the imperial opera and Theater an der Wien to secure similar works from the likes of Cherubini, Nicolas-Marie Dalayrac, André Modeste Grétry, Jean-François Le Sueur,

Etienne-Nicolas Méhul, and Pierre-Alexandre Monsigny. The contest reached its bizarre climax with the simultaneous programming of the same opera by Cherubini in two theaters at once. Braun had advertised the premiere of *The Water Carrier* (*Der Wasserträger,* the German version of his opera *Les deux journées*) for August 14, 1802. In the meantime, Schikaneder had sent his conductor, Seyfried, to Munich to manufacture a transcription of the score, which was subsequently used to rehearse the opera in total secrecy. It was then presented, with extensive alterations and under the new title of *Count Armand, or The Two Unforgettable Days* (Graf Armand oder Die zwei unvergesslichen Tage), on August 13, 1802—one day before its scheduled premiere at the imperial theater. Braun did score a subsequent coup by obtaining the exclusive rights to Cherubini's smash hit *Medea,* after which Schikaneder retaliated with *Elisa.* This game of operatic ping-pong continued for some time, until Braun gained full control of all the Viennese theaters in February 1804. After that, in the summer of 1805, it was no trouble for him to travel to Paris himself and persuade Cherubini to come to Vienna and write a new opera, *Faniska.*

In the midst of this battle to win the public's favor, Schikaneder executed one spectacular maneuver: he welcomed Beethoven with open arms and, in January 1803, appointed him "Composer at Theater an der Wien." Along with this title, Beethoven, his brother Kaspar Karl, and a servant were granted lodgings in an apartment on the second floor of the new theater complex (right above the offices of the directors and the administration), in a wing abutting what was then Böhmisches Gassl. The accommodations were hardly spacious, with only two sitting rooms and access via the kitchen, which did double duty as the servant's sleeping quarters. The windows were also tiny and looked out on to a blind wall, lending the residence an oppressive, slightly claustrophobic quality. Beethoven was unhappy there and made various attempts to relocate within the enormous building. When these proved unsuccessful, he rented a pied-à-terre in town, reserving his rooms in the theater for work purposes only. They still offered indisputable benefits, however. Just as the emperor had direct access to his private box in the Burgtheater via a small doorway in his bedroom, so too could Beethoven easily slip down from his chambers in Theater an der Wien to observe and take in the latest operas. Witnesses have told how the already partially deaf Beethoven would sit at the front of the stalls, lean over the railing, and gaze into the orchestra pit in full concentration. Many of the same witnesses also attested to Beethoven's frequent departure during the intermission, clearly having already seen—and heard—enough.[3]

In return for all of these privileges, Beethoven had promised to compose at least one new opera each year—hardly a burden, as Beethoven had been eager to rectify one of the greatest omissions in his oeuvre for some time. One slightly problematic aspect was the fact that Beethoven had been discreetly advised to select a libretto by Schikaneder for his first opera. After six months of being held in suspense, Beethoven finally received the initial version of Schikaneder's libretto *Vestas Feuer* (Vesta's fire) in October 1803. He was mortified. Over the course of three acts, each containing three scenes, Schikaneder had spun out an impossibly convoluted Roman love epic, peppered liberally with labyrinthine intrigues and cosmic interventions. The purpose of the latter was ostensibly to ensure the story line's moral progression and happy ending, but in truth they merely served to justify the inclusion of outlandish and spectacular deus-ex-machina scenarios. Although Beethoven himself once admitted in writing that Schikaneder could indeed create stunning onstage effects, he also noted that Schikaneder's "realm of light"—a thinly veiled reference to Mozart's *Magic Flute*—was eclipsed by the comparison. Beethoven thus felt no affinity whatsoever with what he deemed the "prattle of fishwives" and had completely abandoned work on *Vesta's Fire* by New Year's Day 1804.[4] Only the opening scene was more or less complete, the finale of which would be recycled in *Leonore* as the grand love duet "O namenlose Freude" (O nameless joy).

By the time Beethoven had decided not to proceed with *Vesta's Fire,* he had already forged plans for an alternative project: an opera based on Bouilly's libretto *Léonore, ou L'Amour conjugal.* Although it remains unclear exactly how Beethoven laid hands on this material,[5] what *is* certain is that he was seriously considering emigrating to Paris at the time and saw the advantage of having an opera ready whose success in the French capital was already guaranteed.

Beethoven's decision to adopt a new libretto was of course expedited by the fact that Schikaneder's days as director were numbered. The deck was indeed completely reshuffled in February 1804, and it is logical to assume that Braun's arrival on the scene would spell only bad news for Beethoven. But Vienna was (and is) known for its fleeting allegiances, and Braun—whose new, peripheral suburban theater was relatively immune to the machinations at court—saw in Beethoven a valuable ally capable of giving a face to his newly acquired establishment. A crucial point in Beethoven's favor was that Braun had appointed Joseph von Sonnleithner as artistic director. The scion of a reputable family of Viennese lawyers, Sonnleithner had been a protégé of Joseph II and thus was of limited practical use to the new regime, resulting in his sideways promotion to the less-volatile realm of arts management. He was appointed artistic director of Theater an der Wien, and shortly thereafter he even became secretary (or in more modern terms, business manager) of the two imperial theaters, the Burgtheater and Kärntnertortheater. This career shift suited him quite nicely, as it gave him some power he could readily abuse in pursuit of his favorite hobby—translating French plays and writing opera libretti according to French models—while moving in the uppermost circles of theatrical society.

Beethoven and Sonnleithner had had dealings in the past. Sonnleithner had given Beethoven free legal advice during the debacle over the Quintet for Piano and Winds in 1802, and Beethoven was a regular guest at the former's musical soirées, most likely having performed there on several occasions. When Beethoven forged plans to compose an opera based on Bouilly's *Léonore* in 1803, it was therefore a logical step for him to approach Sonnleithner for the libretto. Sonnleithner's promotion to manager of Theater an der Wien only weeks later was a windfall, sparing Beethoven the time and energy that would otherwise have been necessary to get him on board. Sonnleithner's dual post would prove useful again later when *Leonore* faced the censors' guillotine; as we will see, the permission granted to allow the contested work on stage owed less to its setting in sixteenth-century Spain and more to the backstage connections of the theater-manager-cum-librettist.

Beethoven had originally been charged with the composition of a new opera every year. He had also been given kind permission to make unlimited use of the establishment's choir and orchestra to organize his own *Akademie* concerts,[6] an opportunity he availed himself of even during schikaneder's reign: on April 5, 1803, he put on a concert not only of his oratorio *Christ on the Mount of Olives* but also of the First and Second Symphonies and the Third Piano Concerto.[7] (Subsequent years would also see the Fifth and Sixth Symphonies, the Violin Concerto, and the Fourth Piano Concerto premiered at Theater an der Wien.)

As usual, the period leading up to this concert was fraught with typical Beethovenian turmoil. The highly competent conductor in residence and friend of Beethoven's, Ignaz von Seyfried, took responsibility for rehearsing the soloists, choir, and orchestra and followed the master's instructions to the letter. The orchestra itself, however, was populated by players of varying ability. Theater an der Wien employed only a small core of permanent musicians, and for larger productions was dependent on a wider pool of freelancers. But because Braun had scheduled a gala performance of Haydn's *Creation* on that same evening, the city's best musicians were already occupied and unavailable for side engagements beyond the city walls. To make matters worse, the music for the oratorio was completed only at the last minute. Ferdinand Ries even reported that on the day of the dress rehearsal (i.e., the day of the concert), he visited Beethoven at five in the morning to pick up additional trombone parts that had only been written out the night before—Beethoven had done so from memory, without even adding the parts to the full orchestral score. After a marathon rehearsal lasting from eight in the morning until two-thirty in the afternoon, Beethoven then insisted on yet another run-through of the entire oratorio. Musicians' unions would today be up in arms at such treatment; on that afternoon, too, resentment stirred. But disaster was averted by none other than Karl Lichnowsky himself, who had been in attendance since the early morning. He saw the storm brewing and soothed the players' discontent by having large baskets of bread, cold meats, and wine delivered to the theater. According to Ries, the musicians fell on the impromptu smorgasbord like wild animals, after which spirits rose tremendously.[8]

The performance commenced at six o'clock. Most critics agreed that the quality of playing varied considerably throughout—hardly surprising given the day's hectic preparations and the inevitably foggy mental state of the exhausted players. Even Beethoven's own performance at the piano was considered "less than successful," with the reviews claiming he had not performed "to the audience's full satisfaction."[9] This too was to be expected: like the orchestra, Beethoven had had a rough day of rehearsal, compounded both by several nights of poor sleep and by the general deterioration in his playing due to his increased focus on composition in the preceding years. The degree of difficulty was also raised by Beethoven's decision—in keeping with the premieres of the First and Second piano concertos—to partially improvise the solo piano part during the concert. Seyfried, Beethoven's assistant and page-turner, later wrote of how he stared in desperation at the "virtually empty pages, only here and there containing some scrawled Egyptian hieroglyphs which, while serving as a reminder to Beethoven, to me remained utterly inscrutable." Poor Seyfried's only aids in his hour of need were the frequent "surreptitious nods" given by Beethoven, as a signal that he should turn the page.[10]

Seyfried's account also states that the problems were due in part to Beethoven's unorthodox conducting style. He said that the master was "hardly a paragon of conducting technique" and that the orchestra needed "unwavering concentration to avoid being misled by its director." The problem was rooted in the fact that Beethoven's gestures pertained exclusively to matters of expression. It was his custom, for example, to mark all accents with an emphatic downbeat, regardless of their metrical position within the bar, thereby completely disorienting the players. He also tended to crouch lower and lower as the music became quieter, sinking behind the lectern and, during pianissimo passages, disappearing completely from view. Conversely, during forte sections, he seemed to swell and take on "gigantic" proportions, flailing his arms wildly and eliminating all possibility of metrical precision. His failure to address ensemble problems during rehearsals also played a role—rather than repeating any messy passages, he would laconically utter, "Things will go better next time," and leave it at that. According to Seyfried, Beethoven could obsess over the tiniest details; discussions on instrumental balance, minor shifts of light and shade, or an effective rubato (a minor fluctuation within the principal underlying tempo) could occupy him for hours. And yet Seyfried did not consign him to "the capricious lot of conductors for whom no orchestra is ever good enough." On the contrary, whenever "he saw the musicians grasp his intent, how they began playing together as one like a rising inferno, how they were absorbed, transported and possessed by the magic of his creations, then his face lit up with joy, and a booming 'Bravi tutti!' was the players' reward." To Beethoven, such moments were far more gratifying than "the thunderous applause of any large, approving audience."[11]

Such applause was limited following the concert on April 5, 1803; the scarce reports from the press were mixed and for the most part reserved. Although both symphonies were said to have been "not lacking in striking moments of brilliance," the "effortlessness" of the first symphony still met with greater appreciation than "the more obvious attempts to surprise and impress" in the second.[12] Opinions of the oratorio in particular varied considerably. A review in the *Freymütighe* stated that the work "in its entirety was too long, drawn-out, contrived, and lacked the proper expression, particularly in the vocal parts."[13] Criticism by a fellow reviewer in the *Zeitung für die elegante Welt* was directed primarily at the libretto. The same critic believed that the music contained "several excellent passages" and that "a composer of such genius can create great work from even the poorest of material."[14] The authoritative *Allgemeine musikalische Zeitung* sparked controversy. An initial critic wrote that the oratorio enjoyed "widespread acclaim" and that Beethoven "was capable, given some time, of effecting a bona fide musical revolution, as Mozart had done." Three months later, however, a second critic claimed that "Beethoven's cantata was—disappointing."[15]

Oddly enough, considerable media attention was devoted to Beethoven's unusually high ticket prices: double the norm for seats in or near the front row, triple for a reservation, and twelve times (!) the usual sum for a box seat.[16] Rumors circulated that Beethoven made a profit of 1,800 guilders from the entire operation, equivalent to the annual salary of a senior public servant—an exorbitant figure in the eyes of the critics.

The warmer reception of the First Symphony relative to the Second is logical, given its established popularity—it had already seen performances in Leipzig, Berlin, Breslau, Frankfurt-am-Main, Dresden, Brunšvik, and Munich. But it is also representative of a new trend that would come to dominate classical music, and still does to this day: the general skepticism of the public in the face of new works. Beethoven's predicament in this sense was twofold. First, "new music" is by its very nature "unheard-of," and only a tiny minority of specialized listeners can surmount their immediate perceptions on a first hearing to construct a full mental overview of the work as a whole. Music cannot escape its temporal dimension, and memory plays a crucial role in recognizing structural links that extend through time. The less proficient a listener is in the language of music, the more hearings are required for memory to do its job. Second, Beethoven's latest works were not only newly composed but also newly conceptualized, presenting the listener with an entirely new set of rules and expectations. Grasping such new "rules of engagement" on the fly is often beyond the capacity of even the most specialized experts.

Beethoven's Second Symphony was "new" in both of the above senses. Our modern perspective gives us a better understanding of Beethoven's development since the First Symphony and of the importance of the Second Symphony as a springboard to the *Eroica*. Not only that, but the rapid development of Beethoven's orchestral style between 1800 (the year of the First Symphony) and 1804 (the birth of the *Eroica*) is in no small measure attributable to the composition of the Second Symphony.

It was in this work that Beethoven hit upon the orchestral color that would come to typify his symphonic style. From the initial opening chord and throughout the slow introduction, it is clear that we have bid adieu to Haydn's orchestra. The sound carries more weight, with greater depth and richer contours, creating an unparalleled dramatic intensity. This latter quality in particular comes to the fore in the ensuing Allegro, which boasts powerful sonorities, extremely long phrases (there are few cadence points allowing the music to come to rest), and sweeping gestures that conjure up a wide variety of moods. Such energy and momentum also give rise to inevitable structural consequences: the coda—an addendum that until Beethoven's time had been nothing more than a negligible "tail end"—became not only the conclusion of the movement but also its climax, and the associated richness of ideas also made it substantially longer (Beethoven clearly understood the laws of musical inertia: as the size and speed of a moving body increase, so too does the braking distance). The same applies even more to the final Allegro molto, whose main theme is defined by a rapid tempo, erratic bursts of sound, hectic rhythms, and disorienting accents, trills, and sforzati, invoking a primal quality hitherto unprecedented in orchestral playing. One critic from the *Allgemeine musikalische Zeitung* characterized the movement as "bizarre, wild and shrill," while another compared it to "a rough-hewn monstrosity, an impaled dragon resolutely battling on and refusing to perish, blindly and savagely thrashing its tail as it bleeds to death."[17]

It is the second movement, however, that most clearly embodies the soul of Beethoven's new, rich, and flexible orchestral sound: a Larghetto conjuring up a poetic atmosphere that until that time had only been possible in the more intimate genres of piano repertoire or chamber music. Here the progression of orchestral colors and moods becomes an integral component of the musical narrative. The pace of the Larghetto is, quite literally, "a little slow," creating the illusion of movement in slow motion—elegant and ponderous, with an intensity that nonetheless maintains forward momentum. It is unsurprising that the beauty and sumptuousness of the movement inspired great admiration, giving rise to a range of poetic associations and lyrical interpretations over the course of the nineteenth century. Berlioz reported feeling "deeply moved," describing the Larghetto as "the enchanting portrayal of innocent bliss" (1835); Ulybyshev, a Russian expert on Mozart and Beethoven, compared it to "a long conversation with a charming and tender lady" (1857); his German fellow Adolf Bernhard Marx heard in it "the innocence of a young maiden's song" (1884).[18] The Englishman George Grove mentioned the work's "elegant, indolent beauty" (1898).[19]

However, most ears during the concert on April 5, 1803, were fixed on Beethoven's oratorio *Christ on the Mount of Olives,* not least since—leaving his two unperformed Imperial cantatas aside—it was Beethoven's debut in the field of vocal music. The oratorio served a dual purpose for Beethoven: it was both the calling card of the new composer in residence at Theater an der Wien, as well as a test bed for his operatic aspirations. But despite numerous performances during its first years,[20] the *Mount of Olives* was controversial from the outset. This reputation has encumbered the work ever since, as even Beethoven partially distanced himself from it in 1811, saying, "I would now set about writing an oratorio very differently, that much is certain."[21]

Beethoven would later plead special circumstances, claiming that the *Mount of Olives* was composed in great haste. While it is true that the oratorio was written within the space of only a few weeks, this is hardly a valid excuse: the First Piano Concerto, the Violin Concerto, and the Mass in C are all evidence of Beethoven's ability to produce marvelous works under pressure. Other apologists say that the libretto was not up to snuff, but this too can be refuted: librettist Franz Xaver Huber was experienced and had a fine reputation, and his collaboration with Beethoven was open and constructive. Furthermore, Beethoven himself believed that a good composer should always be able to produce good work, even with a poor text as the basis.[22]

A far more pressing issue was that for some decades, aside from Haydn's highly popular *Creation* and *The Seasons,* no quality oratorios had been written that Beethoven could use as a point of reference. After Handel, the genre had all but fossilized and would need to wait at least until the time of Mendelssohn for any new stylistic inroads. Beethoven therefore had no choice but to forge a path through terrain that was not his own and without any convincing models as landmarks. He also made some fundamental errors of judgment. Over the course of six scenes, he and Huber had decided to cover two Gospel excerpts: the story of Christ and his disciples on the Mount of Olives, and Jesus's arrest. Both narratives were treated fairly loosely: some Bible passages were blended together; others abridged or left out entirely; and it was clear that the creators had chosen to emphasize the saga's lyrical qualities over its epic aspects. Since they were clearly more interested in the protagonists' emotional lives rather than the historic details, they also broke with previous convention and eliminated the role of the evangelist—an initial strategic choice that met with broad disapproval. The portrayal of Christ in particular is highly psychoanalytical. Even in the first scene, which begins in medias res, the audience meets Jesus as an anguished figure, torn between his duty to redeem humanity and his fear of death and suffering. As the oratorio progresses, instead of depicting the biblical and duty-bound son of God who ultimately accepts the will of his father, Beethoven paints a man of flesh and blood, full of doubt and desperation, vacillating between feelings of fear, hope, surrender, and resignation. This too rubbed early-nineteenth-century audiences the wrong way. Not only was it a theological aberration to grant Jesus dual status as both the son of God and a human being, but to give his humanity a concrete form onstage was an act of the purest blasphemy.

It cannot be denied that Beethoven, as one might expect, was indeed carried away by the lyrical possibilities offered by such a gripping psychological drama, and deliberately pushed (now and again overstepping) the boundaries of the oratorio genre. Indeed, many fragments are so expressive as to seem more at home in an operatic setting: Christ's first monologue is a rather unapologetic, heroic tenor aria; the trombones during the oracle of the Seraph conjure up associations with the *Magic Flute* and *Don Giovanni;* the Seraph's aria is highly reminiscent of the Queen of the Night; the duet between Christ and the Seraph resembles a love duet from a sentimental rococo opera; and the final numbers—the large choruses sung by the soldiers and disciples—might easily have been lifted from any French lyric tragedy. Occasionally, various elements are jumbled together. The opening aria, for example, is a German text sung to an Italian melody, with a French orchestral accompaniment. Although this stylistic potpourri is to a large extent responsible for much of the oratorio's charm, it is understandable that such musical and dramatic intensity had nineteenth-century audiences scratching their heads. Having been presented with such a libretto, however, it is hard to imagine Beethoven having written anything else, and every note testifies to the composer's deep and personal commitment to the subject matter. The *Mount of Olives,* after all, somewhat reflects Beethoven's own life story, and he was clearly struck by the parallels between Christ's fate and his own destiny. Although originally conceived as a strategic career move, the *Mount of Olives* grew into an emotional and ideological confession piece.

Most concertgoers likely found the approach too arrogant and therefore presumptuous.

Breitkopf & Härtel responded with similar reservations. After some initial failed attempts to publish the *Mount of Olives,* Lichnowsky increased pressure in the spring of 1805 by traveling to Leipzig to deliver the manuscript in person. Still the response was lukewarm—ostensibly because oratorios were slow sellers, but in reality because Beethoven's intensely emotional approach to the Gospel was deemed unacceptable by the Protestant-Reformationist publishers in northern Germany. The decision was finally made to publish the work in 1811 but with a completely revised libretto. Only at the last minute was Beethoven able to prevent the alteration of the text, which he had not himself authorized. As it transpired, the publisher had engaged the services of one Christian Schreiber to substantially rework the libretto to the *Mount of Olives* (several months later, and to Beethoven's immense satisfaction, Schreiber would supply a German version of the Mass in C, opus 86). Schreiber was not only a poet and composer but also a philosopher and theologian, making him the perfect candidate to remove the political and religious barbs from Beethoven's oratorio. He un-dramatized the work, removing the linguistic and stylistic peaks and valleys (emotive words such as *blood, fear, hell, death, pain, exile, enemy, rage,* and *hate* were systematically avoided) while simultaneously ensuring an overall tone of moralistic contemplation. Occasional modifications to the music itself were considered a necessary evil. When Beethoven got wind of this scheme, he wrote an angry letter to Leipzig, admitting that the libretto was lamentable but insisting that it remain unchanged. He emphasized the inextricable interwovenness of the text with the music, implying that any alteration—be it of a single key word—would derail the entire composition.[23] The revised libretto was thus withdrawn, although Breitkopf & Härtel could not resist making several small changes despite Beethoven's clear position on the matter. Beethoven was incensed: "I see that, despite my letter to the contrary, you have opted for the <u>unfortunate</u> alternate version of the text in the chorus 'Wir haben ihn gesehen.' Dear God in heaven, do you in Saxony really believe that the words are what make the music?"[24]

The Anglicans, too, were affronted by the "humanization" of Christ and his apostles on stage and censored the oratorio. A performance took place in London on February 28, 1814, for which an English "translation" had been produced, with all roles sung in the third person. In 1842 a version was even released with a completely new story from the Old Testament—the persecution of David by Saul. We can only imagine Beethoven's fulminations at such a shameless lack of respect.

The concert on April 5, 1803, at Theater an der Wien was in many ways an ego statement, in which Beethoven made a declaration about himself and his status as a composer. He was the star attraction in a program comprising exclusively his own music (during his first *Akademie* in 1800, he had hidden, at least partially, within the thickets of Haydn and Mozart), and by identifying so strongly with the main character in his oratorio, he had infused it with the significance of a personal creed. Beethoven thus set a new tone for music in general. The nineteenth-century Romantic composer would thenceforth put Himself and His feelings in the spotlight, imbuing music with grander gestures, greater resources, and more emotional and intellectual intensity in order to practice Art and convey a Message. Conversely, this development is also what consigned Haydn and Mozart forever to the ranks of the "classical" composers.

27

Salieri's Opera Lessons

BEETHOVEN DID NOT CLIMB THE *Mount of Olives* unprepared. He realized early in Vienna that his experience in the field of vocal music was too limited to ensure the success of a major project. On the scarce occasions when he had ventured into vocal terrain (such as the two Imperial cantatas), he had done so armed with nothing more than his intuition. But real operas and grand oratorios require specific expertise, and Beethoven had spent enough time in the opera orchestra in Bonn to know that opera houses were unforgiving, vicious, and cutthroat places where there are rarely any second chances. In 1801, he therefore decided to take lessons in opera from imperial Kapellmeister himself, Antonio Salieri.[1]

The choice was a logical one. Although Salieri's star was fading, he remained one of the most prominent composers in Vienna and enjoyed Joseph II's unconditional support until his death. They would often be seen together, and their rapport even bordered on friendship (they were on the very verge of using the familiar *du* form of address with one another). While Salieri's influence in the opera world had vastly declined, as vice president and conductor in residence at the Tonkünstler-Sozietät (Society of Musicians) he belonged to the select group in Vienna who determined the prevailing musical tastes. He was a professional and knew the tricks of the opera trade. After training under Florian Gassmann (the director of the imperial Hofopera and thus the definitive authority on opera in Vienna), he had collaborated with theater giants such as Da Ponte and Beaumarchais, and celebrated triumphs in Vienna, Paris, Milan, Venice, and Rome. Salieri had seen his fair share of debacles, certainly; but while some of his productions were indeed utter failures, they did furnish him with a wealth of useful experience on the pitfalls of opera composition.

Salieri has an unfortunate reputation as a villain who elbowed his way to the top, an image reinforced by the unwholesome and often exaggerated tales of his supposed conflict with Mozart. Contrary to this portrayal, Salieri was a very affable fellow. He never forgot how as a fifteen-year-old orphan he received not only tutelage but also room and board from Florian Gassmann, and he considered it his duty to pass on his knowledge and experience to all young musicians—composers and singers alike. There are records of him having taught over one hundred pupils, usually free of charge (only children of the wealthy were asked to pay). The list of his pupils is impressive. Alongside the many unknown aristocrats and a few local celebrities, it boasts the likes of Carl Czerny, Johann Nepomuk Hummel, Franz Liszt, Giacomo Meyerbeer, Ignaz Moscheles, and Franz Schubert.

Beethoven's lessons with Salieri were intensive but sporadic, given the sheer quantity of work that Beethoven had on his musical plate. Salieri did not apply a fixed method but took an ad hoc approach. He had his pupil set texts by Metastasio and other Italians, corrected the errors, and notated the alternative versions neatly above Beethoven's draft, teaching him the ins and outs of vocal writing in a tangible and practical fashion. A striking aspect is the fact that Salieri used only Italian texts, due to his inadequate proficiency in German (despite having lived in Vienna for decades). His assumption was that once mastered, the fundamental rules and principles of the art could be applied anywhere. Beethoven wrestled greatly in the beginning with the specific rules of Italian prosody, a struggle that was chiefly attributable to his poor knowledge of the language—a deficiency that he would not rectify until 1813 by taking private Italian lessons with university professor Anton Filippi.

Essentially, the lessons with Salieri boiled down to ensuring that the musical meter matched that of the text. To achieve this, Salieri swore by the proven method of declaiming the text aloud as much as possible until the melody virtually presented itself, according to the old adage "Well spoken is half sung." He then taught Beethoven how to mold the character of a melody to suit the meaning of the lyrics, with key words receiving the highest (and in rare cases the lowest) tones, and how to adapt the structure of a melody to the punctuation—an exclamation mark requires a different contour than a question mark, for example. Lastly, he offered practical guidelines regarding the placement of rests and breaths, as well as the use of vowels, about which Beethoven once noted in the margin of a notebook, "U, I and O are ungrateful vowels, on which long melismas or coloraturas are to be avoided."[2]

Beethoven in 1815

St. Augustin's and the Palais Lobkowitz in Vienna

St. Michael's Square and the riding school in Vienna

The Kärtnertortheater

Theater an der Wien

University Square in Vienna

The Razumovsky Palace

Josephine Deym von Stritetz (née von Brunsvik)

Joseph Deym's palace on Rotenturmstrasse

Antonie Brentano and children Georg and Fanny

Giulietta Guicciardi (presumed)

Therese Malfatti

Christine Gerhardi

The bathhouse in Teplitz (Teplice)

Inside the main bathhouse in Karlsbad (Karlovy Vary)

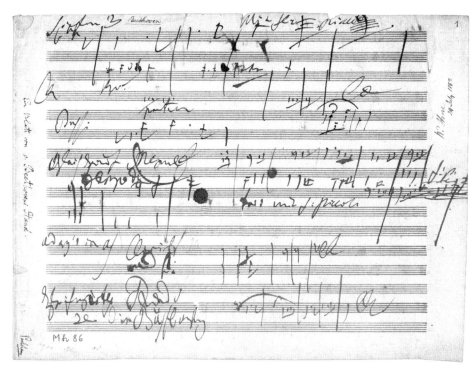

Sketch of the Eighth Symphony (op. 93)

Sketch of the incidental music for *King Stephan* (op. 117)

Beethoven's lessons concluded after two years, at which time Salieri had Beethoven write three more "masterpieces": the soprano aria "No, non turbati" (WoO 92a), the duet "Ne' giorni tuoi felici" for soprano and tenor (WoO 93), and a trio, "Tremate, empi, tremate" for soprano, tenor, and bass (op. 116). The aria and duet were reviewed, corrected, and approved by Salieri, but neither ever received a full orchestration. This is the reason why, of these three works, only the trio ever found its way to the concert stage.

While Beethoven's lessons with Salieri undoubtedly bore fruit, a void remained that Beethoven would have to fill himself. Salieri may have had a nose for the theater and a flair for the dramatic, but what he lacked was the capacity to harness his imagination and distill it into a musically coherent whole. To us, his music flits capriciously from one moment to the next; in this respect, Salieri was forced to recognize his infinite better in Mozart, who succeeded in taking the principles of the "Viennese classical school"—which he had developed extensively in his piano concertos and chamber music—and extrapolating them to opera. Mozart's arias and ensemble pieces are perfectly structured, well proportioned and fleshed out, and retain their musical effect even if the text goes unheard. Salieri was unable to impart this key aspect of opera composition to Beethoven, who would need to develop a sense for it later—independently and via many byroads—during his work on *Leonore*.

Beethoven learned what he could from Salieri and always showed his teacher the greatest deference and gratitude. He dedicated the Violin Sonatas in D, A, and E-flat (op. 12) to Salieri, putting him on equal biographical footing with Beethoven's other ex-teacher, Haydn. At around the same time, Beethoven also composed a set of variations on "La stessa, la stessissima" (WoO 73), one of the hits from Salieri's *Falstaff*. While capitalizing on the tragicomedy's success in Vienna, Beethoven's tribute was undoubtedly intended to charm his former teacher.

The typical frictions that existed between Beethoven and all of his close friends were of course unavoidable. In 1808 Beethoven even accused Salieri of sabotaging his grand *Akademie* on December 22 by scheduling a competing concert by the Tonkünstler-Sozietät that same evening. This was manifestly untrue,[3] and Salieri might have made the reverse accusation on the very same grounds.[4] But all other reports indicate a very amicable relationship. Beethoven took the problems surrounding *Leonore* to his ex-teacher (whose advice, incidentally, he patently ignored), and Moscheles once reported finding a note on Salieri's desk saying, "Beethoven—your pupil—was here!"[5] We also have the endearing tale of Salieri's appearance as assistant conductor to Beethoven during two concerts held at the university hall in 1813 when, as a nearly sixty-five-year-old *Hofkapellmeister,* he conducted the offstage trumpets and percussion (representing the clamor of weaponry) during performances of *Wellington's Victory, or the Battle of Vitoria* (op. 91).

When Salieri was admitted to the Vienna General Hospital in 1823, by then very ill and half insane, Beethoven was immediately informed by Schindler, who also reported Salieri's confession that he had poisoned Mozart. Beethoven would hardly have believed such a thesis: not only did Salieri have no motive, but Beethoven knew him too well to even think him capable of committing such an act.

The Mystery of the Eroica

ON AUGUST 6, 1803, FERDINAND RIES wrote a letter to publisher Nikolaus Simrock in Bonn, announcing Beethoven's plans to move to Paris within eighteen months (by the winter of 1804–5). The decision cannot have been a flight of fancy, as Ries raised the subject twice more several months later.[1] Beethoven himself also implored Joseph Sonnleithner to make haste with the *Leonore* libretto in March 1804, not only because of the timing he had envisaged for the Vienna premiere but also because he wished to take his new France-based opera with him to Paris as a musical and dramatic calling card.

The decision to emigrate to Paris was certainly an escape of sorts, as Beethoven's career opportunities in Vienna had remained limited despite his successful *Akademie* at Theater an der Wien. However, it also represented a positive and conscious choice to move toward the grandeur and the *élan et éclat*—the spirit and shine—of musical life in the French capital. This in turn was due in no small part to the rise of First Consul Bonaparte, who since the Coup of 18 Brumaire in the year VIII (November 9, 1799) had also taken the musical reins firmly in hand. Napoleon believed that music was deserving of government support, since of all the arts it exerts the greatest influence on the mind. He oversaw everything—the opera, conservatory, and the Académie française, where he appointed the composers François-Joseph Gossec, André Grétry, and Etienne Nicolas Méhul. He also issued new intellectual property laws and saw to the institution of a pension system for orchestral musicians. Lastly, he ensured that future composers would also be eligible to compete for the famous Prix de Rome, alongside painters and sculptors. Opportunities in Paris were thus plentiful for those with musical ambition.

Beethoven was not lacking in ambition, and the fact that Parisian audiences had already been introduced to some of his works gave him a head start.

On November 21, 1801, for example, his First Symphony was performed at a concert run by the Société des concerts français under the auspices of Madame Bonaparte; other sources report a concert that included the Second Symphony. Both were successful, despite claims by some critics that certain orchestral effects resembled the cries of pigeons and crocodiles.[2]

Beethoven planned his relocation thoroughly. He had Nikolaus Simrock (whose brother Heinrich had opened a publishing branch in Paris in 1802) release several piano sonatas and chamber works in an attempt to boost his renown among the general public. His reputation among professionals was of course already secured—Parisian piano builder Sébastien Erard had gifted a magnificent grand piano to Beethoven in 1803. Beethoven believed that the French violinist Rodolphe Kreutzer had facilitated the gesture, and decided to dedicate to him the newly composed Violin Sonata in A (op. 47), which he and Bridgetower had premiered several months earlier in Vienna.[3] Beethoven's aim with this diplomatic maneuver was to gain the favor of Kreutzer, who was a professor at the conservatory and the concertmaster at the opera and whose opinion was influential throughout Paris. Whether the ploy was successful is unclear—what we do know is that Kreutzer never publicly performed the sonata that bore his name. Some say it was because the sonata's technical demands, which include many staccato and spiccato passages, exceeded Kreutzer's ability; others claim that he was simply averse to Beethoven's music in general, describing it as "outrageously unintelligible."[4]

The keystone in Beethoven's propaganda offensive was to be a grand symphony dedicated to Napoleon, a move whose significance was more pragmatic than ideological. As with many intellectuals in Bonn, the enthusiasm with which Beethoven had followed the developments in Paris gradually made way for increasing distaste, and he also had mixed feelings regarding Napoleon's political career. On the one hand, Beethoven could appreciate the ingenuity, willpower, and peerless determination with which the Corsican had worked his way up from humble beginnings; on the other, he could not close his eyes to Napoleon's opportunism and blind lust for power. When the German countess von Kielmansegge tried to commission a sonata from Beethoven in November 1801 that was to depict the events of the French Revolution, Beethoven declined, claiming to have been disillusioned by the Concordat with the pope that Napoleon had signed several months before on September 25, 1801, thereby turning back the clock: "Gentlemen, have you gone utterly insane? Asking me to write such a sonata, with things as they are? While the revolution still blazed, perhaps, it might have been appropriate. But now, when everything seems to be going backwards, and Napoleon has signed a Concordat with the Pope? *Now* you would have such a sonata?"[5] This was Beethoven through and through: simultaneously critical, ironic, and verging on the sarcastic. It should be noted here that he did not decline the proposal outright; he merely drove up the price, after which the countess let the matter rest.

Beethoven's indignation at Napoleon's realpolitik was of short duration, however, and on October 22, 1803, Ries informed Simrock of Beethoven's plans to dedicate his new symphony to Bonaparte. It was a perilous initiative, as Beethoven risked losing the goodwill that he had so carefully cultivated among the Viennese aristocracy, who themselves harbored a deep-seated aversion to anything associated with contemporary France. Partly they were fearful of the—in their eyes—deviant ideas brewing there regarding the organization of people and society, but the horrendous image of a beheaded Marie Antoinette (the youngest sister of Joseph II and Leopold II, and the aunt of the reigning emperor) was also still firmly etched in their minds. Despite these reservations, Beethoven sensed that the political climate had indeed been changing in recent months and that he could afford to hedge his bets, despite the persistent anti-French sentiments among the most conservative aristocrats.

Keep in mind that the cards in the geopolitical European power play had been thoroughly reshuffled since the Treaty of Lunéville on February 9, 1801, which had put an end to the War of the Second Coalition. In the wake of several dramatic defeats by Napoleon's armies in northern Italy, Austria had been forced into an agreement involving the surrender of a vast amount of territory, including the Austrian Netherlands (modern-day Belgium), the Left Bank of the Rhine, and Lombardy. The agreement was nonetheless welcomed in Vienna, due to a rather perverse line of reasoning: Napoleon's strength was still the best bet for erasing the ghost of the revolution, and stability in France was a precondition for peace in Europe. From that moment on, all of Austria's international policy concentrated on maintaining friendly relations with Paris.

Beethoven therefore had good reason to dedicate the Third Symphony to Napoleon. There was one important man, however, who stood in the way of Beethoven's well-laid plans: Prince Lobkowitz. He must have caught wind very early on that Beethoven had an exceptional symphony in the works, and—given his advocacy of modern music and the success of Beethoven's

String Quartets (op. 18)—expressed a natural interest in the new symphony project. He offered Beethoven rehearsal and run-through facilities in his "center of excellence," helped organize the first semipublic performances, and took care of the necessary advertising. In return he claimed all of the performance rights for a half-year period, even laying four hundred guilders on the table to secure the commission (he would later extend the exclusivity period to one year, raising the compensation to seven hundred guilders and eighty additional gold ducats, themselves amounting to another 360 guilders). It was an attractive offer, but it thwarted somewhat Beethoven's Bonaparte plans. As a canny member of the middle class, Beethoven cleverly circumvented the problem by applying a "marketing mix": the new symphony would be dedicated to Lobkowitz but titled "Bonaparte."

Initial rehearsals were held chez Lobkowitz in late May and early June 1804.[6] Recently discovered financial records show that the orchestra numbered a mere twenty-seven players.[7] We also learn that the sessions were billed as rehearsals (paying players two guilders each) rather than as concerts (at three guilders each)—a point of contention since there was a small audience present—and that the double-bass player received an additional allowance for the transportation of his instrument. During the first rehearsal, Ries also felt compelled to make a pertinent observation regarding the second horn's uncommonly dissonant entry before the recapitulation in the first movement: "That blasted horn player! Can he not count? That entry is disgraceful!" According to the same account, Beethoven threatened to give Ries a clap across the ear.[8] Further sources indicate that Beethoven's rancor at the lack of appreciation for his symphony persisted for some time.

Aside from this one incident, the rehearsal atmosphere was more one of strained concentration than nervous tension. Concertmaster Anton Wranitzky led the orchestra from the first chair; Beethoven sat in the auditorium and regularly halted the proceedings to dictate various changes, which Wranitzky carefully noted down. Afterward Beethoven collected all of the orchestral parts and took them home to make the corrections, allowing him to hear the improved version the following day, when the parts were further retouched as needed. Beethoven greatly welcomed this feedback loop, as he had grave doubts regarding the timing of certain effects and the proportions of the work in general. He was unsure, for example, about whether he should stick to tradition and repeat the exposition in the first movement, fearing that the work might become too long. The run-throughs with

Lobkowitz helped him realize that the omission of the repeat actually made the symphony seem even longer.[9]

Lobkowitz later made extensive use of his exclusive rights. Several weeks after the rehearsals in Vienna, he organized a concert at his estate in Eisenberg (Jezeří) that included Beethoven's symphony. Beethoven himself did not attend, and Wranitzky was left to conduct the orchestra.[10] In late September 1804, when Prince Louis Ferdinand of Prussia spent the final days of a diplomatic mission to Austria and Bohemia with Lobkowitz, the Third Symphony was performed privately once more—again in Beethoven's absence. Louis Ferdinand was so delighted to be one of the first to hear his idol's latest creation, he had the work played through three times in its entirety. He had called on Beethoven in Vienna earlier that month, the pair having not seen each other in some time. Their previous meeting had taken place in May 1796 during Beethoven's concert tour in Berlin, when the prince treated Beethoven with the amicable deference of a subordinate acknowledging his superior. During an official dinner, for example, Louis Ferdinand allocated Beethoven the seat beside him, while an aristocratic lady (who had slighted Beethoven the day before) was seated opposite. Beethoven was always extremely sensitive to such attentions and decided on the spur of the moment to dedicate the Third Piano Concerto (op. 37) to his noble Prussian friend.

The September conversations with Louis Ferdinand undoubtedly went beyond the musical, extending to the disturbing shifts within the political landscape that were of considerable relevance to Beethoven's future plans. Tempers between Vienna and Paris had flared anew. Razumovsky, after a sojourn of several months in St. Petersburg, had returned to Vienna with clear instructions to increase Russian pressure on the Austrian government to support a third anti-French coalition. The emperor was indifferent, and Cobenzl—the deputy First Minister and Minister for Foreign Affairs—expressed some doubts. Only Archduke Karl Ludwig vehemently opposed any renewed confrontation with the French. Any arguments for peace were rendered moot, however, by Napoleon's increasingly rash behavior. The manner in which he had the Duke of Enghien, the supposed orchestrator of a failed conspiracy, executed in March 1804 had instilled terror into the hearts of the people, and his self-proclamation as emperor of France on May 18, 1804, came across as particularly antagonistic and menacing to those who opposed him.

Francis II responded in August 1804 by founding the Austrian Empire, thus upgrading himself from "archduke" to "emperor." This allowed him to retain his status as a "dual emperor" for two more years, as both Emperor Francis II of the Holy Roman Empire and the German Nation, as well as Emperor Francis I of Austria. Only when the Holy Roman Empire came to an end in 1806, and he was deposed as emperor, was he finally in a position to manage a realm whose scope was more commensurate with his talents.

According to Ries, Beethoven too was outraged at Napoleon's self-appointment as emperor and was once heard to cry out: "Is he not an ordinary man? Now he will trample over all human rights, serving nought but his own ambitions. He will rise higher and higher to become, as everybody says, a tyrant!" Ries goes on to tell how Beethoven then ran to his desk, snatched up the title page of the symphony, tore it to shreds, and threw it to the floor.[11]

This anecdote has taken on a mythical allure and would later come to symbolize the resistance of all artists against tyranny, as well as the more general frictions that exist between art and politics. The ideological implications of the tale should be put into perspective, however, as the Concordat had long since disabused Beethoven of any illusions regarding Napoleon's integrity. Beethoven's outburst in May 1804 was more likely related to the fact that Napoleon's accession as emperor put an irreparable end to any amicable French-Austrian relations, simultaneously laying to rest his own two-pronged strategy of conquering Paris without turning his back on Vienna. This imposed strategic about-face was reflected in the hesitation with which he thenceforth referred to the "Bonaparte" attribution. On October 22, 1803, Ries had written to Simrock: "[Beethoven] is eager to dedicate the symphony to Bonaparte, but because Lobkowitz is prepared to give 400 guilders for half a year, it will be titled 'Bonaparte' instead." A subsequent communication, on August 26, 1804, states, "The symphony is *actually* titled Ponaparte [*sic*]."[12] Far more telling, however, was the manuscript he sent to Breitkopf & Härtel, as the name "Bonaparte" had been erased so vigorously that the paper was completely worn through.

Events unfolded rapidly thereafter. Taking Russia's lead, in September 1804 Prussia also urged Austria—via special emissary Louis Ferdinand—to enter into a new anti-French coalition. Eventually the war hawks got their way, and on November 6 an agreement was signed with the Russians (behind the back, incidentally, of Archduke Karl, who was forced to step down only months later). On August 9, 1805, Austria joined the Third Coalition, and a new war began. The French marched on Vienna, met with negligible resistance, and took the city on November 13. Napoleon made the city's humiliation complete by spending the night in Schönbrunn castle, in the bed of

Empress Maria Theresa, the mother of all Austrians. The allied troops continued to offer resistance but were forced to surrender on December 2 following a grim battle at Austerlitz (around a hundred kilometers north of Vienna). The Treaty of Pressburg, signed on December 26, brought a provisional end to French-Austrian conflict.

After conversing with Louis Ferdinand and armed with inside information received from Breuning, sometime around New Year's Day 1805 Beethoven finally decided to shelve his Paris plans entirely and remove any association of his symphony with Napoleon. He switched targets and instead launched a major publicity campaign to introduce the Third Symphony to the Viennese public. Initially two semiprivate concerts were given to warm up a select group of well-disposed and musically inclined listeners (i.e., aristocrats). The first of these was held on January 20, 1805, at the home of banker Joseph Würth, and the second followed three days later in Lobkowitz's concert hall. No extant sources can explain why Lobkowitz waived his hard-won rights, allowing the work to premiere outside his own home. Some believe it was merely the outcome of the latest spat between Beethoven and his sponsor-patron; others suggest that Würth may have loosened his purse strings to secure the rights to the premiere. He was, after all, a new, ambitious, and wealthy player in high-society circles: he had married up, refurbished the Hoher Markt residence of his in-laws into a lavish *palais* in 1801, and made earnest attempts to add an intellectual and cultural sheen to his new material status. In the winter of 1803 he began hosting regular Sunday morning concerts of such high caliber that they were occasionally reviewed in the *Allgemeine musikalische Zeitung.* The orchestra was assembled from the ranks of freelance professionals and quality amateurs and led by Franz Clement— the concertmaster at Theater an der Wien and a Beethoven expert.

Beethoven's strategy seemed clear. His aim with the first two January concerts was to win over a select group of opinion makers, to familiarize them with the symphony's more unexpected twists and turns, and to train their concert-going endurance and stamina. A favorable reception among the experts and the initiated, he hoped, might spread favor throughout the wider lay population over the ensuing months, encouraging them to flock to the first public performance in a positive and curious frame of mind. The premiere was held on April 7, 1805, at Theater an der Wien during a benefit concert for violinist Franz Clement. Turnout was high, but responses were mixed despite

Beethoven's calculated efforts to prime the audience beforehand. Beethoven must have sensed as much during the debut, particularly when an audience member screamed from the balcony, "I'll pay extra just to make it stop!"[13] Afterward Beethoven left without saying a word to the public. One critic reported: "On that evening the audience and Herr v. Beethoven, himself on the conductor's stand, were not pleased with one another [...] Beethoven [...] found the applause to be somewhat lacking." Precious few members of the audience would have been able to appreciate such a "masterpiece" in any case, and for the majority the symphony had little to do with art at all. It was "too long and ponderous," and "the juxtaposition of heterogenous elements produced strange modulations and violent transitions," lending the work an "originality that one would hardly wish to pursue," characterized by "transparently desperate attempts to stand out and be noticed." The optimists claimed that it would be "several thousand years" before the public were sufficiently schooled in the arts to comprehend the symphony's beauty; the pessimists feared that "if Beethoven continues along this path, things will not end well between him and his audience."[14] Only Haydn expert Griesinger glimpsed the symphony's true import, referring to it as a "work of genius."[15]

The concerts presenting the Third Symphony, and their painstaking preparation, illustrate Beethoven's intention to continue pursuing his career in Vienna—for the time being. The decision was set in stone in October 1806 when he had the score and parts printed in his city of residence, thus putting an end to more than three years of psychological warfare among various publishers, the history of which—as we will see—mirrors the progression of the Bonaparte story in virtually every respect.

In May 1803, when the Third Symphony was still far from complete, Beethoven's brother and personal secretary Kaspar Karl began negotiations with two publishing houses: Breitkopf & Härtel in Leipzig, and Simrock in Bonn. It hardly needs mentioning that Kaspar Karl played one off against the other to drive the price up as high as possible. In December 1803, however, negotiations ceased, as Beethoven was so sure of his plans to relocate that he thought it made more sense to release the symphony in Paris. After a hiatus of over half a year, Kaspar Karl revived talks with Breitkopf & Härtel in August 1804, shortly after his brother had torn up the "Bonaparte" title page. The Third Symphony was to be part of a package that also included the Triple Concerto, the Piano Sonatas in C Major, F Major, and F Minor (opp. 53, 54, and 57), and the *Mount of Olives.* In December 1804—coincidentally the moment when his focus had switched back to Vienna—Beethoven suddenly began stalling for time; the negotiations took on a more acrid tone, and both sides seemed to be waiting for the right pretext to back out of the deal. On December 22, 1804, Breitkopf & Härtel first threatened to cease collaboration if Beethoven failed to meet certain delivery deadlines, following up several days later with complaints about the unpleasant "intermediary" (Beethoven's brother) who was "making the matter difficult to resolve."[16] Beethoven played dumb, and on February 12, 1805—again, via Kaspar Karl—formulated several demands for corrections to the score, insisted on the repeat of the exposition in the first movement, and asked Breitkopf & Härtel to release an additional version of the score in pocket format, analogous to similar editions of Haydn's symphonies that had appeared in Paris.[17] Lichnowsky briefly stepped in as a go-between, but Breitkopf & Härtel's patience had run out, and in June 1805 they sent all of the materials back to Vienna, bringing the chapter to a final close.

Beethoven was now free to negotiate with a young but very promising Viennese publishing house: the Agency of the Arts and Industry (Kunst- und Industrie-Comptoir), better known as the Bureau des arts et d'industrie. This enterprise, whose Kohlmarkt offices were within walking distance of Beethoven's lodgings, was founded in 1801 and initially specialized in the visual arts, scientific publications, and cartography. Its core business gradually shifted toward music, however, and within a few years the Comptoir could compete with other key players in the market. One of the shareholders was Joseph von Sonnleithner—which goes some way to explaining his eagerness to assist during the 1802 Quintet conflict with Artaria—and we can safely assume that his role was pivotal in putting the publisher in touch with Beethoven. From 1802 on, the Comptoir released over forty of his compositions, including such major works as the Violin Sonatas in A Major, C Minor, and G Major (op. 30), the Second Symphony (op. 36), the Third Piano Concerto (op. 37), the Romance for Violin and Orchestra (op. 50), the Piano Sonatas in C Major, F Major, and F Minor (opp. 53, 54, and 57), the Triple Concerto (op. 56), the Fourth Piano Concerto (op. 58), the Three String Quartets in F Major, E Minor, and C Major (op. 59), the Fourth Symphony (op. 60), the Violin Concerto (op. 61), and the *Coriolan* Overture (op. 62). The Comptoir was Beethoven's preferred publisher for many years, until the business succumbed to financial difficulties in 1808 and Beethoven was forced to return to Breitkopf & Härtel.

Beethoven's fondness for the Comptoir was not entirely due to Sonnleithner. Unlike other music publishers, the founders of the Comptoir focused exclusively on "serious" music and turned their noses up at what they called "humdrum entertainments."[18] Beethoven valued their dedication, and so it was only logical that he turned to them for the publication of his Third Symphony. It was released in the autumn of 1806—the first time that the title page of the symphony bore the name *Sinfonia Eroica*. Below the dedication to Prince Lobkowitz, the following comment was added: *composta per festeggiare il sovvenire di un grand Uomo* (composed to celebrate the memory of a great Man).

The Third Symphony had remained untitled since the concerts in January 1805, and all references to Napoleon had been removed. The symphony now bore the epithet "Heroic," and at roughly the same time, Beethoven penciled in above the second movement, *Marcia funebre sulla morte d'un Eroe* (Funeral march on the death of a Hero). Once again we see both the hand of Lobkowitz and a direct reference to the contemporary political landscape. Immediately following Austria's capitulation to France in December 1805, Lobkowitz wrote two extended letters to Prince Louis Ferdinand of Prussia, encouraging him—by force or other means—to seize power in Germany.[19] Lobkowitz believed that golden child Louis Ferdinand had all of the qualities necessary to become a true leader (in Lobkowitz's own words, *der Führer*) and was the alliance's only hope for halting Napoleon's otherwise inexorable advance. Louis Ferdinand took the recommendation seriously and set about writing a critical manifest on the state of affairs in Prussia, which generated some friction within his own circles. But the one thing they all agreed on was that Prussia ought to step up as the driving force behind the new anti-French coalition. Before any such alliance was formed, Prussia sent an ultimatum to the French on August 26, 1806, demanding their retreat beyond the Rhine. Prussia then began preparing for war. On September 23, Louis Ferdinand left Dresden to lead the Prussian troops. He made a small detour via Bohemia where, along with the crème de la crème of the Viennese aristocracy and several astonishingly beautiful young ladies, he spent two very enjoyable days at Lobkowitz's castle. On October 10, 1806, exactly a fortnight after his emotional farewell from Lobkowitz and one day after war was officially declared, he perished during the battle at Saalfeld. When news of his death reached Vienna, the mourning was widespread and his heroism took on mythical proportions. Commissioned by Lobkowitz, Louis Ferdinand's longtime private pianist Johann Dussek composed an "Elégie harmonique sur la mort de

Son Altesse Royale, le Prince Louis Ferdinand de Prusse" (Harmonic elegy on the death of His Royal Highness, Prince Louis Ferdinand of Prussia). At the last minute, Lobkowitz also succeeded in convincing Beethoven to give "his" symphony its heroic title.

The decision to remove the inopportune association with Napoleon from the *Eroica* in the autumn of 1804 is not what caused Beethoven to distance himself from the general entirely. Beethoven would later make equivocal and often contradictory statements about the most infamous politician of his day. On the one hand, he abhorred the manner in which Napoleon had decimated the allied troops in Jena on October 8: "A pity that I am not a master of war as I am of music! Otherwise I would vanquish him."[20] But when he was visited in 1809 by French emissary and music lover Baron de Trémont, Beethoven welcomed him with open arms. He inquired about the etiquette at court, expressed his admiration for Napoleon's ascension through the ranks, and tested the waters—all but discreetly—regarding the possibility of being honored and raised to the peerage by Napoleon. Trémont put this unexpected show of ambition down to the general human tendency to sacrifice pride for flattery.[21] At around the same time, Beethoven was equally willing to negotiate with Napoleon's brother Jérôme Bonaparte—who had been bullied into a post as king of Westphalia—and angled for a position as Kapellmeister at his court.

Later, too, Beethoven continued to drift with the meandering political current. When Napoleon married Marie Louise (the eldest daughter of Francis I) on April 2, 1810, Beethoven briefly considered dedicating his Mass in C (op. 86) to him. By contrast, when Napoleon's inevitable downfall became clear several years later, and Vienna was swept up in a wave of unbridled nationalism, Beethoven saw fit to compose an anti-Napoleonic work for the occasion, the roof-raising *Wellington's Victory, or the Battle of Vitoria* (op. 91), which earned him a great deal of money and fame. His outlook changed once again toward the end of his life, and in 1824 he is reported to have said to Czerny: "Napoleon! [...] There was a time when I couldn't stand him. But my thoughts have now changed completely."[22] This sentiment is completely in line with a nostalgic remark left by a contributor to one of Beethoven's 1820 conversation notebooks: "If Napoleon were to come again now, he would enjoy a better reception in Europe. He understood the *Zeitgeist,* and knew how to take a firm hold of the reins. Future generations will have a better appreciation of him."[23]

Matters are further complicated by another remark made by Beethoven on the death of Napoleon on May 5, 1821, when he said that he had already composed the music (referring to the funeral march from the *Eroica*) befitting what he termed a "catastrophe." Some time before that—nobody can say precisely when—Beethoven scribbled in pencil "Written for Bonaparte" where the work's title had previously been erased. Our befuddlement is thus complete.

Despite its convoluted history, the true "mystery of the *Eroica*" is more musical than historical in nature. For over two hundred years now, Beethoven experts and music lovers alike have struggled with the conundrum of whether the symphony's title is at all pertinent to its content. Is knowledge of an extra-musical program necessary to fully understand the work? Is the hero after whom the symphony may or may not be named—or whose death prompted its composition—also the hero to which the symphony pertains? Is it a reference to a conglomerate of heroes in various scenarios? Does the "hero" perhaps represent all humans, struggling and suffering, Beethoven first and foremost? Delving deeper, is the symphony even *about* a hero? Is it about anything at all? In the pursuit of such highly existential questions, there are as many opinions as there are commentators.

Beethoven left us with quite a riddle. From Czerny we know, for example, that when starting a new work Beethoven often took extramusical inspiration; to English musician Charles Neate, Beethoven reportedly said that he always composed with a picture in his mind, which served to guide his compositional efforts.[24] In some cases, the imagery is clearly audible: the second movement of the String Quartet in A Major (op. 18, no. 5) depicts the tomb scene from *Romeo and Juliet;* a galloping horse is heard in the finale of the Piano Sonata in D Minor (op. 31, no. 2); and the slow movement of the String Quartet in E Minor (op. 59, no. 2) paints a glorious sunlit sky.[25] At the same time, Czerny noted Beethoven's reluctance to divulge the source of his inspiration, as he believed that knowledge of it did nothing to enhance the listening experience.

In the case of the *Eroica,* we are presented with the manifest and unavoidable connection to *The Creatures of Prometheus*—music which, at least at the outset, is undeniably programmatic. Both the famous "Basso del Tema" and the *Kontretanz* theme on which the finale of the *Eroica* is built are taken directly from the ballet's exalted and climactic final scene. Musicologists

Floros, Geck, and Schleuning hence conclude that the *Eroica* is essentially a remake of *Prometheus,* and because they are likewise convinced that the ballet is a Napoleonic work, they take the presumed scenario for the ballet as the basis for their interpretation of the symphony.[26]

Many other musicologists have similarly allowed their interpretations of the *Eroica* to be led (or misled) by the potential association with Napoleon. Adolf Bernhard Marx and Alexander Ulybyshev, two highly authoritative nineteenth-century Beethoven biographers, see in the symphony's opening a depiction of dawn on the battlefield, the rising sun, the tableau of Napoleon mounting his horse, and lastly the hero's trepidation at the challenge ahead. Their musings continue in the same vein: the second movement is reconceptualized as a march for the dead, followed by the resurrection of the hero in the third movement, and the ultimate apotheosis in the fourth.[27] Others posit that the *Eroica* tells Prometheus's own tale, or that of Hector from the *Iliad;* a final cohort draws the line at a portrait of the "universal hero," who may or may not be Beethoven himself. Among this group, associations with Beethoven's own personal martyrdom and resurrection following the Heiligenstadt Testament are never far away.[28]

The *Eroica* is generally viewed as the secular counterpart to the *Mount of Olives,* and Beethoven himself even advised programming both works as a pair.[29] Unlike the oratorio, however, and flying in the face of the above speculations, the merits of the symphony do not lie in its potentially biographical or autobiographical nature. The *Eroica* Symphony is first and foremost precisely that—a symphony—an autonomous piece of auditory architecture, which Beethoven used as a lever to heave instrumental music out of the previous "classical" era and into a new century. Its exceptional length alone (more than fifty minutes) sets it apart from all previous works in the symphonic genre. Although only ten minutes longer than Mozart's *Jupiter* Symphony, those ten minutes make a world of difference, for they can no longer be smuggled in by making small temporal concessions here and there, but instead demand a complete reorganization of form and content. Just as bridge builders must develop new principles of construction when distance or depth exceeds a certain critical threshold, so too was Beethoven forced to go in search of alternative logical constructs to prop up his gargantuan edifice. Civil engineers solve this problem by increasing tension and reducing the number of supports. As a musical technician, Beethoven likewise discovered a new and seemingly paradoxical law of composition: the longer a work goes on, the fewer themes it can accommodate and the greater the necessary cohesion between them. With his new blueprints in hand, Beethoven thus elevated the art of composition to new heights. While his predecessors were looking for creative ideas with which to populate a more or less fixed framework, Beethoven went in search of innovative frameworks that were capable of supporting his ideas. In this sense Beethoven—far more so than Haydn or Mozart—was an emancipated composer, who established his own set of rules for the game he wished to play. In so doing, Beethoven had not only mastered his art—he had become a master over that very art.

The *Eroica* is thus a heroic compositional act in and of itself. It ushered in a new era by redefining the relationship between means and end and introducing an alternate perception of space and time. Beethoven was also fully aware of the new demands he was placing on his audience; given the symphony's abnormal duration, he recommended programming it at the start of a concert rather than after an overture, aria, or concerto, in the belief that much of its impact was lost if heard by an already fatigued public too late in the evening.[30] Perhaps here, in the new active role it places on the listener, is where the true mystery of the *Eroica* lies.

29

The Immortal Beloved

EPISODE TWO

BEETHOVEN'S VACILLATIONS OVER THE TITLE and dedication of the *Eroica* reflected his career doubts, and the inevitable stress he felt as a result can be observed in one typical parameter: the frequency with which he moved house over the course of several months. In May 1804, the change in management at Theater an der Wien meant that Beethoven had to give up his official rooms there, which in itself was hardly regrettable. He moved to an apartment in the Rothes Haus in Alservorstadt, where he remained for only a few weeks. Without even an official notice to the owner (none other than Prince Nikolaus Esterházy), he then vacated the premises to move in with his Bonn friend Stephan Breuning, who occupied a separate apartment within the same residential complex. As noted earlier, the two exchanged heated words in July of 1804, and Beethoven left for the exclusive spa town of Baden to recoup his strength. After briefly considering a summer in Hetzendorf near Schönbrunn, in late July he decided instead on Unterdöbling, a winemaking village just south of Heiligenstadt. From there he had Ries scout for a new inner-city home, and on October 1 he finally took lodgings in the Pasqualatihaus in Mölker Bastei. Though this new apartment was on the fourth floor, any inconvenience was more than compensated for by the glorious views of the nearby forest, the Wienerwald. To enjoy more of the panorama, Beethoven had one of the neighbor's walls demolished without obtaining permission first, which sparked the usual to-do. The Pasqualatihaus would become Beethoven's preferred residence over the next ten years. He moved in and out several times, but the owner of the building—banker and art collector Johann Baptist von Pasqualati—was a staunch Beethoven devotee and always insisted that the rooms be left unoccupied until Beethoven's return.[1]

Meanwhile, Beethoven's Paris plans seemed increasingly unlikely to materialize. Although his final decision to remain in Vienna was motivated by both political and career considerations, he was undoubtedly also influenced by one factor that routinely deprives otherwise rational people of their senses: love. Josephine von Brunsvik, who in 1799 had become Josephine Deym, came into Beethoven's life for the second time in the summer of 1804. They had never completely lost sight of each other, not even after the Deyms had moved to Prague to take advantage of the city's lower cost of living. But on January 27, 1804, Joseph Deym died unexpectedly of severe pneumonia, and the life of the twenty-five-year-old Josephine—who at the time was pregnant with her fourth child—took a new turn. Shortly before his death, Deym had drawn up a will and testament granting his wife custody of the children and full authorization to manage the family's real estate portfolio—quite an uncommon bequest to a widow in those times. While Josephine was certainly appreciative of her husband's final act, she felt saddled with an enormous responsibility (the more so since, on closer inspection, inheriting the Deym "fortune" proved to be more of a "misfortune"). She returned to Vienna to put her affairs in order, to increase the revenue from their Rotenturmstrasse premises, and also to seek support from family and friends. Even the emperor granted her and her children an audience, making an attempt at consolation with the words, "Do not weep, for your children are my children."[2] This declaration would later prove to be more rhetorical than practical in nature, although in his defense the emperor did have more important matters to attend to at the time.

The mental burden on Josephine was by no means trivial. She quickly fell ill, and teetered on the brink of a nervous breakdown. In June 1804, on the advice of her younger sister Charlotte, she reestablished contact with Beethoven, who until that time had maintained the respectful distance befitting for a young widow. (Josephine herself seems to have taken a rather different view of her year of mourning, as the rumor quickly spread throughout Vienna that the comely widow Deym had designs of marriage on one of her departed husband's friends, a certain Swirby.) On hearing from Josephine, Beethoven hastened to her side to offer his services as a music therapist and to pick up where they had left off five years before. Despite his mounting professional commitments and the fact that he was utterly preoccupied by his opera *Leonore,* Beethoven gave Josephine piano lessons nearly every day. He was most obliging, performing hour upon hour of the most beautiful music for his "patient" without ever needing to be asked. Josephine was reinvigorated, made progress with her playing, and once again started organizing musical soirees, charming the company—if her girlfriends are to be believed—with her modest elegance, impeccable taste, and ever-irresistible radiance.[3] Sparks flew between Beethoven and Josephine, as they had five years before, and their time apart had only served to reinforce the sense that they were kindred spirits. Beethoven's letters to her speak of their "many similarities in thought and feeling" as well as of "mutual admiration and friendship."[4] Such sentiments were completely new to Josephine. Shortly after entering into her first marriage, while she had written to her sister of her husband's praiseworthy character, she also complained of the age difference, and of the fact that his "upbringing, opinions and age" differed so from her own.

Beethoven fell head over heels, this time feeling unimpeded by any social barriers that might have stood in the way of a relationship with Josephine. He wrote impassioned letters, gushing of his love and signing off with romantic phrases such as "Your adoring Beethoven," "Your admirer Beethoven," or "Your—your—your—Beethoven."[5] In Beethoven's eyes, Josephine was the perfect woman. He nurtured an idealized love for her that inspired him to great lengths and sacrifice: "I shall redouble my efforts, and—this I promise truly and dearly—will soon be worthier, both in your eyes and my own."[6]

In the autumn of 1804, Beethoven gave his love a very special gift: a song setting of Tiedge's lyrical and didactic poem "Urania," titled "An die Hoffnung" (To hope; op. 32).[7] Josephine handed the song proudly over to her two sisters, who diligently studied and performed it at several soirees but on the express condition that they would not show the score to a single living soul. Of course, Josephine had good reason for her request, as the song was an unabashed and outright declaration of love. Turn-of-the-century etiquette had subtle but strict vocabulary guidelines when it came to matters of love, engagement, and marriage, which nobody—not even those rendered senseless by their infatuations—could afford to break. Even Beethoven knew precisely what he did, said, and wrote. By giving voice to the notion of "hope" and certainly by dedicating a musical work to it, Beethoven consciously and deliberately crossed the threshold from "admiration" into the various stages of more palpable love.[8] This placed Josephine in a predicament. She gratefully accepted the gift and thus fueled Beethoven's hopes. At the same time, she wanted their relationship to remain secret, and she pleaded for the utmost discretion on multiple occasions. She was well aware that her family looked disparagingly on her close relationship with the famous, somewhat eccentric composer. Josephine's sister Charlotte wrote on December 19, 1804:

"Beethoven visits very often, and gives lessons to Pepi [Josephine]. That is rather *dangerous,* I must confess."[9] Two days later, a similarly alarming report reached their brother Franz: "Beethoven is here nearly every day to teach Josie—you understand my meaning, dearest!" Some time later, Theresa wrote to Charlotte: "But tell me, Josephine and Beethoven, what is to become of them?"

An unfortunate incident followed shortly thereafter involving Lichnowsky, who had glimpsed the score of "An die Hoffnung"—complete with dedication—lying on Beethoven's piano. As a seasoned profligate himself, Beethoven's patron had developed an uncanny, almost seismographic sense for subtle shifts in erotic and semi-erotic terrain and immediately felt a tremor. He asked Beethoven for clarification—fearing that he might one day lose his exclusive grip on his protégé—and deliberately set a well-orchestrated campaign in motion to undermine their relationship. He assured Beethoven that he approved of their association, as it no doubt aided Beethoven's creative endeavors. In passing, he then muttered something about whether Josephine's friends and family members—of which he himself was one— would approve of their blossoming connection. In any case, Lichnowsky promised not to tell a soul, and on this count at least, he kept his word. He merely posed one or two pointed questions to Beethoven's friend Zmeskall, who in turn confided in Josephine's aunt Guicciardi, after which news of the affair spread through the Viennese aristocracy like wildfire.

The Brunsvik family, and their dear mother first and foremost, were now forced to take action. They tried to dissuade Josephine from a relationship that in their eyes could only end in disaster. But Josephine was no longer susceptible to family pressures: she was a free and independent woman and would be dictated to no longer. Beethoven and Josephine thus continued to see one another but were forced underground; they met in secret and communicated via coded messages and through letters hidden in books. They are rumored to have spent the summer of 1805 together in Hetzendorf, a short distance from Schönbrunn. In those times the local surroundings were quite rustic and peaceful, though Hetzendorf's main appeal was its lack of popularity compared to other retreats (such as the elitist Baden), which guaranteed greater discretion. An unsubstantiated anecdote tells how Beethoven composed the final scenes of his opera *Leonore* beneath an oak tree in Hetzendorf, and that Josephine was the first to become acquainted with their beauty.

Their shared secret—the unspoken knowledge of that which may not be known—created a strong bond between the two lovers. Josephine was walking on air, and over the ensuing months Beethoven composed many of his most beautiful works: the Fourth Piano Concerto, the Fourth Symphony, the *Razumovsky* Quartets, and the Violin Concerto. But the situation was volatile, if only because Beethoven longed for more physical intimacy which Josephine—who was known to be easily excited—could not allow. Her sisters sent her frequent warnings: "Be sure never to meet with him alone" or, "Make it a rule never to see him by yourself. It would actually be far better never to receive him at home."[10] Promiscuous nineteenth-century Vienna was particularly hypocritical on this count. In a city where the number of illegitimate children was extraordinarily high, accidental pregnancies among widows were always tremendously stigmatized.[11] Beethoven and Josephine would therefore need to marry, which was, alas, impossible: not only had the Brunsvik family vetoed the prospect, but Josephine herself did not desire it. Despite the admiration and love she felt for Beethoven, she could not envisage him as the stepfather to her four children. She felt an intuitive reticence, which, given what would later transpire between Beethoven and his nephew Karl, we now know was not entirely unfounded. Josephine, as both a conscientious mother and a woman in love, was conflicted. Having solemnly sworn at her husband's deathbed to do all she could to ensure their children's happiness, Josephine, like a "New Héloïse," informed Beethoven of her decision to put her motherly obligations first and her feminine desires second. She hoped that Beethoven would accept her argument, and as a demonstration of his love for her, agree to keep that love at a platonic level: "You had my heart long ago, and the greatest proof of my love—my respect—is yours through this admission, and my trust! [...] Prove to me that you know its worth. If you can be satisfied—do not break my heart—or press me further— I love you beyond words—from one kindred spirit to another—Are you incapable of such a bond?—For currently I cannot love you any other way."[12]

Her plea was too much for Beethoven, not least because he knew only too well that Josephine was manipulating her own feelings. He felt egregiously wronged and made a strategic blunder by believing that it is possible to convert a woman's refusal into acceptance by bombarding her with letters, supplications, and recriminations. From then on, their correspondence would occasionally take on a bitter tone. When Beethoven heard in 1806 that a third-rate Tyrolean nobleman, Anton von Wolkenstein, had importuned her with courtly attentions—and that she had tolerated them—he accused her of betrayal. Josephine protested her innocence, seeking refuge (as befitted a lady of the aristocracy) behind a screen of moral outrage: "I despise this base, vulgar behavior exhibited by others of my gender! It is beneath me and I have no need of it. *Coquettishness* and childish vanity are both alien to me."[13]

Ultimately they both agreed to spend some time apart; just how long they managed to do so is unknown. We know, for example, that Josephine traveled to Baden in July 1807 with her mother and four children and that Beethoven was spotted there at around the same time. In September, on his return from Eisenstadt after the premiere of the Mass in C, he could bear it no longer and insisted on a reunion: "A thousand voices whisper constantly to me that you are my only love, and the only woman for me. I can no longer tolerate this self-imposed burden [. . .] Tomorrow, or the day after, I shall come to see you. May the heavens grant me one undisturbed hour, wherever we may be, that I may finally talk with you as I have wished to do for so long, that my heart and my soul may join with you once more."[14] Beethoven was, after all, utterly convinced that Josephine was suffering no less from their amorous abstinence, and hoped that she might still capitulate: "When I decided to put distance between us, I did so because I thought it was what you wanted [. . .] later, however, I started wondering whether I had misread your intentions."[15]

When he came to visit, Josephine shut Beethoven out both literally and figuratively, sending a servant to fend him off at the door. Her need to lock herself away from Beethoven like this is perhaps proof of just how much she feared losing her self-control.

We will never know what might have happened if Josephine and Beethoven had decided to marry in September 1807, nor what it would have meant for Beethoven's life as a composer. Would he have written more music? Less music? Would his music have been any different? And in what way?

In any case, Josephine and Beethoven went their separate ways in September 1807, to all appearances for good, and set their respective bars for romance pragmatically (almost cynically) low. At first Josephine focused entirely on her children. Accompanied by her two sons Fritz and Carl, and her sister Therese (who was starting to take her role as a surrogate father more seriously), in 1808 she traveled to Yverdon in Switzerland, having resolved to find a suitable teacher for her children at the private school run by contemporary pedagogical guru Johann Heinrich Pestalozzi. It was there that Josephine and Therese fell in with Pestalozzi's educational philosophy, in many ways because it was a natural extension of how they themselves were raised. Therese in particular would be inspired, and the philosophy underpinned a future charitable initiative of hers aimed at poor children in Hungary. But Josephine too became an avid follower of the method that she felt offered the best guarantee for her children's happiness. An initial Swiss candidate declined the position due to the uncertainty of leaving his home country in a time of war. She was therefore delighted when another of Pestalozzi's assistants, the Estonian baron Christoph von Stackelberg, volunteered his services. Stackelberg was a charming gentleman, who impressed others with the erudition and eloquence with which he debated his pedagogical theories. On the return journey to Martonvásár (which due to the war, no longer went via Germany but instead traversed the Alps, northern Italy, and Trieste), he also proved to be a most genteel and attentive travel companion. The journey was near-fatal, as during their trek across the snow-covered Alps, they were almost driven into a ravine by caravans of heavily laden mules and were forced to cross enemy lines on more than one occasion. Josephine then became seriously ill and fought for her life for four weeks. But fate struck a far more insidious blow during a sojourn in Pisa, when Stackelberg took more than an amicable liking to Josephine and she reciprocated, although their mutual affection seemed to be as superficial as it was transitory. Nonetheless, their brief flirtation seemed compromising enough for Stackelberg to exact marriage on Josephine, who one year later—on February 13, 1810—was again forced to wed a man she did not love. While her family was hardly brimming with enthusiasm, they offered little objection. Stackelberg may have been a Protestant, but he was also a baron, and that seemed to suffice.

Thick mists of hypocrisy obscure this period in Josephine's life. Marie-Elisabeth Tellenbach, whose in-depth research produced a long list of arguments for proclaiming Josephine as Beethoven's one true love (the "immortal beloved"), concluded from Therese's diaries and letters that Josephine's second marriage took place under "dark and mysterious circumstances." Tellenbach claims that Stackelberg had the means to force Josephine into marriage, but exactly how an awkward, thirty-three-year-old educator of limited means was able to exert any pressure on a seasoned, thirty-year-old emancipated widow goes unexplained. Josephine also went into hiding for nearly a year before the marriage was officially concluded. For this, Tellenbach offers only a simple hypothesis: "Perhaps Josephine wanted to avoid living in Vienna, so as not to run into Beethoven?"[16]

In 2001, Rita Steblin made discoveries that shed greater light not only on the above affair but also on Josephine's personality in general.[17] Steblin ascertained that the biographical details of Josephine's two eldest daughters from

Stackelberg had been doctored (their third daughter will be discussed later). In contrast with the prevailing theory, Josephine's daughter, Laura, was not one year younger than her sister Theophile (who was born in November 1810) but a year older. This puts her birth in December 1809 and her conception in the spring of that same year—precisely the period of Josephine's brief flirtation with Stackelberg. The puzzle pieces now suddenly fall into place: following a period of seclusion in the family's country estate, Josephine was forced to marry the father of her illegitimate child, whose birth was first kept a secret and later postdated.

Some sympathy can be mustered for the Brunsviks' desire to conceal this sordid episode. According to Steblin, the current heirs to the Brunsvik estate continue to sabotage research efforts into this delicate affair to this day. But even Josephine biographers have, until now, tended to ignore this "mishap," which undermines somewhat the image cultivated of Josephine—by her elder sister Therese in particular—as the very paragon of motherly virtue and morality. By contrast, Steblin has unearthed evidence, in Josephine's letters to Stackelberg for example, suggesting that Beethoven's great love was far less virtuous than is either generally assumed or was deemed commensurate with our highly romanticized image of the composer. Steblin even goes so far as to describe Josephine as a "femme fatale."[18]

Whatever the case, the dramatic events leading up to Josephine's second marriage cast a dark pall over the rest of her life. Things went downhill very early on, as the result of embezzlements made during the purchase of a farm in Moravia. Stackelberg believed that it was important to have the children grow up in an idyllic country setting in harmony with nature. Ignoring the fact that Stackelberg was just as ill-suited to farming life as Beethoven, the enterprise failed purely due to a lack of finances. When it became apparent that Stackelberg's family was not prepared to help with the necessary investments, Josephine turned to her aristocratic friends the Trauttmansdorffs. This family—and with a degree of cynicism rarely observed—caused her to sink ever more deeply into the financial morass. In the end, Josephine could only turn to her own family, who first asserted that she was in no way to be held liable for the corruption of Stackelberg and his kin. Ultimately it was Josephine's brother Franz who came to the rescue. Despite the unstable economic conditions, and using the family's entire real estate portfolio as collateral, he took out loans that ran him to the very brink of ruin.

A far more devastating factor was that as a pedagogue, Stackelberg exhibited a far more theoretical than pragmatic approach to life. Expressed in less delicate terms, he was psychotic, egocentric, and lazy; the long hours he spent reading esoteric volumes were punctuated by tyrannical outbursts targeting everyone and everything in his vicinity. The diary entry on April 3, 1812, by the eldest of the Deym daughters, twelve-year-old Vicky, tells the dire tale of the terror unleashed on the family by her stepfather, of how at the most unexpected moments and at the slightest provocation he threw himself at her defenseless mother, denouncing her as the source of all the failures in his life and an impediment to his intellectual aspirations.[19] Josephine's sister Therese would later attest to what Josephine endured in her marriage to Stackelberg, and the extent of her suffering. In June 1812 Josephine could bear it no longer, and she threw her baron out. He moved into a small room in the city center, the timing of which is not without import for the rest of our story.

Beethoven fared differently in love but hardly any better. His new financial situation, which had improved tremendously in 1809, had also bolstered his hopes on the marriage market. In March 1809 he asked his friend Ignaz von Gleichenstein—only half-jokingly—to aid him in his search for a wife: "If you should encounter a belle there in F. [Freiburg] who might grace my harmonies with a tender sigh now and then, [. . .] go ahead and make contact—she must be beautiful however, for I can love nothing that is not beautiful—otherwise I should love myself."[20] His search proved largely fruitless. Starting in 1810 (coincidentally or not, the year of Josephine's second marriage), Beethoven tumbled from one love affair into another. The caliber of the ladies in question varied as much as the effort exerted by Beethoven to win them over, and he became ever more resigned with each successive rejection.

The tale of Therese Malfatti will serve as a prime example. She was the eldest daughter of a refined, culturally active, and meritocratic family of bankers who kept a beautiful home on Rotenturmstrasse only a few houses down from Josephine's own apartment complex. Introductions were made in 1810 by the above-mentioned Ignaz von Gleichenstein—the suitor and later husband to the family's youngest daughter, Anna—and Beethoven soon became enchanted by the elder sister, Therese. By all accounts the Malfattis were beautiful girls: brunettes with tanned skin and dark eyes, intelligent and spirited, but also a little coquettish and, according to some, a tad superficial, which was not without its charms. The rest of the story should sound familiar: a dapper, freshly bathed, and clean-shaven Beethoven made frequent visits, gladly performed for the family, taught the girls piano, impressed the company with his knowledge of literature and philosophy, and advised the father on the purchase of a new instrument. The parents were initially very honored by their eminent guest's appearances, and Beethoven began to entertain sincere notions of marriage with Therese, with whom he felt at ease despite the fact that she could have been his own daughter (Therese was more than twenty years his junior) and, like Josephine, was beyond his social standing. He even set the nuptial formalities in motion, asking his friend Wegeler to procure an official birth certificate from Bonn—a bold and hasty move, as he was quickly made to realize that he should not harbor any such illusions. When the Malfatti family left in late May for their summer residence near Krems, Beethoven wrote Therese a long letter, excusing himself for his advances and asking her to "please forget my craziness." He also made a few literary recommendations, saying she must absolutely read Goethe's *Wilhelm Meister* and Schlegel's translations of Shakespeare, and lastly asking whether he might still pop by "even just for half an hour."[21] Therese's parents responded by having Gleichenstein inform Beethoven in no uncertain terms that he was still welcome in his capacity as a musician but not as a suitor. A younger Beethoven would never have tolerated such an affront; but his skin had clearly thickened in the meantime, and without so much as a riposte he promptly resigned himself to the new state of affairs. Despite the fleeting nature of this love story, it is nonetheless the reason the rather unprepossessing, four-minute-long Bagatelle in A Minor (WoO 59), composed and presented by Beethoven to Therese Malfatti in April 1810, has assumed a significance in Beethoven's oeuvre that is utterly disproportionate to its musical import. It is generally known by the nickname supposedly given to it on its posthumous publication in 1867: *Für Elise*. Since that time, discussion has been rife surrounding the origins of the name and the possible contradictions between it and the identity of the work's dedicatee. The conundrum disappears when we consider that in German poetic tradition, "Elise" is often used as a synonym for "the beloved" (or literally, "the chosen one"). Sooner or later any Maria, Josephine, or Therese could therefore be dubbed "Elise."[22]

Beethoven's ability to recover from this amorous setback was partly due to his embroilment in another affair, this time with the lucky Elisabeth (Bettina) Brentano. Exactly who pursued whom remains unclear. Bettina Brentano was a prototypical groupie: a person who, regardless of her own marital status, pathologically seeks out the companionship of famous figures in order to boast of an important role in their lives—a behavior often accompanied by an inability to separate fact from fiction. Bettina Brentano was well suited to the part, as she was well read, spoke various languages fluently, could recite contemporary poetry for hours, and was also a reasonable painter and a sometime composer. Her intellectual arsenal thus allowed her to engage on a wide range of topics and draw attention to herself with charismatic ease. She was eminently charming and had a physique to match (although it was supposed that her strict, cloistered upbringing had perhaps denied her the regular use of a mirror, a deficiency that she felt the irritating need to make up for later in life). Bettina's list of conquests was impressive and included two great pillars of European culture, Beethoven and Goethe. She was even permitted to address the latter with the informal German *du* in public, an honor conferred only seldom by the conservative and rather pedantic poet. She thus followed in the footsteps of her mother, Maximiliane de la Roche, who had had a liaison with the young Goethe nearly forty years prior. When Bettina heard that it was Beethoven's greatest wish to meet the famous author from Weimar and he asked her for an introduction, she felt that her time had come to earn a place in history, and showed not a moment's hesitation in putting her privileged position to work for the cultural and greater good. She did so in such an officious and supercilious manner, however, that an exasperated Madame Christiane von Goethe-Vulpius had her forcibly removed from the house.

Famous men are seldom inclined to forego the attentions of such women, and Beethoven was no exception. But while Bettina's account of their relationship should be taken with a sizeable grain of salt (the overromanticized circumstances of their first meeting, for example, are a barefaced lie[23]), she and Beethoven must have at least spent several weeks together. They walked the streets hand in hand; he took her to society gatherings; and she was even permitted to gaze on admiringly from a front-row seat during rehearsals, no doubt to the wry amusement of the orchestral musicians. Bettina later described the imprint that Beethoven the "conductor-composer" had left on her, and it was partly her high-blown, overaestheticized, idealistic, and partially fabricated account that laid the foundations for the modern romantic image of Beethoven as a "genius," "magician," and "high priest of the arts."[24]

This relationship, too, was of short duration, and it is uncertain whether either party ever seriously entertained notions of marriage. Bettina had already promised her hand to the German poet Achim von Arnim (who had collaborated with her brother Clemens on *Des Knaben Wunderhorn*), and she may have rushed her engagement and marriage in December 1810 to prevent her dalliance with Beethoven from escalating needlessly. They did have dealings several times afterward, however. In February 1811, Beethoven asked her to relay that he did not wish to be involved in the memorial cantata project for the recently deceased Queen Louise of Prussia being organized by her brother Clemens, and they also met once again in Teplitz (Teplice) in the summer of 1812. After that, nothing.

During the Second Josephine Era (1804–7), Beethoven's compositional efforts were focused principally on *Leonore*. It was during this period that he also wrote his greatest piano sonata until that time, the *Appassionata* (op. 57), a work whose marked expressiveness and emotional tension strongly suggest a link with the Josephine saga.[25] Although *"Appassionata"* would seem to reinforce this association, the title was only added later, in 1838, by Hamburg publisher Cranz as a marketing ploy to boost sales of an arrangement of the work for piano duet.[26] The epithet is also somewhat superfluous, as almost all of Beethoven's piano music can be labeled "passionate." An alternative, such as "tragic" or *"pathétique,"* might have been more appropriate.

The *Appassionata* was a masterpiece without precedent. It can be regarded as an epic melodrama with wild outbursts of fear, lamentation, rage, and willful rebellion against the diabolical forces of destiny. There is little room for hope or optimism, and any glimmers of liberation or redemption—such as the second theme from the first movement, or the conclusion of the central theme and variations—are always abruptly and brutally extinguished. The *Appassionata* has no happy ending; quite the contrary, the negative forces retain the upper hand, and the keys are not so much struck as hammered. By writing this way, however, Beethoven was capitalizing on the broader sonic capabilities offered by the newest pianos of his day. The sonata's predominantly dark character becomes a key characteristic of the work, a fact evident in the opening theme's emergence as it rises up from the depths of the instrument, traversing a large part of the instrument's tessitura:

The opening theme also immediately sets the tone, and Beethoven's clearly deliberate choice for a two-octave range gives it a tinge of Verdian ominousness. In the second movement, too, it is the timbre that carries the musical import, as the scant melody is enriched by chords dark and lush, lending an expressiveness that pulls at the heart strings:

Here Beethoven develops an acoustic fingerprint that is entirely his own. He meticulously selects the chord tones that are to be doubled, distributing them across the hands and fingers in such a way as to maximize breadth, depth, and musical weight, but without compromising on flexibility, transparency, or legato.[27] This was Beethoven's great strength and one which also extended to his orchestral music, for while the full tutti passages of his contemporaries (Clementi, Weber, Spohr—even Schubert) tend toward monochromatic and monotonal opacity, Beethoven's characteristic harmonic and tonal distribution always ensures a crystalline transparency.

In the final movement, Beethoven unleashes his full rage and fury. Ferdinand Ries provides a detailed description of how this unhinged work came into existence. During a long walk together, Beethoven had been completely preoccupied and withdrawn, incessantly murmuring a new theme for his sonata. On their return home, Beethoven took no time even to remove his hat or coat, instead rushing straight to the keyboard to develop the new idea further. After an hour of hammering like a madman in a trance, he eventually looked up in a daze at his student, who stood rooted to the spot, watching the scene unfold in bewilderment.[28] The music bears the stamp of its genesis—that is, if the loud, drawn-out cry of desperation and defiance it resembles can even still be described as "music." If we extend this comparison, the pianist likewise resembles a kind of shaman, trapped in a futile attempt to hold destiny at bay.

But despite the storm and tumult, Beethoven still retains control, reining in the psychodramatic turbulence through architectural precision. The first movement in particular is cast within a clear mold following a compelling musical logic. The four traditional components of sonata form—the exposition, development, recapitulation, and coda—are not only equal in length (a feat that no other composer had achieved until that time) but also of equal musical import, and they embody a formal symmetry. In other words, in the *Appassionata* the conflict between general optimism and individual powerlessness did not result in skewed compositional proportions (unlike the later piano sonatas and string quartets), as though Beethoven still cherished hopes of liberation and redemption through the power of reason. This intriguing interplay between the emotional and the rational is what makes the *Appassionata* such a masterpiece. Beethoven himself thought the same, and for some time he felt he had said all that needed to be said in the genre.

The *Appassionata* was published in February 1807 and was dedicated to Franz von Brunsvik.[29] Sister Therese would receive her dedication three years later, the Sonata in F-sharp Major (op. 78); only Josephine was left empty-handed. But by neglecting to dedicate a single serious work to her, Beethoven actually achieved the opposite of what he had intended, further fanning the fire of speculation regarding the intensity of the Josephine affair. Even the *Andante favori* in F Major (WoO 57)—a Josephine work if ever there was one—was not officially dedicated to her. The piece started life as the central movement of the Sonata in C Major (op. 53, more commonly known as the *Waldstein*). As the story goes, several of Beethoven's friends told him that they found the sonata too long, whereupon Beethoven replaced the movement with a brief Introduzione in an adagio molto tempo. This version of events is barely credible, however, as Beethoven had never before displayed even a shred of interest in his audience's opinions regarding the length of a work. A far more plausible theory is that he simply realized the character was not a proper fit for the rest of the sonata, after which he sent it to Josephine as the *Andante favori*, with the accompanying note, "Here is your—your—Andante."[30]

Josephine must have been very pleased with "her" *Andante*. It is a strikingly beautiful miniature with a befitting character, designated by Beethoven himself as grazioso. We might also imagine that Josephine, with a little imagination, could even hear her own name (which is four syllables long in German) being sung to the notes of the opening theme:

Andante grazioso con moto

[Jo - se - phi - ne, Jo - se - phi - ne]

Beethoven's own fondness for the work is evident from his overreaction to a seemingly harmless prank played on him by Ries and Lichnowsky. Ries had heard the *Andante* at Beethoven's home several times; he had memorized it and then taught it to Lichnowsky. The next day Lichnowsky called on Beethoven, saying he had been composing with some success, and proceeded to play a horribly mangled version of the *Andante*.[31] Beethoven was incensed and decided then and there never to play a single note in Ries's presence again.

30

In Search of the Perfect Piano

BEETHOVEN'S *APPASSIONATA* PUSHED CONTEMPORARY pianism to its very limits. It placed high demands on the player, who in turn also demanded the utmost from the instrument. Beethoven had not yet reached the point of pianistic maltreatment or abuse—that would come later when he tried to compensate for his lack of hearing. Until then, he remained mindful of the old adage that a musician cannot ask of an instrument what it cannot give. "Loudness" is a relative concept after all, an emergent property of both absolute volume and compositional texture (a dense chord, for example, will always sound louder than a single note struck with great force). Still, we cannot escape the impression that Beethoven had music in mind that exceeded the capabilities of contemporary instruments. Essentially, he wished to square the pianistic circle: to generate a piano tone that was lyrical, sustained, and even powerful while simultaneously remaining articulated, flexible, and responsive. Beethoven searched his whole life for this impossible combination, sampling a wide range of instruments and putting constant pressure on piano builders to move in the direction he wanted. The resulting symbiosis was fascinating, for Beethoven's piano music was largely guided by developments in early-nineteenth-century instrument manufacture, themselves driven in part by Beethoven's musical and pianistic ideas.

Two crucial figures in these developments were Anna Maria (Nannette) Stein, the daughter of Augsburg piano builder Johann Andreas Stein, and her husband, Andreas Streicher. Nannette Stein and her brother Matthäus had continued to run the factory they had inherited from their deceased father. In 1794, they moved to Vienna, where they hoped to capitalize on the exponentially growing piano market. Shortly beforehand Nannette had married Stuttgart pianist, teacher, and arranger Andreas Streicher, a fascinating personality who had already made history in September 1782 by risking his life (and his life savings) to help his friend Friedrich Schiller escape from Stuttgart. Together they journeyed under cover to Mannheim where they parted ways, but not before swearing a solemn oath not to meet again until one had become a minister and the other a Kapellmeister. Although neither ever fulfilled the bargain, we can only imagine Beethoven's captivation at Streicher's tale of heroic bravery.

The siblings' business, Frère et Soeur Stein à Vienne, was a great success. Nannette Stein cultivated an impressive network of sales representatives, which considerably boosted revenue from the German market (Breitkopf & Härtel purchased the exclusive rights for Saxony in 1802). However, that same year saw the escalation of a conflict that had been brewing between the siblings for some time, leading to a fallout and Nannette's decision to exit the partnership. Andreas Streicher, who one year earlier had written a most interesting instruction manual and maintenance guide for his wife's instruments ("Brief Remarks on the Playing, Tuning and Maintenance of Fortepianos"[1]), retrained as a piano builder and joined the business that was run by and named after his wife, Nannette Streicher née Stein. From that point on, the Streichers organized weekly private concerts in their Landstrasse studio. Officially their purpose was to provide a forum for young and promising pianists; in reality, of course, the enterprise revolved around the promotion of their newest instruments. The concerts were so well attended that in 1812 the Streichers could afford to build a dedicated three-hundred-seat auditorium, with a stage that could even accommodate a large orchestra. The wings were decorated with busts of eminent composers, who cast their gaze on the music making with benevolent approval. The ceremonial opening was held on April 12, 1812, in the presence of Archduke Rudolph and notable members of the aristocracy. Schuppanzigh directed a program that included two Dussek piano concertos; the real show-stopper, however, was Beethoven's *Coriolan* Overture.

Beethoven had already become acquainted with the Stein pianos in Bonn, where virtually everybody played a Stein instrument. He himself had been gifted one by Count Waldstein in 1788 and was thus already familiar with the instrument's strengths and limitations. As mentioned earlier, Beethoven had visited father Stein's studio on his way back from Vienna in 1787, and he was not only impressed with the builder's work but also became acquainted with Stein's daughter, Nannette. A future meeting in Vienna was therefore to be expected. In the meantime, Beethoven became steadily more critical of the Streicher-Stein instruments. In the summer of 1796, his outlook was still complimentary: "The art of playing the piano remains the most uncultivated to this day, that much is certain. One often believes to hear no more than a harp, and I am happy to see that you are one of the few who sense and understand that the piano is also capable of song, if one can only nurture the proper feeling. I long for the day when the piano and the harp are viewed as two completely separate instruments."[2] Several months later, however, after playing one of Streicher's instruments during a concert in Pressburg, he expressed some (albeit veiled) reservations: "Two days ago I received your fortepiano—the result is truly excellent, and anybody else would no doubt endeavour to keep it for themselves. But—and laugh if you will—I would be lying if I did not confess that the instrument is simply too good for me. Shall I tell you why? Because it robs me of the freedom to create the tone myself. But this should in no way discourage you from continuing to build such instruments, for there will be few out there who are as particular as I."[3]

Beethoven's more critical outlook was no doubt prompted by his enjoyment of another piano that he had received on loan around the year 1800 from Anton Walter, Streicher's key competitor. Beethoven was so happy with the instrument in fact that two years later he tried to wheedle another from Walter at a negligible price, arguing that any other builder would jump at the chance to gift him an instrument outright. Walter built pianos with a more robust sound and a heavier action, both of which appealed to Beethoven. Although the mechanics of Walter's instruments did not vary greatly from Streicher's, all components were designed specifically to boost resonance and volume: the ribs on the soundboard were placed differently; the strings were thicker; the upper registers were triple-strung; the hammers had almost doubled in weight; and the key-beds were deeper.[4] Despite the heavy machinery, the sound of a Walter piano was very transparent, hardly a trivial matter to Beethoven given the compact chord voicings in his music. Even the trills in the lowest registers retained their clarity, and Beethoven must have been delighted to hear that the characteristic timbre of all registers—from treble to bass—was preserved. Despite its more imposing sound, a Walter piano could always still convey the distinct inner voices of a four-part choir—with sopranos, altos, tenors, and basses—or a string quartet.

A Walter therefore required a different touch from a Streicher, so much so that the Viennese even spoke of two "schools" of pianism. The Walters took an approach that was more athletic, brilliant, and virtuosic and, in the eyes of the Viennese, somewhat superficial. The Streichers, on the other hand, were more sensitive, played with greater nuance and clarity, and—again, according to the Viennese—thus had more audience appeal. Beethoven was somewhat unjustly consigned to the former.

Beethoven's preference for Walter pianos was attributable not only to their greater power and speed but also to the more sustained tone and the smooth legato he could extract from them. Yet even these qualities ultimately proved inadequate, and he eventually turned to instruments built after the English model. This step was hardly surprising, given the influence on his music hitherto by composers belonging to what was known as the "English" school, founded by Clementi and Dussek. Many of the virtuosic passages from his sonatas even seem to have been inspired—from a technical perspective—directly by the work of his two elder colleagues. But what fascinated Beethoven most about Clementi and Dussek was their sound ideal, which had clearly been shaped by the instruments on which their music was most often performed. These instruments were incomparably louder and could "sing" more than any piano in Vienna.

This major difference could be assigned to the alternative mechanism used to strike the strings in English pianos. Unlike the *Prellzunge* mechanism of the Viennese instruments, which "flipped" the hammers toward the string using a double lever, the English instruments used a *Stosszunge* system, which effectively "thrust" the hammers into the strings directly. This system required longer keys, a deeper action, and greater strength to operate, necessitating an additional impulse from the wrists and sometimes even the arms. The instrument's other components—the soundboard, strings, and so on— were all modified accordingly to suit the same purpose. The English had also far surpassed the Viennese in experiments with pedal and damper effects and had extended the range of the piano to six octaves or more. Unsurprisingly, the English pianos were therefore literal "heavyweights" and far more expensive than their Viennese counterparts.

English pianos thus had a wider dynamic range capable of sustaining broader melodic arcs, and as such met the needs of the more modern "romantic" pianists and composers.[5] These included Beethoven, although his thoughts on the matter were far more nuanced than later commentators wished to admit.[6] The broader acoustic palette came at a price: English pianos had a rough tone; repeated notes and dampers were slow to respond; and the instruments offered little variety in articulation.

Paradoxically, Beethoven was introduced to English pianos via a Parisian builder, Erard, who—for lack of a French tradition—had been building pianos according to the English model for decades. He thus had access to the London market, and the branch he opened there in 1792 remained one of the capital's most high-quality and productive piano studios into the 1890s. Encouraged by his success, Erard attempted to conquer the lucrative Viennese market with his "English" instruments. And just as the modern music industry devotes a sizeable portion of its budget to sponsoring the equipment of its most famous exponents, Erard sought promotion by donating one of his newest pianos to the most notable Viennese pianist of the day, in the hope that he would sing the instrument's praises far and wide.[7] Beethoven was understandably flattered by the gesture and believed that the Paris connection might also aid his chief ambition at the time, which was emigration to France. Yet Beethoven's primary interest was in the musical possibilities offered by the new instrument. He sensed instantly that the difference between an Erard and a Walter was greater than that between a Walter and a Streicher, and realized that a hybrid French-English instrument offered more possibilities than a German-Viennese breed. So he pounced on the Erard and wrote on it a number of his greatest piano works (the *Waldstein* Sonata, the *Appassionata,* and the Fourth and Fifth piano concertos), in which the new resonant dimensions and a powerful, more legato-oriented tone constituted an integral part of the overall musical concept.

Ultimately, though, the new Erard could not meet Beethoven's high expectations, and Beethoven could not adapt to the English mechanism. Despite the fact that—unlike many of his colleagues—he increasingly favored a curved finger technique that offered greater force, he continued to struggle with the action's depth and heaviness. Even the tone was not entirely to his liking. And so he contacted Streicher with a request to modify the Erard, a delicate operation that yielded poor results. Beethoven decided to sell the instrument in 1810, and when that too was unsuccessful he gifted it to his brother Johann.[8]

It was then that Beethoven returned to his first piano love. The Streichers had long built pianos according to established tradition, producing instruments with a light action and a sound that was crisp, tender, and intimate. They were utterly convinced that if the piano were to drift too far from the instruments of old, at least 90 percent of amateur players would give up playing the piano altogether. As time went on, however, it became harder and harder to ignore the demand for instruments with a broader—and louder—

timbral spectrum and an action to match. Their business partner Breitkopf & Härtel insisted that they modernize, and Beethoven also exerted some pressure. Streicher capitulated only under immense protest, as he knew that a heavier and deeper action was fundamentally at odds with his desire to ensure responsiveness and transparency. It would take until 1809 for him to find an acceptable middle ground, and his many talks with Beethoven, including those regarding his work on the Erard grand, were of crucial importance. This brings us to yet another paradox: it was the search for ways to lighten Beethoven's Erard that actually taught Streicher how to add "weight" to his own instruments. The result was a brilliant success. Johann Friedrich Reichardt claimed that the new piano sounded like an orchestra,[9] and Beethoven promptly ordered a new instrument on September 18, 1810.

Beethoven remained satisfied with his new Streicher for years, and his relationship with the Streichers during that time was also warm and open-hearted. He even lived in their immediate vicinity for some time, on Landstrasser Hauptstrasse, when Nannette would drop by almost daily to help with his personal affairs. For several years, no housekeeper or cleaning lady entered the Beethoven residence without Nannette's prior approval, and it was she who often mediated whenever Beethoven had once again mis-treated his staff.[10]

On July 7, 1817, Beethoven asked Nannette Streicher whether her husband might build him a new piano. This time the problem lay not with the instru-ment but with himself, a fact that Beethoven took no pains to obscure: "Please ask him [Streicher] whether he would be so kind as to build one of your pianos to accommodate my poor hearing, and to make it as powerful as is humanly possible."[11] By that time, the piano also fulfilled a completely different role in Beethoven's life. It no longer served as a practice instrument for concert per-formances, and it is even contested whether the instrument was of any help in his search for coloristic and brilliant virtuosic effects in his new piano works. In reality, Beethoven only used it as a sounding board and touchstone for his new orchestral works and string quartets. And it showed: Beethoven's guests reported that he neglected his instrument, that it was rarely ever tuned, and that any snapped strings were left dangling for some time.

In the end, Streicher was spared the trouble of producing such an instrument, as shortly after issuing the request Beethoven received a state-of-the-art English piano made by Broadwood, the Rolls Royce of piano builders.

Within a matter of decades, by effectively combining a strong business acumen with a keen interest in cutting-edge technology, the company's founder, John Broadwood, successfully grew his business into the largest manufacturer of the finest pianos in London.[12] His son James and his grandson Thomas continued the success story, until "John Broadwood and Sons" had become the European market leader. In an effort to win Vienna's favor as part of the business expansions, Thomas Broadwood decided to gift an instrument, as Erard had done in 1803, to the preeminent composer of the day. Broadwood visited Beethoven personally in Vienna, officially announcing the prized gift on January 3, 1818.[13] Beethoven, in response, composed a letter of thanks in the most dignified French he could muster:

> Mon très cher Ami Broudvood!
>
> J'amais je n'eprouvais pas un plus grand Plaisir de ce que me causa votre Annonce de l'arrivée de Cette Piano, avec qui vous m'honorèe de m'en faire présent, je regarderai Coṁe un Autel, ou je deposerai les plus belles offrandes de mon Esprit au divine Apollon. Aussitôt Coṁe je recevrai votre Escellent Instrument, je vous enverrai d'en abord les Fruits de l'inspiration des premiers moments, que j'y passerai, pour vous servir d'un Souvenir de moi à vous mon très cher B., et je ne souhaits ce que, qu'ils soient dignes de votre Instrument.[14]

The new piano was shipped to Vienna via Trieste, sustaining so much damage along the way that it first needed repairing by Streicher before Beethoven could use it. Later, too, Beethoven would send the instrument in for major refurbishments, subjected as it was to such intensive use by its owner. Occasional attempts were also made to increase the piano's dynamics, although it already offered the widest range of any piano available.

Broadwood's instruments were of very high quality and had a typically English sound: full, resonant, lacking in overtones yet extremely lyrical. Although we will never know the extent to which Beethoven was able to appreciate and employ the instrument's unique qualities, still a connection seems evident between the grandeur of Beethoven's late piano sonatas and the sonorous allure of the Broadwood piano. And certain piano and pianissimo effects (either alone or in combination with markings of *una, due,* or *tre corde,* as indicated in the slow movement of the *Hammerklavier* Sonata or the recitative of the Piano Sonata in A-flat Major, op. 110) were undeniably inspired by the exciting new capabilities offered by the soft pedal of Beethoven's new instrument.[15]

Beethoven's experience of his new Broadwood was thus more tactile than auditory. The same applies to the final instrument he was to own, a grand piano built by Conrad Graf in 1826. Graf was the leading light among the younger generation of Viennese builders to succeed Streicher and Walter. His immense commercial success can be attributed to two factors: the ease with which he incorporated the English style of construction without compromising on the Viennese character of his instruments, and the flair with which he industrialized his business—with conveyor belts and external suppliers—without sacrificing traditional craftsmanship. His success in straddling two major divides earned him the title of Royal Fortepiano and Keyboard Maker to the Imperial Court in 1824. Once the court had issued a royal seal of approval for the quality of his instruments, Graf hoped that the Emperor of Music himself would follow suit, and delivered to Beethoven a magnificent instrument for his personal use in 1825.[16] Alas, by that time Beethoven's hearing had abandoned him completely, and his ability to evaluate the instrument had dwindled to that of the average musical philistine in the Hofburg.

There is therefore little sense in discussing the construction, performance, or acoustic properties of Graf instruments in detail here, especially since Beethoven ceased composing piano music entirely after 1824 (besides two trivial waltzes and an ecossaise, WoO 84–86), thus putting an end to any potential interaction between his instrument and his music. One detail should not be omitted, however: Graf's pianos, even in their earliest incarnations, were triple-strung across their entire compass. In 1812, a fourth string was added to the middle and upper registers in an attempt to further bolster the volume, a factor that was understandably of great interest to Beethoven. Unfortunately, the law of diminishing returns dictates that the added value of supplementary strings is inversely proportional to their number, a fact that Streicher's brother-in-law Matthäus Stein pointed out to Beethoven in 1820.[17] The difference made by the addition of a fourth string was therefore of a negligible order and of no help whatsoever in solving Beethoven's fundamental hearing problem. We might therefore surmise that the fourth string served only as a spare for when Beethoven had hammered one or two of the others to death. Thus it was that Beethoven's fascinating search for the ideal piano, undoubtedly the most important instrument of his career, faded—literally—into silence.

Leonore

A WORK IN PROGRESS

IT IS A STRIKING COINCIDENCE that the Second Josephine Era (1804–7) coincides almost exactly with the genesis of Beethoven's only opera. And not just any opera, but one about the power of unconditional love. Yet despite the apparent serendipity, the opera's subject matter had already been chosen in the autumn of 1803 and predates Josephine's tumultuous return into Beethoven's life. Beethoven worked on the first version of his opera for nearly two years—an eternity by the standards of his day. In March 1804 he was still harassing the librettist, Sonnleithner, to supply the book by no later than mid-April so that he might press on and have the opera ready for a premiere in June at the latest. It would be autumn 1805, however, before he would inform Sonnleithner that his own work was complete. Only later did it transpire just how optimistic Beethoven's announcement had been, as several of the movements (including the overture) were not ready until the very last minute, and Beethoven's merciless self-criticism is evidence that the opera, despite its many revisions, was never truly finished at all. It is for this last reason that *Leonore/Fidelio* will always bear the label of a "work in progress."

Several months before his death, Beethoven allegedly said that "of all [his] mind's children, Fidelio's birth was the most difficult."[1] One explanation of course was his lack of opera experience; another was the nature of the subject matter and Beethoven's determination to elevate both it and the music to a level beyond that of the original French production. The French libretto, based supposedly on a true story, was written by Parisian Jean-Nicolas Bouilly,[2] and was first produced at Théâtre Feydeau in 1798 with music by tenor and composer-poetaster Pierre Gaveaux. The original *Leonore* was officially an opéra comique, a designation that at the time served as a collective name for all works that were neither purely spoken theater nor fully sung opera (or *tragédie lyrique*). In practice the form was always a hybrid, in which spoken dialogue alternated with musical numbers of diverse caliber. Originally the dialogues were used to propel the narrative, while the music—which often parodied existing opera arias—provided opportunity for commentary or general social (or even political) reflections. After some time, and especially under the influence of consummate dramatists (and melodramatists) such as Cherubini, Grétry, Le Sueur, and Méhul, the music took on a weightier role, eventually including ensemble pieces and finales deserving of comparison with their Italian equivalents.

Contrary to what its name suggests, the opéra comique was seldom about laughter. The label was only intended to reassure the audience that they could count on a happy ending, or a *lieto fine*. Other than that, there was drama—and even melancholy—aplenty. Moreover, French citizens in the late eighteenth century resented being the butt of the theater's jokes and viewed the sincere portrayal of their own trials and tribulations alongside those of kings and aristocrats as a sign of emancipation. As the same time, they still wished for their bourgeois ideals to be clearly identifiable. All in all, decency and virtue still met with greater appreciation than heroism and bravery.

The postrevolutionary time of terror, fear, and uncertainty in France had darkened the tone of the opéra comique, providing fertile ground for musical theater of a less sentimental and more tragic character. This genre would later be defined as the "rescue opera," a formula whose plot always involved one or more persons being liberated from the clutches of an egomaniacal and vengeful despot. Like the opera seria, *semiseria,* and opera buffa, the rescue opera made grateful use of familiar patterns and arrangements of protagonists—the oppressor and his accomplice, the oppressed, the liberator, the sidekick—thus guaranteeing sufficient variety and contrast in the characterization. But despite these stereotypes, every scenario retained its individuality, and the tragic events of postrevolutionary France ensured that authors were never short of new material to draw from.

Leonore too had its own special charm, if only because the role of the liberator was played by a woman. This element introduced several dramaturgical consequences. Although the time may have been ripe for Eurydice to go in search of her Orpheus, the public was still not ready for a heroine to be driven by ethical motives (let alone political ones). The subtitle to the original

Léonore—L'amour conjugal—leaves no doubt that her actions are motivated by a white-picket-fence brand of "marital" love.

To understand Beethoven's *Leonore,* some knowledge of the background story is required. The eponymous character, Leonore, is convinced that her husband, Florestan—a Spanish official who had disappeared two years before—had been abducted just as he was about to expose certain abuses in the prison system. Unlike her friends, including the minister Fernando, Leonore maintains hope that Florestan is still alive somewhere, and decides to risk life and limb to go in search of him. Her quest leads her to the prison in Seville, whose warden (the "governor") is the corrupt Pizarro. Driven by boundless love, she overcomes her fear and attempts to infiltrate the prison. Disguised as a man under the pseudonym of Fidelio, she takes a post as assistant to Rocco, the prison guard. It is at this point that the opera begins. It does take some time to get off the ground, however; the main purpose of the first two acts is to set the stage and provide some psychological portraiture, creating an effective framework for the developments in act three.

Act 1 takes place entirely within the lower-middle-class confines of prison guard Rocco's family home. Disguised as Fidelio, Leonore offers her services and tries to win Rocco's trust so that she might be charged with more serious duties and thus gain access to inmates at all levels within the prison. To do so, she is prepared to feign a love interest in Rocco's daughter Marzelline; her ruse both confirms the effectiveness of her disguise and awakens the chagrin of Marzelline's real admirer, Jaquino (the porter). The rather spineless Rocco offers no resistance and accepts every proposal made to him.

The fact that Beethoven was willing to devote a full twenty-five minutes of music to a tawdry side plot that would be more at home in a tacky novel is only partially explained by the *opéra comique* origins of the work. Though necessary as a dramaturgical launching pad for the acts to follow, Beethoven's real purpose is more closely connected to the general concept underpinning the entire opera. The music composed for the first six items draws heavily from the style of the singspiel and opera buffa (it bears a striking resemblance to the opening scene from Mozart's *Marriage of Figaro*), and symbolizes the baser and more trivial aspects of human nature that the main character must overcome as the opera progresses. Nevertheless, the opening does remain rather bland, in part because much of the character appeal from the original French was lost in the German translation. In Bouilly's original, each population group retains a unique patois, such as the crude dialect of the working classes, which Sonnleithner had emulsified into a homogenous, gentrified, somewhat soulless form of stage German. Vienna was not as tolerant as Paris, after all, and the characters' sharp edges needed dulling down, which came at the expense of theatrical interest.

Act 2 is of a different caliber and is where the real main characters—Pizarro and Leonore—truly come into their own. After hearing that the minister is planning a surprise inspection at the prison to investigate the reported abuses for himself, Pizarro decides to have his compromising inmate, Florestan, executed. He calls on Rocco to do so, who is not at all enthusiastic. Nothing can persuade him to commit the murder, but he is prepared to dig the grave under the mollifying pretext of helping to end the prisoner's suffering. Leonore is privy to the entire conversation and is given permission to accompany Rocco throughout the prison. She prepares herself for the ordeal but balks on hearing that the only way to get close to her beloved Florestan is to help dig his very grave. At the end of act 2, Rocco and Leonore allow the prisoners to leave their cells for a brief recess and are reprimanded by a restless Pizarro, who is eager to make haste with his enemy's execution.

In addition to providing a change of scenery, act 2 transports us into a new musical realm, where we land in the midst of a dramatic and heroic opera. One crucial modification introduced by Sonnleithner and Beethoven was the transformation of Pizarro into a singer (he only had a spoken role in the original Bouilly-Gaveaux version). Doing so opened up a wealth of new possibilities: it allowed the final dénouement to be realized by entirely musical means, and a singing Pizarro—representing the evil in all of us—could take on a more dominant role in act 2, further deepening Leonore's character and making her final victory all the more glorious. It is no coincidence that Beethoven had some difficulty with Leonore's central aria, which had become sandwiched between Pizarro's outbursts of rage.[3] An initial version carried far too little textual and musical weight, and at Beethoven's request Sonnleithner wrote a completely new text departing entirely from the French original. Beethoven took the new version and crafted a sweeping aria, carried by three mighty *Eroica* horns. With Josephine in mind, the new lyrics "Komm, Hoffnung" (Come, o hope) must have offered a powerful source of inspiration.

The drama reaches high intensity at the conclusion of act 2, where the music speaks louder than the words. One such iconic moment is the prisoners' chorus, where the music afforded the inmates by Beethoven is of such astonishing beauty, we can be certain that these are no criminals who are yearning for their freedom. Beethoven's unequivocal message therefore seems to be that *all* prisoners are wrongfully incarcerated. In direct opposition to the case made later by Sonnleithner to the censors, in this respect the opera most certainly levels accusations at the injustices of a political system.

For the opera's resolution, we descend ever deeper into the underground catacombs of the prison. The dark cavern where Florestan lies languishing is the very cradle of loneliness, symbolizing the desperation of a man who has been robbed of all selfhood. To set the scene, Beethoven draws from the music he composed more than fifteen years earlier on the death of Emperor Joseph II, in which the low orchestral instruments (horns, bassoons, cellos, and double basses) conjure up a hair-raising and chilling harmonic atmosphere. Nearby, Rocco and Leonore start digging a grave; the mood is stifling, heightened by the use of the historical melodrama technique which, as in film, employs suggestive, sinister music to underpin the spoken dialogue. Only on hearing Florestan's voice is Leonore convinced that the moribund prisoner really is her beloved husband. She offers him bread and wine as a token of her love—a gesture laden with symbolism— but he fails to recognize her. The pace then picks up drastically (as though Beethoven has lost interest in the remaining details), and over the course of a highly dramatic musical quartet, the narrative explodes: on Rocco's signal, Pizarro enters the dungeon to kill the prisoner, whereupon Leonore flings herself onto Florestan, revealing her true identity with the words "Töt erst sein Weib!" (Kill first his wife!). Just as she plans to draw a pistol, musical sunlight shines through in the form of a distant trumpet fanfare, announcing the minister's imminent arrival. Leonore and Florestan are briefly bereft of all hope and sing a lengthy farewell love duet (the unused duet from *Vesta's Fire*). But the minister liberates them, symbolically handing over the keys to Leonore, who uses them to unchain Florestan. All then sing a monumental hymn to joy and justice. At this point, as in the act's opening, Beethoven recycles another of his favorite excerpts from the *Joseph* Cantata: "Da stiegen die Menschen ans Licht" (And they ascended into the light). The metaphor needs no explanation.

Pizarro is then exposed and in turn incarcerated. Leonore and Florestan plead for leniency on his behalf, but the minister will not hear of it, proclaiming "Der König wird dein Richter sein" (The king shall be your judge). The opera concludes with a hymn of praise to marital love and fidelity.

The premiere of *Leonore* was originally scheduled for October 15, 1805, the name day of Emperor Francis II's wife, Maria Theresa of Naples and Sicily.

This timing would have allowed her to identify with the opera's heroine and see herself as her husband's savior, himself having been driven into ever-deeper political entrapment. On September 30, however, the censors issued a ban on the work, which must have come as quite a surprise to Sonnleithner—we can assume, after all, that he was close enough to the source to know just how far the envelope could be pushed. The opera's subject matter was indeed quite volatile, as it openly criticized all forms of tyranny and oppression, a message that could be taken personally by any heads of state with a guilty conscience. But Sonnleithner had anticipated this problem and transplanted the events in both time and space to sixteenth-century Seville. (He obviously also counted on the Austrians' poor historical memory, as the sixteenth-century Spanish kings were Hapsburgs.) As the opera's setting gave no cause for discontent, the primary objection must therefore have come from behind-the-scenes dealings at court.

Sonnleithner then wrote an apologetic letter to the board of censors in an effort to turn the tables and gain approval for *Leonore*. His most substantial argument was the claim that the corrupt warden's abuses were committed in his own name and were thus of an incidental nature and in no way attributable to the systemic failures of an inhuman regime. Sonnleithner also reiterated the empress's keen interest in the work (here he was treading on dangerous ground), made reference to unproblematic productions by Ferdinando Paër in Prague and Dresden, and begged consideration for the immense effort already expended by Beethoven on the work's composition.[4] His arguments were weak, and in all likelihood Sonnleithner discreetly approached and persuaded some key figures behind closed doors before proceeding with the formalities and submitting a new application. Whatever the case, on October 5 the censors approved the libretto on the condition that the "most flagrant scenes" be removed.[5] Exactly what is meant by "flagrant" remains unclear, as analysis of the sketches and early manuscripts shows unequivocally that none of the musical material was altered. These "flagrant scenes" must therefore have been in reference to the spoken dialogues, but because the playbook merely served as a framework for the actors' improvisations on stage, no liability could be taken for any politically charged ad-libbing by the performers.

Valuable time had been lost due to the censorship issues, and the premiere was postponed until late November. Beethoven had no cause to complain, as he himself still had several items to complete. The instrumental sections in particular—the overture and the introductions to the second and third acts—were, in true Beethoven style, composed and delivered only at the last minute.[6] It is also a known fact that when major new orchestral works and operas are being prepared, much time is lost on correcting the many transcription errors in the parts, and that the already rattled nerves of the conductor and players are further shaken by the inevitable missing bars, wrong notes, and unclear accidentals. Usually, the only person who can resolve these matters is the composer. Things were no different in 1805, and in the days leading up to the premiere Beethoven was forced to divide his precious time between composing the final items and making mundane corrections. To make matters worse, he also fell ill. As was usual for him in stressful situations, it was his digestive system that sounded the alarm.

The rehearsals also involved the classic Beethovenian frictions, and altercations with frustrated singers who faced uncommon technical challenges. At the close of act 2, for example, bass Sebastian Mayer (the first Pizarro) found it impossible to hold his note against the—dramatically very effective—dissonant seconds in the strings. Mayer, who was more self-important than vocally secure (he was Mozart's brother-in-law and could present an excellent Sarastro), was heard to remark, "My brother-in-law would never have written such wretched nonsense!"[7] The pit, too, had its share of problems. To Beethoven's great consternation, the contrabassoon went absent during the dress rehearsal. Lobkowitz, who was in attendance and ready to help put out any fires, committed the idiocy of pointing out that the two bassoons were present and that that should be enough. Beethoven was so furious that on the way home, outside the prince's palace, he allegedly turned around and yelled, "Lobkowitz, you ass!"[8] Lobkowitz was later graced with a letter from the master, stating: "So this is His Highness's preferred instrumentation? I shit upon it."[9]

One last-minute dispute also arose regarding the title of the opera. It was Braun's opinion that the work should be titled *Fidelio,* to avoid any potential confusion with Paër's *Leonora.* Beethoven was staunchly opposed to the idea, not because of any nostalgic attachment to the name Leonore but because in his eyes Leonore—and not Fidelio—was the opera's true protagonist. He also believed that the subtitle, *L'amour conjugal* (Marital love), was an irrelevant relic from the sentimentality of the French original and thus no longer applied. But Braun was in charge; Beethoven was not in a position to insist and was forced to capitulate to Braun's more pragmatic concerns.[10]

The premiere on November 20 was an unmitigated disaster. The chorus was underrehearsed, and the orchestra's struggles began during the overture with a precarious passage in the winds. According to the critics, the singers could barely cope with their allocated roles: Anna Milder (Leonore) was of fine voice but immature as an actress; Friedrich Demmer (Florestan) sang flat and with a dull tone; and Sebastian Mayer (Pizarro) was hoarse. The singers who played Rocco, Marzelline, and Jaquino were also reportedly unconvincing. Only Johann Michael Weinkopf, who played the minor role of the minister, gave a satisfactory performance. On top of all this, the theater was half empty and was populated—with the exception of Stephan Breuning and the Brunsvik sisters—by the wrong people. French troops had stormed their way into Vienna one week earlier, and most of Beethoven's loyal supporters—the aristocrats—had fled to their country estates. For those remaining, attending the theater was the last thing on their minds, and so Braun madly began offering free tickets to any French soldiers who happened to be passing by. They of course understood nothing of the text and even less of the music, and it is also highly questionable whether they had any affinity with the high moral principles being professed onstage. There was, however, a certain ironic humor to be derived from the situation. In combination with the *Eroica*, Beethoven had initially chosen a French libretto in order to pave his way into the Parisian music scene from Vienna. Two years later, the sands had shifted: Leonore had been written for the Viennese, but their absence during the premiere meant that it was enjoyed, for the most part, by a bunch of uninterested Frenchmen.

The second performance was no better, despite Stephan Breuning's well-meant initiative to scatter pamphlets from the gallery. After the third performance the production was canceled, putting the poor composer out of his misery.

We can only imagine Beethoven's disappointment. For over twenty years, since he had first set foot in the orchestra pit as a young lad, he had lived in anticipation of this moment. It was to be an achievement representing the climax of his career, for while instrumental music had certainly gained in importance, musicians and audiences alike still regarded opera as the pinnacle of all musical genres. For two decades he had dreamt, studied, suffered, and fought to achieve this one goal. In his eagerness and enthusiasm, though, he had become blind to an important truth, namely that virtually no operatic composer ever got it right the first time. Claudio Monteverdi's *Orfeo* is the exception that proves the rule, but would we still be talking about Giuseppe Verdi, Richard Wagner, and Richard Strauss today if all they had ever written was *Oberto, The Fairies,* and *Guntram?*

Beethoven would not be discouraged. The *Leonore* debacle had failed to appease his appetite for opera, but rather than going in search of a new libretto and starting from scratch, he took decisive action and made a commitment to rework his debut attempt. Of course, one primary consideration would have been the time required to compose a completely new opera, which would have eaten into other opportunities for composing new symphonies, concertos, and chamber works. Still, his choice should be viewed chiefly as a vote of confidence in *Leonore.* Beethoven's friend Stephan Breuning also played a crucial role, as it was he who convinced Beethoven that the work—a valuable one, in his view—could be salvaged by making minor adjustments to increase the dramatic pace and help move the action along.

Breuning championed the initiative and—in close consultation with Beethoven—set about cutting and pasting parts of the score. He was of the correct opinion that the opera was too slow to start, that Beethoven and Sonnleithner lingered too long in Rocco's living room, and that the absence of the main characters was too protracted. One aria was scrapped, a duet pushed back, Leonore's grand aria pulled forward, and one melodrama omitted. To create the illusion of momentum, the first intermission was deleted and the first two acts merged into one.[11] Some cosmetic touches were also added: Breuning made the dialogues less cut-and-dried and more sentimental, while Beethoven refined the orchestration and removed superfluous bars here and there. Lastly, Beethoven composed a new overture and fabricated a grotesque march to replace the now redundant introduction to the second act. Breuning believed that the opera had gained in vitality thanks to its newfound brevity, but in fact, due in part to the elongated overture, the duration of the new opera was only marginally shorter than its forebear. It merely *seemed* shorter.[12]

This whole operation was executed without a word to the original librettist, Sonnleithner. We can only guess as to why, but the official reason was that Sonnleithner was too preoccupied with another opera, *Faniska,* on which he was collaborating with Cherubini. But because it was of vital strategic importance that Sonnleithner's name remain on the program, in March 1806 Beethoven sent him a short, polite, but rather undiplomatic letter, explaining why he had not importuned him earlier and asking whether he might sign and return the enclosed document as soon as possible, granting his approval of the modifications that were necessary to give the new opera "a healthy start."[13]

Nowadays, we might be surprised that a musical amateur—Breuning—played such a major role in the realization of *Leonore II*. Two hundred years ago, however, aristocrats drew no major distinction between work and play (to their mind, this division was a rather artificial construct made by the general populace), and the hours that many had whiled away in theaters entitled them to at least some degree of authority. Beethoven did not even contest the point; on the contrary, in return for Breuning's hard work, he gifted him a song composed to Breuning's own text, "Als die Geliebte sich trennen wollte" (When my beloved wished to leave me, WoO 132).

Despite this tribute, the rumor persists that Beethoven later disowned the second version of *Leonore* because it was forced on him by his friends. This story, which in the Beethoven literature has taken on a mythical status equal to that of the title page of the *Eroica,* dates from 1861 and can be traced back to the tenor Joseph Röckel, who played Florestan in the 1806 production. Nearly fifty years after the fact, Röckel alleged that in December 1805, shortly after the opera's disastrous premiere, he took part in a crisis meeting at the Lichnowsky residence. According to Röckel, the attendees included Breuning, the author Collin, concertmaster Clement, some of the principal singers, and of course the Lichnowskys, who had all come together to exchange views on how *Leonore* could be resurrected. Beethoven was forced to endure the well-meant commentary of the assembly on what they considered to be the defects in the opera that he had slaved and struggled over for two years, as well as their suggestions on how it could be improved. The opera was played through in its entirety. Christiane Lichnowsky sat at the piano and Clement played the entire first-violin part from memory, while the other attendees sang the vocal parts. Many omissions were proposed, but Beethoven steadfastly rejected them all. Röckel concludes that after six hours of tiresome discussion, it was only through the "begging and pleading" of the "tender and sickly princess, who had been a second mother to Beethoven and whom he acknowledged as such" that Beethoven ultimately consented to the omission of three numbers.[14]

This "historic" gathering almost certainly never took place. Granted, Christiane Lichnowsky was capable of playing through the whole opera, and we cannot exclude the possibility that Clement played his own part entirely from memory. Whether Beethoven was amenable to changes in the dialogue is of little relevance, but the very notion that he would stand for being lectured to by a pack of amateurs and second-rate musicians is simply preposterous. But the legend took on a life of its own and is responsible for the general misapprehension that Beethoven was never fully committed to *Leonore II*.

The first performance of the revised opera was held on March 29, 1806. Rather than a true premiere, the theater management treated the project as a "revival." Little time was therefore allocated to rehearsals, despite the sweeping changes to the score. Beethoven pleaded with Braun for more time, who flatly refused and even threatened to cancel the production. The outcome was predictable. The chorus was below par, and the orchestra's playing was so lackluster that Beethoven proposed "simply striking out all *p, pp, cresc., decresc., f* and *ff* markings from my opera—the orchestra will ignore them anyhow." He even insinuated that the winds were intent on sabotage. Lastly he added, "I lose all desire to compose when I hear my music thus performed."[15] The second show, which could not take place until April 10 due to Holy Week, fell equally flat. Despite Beethoven's constant pleading, there was absolutely no possibility of an extra rehearsal, and he was so gripped by fear that he handed over the conductor's baton to his assistant, Seyfried. Beethoven himself is reported to have said that he would rather leave the job to someone else than hear his music being butchered from such close proximity.[16]

A heated dispute between Braun and Beethoven put an end to any further performances of the revived *Leonore*. The day after the second performance, Beethoven marched into Braun's office to complain about his compensation. He was paid in royalties—an exception in those times—and suspected that Braun had doctored the attendance figures. Braun countered Beethoven's claims, arguing that while the parterre and boxes were reasonably full, the galleries had remained empty. Beethoven fumed in response, "But I do not write for the galleries!" When Braun remarked that not even Mozart considered the galleries beneath him, Beethoven lost all decorum, demanding immediate cancellation of the production and the return of his score. Braun needed no convincing; he called an assistant to fetch the score, and Beethoven stormed out in a huff.[17]

This vivid account also comes from Röckel, and although it does seem more plausible than that of the emergency meeting at the Lichnowskys, it should nevertheless be treated with some circumspection. In any event, *Leonore* remained untouched for eight years thereafter, despite the positive response from audiences and the media—a critic from the *Journal des Luxus und der Moden* even wrote that an air of genius enveloped the work.[18] An attempt to organize one or more additional performances at the Lichnowsky residence in 1806 failed, along with similar initiatives in Prague and Berlin.

Beethoven's "sudden" decision to withdraw *Leonore* turned out to be in Braun's favor. Theater an der Wien had been underperforming for some time. Operas had become a particular liability, debts were mounting, and bankruptcy seemed inevitable. In July 1806, Braun informed the emperor that he wished to liquidate or otherwise close the theater doors as of September 1. There was a backlash, and the head of the Police Bureau (the *Polizeihofstelle,* also the seat of the Viennese secret police) in particular refused to accept such an outcome. In a letter to the emperor, the chief argued that the atmosphere in the city had so deteriorated due to the relentlessness of war, that it would be folly to close the theater and deny the people their primary source of relaxation and entertainment. To him, it was a clear-cut case of *panem et circenses.* His arguments also underscored that in the event of a closure, "around 300 people from all walks of life would lose their livelihoods, and the general public shares a concern for the welfare of many of these 300 people."[19] The emperor sympathized with their plight and called on Count Ferdinand von Pálffy—an immensely wealthy second-rank nobleman—to rally the aristocratic troops and come to the rescue. Pálffy founded a noble consortium titled the Theater-Unternehmungs-Gesellschaft (Theater Enterprise Committee), and raised 1.2 million guilders with which to purchase Theater an der Wien and lease out the imperial Burgtheater and Kärntnertortheater. Nine members of the aristocracy made financial contributions, and divided the leg work among themselves: Esterházy became general director, Lobkowitz managed the opera, Pálffy took charge of spoken theater, and Zichy ran the ballet. The "smaller fry" were assigned duties in the technical departments, and the richest of them all, Prince Schwarzenberg, did nothing but grace the shows with his presence. This aristocratic rescue squad had only the vaguest notion of what they had let themselves in for. The entire operation would prove to be a costly one—it ran Lobkowitz virtually into the ground—and the committee members would gradually drop out one by one. Pálffy himself was the last man standing, but despite having set off in his own direction with commercial theater and cheap forms of entertainment, he was forced to concede defeat in 1826 and threw in the towel, exhausted and penniless.

Pálffy's promotion to the mogul of Viennese theater on January 1, 1807, was initially of little use to Beethoven, as the two men still had an old score to settle. In 1803, Beethoven and Ries had performed some piano duets during a concert at the Browne residence. Pálffy talked loudly with one of the lady guests throughout the entire performance, and after asking him in vain to keep quiet, Beethoven eventually stopped playing, got up, and yelled, "I refuse to play for such swine!"[20] We can assume that an aristocrat would not tolerate such insolent behavior and that old grievances likely resurfaced in 1807 when Beethoven took Lichnowsky's advice and applied for a new contract with Theater an der Wien. In a petition to the theater management, Beethoven proposed committing to "the composition of at least one major opera per year" for a "fixed annual salary of 2400 fr. alongside the free revenue [. . .] from the third performance onwards." In addition, he offered to produce—annually and without any extra compensation—a "small operetta or *divertissement,* several choral works or other occasional pieces." In return for this extra work, he did expect to be "granted permission to organise one benefit concert or *Akademie* per year."[21] Beethoven was quickly informed that his proposal was unacceptable. Old grudges were not the sole motivation behind the management's refusal, however, as Beethoven's offer was also presumptuous and one-sided. His proposed compensation—twice that of Salieri's stipend—was grossly disproportionate to the services on offer, and Beethoven could not offer any assurances for their fulfillment. It thus seemed as though Beethoven was angling for an exemption from the limitations of such a post, and the new management was—understandably—not in any position to issue a carte blanche. They did leave the door slightly ajar, stating that freelance engagements remained a possibility, that Beethoven was always welcome to propose new opera projects, and an *Akademie* could certainly be negotiated. Beethoven undoubtedly sensed that the opera invitation was a diplomatic red herring. He did get his *Akademie* in the end, although it would be a year before he did so.

The Golden Years

SHORTLY AFTER *LEONORE* CAME TO ITS ABRUPT END, Beethoven fell
into a conflict with his brother Kaspar Karl. Karl had informed him of his
intention to marry Johanna Reiss, a wallpaperer's daughter from Alservorstadt,
with whom he had fallen madly in love. As paterfamilias, Beethoven felt he
had to intervene. His opposition to Kaspar Karl's marriage was in fact merely
the latest manifestation of a well-intentioned sense of responsibility that presented time and again throughout his life as meddlesomeness in others' affairs.
It was also strongly reminiscent of grandfather Louis's opposition to his son
Jean's marriage, which had been fueled by fears of a disruption to the family
balance. (Six years later, Beethoven would respond in exactly the same fashion
to the marriage of his other brother, Johann.) To justify his complaint,
Beethoven officially cited his imminent sister-in-law's reputation as a thief; she
had been formally indicted in 1804 but never convicted.[1] Beethoven's real
objection, however, was to the hurried nature of the marriage and more specifically to the fact that the bride-to-be was already four months pregnant. In
those times the scenario was hardly uncommon, as marriage was subject to so
many legal and bureaucratic barriers, and monitoring by priests so strict (candidates were assessed on criteria such as upbringing, proper conduct, loyalty
to the regime, and a minimum of material wealth), that many young people
from Vienna and surrounds were effectively doomed to a life of concubinage.
Among the common people, an unmarried pregnant woman was therefore
never cause for any moral recriminations. This view was not shared by
Beethoven, who held to different moral principles (although his own unfulfilled romantic desires doubtless played a part). Another potential trigger was
that Beethoven—who at this point still hoped things might work out with
Josephine—may have been overcome with embarrassment at the prospect of a

floozy from the Viennese working class becoming the sister-in-law to a proud descendant of the Brunsvik name.

Kaspar Karl and Johanna were married on May 25, 1806. Family relations returned to normal thereafter, although Kaspar Karl could no longer work as his brother's secretary, which saddened Beethoven a great deal. From that point on, they had their ups and downs. Beethoven took refuge with Karl and Johanna during the siege of Vienna in May 1809, and there are several accounts of Beethoven protecting his sister-in-law from maltreatment by her husband. After his brother's death in 1815, Beethoven fought a grim legal battle with Johanna for the custody of their only son, Karl—but more on that later.

COMPOSING FOR A PROFESSIONAL STRING QUARTET

Beethoven began composing again the day after his brother's wedding, on May 26, 1806 (the date is carefully marked in the autograph). He resumed work on three quartets that he had started in the summer of 1804, which had been set aside to make way for *Leonore*. But contrary to what their ultimate namesake might suggest, it was not the dedicatee—Count Andrey Razumovsky—who provided the impetus for the new set of quartets, but rather violinist Ignaz Schuppanzigh.

Schuppanzigh was one of Beethoven's key musical allies in Vienna. Originally a professional violist, after several years he made the rather unconventional switch to the violin (conversions between these two instruments usually only occur in the opposite direction). Although Schuppanzigh had taken instruction from the greatest masters, including Mozart, Haydn, Albrechtsberger, and Anton Wranitzky, he remained unable to secure a permanent post with any of the local orchestras. This is not as surprising as it may seem, given the limited number of available positions. In 1795, for example, the court ensemble offered contracts to a mere five first violins, five second violins, and two violists; in that same year, the city's theater orchestras employed only thirty-three violinists and twelve violists between them.[2] Driven by necessity, Schuppanzigh turned to chamber music, and fortunately he found enough rich aristocrats who were both fond of music and willing to help. Lichnowsky in particular was a rich source of income, due in part to his regular Friday-morning chamber music concerts (which were always followed by a richly laden table). Lobkowitz likewise availed himself of Schuppanzigh's services in order to try out new works in his "center of excellence"—the first run-throughs of Beethoven's String Quartets (op. 18) were held under his aegis. Schuppanzigh always performed with the same companions, and so it was that he ultimately, and accidentally, became the leader of the world's first-ever professional string quartet. The advent of the Schuppanzigh Quartet also gave rise to a productive form of musical reciprocity. The ensemble's ongoing collaboration with the eminent composers of the day—Mozart, Haydn, Förster, and later also Beethoven—allowed them to develop a new wealth of expertise, which in turn was put to use by composers in their further exploration of the genre.

From 1795 on, Schuppanzigh began expanding his sphere of operations. He first became the conductor—and later the manager—of the outdoor concerts in the Augarten park and persevered in this dual role for several years. Later, however, he was gradually forced to admit that the financial losses were simply too great, and he abandoned the enterprise in 1806. Meanwhile he had developed a taste for management and in the summer of 1804 hatched a plan to present and run his own subscription series of string quartet concerts. Originally held in private residences, the series ultimately moved to Zum Römischen Kaiser in Rennweg, where Schuppanzigh's group became the quartet in residence (in altered form, as the second violinist and violist were replaced). Their new status was what moved Russian ambassador Razumovsky to offer the quartet a permanent engagement two years later, on the opening of his opulent new palace in Vienna's Third District. The quartet was promised a lifelong pension, and it was also tacitly agreed that Razumovsky might occasionally stand in for the second violinist (Schuppanzigh could not refuse but can hardly have been thrilled with the idea). With this initiative, Razumovsky became competition for his brother-in-law Lichnowsky, who sank ever further into dire financial straits and was gradually forced to withdraw from musical patronage altogether. The period thereafter was a golden age for Schuppanzigh Quartet (although the members had changed again). They held plenty of concerts, most of which sold out. They also stepped up their rehearsal regime, and refined their expertise as performance standards rose. Their heyday was abruptly cut short in 1814, when Razumovsky's palace was almost completely destroyed by fire on New Year's Eve, putting an end to the residence's cultural activities, as well as a major dent in the Schuppanzigh Quartet's income. The ensemble eventually disbanded in the spring of 1816, although Razumovsky did keep his promise and continued paying their pensions. Schuppanzigh later made some concert tours through Europe, and after perambulations through Germany,

Poland, and especially Russia, he returned to Vienna in 1823. He immediately set about founding the fourth Schuppanzigh Quartet, which ultimately became the platform for the revolutionary string quartet writing that Beethoven would pursue toward the end of his life.

Beethoven and Schuppanzigh had met very early on at the Lichnowskys. Beethoven initially even took violin lessons from Schuppanzigh (who was six years younger), and they quickly forged a bond that remained intact for the rest of their lives. While this exceptional instance of long-term friendship was certainly related to the fact that Schuppanzigh's violin presented no threat to Beethoven as a pianist-composer, it was also due in part to the violinist's character. Schuppanzigh was Beethoven's polar opposite. With a candidness matched only by his corpulence, he was a generous bon vivant, who knew how to roll with the diplomatic punches. The real secret to their sustainable relationship, however, lay in its intermittent and businesslike character. To Beethoven, Schuppanzigh was someone in whom he had confidence, but never confided[3]—nothing more and nothing less.

They gave many concerts together, in various formations. On occasion, Schuppanzigh would give Beethoven advice on how to tailor his musical ideas properly to strings, an idiom to which Beethoven was less accustomed. When it came to string quartets in particular, Schuppanzigh's expertise was invaluable to Beethoven. And when Beethoven got wind of Schuppanzigh's plans to launch an independent subscription series in 1804, he resolved to compose a new set of three quartets. Despite mountains of pressing work, he immediately sketched the contours of what would later become the String Quartet in F Major (op. 59, no. 1).

It is unclear precisely when Razumovsky entered the picture. We know that Kaspar Karl offered the three new quartets to Breitkopf & Härtel on October 10, 1804, suggesting that at that time there was still no official patron. But when Beethoven resumed work on the quartets in May 1806 (after a mandatory hiatus due to *Leonore*), he must have been assured of Razumovsky's support, a theory supported by the presence of Russian folk melodies in the first two quartets.

Work progressed quickly after that, and by November the three quartets were complete. The first airings were held around New Year's Day 1807, and an initial review appeared in the *Allgemeine musikalische Zeitung* in February. The commentary was overwhelmingly positive, although the critic did note that the quartets were long and difficult, and would not be fully understood by everybody.[4] It would be a full year—the period of exclusive ownership by

Razumovsky—before the new quartets were published by the Kunst- und Industrie-Comptoir under opus number 59.

Beethoven's *Razumovsky* Quartets ushered in a new era of string quartet writing. The *Eroica* and the two great piano sonatas (the *Waldstein* and the *Appassionata*) had clearly influenced his conceptualization of the string quartet, where we now also see a considerable broadening of the dimensions, the familiar gravitas conferred to the development and coda sections, and considerable enrichment of the harmonic spectrum. Far more drastic, however, was the influence of Schuppanzigh's professional ensemble. While the opus 18 String Quartets had been tailored to their consumers, placing high but attainable demands on amateur musicians from the aristocracy and upper middle classes, the *Razumovsky* Quartets were conceived with professionals in mind, which in practice meant that Beethoven abandoned all consideration for anybody. Certain passages were technically so challenging that they could only be played by the greatest virtuosi and seemed more at home in a dazzling concerto than in an amiable quartet. Occasionally Schuppanzigh was pushed to the limit, and when he complained to Beethoven of unplayable passages, the master replied, "Do you really think that I give a damn about your miserable violin when the spirit speaks to me?"[5]

Perhaps of more profound importance was the transplantation of the string quartet from private salons to the concert hall, and the altered dynamic between players and public that was first initiated by Schuppanzigh and later effected by Beethoven. In traditional eighteenth-century string quartet practice, audience and performers were blended together: the four musicians would sit in a closed circle—sometimes surrounding a specially made table with collapsible music stands—and just like four friends playing cards would engage in several enjoyable hours of musical conversation. Quartets were composed with this purpose in mind; they were extended games of call and response, of concurrence and conflict, of tension and resolution (not coincidentally, many bore the title *Quatuor dialogués*). Generally the dialogue also took place without an audience. While others were of course welcome to listen, their presence was incidental and by no means necessary. Schuppanzigh's subscription concerts were another matter entirely, conceived primarily for the paying public. During these concerts the players now oriented themselves both mentally and physically toward the audience; players sat in a half-circle with instruments facing the listeners.

Beethoven needed to develop a new quartet idiom, one in which the projection of sound became an important parameter. Counterpoint—the juxtaposition of independent lines—of course remained a potent element at the heart of the genre; however, the instances of doubled or parallel voices increased dramatically, creating powerful eruptions of sound. The string quartet took on an utterly different character, and for decades this new, "compact" idiom became the norm for players and composers alike. It is interesting to note that the impetus for the development was more sociological than musical in origin.

CONCERTO PAR CLEMENZA POUR CLEMENT

On December 23, 1806, an *Akademie* was held at Theater an der Wien for Franz Clement, the establishment's concertmaster and since 1805 also its musical director. In addition to overtures by Méhul and Cherubini, the program included several vocal fragments from works by Handel, Mozart, and (once again) Cherubini. Toward the end of the concert, Clement gave an obligatory improvisation, astonishing the audience with his legendary trick of playing the violin while holding it upside-down. The highlight of the evening, however, was the premiere of Beethoven's Violin Concerto in D (op. 61), written specially for the occasion. During a previous *Akademie* on April 7, 1805 (which included the first public performance of the *Eroica* Symphony), Clement had performed a concerto of his own in the same key and had asked Beethoven to compose a new work for his own *Akademie*.

Beethoven was greatly indebted to Clement, who had not only premiered all of Beethoven's major works as concertmaster (the Second and Third Symphonies, the *Mount of Olives* and *Leonore*) but also staved off many a catastrophe with his combination of musical expertise and diplomatic aplomb. He could filter and interpret Beethoven's idiosyncratic directions like no other and often served as the virtuosic buffer between the cantankerous conductor and his overwrought orchestra. Beethoven was therefore only too happy to compose a new concerto for Clement, and expressed his sincere gratitude through a clever dedication on the title page: *Concerto par Clemenza pour Clement.*[6] Beethoven had little time—just over a month—to write the concerto, and some even assert that Clement sight-read the solo part during the premiere.[7] This is most likely an exaggeration; Clement may have been an astonishing sight-reader, but since he had been involved in the concerto's genesis from its inception and Beethoven had regularly consulted him on its technical aspects, we can safely assume that Clement was privy to—and had already mastered—the most difficult passages ahead of time.

In the autumn of 1806, Beethoven thus collaborated intensively with two eminent violinists, Schuppanzigh and Clement. Clement was of an entirely different musical order than his string quartet colleague, not least because he had enjoyed a young career as a wunderkind, prompting many to draw a comparison with Mozart. Clement's father set him on the path to violin virtuosity very early on. No sooner had he made his stunning debut in Vienna as an eight-year-old than he embarked on a three-year European concert tour. Just like Mozart, he spent an extended period in London, living there for over two years and astonishing listeners everywhere with his musicality and extraordinary memory. The turbulent political climate then prompted Clement to give up traveling, to reestablish himself in Vienna and to take on a permanent position, first at the Hoftheater and later at Theater an der Wien. Only in 1811 did he set off once again, and even served as concertmaster for a time under Carl Maria von Weber.

The decline in Clement's solo career was due chiefly to his failure to move with the times and keep up with the latest trends in violin development. The turn of the century saw far-reaching changes to the construction of both the instrument and the bow, sending out major ripples in playing technique, sound production, and style. All changes to the instrument—the raised bridge, longer strings, the angle of the neck relative to the body, and the elevated and elongated fingerboard—were conceived in the service of a more brilliant sound with greater projection. The biggest game-changer, however, was the bow. At the end of the eighteenth century, the French brothers François and Léonard Tourte developed an entirely new construction, and their design has remained the standard prototype to this day. While they made technical alterations to virtually all of the bow's components—the tip, frog, and hairs—their main innovation was the conversion of the bow's arch from a convex to a concave form. Unlike the baroque bow, which (as noted by Leopold Mozart in his treatise on the violin) always occasions a barely audible but unavoidable weakness at the beginning and end of each tone, thus limiting the region in which the bow can truly "speak," the modern bow equalizes the tone across its entire length, guaranteeing a more continuous legato and enabling more agitated, staccato-articulated playing.

Most musicians in Vienna had little regard for these developments. Among the members of the ad hoc orchestra assembled by Clement for his

Akademie, quite a rag-tag bunch to begin with, made up of moonlighting professionals interspersed with the city's more accomplished amateurs, it was chiefly the latter who had converted to the Tourte bow. Most professional musicians continued to swear nostalgically by the old design, including Clement, whose tone had been described as thin and even somewhat shrill. By contrast, his left hand is purported to have been phenomenal, with a spectacular mastery of the upper positions in particular. But he was limited by his bowing technique; his phrases were shorter and less sustained and also lacked the virtuosic flair that audiences had come to know and admire from the likes of Viotti, Kreutzer, and Baillot.

Given his conservative leanings, Clement may not have been the ideal consultant when it came to violin technique. Although Beethoven had taken violin lessons in Bonn and Vienna from Krumpholz, Schuppanzigh, and others, and while his experience with string quartets and orchestras had given him a certain knowledge of the idiom, still he lacked the level of familiarity required to produce a modern and attractive concerto. Piano concertos were another matter entirely: Beethoven's musical ideas were so inextricably interwoven with his pianistic ability (and vice versa) that pushing the boundaries of the keyboard genre was an entirely natural process for him. In other words, at the piano he never needed to devote any conscious thought to the performability or effect of any particular idea. The violin concerto, on the other hand, pushed him out of this "comfort zone," making him principally reliant on input from Clement. And it shows, for Beethoven's violin concerto is technically rather biased, emphasizing the instrument's more lyrical qualities and leaving much of the technical terrain unexplored. The work is also hard to play, as some passages that sprouted from Beethoven's non-violinist mind are not idiomatic to the instrument—the terrifying opening solo, for example, has bested many a violinist. While it is no problem for a concerto to be easier than it sounds, the reverse is never true and indeed is highly unproductive.[8]

The musical discourse between soloist and orchestra might easily have been impoverished by such a one-sided technical approach. Beethoven resolved this problem by simply redefining the relationship: rather than an accompanying instrument, the orchestra was treated as an equal partner in the music making. One might even say more than equal: the purely "neutral" orchestral passages constitute only 20 percent of the opening movement, and there are myriad instances where the principal thematic material appears in the orchestra, turning the solo part into an interesting but nonetheless secondary addition to the orchestral palette. One added bonus of the orchestra's active role allows the well-known timpani figure,

to dominate and lend a more rhythmic focus to the music, which was originally conceptualized lyrically.

As mentioned above, the Violin Concerto was composed in haste and Beethoven was not fully satisfied with the result. In the months following the premiere he continued to tinker with the solo part—the orchestral score remained untouched. He made a host of corrections, the purpose of which is not always immediately clear. Some passages in the manuscript exist in three different versions, stacked one on top of the other. How should these be interpreted? As express improvements by Beethoven? Simplifications requested by Clement that Beethoven grudgingly accepted? Or merely alternative ossia bars, from which the performer is free to make a personal selection?[9] The matter is further complicated by the transcription for piano made by Beethoven in the summer of 1807 at Muzio Clementi's request for publishing in England, a task that later inspired him to introduce even more changes to the original violin part.[10] A version of the concerto was thus finalized in the summer of 1807 and used as the basis for the first published edition in Vienna (released in 1808). This version is still taken as definitive today; however, all Beethoven experts agree that—of all the various incarnations of the Violin Concerto, and more so than with some of the piano concertos—this "definitive" version is still a far cry from the "ideal" version that Beethoven had in mind.

These ins and outs were still of little concern to most early-nineteenth-century performers. The concerto was approached with some trepidation, giving rise to a familiar vicious circle: because it was rarely performed, it never gained sufficient popularity, which in turn limited the public demand for it. Change would not come until the 1840s, when famous violinist Joseph Joachim—the evangelist of the Brahms violin concerto—undertook a grand tour with conductors Mendelssohn and Schumann, helping the concerto to find its way into the concert halls of Europe.

While Beethoven's work on the *Razumovsky* Quartets and the Violin Concerto undoubtedly brought him a great deal of satisfaction, at the same time he itched to return to his "core business" of writing for the orchestra. In the years following the *Eroica,* his symphonic mind had not lain idle: many ideas for the Symphony in C Minor and a pastoral symphony were first penned in 1803, while he was still working on the *Eroica.* Sketches have since revealed concrete and identifiable material for the Symphony in C Minor—the later Fifth—dating from as early as 1803. The contours of the well-known motif said to be reminiscent of "fate knocking at the door"

were firmly established at the outset, although Beethoven still had no clear notion of exactly where things would go from there.

Beethoven's concrete plans for these two symphonies thus percolated in his mind for nearly three years. But before giving them an outlet, he first composed—without any lengthy preparations and within a very short space of time—the completely new Symphony in B-flat Major (op. 60). The impetus for this work came from the Silesian count Franz von Oppersdorff, a musical fanatic who maintained his own orchestra. Although the ensemble consisted, for the most part, of amateur musicians recruited from among his own staff,[11] it was said that when hiring new personnel he valued their musicianship over any other credentials, allowing him to groom an ensemble that was highly capable of performing even the latest contemporary works. Beethoven met Oppersdorff in September 1806 during a stay with the Lichnowskys in Grätz, when he and his host traveled fifty kilometers north to spend several days in Oberlogau (Głogówek), where Oppersdorff owned a castle. For the occasion, Oppersdorff's Kapelle performed Beethoven's Second Symphony. The choice was very well considered, and to this day we might wonder who could lay claim to the greater flattery: Beethoven, the composer of the symphony, or Lichnowsky, to whom it was dedicated. The count then placed an immediate order with his honored guest for two new symphonies. Because Beethoven feared that both his Symphony in C Minor and the *Pastoral* Symphony might be destined to cause him some headache, he decided to compose at least one completely new work straight away. He succeeded, and the Symphony in B-flat Major was finished in record time. The count received the manuscript around New Year's Day in 1807, paid the agreed five hundred guilders in cash for the work and the exclusive rights, and then made the generous gesture of paying nearly the full fee for the second symphony in advance. In hindsight, this was a tremendous blunder, as the scarce correspondence with Oppersdorff regarding the second in the pair clearly shows how Beethoven began stalling for time. In March 1808 he announced that it was virtually complete and would be sent with the next post; six months later, he sent a cursory note stating that he had regrettably been forced to sell Oppersdorff's Symphony in C Minor to another buyer,[12] and assured the count that he would replace it with another. He never did, nor was the advance ever repaid. There is a simple explanation for this rather tactless conduct on Beethoven's part: on September 14, Beethoven had concluded a lucrative contract with Breitkopf & Härtel, for which both the Symphony in C Minor and the *Pastoral* Symphony had served as bait. He had also suddenly realized that he could dedicate each of the symphonies to both Lobkowitz *and* Razumovsky, doubling his income. These were opportunities that Beethoven could of course not pass up, even if it meant falling into disfavor with Oppersdorff.

Although not Beethoven's original intention, the Symphony in B-flat Major thus became known as the Fourth Symphony. It was first performed during a pair of Beethoven concerts held at the Lobkowitz residence in March 1807. The program included not only excerpts from *Leonore,* an unspecified piano concerto, and the brand-new *Coriolan* Overture, but also a complete performance of all four symphonies composed thus far. Our modern view of this odd and somewhat overblown program differs from that of the contemporaneous concertgoer: by presenting all four of Beethoven's symphonies together for the first time, Lobkowitz propagated the idea—consciously or otherwise—that they could be understood as a set, a notion that would later come to dominate much of Western musical culture. In this sense, these concerts can be ascribed a significance at least as great as that of Beethoven's *Akademien,* which ordinarily derive their import from the strategic impetus they lent to his career.

For the most part, the press overlooked the premiere of the Fourth Symphony, and it would be 1812 before the *Allgemeine musikalische Zeitung* devoted an article to it. The critic in question found it to be "brimming with the originality and energy of his earlier works, but without marring the clarity with any bizarre antics."[13] The critic was thus clearly hiding some reservations, and even today commentators have difficulty orienting the Fourth within Beethoven's wider symphonic oeuvre. Often they resort to the general proposition that the "even" symphonies are overshadowed by the "uneven" ones. This would seem to apply to the Fourth in particular, which is wedged tightly between the momentous Third and Fifth symphonies. Robert Schumann equated the symphony to "a slender Greek maiden between two Nordic giants,"[14] a view arising from the symphony's modest dimensions, less complex structure, and the inclusion of several lush, sultry themes reminiscent of the Mediterranean summer, such as the second subjects from the first and last movements.

And yet the Fourth is such an energetic work that it need not be considered inferior to the *Eroica*. It generates tremendous drive through syncopations (disorienting emphases placed on unstressed beats) and the dominant presence of the timpani. At the same time, the music is characterized by an intriguing fluidity, as there are episodes where the music stills and the momentum fades, only to pick up again immediately afterward. It concludes with a maniacal perpetuum mobile, leaving performers and audience breathless at the finish line. What is astonishing about this symphony is the compact format into which all of its elements are condensed. Though the dimensions were for the most part dictated by circumstances (including the limited timeframe), it is nonetheless possible that after his titanic work on *Eroica* and *Leonore*, Beethoven embraced the challenge of constructing a powerful narrative within the context of a self-imposed limitation. A little contrary to his nature, to be sure, but there is a first time for everything, including the realization that "less" can sometimes be "more." The Fourth Symphony is thus a tour de force of a different kind and undeserving of a status inferior to the *Eroica*.

In addition to the Fourth Symphony, the March 1807 concerts at the Lobkowitzes' also premiered the *Coriolan* Overture in C Minor (op. 62). Beethoven composed this overture within the space of a few weeks, immediately on completion of the Fourth Symphony. His exact motivation for doing so is a mystery. What we do know is that it can never have been his original intention to have it performed as the introduction to Collin's stage tragedy, which had already left theaters in 1806, four years after its premiere at the Burgtheater. The only time the overture actually ever preceded the play (on April 24, 1807) was as a result of the acclaim it had already received as a concert piece. The drama was therefore appended to the overture, and not the other way around.

Although its exact origins are unknown, Beethoven's idea to write an independent concert overture did not come entirely out of the blue. In Vienna it had become a trend for concerts to open with well-known opera overtures, a practice first instituted by Baron Würth. Some composers later went one step further, composing a new overture specially for the occasion. Thus the concert overture was born, a genre that would see its heyday under Mendelssohn and Schumann and later feed into the development of the symphonic poem. Concert overtures of this type were a prime vehicle for the more vivid, expressive (shall we say "romantic") style of composition. Part of what made this possible was the very absence of any ensuing opera or theatrical work, allowing the narrative drama to play out fully without any fear of "spoilers"—a danger that had plagued Beethoven when writing his initial *Leonore* overtures, and later also the overture to *Egmont*.

The temptation is therefore great to interpret the *Coriolan* Overture in a strictly narrative sense. But at a certain point—nobody knows when—Beethoven himself actively combated such an interpretation by striking out the words "zum Trauerspiel Coriolan" (on the tragedy of Coriolan) on the work's title page, simply titling it "Overture." His desire was therefore perhaps to portray not Coriolan's tragic history but rather the emotional pitfalls to which the hero fell victim.[15] Beethoven paints a psychological portrait of the heart-wrenching dilemma between high moral principles and human fallibility. Coriolan wages war on his native city of Rome to seek vengeance for the injustice done to him, but is urged to reconsider by his mother and wife. Rather than representing characters in the story, the contrasting main and second subjects might thus stand for the conflicting emotions that plague Coriolan and bring about his undoing. This interpretation explains the disintegration or fragmentation of the main theme at the end of the overture—with echoes of the *Eroica* funeral march clearly audible—until finally only unison pizzicato notes remain in the strings, symbolizing the hero's downfall. Their significance is profound, for looking back we see that the overture began with the very same unison tones in the strings, but in a firm, drawn-out fortissimo legato, proclaiming Coriolan's determination to realize his plans. The metamorphosis of these simple tones underpins the entire concept on which Beethoven built the overture, a structural feat that he was the first to achieve.

The two Lobkowitz concerts came about after failed attempts to organize an *Akademie* in one of Vienna's major theaters. The management had initially agreed, but when it became apparent that the Burgtheater had been double-booked and that Theater an der Wien was likewise unavailable, Beethoven was offered one of the Redoutensaal halls in the Hofburg. When he adamantly refused, Lobkowitz came to the rescue. One advantage was that Beethoven knew what to expect: adequate rehearsal facilities and a cultured audience. At the same time, he knew that the financial side left much to be desired in comparison with an *Akademie* in one of the major theaters.

And Beethoven's financial need was great. The withdrawal of Lichnowsky's support and the failure of *Leonore* meant that he was sinking fast—so fast that he was forced to borrow money from his youngest brother, Johann, a move that both would regret later when Johann desperately needed the funds to purchase his pharmacy in Linz. While waiting for a lucrative *Akademie*, Beethoven's attention was focused more than ever on tapping into alternative sources of income and conquering new markets. He had clear ideas on how to do so but first needed a new secretary who could convert his schemes into well-worded letters and signed contracts. His savior this time was Ignaz von Gleichenstein, a lawyer ten years Beethoven's junior who had moved to Vienna in 1800 and who worked under Stephan Breuning at the Ministry of Defense. Beethoven had known the Gleichensteins for some time, and some sources claim that Ignaz even took music lessons from Beethoven, although this remains uncertain.[16] Gleichenstein was known as a man of charming and upright character, who represented Beethoven's interests from 1807 on with a style and efficiency that differed markedly from that of his predecessor. He would do so until the spring of 1811, when he married Anna Malfatti and left Vienna for good, unable to be of any further service to Beethoven. Leaving aside one minor incident involving women—Beethoven "shot the messenger," as it were, when Gleichenstein came to inform him that a relationship with his own future sister-in-law, Therese Malfatti, was out of the question—both gentlemen were perfectly well disposed to one another. It was with much warmth and affection that Beethoven dedicated his Third Cello Sonata (op. 69) to Gleichenstein in April 1809.

Gleichenstein's first order of business was to draw up a publishing contract with Clementi in April 1807. Although of Italian origin, Clementi had settled in London fairly early on and set up a piano and sheet-music business that was so lucrative, he could easily have given up his successful career as a composer and concert pianist. Beethoven admired him a great deal, and most commentators agree that traces of Clementi's influence are clearly present in both the technical and compositional aspects of his piano music. What is certain is that Beethoven thought very highly of Clementi's modern piano method, the *Introduction to the Art of Playing on the Piano Forte* (1801), and carried it with him as a reference wherever he went.[17]

Clementi was a charismatic businessman and was very dedicated to broadening his network. Between 1802 and 1810, for example, he visited Vienna four times to meet with the most eminent musicians of the day. Beethoven was certainly on his list, although it would be 1807 before they came to any kind of agreement. Initial attempts to make contact in 1804 were derailed in a hilarious fashion: multiple witnesses have reported that while Beethoven and Clementi both dined in the same restaurant on many occasions—Zum weissen Schwan (The White Swan) on Kärntnerstrasse—neither dared make the first move, each holding the belief that the other should take the initiative according to the etiquette of social hierarchy. Clementi boasted seniority, but Beethoven's fame was more illustrious. In the end, both Beethoven and Clementi acknowledged their mutual interests, abandoned their game playing, and quickly reached an accord.[18] On April 20, 1807, Gleichenstein presented a contract offering Clementi—for two hundred pounds sterling, or around eighteen hundred guilders—the exclusive English rights to the Fourth Piano Concerto, the *Razumovsky* Quartets, the Fourth Symphony, the Violin Concerto, and the *Coriolan* Overture (opp. 58–62) for six months. Beethoven was also to produce a special piano arrangement of the Violin Concerto and was commissioned to write two additional piano sonatas and a fantasy (the later opp. 77–79). Clementi benefited enormously from the enterprise, as after only several years he had recouped his investment fifty times over.

With that, the London market was covered and Beethoven turned his attention to finding a similar partner in Paris. Six days after concluding the contract with Clementi, Gleichenstein wrote two standard letters to Pleyel in Paris and Simrock in Bonn (who also had operations in Paris), offering the rights to the same works, albeit for a lower price. Neither took up the offer, ostensibly because international trade was suffering from the perpetual state of war. In reality, neither Simrock nor Pleyel dared to make a commitment due to the lack of any legal security regarding intellectual property or publishing rights, a field in which England had its own, more protectionist policies.

As a negotiator, Gleichenstein was also charged with less pleasant duties, or "horse trading" as Beethoven put it. One such job involved extracting an advance payment from the Kunst- und Industrie-Comptoir, to which Beethoven had sold the European rights for the aforementioned orchestral and chamber works in May 1807. Advances were rare in those days, and though asking for them was slightly demeaning, Beethoven was desperate for funds due to delays in payments from London caused by the continental blockade on trade relations with England, imposed by Napoleon on November 21, 1806.

A MASS FOR THE CONCERT HALL

Beethoven, meanwhile, had been offered a commission from Prince Nikolaus Esterházy to compose a celebratory Mass for his court. Esterházy was the general director of the aristocratic consortium managing the city's principal theaters at that time and may have felt somewhat embarrassed by the recent dismissive treatment Beethoven had received.

The honor of this invitation was, in any case, commensurate with the challenge. Nikolaus Esterházy (Nikolaus II) came from an illustrious family, one that had helped shape the cultural scene in Vienna for generations. His grandfather in particular, Nikolaus Joseph Esterházy (Nikolaus I) —rightly nicknamed "the lover of splendor"—had successfully transformed his residences in Eisenstadt and Fertöd into the most powerful cultural attractors in Europe. It was there that he cultivated the perfect environment for Joseph Haydn to develop his own symphonic style, thus indirectly laying the foundations for the next two centuries' worth of orchestral music. Nikolaus's son, Anton I, was cut from different cloth. He was far from culturally minded and disbanded almost the entire Kapelle in 1790, though he still granted Haydn his pension, which enabled him to make a fresh start at almost sixty years of age. Anton Esterházy thus had an oblique hand in Beethoven's career, for it was his initiative that allowed Haydn to travel to London, which ultimately also led to Beethoven's departure from Bonn.

When Nikolaus II acceded to the throne following the untimely death of his father in 1794, his main preoccupation was the expansion of the enormous library and picture gallery at his summer residence in the Viennese suburb of Mariahilf. But despite his more conservative tastes and relatively limited musical understanding (he himself was only an amateur clarinetist), he made several attempts to welcome the winds of change in Eisenstadt—a mandate he interpreted rather literally by taking a six-piece wind ensemble and three trumpet players into his employ. He had a particular soft spot for church music, for which he sourced additional players from Vienna now and then. The annual public highlight of musical life at court were the September celebrations of his wife's name day, which regularly involved the commission of a new Mass. Haydn was the obvious choice between 1796 and 1802, after which the baton passed to Johann Nepomuk Hummel, the new concertmaster in Eisenstadt. In 1807, the honor fell to an outsider, and Beethoven was granted the commission.

Beethoven was enthusiastic but felt slightly out of his depth, having never composed a Mass before. While he had performed many a Mass in Bonn, those days were long behind him, as were his stile antico counterpoint exercises with Haydn and Albrechtsberger. He was also daunted—for the first time in years—by pressures to measure up to his former teacher, who had established a lasting reputation with the Esterházys. Paralysis set in; he made slow progress and was eventually forced to write an apologetic letter to his benefactor, brimming with excuses. Among other things, his problems included a "head ailment," proof of which was provided by an accompanying letter from Dr. Schmidt. He also mentioned the high standards to which he held himself, given the prince's custom of "having the inimitable masterpieces of the great Haydn performed."[19] Esterházy gave a cool and polite response, stated that he looked forward to the prompt arrival of the score, assured Beethoven that any comparison to Haydn could only lead to a greater appreciation of his efforts, and wished the composer a speedy recovery.[20]

As usual, Beethoven's work was not finished until the last minute.[21] But this is not the only reason the production was a disaster. There had been little time to rehearse, and the absenteeism among the choir and orchestra was so great—even at the dress rehearsal—that Esterházy urged vice Kapellmeister Fuchs to ensure at the very least that all the parts be accounted for during the performance.[22] His entreaties bore little fruit: Beethoven's Mass in C was unconvincing, and the prince was displeased. According to Schindler, Esterházy approached Beethoven at the end of the Mass rehearsal and was heard to remark, "But my dear Beethoven, what is it you have done now?" This slight, alongside Kapellmeister Hummel's snigger of agreement, pushed

Beethoven over the edge. He respectfully nodded his head, turned abruptly, and marched off, leaving a bewildered prince and his entourage behind.[23] Hummel would later Jesuitically declare that his chortle was in response to the imbecility of Esterházy's comment, but by then the damage was done. When Beethoven had the Mass published in 1812, he took his revenge by dedicating it to Ferdinand Kinsky. Esterházy remained unmoved, however, writing in a letter to Henriette Zielinska (in French), "Beethoven's mass is insufferably ludicrous, simply awful [. . .] I am enraged and ashamed."[24]

It is tempting to think that Esterházy's reaction was a knee-jerk response, that he was perplexed by unfamiliar music which had taken him by surprise. Indeed, perhaps he was ill-equipped to pinpoint exactly how Beethoven's Mass contrasted with Haydn's works (to which his ears were already accustomed), and failed to comprehend why Beethoven had written anything different at all, let alone how he could approve of it. There is a possibility, however, that he understood only too well what he had seen and heard, for Beethoven had—consciously or otherwise—made a profound statement about the identity of church music, and by extension the church in general, which can only have discomfited the members of the aristocracy.

For many years, Mass performances in Vienna had been discontinued as a result of the austerity measures imposed by Emperor Joseph II in the 1780s. By the time the genre was revived by Leopold II and later by Francis II, the new generation of composers had been cut well adrift from the centuries-long tradition of Mass composition, whose roots stretched back to Palestrina. What is more, during this hiatus all of these composers had been working to advance the Viennese style, which at its core was a purely instrumental genre. Consequently, when composing Masses, Haydn and his contemporaries were forced to use the grammar, vocabulary, and rhetoric of a language which—despite their mastery of it and its undisputed success in the concert hall—was, in essence, "a-religious." Indeed, many of the instrumental introductions to Haydn's Mass movements were indistinguishable from the opening of a symphony or concerto, and the development of the themes was governed principally by a harmonic and tonal logic. The text was kept emotionally at arm's length—"grafted," as it were, on to the existing framework—and repetitions of words and phrases were used to underpin the prefabricated and well-balanced musical structures. Viennese Masses themselves thus had negligible religious content and sourced their legitimacy purely from their inclusion in the liturgy. While the music certainly glorified the services in this manner, it offered little to no spiritual or emotional depth.

Beethoven could not be contented by following such a tradition. Even before leaving Bonn he had developed an aversion to the church as an institution, and his letters regularly contain such ironic pronouncements as "Read the gospels daily, keep Paul and Peter close to your heart, travel to Rome and kiss the Pope's slippers" or "Christian though I am, one Friday a week is enough for me."[25] Beethoven believed that all people were capable of a personal relationship with God, and that third-party intervention by individuals or institutions was unnecessary. He nurtured a particular sympathy with the Christ figure from the *Mount of Olives,* who had undergone suffering not because he was the son of God but from a commitment to fulfilling his duty. This is why Beethoven was not a churchgoer: religious ceremonies were, in his eyes, no more than theatrical (and thus superficial) public displays, and his moral appraisal of the highest officiating members of the service left much to be desired.

When composing the Mass in C, Beethoven made a radical ideological statement by composing music whose splendor far outshone that of the liturgical decor. He wished for his music to both express and evoke deeply religious sentiments in his listeners, and as such the text of the Mass took pride of place. Each word and phrase received the proper expression, any repetitions or elongations being dictated purely by the subject matter or emotional subtext. The Mass thus became an extended dialogue with God, which Beethoven infused with prayer in all its forms: laudation, adoration, supplication, and gratitude. Looking through a different lens, Beethoven also seized every opportunity to highlight—by musical means—his skepticism of the institution and its doctrine. The *Credo,* which traditionally embodies the more militant character of the church, begins here with a tentative crescendo, as though Beethoven himself was hesitant to declare his own faith. Furthermore, most attention is devoted—in an adagio encompassing around one third of the movement—to the mystery of Christ's incarnation and crucifixion.

As a further departure from Haydn's style, in this Mass it is the choir that provides the momentum, while the orchestra is relegated to a secondary, supporting role. Perhaps even more drastic, however, was the fact that Beethoven reversed the hierarchy of the music and the liturgy. Whereas in Haydn's works it was the latter that legitimized the former, Beethoven's treatment of the text was dramatic and vivid enough in its own right to afford the Mass a life outside the church. Beethoven knew this, and during negotiations with Breitkopf & Härtel in 1808, he suggested having Christian Schreiber (the man who rewrote the *Mount of Olives*) produce a German translation of the text. The Mass was thus transformed into a series of hymns, facilitating concert performances and boosting its popularity, especially in the more Protestant German states. Vienna was not kept waiting: in an *Akademie* held at Theater an der Wien on December 22, 1808, the *Gloria* and *Sanctus* of the Mass were performed within the context of an otherwise entirely secular program. Aristocrats generally recoiled from this type of secularization, and Esterházy likely feared recriminations for having been responsible for its genesis.

Again, Beethoven was ahead of his contemporaries. Ironically, this time he led the way by treating the text in a manner that could even be described as "old-fashioned," in which the use of resources is so economical that every note is imbued with profound depth and emotional impact. To Beethoven, this approach was nothing new. During the turbulent years between 1798 and 1802, when he felt compelled to set several texts on the subject of death for voice and piano (which would later become the *Gellert* Lieder, op. 48), he developed a vocal style based largely on expressive declamation. The first of the central songs in particular, "Vom Tode" (On death), lacks any suggestion of melody whatsoever, and many fragments from the Mass in C are recollections of this detached style, which is precisely what lends the work its emotional substance.

Taking this idea further, the Mass in C could be viewed as a commentary on the Heiligenstadt Testament, making it the final panel in a triptych and a contemplative counterweight to the psychological drama of the *Mount of Olives* and the *Eroica*.

BACK TO BUSINESS, PART TWO

On his return from Eisenstadt (before September 20, 1807), a slightly overwrought Beethoven knocked frenetically at his beloved Josephine's door, with hopes of convincing her to change her mind and marry him. As we already know, his plan backfired and Josephine only became more distant, leaving him to pass the dreary autumn and winter months in lonesome solitude.

Beethoven threw himself into his work once more. He was determined to finish both his Symphony in C Minor and the *Pastoral* Symphony, for which he had already completed several years of preparatory work. At the same time, he also needed to continue lobbying to have his existing music performed. His chief aspiration remained an *Akademie* in one of the major theaters—not least because with a little luck he could earn the equivalent of a year's salary in one fell swoop. He needed the cooperation of the management, however, which had recently proven to be an unreliable partner. Multiple times Beethoven's applications had been approved, some even in writing, and in several instances he had even obtained police authorization. But for some reason the plans always fell through, so much so that at one point Beethoven even threatened to go to court. He ultimately decided on a policy of patience and persistence, and earned goodwill by collaborating with others on benefit concerts (those featuring his own works, of course).[26] He generally left the solo parts to others and restricted his involvement to conducting the orchestra, further evidence of his resolution to focus more on his image as a composer rather than a pianist. This telling mental shift is also illustrated by the original programming of Beethoven's newly composed Fourth Piano Concerto during a concert on November 15, 1808, at the Burgtheater.[27] Ferdinand Ries was originally approached to premiere the work but feared that five days might not be sufficient time to master the part. The young pianist Frederich Stein—Nannette's cousin—was therefore asked to replace him. He initially agreed but changed his mind on the eve of the concert, deciding instead to play the Third Piano Concerto. Contrary to the original plan, Beethoven ultimately had no choice but to premiere the Fourth Piano Concerto himself at his own *Akademie* five weeks later. Equally curious is the fact that, going against all previous convention, the Fourth Piano Concerto had been in print for months leading up to its premiere and was thus already known to both experts and amateur music lovers. Up until that time, Beethoven's greatest concern had been that others might make off with his music, a scenario that he tried to prevent by delaying the publication of his concertos for as long as possible. His new strategy fit within a broader, more fundamental shift that was already underway in the concerto genre and which manifested even more strongly with the fifth concerto—but more on that later.

Beethoven's metamorphosis from a pianist into a composer also took place in the minds of his listeners, for whom his writing had become more important than his playing. When several Viennese music enthusiasts launched a new concert series in the autumn of 1807—known as the Liebhaber-Konzerte, or

Friends of Music Concerts—they proclaimed Beethoven as the series's composer in residence. Not only that, but he was also asked to join the committee that decided on the programming and the soloists. Beethoven, who was hardly known for his love of the consultation process, leapt at the opportunity: not only, we might surmise, because he saw a chance to expand his listening public, but also to prevent any of his competitors from doing the same.

The winter concerts held by Baron Würth from 1803 to 1805 revealed that Vienna supported a (chiefly middle-class) concert-going public with a desire to attend regular orchestral performances. And although the French occupation in November 1805 put an end to his original concert series, the idea was not forgotten. Count Moritz von Dietrichstein, who as a young lad had attended the soirées organized in the good-old days of the aristocracy by his aunt, Countess Thun, and who had thus developed an affinity with cultural events, rallied together seven members of the nobility in 1807 (headed once again by Lobkowitz) to continue Würth's initiative, now on a far grander scale. The business model was simple: seventy members of the aristocracy and the nouveaux riches signed up and purchased at least ten tickets each, either to be sold or distributed among family, friends, and business relations. Unused tickets were to be returned so that they could be resold a second time. Profitability was thus guaranteed, as the seats were exclusive and therefore in high demand. They were also numbered for the first time in Viennese concert history, further adding to their status. At the same time, overheads were low as the orchestra was made up chiefly of amateurs whose compensation was the honor of a seat on the stage rather than in the audience. (Only the sections that were traditionally problematic—double basses, oboes, bassoons, and horns—were populated with moonlighting members from the opera.) The same was even truer of the soloists, who were recruited from aristocratic circles and in all likelihood were even required to pay for the privilege. The success was enormous. At noon on November 12, 1807, over thirteen hundred eager listeners fought their way into the (now demolished) Mehlgrube, whose capacity was of course grossly inadequate. The second concert was moved to the university's upstairs auditorium, but there too some attendees were still forced to either stand or sit on the floor. The series ultimately saw twenty orchestral concerts, the last of which was a gala event: on March 27, 1808, Haydn's *Creation* was performed in the presence of the aged and ailing composer himself. Renewed war with France was the reason no second Liebhaber series was organized the following year.

But we are getting ahead of ourselves: Beethoven had been appointed as an artistic consultant, could suggest works for inclusion in the program, and was charged with the effective running of rehearsals (of which there was usually only one). The society running the Liebhaber-Konzerte considered itself a "Musical Institute," whose aim was to "present the works of great masters in their entirety, and give virtuosos the opportunity to display their art."[28] Beethoven obviously cared about this work a great deal, and certainly in the beginning he derived much enjoyment from piecing together fitting combinations of works, ensuring a proper mix of symphonies, overtures, concertos, and arias and finding the right balance between challenging masterworks and "easy listening." It is certainly no coincidence that the only symphonies on the program were those by himself, Haydn, and Mozart and that Messrs. Andreozzi, Guglielmi, Liverati, Vogel, and sundry others had to be content with operatic arias and the occasional wayward concerto. During that first season, Beethoven's symphonies were nearly all performed twice, provoking criticism of excessive self-promotion. He was also accused of devoting too little rehearsal time to the works of his fellow composers. Beethoven was likewise quite vocal in his own dissatisfaction and even threatened to quit when some aristocratic dolt made a public mess of his First Piano Concerto. Although things never came to such a head, we can only imagine Beethoven's frustration at a troupe of amateurs whose enthusiasm was, at times, inversely proportional to their ability.

Beethoven invested a great deal of time in his committee role. It was a sideline in which he rarely dabbled and for which—as far as we know—he was never paid. He did receive twelve complimentary tickets per concert, a privilege of which he availed himself fully. Of far greater importance, however, was the goodwill that his participation generated among members of the Viennese cultural establishment and the vast expansion of his listener base, which he hoped would bear fruit if and when his *Akademie* finally came.

When it did come, on December 22, 1808, at Theater an der Wien, Beethoven organized what he hoped would be a festive celebration of his music, a glorious moment that he had been dreaming of for over five years. Alas, fate had other plans. Having been denied for so long, Beethoven behaved like a starving man at a banquet, gorging himself beyond all measure. In his blind determination to offer a representative sample of his work from the previous two and a half years, he forgot one of the cardinal rules of concert programming and failed to think from the audience's perspective. The concert thus took on unseemly proportions and included not only the *Pastoral* Symphony (billed as the Fifth) and the Symphony in C Minor (billed as the Sixth) but also the Fourth Piano Concerto, the concert aria "Ah! Perfido," and the *Gloria* and *Sanctus* from the Mass in C. And because the *Sanctus* was not a brilliant enough conclusion in Beethoven's view, he also insisted on a fitting climax that would unite all performers onstage together in a triumphant finale. To that end, he dashed off a set of variations on a theme dating from over ten years before,[29] had court clerk Christoph Kuffner whip up a text on a lofty subject to match it (namely, the power of music to dispel humanity's ills), and true to form, improvised a long solo introduction during the performance itself. Thus the *Choral Fantasy* (op. 80) was born, which, despite bearing the hallmarks of its hasty genesis, sports many charms.

The public's patience was sorely tested. A Siberian chill filled the hall, and the concert seemed to go on forever. Even the more experienced concertgoers later complained of having to wade through nearly four hours of music. They seemed to have forgotten that Beethoven's first *Akademie* on April 2, 1800, had lasted even longer. The concert's duration had clearly not been a problem the first time, perhaps due to the less monolithic nature of the programmed works. But its duration aside, by all accounts the performance was also substandard. The orchestra left much to be desired, and Beethoven himself played poorly (it was to be his final public concerto appearance).[30] Because of a benefit concert being held by Salieri in the Burgtheater that same evening, which according to Beethoven was no coincidence, most of the available musicians were second-rate. As usual, there had been little rehearsal time, and tensions ran high between the orchestra and the hypermotivated, over-concentrated composer-conductor—so high in fact that at one time he was forcibly removed from the hall. Lastly, things went horribly wrong during the *Choral Fantasy*. Some argued that there had been a misunderstanding regarding the observation of the repeats; others blamed the myriad transcription errors in the orchestral parts, the ink of which was still wet on the page. The precise reason matters little, for at a certain point the performance was derailed and the resulting chaos left no option but to call a halt and start again. A very frustrated Beethoven put the blame—predictably—on the musicians.

And so it was that the concert, intended as the crowning achievement of two and a half years of uninterrupted creative endeavor, came to a sad end. It was the anticlimax to a golden age in which Beethoven had reached critical velocity and composed music not only of great scope, but also of great stature.

It became symbolic of the difficulties that he encountered time and again when putting his ambitious ideas into practice in an attempt to achieve greater material and social status. His disillusionment was bitter in the extreme.

Because the Symphony in C Minor and the *Pastoral* Symphony appeared together on the concert program of December 22, 1808, they have lived a paired existence ever since. The symphonies were written virtually concurrently; they were dedicated to the same aristocrats (Lobkowitz and Razumovsky) and were published the following year with successive opus numbers (67 and 68). But despite these historical parallels, Beethoven actually commenced work on the Symphony in C Minor immediately after completing the *Eroica,* with the intention of using the symphonic pair to conquer Paris. Although his plan fell through for various reasons, the Symphony in C Minor still contains auditory evidence of the work's political undertones. The entire composition is conceived as a gradual transition from the dark and ominous opening in C minor to the open and positive character of its C-major conclusion. C major is traditionally the key of light, and so the transition from the "darkness" of the past into the "light" of the future confers a political dimension to the work, especially when its instrumentation is also taken into account. While the symphony opens with a prototypical Austro-German sound, for the final movement Beethoven adds a piccolo, contrabassoon, and three trombones, all of which were typical of what was then known as the "French Revolutionary style." Beethoven seems to be suggesting that a bright future would have a French veneer, and we might imagine that it was with this vision that he hoped to win over the hearts of Paris.

But it was not to be, and Beethoven set the symphony aside for over two years. Not until the autumn of 1806 did he resume work on it, and because the Symphony in C Minor was immediately followed by the *Pastoral* Symphony in F Major, a different connection was forged. There are indeed many arguments for regarding these two new symphonies as compositional fraternal twins. The structural similarities are striking: both opening movements are relatively short; each commences with a four-bar motif, or "motto," that ends with a fermata; and each motto constitutes a germinal figure that undergoes development but never truly takes on any clear thematic contours. The final movements, by contrast, are relatively long and hymnlike, representing the carefully prepared culmination of each work and emerging organically from the previous movements.

It is not only their similarities, however, but also their internal complementarity that binds the symphonies together and gives them their unique character. The Symphony in C Minor is an auditory onslaught, in which the obsessive rhythms of the familiar opening motif are repeated incessantly, propelling the symphony and the listener inexorably forward.[31] We are plunged into the symphony's depths; details blur and one becomes oblivious to the many abrupt transitions, sudden modulations, and dynamic explosions. Players and public alike fall into a delirium, and the fear arises that at any moment, "the house might collapse" (Goethe).[32] Beethoven was well aware that the symphony's "power" was due chiefly to its "drive," and wrote that the final movement made "more of a racket than six kettledrums, and a better racket at that."[33]

The *Pastoral,* on the other hand, is the polar opposite. Time glides by slowly, allowing for the transcendence of inner peace, and there is barely any sense of "development." Momentum is scarce; the tonal progression is gradual; and modulations are unassuming, due to the lack of any pronounced leading tones or dominant chords. Dramatic development is equally lacking, and even the temporary eruption of the storm in the fourth movement serves primarily to emphasize the ensuing serenity, with the final movement emerging as an extended prayer of thanks.[34] But contrary to what the symphony's subtitle might suggest, Beethoven's intention was not to evoke the visual image of a musical landscape. His note to listeners on the title page asserts that the symphony is "more an expression of sentiment than a painting."[35] The fourth-movement depiction of the storm, and the literal citations of the nightingale, quail, and cuckoo at the end of the second movement, are exceptions to be interpreted within the context of the *Pastoral* tradition and should not be taken too literally. (The fact that Beethoven's cuckoo sings a major third, while real cuckoos prefer a minor third, is an endearing blemish on the composer's oeuvre that serves to underscore the symbolic character of the reference.)

The Symphony in C Minor and the *Pastoral* address two diametrically opposite forms of temporal perception and existential experience. Nineteenth-century commentators observed a dichotomy between exaltation, struggle, and triumph on the one hand, and beauty, comfort, and thanksgiving on the other. Looking at Beethoven's own commentary, one might also describe this antithesis in terms of city versus country, modernity versus nostalgia, or intellectualism versus spirituality. In short, the symphonies are bound together like yin and yang: each can only be fully understood in the complementary presence of the other. With this in mind, Beethoven's eventual decision to reverse the order—turning the *Pastoral* into a reflection on the Symphony in C Minor—becomes a powerful musical statement.

PART FOUR

Crowds and Power

(1809–1816)

33

A New Social Status

FOR SOME TIME AFTER THE CONCERT on December 22, 1808, it seemed as though Beethoven might leave Vienna. Several weeks beforehand he had been offered the post of Kapellmeister in Kassel, a position that he was inclined to accept. His chances of finding a permanent post in Vienna were virtually nonexistent: the negotiations for a new opera had run aground; the resistance he encountered when trying to organize his *Akademien* was enormous; and because he had signed a new exclusive publishing contract with Breitkopf & Härtel in September, any future collaboration with the Viennese Bureau des Arts et d'Industrie (the Comptoir) had been rendered unnecessary. Nothing seemed to stand in the way of Beethoven leaving what had become his second hometown.

Kassel was the capital of the new kingdom of Westphalia, an administrative region created by Napoleon as part of a large-scale employment program intended to consolidate his power outside France and to manufacture European posts for his many brothers and sisters. The youngest of the Bonaparte siblings, Jérôme, was thus inserted as king of Westphalia on August 18, 1807. But while his elder brothers and sisters had not completely forgotten their Corsican roots and had continued to exercise some restraint when performing the duties of their "office," Jérôme's grip on reality was tenuous, so much so that historians are often at a loss for words when describing the delinquency, extravagance, and moral corruption of his despotism. *Morgen wieder lustig*—more merriment tomorrow—seems to have been the only phrase he was capable of uttering in the language of his subjects. They were forced to look on in dismay as their taxes were squandered on *Wein, Weiber, und Gesang*—women, wine, and song—and on their new sovereign's lavish "Louis XV" lifestyle. Even Napoleon would have been ashamed of his little brother's excesses; however, his admonitions were limited to the occasional murmur of disapproval and nothing more.

The German composer Johann Friedrich Reichardt was recruited to provide the *Gesang,* and on January 1, 1808, was appointed as "general director of the theaters and the orchestra." A mere ten months later he was shown the door, and as is often the way, negotiations with his successor had already begun; in a letter to Count Oppersdorff dated November 1, 1808, Beethoven wrote that he had generously been offered the position of Kapellmeister in Kassel. There are indeed historical indications that Count Truchsess-Waldburg, Jérôme's right-hand man, had made initial contact earlier that summer. Reichardt would later claim that he himself had been charged with the duty of officially asking Beethoven to take his place, during a visit to Vienna in November 1808, and that he strongly urged Beethoven not to do so. Beethoven emphatically denied this version of events, even publishing a general notice to that effect in the *Allgemeine musikalische Zeitung.*[1] A known fact is that Reichardt did suggest Ferdinand Ries as a possible candidate for the position, under the apprehension that Beethoven was not interested. The ever-proprietous Ries contacted his former teacher straightaway to verify his position and to chart a course moving forward. Beethoven, who in reality was still undecided at this point, suspected a conspiracy, and for weeks Ries was given no chance whatsoever to relay his own version of events. Only following a fracas at the door to Beethoven's apartment (reports say that Ries seized Beethoven's servant by the throat and hurled him to the ground) was Ries able to clear the air and resolve the matter. Still, it took some time before Beethoven—having since decided against Kassel—would support his former pupil's candidacy, perhaps on the supposition that Ries was unlikely to obtain a post that had originally been intended for him. Alas, valuable time had already been lost, and Ries was beaten to it by a certain Felice Biangini.

For some time, at least, Beethoven certainly did intend to make the move to Kassel. In a letter to Breitkopf & Härtel dated January 7, 1809, he even claimed officially having accepted the offer, and felt forced to leave so he could "escape the constant plotting, scheming and fighting" in Vienna.[2] He then tasked the organization of the contract to his secretary, Gleichenstein, who managed to salvage an agreement consisting primarily of entitlements (an annual salary of six hundred ducats and a travel allowance) and with few obligations (mostly related to conducting). At the same time, Gleichenstein also lent his collaboration behind the scenes to an emergency plan concocted by Countess Erdődy, the aim of which was to keep Beethoven tethered in Vienna.

Anna Maria von Erdődy was a thirty-year-old countess from the ancient Hungarian nobility, who had been residing in Vienna for some time. She was married to a relative of the Esterházys, who had deserted her after an acute rheumatic condition had left her bedridden. But despite being in a constant drug-induced stupor (she was essentially addicted to opium), she managed to raise her three children and continued to play the piano and organize salon concerts, where Beethoven made regular appearances. He felt comfortable in her presence, was willing to exchange ideas with her in candor and confidence—according to Schindler, Beethoven often referred to her as his "confessor"—and he even lived with her family for a time during the autumn of 1808. As far as we know, the two never had an affair. Far from it: Beethoven himself even alluded to the fact that the children's private tutor, Master Joseph Brauchle, was the one who took his role as a surrogate father perhaps a little too seriously.[3] In March 1809, things came to an all-too-familiar head. This time a heated exchange concerning one of the servants prompted Beethoven to seek new lodgings less than a hundred paces away, on the same street.[4] This typical Beethovenian *raptus* was followed by an equally typical letter of apology, after which the incident was considered closed.

Officially, the story goes that Countess Erdődy and Gleichenstein went begging among the Viennese aristocrats—unbeknown to Beethoven—in an effort to thwart his relocation plans. This hypothesis has little credence, however; they probably tried to convince him themselves first that moving to Kassel was hardly a sensible idea (if only for fear that the values espoused by the fledgling king were not in line with postrevolutionary ideals), and suspected that the days of the Napoleonic regime shielding Jérôme from recriminations were numbered.[5] After that—with Beethoven's approval, though without his knowledge—they then used the imminent contract with Kassel as a bargaining chip to forge similar working conditions for him closer to home.

In former times, Countess Erdődy and Gleichenstein would have taken the matter directly to the emperor. In early 1809, however, Francis I was busy preparing for a new war against Napoleon, and his mind—which was hardly culturally oriented even at the best of times—was not receptive to such a relatively trifling matter. A further complication was the fact that composers with Jacobean sympathies (which in his view was virtually all of them) were not on his list of favorites. The aristocrats therefore turned to his youngest brother, Archduke Rudolph. This black sheep of the royal family was known to have a strong affinity with music and was a great admirer of Beethoven's.

Not only that, but Beethoven had dedicated the Fourth Piano Concerto to him in the summer of 1808, and the archduke also nurtured a wish to take composition lessons from the great master. He therefore had a vested interest in Beethoven remaining in Vienna and pledged his financial support. Erdődy and Gleichenstein then turned to Lobkowitz, who as a member of the theater management committee had himself already made previous attempts to secure Beethoven a job. Lastly, they called on Prince Ferdinand Kinsky, who was prepared to contribute in order to prevent the need for Beethoven—in his own words—to "eat from the Westphalian ham."[6]

The three aristocrats quickly reached an accord and resolved to lay out an annual sum of 4,000 guilders to keep Beethoven on Austrian soil: 1,800 from Kinsky, 1,500 from Rudolph, and 700 from Lobkowitz. It was more than Beethoven could earn in Kassel, and money enough to freely live and work from in Vienna. Next, Gleichenstein drew up a draft contract stating that Beethoven would bear the title of "Imperial Kapellmeister," which at that time was little more than an empty accolade. He was also afforded unlimited travel for the purposes of promoting his work abroad and was guaranteed permission to organize an *Akademie* every year on Palm Sunday. Beethoven's obligations under the contract were less clearly formulated. He was required to conduct one benefit concert annually and was bound to residing in Vienna or one of the Austrian succession states. In the final version of the contract signed by Beethoven on March 1, 1809—which came to be known as the "decree"—most of these conditions were omitted, leaving only vague formulations such as: "Beethoven's extraordinary talents and genius [. . .] give rise to a desire for him to exceed the greatest expectations that might reasonably be placed on him, based on experiences up until now. Since it has been demonstrated, however, that only a person living entirely free from care can dedicate himself fully to a single pursuit [. . .] and produce sublime works of such grandeur that they pay tribute to art itself, the undersigned thus undertake to put Herr Beethoven in a position such that his most basic needs will no longer be of concern to him, leaving his powerful genius unfettered."[7] Several clauses also addressed the term of the contract—which in principle was lifelong, even should Beethoven no longer be able to compose—as well as the conditions in the event of an additional appointment.[8] This last point was no trivial matter, as all parties had assumed that Archduke Rudolph would one day become either a governor (*Vogt*) in Hungary or archbishop of Olmütz, and when that time came would take both Beethoven and the contract with him.[9] There are even indications that the archduke had made explicit promises to Beethoven to this effect, a scenario that was in any case far more attractive to Beethoven than the Kassel appointment. Olmütz (Olomouc) lay a mere 180 kilometers from Vienna, and the archbishop was generally only required to physically occupy his seat for six to eight weeks a year, leaving ample occasion for both the archbishop and his Kapellmeister to maintain ties with Vienna. Beethoven was mentally prepared for this scenario; we know that he eagerly combed the real estate listings in 1810 and that he considered purchasing a country property in Hungary.[10] Rumor has it that he even planned to breed horses . . .

Countess Erdődy and Gleichenstein thus secured a major triumph. Beethoven did not leave for Kassel and felt assured of a future carefree life as a composer in Vienna. He was tremendously grateful to the aristocratic triumvirate, and as an expression of thanks dedicated to them the newly composed Piano Trios in D Major and E-flat (op. 70), and the Cello Sonata in A (op. 69).

Beethoven would later condemn the contract he had signed on March 1, 1809, as an "accursed decree" and a "siren's call," declaring, "I ought to have had myself tied down and my ears plugged with wax, so as never to have signed it."[11] The contract—the primary purpose of which had been to render him free of material day-to-day cares—quickly proved to be an enormous Trojan horse that saddled him with even more troubles, ongoing stress, and mounting legal bills. The first mishap occurred before the decree even took effect, when Kinsky, in his haste to reach the war front in Bohemia, forgot to issue the requisite authorizations so that payment could commence. Because Kinsky's share was the largest, Beethoven fell into difficulties straightaway. He sent multiple letters to Kinsky's chargé d'affaires in Vienna, who was nonetheless powerless to undertake any action. Even Kinsky's wife, who was staying in Prague at that time, had no power of attorney. It would be over a year, on June 20, 1810, before Kinsky issued a written authorization, and another month before Beethoven received his due.

The complications did not end there. Although the three-monthly payments were made from then on as agreed, the resulting sum had lost most of its value due to the economic crisis that had gripped Austria since 1809. Once again, the Hapsburgs had overplayed their diplomatic hand, and once again, it was the common people who paid the price. In the spring of 1809, the Austrians had felt compelled to rush in and call a halt to the advance of the

French military, unaided by any other major powers. They had been misinformed in this respect by their ambassador in Paris, the young Klemens von Metternich, who had sent reports to Vienna of the French army's waning forces, saying that the police and the populace had grown weary of their ongoing military exploits. He even declared that the time was ripe for a coup and that Napoleon was only one defeat away from deposition. Metternich, in turn, was unaware of how he had been misled by his own informants. These mostly numbered opposing members of the ancient nobility who already saw their dreams coming true, but they also included Napoleon's sister Caroline, with whom Metternich shared a bed for several months. On April 9, 1809, Austria declared war on the French, who one month later showed that they were not to be trifled with, and marched on the gates of Vienna. Unlike the previous occasion, the metaphorical gloves were now off, and on the night of May 11 the French army bombarded the city center with mortar grenades. Beethoven was physically and mentally unable to cope. He fled to his brother's house on Rauhensteingasse and sought refuge in the cellar, where he sat hunched for hours, burying his head and oversensitive ears in a pile of cushions. Not until two-thirty in the afternoon did the Austrian authorities officially concede defeat.

For the next five months, the French effectively terrorized the city. Napoleon may have suffered a defeat in Aspern, but after the battle of Wagram Austria's resistance was crushed entirely. The French then forced the Hapsburgs into a disadvantageous peace treaty, after which the armies vacated Vienna in October 1809. Before doing so, they exploded a few defensive walls for safety's sake, including those abutting the Hofburg. Supreme humiliation followed one year later, when Napoleon asked for and received the hand of Archduchess Marie Louise; a year after that, the Hapsburg emperor became grandfather to Napoleon's successor and heir. To the Austrian nobility, who still had the untimely demise of Marie Antoinette fresh in their minds, it was as though "a virgin had been offered to a Minotaur."[12] But there was no alternative. Metternich, to his credit, at least pointed out that Napoleon otherwise might have wed the daughter of the tsar, which would have left Austria hopelessly wedged between the French and the Russians.

This political and military fiasco gave rise to some dramatic economic consequences: Austria was forced to pay enormous war reparations. It had also lost one third of its territory along with one third of its taxpayers, and rebuilding the city was a costly enterprise. The national debt skyrocketed, and Austrian currency—the *Bancozettel*—lost value by the day.[13] Prices soared, and several failed harvests led to a market shortage that affected basic food items. In an attempt to stop inflation spiraling out of control, on February 20, 1811, the Austrian government issued the *Finanzpatent,* a financial decree dictating that on March 11, 1811, the old paper guilders would be replaced with *Einlösungsscheine* (exchange vouchers) at a rate of 5 to 1. In practical terms, this meant that all prices—thenceforth expressed in *Wiener Währung,* or Viennese currency—were to be lowered by four-fifths. To help soften the blow for the working class (whose savings had already run dry), a simultaneous decree stated that all contracts concluded before 1811 were to be recalculated according to an official table taking account of the "gradual" devaluation of the original *Bancozettel* between 1796 and 1811. Under this mechanism, Beethoven's retainer of 4,000 old *Bancozettel* would not be reduced to 800 new guilders under the *Wiener Währung* (4,000 divided by 5), but instead to 1,612.9 (4,000 divided by a mere 2.48, a figure more accurately reflecting the ratio between the devaluation of the *Bancozettel* when the contract was signed and when the decree was issued). A wily Beethoven, however, claimed that the amount originally agreed upon was no longer accurate (since the devaluation of the *Bancozettel* was already underway when the contract had been signed), and requested additional compensation for the devaluation that had occurred prior to 1809. In other words, he demanded that his 4,000 old *Bancozettel* simply be converted to 4,000 new *Währung* guilders, amounting to a veiled salary increase. Archduke Rudolph, in a fit of religious charity, shut his eyes to Beethoven's skewed logic, raised the figure, and promptly paid in full.

Kinsky took a different stance. Although he had given the order on January 16, 1812, to raise his contribution to 726 new guilders (1,800 divided by 2.48 and rounded up), for some unknown reason his Viennese bookkeepers became hesitant to make the payments. Beethoven also tried to persuade Kinsky to follow Rudolph's example and simply start paying 1,800 new guilders, to which Kinsky is supposed to have agreed several times over the summer of 1812—on one occasion to Beethoven himself during a sojourn in Prague in early July on the way to Teplitz. In a further calamitous turn, Kinsky lost his life on November 3, 1812, in a tragic road accident. Officially, the brave Kinsky fell from his horse while riding to his regiment in Weltrus, and broke his neck.[14] According to the Viennese rumor mill, however, the prince—reckless and half drunk following a pit stop at a roadside restaurant—insisted on riding a traveling companion's horse no matter the cost, with the resulting dramatic conclusion.[15] The precise circumstances are of little consequence; suffice it to say that Beethoven, who had not received a single guilder from Kinsky since September 1811, was now forced to deal with Kinsky's Viennese accountants directly, who knew nothing of any agreement on the prince's part to raise the payments. What is more, Kinsky's untimely death meant that they were no longer authorized to make payments of any kind whatsoever. Even writing to the deceased's widow brought no solace, as her leeway was markedly restricted by the shared custody of her children with her brother-in-law Franz Anton von Kolowrat, who in turn was reliant on the district court in Prague (the *Landrecht*, of which he was incidentally also the president). This was the beginning of an extended legal and administrative back-and-forth, whereby the court in Prague demanded that Beethoven submit a new dossier, including all manner of documents, proofs of payment, extracts certified as true and faithful copies by the Viennese court, as well as certified personal attestations to verbal agreements. And all in duplicate: one set for the arrears already accrued, taking into account the payment increase as had purportedly been agreed to, and another pertaining to the continuation of the contract (following Kinsky's death on November 3, 1812). Beethoven did not receive his first arrears payment until December 1813. The postmortem contract extension was a more complex issue, and addressing it required Beethoven to deploy an army of lawyers in both Vienna and Prague. He was forced to lodge his claim with the district court in Prague twice (lowering it the second time to 1,500 guilders), and each instance demanded a new set of papers—hardly a trivial matter in an age before photocopiers. At one point Beethoven even recruited Archduke Rudolph to mediate on his behalf. For a time it seemed as though the affair might be taken to a higher court, but both parties eventually settled on a compromise: the Kinsky family would pay Beethoven 1,200 guilders per year, with retroactive effect from November 3, 1812. After a grim and nerve-racking ordeal lasting over two years, Beethoven, on March 26, 1815, became the glad recipient of nearly 2,500 new guilders in cash.

Beethoven was in dire financial straits during these two years, since the third benefactor, Lobkowitz, also failed to meet his financial obligations. He too is supposed to have promised to continue paying the agreed figure in new *Währung* guilders (a highly optimistic commitment in view of the dizzying speed with which he orchestrated his own financial demise). Beethoven raised the matter with him on several occasions, initially maintaining courtesy and respect (though still making the occasional mocking reference to Prince Fizly-Puzly or "His Royal Roguishness"[16]), but later giving in to aggravation and even rage, especially when put under pressure by his own creditors, who were threatening legal action of their own. When in July 1813 he heard that Lobkowitz had been placed first under familial supervision, later under guardianship, and had subsequently fled Vienna, Beethoven initiated legal proceedings against his former patron. Lobkowitz's obligation to pay was a foregone conclusion—the only question was how much, as Lobkowitz officially denied ever having promised to increase the original sum. When both were summoned to court, each to present their word against the other, Lobkowitz's lawyers argued valiantly that any "verbal" agreement made with a man whose deafness was "notorious" was legally null and void. Lobkowitz eventually relented and on May 9, 1815, paid out both the agreed sum and the accrued interest in arrears.

From that point on, and for the first time since signing the "accursed decree" in March 1809, Beethoven was paid his proper due—a boon that had cost him over six years of suffering and had driven him more than once to the very brink of desperation. In a letter dated February 19, 1812, he despondently writes, "I am no Hercules, unable to help Atlas bear the weight of the world, let alone do so in his stead." And a year later, "What an awful business for an artist, to whom nothing is so dear as his art." Beethoven's distrust of people in general was augmented as a result: "These days it seems that nobody feels bound by anything—honour, oath or written word."[17]

The resolution of the decree did not solve all of his financial problems, however. The Austrian government had still failed to get inflation under control, which was due in no small measure to the massive sums it had spent on organizing the Congress of Vienna. Only by 1818 did it succeed in (more or less) stabilizing the economy, although the *Wiener Währung* had plummeted in value by over 250 percent since 1811. The annual sum of 3,400 guilders that Beethoven had received since May 1815 was in reality worth far less, placing him in greater need than ever to seek funding elsewhere.

34

New Prospects

DESPITE BEETHOVEN'S DIFFICULTY in holding his benefactors to their word, and the limited extent to which the "accursed decree" actually freed him of any financial concerns, the signing of the new contract represented a milestone in Beethoven's life. From that point on—at least in theory—he was free to write whatever music he wanted. And even though in practice this freedom proved less liberating than he had imagined, his three Viennese aristocrats had opened up some new and exceptional career prospects. Besides earning themselves a place in the music history books, the sponsors had thus added a key sociological facet to Beethoven's reputation and, although the side effect was probably unintended, pushed his musical thought in a new direction.

Despite first appearances, it was not artistic or idealistic principles—let alone generosity or altruism—that prompted the initiative by Rudolph, Lobkowitz, and Kinsky. The decree was first and foremost a political and ideological statement, and one with inextricable ties to the nationalist revival that had pervaded Austria for several years. To understand it fully, we must return to the year 1805 when the French seized Vienna and, after meeting with limited resistance, concluded a most favorable peace treaty with the Hapsburgs. Austria's military weakness at the time was due in part to the fact that the war—like most eighteenth-century conflicts—was based chiefly on the concerns of the Austrian government, not of the Austrian soldiers and certainly not the Austrian people. If anything, the opposite was true: when the French entered the city, they met with more curiosity than enmity, prompting them to adopt an occupational strategy based uncommonly on respect and courteousness. It is with some sense of irony that Napoleon, on his departure from Vienna, thanked the Viennese for having lived up entirely to his genteel expectations of them.

After the bitter defeat in Austerlitz in December 1805 and the Peace of Pressburg, both of which put the Austrian government in a weak position, policy took a different course. The new minister of foreign affairs, Johann von Stadion-Warthausen, believed that a war of retaliation could only succeed if the support base was sufficiently broad; or, to be more specific, if the underlying rationale was based on idealistic rather than dynastic or territorial concerns, and had the appearance of seeking to restore the old empire founded on Catholic, aristocratic, and conservative values. He launched an enormous propaganda offensive that combined patriotic enthusiasm with a revival of the old morals. New journals were created, boasting such overblown titles as *Pages from the Fatherland* (Vaterländische Blätter) and *The Austrian Plutarch* (Österreichischer Plutarch), the latter growing into a twenty-volume encyclopedia containing portraits of all Austrian rulers as well as the most illustrious generals, statesmen, scholars, and artists. Patriotic poets and playwrights—led by Beethoven's favorite, Collin—gathered in the salons of Fanny Arnstein, Henriette Pereira, Caroline Pichler, and Eleonore Schwarzenberg to spur each other on with mutual ideological support and profess their restorationist principles with renewed confidence. (It was through this process, however, that the emancipation of women, as propagated by Germaine de Staël and Rahel Levin, was dismissed as an abomination against nature.) Traditional Austrian national costume (the *Tracht*) was restored to its former glory, and communal singing events were held in the Redoutensaal, where costumed throngs in their thousands gave renditions of patriotic songs under the motto of "Österreich über alles!"—a rather graceless text that even Beethoven considered setting for a time. This subtle form of psychological mass conscription was a success. When Austria declared war on France on April 9, 1809, the population was willing to defend their city tooth and nail, and the Hapsburgs mustered the largest army in their country's history. But although the enterprise was doomed from the outset and resulted in incalculable damage, much of the people's suffering was compensated for by the strength of their convictions.

Under these conditions, the notion that Beethoven—the very icon of Western musical culture—might take a position at a French-run court in Germany was tantamount to a slap in the face and is the reason Archduke Rudolph, Lobkowitz, and Kinsky did their utmost to keep him in Vienna.

The fact that Beethoven pledged to remain there on March 1, 1809, was thus a major coup in the preparations for the war to come.

As already mentioned, the decree gave Beethoven more rights than obligations. He was not entirely free to do as he pleased, however. Beethoven was a subscriber to the same ideological agenda as the other three signatories and had essentially agreed to being proclaimed the unofficial "state composer." By extension, the choice logically fell to him many times during the ensuing years whenever regime-friendly works were required, such as the opening music for the theater in Pest in 1811 (opp. 113 and 117), the many occasional pieces for use during the Congress of Vienna, and the grand mass for the inauguration of Archduke Rudolph as archbishop in Olmütz. These commissions also had certain artistic repercussions; whereas formerly Beethoven had taken a great deal of his inspiration from the French music and sound of Cherubini et al., he now had no choice but to align firmly with the Austro-German music tradition, having just been proclaimed its preeminent exponent. His status was reinforced when during this period—on May 31, 1809—Joseph Haydn passed away.

To meet these high expectations, Beethoven madly began studying the music of his forebears. On July 26, 1809, he asked publisher Breitkopf & Härtel to send him regular batches of scores by Mozart, Haydn, the Bachs (both J. S. and C. P. E.), and others. In the same letter we also read of Beethoven's great enjoyment in organizing weekly singing gatherings (which he called *Singmusik*), where a select group of music lovers gathered to perform German works of which he had little to no previous knowledge.[1]

Beethoven's new fascination for the past was also manifest in the many hours he spent in libraries, consulting old counterpoint treatises. This was, of course, partly due to the new teaching remit he had received from Archduke Rudolph (discussed in greater detail in the following chapter). But his sudden interest in tradition was more than purely artistic. The stile antico, as it was dubbed and propagated by Viennese church composer Johann Joseph Fux in his famous *Gradus ad Parnassum* (1725), was well known as a bulwark of orthodoxy and conservatism. It was viewed by its author as a remedy to the decadences of an age "in which music has become almost entirely arbitrary, when composers no longer wish to be bound by rules and principles, and shun all adherence to school or law as though they represented death itself."[2] It needs no explanation that this "learned style" was still highly esteemed in

Vienna, and the fact that Beethoven returned to the discipline in 1809—coincidentally also the year in which Albrechtsberger, his other counterpoint teacher, passed away—says much about his mental reorientation during this period. But although it would take ten years for him to integrate this learned style into his later keyboard works, from 1809 on we find subjects intended for fugal treatment scattered haphazardly throughout his sketchbooks. For a short time he even considered writing a complex fugue he called Monument to Bach, featuring "ever-shorter note values, right down to demi-semiquavers."[3]

The war of 1809 had taken its toll on Beethoven—mentally, physically, and most of all aurally. On July 26, he wrote to Breitkopf & Härtel complaining of "Such devastation and destruction all around . . . nothing but drums, cannons, and human suffering in all its forms." Several months later: "At last, some peace following the savage destruction, after all the unthinkable hardships we have endured."[4] The latter was a clear reference to the demolition of the defensive walls by the French, two days after the Treaty of Schönbrunn was signed on October 14. Just like the bombardment on May 11 and 12, the explosions must have been torture to Beethoven's hypersensitive ears.

Beethoven's hearing problem was clearly twofold. On the one hand, his "normal auditory capacity" was weakening. Indeed, Beethoven was clearly having greater and greater difficulty carrying on normal conversations. Louis Spohr attested that conversing with him was hard labor, requiring such loud bellowing that one could be heard three rooms away.[5] Many anecdotes also tell how his capacity as a performing musician, pianist, and composer was sorely impeded by his poor hearing, and that he came to rely more and more on his senses of sight and touch, with predictable outcomes. Far more painful, though, was the realization that while Beethoven was "hearing less and less," he became more and more sensitive to the noise that he *could* still hear, imagined or otherwise. In the summer of 1811, he noted in one of his sketchbooks, "Cotton in my ears dampens the sound of unpleasant crackling while at the piano."[6]

Beethoven thus had no choice but to try to escape the cacophony of war—an act that coincides rather symbolically with attempts to distance himself from the crossfire of the establishment. It is one of the most curious paradoxes of Beethoven's life that, precisely at one of the rare times when he chose to associate with the conservative powers-that-be, he abandoned his grand "heroic style" and sought out more small-scale yet robust forms of expression. The Fifth Piano Concerto (op. 73), which was drafted before the war and completed in the summer of 1809, represents the definitive end to this period.

Immediately afterward, he wrote a number of more introverted chamber works—first the String Quartet in E-flat Major (op. 74), nicknamed the *Harp,* and later the Fantasia in G Minor (op. 77), followed by the Piano Sonatas in F-sharp, G, and E-flat (opp. 78, 79, and 81a). These charming pieces are awash with intimate colors, contrasting starkly with the monumental and overbearing nature of his more "heroic" works. They are bathed in a lyrical ambience affording the free development of melody which, while tranquil and introverted, is nonetheless self-assured. Beethoven would never abandon this newfound sense of lyricism, and it would become a strong foundational pillar for his final works: the late piano sonatas and string quartets.

The *Harp* quartet, moreover, is the first work whose lyrical exterior leads an existence entirely separate from the underlying musical and compositional logic. While the broken triads characterize and provide the structural cohesion between the movements in this string quartet, they no longer determine the physiognomy of the themes themselves. No such discrepancy was evident in the *Eroica,* for example, where the superficial form of the themes and their motivic underpinnings were one and the same—the music's external and internal features were, in other words, congruent. In the opus 74 quartet, however, an underlying level of cohesion emerges which, while essential to the musical structure, is no longer relevant to the auditory experience and thus escapes the listener's attention. The presence of such deeply embedded structure is known to musicologists as "subthematicism."[7] It is a kind of musical straitjacket, donned voluntarily by composers to achieve greater freedom of expression, and is an important key to understanding Beethoven's late chamber works.

While the String Quartet in E-flat Major (op. 74) has a reputation as one of Beethoven's more accessible and conservative works, it also represents a profound turning point in his career as a composer. It carries within it the seeds of a new compositional offshoot, and for that reason—at least within the context of Beethoven's life—can be considered prophetic.

35

An Imperial Pupil

ARCHDUKE RUDOLPH PLAYED A PIVOTAL ROLE in the saga of the "accursed decree," and it was through his involvement that the initiative by Countess Erdődy and Gleichenstein was brought to a fruitful conclusion. More than once he acted as diplomat to resolve conflicts, exerting pressure on the two other benefactors to ensure they kept their word and offering Beethoven a refuge in times of crisis. Even after the financial situation had been resolved in 1815, the archduke—not least to further his own interests as the master's composition student—continued to give Beethoven his full support. We know, for example, that Archduke Rudolph financed Beethoven's holiday in Baden and that he acted as guarantor for some loans. He occasionally covered the costs for producing orchestral parts, made his rooms at the Hofburg available for rehearsals and concerts, and prevailed on the university rector for the use of his hall.[1] Archduke Rudolph was by far Beethoven's greatest sponsor and patron, and evidence of Beethoven's gratitude can be found in the long list of important works dedicated to him: the Fourth and Fifth piano concertos, the Piano Sonata in E-flat (op. 81a), the Violin Sonata in G Major (op. 96), the Piano Trio in B-flat (op. 97), the *Hammerklavier* Sonata (op. 106), the Piano Sonata in C Minor (op. 111), the *Grosse Fuge* for String Quartet, including its arrangement for piano four-hands (opp. 133 and 134), and of course the *Missa solemnis* (op. 123). No other aristocrat can boast such a record. The vast body of correspondence between the composer and his benefactor—one hundred letters of which have been preserved—also suggests a close bond. As one might expect, there is evidence of Beethoven having made "unofficial" scornful remarks about the archduke, but overall their contact was respectful and, to a certain degree, intimate. Rudolph was also the only aristocrat before whom Beethoven was known to grovel on occasion.

Like many of the Hapsburgs, Archduke Rudolph was hardly bursting with charisma. In all portraits ever painted of him, he is depicted with a dull, vacuous, and somewhat lachrymose expression. After losing his father at the age of four (the then emperor Leopold II), he was taken in and raised by his elder brother, the new emperor Francis II. He thus became grist for a pedagogical mill that had actually been designed to churn out crown princes destined to be emperors, and which was entirely unsuited to the needs of those on the lower rungs of the succession ladder. He prepared initially for a military career, but because of his poor health—he suffered from epilepsy and chronic rheumatism—he was later steered toward a position in the higher clergy and appointed coadjutor in Olmütz as a seventeen-year-old in 1805. But when Archbishop Anton Theodor von Colloredo died on September 12, 1811, leaving the road to succession wide open, Rudolph let the cup pass from him. It was then than Beethoven realized that he had made a gross miscalculation, as evidence suggests that the archduke had always promised to take him along as Kapellmeister to Olmütz.[2] Under the assumption that his benefactor would soon become the archbishop, or at the very least Prince-Primate of Hungary, Beethoven dropped everything on hearing of the incumbent's death, cut short his holiday in Teplitz, and sped to Vienna in readiness to assume his post and perhaps even start work on his *Missa solemnis*. Bitter was his disappointment when he heard that Rudolph's accession had been postponed indefinitely, and he wrote to Breitkopf & Härtel, "I have just heard the shocking report that our gracious ruler has abandoned all his plans for Popery and Primacy, and that the whole affair will come to naught."[3] For a time he even considered rescinding the dedication of the Sonata in E-flat that he had composed for the archduke (*Les Adieux,* op. 81a). Not until 1819 would Rudolph assume the post in Olmütz, by which time Beethoven was no longer fit for the duties of a Kapellmeister.

Rudolph's refusal to accede as archbishop in Olmütz in 1811 had nothing to do with a lack of religious conviction. Rather, at the age of twenty-three, the archduke did not yet feel ready to dedicate his life to such a high office, despite the fact that the position was not even full-time. Deep in his heart he was, after all, an artist; he had some skill as a painter and was an excellent pianist. He was also a reliable supporter of charitable musical initiatives, a cofounder of the Society of Friends of Music in Vienna (the Wiener Musikfreunde), as well as an avid collector of scores and books on musical subjects.[4] The claims of his pianism must of course be first denuded of their panegyric mantle; but anyone capable of performing Beethoven's piano concertos and holding their own alongside world-famous French violinist Rode in a performance of the demanding Violin Sonata in G Major (op. 96) cannot have been without talent.

It is unclear exactly when and where Archduke Rudolph first met Beethoven. Schindler posits a date as early as 1803/1804, when Beethoven was thought to have composed the Triple Concerto for the archduke; however, this theory has since been disproven.[5] A new hypothesis puts their first contact in 1808 at the Lobkowitz residence, after which Rudolph quickly expressed his desire to take composition lessons from Beethoven.[6] The aspiring pupil's high social status meant that Beethoven could hardly refuse, despite his total lack of experience—and interest—in teaching composition. The first lessons were delayed by a year, since the royal family fled to Pest on May 4, 1809, to escape the encroaching French armies. To mark the occasion, Beethoven gave his patron a parting gift, *Das Lebewohl* (The farewell) for piano. On the archduke's return in January 1810, he added two more sections—*Abwesenheit* (Absence) and *Das Wiedersehn* (The return)—forming a complete *sonate caractéristique* that was later published and released under the title *Les Adieux* (op. 81a).[7]

Beethoven was probably happy that Rudolph's lessons did not start straightaway, and made good use of the hiatus to prepare. During the summer of 1809, he selected and copied excerpts from the preeminent composition treatises of the day—by C. P. E. Bach, Daniel Gottlob Türk, Johann Philipp Kirnberger, Fux, and Albrechtsberger, for a total of over two hundred handwritten pages—with the intention of distilling the material into a course of his own.[8] It was this material that provided the theoretical basis for the archduke's lessons. Beethoven also returned to the tried and tested method of teaching by example: he had the archduke transcribe and arrange existing musical masterpieces, an exercise made all the easier by Rudolph's well-stocked library. Eventually the pupil lay his first attempts before the master, who set to work both intuitively and diplomatically. He first corrected the most glaring errors and followed up by suggesting more subtle changes, while always being sure to maintain a balance between praise and criticism. After some time, the archduke made his public debut as a composer. And like Beethoven, he did so with a set of variations: *Forty Variations on a Theme by Ludwig van Beethoven*. There were certain advantages to the fact that the short theme was from the master's own hand (it was a paraphrase of an earlier vocal setting of the ambiguous text "O Hoffnung" [O hope] from Tiedge's *Urania;* WoO 200). Nobody, after all, could more ably envisage the possibilities for variation than the theme's own creator, and there can be no doubt that Beethoven subtly but surely guided the composition process. He eventually also found a publisher and made sure to point out his own share in the enterprise: the title page of the 1819 edition—clearly stating that the theme was composed by Beethoven and that the variations were dedicated to him by his "pupil R.E.H."[9]—implies a social role reversal of the highest order. Financially dependent on his betters though he was, Beethoven left no doubt that when it came to music, he still firmly held the upper hand.

The *Forty Variations on a Theme by Ludwig van Beethoven* were simultaneously *première* and *dernière* for the archduke, representing both the climax and the conclusion of his career as a composer. Aside from a set of Variations for Clarinet and Piano, none of his other projects (including several religious works) ever made it past the drafting stage. In his defense, we should remember that the archduke was appointed archbishop in Olmütz immediately on completing his magnum opus, after which much of his time was divided between exercising the duties of his office and caring for his fragile health in various luxury spa towns.

The limited scope of the archbishop's oeuvre is in truth an inaccurate reflection of the time and effort invested in him by his famous teacher. To Beethoven, the lessons were time-consuming and exhausting—he always complained of such fatigue afterward that he was no longer able even to think, let alone compose. Etiquette also demanded that the teacher travel to the student, and an invitation (or more accurately, a summons) to spend several days at the imperial residence in Schönbrunn made serious inroads into Beethoven's time. It is hardly surprising, therefore, that Beethoven did all he could to wrest himself free of his honorable appointment, especially during its final stages. There are scores of letters from Beethoven to the archbishop offering flimsy excuses and apologies for his absence. If they are to be believed, then not only was Beethoven constantly and chronically ill but Vienna was in the midst of a climate catastrophe, and public transport was in a state of utter chaos.

Beethoven's hands were tied, however, especially after having renewed his promise in 1819 to compose a *Missa solemnis*—a work that would occupy him for four years while he strung his benefactor along with a litany of broken promises. The balance of power between Beethoven and his imperial student is illustrated by the patience exercised by the archbishop in anticipation of what would be the greatest reward for his years of support to the composer— but more on that later.

The archduke's tolerance of this treatment stemmed from his unwavering belief in Beethoven's great genius, which occasionally took on idolatrous proportions. In 1814, for example, he made his own transcription by hand of Beethoven's new Sonata in E Minor (op. 90), even going so far as to imitate Beethoven's handwriting and thus inhabit his teacher's compositional mindset as authentically as possible. When Beethoven died in 1827, Rudolph collected every article and notice that appeared in the newspapers and journals.

In the spring of 1809, when Beethoven signed the "decree," he also put the finishing touches on a new piano concerto, the Fifth Piano Concerto in E-flat (op. 73), which he dedicated (along with the Fourth) to his imperial composition pupil. Beethoven never performed the concerto himself before an audience. It was premiered—and to great acclaim—in November 1811 at the Gewandhaus in Leipzig by a certain Friedrich Schneider; the Viennese premiere followed in February 1812, featuring Carl Czerny as soloist. The latter performance enjoyed a lukewarm reception, though due in no way to the soloist and certainly not to the composition. Rather, the circumstances were at fault: the audience had gathered primarily for a society event—the opening of an art exhibition including works by Raphael and others—which was to be accompanied by a modest musical performance and a hearty drop of wine, all in support of a noble cause. By all accounts, the *Variations on "Aline"* by violin virtuoso Joseph Mayseder, which also graced the program, did find favor with the attendees.

The Fifth Piano Concerto, like its predecessor, had actually already been published many months prior to its public debut—first by Clementi in London in 1810, and by Breitkopf & Härtel in Leipzig in 1811. The true musical connoisseurs, Archduke Rudolph first and foremost, had thus had more than an ample opportunity to become familiar with the new score. The move was a continuation of the strategy employed for the fourth concerto, which originally was no longer intended for Beethoven's personal use. Beethoven was thus targeting not only professional concert pianists (such as Czerny) but also the more accomplished amateurs (such as Rudolph), a fact that was clearly evident in the printed piano part. Ordinarily, orchestral tutti passages were represented in piano scores by a cursory figured bass line, indicating the harmonic contours and allowing the soloist to follow the parts and play along if desired.[10] Now, however, these passages were given as a full piano reduction, so that amateur pianists at home could play through the entire concerto without an orchestra. What is more, Beethoven also had alternative versions of some passages printed that were either technically far less demanding or playable on smaller instruments with a limited range. The printed edition of the Fifth Piano Concerto also bore many more performance instructions such as articulation and pedal markings, and directions regarding timbre and expression. Nothing was left to chance. Even the cadenzas, which were traditionally left entirely to the soloist's discretion, were now fully written out to the very last note. To prevent any misunderstanding, at the end of the first movement—where a cadenza would normally be improvised—Beethoven includes the following clear warning: "Non si fa una Cadenza, ma s'attacca subito il seguente" (Do not play a cadenza here, but continue on immediately).

Beethoven appears to have had little confidence in the talent of modern pianists. Several years later, in 1814, he would speak to Bohemian pianist and composer Johann Wenzel Tomaschek of how greatly he feared pianists with too little knowledge of composition and who, according to him, would simply "run up and down the keyboard with nothing but meaningless, memorised clichés."[11] Beethoven wished to safeguard his music against the offenses of such pianists and thus introduced a new musical schism between the creative act of composition and the postcreative act of interpretation. Until that time, the solo concerto had been not so much a vehicle for dazzling displays of technique or virtuosity, but rather one for feats of imagination and surprise. The "unexpected" was Beethoven's specialty and was initially what had allowed him to stand out as a concert pianist and make his way to the top. By contrast, in his Fifth Piano Concerto Beethoven straps the soloist down, eliminating the natural tension between unpredictable and accidental elements on the one hand, and predetermined and definitive elements on the other. The concerto thus attained the status of an "artwork," whose substance took on a separate, more elevated hierarchical identity that transcended the incidental nature of individual performances. The score thus ceased to be a guidebook and instead became a script.

By thus satisfying the appetites of amateur pianists, Beethoven expanded his target audience appreciably. He also continued to cater to the needs of modern concert pianists, however, who demanded a piano sound to match their copious egos and wished to captivate their audiences from the very outset—it is no coincidence that this concerto, flying in the face of tradition, opens with a brilliant and extended cadenza. Beethoven also invites the soloist to explore the rich timbral spectrum between piano and pianissimo to an unprecedented degree, demanding a highly refined piano technique. (The orchestra's palette is enriched in a similar fashion, which is why this concerto only really comes into its own with an *Eroica* instrumentation. The other piano concertos require no such forces.)

The rather "heroic" tone of the Fifth Piano Concerto is what gave rise to the nickname that it acquired in England—the *Emperor* Concerto—which was later translated into German as *Kaiserkonzert*. Not only is this epithet a testament to poor taste (though precisely which emperor is being referenced remains unknown), but it also reinforces the cliché of a certain "Germanness" in Beethoven's works and serves to eclipse the work's true virtues: its innovations in the field of concert pianism.

No sooner had Beethoven completed the Fifth Piano Concerto than he began writing out the cadenzas for the other four. Although he was chiefly prompted to do so by a request from Archduke Rudolph, it is clear that this decision (which, again, essentially contradicted the traditional improvisational character of the cadenza) fits within the new concept that Beethoven envisaged for his concertos.

The cadenzas have since become so established that there is hardly a pianist alive who would dare to play anything else. An enormous stylistic chasm also gapes between Beethoven's earliest piano concertos and their associated cadenzas, which were conceived much later. The second concerto makes for a particular roller-coaster ride, as listeners and interpreters alike are jerked back and forth between the Mozartian style of the concerto body and the *Appassionata* character of the cadenzas, eliciting simultaneous feelings of euphoria and disorientation.

36

Beethoven and Goethe

WITH THE FRENCH OCCUPATION UNDERWAY, Beethoven spent most of the summer of 1809 in Vienna instead of the countryside. As previously mentioned, he took advantage of this circumstance by conducting research in preparation for his lessons with Archduke Rudolph. He also read a great deal in order to work through the literature backlog that he had amassed during the preceding years of fervent compositional activity. Beethoven immersed himself in a wide range of cultural and historical topics and developed a particular fascination for writings from Greek and Roman antiquity. The teachings of the era were very important to him, and he set high standards for himself; on November 22, 1809, in a letter to Breitkopf & Härtel, he wrote that it had been his mission since childhood to "seek an understanding of the wisest and most exemplary figures from all eras," and that any artist should feel ashamed who felt no deep obligation to do so.[1]

That same summer, Beethoven received an official letter from the Royal Netherlands Institute of Sciences, Literature and Fine Arts, announcing that he had been elected as one of the illustrious organization's "corresponding members." The appointment entailed neither obligations nor rewards, and its significance was thus chiefly symbolic. Still, Beethoven—who had scarcely even attended primary school—felt particularly flattered by such a high academic distinction. It was one that he shared with renowned musicians and writers such as Johann Friedrich Reichardt and Friedrich Rochlitz and which he happily broadcasted at every opportunity.

Several weeks later, he received another invitation that he recognized immediately as a potential stepping-stone to realizing his long-cherished desire to meet one of the greatest intellectuals of his day, Johann Wolfgang von Goethe. The invitation was a commission to compose the incidental music to

Goethe's stage play *Egmont*. The management of the Hoftheater had elected to ride the wave of nationalistic sentiment in Vienna and planned to stage two productions centering on the people's rebellion against foreign occupation: Schiller's *William Tell*, and Goethe's *Egmont*. Generous funding had been made available, lubricating significant investments not only in costumes, scenery, and professional direction but also in new music. Two eminent composers—Beethoven and the Kapellmeister of the Hoftheater, Adalbert Gyrowetz, were granted the privilege. It is unclear why Beethoven was chosen for Goethe and Gyrowetz for Schiller, but Beethoven later declared that he had composed his *Egmont* music out of love for the poet and for that reason had requested no payment. In reality, his motives were probably slightly more complex, as Beethoven is reported to have said, among other things, that Goethe's texts were more music-friendly; *Egmont*'s setting in Flanders—the land of Beethoven's forebears—means that nostalgic arguments cannot be entirely refuted either. The fact that the work's eponymous hero was put to death on precisely the spot where, thirty years later, Beethoven's five-times-great-grandmother would also be executed, is another seductive (but completely unfounded) theory as to why his choice may have fallen to *Egmont*.

In *Egmont*, Goethe tells the tragic tale of the Flemish *stadholder* who led a snowballing resistance movement against the occupying Spanish forces. Unlike his northern counterpart William of Orange (who saw little point in negotiating with new custodian Alva, and instead fled to Germany), Egmont remained in Brussels in an effort to reach a compromise with the oppressors. This decision ultimately led to his downfall, when he was wrongfully incarcerated and sentenced to death for high treason. After a futile attempt by his beloved Claire (Klärchen) to mobilize the populace to rescue him, she poisons herself. Shortly before his execution, Egmont experiences a vision of Claire prophesying that Flanders will one day be liberated.

It is entirely conceivable that the Viennese sympathized with Egmont, not least because the Flemish rebellion was motivated by ideological considerations similar to their own. It was not so much the act of occupation but rather the Spanish oppressors' desire to impose a new social order and limit the powers of the privileged upper classes that incited their rebellion. The Viennese nobility in particular were well acquainted with this notion, as well as with Egmont's constant tendency to vacillate between lofty political discourse on the one hand, and his own base, private opportunism on the other. But despite these very relatable themes, the work failed to gain purchase. Goethe's contemporary, Schiller, had already pointed out the weaknesses of the tragedy in a review in the Jena-based *Allgemeine Literatur-Zeitung*. According to Schiller, *Egmont* was nothing more than a dreary succession of anecdotes and static tableaux, without any intrigue or dramatic structure and manifestly lacking any sense of depth in the main characters—Egmont is certainly no Macbeth, Richard III, or Götz von Berlichingen. Schiller wrote that Egmont is a typical Flemish hero, one who refuses to let the injustices of the world rob him of his complacency and who enjoys his food and drink too much to be capable of true passion. His goals may be ambitious and lofty, but they do not stop him from seeking to fulfill his many personal—and often physical—desires. Again, according to Schiller, the Flemish Egmont differs from the cool and calculating William of Orange through his naïve confidence in both himself and others. Egmont believes that everything will work out fine in the end, and it is for this reason that he cannot choose between resistance and collaboration. Schiller sees a similar two-dimensionality in Claire, a beautiful but innocent middle-class girl whose sole purpose is to embody the promise of a utopian freedom at the play's conclusion. A promise is, in the end, all the Flemish are left with—unlike the Swiss, who are genuinely rescued by William Tell. So while Egmont and Claire may elicit some sympathy and occasionally compassion, Schiller believes that their tribulations are simply too weak to carry a full evening of theater.[2] As a Flemish expert, Schiller took his cue from these conclusions, and in his *Don Carlos,* which shares *Egmont*'s timeline exactly, the eponymous role is given to a Spaniard with Austrian roots.

For Beethoven, it would have been very out of character had he not tried to improve the play's cohesion through his music. As was customary, he was expected to provide an overture, several ariettas, four entr'actes, and a finale. But in addition to these, he also furnished music for the key dramatic scenes: Claire's death and the vision of Egmont, who falls into a delirium similar to Florestan's in *Fidelio*'s dungeon scene. Beethoven also heightened the drama by deploying the full arsenal of motivic and thematic developmental techniques, making all of the fragments interconnected and providing an impetus to propel the drama forward. Whereas the entr'actes composed by most of his colleagues were empty intermezzi whose main purpose was to provide auditory distraction during the scene changes, Beethoven's transitions offered a deeper and more interpretive commentary. The impression thus emerges that the drama's principal development occurs during these very interludes; Beethoven's sketchbooks testify to both the tremendous effort he put into the entr'actes as well as the obvious importance he assigned to them. The same applies to Claire's two ariettas, which also transcend the ordinary melo-drama style. For one thing, Beethoven took kind consideration of actress Antonie Adamberger's limited vocal technique. (Much later she would recount how Beethoven first tested her musical abilities and was charmed by her uncultivated, somewhat throaty voice. Three days later he brought her the two ariettas, patiently rehearsed them with her due to her inability to read music, and afterward implored her never to be dissuaded by anyone from her own rather idiosyncratic interpretation.[3]) At the same time, he composed a rich and complex orchestral accompaniment that even included references to the other musical items, elevating Claire's personality to a higher dramatic echelon. As the story goes, when a heckler in the hall called out that such songs were only supposed to have guitar accompaniment, a good-humored Beethoven—most likely under the spell of the beautiful actress—turned and quipped in response, "Well now, this gentleman clearly knows what he's talk-ing about!"[4] E. T. A. Hoffmann, however—who certainly did know what he was talking about—criticized Beethoven's failure to observe the stylistic dif-ferences between genres, and held that the character of the *Egmont* music was too operatic.

As with *The Creatures of Prometheus* ten years before, Beethoven had over-stepped his compositional mandate and delivered work that was both dispro-portionate and dysfunctional. The writing itself also took far longer than had been anticipated, with the now all-too-familiar consequence: rather than sharing its debut with the play—on May 24, 1810—the music instead pre-miered during the fourth performance on June 15. That it never found broad public acceptance thereafter is due in part to the complex reception history of the play itself. The music's close interconnectedness with the drama also made it unviable as independent concert music.[5] Most fragments are open-ended and dissolve seamlessly into the following scene—an extremely effec-tive dramaturgical device but simply unworkable in a concert context. Breitkopf & Härtel pointed this out to Beethoven immediately, urging him to compose alternate endings, but the entreaty elicited only a brusque, sarcas-tic reply: "If you wish to clamp endings onto the *entr'actes* here and there, be my guest. But you are welcome to enlist one of your Leipzig music correctors for the task; I have no doubt they will do an excellent job."[6]

Egmont would not be Beethoven's last foray into incidental music. One year later he received an invitation to compose a celebratory work for the opening of the new imperial theater in Pest. In truth, the offer could not have come at a worse time, for Beethoven was desperately in need of rest and his personal physician, Dr. Johann Malfatti, had urged him to spend several months recuperating in Italy. Beethoven lacked the means to finance such a luxurious escape, and so for the first time in his life he spent the summer in the nearby Bohemian spa town of Teplitz. A similar effort had been interrupted one year before (when he had rushed to Vienna in anticipation of Archduke Rudolph's accession), and this year, too, his plans were potentially threatened by the lucrative commission from Pest, which arrived the day before his scheduled departure on August 1. But despite the tight timeline (the new theater was due to open during the emperor's name-day celebrations on October 4), Beethoven felt he could not let the offer slide. He accepted the commission and decided first to take three weeks' rest in Teplitz regardless.

The opportunity in Pest was a prestigious one. For the text, popular German poet August von Kotzebue had been approached to provide a treatment of an episode from Hungary's history, along with the usual abundance of imperial praise.[7] He was expected to design nothing short of an extravaganza, including spectacular scene changes and stunning visual effects to put the theater's new technical capabilities on fine display. Kotzebue originally proposed a theatrical triptych: *Hungary's First Protector (King Stephan)*, *Béla's Escape*, and *The Ruins of Athens*. The central component was quickly ruled out, however, due to its precarious associations with the Austrian royal family's own recent lack of heroism during the war of 1809.

Beethoven's duty was to compose nineteen separate musical items, totaling over ninety minutes of music. Despite the limited timeframe—and contrary to all expectations—he actually succeeded in meeting his deadline and on September 13 proudly announced that he had sent off the scores with the post. The premiere's postponement until February 9, 1812, thus had nothing whatsoever to do with any tardiness on Beethoven's part but was attributable to incomplete construction work on the building itself.

Paradoxically enough, it was the very shortage of time that led to Beethoven's timely success. Because he had not been afforded the luxury of overcontemplation (as opposed to the *Egmont* commission), he was forced to comply with the prevailing limitations and expectations and to rein himself in across the board. He created short and compact pieces based on themes that were simply structured and occasionally cliché, sought effective contrasts, and sacrificed convoluted motivic treatment and thematic development for a mixed assortment of pleasing melodies. He drew heavily from material he had composed over the previous twenty years, and the attentive listener to *King Stephan* and *The Ruins of Athens* will recognize fragments from *Leonore,* the *Mount of Olives,* and even the Imperial cantatas from his Bonn years. It is precisely this potpourri approach that makes the music sound so incredibly spontaneous and uncontrived, at times even imparting a Schubertian charm. It nonetheless remains incontrovertibly Beethovenian, with violent contrasts between brilliant fortes and extreme pianissimos, glorious lyricism in the choral and hymnic writing, and exuberant final orchestral tuttis. And of course, parody and sarcasm are never far away, abundant opportunities for which are provided by the presence of the hostile and culturally threatening Turkish, whose musical representation by Beethoven is more cacophonic than symphonic.

Despite these many charms, *King Stephan* and *The Ruins of Athens* still bear the hallmarks of their incidental nature, and except for a reprise of *The Ruins of Athens* at the opening of the Josephstädter Theater in Vienna in October 1822,[8] they have all but vanished from the concert repertoire, never quite surmounting the prejudice that "quick Beethoven" must, by definition, be "bad Beethoven."

The completion of Beethoven's work on *King Stephan* and *The Ruins of Athens* coincided with the end of his holiday in Teplitz. En route back to Vienna, Beethoven took a detour via Lichnowsky's castle in Grätz to oversee the rehearsals and performance of his Mass in C. His confrontation with the harsh reality of day-to-day music practice could not have been more brutal: Lichnowsky had recruited his entire household for the ambitious project, resulting in a musicians' collective of mixed ability. One extreme and hilarious case was that of Lichnowsky's physical instructor, who had been entrusted with the timpani part and was so inexperienced that Beethoven had to teach him the solo in the *Sanctus* beat by beat, note for note. But Beethoven, well rested and relaxed from his time in Teplitz, remained unruffled, and after the performance he conceded to a general request by those present—to their great enjoyment—by improvising for half an hour on the organ.[9]

On or around October 1, Beethoven returned to the familiar surroundings of the Pasqualati house in Vienna. It was there that he began work on his Seventh Symphony and on what was originally conceived as a new piano concerto but later became the Eighth Symphony.

While Beethoven thus spent half of his Teplitz holiday working, it is doubtful whether it did him any harm. As a somewhat socially inept and more cerebrally (rather than physically) oriented nonconformist, Beethoven found the Bohemian baths hardly the ideal environment to relax and find inner calm. For centuries, the ill and disabled of every stripe—including the hearing-impaired—had flocked to Bohemian spa towns in the hope that the salty, alkaline qualities of the local spring waters would cure (or at least alleviate) their suffering. The hope that towns such as Karlsbad and Teplitz would offer relief from acute maladies was based on old medieval tales of emperors and kings, who attributed their salvation to the healing powers of the mysterious waters bubbling up from the depths. The early-nineteenth-century summer clientele who frequented Karlsbad, Teplitz, and the new Maria and Franz baths included not only the higher aristocrats but also large numbers of nouveaux-riches, from Russia and Poland in particular. Although the luxury spa therapies offered the greatest benefits to sufferers of rheumatism, gout, and sciatica, most visitors came with digestive complaints; that is to say, they suffered the consequences of an indulgent lifestyle involving too much alcohol and fatty food. The largest demographic, however, were the snobs who visited the baths for the annual rendezvous of the rich—a refined society ritual with wellness as a pretext.

In 1759 and 1793, Karlsbad and Teplitz had respectively both burned to the ground, after which the authorities took advantage of the opportunity to give the towns a thorough facelift and provide a suitable decor. Infrastructure was reconceptualized to serve the cities' core business: the streets were paved, night lighting installed, colonnades built around the springs, and new hotels established, including exclusive boutiques and small souvenir shops. Transport connections to and from Prague were also improved. Generally the weather was fair, with sunshine and clear skies, and the permanent presence of water meant that temperatures, though high, were never oppressive. Despite the many tourists, the hustle and bustle was more lively than hectic, due in part to the more relaxed social etiquette. The dress code was less prescriptive; ladies were permitted to wear more comfortable, loose-fitting clothing; and while gentlemen still always wore a hat, they were exempt from mandatory glove wearing. Carrying a dagger was strictly forbidden.

But even the unconventional behavior typical of fashionable holiday destinations is subject to the stringency of social controls. In Karlsbad and Teplitz, with feigned spontaneity and enthusiasm, the tourists followed a strict and rigorous daily program, from which nobody dared deviate. Mornings were devoted exclusively to bathing and the consumption of medicinal beverages, the latter being anything but a pleasure; the spring water was horribly bitter, making cod-liver oil seem like a delicacy, and the most intensive prescribed treatments stipulated twenty cups per day. As a wind ensemble provided "pleasant background music," the guests would slowly revolve around the colonnade like ponies on a carousel. On arriving at the entrance to the spring, they presented their cup to one of the white-clad maidens, who would graciously refill it. After imbibing the substance—and making facial contortions to rival those of Hieronymus Bosch—they resumed their strolling orbit until they once again arrived at the spring, where their cup was filled once more. This parade continued until noon. After lunch, which was usually a modest affair, the guests would socialize by taking communal walks or converging in the coffeehouses. Dinners, by contrast, were lavish affairs followed by parties and dances in the locale's exclusive salons. Cultural events were organized now and again but were nothing to write home about—it is known, for example, that Lobkowitz took part in several theater productions.

The social goings-on at the resorts were therefore just as important as their therapeutic value. Everybody was under constant surveillance, and the tiniest shifts in the social sands gave rise to the most overblown commentary. At one time, Vienna even saw the publication of a tabloid—*Strudel*—that included paparazzi-style reports on celebrity comings and goings in Karlsbad and Teplitz. Most of the guests were only too happy to put themselves through this grisly social wringer, the privilege of which was considered a status symbol in itself.

The mind boggles when attempting to slot Beethoven into this picture. At the very least, we can surmise that he belonged to the minority of patients for whom health resorts actually did more harm than good. His various letters to Breitkopf & Härtel sent from Teplitz and Franzensbrunn leave no doubt as to his own lack of confidence in any physical benefits. And although he meticulously followed his doctor's orders—from his "Aesculapius," as he put it—he did so under extreme duress: "I must go and splash around in the water again. Hardly have I filled my insides with a decent quantity than I am required to drench my outsides with the same."[10] The "Muzak" played in the colonnades, furthermore, must have driven him half mad, and the booming chatter of the indoor baths have tortured his poor ears—ordinary conversation was often more than he could bear, let alone hours of reverberating small talk.

We do know that he met a number of fascinating individuals, with whom he shared many pleasant moments: the poet couple Christoph August Tiedge and Elisabeth von der Recke; German diplomat Karl August Varnhagen von

Ense and his strikingly beautiful and eccentric love (and later wife) Rahel Levin; lawyer and concert organizer from Graz, Joseph von Varena; and the young singer from Berlin, Amalie Sebald. As a rule, though, Beethoven gave the baths' bustling social scene a wide berth. Only once did he seek out the spotlight: during his second visit to the Bohemian springs in the summer of 1812, Beethoven collaborated with Italian violin virtuoso Giovanni Battista Polledro on a benefit concert held in Karlsbad, in support of the victims of the great fire in Baden. Beethoven was a loyal patron of the tiny resort town to the south of Vienna and had many acquaintances there. The catastrophic blaze that engulfed the city on July 26—destroying the town hall, church, school, ballroom, theater, and the homes of 117 ordinary citizens—must have grieved him deeply. Despite the marked drop in visitors to Karlsbad because of the war, the concert raised nearly one thousand guilders.[11]

That same summer of 1812 was when the two behemoths of German culture—Goethe and Beethoven—met for the first time. Goethe was a regular at Karlsbad and Teplitz and, unlike Beethoven, thoroughly enjoyed moving with deftness and grace amid the nineteenth-century beau monde. He relished the attention to be garnered from the holidaymakers, many of whom had avidly studied his newly published *Theory of Colours*. The empress Maria Ludovika of Austria-Este, the third wife of Emperor Francis I, was one of his most devoted acolytes, and the sixty-three-year-old womanizing Goethe objected little to her attentions. During that summer of 1812, Goethe and Maria Ludovika spent time together daily—officially, according to the great poet, to give the originally Italian empress some recommendations for what to read in German. In the cafés and bathhouses, however, there were sneers about ulterior motives.[12] Goethe himself would later reflect nostalgically and with affection on these meetings with the young empress.

Beethoven thus found Goethe in good spirits. He had dreamed of being able to shake the hand of his "classical" German literary idol, and the wait had been long. After completing *Egmont* in 1810, Beethoven had made further overtures of his own to Goethe, enlisting the help of go-between Bettina Brentano. Sensing her chance to earn a place in history, she switched into overdrive and visited Goethe in Teplitz in August 1810 armed with Beethoven's Three Songs (op. 83), which he had composed specially for the occasion. Although Goethe generally kept his correspondence in good order, on this occasion he failed to congratulate or even thank Beethoven for his gesture. The cause of this oversight is usually attributed to the opinions of his friend Carl Friedrich Zelter, a composer and music scholar from Berlin on whom Goethe relied utterly when it came to matters of music (his ears were infinitely less perceptive than his eyes). Zelter was a disciple of the old ways and swore by the values of traditional craftsmanship, an attitude that held great appeal for Goethe. Needless to say, Zelter did not hold Beethoven in terribly high esteem. He believed that his music was the product of a "masculine mother and a feminine father," and compared his adherents to those of "Greek love."[13] It is therefore entirely possible that Zelter's views lay at the basis of Goethe's unresponsiveness to Beethoven's latest song cycle.

A more likely cause for the communication problems between Beethoven and Goethe was the disintegration of the relationship between Goethe and Bettina Brentano (as described earlier). Because Beethoven had thus lost his "ambassador," in April 1811 he had no choice but to take matters into his own hands. He wrote an exalted and submissive letter, expressing his great admiration for the master poet and his hope that Goethe might be so gracious as to permit an audience. Beethoven had the letter delivered personally by his new secretary, Franz Oliva,[14] who returned to Goethe multiple times over the ensuing days and once even performed several of Beethoven's songs at the piano. Contemporary accounts tell how Goethe paid hardly any attention but rather was far more interested in the remarks of the other guests concerning his art collection. In reply, he did have Oliva relay that he was certainly interested in hearing Beethoven's *Egmont* music and that he looked forward to welcoming him in Weimar, an intention that he confirmed in a beautifully written letter to Beethoven some weeks later. He even claimed that he would be honored to introduce Beethoven to several of the city's important dignitaries.[15]

The coveted meeting with Goethe would not come about until the summer of 1812, when Beethoven heard on July 14 that Goethe had been spotted in Teplitz. In a letter to Breitkopf & Härtel dated July 17, he wrote, "Goethe is here."[16] Two days later, the historic rendezvous took place between these two artistic giants. They met again almost every day thereafter, taking walks together as well as a boat trip on the Bílina, and there was at least one evening when Beethoven improvised for Goethe at the piano. On July 27, Beethoven left for Karlsbad—the precise date on which an unsuspecting Bettina Brentano arrived in Teplitz. How enraged she must have been to discover that she had so narrowly missed the tantalizing opportunity to witness their historic meetings! Beethoven and Goethe crossed paths once more in

September—it was to be their final encounter. All sources indicate that they never corresponded again after that, with one exception: many years later, in February 1823, Beethoven asked Goethe to plead with the Grand Duke of Saxony to become a backer for the publication of the *Missa solemnis.* There was no reply from Weimar.[17]

Clearly, the two gentlemen never truly "hit it off." Goethe undeniably held Beethoven in high esteem and wrote home to his wife, "Never before have I met an artist who is so resolute, so energetic, so earnest."[18] To Zelter, however, he noted that Beethoven was "sadly a very wild personality, and although he is not wrong in finding the world a detestable place, this attitude certainly does nothing to make it a better one, either for himself or others." To mitigate his criticism somewhat, he added, "He is to be excused and pitied, however, for the fact that his hearing is abandoning him, an impediment which, in his case, may present more social difficulties than musical ones."[19] Beethoven, in turn, wrote, "Goethe is too fond of the air at court, more than is beseeming for a poet."[20]

While their considerable age difference certainly cannot have helped (Goethe could have been Beethoven's father), more relevant was the fact that both were the products of different times and different worlds. Goethe was a man of the eighteenth century, with an unshakable belief in a hierarchical society, evinced by his efforts to seek favor and approval from the epicenters of power. Beethoven was a "new age" man, devoted to the primacy of the individual, unwilling to submit to the authority of the establishment, and who spurned the style and etiquette of the old elite. This contrast is illustrated perfectly by an incident that supposedly took place on the cobblestoned avenues of Teplitz on Sunday, July 26, and which has since become one of the classics in the Beethoven literature. While on a walk together, Goethe and Beethoven encountered the empress and her extended retinue, which included Archduke Rudolph. Goethe stood aside, removing his hat and bowing his head deeply in a gesture of respect. Beethoven, on the other hand, remained patently steadfast in the middle of the road, forcing the imperial retinue to make a wide circle around him—much to the embarrassment of Goethe, who was then subjected to a Beethovenian diatribe on the hierarchy of people and values in society. Although there are doubts as to the veracity of this tale (the primary source is Bettina Brentano), it not only serves to illustrate the divergent social outlooks of Goethe and Beethoven, but it also exposes the paradox that Beethoven—thanks to his royal pupil Rudolph, and despite his relative indifference to God and religious command—nonetheless enjoyed a level of personal intimacy with the imperial court that trumped Goethe's wildest dreams. And if the incident with the empress was not embarrassing enough, Beethoven also had the audacity to brag of it to any who were willing to listen. This too undoubtedly frustrated Goethe a great deal.

Goethe and Beethoven were also cut from entirely different cognitive cloth. Whereas Goethe took possession of thoughts, associations, and images, these were notions by which Beethoven was, himself, possessed. Goethe's formulations were correspondingly more refined and circumspect and always contained their own mitigating, contrasting perspective. Beethoven did precisely the opposite, magnifying his thoughts beyond all proportion and leaving little room for doubt or interpretation. Not only as thinkers but also as artists, Beethoven and Goethe were worlds apart. Goethe was a generalist with a panoramic lens and seemed able to flit effortlessly from one discipline to another. He might write further on his *Faust* one day, then study human anatomy the next, then philosophize on the nature of color in art. This artistic versatility suggested a certain arbitrariness, for while all disciplines were equally important and interesting, none of them thus seemed essential. To Beethoven this was the hallmark of an amateur. He himself was the prototypical modern artist: specialized, monolithic (and occasionally monomaniacal), dynamic and idealistic, insatiable and uncompromising, restless and obsessive. These two worlds were clearly destined to collide. And though we can only speculate on what might have happened if Beethoven had met the *other* towering figure of German literature—Friedrich Schiller—the likelihood seems far greater that they would have formed a closer and more immediate bond.

37

The Immortal Beloved

EPISODE THREE

IN MANY BIOGRAPHIES, BEETHOVEN'S ENCOUNTERS with Goethe in the summer of 1812 are eclipsed by a rather more cataclysmic event that took place on the evening of July 3, 1812. The dramatic and passionate character of this incident speaks far more to the imagination and is documented in a three-part letter—the infamous "Letter to the Immortal Beloved"—that was written by Beethoven in the days thereafter. The letter's importance is underscored by the fact that it was found, together with the Heiligenstadt Testament, as part of his estate after his death. This fact alone has afforded both the document and its import a legendary significance.

En route to Teplitz, Beethoven stopped in Prague on July 1 to attend to an urgent matter: to meet with Kinsky and come to definitive terms regarding the "accursed decree." The road to this negotiation had been paved by the efforts of German diplomat and man of letters Karl August Varnhagen von Ense, whose acts of heroism during the war of 1809 had earned him some standing among the nobility. Beethoven had met Varnhagen during his previous summer holiday in Teplitz; they became good friends, and briefly there was even talk of them writing a new opera together. In the interest of full disclosure, it should be added that Beethoven was particularly enamored of Varnhagen's love interest, Rahel Levin; she was the only one he was still prepared to play for, on the condition that she spoke of it to no one. Beethoven's excessive interest in Rahel would later lead to a falling out with Varnhagen.[1]

Varnhagen lived in Prague, making him the perfect go-between in the dealings with Kinsky. On June 9, 1812, he announced triumphantly to Beethoven that the matter had been resolved over dinner at his residence. Kinsky had given the order to pay out the agreed sum plus interest in the new

Währung, and Beethoven was invited to call on Kinsky for the necessary papers and an advance of sixty ducats so that he might at least enjoy his holiday.[2] Beethoven met with Kinsky on the morning of Friday, July 3, and had arranged to visit Varnhagen that evening to thank him for his assistance in the matter. He never made it. It took him until July 14 to write a letter offering his apologies, in which he also made vague promises to provide more detailed explanations later.[3]

On the early evening of that third of July, Beethoven left his hotel, The Black Steed (Zum schwarzen Ross) on Alter Allee, and was on his way to see Varnhagen, when he chanced unexpectedly upon a woman who over the ensuing hours would become his "immortal beloved." Beethoven had evidently known the lady—and been in love with her—for some time. Needless to say, there is no official record detailing the events that transpired that night, but from the voluminous letter composed by Beethoven over the ensuing days we can infer that the encounter was of such a passionate nature that he "forgot" about his date with Varnhagen. The identity of the "immortal beloved" has, alas, never been conclusively proven. From the famous letter we can ascertain that it was a lady with whom Beethoven had shared an amorous history and that she was also married, which seemed to preclude any official relationship with him.[4] Her marriage also seemed to be in jeopardy, however, leaving both her and Beethoven free to express and partake of their mutual affections.

For nearly two centuries, there has been speculation as to the identity of the "immortal beloved." Beethoven expert Marie-Elisabeth Tellenbach, who has conducted extensive research on the subject, sees Josephine von Brunsvik as the primary candidate.[5] Josephine meets all of the above criteria: she had known Beethoven since 1799 and had enjoyed an intimate friendship with him between 1804 and 1807, after which she entered into a second marriage, which had all but fallen apart in the meantime. There is no hard evidence that Josephine was in Prague in early July 1812, but there is no proof to the contrary either.[6] In the diaries of the eldest Brunsvik sister, Therese—which constitute the primary source materials documenting the activities of the Brunsviks—the pages pertaining to these dates have been destroyed, giving rise to the wildest of speculations. One compromising fact is that on April 8, 1813, Josephine gave birth to her seventh child, a daughter, who—if carried to full term—would have been conceived around July 3, 1812, a time when its legal parents were for all intents and purposes separated. Josephine gave her youngest daughter a fitting name, Minona, which in reverse reads Anonim,

German for "anonymous." Josephine Brunsvik-Deym-Stackelberg knew her literature: in the cult classic *The Sorrows of Young Werther,* Werther himself reads a passage from *The Poems of Ossian* to Lotte—with whom Josephine could identify only too well—making mention of a certain Minona, "the daughter of a Celtic singer." In her memoirs, Therese also confessed that her niece and foster child Minona had a more robust build than the other Stackelberg children, as well as "the most gifted intellect." There are even indications of some musical talent . . .[7]

Recent research by Rita Steblin has provided additional support for the hypothesis that Josephine is indeed the "immortal beloved." On the basis of available evidence, Steblin has made the following reconstruction of events. On June 9, 1812, Josephine sent her husband packing—not with immediate divorce in mind but rather to acquire a greater degree of independence within her marriage. She understood, however, that in return for the custody of her six children and some mental freedom and peace of mind, she had also shouldered full financial responsibility for her entire family—hardly a trivial matter given her real estate troubles in Moravia. She therefore traveled to Prague in early July in the hopes that her brother-in-law and his wife (the Deym-Goltzes) could alleviate her most pressing financial needs. At the same time, she hoped for a brief audience with the emperor, who she had heard was sojourning in Prague with his entire household on their return from a congress in Dresden. We remember that when Josephine's first husband, Joseph Deym, died in 1804, the emperor had generously pledged his ongoing support, and Josephine felt that the time had come to remind him of his promise. The legal proceedings with the Trauttmansdorff family concerning her property in Moravia were also still underway, and she knew enough members of the imperial court whom she could call on to lobby for a just outcome on her behalf. Sadly, the emperor had already left for Karlsbad on July 1; Josephine briefly considered following him there but ultimately decided against it—due, Steblin argues, to the events on the night of July 3.[8]

If so, the following scenario in Prague emerges. As always, Josephine lodged with her brother-in-law's family on Neuer Allee—an extension of Alter Allee, where Beethoven was staying. Neither was aware that their accommodations were in such close proximity, and when Josephine went out to "take a turn" on the evening of July 3, she unexpectedly ran into Beethoven, who was on his way to see Varnhagen. They had been avoiding each other completely since 1807; only in 1809 was their correspondence briefly revived when they cautiously exchanged pleasantries. All communication channels had been cut off on Josephine's marriage to Stackelberg in 1810, but Beethoven—who maintained close contact with Josephine's brother Franz— knew full well that she was experiencing marital difficulties. The surprise nature of their encounter served only to heighten its emotional intensity, and because Josephine and her husband had effectively been separated for several weeks (legally the matter was far from resolved, but psychologically and morally she considered herself a divorced woman), any barriers of hesitation or guilt were quickly overcome.

Naturally, we can only guess as to the exact course of events that night. We might safely assume, however, that Beethoven and Josephine at the very least talked and that one topic of discussion was their potential future together. The Letter to the Immortal Beloved indicates that Beethoven strongly urged Josephine—one might almost say he gave the order—to spend the rest of her life with him and to set divorce proceedings in motion: "I must either share my life entirely with you, or not at all." Of course, he realized that the procedure could be a lengthy one and that he would need to keep a respectful distance in the meantime. This was a sacrifice he was willing to make.

Their parting must have been heartrending. Beethoven promised to write to her soon, and Josephine gave him her favorite pencil as a pledge—a keepsake which, according to the conventions of the day, was almost tantamount to an engagement ring. Beethoven left for Teplitz the following day; for reasons unknown, rather than taking the usual easterly road via Budin, the coachman instead chose the far more treacherous western route via Louny and Bílina. The consequences were disastrous: the journey took nearly twenty-four hours, and the constant downpour made the unpaved roads all but impassable—the post chaise even broke one of its wheels. Beethoven did not arrive in Teplitz until four in the morning and found temporary accommodation at The Golden Sun (Zur goldnen Sonne). He could not check into The Oak (Zur Eiche) until the next day. It was there that he took Josephine's pencil and, in three sittings, composed a heartfelt confession to the woman who would thenceforth be known as his "immortal beloved."

Beethoven clearly wrote the Letter to the Immortal Beloved in an intensely emotional state; the language is impassioned, the thoughts erratic. As with the Heiligenstadt Testament, multiple rhetorical levels are interlaced with one another, alternating between internal and external observations, rational considerations and heartfelt outpourings. Beethoven is simultaneously hopeful and fearful. He hopes that his beloved will not desert him again (as she did in 1807), but at the same time he is aware that his fate lies entirely in her hands. His insecurity is palpable, and he clings desperately to her, concluding with the following dramatic plea:

> Calm yourself, for only by reflecting calmly on our existence can we attain our goal of living together—be at peace—love me—today—yesterday—Oh how tearfully I long for you—you—you—my life—my everything—farewell—Oh continue to love me—never deny this, the most faithful heart of your beloved
>
> > Forever yours
> > Forever mine
> > Forever us.[9]

But Beethoven's greatest fears were eventually realized, and for the third and last time he was forced into a confrontation with an impossible love. News must have reached him quickly of Josephine's decision not to travel on to Karlsbad as she had originally planned but instead to return immediately to Vienna (which adds some support to the theory that the Letter to the Immortal Beloved was never sent). Yet rather than owing to her capricious nature—which lay at the root of Beethoven's fears—her sudden change of heart may instead have been the result of cool calculation. Rita Steblin assumes that in all likelihood the evening of July 3 got quite out of hand, and Josephine—who knew only too well where a night of wild abandon could lead—may have harbored serious concerns of a second illegitimate pregnancy. Under these circumstances, the most logical option was to drop everything and return to Vienna, in order to fool Stackelberg and the rest of society into thinking that he was the father of her seventh child. If at that stage of the divorce proceedings it became apparent that she had committed adultery, not only would she face an enormous scandal but she would lose all hope of a favorable ruling, as well as custody of Joseph Deym's children and of the unborn corpus delicti that she carried within her.

Steblin posits that Josephine therefore had little choice but to rush home and save her marriage. A set of memoirs discovered later by her eldest son, Fritz Deym, testifies to her tremendous efforts in this regard—including a nostalgic holiday to Italy for the whole family—and to her success in convincing Stackelberg that he was the proud father of Minona. Fritz Deym writes of a period of warm tenderness between the parents, whose bond grew closer through the birth of the new child.[10]

Meanwhile, Beethoven waited in Teplitz for a sign from his "immortal beloved." It never came. He traveled on to Karlsbad, where he stayed at the same hotel as banker Franz Brentano and his wife, Antonie. Antonie was fifteen years younger than Beethoven and offered him some comfort in his distress. The Brentanos then invited Beethoven to travel with them to Franzensbad, where he could spend the remainder of his holiday in their company. Antonie Brentano's pronounced warmheartedness toward Beethoven has since generated intense speculation and will be the topic of later discussion.

Beethoven arrived back in Teplitz on September 10, 1812, where he continued work on his Eighth Symphony, met with Goethe, and engaged in some playful note writing with Amalie Sebald. He was sick for most of the time—presumably the stress of the episode with Josephine had taken its toll. He left Teplitz on September 29 and would never return.

After a detour via Linz and a visit to his brother Johann, Beethoven arrived back in Vienna around November 10. We can only imagine his dismay at the upward turn that the Stackelbergs' marriage seemed to have taken in the meantime, and at Josephine's abandonment of any plans to enter a long-term relationship with him. Beethoven was dealt a terrible blow.

It was then that Beethoven began keeping a diary, the first entry of which concludes with the following desperate cry:

If things continue in this manner with ⟋ then all is lost.[11]

This statement has since become legendary, and in the eyes of Beethoven experts it is one of the most crucial clues in unraveling the identity of the "immortal beloved." It seems entirely plausible, after all, that the person whose name begins with the letter shown above must be the one responsible for Beethoven's woe and can thus be identified as the "immortal beloved." Most researchers have interpreted this truncated letter as an *A*, which immediately suggests either Antonie (Brentano), Amalie (Sebald), or Almerie (Esterházy).[12] One problematic aspect, however, is that Beethoven's diary has not come down to us in its original form—that is, in his own handwriting—but instead as a transcription made shortly after his death.[13] This gives rise to a host of speculations regarding the copyist's reading, or rather interpretation, of the letter in question, and any doubts he himself may have had. The present reader will be spared the litany of arguments for and against the numerous theories proposed over the years. Rita Steblin, however, recently demonstrated the striking similarity in Beethoven's handwriting between an uppercase *A* and the abbreviation *St.*, which in all likelihood may have led the copyist astray. Given that Josephine was in the habit of always abbreviating her husband's surname, Steblin proposes that the mysterious sentence be completed thus: "If things continue in this manner with St[ackelberg] then all is lost." Following this logic, the resulting hypothesis would seem watertight: Josephine is the "immortal beloved," and in Beethoven's eyes her husband is the bête noire.[14]

Beethoven was now forced beyond all doubt to abandon any hopes of marriage with Josephine and felt doomed to a life of loneliness, a condition that he would lament time and again. In May 1816, for example, he wrote to Ferdinand Ries: "Give my love to your wife—alas, I have none, I found only one woman, whom I shall certainly never have."[15] Fanny Giannatasio del Rio, the daughter of the principal at the school where Beethoven had sent his nephew Karl, made a similar observation about Beethoven in her diary: "Five years ago [*sic*] he met someone, a closer relationship with whom he would have considered his greatest happiness. But it was out of the question, an impossibility, a chimera."[16]

Opinion on the situation was divided among the Brunsviks. Josephine's brother Franz, who in the past had vehemently opposed any impulsive marriage plans, stayed in touch with Beethoven (who even addressed letters to him as "Dear friend and brother!"[17]) but offered no further opinion on the matter. Josephine's sister Therese, on the other hand, was prepared to speak her mind. In 1817 she wrote in her diary: "Is Jo[sephine] not being punished for the hurt she has caused poor Ludwig? Imagine, his wife! What she could have made of such a hero!"[18] In 1846 she wrote: "Beethoven! Was it not a dream that he was such a trusted friend and guest in our home? Such a great mind! Why did my sister not take him as her husband when she was a widow? She would have been far happier with him than with St[ackelberg]. It was a mother's love that caused her to sacrifice her own happiness."[19]

38

Se non è vero ...

WHEN SCHINDLER PUBLISHED HIS BEETHOVEN biography in 1840, revealing the unaddressed Letter to the Immortal Beloved that he had found among Beethoven's papers together with the Heiligenstadt Testament, panic broke out in the Brunsvik household. Immediately they destroyed any and all incriminating materials, such as letters and diary entries, in the hopes of shifting suspicion elsewhere—preferably to their young cousin Giulietta Guicciardi. Schindler, who knew the Brunsviks and in all likelihood was aware of the situation, had actually already put Giulietta forward as the prime suspect and the letter's addressee. Therese, on the other hand, had her doubts, even without having read the letter in question. No sooner did Schindler's biography appear in 1840 than she wrote in her diary: "Three letters by Beethoven, apparently to Giulietta. Could they be fakes?" Six years later, she was far more steadfast in her views: "Those three letters by Beethoven to Giulietta—I'm sure they were meant for Josephine, whom he loved passionately." She felt an obligation to keep quiet, however: "Speech may be silver, but silence, silence at the right time is pure gold!" To which she added the poignant remark, "This beautiful epigram was once set to music by Beethoven."[1]

For some time, the Brunsviks' attempts to remove Josephine from the spotlight seemed effective. Nowadays, one could fill entire bookshelves with the writings reflecting and speculating on the identity of the lady with whom Beethoven spent the night on July 3, 1812; the list of possible candidates is equally long. For many years, the bookmakers saw Josephine as no more than an outside chance—until 1949, when Swiss collector of Beethoven manuscripts Hans Conrad Bodmer came into possession of thirteen letters sent by Beethoven to Josephine between 1805 and 1807.[2] This discovery not only allowed Beethoven scholars to reconstruct a large portion of the romance between Beethoven and Josephine but also shed new light on the mysterious letter from the summer of 1812. The new trove of correspondence provided a sudden new context, conferring additional meaning and significance to the myriad subtle references hidden within the Letter to the Immortal Beloved. Comparative stylistic studies have also enabled the letter to be interpreted as a continuation of its thirteen predecessors.

The previous chapter already set out how first Marie-Elisabeth Tellenbach and later Rita Steblin put together the few available puzzle pieces to formulate a detailed hypothesis from this perspective. Their proposed scenario seems possible, though their reconstruction of the events in 1812 and 1813 does strike a precarious balance between fact and fiction on more than one occasion. The frequent lack of hard evidence is unsurprising given the nature of the events, yet the absence of certain proofs undermines the plausibility of their version of the love story. As long as Josephine's actions and whereabouts in July and August of 1812 remain undocumented, the nonbelievers have just cause to cast doubt on her candidacy as the "immortal beloved." DNA testing could theoretically prove that Minona was a Beethoven rather than a Stackelberg, but until such testing becomes a genuine possibility, we must wait.

By carefully concealing the identity of his "immortal beloved," Beethoven complicated matters a great deal. Attempts to solve the mystery were also thwarted for a long time due to the ambiguity of the letter's dates—July 6 and 7, but no year—and its intended destination, simply given as "K." All commentators now agree, however, that the letter dates from 1812, the principal argument being Beethoven's claim that July 6 was a Monday and that the sixths of July falling on a Monday in 1795, 1801, 1807, and 1818 are all ruled out for various reasons. The use of "K." as an abbreviation for Karlsbad is now also a certainty. But many questions still remain unanswered, such as how the letter found its way into Beethoven's posthumous estate. Did Beethoven ever send it? If so, when, how, and why did his secret lover ever return it to him?

The movements of virtually every married or engaged woman known to Beethoven during the summer months of 1812 have since become the subject of meticulous scrutiny, and especially of those who can be placed with certainty in Prague or in any of the surrounding spa towns. Any who were of the aristocracy and experiencing marital difficulties are taken very seriously indeed, and if any of them should have given birth to a child on or around April 1, 1813, the case would be considered closed.

Aside from Josephine, virtually all other candidates have since perished on the battlefield of historical criticism.[3] There is one important exception: Antonie ("Toni") Brentano, who enjoys great popularity among no small number of Beethoven specialists and whose most fervent advocate is Maynard Solomon. According to him, it is "all but certain that Antonie Brentano was the woman to whom Ludwig van Beethoven wrote his impassioned letter." She meets all of the criteria to qualify as the letter's intended addressee, including a close relationship with Beethoven and her established presence in Prague and Karlsbad during the period in question. Her name was first proposed in 1972, and because since then "no data speaking against her candidacy has emerged, [. . .] the case in her favour has advanced from plausibility to near certainty."[4] As mentioned above, we ourselves are not so sure.

Antonie Brentano was the daughter of Johann Melchior von Birkenstock, an Austrian diplomat and one of the preeminent intellectuals in Vienna during the late eighteenth century. He was a trusted advisor of Maria Theresa, and along with his brother-in-law Joseph Sonnenfels was responsible for the far-reaching education reforms implemented under Emperor Joseph II. His advocacy of the reforms was subsequently held against him by the conservatives, who later acquired power under the successors of Joseph II, after which Birkenstock retreated to his *palais* on Erdberggasse, a protective cocoon composed of books, scientific objects, and magnificent artworks.

As was customary for the time, when marrying off his daughter Birkenstock allowed practical and even political considerations to take precedence over matters of the heart. By securing a match with Frankfurt-based private banker Franz Brentano (a half-brother of Clemens Brentano), he succeeded in forming an alliance with one of Germany's richest citizens. But money cannot buy happiness, and despite Brentano's engaging personality, Antonie never felt truly at home with him in Hessen. By all accounts, it even took her several months before she dared to address her husband with the familiar German *du*. To make matters worse, Brentano was a workaholic and seldom at home, and so Antonie was left both to raise her own rapidly growing family—she produced five children between the years 1799 and 1806—as well as to provide for the twelve younger Brentano brothers and sisters, of whom her husband had taken custody. She was thus thrust into the role of wife, mother, and surrogate mother all at once; as a result, she became ill, melancholic, withdrawn, and was consumed by homesickness. When Antonie heard in

September 1809 that her father lay on his deathbed, she was only too happy for an excuse to make haste for Vienna, with the eldest children in tow. She would continue to reside there even for some time after her father's death, principally to deal with matters pertaining to his estate but also because she was simply too unwell to make the return journey to Frankfurt. Her husband later came to join her along with the youngest children and was thus forced to handle his business affairs while living in Vienna—a precarious undertaking in a time predating e-mail, fax machines, and even telephones. For three years he persevered, and when the last of father Birkenstock's possessions were auctioned off in the autumn of 1812—representing the symbolic conclusion to Antonie's mourning—it was high time to return to Frankfurt.

For over a century now, Beethoven experts have been discussing exactly how, and at what point in time, Beethoven was first introduced to the Birkenstocks and thus to Antonie. Theories range from very early on (immediately on Beethoven's first arrival in Vienna in 1792) to quite late (at Johann Melchior's deathbed in the autumn of 1809). Some even go so far as to posit that Franz's half-sister Bettina Brentano, who was in regular contact with Beethoven for several months in 1810, was the one who introduced her famous friend to the Birkenstocks. In any case, it seems unlikely that Antonie—who moved almost directly from St. Ursula's convent school in Pressburg to her gilded matrimonial cage in Frankfurt—could have met Beethoven any earlier than 1810.

Once they were acquainted, however, matters proceeded in the usual manner. In Vienna, the frail and ailing Antonie was often confined to her room and bed for days at a time and looked forward to regular visits from the great master, who would do his best to cheer her up at the piano. One thing led to another: kindheartedness became warmheartedness, and empathy became sympathy, which, nourished by affection, grew into something more. Beethoven gave piano lessons to Antonie's gifted daughter Maximiliane (to whom he would later dedicate the Piano Sonata in E Minor, op. 109) and ran rampant with the other children, who presented him with fruit and flowers and accepted his gifts of sweets in return. He also facilitated the sale of the most valuable musical manuscripts from the Birkenstock collection to Archduke Rudolph. Slowly but surely, Beethoven became a true friend of the family. As previously noted, in the summer of 1812 he even spent a large part of his holiday in the Brentanos' company. He made the first part of the journey alone (from Prague to Teplitz), but they all stayed in the same hotel in Karlsbad and traveled on together afterward to Franzensbad.

It is during this time that Solomon believes matters came to a head between Beethoven and Antonie. On July 3 the Brentano couple, their youngest daughter Franziska, and a small entourage arrived in Prague—one day after Beethoven—where they sojourned for several days, partly to visit friends but also to find a suitable tutor for their eldest son, Georg. The Brentanos' presence in the Bohemian capital is an established fact: on June 26 they had requested their passports from Vienna and underwent mandatory registration in Prague on July 3—as a common citizen, Brentano was naturally subject to more stringent migration protocols than were aristocrats. Solomon views this incontrovertible proof of the Brentanos' whereabouts as sufficient to present Antonie as the woman with whom Beethoven experienced the throes of ecstasy that gave rise to the Letter to the Immortal Beloved. Others, however, consider it highly unlikely that the Brentanos' travel plans were unknown to Beethoven, a circumstance that would seem at odds with the unexpected, overwhelming, and seemingly bewildering nature of the encounter, as suggested in the very same letter. Beethoven biographer Ernst Pichler, furthermore, points out the obvious difficulty in imagining how Beethoven and Antonie could have escaped the attention of her entire family (including the servant and the nanny); how during dinner—between mains and dessert, as it were, and before putting Antonie's daughter to bed—they "popped off to the lavatory for an unforgettable romp."[5] And what to think of the weeks thereafter, when Beethoven was almost constantly in the presence of his "immortal beloved" and her supposedly cuckolded husband? Were Beethoven, Antonie, and Franz Brentano the protagonists in a complicated ménage à trois, where the husband feigned ignorance? Or did the trio, as Solomon suggests, come to a reconciliation and use the crisis to elevate their relationship to a new plateau, thus sublimating passion into "exalted friendship"?[6] In view of Beethoven's lofty principles regarding marriage, the latter seems hardly likely. The members of the Josephine camp, on the other hand, turn the argument on its head, claiming that the only reason Beethoven was able to commune so closely with the Brentanos in July and August of 1812 was because he was *not* embroiled in a love affair with Antonie. Given the circumstances, the Brentanos were probably the only ones in a position to give Beethoven the emotional support he needed.

The Brentanos moved back to Frankfurt for good in 1812, and Antonie was delivered of her sixth child on March 8, 1813. Beethoven never saw them again, although they continued to correspond. Their letters, written without the slightest trace of bitterness or rancor, contain no allusions whatsoever to anything that could be considered an "affair." And when Beethoven begged them for his first loan in 1814, the considerably wealthy Franz Brentano showed not a moment's hesitation in aiding his wife's supposed ex-lover. It would not be the last time, and their close friendship was cemented in 1820 by a portrait of Beethoven commissioned by Brentano from the artist Joseph Karl Stieler. Beethoven undoubtedly felt very flattered, and the Brentanos, too, must have greatly appreciated the trouble taken by Beethoven—who hated having his portrait painted—to sit still for hours as a favor to them.[7]

Whoever the "immortal beloved" may have been, the fact remains that in the summer of 1812, Beethoven was disabused of any cherished notions of a happily married life. It was a harsh blow, and his bulldog-like determination in the battle for custody of his nephew over the ensuing years seems to have been fueled, to a large extent, by his need to compensate for this sense of emptiness.

Sporadic writings suggest that from this time on, Beethoven sought solace with sex workers. The experts' opinions differ widely, though all suspicions revolve around the exegesis of certain passages in letters by Beethoven to his friend Zmeskall, passages such as, "Treat our national establishments with care; for as you know, they are no longer virginal and have been subjected to many an invasion," or, "I thank you, dear Z., for your kind information; however concerning the establishments, I thought you knew that I have no desire to spend time in marshy areas?"[8] His thinly veiled references to the "establishments"—the houses where many a Viennese gentleman's sexual needs were met—might indeed suggest a certain lack of inhibition when it came to the services of sex workers. On the other hand, his allusions might just as easily be interpreted as a warning, as in the following diary entry from 1817: "Pleasures of the flesh without a unification of the souls is, and always will be, animalistic. Afterwards one has no sense of any noble feeling—only regret."[9] Proponents of the bordello hypothesis claim that Beethoven's description of a *post-coitum-omne-animal-triste-est* feeling is evidence of his expertise in the field, while opponents interpret it as a reaffirmation of his robust ethical principles. A different picture is painted by a certain Janitschek in one of the conversation notebooks from 1820, whose remark leaves far less to the imagination: "So where were you off to earlier, on the hunt near *Haarmarkt* at around 7 o'clock?"[10]

Maynard Solomon goes out on the longest speculative limb concerning Beethoven's sexual morals and is easily swayed by the "pub talk" of the various men in the conversation notebooks. He believes, for example, that the Lobkowitz household's tutor in residence, Karl Peters, sent several ladies along to his friend Beethoven and once even proposed that Beethoven spend the night with his own wife. Likewise, he suggests that Beethoven also slept with Mrs. Janitschek, who had apparently already removed Peters's clothing, "As Potifar's wife did to Joseph." To Solomon, all of these anecdotes constitute proof of Beethoven's promiscuity. The interpretation along the same lines of a marginal note in one of Beethoven's sketchbooks, "*34 xr* [Kreutzer] *am Lusthaus*" (where *Lusthaus* can potentially be read as "house of lust"), merely exposes Solomon's limited knowledge of nineteenth-century Vienna, as Lusthaus was the name of a popular café-pavilion in Prater Park.[11]

Nevertheless, the lascivious temptations of a bustling metropolis were never far away, a fact of which Beethoven must have been well aware. In 1819, he purchased a copy of Lagneau's seminal work on sexually transmitted infections, "How to Identify, Cure and Protect against All Types of Venereal Disease" (Die Kunst, alle Arten der Lustseuche zu erkennen, zu heilen, und sich dafür zu sichern).[12] We have already refuted the theory that Beethoven may have contracted syphilis, although it must be said that anyone who believes that Beethoven purchased the volume out of a general interest in medical science (as proposed by Marie-Elisabeth Tellenbach) is naïve indeed.[13]

39

The End of the Classical Symphony

ALTHOUGH THE TUMULT of the "immortal beloved" affair and Beethoven's subsequent devastation took a strong mental toll, it was not his only source of distress during that time. The autumn of 1812 was also over-shadowed by conflicts with his brothers and a litany of financial woes. On the return trip from Teplitz to Vienna, Beethoven took a detour to the south via Linz to visit his brother Johann, who had opened a pharmacy there in 1808—the Apotheke zur Krone. Johann's business was flourishing: he earned a pretty penny by making deals with the French occupiers, and just like his great-grandfather in Mechelen he had ventured into the real estate market. He became so rich in fact that he could later afford a magnificent country estate in Gneixendorf near Krems, known as the Wasserhof.[1] To Beethoven, however, Johann's commercial success was tarnished by what he considered to be a debauched and unacceptable lifestyle. For some time, Johann had been intimately involved with Therese Obermayer—the upstairs neighbor's sister-in-law and long-term houseguest—who already had an illegitimate daughter of her own. As the eldest brother and head of the family, Beethoven felt outraged and duty-bound to intervene. He tried to force Johann to put an end to his indecent conduct, and the brothers even came to blows. Next he called in the cavalry, abusing his influence with both the religious and civil authorities to have Therese Obermayer banished from the city by local decree. Johann's canny response was to legalize his situation: on November 8, he married Therese and adopted her daughter, and a livid Beethoven promptly returned to Vienna. Nearly ten years would pass before communication nor-malized between Beethoven and, by that time, his only surviving brother.

His other brother, Kaspar Karl, was a further source of concern. He was suffering from tuberculosis, an affliction that was all but untreatable in those times. Kaspar Karl and his wife, Johanna, also proved to have been altogether careless with money, which in their case had driven them to several desperate acts of embezzlement. Johanna was sentenced, the abyss was beckoning, and Beethoven felt compelled to lend financial aid.

It was then too that the bad tidings of Kinsky's death arrived on November 3, and all hopes of an expeditious payment of the sum agreed on in March 1809 were dashed. Other sources of funding had also run dry, and all prospects of an *Akademie* had evaporated since the economic crisis had brought Viennese sociocultural life to a standstill. The aristocrats who had hitherto supported Beethoven's career had virtually disappeared from the public sphere and, with the sole exception of Archduke Rudolph, received only bad press. The common populace was also otherwise preoccupied, and ultimately Beethoven's music was only performed during charity events or benefit concerts. In Graz, for example, four Beethoven concerts were held to raise money for St. Ursula's convent school. Beethoven had met the organizer of these concerts, the lawyer Joseph Varena, during the summer of 1811 in Teplitz. He showed an interest in Varena's charity projects and offered whatever services he could provide, including the collection and delivery of orchestral parts. This typical Beethovenian generosity earned him much goodwill but left him financially no better off.

Beethoven's mounting problems weighed on his mind, and he confessed his poor mental and physical state to Archduke Rudolph on more than one occasion. Nannette Streicher described his appearance as unkempt, and his lodgings even more so. He also avoided all contact with friends and acquaintances; he still visited his regular haunts but isolated himself from the crowd, and it was obvious to all present that there was little use in disturbing him (although it should be admitted that the many unsociable eating habits Beethoven had cultivated in the meantime hardly aroused the appetite of his scarce table companions). Beethoven also had difficulty working. It was imperative that he finish the folksong arrangements he had promised to Scottish publisher George Thomson, and the Violin Sonata in G Major (op. 96) was completed in haste: a messenger collected the parts—the notes still glistening on the page—only two days before Archduke Rudolph and the famous French violinist Pierre Rode were to perform the work at a concert on December 29 at the Lobkowitz residence. After that, Beethoven's sputtering engine fell silent.

For ten years since his Heiligenstadt crisis, Beethoven had battled relentlessly against the limitations imposed on him by contemporary instruments, musicians, audiences, and society, as well as those of his own body and of music itself. Over the course of an opera, an oratorio, a Mass, three stage productions, seven symphonies, five concertos, five string quartets, seven piano sonatas, and several other chamber works, he had used grand gestures to depict gods, heroes, and the most noble deeds of which humanity is capable. Now he had no more to give. Over the next several years he might still put pen to paper, but it would take all his strength to write any music that was truly his own.

His collapse was swift. Earlier, in the summer of 1812, Beethoven wrote an enthusiastic and passionate response to a piece of fan mail he had received from a young pianist, the ten-year-old "Emily M. From Hamburg": "Forge ahead, do not only practice art, but also try to fathom its greatest depths; it is a worthy occupation, for only through art and science can humanity attain divine transcendence [. . .] A true artist has no pride; he sees, alas only too well, that art is limitless, he senses grimly how far removed he is from his goal, and although others may admire him, he laments nonetheless at not yet having reached the point where his genius beckons to him, twinkling like a distant sun."[2] Only one year later, in a letter to Franz Brunsvik, his despondent tone was palpable: "Higher, nobler ideals begone—though our striving be unending, mundanity puts an end to all things!"[3]

The diary he had started in the meantime now served as a welcome outlet for all his pent-up frustrations from the year 1812. The sudden decrease in normal modes of communication with others also made the diary an important vehicle for reflection, for establishing structure and finding stability. It reads as an extended soliloquy on the meaning of life, delivered by a resolute but increasingly lonely protagonist—a collection of quotes, paraphrases, and personal observations, compiled in search of consolation and inspiration. At the same time, it also illustrates how mundane life could be, even for Beethoven, for alongside lofty expostulations and poetic musings we find personal reminders and short notes on banal trivialities, such as "Shoe brushes, to polish for when guests come," "34 bottles from Countess Erdődy," "15 bottles in the maid's room. 18 shirts," and "Take pills again on Saturday or Sunday."[4]

Beethoven's completion of the new Violin Sonata in G Major (op. 96) on December 29, 1812, represented the conclusion not only of the year but also of a decade of work, and offers a telling reflection of Beethoven's state of mind at the time. Particularly striking is the sonata's opening, with a solo trill in the violin:

In earlier times, a trill served merely as an ornament to a given tone; it had an expressive but no substantive purpose. Here, however—and increasingly in Beethoven's later work—the trill takes on its own motivic significance. The vibration imparts both sensitivity and insecurity, embodying a brittle, vulnerable quality. The opening tone floats freely in space, completely disoriented and without purchase, evoking feelings of simplicity, ease, innocence, and peace, and invoking a general ambience of fragile melancholy. Various commentators have thus described the sonata as "pastoral,"[5] an epithet that is not entirely superficial; for romantic composers, after all, the *pastorale* carried highly nostalgic connotations of loss, wistfulness, resignation, and consolation. "Pastoral" music expressed an insatiable longing for bygone happiness, for a lost Arcadia. The same applied, in his vulnerable state, to Beethoven who in the summer months—with reason but lacking purpose—began work on the sonata. It is not so far-fetched to surmise that the utter introversion, compositional succinctness, and absence of drama in the opening Allegro moderato are symptoms of Beethoven's nostalgic resignation following the "immortal beloved" affair. The ensuing Adagio espressivo, composed later, is also characterized by sentimentality and a tender beauty. For the final movement, Beethoven had a fortuitous stroke of inspiration, as the arrival of Pierre Rode in Vienna in mid-December not only motivated Beethoven to ready the sonata for a public performance but also dropped in his lap a violin virtuoso who was not obsessed with bravura or flashy showmanship. After some initial apprehension, Beethoven eventually hit upon a fitting solution: a set of variations on a relatively simple tune. But instead of resorting to the robust artillery of techniques he had developed previously in the genre, he instead opted for five more reflective "commentaries" on the theme. The sonata's overarching concept benefited greatly from this treatment, since a virtuosic "concertante" finale (as in the *Kreutzer* Sonata, op. 47) would most likely have torn apart the more delicate fabric woven by the previous movements.

After its premiere, the sonata was performed a second time on January 7, 1813, once again in the Lobkowitz home. On the previous evening, the archduke and Rode had held an extra rehearsal. Beethoven was present, and he took advantage of the opportunity to make some alterations. The sonata lay dormant for some time afterward and was not published until 1816. Curiously, Beethoven had to borrow the archduke's copy to prepare the publication, as his own had somehow gone missing.

Clearly, the public at large was not terribly interested in the Violin Sonata in G Major (op. 96). The same was even truer of the String Quartet in F Minor (op. 95), which Beethoven had composed in the autumn of 1810. Although we can safely assume that the quartet's dedicatee, Nikolaus Zmeskall, played it at one of the many chamber music events held at his home, its official public debut by the Schuppanzigh Quartet did not take place until 1814, with publication following two years later. Here the long timeline was occasioned not by any practical obstacles but by the music itself, which was uncommonly terse and introspective and, as a result, lacked audience appeal. Beethoven placed high demands on his listeners, confronting them suddenly with an entirely new musical grammar. The most disorienting factor was not that the traditional forms—such as sonata, rondo, binary, or ternary form—were now barely recognizable, but rather that the new dramatic and temporal proportions were beyond the average listener's frame of reference. Until opus 95, this had not been the case. The logic of the old classical style was based, after all, on the juxtaposition of categorical opposites that held each other in check: thematic vs. nonthematic, static vs. dynamic, structured vs. rhapsodic, compact vs. ethereal, dramatic vs. lyrical, and so on. To the listener these elements were easily recognizable, understandable, and offered a certain reassurance. Even Beethoven had long been consistent in his application of these fundamental principles. At a certain point, he began painting with broader strokes on a bigger canvas; his compositions became longer, and the transitional passages in particular took on greater substance. But although the audience's patience was sometimes sorely tested, the music remained inherently intelligible. The String Quartet in F Minor (op. 95), on the other hand, represented a complete about-face. The music was reduced to its very essence; movements became suddenly shorter; themes were denuded of all ornament; musical ideas followed in rapid succession and without preparation; modulations were brusque, tonal relationships loose, and the drama fleet-footed. Time was short and the learning curve steep, and listeners were forced to either keep pace with the composer or give up entirely. The latter was not an uncommon occurrence.

Beethoven was well aware of the quartet's challenges, and in a letter to English conductor and concert planner George Smart in 1816, he writes, "The Quartett is written for a small circle of connoisseurs and is never to be performed in public."[6] This warning should be taken more as a recommendation than as a prohibition, a summation supported by the title given to the work by Beethoven himself, *Quartetto serioso*. Initially, the epithet referred exclusively to the third movement; unlike traditional third movements, it was to be performed not in a light, scherzando manner but rather with gravitas, hence the tempo indication "Allegro assai vivace, ma serioso." This specific indication aside, the title also very aptly describes the character of the other movements, as well as the quartet as a whole.

The *Quartetto serioso* in F Minor (op. 95) and the Violin Sonata in G Major (op. 96) symbolize a turning point in Beethoven's career. Although he would certainly continue to write major works for the concert hall—and earn a great deal in the process—deep inside he had once again veered onto a new artistic course. It is no coincidence that this monumental change in direction coincided with dramatic events in his personal life.

The Seventh and Eighth symphonies, on which Beethoven placed the finishing touches in October 1812, mark the same turning and end point, albeit each in its own way. The Seventh Symphony in particular gives the impression that Beethoven had reached the limits of the genre. The previous six symphonies saw him agonize over how to fully exploit the melodic, harmonic, and tonal potential of the classical orchestral tradition that had been handed down to him. With the seventh, he seems to have reached the bottom of the symphonic barrel, for with precious few exceptions (the slow introduction and the middle sections of the Allegretto and the Scherzo), the Seventh Symphony is essentially a nonmelodic, nonharmonic, and nontonal symphony, being dominated instead by rhythmic elements. Until that time, this musical terrain had remained utterly unexplored, and such a path would not be trod again until the twentieth century by such composers as Igor Stravinsky.

Each section of the symphony opens with a germinal rhythmic "cell" that is subsequently repeated and strung out in seemingly endless concatenations, culminating in exhilarating eruptions of sound. The timpani play a particularly crucial role, hammering out the rhythms and goading the orchestra into ever-increasing crescendos, explosions of energy, vitality, and bursts of primal force, celebrating the climaxes in moments of trance and orgiastic abandon.

The ebullient final movement carries this idea to the extreme; on hearing the Seventh Symphony, Carl Maria von Weber is said to have remarked that Beethoven was ripe for the asylum. And Friedrich Wieck, the father of pianist Clara Wieck (later Clara Schumann), believed that Beethoven must have been drunk when he wrote it.[7] But madmen and drunkards often speak the truth. The obsessive character of the Seventh is indeed difficult to deny: the string players in particular must often stretch their physical capabilities—and those of their instruments—to the limit in an effort to withstand the onslaught of the winds and timpani, and their struggle to push ahead with sore, cramped arms is analogous to Beethoven's own dogged battle against the limitations of the classical symphonic language. It is hard to tell what is embodied more by the symphony's masterfully measured conclusion: rapture, or relief?

The Eighth Symphony, too, harbors moments of internal orchestral struggle. In the first movement, for example, the return of the main theme in the bass parts is completely obscured by forte-fortissimo entries elsewhere in the orchestra. This is no error of instrumentation committed by a Beethoven hard of hearing; on the contrary, it is a clear and unmistakable artistic statement. In the final movement, the musicians must contend with rapid triplet tremolos, which due to being either extremely loud or incredibly soft are nigh impossible to play—a denial of crucial musicospatial "elbow room" that can also be taken as a deliberate statement. The movement's three-part piano opening (which leaves us wondering whether it contains a theme at all) is also rudely interrupted by an abrupt C-sharp, which has no business whatsoever in F major and thus leaves a comical impression. Eminent violinist Louis Spohr once remarked that it sounded like a person sticking their tongue out in the middle of a conversation.[8] Beethoven continues to toy with both the musicians and the audience throughout the rest of the movement. It is also noteworthy that musicologists have long debated whether the symphony's conclusion is in sonata or rondo form and, in the case of a hybrid, what the proportions might be. It ultimately matters little, as an excess of organization is often indistinguishable from a lack thereof. Be the form what it may, the overall impression is that chaos wins out in the end.

The two central movements are also possessed of a grotesque and slightly alienating quality. On first hearing, the Allegretto gives the impression of sweetness, elegance, and charm, and the persistent staccato chords in the winds have led many commentators to associate it with the slow movement from Haydn's Symphony no. 101, nicknamed "The Clock." Beethoven's timepiece, however, constantly skips and stalls, and by the end the malfunctioning mechanism simply falls to pieces. The Tempo di Menuetto, too, is disorienting due to the many deliberately misplaced accents. This quality has often been described as "humor"; in reality, it tends more toward the interpretation offered by the poet Jean Paul—the enfant terrible of romantic German culture—who puts it closer to satire. Or worse: sarcasm.[9]

Richard Wagner described Beethoven's Seventh Symphony as the "apotheosis of the dance." But rather than a reference to "ecstatic" or "heavenly" dancing (the Allegretto more closely resembles a funeral march), his comment instead suggests that in the Seventh, the symphonic genre—which had its origins in the suite and dance forms—had reached a point of perfection. An apotheosis is both a culmination and a climax, and Wagner believed that the time of the dance-based symphony was over. From then on, narrative would constitute the symphonic substrate. According to Wagner, this was also why Beethoven abandoned his original intention to compose a symphonic triptych, complementing the Seventh and Eighth symphonies immediately with a Ninth Symphony in D Minor. While the sketches for the D-minor symphony do indeed date from the same period, it would be more than ten years before Beethoven would hit upon the innovation to incorporate a text. From this perspective, the relentless pounding of a single harmony—for fifty bars—at the end of the Eighth Symphony can be viewed as an elongated final chord, symbolizing the end of an era.

On December 30, 1812—one day after the Hapsburg prince and a Parisian violin virtuoso premiered a work marking the culmination of a significant period in Beethoven's life and his work—the Prussian general Yorck and his Russian colleague Diebitsch signed an armistice convention in the Lithuanian town of Tauroggen that would be of great symbolic import throughout nineteenth-century Europe. Although both gentlemen acted of their own accord (not until several weeks later would their superiors, the Prussian king Frederik Willem III and the Russian tsar Alexander I, convert the intent of the Tauroggen convention into the Treaty of Kalisz), their initiative provided enormous leverage. Their act was the catalyst that caused Prussia to gravitate away from the French and toward the Russians, in turn encouraging many of the German states to do the same and triggering a resurgence of German nationalism that would enable large swathes of the population to be mobilized against Napoleon and in favor of freedom. Only Austria spent an extended period on the fence, successfully dodging the military turmoil under the direction of master strategist Metternich. In his own words, this was achieved through the deployment of "shrewd manoeuvring, evasion and flattery."[10] On the one hand, Austria needed to stay in Napoleon's good books (one need only recall how the Austrian emperor's eldest daughter was served up as an appeasement to Paris). On the other, ties with the anti-French camp were never truly severed, and Austria continued to collaborate secretly on efforts to destabilize Napoleon's rule and redraw the battle lines.

The Tauroggen convention was an even greater milestone, as it was the very first act of diplomacy to take place after Napoleon's military debacle in Russia. His march to and from Moscow had cost him great numbers and even more authority, and it was at precisely this moment that two generals placed their signatures on a contract that would bring about the rapid desertion of his allies en masse. Weakened and isolated, Napoleon's forces were quickly reduced to a numeric minority, which despite his superior military and strategic acuity would ultimately bring about his rapid downfall. Still, he refused to capitulate, and all attempts to reach an agreement—by Metternich in particular, since Austria had every interest in a prosperous France—met with blind stubbornness. On New Year's Day 1814, under the command of Prussian general Blücher, the allied troops crossed the Rhine and then took Paris on March 31. Napoleon was deposed on April 4 and banished to the island of Elba, with a modest allowance and a household one-thousand strong. He was permitted to retain his title of emperor, and his wife was relocated to the duchies of Parma and Piacenza.

Two days later, on April 6, the French senate decided to retrieve Louis XVIII, the youngest brother of the guillotined king Louis XVI, from his own banishment and reinstate him as king. The allies—led by Metternich and his conservative English counterpart and kindred spirit, Robert Stewart Castlereagh—were in full agreement that the Bourbons should return to sovereign power once more. The allies may have driven the French back to their historical borders from before 1792, but they eschewed all other forms of belittlement. After all, they saw an important role for France in the new balanced configuration of Europe that they sought to attain. The exact nature of this balance was still unknown, however, necessitating the organization of a major congress in the summer. Metternich, a diplomatic force to be reckoned with, insisted that the congress be held in Vienna.

Twenty-five years after the revolution broke out in Paris, peace thus returned to Europe. With the coronation of King Louis XVIII, the ideological clock was turned back, and the circle was complete.

40

Music for the Masses

VIENNA, DECEMBER 8, 1813. IT IS A WEDNESDAY, and a bustling society event is underway in the first-floor auditorium of Vienna University: a benefit concert for wounded Austrian and Bavarian servicemen who have returned from the Battle of Hanau (October 30 and 31). The event was far more than a simple show of solidarity with a small group of unfortunates, for it celebrated the return of nationalistic pride, and nobody, rich or poor, would be kept away. The cream of Viennese society had flocked to the event en masse and were crammed into the magnificent hall like sardines. Many attendees were unable to secure a seat and simply remained standing in the central aisles or leaned against the walls. On stage, too, space was at an absolute premium; over one hundred musicians occupied the small raised dais, where the winds could hardly breathe and the strings barely had room to maneuver their bows. The podium literally groaned under the weight of two orchestras. All the winds were doubled, and the string sections had been scaled up accordingly. The side corridors and stairwells housed even more musicians. On each side were multiple trumpet players, percussionists, and the operators of the "cannon and gunfire-machines"—essentially large drums (the largest that could be found in Viennese theaters, on the composer's express instruction)—and ratchets. This entire arsenal had been procured to supply the special effects for the final and most pertinent work of the evening's entertainments: *Wellington's Victory, or the Battle of Vitoria* (op. 91) by Ludwig van Beethoven.

The opening work, however, was Beethoven's Seventh Symphony, which Viennese audiences had no doubt awaited with keen anticipation. It had been nearly five years since they last heard a new symphony by the master, an eternity by the prevailing standards. Beethoven himself conducted—or rather,

353

concertmaster Schuppanzigh held the metrical reins while Beethoven flailed his arms in a windmill-like fashion and pulled faces by way of musical inspiration. Beethoven, who was already hard of hearing, needed to coordinate his gestures visually with those of the orchestra, keeping track of the musicians' progress by observing their bowing and body language.[1] But despite the musical guesswork, the performance was a resounding success. The audience was enthusiastic and applauded so generously after the second movement that it was immediately reprised. The *Allgemeine musikalische Zeitung* proclaimed the new symphony as "the latest work by the genius Beethoven."[2]

The next items on the program were brief but sensational: two marches for trumpet and orchestra by Johann Dussek and Ignaz Pleyel. According to the program, the solo part was to be performed by "Mälzel's famous mechanical bugler." The bugler was not a musician of flesh and blood but an automaton, a musical robot, a member of a small but slowly growing genus stemming from the minds of many an eccentric European gadgeteer. Such wonders had hitherto only been demonstrated at exhibitions and in art galleries; now, Vienna was given the opportunity to see how such a contraption performed under concert conditions. The level of musicianship may have been questionable, but some compensation was offered by the audience's enthusiasm for the seemingly limitless possibilities offered by the innovation. Alas, there is no record of what Beethoven thought of it all.

Then came the work that all had been waiting for: *Wellington's Victory, or the Battle of Vitoria.* The Viennese were well acquainted with the *battaglia,* a musical genre used to depict scenes of war. Generally it followed a fixed structure, illustrating the preparations for battle, the battle itself, the lamentations of the wounded, and then the final celebration of victory. *La Bataille de Prague,* by little-known Bohemian composer František Kočvara, was a particular favorite and held pride of place on many a Viennese piano stand. But unlike the Austrians—whose only celebrated conquests were bygone victories against the Turks—the average Parisian music lover's library contained the musical evocations of battles at Jemappes, Austerlitz, Jena, Auerstedt . . . the list goes on. Now, however, the political landscape had changed. On June 21, 1813, the allied troops, led by the Duke of Wellington, had scored a major victory against the French in Vitoria (in northern Spain), breaching Napoleon's blockade and reopening the doors to the continent. The victory also had a great psychological impact. While Napoleon's downfall had already begun in Russia the previous winter, in that instance everybody agreed that Napoleon had been bested first and foremost not by the Russians themselves, but by the icy weather and his own ambition. In the Basque region of Vitoria, on the other hand, the allies had fought an honest fight and emerged victorious all on their own, which gave hope for the future. (It should be admitted, however, that the success in Vitoria was expedited somewhat by the inept leadership of Napoleon's brother, Joseph Bonaparte.) At any rate, Wellington's triumph in Vitoria became symbolic of a definitive turning point in the war and of Europe's imminent liberation from twenty-five years of Parisian tyranny. Any piece of music devoted to this glorious battle was virtually guaranteed to spark enthusiasm and win approval.

Imperial engineer Mälzel, the father of the mechanical bugler and the initiator of the concert, succeeded in rallying Vienna's best musicians, and it was Beethoven's *battaglia* in particular that benefited from their presence. The one-hundred-plus musicians onstage had been sourced from the city's musical elite, and even eminent concert violinist Louis Spohr—who had appeared as a soloist in Europe's most prestigious concert halls—was assigned a tutti chair. Yet the real crème de la crème were not on the podium but off-stage to the left and right. None other than imperial Kapellmeister himself, Antonio Salieri, conducted one of the two brass and percussion ensembles hidden in the wings, and the large drums and cannons were manned by such celebrities as Hummel, Moscheles, and the young Meyerbeer. In his "performance notes," Beethoven had expressly prescribed that the percussion parts be entrusted not to any ordinary percussionists but to "very good musicians" and "men of understanding."[3] For although the gunfire during the real battle may have been haphazard, in Beethoven's score the cannons and other explosions were timed precisely to within fractions of a second. Meyerbeer, whose cannon blasts on the massive drum were always a little too late, bore the brunt of Beethoven's fastidiousness during rehearsal. The poor lad failed to realize that his distance from the orchestra necessitated a slight anticipation of the beat, which earned him a dressing-down from the master.

The audience was eager to witness just how originally the Viennese enfant terrible would treat this somewhat unconventional material. In any case, the German title—*Wellingtons Sieg oder die Schlacht bei Vittoria*—was promising: Beethoven had transported the battle from the Basque region of Vitoria to the more symbolically laden "Vittoria." And right from the opening bars Beethoven hit home. The sound of unseen drums and trumpets making a gradual approach from the left, followed by a rendition from the same side of the well-known "Rule Britannia," made it clear to all where the English camp was stationed. The same procedure was then repeated on the right-hand side for the French, who were represented musically not by the "Marseillaise" or the popular "Ça ira" but instead by "Marlborough s'en va-t-en guerre" (Marlborough has gone to war). The significance of this tune cannot have gone unnoticed, as it was a song used by the French to mock a former painful retreat by the English under the command of the Duke of Marlborough. By all accounts, Napoleon would hum this tune as a personal anthem in times of crisis, and Beethoven's inclusion of it suggests a portrayal of the French as arrogant, haughty, and vainglorious. At the same time, their intrada had been cast meaningfully in the key of C major, which—relative to the E-flat entrance of the English—brought them down not one but two musical pegs. After an exchange of trumpet fanfares, the hostilities were then officially opened by the French. The next five minutes paint a raging battle scene: the orchestra first outlines the ballistic contours, followed by the arrival of the cavalry, and lastly the increasingly deafening infantry fire (the eventual fading of which is reminiscent of the abating storm in the Sixth Symphony). The Marlborough theme then slowly resurfaces in a soft, minor variant and suffers gradual fragmentation and disintegration. The similarity of this section to the close of the funeral march from the *Eroica* Symphony conveys unequivocally that the French had come off second-best, and left the battlefield injured and fighting for their lives. The cannons and gunfire resounding from the wings were meticulously coordinated with the raging of the orchestra—like a consummate veteran, Beethoven had reconstructed and distilled the entire battle into a carefully timed playbook (which explains his stipulation for reliable players). Even the work's conclusion was realized in high fidelity. When, at six in the evening on June 21, 1813, the French crept off in defeat leaving their weapons behind, the English—acting contrary to all war etiquette—continued to bombard their retreating opponents. Even these final, indecorous cannon shots are notated in the score.

After a short break, part two of the work followed in the form of the *Victory Symphony* portraying the victors' jubilation. With trumpets blaring, a festive intrada precedes two exhilarating (but otherwise unremarkable) victory marches interspersed with three separate renditions of "God Save the King": the first in a sparse wind instrumentation, including somewhat curious pizzicati in the strings; the second also in the winds but interrupted periodically by brash pairs of trills; and finally as a fast-paced, erratic fugato. Pessimists might have viewed such treatment as a critical commentary by the composer on the entire affair; these naysayers were not in attendance, however, and the audience interpreted Beethoven's piecemeal setting of the

English anthem as a humble gesture of deference to Vienna's own emperor. The trills were taken to represent the applause of the population on the home front, and the closing fugato as a collective and delirious climax.

When it was over, the dazed audience sprang to its feet and let forth a salvo of its own—the orchestral musicians were applauded, Beethoven adulated, and all returned home feeling deeply satisfied.

The concert was repeated four days later, with the same program, the same performers, and for the same noble cause. Once again, Beethoven emerged victorious, and his success prompted him to organize another *Akademie* on January 2, 1814, in the main Redoutensaal of the Hofburg. This time the program included exclusively his own works, of course—the pieces by Dussek and Pleyel for mechanical bugler were replaced by selections from *The Ruins of Athens*. In the meantime, Beethoven had clearly realized that *Wellington's Victory* was open to interpretation as an ode to the English (and by extension to their democratic political system), and thus deemed it prudent to include a respectful nod to the emperor, the more so since the concert took place in one of his prestigious halls. The insertion of the final chorus from *The Ruins of Athens*—"Heil unserm König, Heil!" (Blessed, blessed be our king!)—was particularly intended to curtail any such conjecture. To be doubly sure, a small but effective piece of theater was integrated into the preceding aria. A few moments before the bass launched into "Er ist's! Wir sind erhört! O Vater Zeus! Gewährt ist unsre Bitte!" (It is he! We have been heard! O father Zeus! Our prayer has been answered!), at Beethoven's express request and to the astonishment of all those present, a specially hung curtain was whisked away, revealing a bust of Emperor Francis I.

Once again, the wings and side corridors were put to good use for the stereophonic effects in *Wellington's Victory*. Once again, a mammoth orchestra occupied the stage. An entry in Beethoven's diary makes mention of sixty-nine (!) musicians in the string section: eighteen first violins, eighteen second violins, fourteen violas, twelve cellos, and seven double basses. Once again, the composer "conducted" the work energetically and in his usual style, despite the inherent and frequent risk of derailment. And once again, the audience responded with great enthusiasm. Press reports did note, however, that some members of the audience—especially the morbidly curious who had come almost exclusively for the war spectacle—were bored to tears during the symphony, with special reference made to "several members of the fairer sex."[4]

Beethoven saw that there was money to be made, and organized yet another concert on February 27, again to be held at the Hofburg. Naturally, the Seventh Symphony and *Wellington's Victory* were on the program, but this time they were flanked by the trio "Tremate, empi, tremate" (op. 116) and the Eighth Symphony—its first airing in public. The debut was not a success, however. According to a critic from the *Allgemeine musikalische Zeitung,* the Eighth Symphony was dwarfed by the presence of the Seventh, and the audience's heightened expectations went unfulfilled. The same critic advised the composer thenceforth to program the two works separately. Beethoven was greatly irritated and believed that the limited success of the Eighth was due simply to its superiority to the Seventh.[5]

The success of *Wellington,* on the other hand, seemed to know no bounds. The Viennese could not get enough of it, and repeat performances followed on March 25, November 29, December 2, and December 25. In England, too, the work found fertile soil. In mid-April 1814, Beethoven had sent a copy to the then prince regent (the later King George IV), asking whether he might condescend to accept the work's dedication. The prince regent never sent a reply but did pass on the *Wellington* score to the director of the Theatre Royal in Drury Lane, with the order to include it on the program. The director did so on February 10, 1815, and the English snowball started rolling. More performances followed, and *Wellington's Victory* became immensely popular, not least because Wellington's own fame had taken on mythical proportions since winning the Battle of Waterloo on June 18, 1815, sealing Napoleon's fate for good. Beethoven, meanwhile, only heard "on the grapevine" how enraptured the English had become with his war tribute, and was incensed at the lack of any forthcoming compensation. He subsequently pleaded with the prince regent several times, applying a blend of courtesy and pressure to be reimbursed for the costs of producing the score, but these entreaties, too, met with silence. His experiences in Vienna had clearly led him to misjudge how the world's other sovereigns communicate with mere mortals—even those named Beethoven.

The tremendous popularity of *Wellington's Victory* is perhaps best illustrated by the manner in which it appeared in print in February 1816. The Viennese publisher, Steiner, brought seven different versions to market simultaneously, varying from the original orchestral score to arrangements for string quintet, piano trio, piano solo, and piano duet—even a version titled "Turkish Music." *Wellington's Victory* was also Beethoven's first orchestral score to be published simultaneously with the orchestral parts. Some months later, the *Quartetto serioso* (op. 95), the Violin Sonata in G Major (op. 96), and the "Archduke" Piano Trio (op. 97) also hit the shelves. It is telling that these three momentous and highly sophisticated chamber works had necessarily lain dormant for so many years, until the colossal sales of a popular orchestral monstrosity granted a financial margin wide enough to compensate for the losses they would inevitably cause.

Victory has many fathers, however, and great successes often lead to conflict. *Wellington's Victory* was no exception. In Beethoven's view, Mälzel—who made an early habit of taking liberties with others' intellectual property—had rather too publicly confused his coinvolvement in the Wellington *project* with that of the Wellington *music*. Naturally, Beethoven could not let this equivocation slide, and instigated legal proceedings that dragged on for several years but offered no resolution. Eventually, in 1816, they settled out of court.

Nowadays a figure such as Mälzel would be a prime candidate for the television programs that exploit and ridicule poor souls who dedicate their lives in all seriousness to the zaniest of enterprises. Even the history books vacillate in their evaluations of Mälzel's achievements, which range from "innovative brilliance" to "pseudo-inventive charlatanism." And indeed, the mechanical bugler was but one item on a long list of inventions—original or "borrowed"—that have raised many an eyebrow and included singing, animated canaries, bullfinches and parrots, and chess-playing robots.[6] Alongside these, however, he also produced a vast array of sophisticated musical machines and stood at the forefront of development on the metronome—again, drawing from others' work. Whatever the case, Mälzel captivated audiences, and he was not unique in doing so, as Vienna housed around fifteen studios in 1800 that concentrated solely on the invention of such eccentric curiosities.[7]

Beethoven initially thought highly of Mälzel and in 1812 asked him to fabricate a number of trumpet-shaped instruments for auditory amplification purposes. The pair thus became better acquainted, and in mid-1813 Beethoven borrowed fifty ducats from the inventor. In exchange, he promised to compose a work for Mälzel's "Panharmonicon"—a colossal music machine capable of imitating the sound of an entire symphony orchestra—with the aim of making a joint splash in England. And here lay the roots of the initial dispute over *Wellington's Victory*. Mälzel would later argue that the idea was entirely his, including the work's title and fundamental musical outlines, a claim that Beethoven denied outright. It was later shown that

Mälzel did indeed brief Beethoven on the capacities and limitations of his Panharmonicon, but his input stopped there. Later, Mälzel had considerable difficulty transferring the score of Beethoven's *Victory Symphony* to the barrel (a kind of revolving punch card telling the instruments what to play and when), and it was ultimately rewritten as an ordinary orchestral work. Mälzel had conceived a plan to organize a major charity concert in the university hall on December 8, 1813, to present his "mechanical bugler" to the public. He promised to organize everything—the hall reservation, permit applications, recruitment of musicians, and the advertising campaign—but needed Beethoven as a draw card, preferably with a work of a spectacular nature, and the reworked *Victory Symphony* seemed to fit the bill. Beethoven warmed to the idea. He had spent the previous months trying in vain to organize another *Akademie* to present one of his new symphonies, and he was only too happy with Mälzel's plans to launch a similar project. Composing a spectacular crowd-pleaser was a compromise he was willing to make.

And here was the second bone of contention. Beethoven "rewrote" his *Victory Symphony*—although manuscript research shows that the changes were minimal—and within several days had appended not only an intrada but also the completely new first section depicting the battle itself. Again, Mälzel plucked one too many feathers for his cap, and again it would transpire that his musical contribution was limited to some suggestions with regard to the percussion parts. But Mälzel was no shrinking violet and released posters laying ambiguous claims to the work as his "property."[8] Beethoven found the claims unacceptable and promptly had the posters removed. After the second benefit concert, he also wrote a letter to the *Wiener Zeitung* thanking Mälzel for his exertions in organizing the event but making it abundantly clear that the music was entirely of his own creation.[9] For reasons unknown, the letter was not published at that time. But several weeks later it did appear, in an abridged form, and Mälzel's name was not even mentioned.

Relations soured quickly thereafter. Beethoven adopted the sudden belief that Mälzel was an indecent human being, lacking in any education or proper upbringing.[10] He immediately repaid his outstanding debt of fifty ducats and organized his own *Akademie,* which included *Wellington's Victory* but eliminated all reference to Mälzel. The latter in turn left for London, giving two concerts along the way using his own secret, homemade copy of the *Wellington* score. On hearing this news, Beethoven was livid and offered instant retaliation; as mentioned above, he attempted to dedicate the work to the prince regent in the hopes that the royal appellation would act as a legal force field and protect his legitimate rights. He also wrote a "Declaration and Petition to the Musicians of London," giving them advance warning that Mälzel had never received permission to perform either *Wellington's Victory* or the accompanying symphony.[11] Furthermore, Beethoven issued a reminder that public performances based on stolen scores constituted an act of public deception.

His twofold approach helped little, in part because the prince regent never granted "His High Protection." Beethoven had no choice in Vienna but to initiate legal proceedings, but since there was little to no copyright law at that time, the courts were a dead end. Only in 1816, when Beethoven and Mälzel found a new common purpose—the production and distribution of the metronome—were their differences finally reconciled.

Beethoven's tenacity in the Wellington affair is certainly understandable, as there was both money and glory at stake, both of which were close to his heart. But does his fanaticism carry any implications regarding his own estimation of this rather unorthodox work? The very least that can be said is that he was both pleased and irked by the immense crowds and the widespread acclaim it received. Not long after the premiere of *Wellington,* he made the following remark in his diary: "The likelihood of writing beautifully when composing for the public is obviously the same as when writing quickly!" We also find later derogatory references to such easy pickings: "The world is king, and wants to be flattered. True art, on the other hand, is its own master, and will not be bent to flattery."[12] Within this same context, he also referred to *Wellington's Victory* as an "unprepossessing occasional piece."

Nevertheless, one hallmark of genius is a commitment to one's purpose. Once he had accepted the job, Beethoven came to the table with ambition and appetite, ready to achieve what he could within the precious available creative leeway. It is therefore unfair to judge the results of *Wellington's Victory* by the same high standards that Beethoven applied to himself in other areas, and to which we have become accustomed.

Beethoven's earnest approach to the Wellington project did have one somewhat perverse side effect. Despite all of the inbuilt safety mechanisms, Beethoven had produced a work that was effective, popular, and politically relevant; it reinforced the status quo and can therefore be classified as "reactionary." By so expertly riding the wave of the nationalistic upsurgence,

Beethoven essentially conformed to the role conferred to him by the 1809 "decree." During the Congress of Vienna, which was to commence shortly thereafter, *Wellington's Victory* was given multiple performances; his only opera was revived, and he received several important commissions. On November 16, 1815, Beethoven was even named an honorary citizen of Vienna, which suited him very well at the time, although it is extremely doubtful whether it had ever been a real aspiration of his.[13]

We might consider it an odd twist of fate that Beethoven's rise in status came from his homage to a man whom Heinrich Heine once described as "a dull apparition, with an ash-gray soul in a body of starched linen, and a wooden smile on his frigid face." It irritated Heine exceedingly that Arthur Wellington was "immortalised alongside Napoleon Bonaparte, just as the name Pontius Pilate [became] unforgettably associated with that of Jesus Christ."[14] Had Beethoven been better informed, his opinion of Wellington might well have been the same.

41

A Lucrative Sideline

ALTHOUGH THE EXACT REVENUE GENERATED BY the *Akademie* concerts on January 2 and February 27, 1814, is unknown, it can have been no modest sum. This welcome injection of funds came none too soon. Beethoven's lifestyle was by no means lavish; but by 1813 he was struggling to keep his head above water, a circumstance that weighed on his mind and was hardly conducive to his artistic development. The main culprits were, in his view, the aristocrats who had neglected to meet their commitments from the 1809 agreement. What is more, Beethoven had redirected considerable funds in his ill brother's direction—1,500 guilders in Viennese *Währung*—the retrieval of which ultimately necessitated taking Kaspar Karl's widow, Johanna, to court.[1] Beethoven thus found himself in dire financial straits and was forced to borrow money from Mälzel, his publisher Sigmund Steiner, and the greatest sum from Franz Brentano. Beethoven did so in good faith, as he was convinced that he would be able to pay them back as soon as the problems with Kinsky and Lobkowitz had been resolved.

Now and again the skies cleared: late in 1807, for example, he finally received the promised two hundred pounds from Clementi that had lain trapped behind the continental blockade in London, and in 1813 he received multiple payments from Breitkopf & Härtel. The largest sum, however—250 ducats—came from the Scottish publisher Thomson, as payment for the folksong arrangements that he had commissioned from Beethoven.

The folksong project is a curious blip on the Beethoven radar. It is usually dismissed as a well-paid and fast-earning sideline of little artistic merit and hence often falls through the cracks of music history and concert programming. And yet Beethoven was highly committed to the project; precisely because he was so dedicated, it also exercised his mind a great deal. For this reason alone, the folksong episode is deserving of our attention.

Initial contact with Thomson dates back to the summer of 1803, when Beethoven received the curious request to compose six piano sonatas incorporating Scottish folksong melodies. At that stage, Thomson had already been collecting and publishing folksongs for some time. His approach was devoid of any ethnomusicological or ideological principles—he simply followed his intuition, motivated by a combination of musical enthusiasm, patriotism, and nostalgia. To make his anthologies more palatable and popular for his middle-class audience, he asked certain composers—including Haydn, Hummel, Kozeluch, Pleyel, and Weber—to furnish the original melodies with accompaniments and short introductions and postludes, thus raising the allure of the published songs. In addition, he commissioned eminent poets such as Sir Walter Scott and Lord Byron to write new lyrics to replace the originals, which were usually too crude for prudish, pre-Victorian tastes. Thomson's method was unorthodox: the composers were given only the melodies to work with, and the poets only the original texts, condemning the respective artists to operate in a creative vacuum.

Perhaps Thomson feared that Beethoven would turn up his nose at such menial work, and favored the odds of a more refined project involving sonatas based on Scottish themes. He was gravely mistaken, though, as Beethoven would brook no command regarding the choice of musical material and demanded such an outrageous fee that the project was immediately abandoned. (Two years earlier, we remember, he had used precisely the same strategy to dodge a similar commission for a sonata on the subject of the French Revolution.) In July 1806, Thomson issued a new, even more ambitious proposal: he ordered two sets of six trios and quintets each, and as a side note enquired as to how willing Beethoven might be to arrange some Scottish folksongs. In the rest of his letter, it seemed that Thomson had only half understood Beethoven's previous reply; though his new proposal had uncoupled the folksong project from the ordinary commission, he perpetrated the simultaneous blunder of making suggestions concerning the instrumentation (stating a preference for the flute) and the style (on the "light" side, if possible). Beethoven issued an unequivocal reply, divided into seven discrete sections. These of course addressed the usual matters of money, conditions of payment, and intellectual property; however, Beethoven's principal reservations concerned the musical aspects of the new commission. First of all, he had no inclination whatsoever to write for the flute, an instrument that he regarded as primitive and severely limited. He was also hesitant to commit to six works in each genre. The production of works in sets of three or six was a relic of the ancien régime and had long since lost its relevance to his new, concentrated work ethic aimed at the genesis of original artworks. (Several years earlier, Beethoven had accepted the Lobkowitz commission for six string quartets. He came to regret it, managing to complete two sets of three only with supreme effort. From that point on, he resolved to compose works in sets of no more than three, but even this would later prove unworkable.) Thomson's desire to prescribe the nature of the music itself proved insurmountable: "I shall endeavour to supply compositions that are as uncomplicated and as pleasing as possible, provided this is not at odds with the elevation and originality of style by which you yourself have said that my work is characterised, and to which I will make absolutely no concessions."[2] Full stop. Yet what would prove to be his weightiest remark came in the postscript, in which he agreed to arrange some of the Scottish folksongs. This was a typically Beethovenian contradiction and goes to show once more that he had no objection to an artistic straitjacket—provided it was tight enough. Compositional half-freedom is actually more limiting than no freedom at all.

More than six years would pass before an initial set of sixty-three Scottish, Irish, and Welsh folksong arrangements by Beethoven was ready for publishing. Much of the delay was due to difficulties in communication resulting from the continental blockade—further proof that the embargo was at least as disadvantageous to the mainland as it was to Great Britain. During the blockade, a letter that would ordinarily reach England in around thirty days could take up to nine months, making Beethoven and Thomson's correspondence rife with misunderstandings as the letters passed each other by. Many a package also went astray due to the circuitous routes necessitated by the blockade. An initial batch of songs sent in 1810 never arrived, for example, despite having been sent across three different routes, one of them via Malta. (One of these did ultimately reach its addressee, albeit with a slight delay.) Because Beethoven had neglected to keep a copy for himself, he was forced to start over in 1811. Thankfully, he had taken good care of his sketchbooks, as always.

Another contributing factor to the delay was Beethoven himself, who once again took his remit far too seriously. He himself said that he had worked on the songs "*con amore*"[3]—no prizes for guessing what that means. Whereas his colleagues Haydn, Hummel, Kozeluch, Pleyel, and Weber had been content to write simple accompaniments and short introductions, interludes, and postludes (usually reproducing the first or last line of the melody verbatim), Beethoven instead created new and fully fledged artistic miniatures. In some cases, the purely instrumental sections made up a third of the song's total length and usually constituted an essential, original element of the composition. Beethoven deployed the full arsenal of available techniques for thematic and motivic development, transforming the preludes and postludes into newly composed micro-trios that played an equal part in the musical drama. The accompaniments were far more than cursory harmonizations and maintained their separate identity in the background, often providing a deeper commentary on the simple melodies they supported.[4] Beethoven's job was made even more difficult by Thomson's refusal to supply the lyrics, leaving him to go blindly in search of his own dramatic interpretation and sorely testing his resourcefulness and imagination. Beethoven wrote to Thomson multiple times, begging him to send the accompanying poems in order to help him find the right lyrical expression. Thomson did not capitulate to this—entirely reasonable—request until 1813, when Beethoven threatened that he would otherwise cease collaboration altogether.[5]

Beethoven spent a lot of time on the folksong arrangements. He was therefore stunned to receive an admonishing letter from Thomson in August 1812, over a year after delivery of the initial batch. With true British politeness and charm, Thomson first stated how he had listened to the Scottish, Welsh, and Irish songs in wonder and amazement, how they had garnered much applause, and that he saw them as pearls of composition bearing the hallmarks of genius, profound understanding, and good taste. At the same time, he criticized Beethoven's mini-masterpieces for being too complicated for the broader public for whom they were intended. He then urged Beethoven to rework some of the songs, and even dared to suggest that duplicating the melody would usually suffice for the pianist's right hand; he used a red pencil to highlight the passages in need of correction.[6] This transgression was, of course, unforgiveable. Beethoven had poured his heart and soul into the folksongs, lugging Thomson's tunes around day after day, murmuring them over and over during his walks, searching for just the right illumination to ensure the crystalline clarity of a musical gem. And some Scottish hack dared to lecture him on what notes he could and could not write? Beethoven retaliated with a fiery letter (originally in French): "It pains me to have caused you any displeasure, however I am not accustomed to making any alterations to my compositions. I have never done so, as I am convinced that any partial changes will inevitably affect the compositions as a whole. I am sorry for the losses you have suffered, however you will understand that I am blameless, as you ought to have informed me more thoroughly of the prevailing taste in your country, and of the lack of facility of your intended performers."[7]

Resolute, Beethoven stood his ground and refused to accede to Thomson's wishes. He did, however, declare himself willing, but "with the greatest reluctance" (*avec grande repugnance*), to furnish nine completely new arrangements, for which he charged full price. And so it was that the issue of payment reared its head once more. Beethoven believed he was entitled to a higher fee to compensate for the effort he had devoted to the enterprise. Naturally, Thomson was hardly disposed to accommodate and referred to the remuneration received by the other musical greats—Haydn and Kozeluch—for similar work, usually two ducats per song. Beethoven was unmoved. To him the comparison to Haydn and Kozeluch (the latter of whom Beethoven called a "miserabilis"[8]) was all but irrelevant, since the arrangements they had provided bore no comparison to his own. Beethoven may even have been aware both of the speed at which Haydn worked—completing sometimes eight arrangements per day—and of the fact that he delegated part of the commission work to his pupil Sigismund Neukomm.[9]

In the end, both parties agreed on three ducats per song, a rate that would subsequently be raised multiple times. And despite his insistence to the contrary ("Honour precludes me from disclosing my gains to anybody"[10]), there is no doubt that Beethoven earned a tidy sum from the folksong arrangements. Thomson continued to send Beethoven new folksong melodies regularly until 1820, always accompanied by letters which—while polite—issued the constant reminder to maintain simplicity. Beethoven's patience often wore thin: "You always write saying simple, simple, simple, and I do my best to oblige, but—but—but perhaps the fee could be a little more <u>exacting</u>, or weighty!!!!! [...] When you cry 'simple,' I cry in return '<u>but simple is complicated</u>'!"[11]

In total, Beethoven composed nearly 180 Scottish, Welsh, and Irish folksongs, enough to fill six compact discs. Nevertheless, sales of the folksong arrangements flagged and the enterprise nearly spelled Thomson's financial ruin. He was not to be discouraged, however, and later launched a similar project dedicated to European folksongs, obviously capitalizing on the more relaxed attitudes in Europe following the Congress of Vienna and the renewed communications between England and the continent. On January 1, 1816, he therefore asked Beethoven to collect and arrange a set of twenty-seven new folksongs from Germany, Poland, Russia, Spain, Tyrol, and Venice. Beethoven did so with verve, and within a relatively short time had sent off twenty-seven new arrangements in various configurations. The collection grew into a colorful potpourri, including songs not only from the countries listed above but also from Denmark, Hungary, Ukraine, Portugal, Sicily, and Sweden. Once again, the arrangements testify to Beethoven's commitment to the enterprise. In the end, problems with language and translation seem to have prevented Thomson from ever publishing the European anthology—although it could also be theorized that for the British, Europe was still generally a bridge too far.

In most Beethoven biographies, the folksong project is either trivialized or ignored completely. Of course, Beethoven welcomed occasional opportunities to earn a little extra on the side, and jobs of a "lighter" nature undoubtedly offered respite in psychologically taxing times. But the very fact that Beethoven stayed committed to the project for over ten years, enduring Thomson's nagging and nitpicking for so long, is proof that he must have derived some musical fulfillment from making the most of each song and highlighting the more surprising and unpredictable aspects of each melody. Beethoven's own interest in folklore and folk music doubtless also played a part. And despite not speaking a word of English (Beethoven usually corresponded with Thomson in French and occasionally in Italian), we also know that he had a close affinity with the Ossianic poems and the works of Sir Walter Scott. This too was likely a contributing factor.

First and foremost, the folksong arrangements are a shining example of humble, practical, and musical workmanship and reveal another side to what Thomson described as the "inimitable genius Beethoven."[12] From this perspective, they warrant in-depth study by all students of music. Not only do they offer inspiration to sharpen the imagination, but they also provide a productive training ground for exploring the endless possibilities inherent in even the simplest of melodies, while demonstrating Beethoven's motto that the simple is—oftentimes—complicated.

42

From Leonore *to* Fidelio

FAME OFTEN RESTS ON MISUNDERSTANDING, and when Beethoven achieved immense popularity in 1814 it was at the wrong time and for all the wrong reasons. Since 1812 he had been struggling mentally, and his well of symphonies and sonatas seemed to have dried up. Coincidentally, it was precisely during this trying time that he was appointed unofficial state composer, and his fame among the broader layers of society swelled to new proportions. His earnings matched his newfound notoriety and all because of *Wellington's Victory,* a work that he had thrown together quickly and with the simplest of resources. We might wonder why he never reached such dizzying heights with the nearly one hundred works written over the preceding ten years, into which he had poured his very heart and soul. Some consolation can be derived, however, from meditating on a hypothetical and potentially far greater injustice: the possibility that Beethoven might have pursued fame exclusively through popular kitsch, never producing his other, better works.

We will never know whether these thoughts entered Beethoven's mind when, in the wake of *Wellington's Victory* and going against all expectations, *Leonore* graced concert programs once again in the spring of 1814. The idea was proposed by three singers from the imperial opera—Ignaz Saal, Johann Michael Vogl, and Karl Friedrich Weinmüller—who had been granted permission to schedule their own benefit concert.[1] Programming an attractive opera was vital, due to the ironclad theatrical dictum that the likelihood of a large turnout be inversely proportional to the investment risk. Logic would thus suggest choosing an existing work, but *Leonore*—which no singer or instrumentalist had "ready to go" and which had been controversial from the outset—was a puzzling choice. The three singers were nevertheless a pragmatic bunch. They lived and breathed the theater and had developed an intuitive sense of public demand, and so it must have been with some confidence that they turned to the composer of *Wellington* and asked to borrow the score of his only opera. Beethoven generously agreed and did not ask a fee, stipulating only the express condition that he be permitted to make some changes. The singers clearly had no notion of what that would entail, and naïvely agreed.

To Beethoven, the revival of *Leonore* was in a certain sense a capitulation, the acknowledgment of a prior failure. After the close of *Leonore II* in April 1806 and the rejection of his independent application as imperial opera composer in December 1807, Beethoven had gone keenly in search of a new opera project. But it was a tricky business, and he was oftentimes driven to the brink of desperation. On June 11, 1811, for example, he wrote to the then director of Theater an der Wien, Ferdinand Pálffy: "It is so difficult to find a decent libretto; in the last year alone I have sent back as many as twelve, all financed out of my own pocket, none of which proved to be of any use."[2] There was no shortage of manuscripts offered to him, some even by eminent poets, yet Beethoven always found a reason to reject them. They were either too faddish or outdated, had too many recitatives, were not gripping enough, and so on and so forth. He explained to Gerhard Breuning why he could not find a suitable libretto: "I need a text that speaks to me, something noble and wholesome. I could never use the texts set so successfully by Mozart—I could never feel anything for works of a bawdy nature."[3] Only on a single occasion did Beethoven show some enthusiasm for a potential collaboration with a librettist. In the spring of 1812, the young poet Theodor Körner—a golden child who had moved to Vienna the year before and who had rapidly risen to fame—sent Beethoven a libretto based on the Return of Ulysses. Beethoven was captivated and invited Körner to visit him and flesh out the details. But it would come to nothing, for Körner decided shortly thereafter to join the Lützow Free Corps, a volunteer army whose purpose was to liberate his homeland of Prussia, and died in August 1813.

Beethoven's dream was to tackle the greatest and grandest themes in literature. Sources suggest that in 1808 he had plans to set Goethe's *Faust*,[4] and in a letter from Teplitz in 1812 he proudly announced to Breitkopf & Härtel that Goethe had promised to "write him something."[5] He never did, and we are left in the dark as to why.[6] Beethoven's intention to compose an opera on the other theater classic, Shakespeare's *Macbeth*, met a similar end. The work had found its way into the German-speaking world via the 1800 translation by Schiller. Since Schiller's work—which had been banned by the Viennese authorities for over fifteen years—suddenly became all the rage when the new theater management took control in 1808, Heinrich Joseph von Collin and Beethoven (who had always admired Schiller) wished to capitalize on the resurgence. Collin made it to the middle of the second act with his libretto but called a halt as he found the material too "sinister." His precise meaning remains unclear. Was he, forty years before Verdi and a hundred years before Freud, perhaps afraid of the psychological Pandora's box that Beethoven might open? Whatever the reason, it could be that *Macbeth,* more so than *Faust,* was the greatest of Beethoven's missed opportunities. His sketches show that he had already clearly conceptualized the opening. Unlike *Leonore,* the opera would commence not after but *during* the overture, as the witches and their music emerged seamlessly out of the musical depths. But it was not to be, and Beethoven recycled the fantastical music he had composed for it in the slow movement of the Piano Trio in D Major (op. 70, no. 1), which is now aptly nicknamed "The Ghost."

A further cause for Collin's premature abandonment of *Macbeth* was his desire to work on *Bradamante,* a libretto which—like Handel's *Alcina* and *Rinaldo*—was a derivative of the better-known material from *Orlando Furioso.* Beethoven promptly informed Collin that *Bradamante* held no interest for him, that it contained too much "hocus-pocus" and dulled one's mind and senses.[7] (Beethoven was more than a little upset when he later heard that Johann Friedrich Reichardt, the ex-Kapellmeister from Kassel, was offered the commission.)

More attempts and false starts followed, including collaborations with Kotzebue and Georg Friedrich Treitschke. Finally, in February 1814, the increasingly desperate Beethoven was only too glad at the opportunity to dust off *Leonore.* This time—and with Sonnleithner's permission—he immediately turned to Georg Treitschke, asked him to act as the libretto's reviser, and began tinkering on what he himself called "the stranded ship."[8]

Treitschke was a sound strategic choice. Not only was he an experienced theater producer, but he also held a highly ranked post at the imperial opera, enabling him to mobilize the necessary human and other resources without significant trouble, and to apply pressure where needed. He also had the power to ensure that Beethoven's opera remained on the rotation once the initial benefit concert was over, so that the efforts of the composer and librettist would not have been in vain. Treitschke also knew *Leonore* fairly well, and although the infamous tale of the *Leonore I* rescue operation at the Lichnowskys' was likely an outright fabrication—Treitschke was one of the purported participants—still there were other indications suggesting that he was thoroughly familiar with the opera's strengths and weaknesses.

Such knowledge proved requisite, as Treitschke quickly realized that Beethoven had set the bar high and that hard labor would be required. Again, Beethoven was reminded of how much easier it was to compose a new work rather than edit an old one. He therefore insisted that it was impossible to have the new opera ready within fourteen days and quoted the necessary time at four weeks—another gross underestimation.[9] Ultimately, it would be over two months before Beethoven and Treitschke were ready, and even then the ever-critical Beethoven continued to make changes.

Beethoven took on the revision work with gusto, and on receiving the first proposed amendments by Treitschke, he was only too eager to "rebuild the desolate ruins of an old castle."[10] His work went beyond the usual cosmetic refinements such as scrapping superfluous commentary, eliminating predictable and symmetrical patterns, adding clarity and color to the instrumentation, and making improvements to declamation. Indeed, the duo sought to drastically alter the overall sense of drama. Again there was an attempt to create greater momentum throughout the entire first act: the first two numbers—Marzelline's aria and the duet between Marzelline and Jaquino—were swapped around, allowing the opera to get a running start with a lively dialogue, while two ensemble pieces near the end of the act were discarded. A particularly poignant and dramatic revision was included at the end of act 2. Instead of being part of the prisoners' daily routine, their release became a special privilege granted by Rocco of his own accord, making him a far more sympathetic figure in our eyes. It is touching how, in the exchange with Pizarro, Rocco sheepishly mutters that he released the prisoners in honor of the king's name day. This seemingly minor change was what allowed Beethoven to intensify the music underpinning Pizarro's rage. Whereas previously the first act had ended with a grandiose but hollow "pep talk" delivered by Pizarro to his minions, the prisoners' unauthorized release now enabled a new and engaging conflict to culminate in a dramatic impasse of ever-diminishing light and hope.

Beethoven and Treitschke spent a long time debating the underlying premise of both Florestan's aria and the entire second act. Treitschke later told how Beethoven sent him home time and again, dissatisfied with his proposed lyrics. In truth, their disagreement was of a more fundamental nature, as Beethoven believed that the original aria—which ended with a reverie on bygone domestic bliss and the fulfillment of husbandly duties—was too steeped in bourgeois sentimentality. He wished to portray Florestan in a state of transcendence and ecstasy, delirious with visions of freedom inspired by "the angel Leonore." Treitschke could not reconcile himself to this portrayal, firm in the belief that an emaciated wretch could not possibly sustain such brilliant and demanding vocal theatrics. He forgot that the point of opera is not to be believable—precisely therein lies its charm—and Beethoven stood his ground. The matter was eventually resolved: one evening, having received the latest in a long line of proposed revisions, Beethoven read the text, paced the room up and down mumbling and muttering, then took to the piano and began wondrously to improvise. Treitschke later wrote in his diary that the hours flew by and Beethoven would not be distracted, despite their dinner growing cold on the table. The composer eventually left without food, and the aria was ready the next day.[11]

It is tempting to associate the ecstatic conclusion to Florestan's aria, the oboe's lustrous yearning and the undulating orchestra, with the emotional climax to Beethoven's own "immortal beloved" saga. And while this may certainly have played a role, the aria's new and thrilling conclusion is more directly related to the metamorphosis effected in the close of the opera itself. In the new version, Florestan's freedom can be interpreted as the manifestation of his vision, the realization of a utopian dream. The human drama is thus pushed to the background by the ethical message; the anecdotal elements are minimized and climax further expedited. Instead of celebrating the return of domestic happiness, the opera's conclusion thus becomes a more general hymn to freedom. The protagonists cease to be humans of flesh and blood, and metamorphose into the heralds of abstract and universal ideas. In this manner, the opera ceases to be opera, becoming instead the proclamation of a large-scale vocal manifesto, comparable to the final movement of the Ninth Symphony or the *Credo* from the *Missa solemnis*. Beethoven was skating on thin ideological ice, which ultimately resulted in the quality of the music far superseding that of the text. Not to mention the purely logistical problems that the alternative finale entailed.

Beethoven and Treitschke were naturally more inclined to have the final scene take place not in the dank caverns of the prison but rather in the castle's sun-drenched parade grounds. This scene change—a theater director's nightmare[12]—emphasized the dramaturgical logic underpinning the opera's new premise. While the first act could be viewed as a transition from light into darkness, the second act now portrayed the reverse (keeping in mind that the concluding light was of a very different nature from its initial counterpart). This dialectical development serves as a metaphor for the psychological process undergone by the eponymous heroine, and which is expressed by Beethoven in music—one of the reasons why the title *Leonore* was ultimately exchanged for *Fidelio*. Unlike in 1805, when the suggestion to change the title was motivated by base marketing considerations, it was now supported by the content of the opera itself.

The vocal rehearsals commenced in April 1814. Several days before the premiere, however, the female lead—Frau Hönig—left the production and was hastily replaced by Anna Milder-Hauptmann, who had played Leonore in 1805 and 1806. After ten years, Anna Milder, whose voice had always been powerful but not very agile (she was what one might call a lyric *spinto* soprano), no longer felt confident with the many coloratura passages from the Adagio section of her principal aria ("Komm, Hoffnung"), and she asked Beethoven to remove them. Beethoven, who was quite enamored of the soprano, offered no objection and sacrificed the entire Adagio.

According to Treitschke, who also directed the opera, the rehearsals went without a hitch and the work was well prepared. The dress rehearsal took place on May 22, albeit without the overture, as Beethoven, of course, had once again decided to make a completely fresh start. He felt that the previous overtures revealed too much of the ensuing drama—they were tautological, in other words—and that their character was no longer in keeping with the opera's new opening scene. An additional rehearsal was scheduled for the following morning, but when daylight came Beethoven was nowhere to be found. Treitschke went to Beethoven's home and found him asleep in bed, surrounded by candle stubs, empty wine bottles, and the scattered pages of an unfinished score. In an attempt to burn the midnight oil, he had clearly fallen asleep half drunk and exhausted.[13] The audience at the premiere therefore had to make do with the overture to *The Ruins of Athens*. Three days later, at the next performance, the new overture was ready.

The show was a success. Beethoven conducted with vigor, and concertmaster Michael Umlauf kept a tight hold on the metrical reins. Even at the end of the first act, a rather bashful Beethoven was called on to the stage to receive the audience's loud cries of adulation. In conversation with friends nearly ten years later, he would confess that he had felt flustered at the applause and that he actually found the audience's reaction inappropriate.[14] One of the enthusiastic listeners was a seventeen-year-old who had paid for his ticket by selling some schoolbooks—a young student by the name of Franz Schubert.

Treitschke succeeded in keeping *Fidelio* on the theater rotation. With the exception of a single two-week period in June, when the theater closed its doors in honor of a gala performance celebrating the emperor's return, Beethoven's opera was performed every three days with, in Treitschke's words, "ever-increasing success."[15] Beethoven benefited financially very little from these performances, which was a source of consternation. In a letter to Archduke Rudolph, he once complained that the opera management had put on a performance of *Fidelio* without paying him a cent and that they would have continued to do so had he not "kept a lookout like an old French customs guard."[16] He was therefore aching for an opportunity to organize a benefit concert of his own. He could not do so until July 18, at a time when his target audience—the wealthiest of the Viennese—had fled the hot and dusty city to seek the comfort and relief of a countryside, seaside, or mountain retreat. To mitigate the risk of a low turnout, Beethoven decided on some structural compromises in the hope of generating more popular appeal. Rocco's dreaded "Gold" aria, which had been scrapped after only the first few performances in 1805, was resurrected, and Leonore's grand aria was likewise reinstated. Beethoven composed a new recitative for Anna Milder ("Abscheulicher! Wo eilst du hin?"—Deplorable creature! Whither dost thou hasten?) and after pruning back the ornamentation somewhat, reintroduced her Adagio. Neither intervention was particularly successful, however, as they stalled the momentum in the first act. After only a few shows, the changes were reversed.[17] But these matters were of later concern; Beethoven's objective on July 18 was to fill the hall, and this he did. Although no box-office figures are available, his earnings can only have been appreciable.

Fidelio's victory march did not stop there. Another thirteen performances were held in that year alone, including a festive soirée for the emperor's name day on October 4. *Fidelio* also made regular appearances in 1816, 1817, and 1818. After a lull of several years, a spectacular revival took place on November 3, 1822. The performance caused a furor, not only because the dress rehearsal was marred by a shocking incident in which Beethoven—now virtually stone-deaf—was forcibly removed from the conductor's stand due to his complete inability to lead the production, but also because the fragile, seventeen-year-old Wilhelmine Schröder made her debut as Leonore, a role that she would later play successfully throughout Europe and for which her interpretation would set the standard for decades to come.

Wilhelmine Schröder (later Schröder-Devrient) started her career very early as a ballet dancer and made her public acting debut in the Burgtheater at the age of fifteen. After discovering quite late that she had a beautiful voice, she commenced singing lessons (with Giulio Radicchi, among others, who played Florestan in 1814) and at the age of sixteen took up residence in the Kärntnertortheater, only a few hundred meters from her previous home. She immediately won the hearts of Viennese opera fans with her interpretations of Pamina from *The Magic Flute* and Agathe in *Der Freischütz*—under Weber's own direction. Then, in the autumn of 1822, she was thrown to the lions in her debut as Leonore. Beethoven was extremely skeptical of her ability to master the role, believing that it was folly to entrust such a demanding vocal part to "a child."[18] The opera management, on the other hand, was determined to capitalize on the public demand for new and younger operatic blood, and forged ahead. Wilhelmine would later describe in great detail just how torturous her premiere performance had been.[19] Her mother had helped her diligently study the part, and she embarked rather innocently on the entire enterprise. As the opera progressed, however, the true scope of the role began to dawn on her, and crippling panic took hold. During the performance, her gaze constantly crossed that of Beethoven, who—glaring from behind the conductor, with his head sunk deep into his enormous coat collar, and still rattled from the events of the previous evening's rehearsal—monitored her performance like a hawk. Wilhelmine seized up, her feet turned to lead, and she could barely breathe. She lost control of her voice: all hopes of any legato were lost, and her high notes sounded pinched and forced. Her concentration left her; she was jealous of Thekla Demmer's effortless portrayal of Marzelline and longed to be back at the Burgtheater playing Aricia, Beatrice, Louise, or some other young Ophelia. But strange forces are often at play in the theater, and Wilhelmine, consumed with terror though she was, had no choice but to dive headlong into the opera's gripping finale. Wilhelmine Schröder's fear, frustration, and fury suddenly became those of Leonore. In a state of mental oblivion and unseen frenzy, Schröder/Leonore flung herself upon Anton Forti/Pizarro, abandoning her singing voice in emitting the cry, "Kill first his wife!" The ensuing trumpet signal came as a blessed release to singer and heroine alike; utterly overwrought and drained of all strength, it was all Wilhelmine could do to see Pizarro offstage before the pistol fell from her trembling fingers. She sank to her knees, arched backward, clutched her head with cramped fingers, and—without any premeditation—emitted the famously unmusical and blood-curdling wail that all subsequent Leonores would thereafter seek to imitate. Her loud cry pierced the audience to its very core and served as an outlet for the diabolical tensions that had racked the bodies of both Schröder and Leonore over the preceding hours.

The hall erupted in rapturous applause. Schröder's singing may have been below par, but nobody seemed to care, since never before had the world witnessed such a terrifyingly "lifelike" interpretation of Leonore. Even Beethoven, who had seen it all but heard nothing, was impressed. Afterward he paid a visit to Schröder in her dressing room. He smiled tenderly, patted her on the cheek, expressed his thanks, and promised to write her a new opera.

Wilhelmine Schröder would later go on to give hundreds of performances of *Fidelio* in Europe's biggest theaters, each time seeking to relive and recreate her harrowing experience from that terrible autumn night in Vienna. Her efforts were so successful that her interpretation, right down to the minute gestures and idiosyncrasies, eventually became definitive. Some time later, "La Schröder-Devrient" became Richard Wagner's favorite, and she was the first to sing the roles of Adriano (*Rienzi*), Senta (*The Flying Dutchman*), and Venus (*Tannhäuser*). It was thus that *Fidelio* performers gradually began to favor a Wagnerian over a Mozartian interpretation of the role, and that Leonore came to resemble Senta more than Fiordiligi.

Fidelio's popularity quickly spread beyond Vienna. Several weeks after the premiere on May 23, 1814, Beethoven and Treitschke sent handwritten copies of the score and libretto to ten different opera houses.[20] The response was generally positive, and performances followed in short order. The earliest took place in Prague on November 27 of that same year, followed by Frankfurt (in December 1814), Berlin, Dresden, and Leipzig (in 1815), Breslau, Graz, Hamburg, Karlsruhe, Kassel, Pest, and Weimar (in 1816). Some of the major houses were hesitant—they often had Paër's own *Leonora* on the program— but they eventually came around, with performances in St. Petersburg (1819), Munich (1821), Amsterdam (1824), and Paris (1825, sung in French). It is striking that London (1832), New York (1839, sung in English), and Brussels (1844) were quite late to the party, and the first Italian performance did not take place until 1883 at Teatro dal Verme in Milan. Beethoven and Treitschke of course had no control over the liberties that opera companies took with their text and music; they could only hope that no pirated copies were used in the process. But such was often the case, and there were many royalties that Beethoven and Treitschke never saw.

The international rise of *Fidelio* was staggering and gave signs that Beethoven's career as an opera composer was finally taking off. Alas, nothing was further from the truth. Things took an immediate turn for the worse with a project based on the legend of Romulus and Remus that Beethoven and Treitschke had hoped to realize in the slipstream of *Fidelio*'s success. Beethoven made considerable financial demands—the total revenue from one performance, along with an additional two hundred ducats in cash—which the theater management was disinclined to accept.[21] Matters were further complicated when Beethoven caught wind of a similar commission that Theater an der Wien had offered to a hack by the name of Jonás Fusz, and nobody could give him a straight answer. As the negotiations dragged on for nearly a year, *Romulus and Remus* died a silent death.

At this point, Beethoven turned to Berlin, where Anna Milder-Hauptmann had rescued the October 1815 production of *Fidelio* by replacing the ailing female lead from the second performance onward. Beethoven was so grateful that he promised to write her a new opera and had her ask Friedrich de la Motte Fouqué whether he might provide a libretto. Beethoven added that the opera would be a Berlin exclusive, as he had lost confidence in Vienna's "penny-pinching opera management."[22] This venture also ran aground—exactly why is anybody's guess.

The last of the renewed opera attempts was perhaps the most serious. As mentioned above, following the successful revival of *Fidelio* in 1822, Beethoven had promised to compose a new opera for Wilhelmine Schröder. His chosen librettist was Franz Grillparzer, one of the leading poets of the younger generation. Both had known each other for quite some time. During the summer of 1808, Beethoven had even shared a summer house with the Grillparzers in Heiligenstadt. But despite their personal acquaintance, the initial back-and-forth in the spring of 1823 was mediated by Moritz Lichnowsky—the youngest brother of Karl Lichnowsky—and by theater manager Moritz Dietrichstein. The use of intermediaries hampered communications somewhat, particularly regarding money matters, in which regard Beethoven and Grillparzer were polar opposites. For the subject matter, they ultimately (and remarkably) settled on *Melusine,* a German *Zauberoper,* or "magic opera." *Melusine* was oftentimes rather risqué, included a hefty dose of *couleur locale,* and differed fundamentally from *Fidelio* and the many other dramatic, idealistic works to which Beethoven had always gravitated in the past. Dietrichstein in particular seemed to have insisted on *Melusine.* He had his reasons: a war was raging in Vienna between the proponents of German and Italian opera, and the latter was gaining ground. Vienna was under Rossini's spell, and when impresario Domenico Barbaia, the manager of the well-known Neapolitan San Carlo opera, was also asked to take charge of the Vienna theaters, things looked grim for the German camp. This is the context in which Dietrichstein's imposition must be understood. It also explains why the project failed, as Barbaia—to put it mildly—did very little to ensure any success. Beethoven made a very brief attempt to sell *Melusine* to Berlin, where the notion of a collaboration between Beethoven and Grillparzer did spark some interest. Berlin proposed a change of subject matter, however, claiming that *Melusine* too closely resembled another magic opera—*Undine* by E. T. A. Hoffmann—that had already premiered in 1816. Some purely structural elements may also have contributed to *Melusine*'s demise. Grillparzer had intended to open the opera with a great hunters' chorus, forcing Beethoven to take up unwilling arms against a similar scene from *Der Freischütz*—no mean feat, given the colossal success of Weber's opera. Beethoven briefly contemplated using no fewer than eight horns to trump his younger fellow, but was likely put off by the compelling realization that bigger is not necessarily better. Beethoven was also supremely aware that the implicit rivalry was not limited to the hunters' chorus but also extended to the tone of the opera in general, which is what may have finally dissuaded him in the end.

The absence of any second opera by Beethoven has been the topic of heated discussion. A common tactic is to dismiss the matter by proposing that after his gargantuan efforts on *Fidelio*—which had earned him, in his own words, the "crown of martyrdom"[23]—he no longer had the strength to complete a new work in the genre. In a remarkably astute observation, Grillparzer suggested that Beethoven's creativity had simply become so boundless that no libretto in existence could possibly have served as a vessel to contain the flood of his imagination. The most sober explanation came from the master himself, however, who in conversation with Georg August von Griesinger in 1822 reportedly said: "Although I am fully aware of the worth of my *Fidelio*, I am equally aware that the symphony really is my true element. When I imagine the sound, I hear the entire orchestra. I can demand what I like from instrumentalists, but when writing for the voice I must always ask myself: Can this be sung?"[24]

And so, Beethoven composed only one opera. Or did he? Is *Fidelio* the definitive version of a work whose antecedents—the *Leonore*s from 1805 and 1806—were mere unfinished drafts, necessary byways on the road to the final destination? Or do the two *Leonores*, and the latter in particular, have their own raison d'être and are thus deserving of a status as independent works? Does *Fidelio* represent the culmination of a process, or is there a virtual, fourth version that we shall never know? The repeated inclusion and subsequent removal of arias by Rocco and Leonore is also clear evidence that Beethoven continued to doubt the pragmatic choices he was forced to make in 1814. Looking at his orchestral music, we can see that Beethoven habitually incorporated drastic changes to his music when preparing it for publication. Yet this opportunity was never afforded him with *Fidelio,* and so we must resign ourselves to never truly knowing what the definitive version might have been.

Most specialists now agree that the 1806 version of *Leonore* should be approached from a different perspective from that of *Fidelio* (rather too little is known about the *Leonore* from 1805). Although they share their composer and narrative, the composer's ideas and the context in which they emerged had changed so radically in the intervening period that the two works really should be viewed separately. By 1814, Beethoven had lost much of his optimistic hope for a society free from tyranny and where the principles of brotherhood and liberty were held high. The narrative thus inevitably took on a more universal and reflective character, with a reduced emphasis on the personal, human elements. Consequently, *Fidelio* is less concerned with trifling or anecdotal material—the main characters are more purposeful and defined—and the dramatic momentum is greater than in *Leonore.* The flipside of this coin, however, is a loss of characterization and fine detail. The same applies to the *music* of the 1814 version, which is far more compact and economical than before and clearly embodies the direction in which Beethoven had chosen to develop his musical idiom. But efficiency and efficacy are two different things, and no true expert or music lover can claim with any certainty that the gains in abstraction and musical or dramatic impact can compensate fully for the loss of theatrical and musical spontaneity. From this perspective, there is certainly a life for *Leonore* alongside *Fidelio.*

43

From Coffee and Cake to Congress and Kitsch

BEETHOVEN'S WORK ON *FIDELIO* was temporarily suspended for a brief patriotic intermezzo. On April 11, 1814, the Kärntnertortheater hosted the premiere of *Die gute Nachricht* (O glad tidings), a singspiel celebrating the capitulation of Paris and the fall of Napoleon. Treitschke had already begun work on the text before April 9—the day on which the "glad tidings" actually reached Vienna—proving that in addition to his skills as an accomplished librettist and director, he also had a keen nose for political and social developments. The work was nonetheless thrown together in rather short order, and multiple composers were enlisted to ensure the deadline was met. There were some advantages to the joint approach, which thanks to the involvement of several famous names, increased both the project's allure and its market value. Given the hype surrounding *Wellington's Victory*, Beethoven's inclusion in the line-up was a must. But unlike earlier occasions, when he had steadfastly refused to share the toil, glory, and earnings with his fellow composers, Beethoven now had no objection to working alongside Gyrowetz, Hummel, Kanne, and Weigl and even lent his collaboration completely free of charge. Perhaps, after the success of *Wellington's Victory*, he no longer took a condescending view of such engagements; it remains curious, however, that a man who only two years before had condemned Goethe's excessive fondness for the "courtly air" should himself now compose a bombastic hymn brimming with empty and ecstatic exhortations, such as "Kaiser Franz! Victoria!" and "Germania! Germania!"

Beethoven clearly saw the opportunities offered by the new wave of nationalism. On discovering that Vienna was to be the stage for an enormous diplomatic spectacle attracting all European heads of state, government leaders, and their retinues, he saw his chance to work himself into the spotlight, with hopes of securing international offers of employment. For the first time in years, he remained in Vienna for nearly the whole summer, and in August he set the wheels in motion for several *Akademie* concerts.

Despite Austria's none-too-enthusiastic involvement in the coalition, its capital city—represented by Minister of Foreign Affairs Klemens von Metternich—had been put in charge of the mammoth congress whose purpose was to establish the chalk lines for a post-Napoleonic Europe. It was not without some pride that Emperor Francis I welcomed not only the tsar of Russia but also no fewer than six kings, over one hundred princes, dukes, electors, and counts, and around two hundred diplomats—including their retinues and servants—to the Hofburg, which had been transformed into a luxury hotel specially for the occasion. No expense or effort was spared to make the "Congress of Vienna" a true "Viennese congress." Even the emperor—a born-and-bred Hapsburg, and stingy to the last—was convinced that Vienna could not pass up an opportunity to show the world what it was capable of, provided it could play a "home game" in the fields of culture, ceremony, and amusements. The honored guests were treated to a lavish entertainment program of concerts, opera, and theater shows, banquets, parades, dances and masked balls (called *redoutes*), festive masses, hunting parties, sleigh rides, carousels, and fireworks. The support services were also first-class: hundreds of cartwrights, decorators, tailors, and chefs were rounded up to provide for transport, wardrobe, catering, and various other forms of bodily comfort. The congress committee also called on the hospitality of the Austrian, Hungarian, and Bohemian nobility so that guests might sojourn in an aura of distinction and refinement even when outside the capital. It was not only the magnificent palaces that contributed to this end—the Russian delegation's festivities were held in the Razumovsky residence, for example—but the striking beauty of the aristocratic hostesses also played a part. As a rule, they were tall and slender, had a unique air about them thanks to their peculiar blend of Hungarian, Slavic, and Italian roots, and were praised and admired by all for the elegance and discretion of their conduct. Despite their unblemished reputation, however, it should be noted that Princess Gabrielle Auersperg (affectionately dubbed "la beauté du vrai sentiment") was sighted with alarming regularity in the vicinity of the tsar; that Countess Julie Zichy ("la beauté celeste") was the subject of the Prussian king's attentions; and that equally questionable conduct was displayed by countesses Sophie Zichy ("la beauté triviale"), Maria Theresia Esterházy ("la beauté étonnante"), Caroline Széchenyi ("la beauté coquette"), and Gabriele Saurau ("la beauté du diable").

Not all of the guests were of such distinguished caliber. As is typical of most events on such an enormous scale, Vienna was also overrun with lobbyists, bodyguards, shady dealers, street artists, astrologists, and sex workers, who swarmed like bees around the diplomatic honeypot. At the first ball held in the main ballroom, where three thousand guests were expected, tickets were collected by the porters and then immediately scalped to others in the inner courtyard. Ultimately, over six thousand guests stood jostling at the buffets, and the next morning it was discovered that around fifteen hundred pieces of brand-new silverware had been stolen.

The Austrian emperor paid for the entire congress, a publicity stunt costing an estimated twenty million guilders, or just under one billion euros. The Viennese papers were well informed when they reported that "The King of Bavaria does the drinking for everyone, the King of Denmark does the talking, the King of Würtemberg does the eating, the Tsar does the loving, the King of Prussia does the thinking, Talleyrand does the thieving, and the Kaiser pays for the lot."[1] It was the common people, of course, who ultimately footed the bill. Not long after seeing much of their capital evaporate during the devaluation of 1811, on January 1, 1815, they were also subjected to an additional 50 percent tax increase. One small consolation was that organizing a world congress was still cheaper than waging a war, and no lives were lost in the process.

Beethoven quickly realized that this explosion of pomp and circumstance provided the perfect opportunity to put himself in the European spotlight. And this he did, thanks in part to his close connections with Prince Ferdinand von Trauttmansdorff, who as *Obersthofmeister* was head of the administrative committee and thus had the final say over all cultural events during the congress. It was this association that afforded Beethoven the honor of composing a festival overture for the emperor's name-day celebrations on October 4. But despite the wealth of material he already had available (including sketches of themes with reference to Schiller's "Ode to Joy"), the *Namensfeier* overture was not ready by the deadline,[2] and so the emperor was instead treated to another performance of *Fidelio*. Beethoven was also granted permission to schedule three *Akademie* concerts in the Hofburg's Redoutensaal, the first of which took on a particularly ceremonial character due to the attendance of each and every dignitary at the congress. After being rescheduled three times (for various reasons, leaving Beethoven rather frustrated), it eventually took place on November 29. Count Pálffy—

one of the few remaining members of the aristocratic consortium that had taken control of the Viennese theaters in 1807—was in such dire pecuniary straits that he tried to turn the hire of the Hofburg's public venues to his financial advantage. Originally, he laid claim to one third of Beethoven's takings, but after the inconvenience of having to reissue the same reservation three times in quick succession, he raised the price to half of the revenue. It was only after a polite but incisive letter from Trauttmansdorff that dismissed Pálffy's claim as uncustomary, excessive, improper, and deleterious to Vienna's cultural image that Beethoven was given the hall on far more favorable terms: for free.[3]

On November 29, an audience of fifteen hundred flocked to the Hofburg for an afternoon concert dedicated entirely to Beethoven's music. In addition to the Seventh Symphony and the, by then, ubiquitous *Wellington's Victory,* the concert featured a cantata composed specially for the occasion: *Der glorreiche Augenblick* (O moment of glory; op. 136), with a politically correct and obsequious text by Salzburg surgeon and professor of veterinary science Dr. Weissenbach (the libretto's many saccharine clichés include the rhyming of *Franz* with *Glanz,* German for "resplendence"). Over the course of six movements, the singers proclaimed the glory of Vienna and the unified purpose of the assembled heads of state—a somewhat cynical sentiment, since behind closed doors those very same dignitaries were fighting viciously for every last scrap of European soil. Although Beethoven set the farce to music quickly and efficiently, he had no choice but to produce a work that was fundamentally disproportionate—while proportion was usually his strong suit—and which employed ideas that were too short and spun out for far too long. Aside from a few fleeting moments of refined expression (Beethoven could never lose himself entirely, after all), *Der glorreiche Augenblick* sounds altogether uninspired, incoherent, simplistic, and bombastic. And with good reason: musical profundity was not part of the brief, and the audience responded with palpable enthusiasm. Yet the intended object of their applause remains unclear; when the concert was repeated three days later without the presence of the monarchs, the general populace also stayed away. The third concert was canceled, and the entire project left Beethoven severely out of pocket.

His fame among the crowns and their retinues *was* secured, however. There are tales that during a reception organized by Alexander I in the chambers of Archduke Rudolph, dignitaries were waiting in line just to shake hands with the great master (a conversation with him had become virtually impossible). Beethoven was happy to oblige,[4] and his ego was particularly gratified by the ample attentions of the tsar's wife, Elizabeth Alexeievna. Following the *Akademie* on November 29, 1814, she had a messenger deliver the sum of two hundred gold ducats to Beethoven, accompanied by a request to hear him play in person during a private audience. Beethoven's languishing piano technique meant that he could hardly indulge her request, but to thank her for her generosity, he gifted the tsarina (who also happened to be a princess of Baden by birth) the Polonaise in C (op. 89). Given Russia's obsession with annexing Poland in 1814, the gesture also doubled as a droll and none-too-subtle commentary on the prevailing political climate.[5]

Other royals, too, called on Beethoven's services. The Prussian delegation wished to stage the tragic tale of the young Leonore Prohaska from Potsdam, who had disguised herself in men's clothing and joined the volunteer forces, only to perish in battle. The dramatization by public servant Friedrich Duncker, *Leonore Prohaska,* was a tribute to the strength of the Prussian people blended with some Masonic undertones. Beethoven was invited to supply the score, and with a bare minimum of resources he successfully cobbled together four items. The vocal numbers had little to no orchestral accompaniment, and the funeral march was an instrumental arrangement of the *Marcia funebre* from the opus 26 piano sonata. We might imagine Beethoven's relief when the production was called off, presumably due to anti-Prussian sentiments in Vienna.

In July 1815, one month after the congress had finished, Beethoven was summoned for one final musical contribution, with a commission identical to the project outlined at the start of this chapter. After Paris had been taken for the second time, on July 7, Treitschke composed another singspiel, *Die Ehrenpforten* (The gates of glory), using a framework virtually identical to that of *Die gute Nachricht.* The line-up of composers was the same, and again Beethoven was entrusted with the finale. Here too Beethoven produced an ode to the emperor, a hymn for bass, choir, and orchestra culminating in the acclamation "Gott sei Dank und unserm Kaiser! Es ist vollbracht!" (Thanks be to God and our Emperor! The task is complete!), while fragments of Haydn's "Gott erhalte Franz den Kaiser" (God save Emperor Francis) resounded in the background.

It was thus that Beethoven fulfilled his patriotic duty. In return, in November 1815 he was granted honorary citizenship of the city of Vienna. As an immigrant of Flemish descent from the provincial Rhineland, Beethoven was vain enough to view his appropriation by the Viennese establishment as both an honor and a privilege. Although the distinction undoubtedly conferred some practical advantages, its significance should not be exaggerated; on the contrary, the Viennese authorities continued to treat Beethoven as a benign but marginal phenomenon on the periphery of society. In a secret dossier issued after the *Akademie* on November 29, 1814, a security agent reassuringly reported: "Yesterday's *Akademie* has done nothing to increase the popularity of Herr Beethoven's music. Though Razumovsky, Apponyi, Kraft and others may idolise Beethoven, they are outnumbered by the vast majority of connoisseurs who will not have a bar of him."[6] It is clear that the year 1814 simultaneously represented the quantitative zenith and the qualitative nadir of Beethoven's career. Over the course of a few months, he gave more *Akademien* than during the rest of his life combined, and *Fidelio* received nearly twenty performances. Equally striking, though, is the fact that he owed his public successes to works that demonstrated an atypical lack of substance, and which would later be characterized as "kitsch." In other words, through his participation in the restoration extravaganza, Beethoven had rendered himself unthreatening as a citizen but relegated his artistic self to the sidelines.

This moment of artistic occlusion was accompanied by the downfall and disappearance of several key aristocratic figures who had hitherto been reliable sources of support. In this sense at least, the remark made by the security agent was correct. Kinsky had fallen from his horse in 1812; Lobkowitz tumbled from his pedestal one year later; and Lichnowsky passed away on April 15, 1814. On December 31 of that same year, Razumovsky's palace burned to a cinder. Razumovsky had built a wooden annex abutting his property in order to hold a lavish ball in honor of Alexander I on New Year's Eve. The heating system (which, ironically, was of French manufacture) caught fire, setting the entire palace ablaze. The emperor rushed to the scene and, in an attempt to console the lord of the manor, uttered the celebrated words: "Well, the same might very well have happened to me—I have the same heating system, after all." He later added, "One should keep away from all things French."[7]

Several months later, Beethoven would write to his lawyer Johann Nepomuk Kanka: "And so everything is an illusion . . . friendship, kingdom, empire, all mere mists that can be blown away or transformed by the slightest breath of wind."[8]

But the loveliest flowers often bloom in the face of adversity. And although the "kitsch" produced by Beethoven in the years 1814 and 1815 enjoys little appreciation or understanding among connoisseurs (fueled in part by the moral umbrage they evoke), its purifying effect on Beethoven should not be underestimated. Beethoven had reached a compositional dead end in 1812, and for the second time in his career he was ready to forge a "new way" forward. As in 1802, when his "new path" could not be forged on command, there was no reason to suspect that 1812 would be any different. He first needed to unburden his mind and put production on hold. Something akin to a sabbatical or moratorium would certainly have helped, but such inactivity is difficult to impose on the creative spirit; the imagination can barely even be comprehended let alone apprehended. For an extended period it was therefore essential for Beethoven to dedicate himself to projects whose impetus was external—such as the revision of *Leonore*—or which distanced him from his natural mode of musical expression, such as the overblown congress music.

This period of creative estrangement proved fruitful. During the summer of 1814—in the midst of the *Fidelio* revival and sandwiched between *O Glad Tidings* and *O Moment of Glory*—Beethoven composed the Piano Sonata in E Minor (op. 90), an effortless exploration of a new musical idiom. His motivation for it was entirely materialistic, however, verging even on the banal. In April 1813, Beethoven had loaned fifteen hundred guilders to his brother Kaspar Karl and his wife, Johanna. After a small court case between the two brothers, they agreed that the sum would be repaid in two installments by July 1814 at the latest. Beethoven's generosity had landed him in quite a predicament—he was most likely counting on a speedy resolution to the Kinsky-Lobkowitz fiasco—and in December 1813, his funds ran dry. He turned to his publisher Steiner, who paid him the entire amount as an advance, on the understanding that in the event of his brother's failure to observe the repayment schedule, Beethoven would have three months in which to resolve the matter. Should Beethoven prove insolvent at that time, Steiner would be content with payment in kind: Beethoven would deliver a piano sonata posthaste, and Steiner would acquire the rights to several major works at a bargain price (essentially opuses 90–100). And so it came to pass. But despite not having composed a single piano work in five years—or perhaps *because* he had not composed a single piano work in five years—the new sonata flowed easily from Beethoven's pen without any serious sketch work or substantial intellectual or psychological barriers. The results speak for themselves. Rarely had Beethoven's music ever sounded so natural, and Schubert's spirit feels very close by.

The work's innovative nature comes from an unexpected angle. A clue is provided by the various movements' tempo indications, as this sonata is the first in which Beethoven makes use of extended descriptions in German: "Mit Lebhaftigkeit und durchaus mit Empfindung und Ausdruck" (Lively, and above all with sensitivity and expressiveness), and "Nicht zu geschwind und sehr singbar vorzutragen" (Not too fast, and to be performed very lyrically). Although his choice of the vernacular might initially seem to have sprung from a patriotic or nationalistic reflex, nothing could be further from the truth. Beethoven incorporated German tempo indications because they are more descriptive of the character and performance of the work than their traditional Italian counterparts. At first glance, the instructions seem full of contradictions: the first movement should be fast (lively) yet unhurried (with sensitivity and expressiveness), and simultaneously introverted (with sensitivity) and extroverted (and expressiveness). The second movement, too, inhabits a gray area between fast and not-too-fast, while also requiring lyrical expression. But this apparent ambiguity is exactly what allowed Beethoven to achieve the precision he was looking for. Experienced performers are familiar with the almost transcendental realm in which a faster tempo can *sound* slower, and vice versa, and where the subtlest shifts in timbre are easier to "sense" than to "hear." (Interestingly, Beethoven's new Streicher piano was the instrument from which he attempted to coax this form of "shimmering song.") Set against the deafening hullabaloo of the congress, the Piano Sonata in E Minor demonstrates how Beethoven was able to circumvent a compositional impasse by moving away from music as "organized sound" and more toward the notion of "tonal poetry."

The same tendency is evident in the modest choral work titled *Meeresstille und glückliche Fahrt* (Calm sea and prosperous voyage; op. 112), composed by Beethoven on the heels of *The Gates of Glory*. The work is a setting of two poems by Goethe about a vessel, which after an unsettling period of eerie stillness at sea is once again set in motion toward safe haven and solid ground. Could the timing of this work be a coincidence? The slow, measured, yet fluid tempo of the opening section (note the mixed signals once again: alla breve, yet poco sostenuto) provides the framework for the evocation of the vast stillness and expanse of the sea, to which the captain at first willingly, and later fearfully, surrenders himself. In part two, fresh winds grant energy, momentum, and renewed joy at the prospect of a safe landing after a "prosperous voyage." Although the fortissimi and sforzati come thick and fast, they owe much of their impact and timing to the recurring piano interpolations, and unlike *O Moment of Glory,* the mounting intensity of this gesture is achieved not through force but through restraint. The same can be said of the *Elegischer Gesang* (Elegiac song; op. 118), which Beethoven composed alongside the Piano Sonata in E Minor for his loyal friend Johann Pasqualati von Osterberg, to commemorate the third anniversary of the death of his wife. The grave subject matter of the poetry does of course lend itself to such sober treatment.

A different fate befell the new Piano Concerto in D Major, which Beethoven worked on for some time during the spring of 1815. Alas, he abandoned the work halfway through the opening solo exposition. Perhaps he realized that the fanfare-like themes and strident drum-based rhythms of his old "heroic" style had long become a compositional cliché—a crutch that he would do better to leave behind.

44

The Fight for a Child

LET US BRIEFLY STEP BACK IN TIME. On April 12, 1813, exactly four days after Josephine had been delivered of a daughter (whose real father may or may not have been in the vicinity), Beethoven's brother Kaspar Karl placed his signature on a will and testament that assigned a second, virtual father to his six-year-old son. His act was both hasty and unnecessary; Kaspar Karl's health may have been in decline, but his condition was far from life-threatening. He would live for another two and a half years, and contemporary laws dictated that as the closest male relative, Beethoven would be awarded either full or partial custody of his nephew anyway. What is more, the criminal record of Kaspar Karl's wife would have precluded her from making any case for the exclusive guardianship of her son (two years earlier she had been arrested on charges of embezzlement). Johanna was initially sentenced to a year in prison under the strictest observation, but ultimately her punishment was reduced in both duration and intensity to a brief period under house arrest.[1] With this in mind, the guardianship agreement between the brothers appears less like a decision in favor of Beethoven, and more like a maneuver against Johanna. She undoubtedly perceived it as an act of both provocation and betrayal, especially in light of indications that Kaspar Karl had, if no direct involvement, then at least knowledge of the offense for which she had been convicted. But taking into account that on the same day, Beethoven also loaned his brother a considerable sum of money under strict repayment conditions (for which Johanna also stood surety), we cannot ignore the possibility that Kaspar Karl signed the agreement under strong duress.

Beethoven had never thought particularly highly of his sister-in-law.[2] He held her responsible for his brother's financial troubles and was appalled at the manner in which she had attempted to alleviate them. In a letter to the regional court of Lower Austria (then known as the *Landgericht*), he emphasized her limited intellectual and ethical merits, as well as her licentious, reckless, careless, and overemotional character. He thus saw it as his duty to protect his nephew Karl from her influence.[3] When word reached him on November 14, 1815, that Kaspar Karl—now truly at death's door—had drawn up a new contract allocating partial custody to Johanna, Beethoven made his brother strike out the relevant clause. The terminal patient complied,[4] but no sooner had Beethoven turned his back than Johanna coaxed her husband—who was probably susceptible to a final act of conciliation—into writing an annex to the testament (a "codicil") expressing his wish that Karl be granted unlimited access to his mother, as well as the desperate and, as would later transpire, fruitless plea: "Only through unity can the purpose for which I appointed my brother as sole guardian of my son, be achieved; for the sake of my child, I therefore ask of my wife greater flexibility, and of my brother, greater temperance."[5] Subsequent attempts by Beethoven to nullify the codicil failed, as the lawyer responsible for the document could no longer be reached. Kaspar Karl died the following day, and for all of his surviving relatives—his nine-year-old son especially—a litany of woe began that would last for over eleven years and leave its bitter mark on all those involved.

One week after the death of Kaspar Karl, the court performed its duty and awarded Beethoven and Johanna dual custody of the young Karl. Beethoven refused to accept the ruling, however, and immediately instigated new legal proceedings. The very least that can be said is that this aggressive strategy—however well-intentioned it may have been—was hardly conducive to his relationship with the child whose surrogate father he wished to become, and for two reasons. First, Karl was thus denied any opportunity to grieve for his own father, leaving no space open for a substitute to step in. (As a further consequence, the young Karl clung desperately to his mother, far more than Beethoven would have liked.) Second, Beethoven created such enmity between himself and Johanna that any hopes of harmonious relations within the new family arrangement were dashed at the outset. Young Karl was thus siphoned, as it were, into an already broken family and became the object of a tug-of-war between two hostile partners. Karl was given little opportunity by his stepfather to nurture any kind of loving relationship with his mother, causing major frustrations and standing in the way of a new father-son relationship.

Beethoven clearly felt sure of himself: no sooner had he submitted his appeal than he began asking his friends—Nannette Streicher in particular—to help him reorganize both the running and the layout of his household. At the end of a rather aggressive campaign, in which Johanna's reputation was dragged through the mud, the *Landgericht* court ruled on January 9, 1816, that Johanna be denied all custody of her son. Ten days later, Beethoven signed the official guardianship documents.

Beethoven desired more than mere guardianship, however. His diary literally states, "Regard K[arl] as your own son, let no mundanities or trivialities stand in the way of this solemn purpose."[6] But true fatherhood can only grow naturally through long-term and complex interaction with the developing child, and it was in this respect that Beethoven—who was late to the party, so to speak—still had a great deal to learn. As reference material, his own father was of profoundly little use. Only from the Breunings (who, incidentally, also lacked a functioning father figure) had Beethoven gained an understanding of the more ambitious objectives that qualified as criteria for a good upbringing among the upper middle classes, such as nurturing a career, good health, the importance of honesty and hard work, and the cultivation of good manners. In all other respects he resorted to his own personal set of beliefs, which had originally been garnered from books and subsequently coalesced into an ideology utterly divorced from all practicality. Beethoven's principal aim was to be an enlightened father, who set high expectations for himself and, more importantly, for his child. He had predestined the boy for a life in the arts or sciences—the only way, in his view, to escape the drudgery of an ordinary life.[7] In pursuit of this noble goal, Beethoven drew from a wide range of parenting strategies: patient negotiation, encouragement, preaching, admonition, and punishment, the last of which included various subtle forms of emotional blackmail. Where these methods did not suffice, Beethoven saw fit to employ the ultimate means and administer a good hiding.[8] Occasionally a more experienced outsider would try to goad Beethoven toward a greater degree of pedagogical realism. But such advice generally fell on deaf ears. Only in rare cases did Beethoven deign to follow others' suggestions—he had given the matter a great deal of thought, after all, and knew his personal circumstances like no other. Was the decision therefore not his to make?

In spite of his eagerness, Beethoven still realized that for one reason or another he would be ill-advised to take Karl into his home straightaway. He therefore sent the boy to a boarding school in Landstrasse, run by Mr. and Mrs. Giannattasio del Rio. The original plan was for Karl to stay only three months, but he would remain there for over two years. The Giannattasios' private school had a good reputation in aristocratic circles, for whom it was customary to outsource the upbringing of children. Beethoven was also initially on good terms with the school directors and their family, spending many a cheerful evening at their home, where discussion was not always limited to Karl's academic progress. The family's two unmarried daughters—the twenty-five-year-old Franziska (Fanny) and her sister Nanni, who was two years younger—were particularly enamored of the regular visits by their celebrated guest. Beethoven was drawn particularly to the younger sister, who unfortunately was already spoken for. The somewhat melancholy Fanny, on the other hand—whom Beethoven playfully referred to as "mother superior"—did have strong feelings for Beethoven. Her affections were not returned.

Karl's piano tuition was entrusted to Carl Czerny, who visited the institute three times a week. Until then, Karl had received lessons from his father, and in Beethoven's opinion the boy possessed sufficient talent to make a career as a professional musician. Beethoven kept a close eye on his nephew's musical progress and wrote Czerny a letter setting out some concrete guidelines. Contrary to his own early musical education, he urged a patient and gentle approach, for fear of unduly stressing the young Karl. He also made a point of not focusing unnecessarily on minor errors but concentrating instead on expression, which Beethoven deemed was of the utmost artistic importance. Lastly, he stipulated that there was no strict need for Karl to play his own compositions, saying that he was "not so childish as to desire such things."[9]

Though well-intentioned, the decision to send Karl to boarding school was in some respects detrimental. For one thing, the constant shunting between three different parenting strategies can only have had an unsettling influence; for another, the regular visits from his mother, which were intended to offer the poor boy some comfort in his emotional distress, usually had the opposite effect. The heartbreaking scenes that played out on each farewell prompted the principal to insist that drastic measures be taken. Beethoven was only too happy to oblige, and in a letter to Giannattasio—in which he referred to himself as "Karl's father"—he ordained that under no circumstances should his nephew be allowed to leave the institute without his express consent, and that his mother should first consult the legal guardian prior to any visits. As an "enlightened" educator, Beethoven claimed that it was in his pupil's interests to be shielded from the influence of his "debauched" mother. To justify his position, he also added a juicy anecdote: "This Queen of the Night was at the artists' ball yesterday until three in the morning, where she proved scant not only of intellect, but also of apparel. She could—it was said—be had for 20 guilders!"[10]

The temporary sidelining of Karl's mother solved only one of many problems, most of which were born of Beethoven's erratic conduct, indecision, and inner turmoil. For two years he repeatedly extended Karl's stay at the boarding school—or rather, he repeatedly postponed the decision to take Karl into his own home—for periods of three months at a time. In some respects, he did everything in his power to remain permanently close to his charge. For a while he considered moving into a small cottage in the Giannattasios' garden, for example, but when the time finally came to put concrete plans in place, he changed his mind, saying his health would not permit it. He did remain in the vicinity, but switched lodgings with a frequency uncommon even for Beethoven.[11] Next he decided that Karl would spend three nights per week at his home: the boy arrived at six o'clock, received a piano lesson from Czerny, and departed the following morning at eight. At several crucial moments, however, when Beethoven could have provided Karl with much-needed emotional support—when he underwent a hernia operation, for example, or expressed a desire to visit the grave of his father on the one-year anniversary of his death—Beethoven turned a deaf ear. The same applied to the summer holidays, which Beethoven spent alone for two successive years while his nephew pined away in the lonesome solitude of a boarding school. (As a side note, Beethoven's indecision regarding a shared future with his nephew may have been responsible for his odd response to the proposal by the Philharmonic Society in London. Beethoven was certainly eager to travel there but raised his fee to such irrational heights that the project was destined to fail, illustrating his incapacity to decide between self-interest and what he perceived to be the child's happiness.)

Neither party benefited from the unstable situation. Beethoven contracted chronic pneumonia, showed signs of extreme exhaustion, and was deeply melancholic—some sources even suggest that he was plagued by suicidal thoughts. He also suffered a profound inability to work; proofing and editing tested the limits of his concentration, and composing was entirely out of the question. Karl, too, suffered greatly from emotional instability and lack of affection. Beethoven himself noted that the boy ate little, said nothing, was downcast, and also seemed less studious than usual. As we might expect, Beethoven held the school fully accountable, which occasionally led to heated exchanges with those in charge. Even the charming daughter Fanny, who can certainly not be maligned for any lack of empathy toward Beethoven, was lambasted for delicately suggesting where the real problem might lie.

Beethoven finally bit the bullet in January 1818 and invited his nephew to come and live with him permanently. Nannette Streicher helped him make the necessary alterations to household and personnel, including the appointment of a new private tutor. Beethoven would provide the piano lessons himself, which offered perhaps the safest guarantee for ruining both the boy's musical education and any hopes of a blossoming relationship with his uncle. Unsurprisingly, little information is available on domestic relations between the two Beethovens; however the elder's swift progress on the *Hammerklavier* Sonata in the spring of 1818 is perhaps a sign that they got on reasonably well after all.

In May they both left for Mödling, where Beethoven took a spa treatment. Because Karl's private tutor could not travel with them (he was himself still a student at the university in Vienna), the boy was put up in the local village school run by Pastor Fröhlich. The plan was anything but a success, and four weeks later Karl was out on his ear. Records state that he had disobeyed the Fourth Commandment (that is, he had displayed a lack of respect for one of his parents). He had also been rather too emphatic in his indifference to the religious education lessons and engaged in raucous behavior both in the church and on the street.[12]

The biggest Mödling fiasco, however, was an incident instigated by Karl's mother, who had successfully bribed members of Beethoven's household to allow clandestine meetings with her son. This twofold deceit was enough to destroy all hopes of any cordial relationship with Johanna for quite some time. Yet despite the radical determination of Beethoven's opposition to her, various letters to Zmeskall, Giannattasio, and others point to a deep desire for reconciliation with Johanna, and he had already made several—albeit short-lived—attempts to do so over the previous two years. In May 1817, both had reached a financial agreement before the court regarding Kaspar Karl's estate and the necessary child support payments. Johanna was permitted to sell the house on Alserstrasse and use the proceeds to discharge all outstanding debts. Karl was to receive a sum of two thousand guilders, and Johanna was bound to surrender half of her widow's pension to her son on a quarterly basis—an obligation she would later skirt by simply not collecting her pension at all. Beethoven wrote in his diary that he found the terms to be "respectable" and felt that they would allow Johanna to lead an amply comfortable life. He concluded: "It is time to let go of my scruples; I see now that the widow is well provided for, which I do not begrudge her in the slightest. O Lord, I have done my part."[13]

The Mödling incident marked the beginning of a new episode in the fight for Karl. Both mother and uncle made repeated attempts to secure sole custody of the boy, with varying degrees of success. Initially, they represented themselves legally; as time went on, they received support from friends who were more adept in the courtroom—the debates became grimmer, and the arguments more refined. Beethoven initially retained the upper hand, and Johanna's demands to revoke custody and have Karl moved to the Royal and Imperial Konvikt school (a newly established state-run institute) were denied. Karl was thus left to continue his secondary studies at the local grammar school, or *Gymnasium*. Beethoven had come to the realization that a musical career for Karl was too ambitious after all, and sent him to the *Gymnasium* in preparation for a life in academia. But when Karl fled the school on December 3, 1818, to seek shelter and security with his mother (where Beethoven had the police wrest him away several days later), Johanna turned to the justice system once more. This time, things ended badly for Beethoven. On December 11, a harrowing courtroom confrontation took place, where both mother and foster father were subjected to invasive scrutiny and at times humiliation, and all in the presence of the crushed child, who himself was forced to give compromising answers to suggestive questions. Beethoven was seemingly so disconcerted by the scandalous proceedings that he made an enormous blunder: when asked about his plans for Karl's education, he replied that he would like to send the boy to the Theresianum—the most prestigious school in Vienna—if only he were of noble descent. Although utterly superfluous, this final remark exposed the fact that Beethoven, despite the "van" in his surname, was of mere "ordinary" stock, and he was asked by the judge to repeat his statement verbatim. Leaving the obvious humiliation aside, as a further consequence of his admission his case was transferred to the *Magistrat,* the municipal court for the common populace. Several weeks later, Beethoven—who not five years before had shaken the hands of emperors and kings—took his place among tailors, shoe-shiners, apple-sellers, and maids to have his case heard. (He had no doubt envisaged the noble principles of freedom and equality altogether differently.) Several days after being thus exposed, Beethoven cited the words of famous Lutheran clergyman Christoph Christian Sturm in his diary: "Willingly do I submit myself to all uncertainty, and only in thy unwavering goodness, O Lord, do I place my trust. Be my rock, O Lord, my light; my refuge ever, day and night."[14] It was to be his final diary entry.

The affair gained momentum in March 1819, when joint custody was awarded to the mother and Mathias von Tuscher—a magistrate, and an old acquaintance of Beethoven's. Karl was immediately withdrawn from his uncle's care and taken to the private boarding school run by Johann Baptist Kudlich in Landstrasse, where his mother was granted unlimited visitation rights. Tuscher gave up only three months into his guardianship, however, purportedly due to being "inundated with official business, and for various other reasons."[15] His comment might imply that he felt under pressure to defend Beethoven's interests, which were, by their very nature, at odds with those of the mother and child. We know, for example, that Beethoven had concocted a plan to send Karl to a school run by the modern theologist Johann Michael Sailer in the Bavarian town of Landshut. Antonie Brentano had made preparations by sending a long letter enumerating Karl's endearing qualities, along with Beethoven's good intentions and Johanna's pernicious influence. Sailer agreed to the proposition and was even prepared to take on the famous composer's nephew for a token fee. The acquisition of an exit permit was thus the final remaining hurdle, but proved insurmountable since the authorities were bound to honor the wishes of both guardians, despite attempts by various important figures (including Archduke Rudolph) to intervene.

Tuscher the magistrate was replaced as cocustodian by another civil servant, Leopold Nussböck. In the meantime, Karl—whose studies had suffered greatly due to his erratic movements over the previous year—was sent to a rigorous but well regarded school in Josephstadt run by Joseph Urban Blöchlinger, a disciple of Pestalozzi. The tables had now turned, and Beethoven was denied all access to his nephew. Frustrated and driven to distraction, Beethoven briefly considered hiding Karl away with a friend in Salzburg, the Dr. Weissenbach of *O Moment of Glory* fame. Thankfully, a number of Beethoven's more level-headed friends seem to have dissuaded him from putting his hare-brained abduction plan into action.

Ultimately, Beethoven was left with only one option to win back his nephew: appealing to a higher court. He sought the advice of well-known lawyer and dean of the legal faculty in Vienna, Johann Baptist Bach, who initially proposed a compromise. Given Beethoven's (now severe) hearing difficulties, Bach believed it was unrealistic to put him forward as sole guardian, making dual custody with the mother a tactically appealing option. Bach reasoned that Beethoven would undoubtedly retain the upper hand under any such arrangement, in the belief that a woman was incapable of exerting any influence whatsoever on a fourteen-year-old boy.[16] But Beethoven would hear nothing of the sort and nominated his good friend Karl Peters as cocustodian. It was a sensible choice: as the Lobkowitz family's live-in tutor, Peters was thoroughly experienced in dealing with problem children.[17] Peters and his wife—who was herself a talented singer—also made regular appearances on the Viennese cultural scene. On April 8, 1820, the court ruled in favor of the Beethoven-Peters alliance. Johanna's defense had crumbled before the undeniable fact of her criminal record and proven lack of elementary domestic management skills, along with fears that she would make short work of her son's savings. Beethoven, on the other hand, had his deafness and his unconscionable prior treatment of the mother to contend with, either of which under normal circumstances would have provided just cause for refusal. Several witnesses also testified to the chaos that reigned in Beethoven's own household and to the prior neglect he had shown toward Karl. Ultimately, however, Beethoven's reputation and history of financial generosity won out. Johanna subsequently lodged two appeals—one of them with the emperor himself—but without success, after which she let the matter rest.

Johanna was battle-weary and perhaps also felt that her grip on young Karl—who was now well into his adolescence—was slipping away. But the deciding factor in her resignation probably lay elsewhere: shortly after the court's ruling, she was delivered of a daughter—named, of all things, Ludovika—who went through life with the surname Hofbauer.[18] Ludovika's birth can only have made it easier for Johanna to come to terms with her separation from her son. The other participants in the conflict were also in dire need of respite and for their lives to return to normal. For the next three years, and in relatively comfortable circumstances, Karl devoted himself to his secondary school studies at the Blöchlinger institute. Despite some difficulties with mathematics (now where have we heard that before?) and a crippling fear of failure, he passed with flying colors. On August 27, 1823, he was awarded his diploma, and he enrolled at the university. Now at last, Beethoven was free to dedicate his mind fully to compositional efforts, which included the Ninth Symphony. This period of welcome relief would last for three years, after which the hostilities resumed. This time, however, Karl—who until that time had been a mere pawn in the battle raging around him—was the instigator of the confrontation with his uncle and foster father. But more on that later.

We might ask ourselves what on earth possessed Beethoven to allow himself to become embroiled in a custody battle that lasted so long, that was so mentally and financially draining, and which kept him away from his regular work for so many years? In the field of Beethoven scholarship, the "nephew-conflict" has grown into an entirely independent subdiscipline comparable to that of the "immortal beloved." But while there is now consensus that the frames of reference used by nineteenth-century Beethoven biographers are generally outdated—casting Beethoven as a well-willing and misunderstood foster father, saddled with a morally corrupt sister-in-law and a ne'er-do-well of a nephew—most specialists still differ widely in their opinion of the extent to which the "nephew problem" can be construed as a "Beethoven problem." In no other area of Beethoven research is the range of emphatic views and analyses so diverse, or the polemics waged with such vehemence. Even appraisals of what would seem to be easily verifiable parameters, such as Karl's intellect (some believe him to have been vastly intelligent; others see him as distinctly average and unmotivated) or Beethoven's character (loving and caring versus tyrannical), give rise to violent controversy.

It cannot be denied that Beethoven's plans for Karl's upbringing were ambitious and that his primary aim was to be his adopted son's "spiritual father." In this respect he drew a comparison with Philip II of Macedon, who took charge of his son Alexander's upbringing himself and appointed Aristotle as his teacher, finding all others unsuitable.[19] Beethoven then mapped out a pedagogical route for his nephew inspired by the customary methods used to raise children of the nobility and the strategies employed by the upper middle class, enriched with his own edifying influence. To a large extent, the journey he envisaged with Karl served to compensate for the defects in his own upbringing and the frustrations he had experienced as a result. As such, Beethoven thrust Karl into the role of "narcissistic substitute."[20] He did so with his usual fanaticism, but forgot that human beings are less easy to manipulate than musical themes.

There is more to be said. It is likely no coincidence that Beethoven's manic desire to lead a shared life with his nephew only truly manifested once the "immortal beloved" affair had reached its final close. His quest for custody may have stemmed from a need to fill the resulting void and to compensate for his ruined hopes of raising a normal family. In a sense, the situation also offered certain comforts; Beethoven's interference in Karl's life was, after all, more legal and ethical than practical in nature. During the early years especially, Beethoven was able to postpone the harsh reality of cohabitation and leave the day-to-day responsibilities to others, such as the Giannattasio family—a comfortable arrangement of which Beethoven was only too glad to avail himself.[21]

Some commentators view Beethoven's involvement in the Karl affair as an operation intended to restore relations within the Beethoven clan, which had been dysfunctional for some time.[22] We saw earlier how deeply Beethoven was affected by the deaths of his mother in 1787 and his father in 1792. Some psychologists believe that Beethoven may have felt subconsciously responsible for his mother's terminal illness during his first trip to Vienna and that his father died shortly after his second move to the capital. It is also possible that he felt guilty for leaving his two younger siblings all alone in Bonn, for whom he had assumed a patriarchal role since their mother's death and the collapse of their father's career, and that he thus embarked on a zealous mission to atone for these perceived sins by becoming the "savior" of what remained of the Van Beethovens. The destruction he left in his wake, and on the two sisters-in-law in particular, is undeniable; even had they been paragons of virtue, still they would have posed a threat to Ludwig's family plans.[23] To Beethoven, Karl represented a golden opportunity to effect reconciliation once and for all.

From the "Immortal Beloved" to a "Distant Beloved"

WHILE BEETHOVEN STRUGGLED DESPERATELY TO maintain peaceful relations with one child and his mother, Josephine sought to attain a tenable modus vivendi with her own seven children and the father of the youngest three. She seems to have had some brief success; however, not long after the birth of Minona, her tenuous marriage finally fell apart. Stackelberg left the marital home, traveling first to Germany and later to his estates in Trutnov. He would subsequently return to Vienna several times, usually bringing with him more grief than happiness.

Josephine was thus left to fend more or less for herself. She worked hard to maximize revenue from the property on Rotenturmstrasse—for a time there was even a possibility that Mälzel might set up shop there—and otherwise spent much time with her mother and brother in Martonvásár to keep living expenses to a minimum. Stackelberg reentered the picture in the spring of 1814, demanding that Josephine join him in Trutnov, presumably in the hopes of regaining control over the upbringing of his three children. Josephine refused, citing (among other reasons) a wish not to abandon the four children from her previous marriage. Stackelberg, who was otherwise awkward and lacking in social graces, nonetheless succeeded in wresting his three wailing children from Josephine with support from the Viennese police (in other words, he staged a kidnapping with a legal escort) and took them to Trutnov, where he promptly washed his hands of the matter by depositing them with the local pastor. For a brief time, he also took legal action to try to have Josephine's four eldest children taken away, over whom he had no legal or moral paternal authority whatsoever. To this end, he dispatched to the highest police officials a letter, which although containing no hard evidence employed the far more efficient method of stirring suspicions. According to

401

Stackelberg, not only were the children being neglected by their simultaneously eccentric, overstrung, and apathetic mother, but he also laid claims of incest, stating he had heard rumors that the thirteen-year-old Fritz (Deym) had interfered with his three-year-old step-sister Theophile (Stackelberg). This final accusation was the proverbial last straw for the Brunsvik family. While the male Brunsviks had previously observed rather passively from the sidelines and done little to stand by Josephine (to Therese's mind, their failure to act was tantamount to acting against her), they now leapt valiantly into action, and thanks to an intercession by the emperor, Josephine was spared the loss of her other four children. Severe damage had still been done, however, and the Viennese secret services—which had been on high alert since the Congress of Vienna—now kept closer tabs on Josephine and those in her company.

Another gentleman had crossed Josephine's path in the meantime: the young Fritz's private tutor Andrian (in full, Karl Eduard von Andrehan-Werburg). Rita Steblin describes Andrian as a "charlatan," a brilliant smooth talker with a shady past. In his memoirs, Fritz Deym describes in detail how his mother slowly but surely fell for Andrian's charms; how she disappeared for several months and was beyond the reach of even her own children after accidentally falling pregnant once again; and how, in September 1815, she gave birth to her eighth and final child, Emilie, in a makeshift hut somewhere in the Vienna woods. Seven days later Josephine dumped the child squarely in its father's lap and, undeterred by Andrian's pleading, washed her hands of Emilie forever. She did pay her daughter's way, and when Emilie died at the age of two, she covered the funeral expenses.[1]

For one and a half years, the fate of Josephine's three youngest children remained unknown to her, until she received a letter from the pastor in Trutnov in January 1816. The letter informed her that Stackelberg had placed the children in his care but neglected to pay the agreed maintenance costs, and that he could no longer adequately feed and clothe the virtual orphans. Shocked, furious, and most of all deeply saddened, Josephine wasted no time and had eight hundred guilders sent to the pastor—hardly a trivial sum given her circumstances at the time. When she read in a second heartrending letter how emotionally her children had responded to this first sign of life in years and how desperately they longed to see her again, she and Therese set about organizing their return to Vienna. Raising the necessary funds took the sisters just a little too long, however, giving Stackelberg—who had been well-informed by his Viennese spies—the opportunity to thwart their plans.

Shortly before the children were due to leave, Stackelberg's brother arrived in Trutnov with a monetary sum and a paternal edict forbidding their departure for Vienna. And that was that. It would be 1819 before Stackelberg finally acquiesced and transferred the children back into Josephine's care.

It is impossible to know the extent to which Josephine communicated with Beethoven during this fraught period. The pair would conceivably have done their utmost to conceal any meetings from the all-seeing eye of the Viennese secret police and to cover their tracks as much as possible. (We now know that for many years, Josephine traveled under the pseudonym "von Mayersfeld" and even had a valid passport under that name, allowing her to enter and exit the city undetected.[2]) One known meeting was documented in detail, however: during this period, the violinist Schuppanzigh (whose string quartet had disbanded after the fiery demise of Razumovsky's castle) had decided to leave Vienna and embark on a major concert tour of Russia. On the eve of his departure, on February 11, 1816, he gave a farewell concert in Josephine's Rotenturmstrasse residence, which was home to a multitude of glorious musical memories, many featuring Josephine herself at the piano. On that evening, Josephine played hostess to an event with many of the well-to-do in attendance, and which unintentionally became an homage to Beethoven. The program contained exclusively music by the composer to whom Schuppanzigh owes his eternal fame: Beethoven's String Quartet in C Major (op. 59, no. 3), the Quintet in E-flat (op. 16),[3] and the Septet in E-flat (op. 20). Beethoven arrived late but just in time to hear the Quintet, and became incensed at how Carl Czerny, in his youthful impetuousness, saw fit to embellish the solo piano part with his own brand of technical flair. Beethoven—who had always maintained a clear distinction between the geese and the gander—found his impertinence unacceptable, and when the performance was over he let fly at his ex-pupil, much to the discomfiture of the audience. A letter expressing regret was sent the following day. Beethoven wrote that while Czerny had played beautifully, he begged understanding for the fact that composers do prefer to hear their work the way it was originally intended.[4]

Other encounters are less well documented. Therese's diary entries clearly suggest that given Beethoven's personal experience with custody battles, the Brunsvik sisters regularly turned to him for advice regarding Josephine's children. At Beethoven's recommendation, they ultimately engaged the services of Joseph von Schmerling, a lawyer who was representing Beethoven's interests at the time. There were presumably also meetings during the summer holidays of 1816, when Josephine and Beethoven were both registered in Baden (on July 1 and 5, respectively), a pocket-sized town where they would have had difficulty avoiding each other. When Beethoven's nephew Karl required a hernia operation in September, his (otherwise so doting) foster father felt no need to interrupt his holiday to attend the procedure. On the contrary, he had Karl sent to him in Baden to recover. Many years later, in one of Beethoven's conversation notebooks, Karl would ask the poignant question: "In Helena [the Helena Valley near Baden] you went walking arm-in-arm with a lady. Who was that?"[5]

As mentioned above, it is difficult to guess at just how serious their relationship was at that time. We have nothing more to go on than dim suspicions and a few tiny hints, such as the fact that Josephine once again insisted on being addressed by her former married name—Countess Deym—and the classic telltale sign that Beethoven's personal grooming improved tremendously during the period in question. It is scant evidence, to be sure, but enough to convince many Beethoven researchers that a fourth episode in the "immortal beloved" saga took place between 1815 and 1816. The proponents of this theory mainly constitute a subset of the adherents to the (not undisputed) proposition that Josephine is indeed the "immortal beloved" and that the events during the summer of 1812 constitute episode three of the same tale. Conversely, it is impossible for nonbelievers to interpret the circumstances of 1815–16 as a continuation of the doomed romance. Those who do believe, however, now also claim to have solved a thorny problem that has exercised the minds of many a Beethoven biographer: How is it possible that Beethoven experienced a chronic financial shortage that summer, despite the revenue streaming in from all directions? If the above theory is true, the answer to this burning question is simple: Beethoven not only lent Josephine day-to-day financial support but was also the one who provided the necessary funds to fetch the children back from Trutnov. Josephine of course signed no notice of receipt, and so concrete evidence for this tantalizing theory is lacking.

It is safe to say that by that time, Beethoven no longer cherished any grand illusions of perfect love with the ideal woman.[6] Accepting the situation would most likely have liberated him somewhat, and the possibility is very real that Beethoven and Josephine's relationship became so amicable in 1815 and 1816 for precisely that reason.

Beethoven documented this key moment of resignation and release musically, in the song cycle titled *An die ferne Geliebte* (To the distant beloved; op. 98). Completed in 1816, it is a setting of a text by Brünn medical student Aloïs Isidor Jeitteles. The poetry was never published independently, and it is likely that the author presented Beethoven with the handwritten manuscript in person—it speaks so well to Beethoven's character, in fact, that we might even suppose it was written to order. It is also known that Beethoven personalized the text himself even further by adding a supplementary stanza to the first poem. Later, shortly before publication, Beethoven also tellingly altered the title from *die entfernte Geliebte* (the "distanced" or "removed" beloved) to *die ferne Geliebte* (the "distant" or "faraway" beloved). The cycle's subject matter speaks for itself: after first lamenting his separation from, and subsequent longing for, the absent beloved, the devoted poet goes on in the second song to measure the distance between them in terms of mountains, valleys, and forests. The third song is an entreaty to the birds, clouds, and rivers to communicate his aching and painful longing to her; in the fourth, he begs those same birds, clouds, and rivers to transport *him* instead, that he might embrace her himself. Although the month of May unifies all things living (and loving—such as the birds), the fifth song tells of how this joy is denied him. Lastly, the poet dispatches the songs themselves to his beloved in the hopes that she will sing them and thus bridge the gulf of distance and time by which they are separated.

More than just a simple message to the beloved, this song cycle is an envoy to the entire world. By both setting and publishing this set of poems, Beethoven effectively made a public admission, confirming the existence of, and his separation from, his own "immortal beloved." First and foremost, though, this hymn to love lost is an ode praising art itself as the ultimate means of communication with a loved one—a sentiment that is, in turn, symbolic of Beethoven's noble attempts to surmount his deafness and, through music, remain in touch with the outside world. And just as the singer's final lay is to be sung "artlessly" (*ohne Kunstgepräng*), so too has the music at this stage of Beethoven's compositional development been denuded of all superfluous ornament, standing in sharp contrast to the gratuitous pomp that he churned out during the Congress of Vienna. From this perspective, *An die ferne Geliebte* can be viewed as an artistic testimony of sorts.

The cycle broke new ground in many ways. *An die ferne Geliebte* is officially the world's first true "song cycle" (the title page designates the work as a *Liederkreis,* the German word from which the English term is derived) and is the model on which all the romantic composers, from Schubert to Brahms, based their own similar works. Reference is commonly made to the fact that all six songs are linked together via brief transitional passages, that all of the melodies are derived from motifs present in the first song, and that the initial imagery returns at the end of the cycle. The poet's final words indeed echo the sentiments of the opening, expressing the hope that his message has reached the beloved safely. A striking aspect is that the cyclical motto, repeated with near-obsessiveness at the song's conclusion ("Und ein liebend Herz erreichet, was ein liebend Herz geweiht"—And a loving heart receives another loving heart's dedication),

is a direct quote of the "Josephine" theme from the *Andante favori* (WoO 57):

But despite these major innovations, the cycle's truly groundbreaking character lies elsewhere. While the overall structure demonstrates a robust cyclical complexity, the songs themselves are of a delicate physiognomy. Beethoven pares the music down to such an extent that some sections tend toward melodic impoverishment (which, incidentally, is what makes them less suitable for independent performance). They are held aloft purely by the strength of the piano accompaniment, which gains in importance as the cycle progresses.[7] This newfound simplicity and fragile purity affords significant

Beethoven in 1823

People promenading in Prater Park

The main Redoutensaal ballroom in the Hofburg Palace

Archduke Rudolph

Beethoven's "Wittgenstein" sketchbook

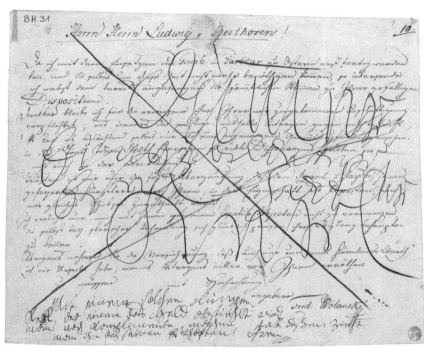

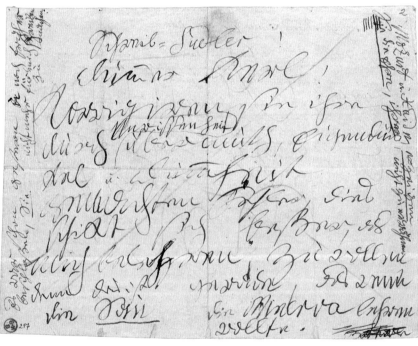

Letter from copyist Ferdinand Wolanek, with Beethoven's response, 1825

Beethoven on his daily walk, ca. 1820

Beethoven's calling card

Small wax seal with Beethoven's initials

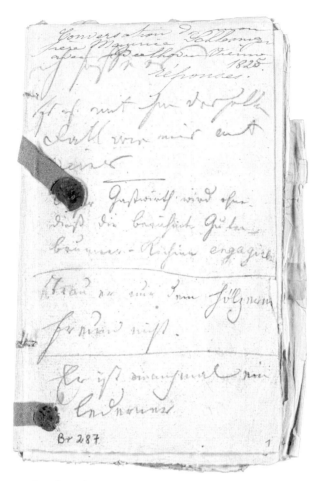

Page from the conversation notebooks, September 9, 1825

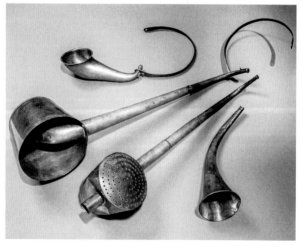

Ear trumpets ordered by Beethoven from Johann Nepomuk Mälzel in 1813

Beethoven's final lodgings on Schwarzspanierstrasse

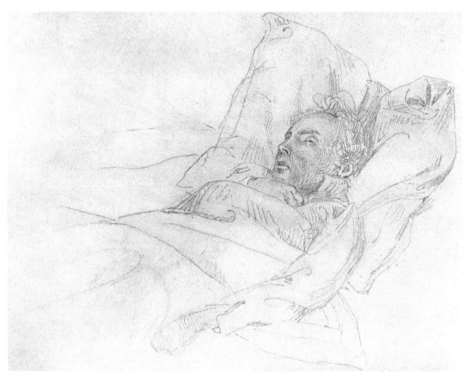

Beethoven on his deathbed, March 1827

The funeral

gains in expressiveness, revealing the direction that Beethoven would later take in the "Ode to Joy" theme from the Ninth Symphony and in certain movements from the late piano sonatas and string quartets, which bear titles such as Arietta, Arioso, Cavatina, and Recitativo. The same can be said of the interplay between tonalities and modulations. *An die ferne Geliebte* is governed by a certain harmonic restraint and ambiguity, imparting a sense of calm and replacing the grand, dramatic, and strident tendencies that so typified Beethoven's earlier music. This, too, presages the reservedness that would come to characterize Beethoven's later works.

An die ferne Geliebte was a milestone, for multiple reasons. It marked the end of a chapter in Beethoven's personal life, while also—after a long, four-year journey through the desert—opening up fresh new musical perspectives. When presented with difficult circumstances, genius minds will, more often than not, intuitively seek out the new horizons ready to be explored. To Beethoven, the Violin Sonata in G (op. 96) and later the Piano Sonata in E Minor (op. 90) were the first glimpses of this new guiding light.

The time has now come for us to bid Josephine a final farewell, but not before revealing how tragically her life came to an end. Soon after the summer holiday of 1816, she slipped into a depression from which she would never recover. On November 5, her sister wrote: "It is such a heart-rending sight, Josephine lying clothed on the bed, surrounded by her three children; her nerves are weak, and her condition so poor that it hardly seems possible that she will improve without intervention."[8] Therese was right. Unlike Beethoven—who changed addresses so often during this period that even his friends and acquaintances lost track of his whereabouts—Josephine barely left her home on Rotenturmstrasse, and her financial situation had become so dire that she was forced to sell her family's treasured heirloom jewelry. Her troubles were exacerbated by the reckless behavior of her eldest son, Fritz, who in the throes of puberty imitated the misogynistic behavior that his stepfather had shown toward his mother and aunt, and which had so deeply hurt Josephine. He took up military service (the parallels with Beethoven's nephew would later prove striking), where he amassed a mountain of drinking and gambling debts, for which Josephine was also held responsible. On top of everything, Stackelberg turned up on more than one occasion to make Josephine's life difficult. His visits were motivated by a pathological love-hate relationship. On the one hand, he claimed that he would die without her, and described the hours he spent in her company as the most precious in his life.[9] On the other, he caused Josephine immense hardship, criticized her parenting, and robbed her of her fortune. When he visited her in 1819, with the three children in tow, Josephine was moved to see them again. But in her exhausted state she could no longer summon the strength to care for them and offered no objection when Stackelberg proposed sending them to his mother in Estonia for good.

Josephine died, forlorn and penniless, on March 31, 1821. Only Therese and her eldest daughter, Vicky, were close by, and the Brunsvik family did not even take the trouble to grant her a final dignified resting place at the Währinger cemetery.

There is one more curious detail. On December 20, 1820, Beethoven had a messenger deliver a rather large sum of money to an otherwise unidentified "sick gentleman" living in the House of the Twelve Apostles on Adlergasse, "directly opposite the residence of Count Deym."[10] In order to do so, Beethoven had secured loans shortly beforehand from the Brentanos and from Carlo Artaria. The identity of the unknown man remains a mystery to this day, but the fact that Beethoven did not even know his exact address (the House of the Twelve Apostles was located not on Adlergasse but on the parallel Hafnergasse) supports a suspicion that the "patient" was a mere straw man whose real purpose was to deliver the sum to the house across the street.

And what of Minona? After Stackelberg's death in 1841, she returned to the Brunsvik family fold. Initially, she moved in with the youngest aunt, Charlotte, and her husband, Count Teleki, in their castle in Siebenbürgen. There she took charge of organizing their sizeable library and made long, solitary treks through the vast countryside on horseback. Ten years later she returned to Vienna where, assisted by her aunt Therese, she made one final attempt at an artistic career (Therese briefly tried to make a pianist of her). Otherwise we know nothing more about Minona, only that she died on February 21, 1897, unmarried and childless.

PART FIVE

The Lonely Way

(1816–1827)

46

Longing for Greater Things

NINETEENTH-CENTURY BIOGRAPHIES are traditionally divided into three parts—youth, adulthood, and old age—a schema that followed the model established by Victor Hugo, who introduced this tripartite career structure in his preface to *Cromwell* (1827).[1] From then on, the triadic model seems to have become more or less the norm for biographers, a straitjacket which, depending on the perspective taken, allowed for some adjustment either to the left or the right.

For over half a century, Beethoven biographers continued to use the *Cromwell* model, although opinions differed regarding the positions of the various peaks and troughs, and the criteria used to identify them. (In 1853, Czerny even devised a schema based on the evolution of his deafness.[2]) In the twentieth century, a need arose to depart from the conventional three-lane biographical motorway. Some musicologists found an emergency exit through subdivision of the existing forms, while others extended the basic structure to include four, five, or even eight sections.[3] Some ultimately abandoned any attempt at periodization altogether, in the belief that biographical compartmentalization is just as futile an endeavor as marking out territorial boundaries in a churning ocean.

Whatever the model, there are many arguments in favor of inserting a caesura at this juncture and for viewing 1816 as a final turning point in Beethoven's life story. On the one hand, by writing *An die ferne Geliebte* Beethoven had set aside all hopes of a shared life with the woman of his dreams. And although the troubled adoption of his nephew was intended to lay the initial basis for a substitute family, from that moment on, loneliness would be his most trusted companion. On the other hand,

the very same song cycle also conveys the essence of Beethoven's transfiguration: associating the idea of "loneliness" with the loftier, spiritual notion of
"detachment" gave it a more positive connotation, laying a mental foundation that would allow Beethoven to bring his renewed artistic mission to
completion.

It was this asceticism that brought Beethoven an alternative sense of comfort and stability, which in turn made it easier for him to sacrifice his social
life for his art. This new attitude was accompanied by new philosophical and
spiritual pursuits. Beethoven took to reading, building up an extensive
library, which alongside classical authors (Homer, Ovid, Plutarch, and Pliny)
and the behemoths of the theater (Shakespeare and Schiller) also included
numerous works by philosophers (Kant and Herder) and some theologians.
He grappled with existential questions in a dedicated effort to conceptualize
God in a manner that he deemed intellectually and emotionally acceptable.
In his readings, he felt an affinity with the opinions of the eighteenth-century
Lutheran clergyman Christoph Christian Sturm (1740–86), whose
Reflections on the Works of God in Nature he turned to almost daily, and in
which he underlined pertinent passages. Sturm's wonderment at the beauty
of nature formed the basis for his praise of the Creator, which Beethoven saw
as an attractive foundation for belief.

Beethoven also perused some spiritual teachings of the East. He became
enamored, for example, of the Rigveda hymns—one of the oldest religious
Hindu texts—and felt especially drawn to the notion of a pure and unchang-
ing consciousness, as well as to the associated daily rituals promoting detachment and inner peace. It was via the East that Beethoven also made the
acquaintance of ancient Egypt. Visitors have reported three fragments of text
that lay on Beethoven's desk, carefully transcribed and displayed beneath
panes of glass so that he could recite them as a daily mantra:

I am that which is.

I am all, what is, what was, what will be.
No mortal man has ever lifted my veil.
He is only and solely of himself, and to this only One
all things owe their existence.[4]

Despite these Eastern leanings, Beethoven did not entirely abandon his
Western (Christian) heritage. The conversation books reveal phrases such as,

"Socrates and Jesus were my examples" and "'The moral law within us, and the starry sky above us.' Kant!!"[5]

No sooner had Beethoven penned the final notes of *An die ferne Geliebte* in 1816, professing renewed confidence in his artistic path, than he immediately put theory into practice: he began working on the Piano Sonata in A Major (op. 101), a work that he had been brooding on since 1813 and for which he had already produced multiple sketches. His retreat into the realm of keyboard music was by now a familiar mechanism, as in the past the piano had proved to be the ideal vehicle for exploring new possibilities.[6] Unlike previous instances, however, Beethoven now made little to no physical use of the instrument; composition had become a cerebral act, performed entirely at the altar of his working desk. The piano had evolved into a virtual acoustic space, whose parameters Beethoven had stored in the "hard disk" of his mind, and which he manipulated and extrapolated on in a manner akin to that of a sound engineer. Beethoven had a well-trained, virtual "inner ear"; not only could he play back a written score perfectly in his mind, but he could also develop musical constructs that were completely new and unprecedented, and distil them with precision on to the page. Testing out certain effects at the piano was a rare occurrence by this stage and must have been quite involved, given the acoustic amplification necessary.

The physical distance imposed between Beethoven and his piano is symbolic of his estrangement from the prevailing musical culture of his time. This fact sparked harsh criticism in itself. Even Czerny—who of all people should have known better—proposed that the apparent lack of continuity and cohesion in Beethoven's late sonatas was attributable to his deafness.[7]

It is true that Beethoven had stopped listening to his contemporaries altogether, both literally and figuratively. At most he would sit and read a new opera, which he found occasionally intriguing but never inspiring. His disregard for performers was even greater than before; although he understood that his new Sonata in A Major was "difficult to execute,"[8] at the same time he believed that "difficult" is a relative concept and does not apply equally to everybody. Ironically he added that while people usually see "difficult" as synonymous with "beautiful," "well-written," and "majestic," this view rested on a misunderstanding: "difficulty only makes one sweat," he said.[9]

Little by little, Beethoven thus distanced himself from both his instrument and the music of his time. But unlike the opinions of some, including

Czerny—who believed that the technical difficulties of the late sonatas also stemmed from Beethoven's deafness[10]—his estrangement did not result in auditory musical abstraction. On the contrary, in the first movement of the Sonata in A Major, with a tempo indication that is "neither fast nor slow," Beethoven had a clear idea of the sound he wanted: sustained but not strained, as though a string quartet had been transcribed for the piano. Occasionally, Beethoven adds articulations which, while not idiomatic for the keyboard, remain practicable nonetheless. The pianist does require extremely subtle finger control; the final note of the three-note motif below, for example, must be both connected to and detached from those preceding it:

In the later sonatas, too, Beethoven occasionally tests the limits of pianism in an effort to win greater expression. A climax occurs in the recitative section of the third movement of the same sonata, with an extreme meditation on the rhetorical power of a single tone:

Here the magical combination of refined articulation and the simultaneous use of both pedals elevates pianism to a point beyond the mere mechanical,[11] creating a seemingly utopian and abstract effect that is vital to the character of the composition. It is the product both of stored memories—distant reminiscences of Beethoven's childhood clavichord seem right around the corner—and of a vision for the future. No competent modern pianist would assert that Beethoven's late piano music is alien to the principles of keyboard technique.

This dichotomy between memory and utopia finds further reflection in the interplay between style and form. We remember that in 1811 and 1812, Beethoven slowly came to the realization that he had exhausted the possibilities of the classical style and was in need of new expressive means. Many of these he developed through the restitution of older styles, which he had come to know through his exposure to Handel and Bach. This process was a lengthy one: Beethoven's affinity with baroque music dates back to his student years under Neefe in Bonn, when he studied Bach's *Well-Tempered Clavier*. Later he regularly attended the soirées at the Van Swieten residence, where he gradually developed a reputation as the leading authority on Bach and Handel. As time went on, Beethoven cultivated a fuller understanding of the craft of the great masters, and his letters to publishers are peppered with requests to furnish him with as much "early music" as possible. Beethoven made a thorough study of these works, both through reading them and by making transcriptions and arrangements—in 1801, for example, he transcribed the Fugue in B-flat Minor from Book I of the *Well-Tempered Clavier* for string quintet (Hess 38). And as mentioned earlier, his interest intensified from 1809 on, when he internalized the hallmarks of the "learned" Viennese tradition.

It would be years before Beethoven succeeded in uncoupling the traditional discipline of the fugue from its baroque roots, integrating it into his own musical language. Beethoven's counterpoint teacher Albrechtsberger had, many years before, thoroughly schooled Beethoven in the principles of fugal writing: the staggered entry of the voices; the composition of countersubjects; the tonal progression to be observed as the subjects are developed; how to position recurring statements to ensure structural clarity; and the more advanced methods of manipulation, including augmentation, diminution, inversion, or retrograde motion. These principles all sound very rational, and they are. The fugue is regarded as the pinnacle of academic musical style: it is strict by default, rigid in structure, businesslike in tone, and therefore no laughing matter. But Beethoven had other ideas. According to Karl Holz, a violinist and Beethoven's greatest source of support in his final years, the master once claimed that while writing a fugue is not difficult per se, the challenge consists in adding an element of poetry.[12] Beethoven clearly wanted the freedom to write fugues on subjects that were dramatic (op. 106) or tender (op. 110), as well as to strip away the rigid frameworks to permit some spontaneity and unpredictability. In some instances he modulated far and wide (op. 106), in others hardly at all (op. 101), and occasionally his fugues ceased to be fugues altogether (op. 110). Beethoven's remark preceding the final movement of the *Hammerklavier* Sonata, while bordering on the sarcastic, is nonetheless deadly serious: "Fuga a tre voci con alcune licenze" (Three-part fugue with some liberties taken).[13]

The final movement of the Sonata in A Major (op. 101) was Beethoven's first successful attempt to integrate the old fugal style naturally into his own language, and to strike a balance between strict organization on the one hand, and seemingly rhapsodic improvisation on the other.[14] Beethoven would maintain this two-pronged approach from that point forward, interweaving objectivity and abstraction with subjectivity and individualization, giving the music a rather timeless character. Here the term "timeless" can be taken quite literally—the occasional absence of clear primary and secondary beats in the final movement of the Sonata in A Major obscures all sense of meter and rhythm. The bar lines are, of course, still visible, but they no longer serve as metrical waypoints, leaving the listener suspended in time. This too is an important form of material detachment that became critical to Beethoven's new style and which would reach its masterful climax in the late piano sonatas and string quartets.

The publisher of the Sonata in A Major (op. 101), Steiner, knew only too well that the work was far beyond the skill of the average pianist. He therefore assigned it to a new series, portentously titled the "Museum of Piano Music" (Musée musical des clavecinistes/Museum für Klaviermusik), which was reserved exclusively for works whose uniqueness and high quality had already been firmly established. Steiner thus emphasized not only that the sonata was intended for professionals—unlike the disposable *Gebrauchsmusik* in vogue among the Viennese amateurs—but also that it had been created to withstand the test of time. It embodied, in other words, the music of the future.

In another bold statement, Beethoven dedicated the sonata to pianist Dorothea von Ertmann, who was regarded as one of the greatest virtuosi of her day; she studied for years with Beethoven and had become a specialist in his music. Her interpretation of her favorite work, the *Moonlight* Sonata, was said to have been unparalleled. When Clementi first heard her play, he exclaimed, "Elle joue en grand maître!" (Her playing is masterful!).[15] Ertmann also had a reputation as a Bach and Handel specialist, owing largely to the influence of her teacher. Ertmann thus had all the qualities necessary to conquer the new pianistic challenges that Beethoven had laid forth, and from opus 101 onward the only pianists capable of doing so would be those with an Ertmann résumé: both technically proficient and historically informed.

Beethoven's request to list Dorothea Ertmann as the dedicatee on the title page of the sonata—at his own expense, if necessary—was made only at the last minute, in a bid to surprise "his Cecilia" with a unique birthday gift.[16] He also wished to take advantage of the opportunity to "Germanize" the name of the instrument, calling it the *Hammerklavier*. Beethoven claimed that several language experts (*conseils* or *Gelehrten*[17]) had persuaded him that the term *Hammerklavier* was the best German alternative to the Italian *pianoforte*. Precisely why the Sonata in B-flat Major (op. 106) and not this sonata came to be known as the *Hammerklavier* remains a mystery.

After completing the Sonata in A Major, Beethoven wrote nothing substantial for an entire year. The pickings from 1817 were slim: three lieder, a new set of folksong arrangements for Thomson, the concise Fugue in D Major for String Quartet (op. 137), and an arrangement of the Piano Trio in C Minor (op. 1, no. 3). It is the dubious quality and erratic prehistory of this latter work in particular that demonstrate how Beethoven's musical path was not always straightforward. It finally seemed, after all, that Beethoven had vowed to renounce all artistic compromises and to concentrate solely on achieving his very best. Yet it was at precisely this point that he agreed to collaborate with an amateur, and we can only hope that he was amply recompensed for the trouble. In July 1817, Beethoven received a call from a certain Joseph Kaufmann: a public servant at the court, violinist, and a member of the Friends of Music Society (Gesellschaft der Musikfreunde) in Vienna. Kaufmann had, most likely for his own personal use, arranged the aforementioned piano trio for string quintet, and prevailed on its composer to make some corrections. Beethoven agreed. First he had the outsider's concoction carefully transcribed by copyist Wenzel Schlemmer, after which he set to work. But Kaufmann's efforts proved dire, the result of methods that can only be described as utterly primitive. The trio's string parts had been allocated verbatim to the cello and the second violin, with the piano part distributed among the three remaining instruments—the first violin and the two violas—creating problems due to the lack of an additional low bass voice to simulate the pianist's left hand. Kaufmann's transcription was also rather literal and bland (with the exception of several rather bold contrapuntal additions to Beethoven's original). Beethoven, who nurtured a well-known disdain for unimaginative arrangements, did not bat an eye; he thoroughly reworked Kaufmann's transcription, in many places fabricating an entirely new version above Kaufmann's original. Despite these improvements, Beethoven still left plenty of mediocre passages unchanged, and altered hardly any of the bizarre fancies added by his "admirer." The end result is thus highly inconsistent, and here and there even second-rate. Surprisingly, Beethoven was not discouraged from having the new version published, and he even permitted the designation of an official opus number (104)—a decision he had never taken lightly in the past. To protect his reputation somewhat, he added the following comical note to the manuscript: "A trio, originally arranged for 3-part quintet by Sir Wellmeant, then reworked from the semblance of five parts into five actual parts, brought up from the miserable depths and restored to some level of regard by Sir Benevolent."[18]

In a postscript, he added that Kaufmann's original five-part arrangement had been burned "to appease the gods of the underworld." A letter sent to his publisher several days later, however, revealed that his strategy had been a literal "smokescreen" and that Beethoven had destroyed the original to erase all traces of the work's initiator in an effort to present himself as the sole arranger. In this instance, mercantile considerations clearly weighed more heavily than matters of professional integrity.

Beethoven's 1817 drop in productivity was due primarily to problems with his health. The previous year, in the third week of October, Beethoven had suffered from what he first termed a "catarrh infection," and later a "lung condition." A simple head cold had developed into a common bout of influenza, from which he ordinarily would have recovered within the week (or, with the help of a doctor, within seven days). Whether the pneumonia was present from the very beginning is unclear; in any case, the viral infections ultimately gave way to chronic bronchitis, which plagued him for many months and did not abate until June 1817.

Many possible reasons come to mind as to why Beethoven remained ill for so long. It cannot be denied that his physical condition and immune system had deteriorated markedly, doubtless aided by his immoderate consumption of alcohol. And as usual, Beethoven afforded himself too little time to convalesce, resuming his normal activities far too soon. On December 25, 1816, for example, he conducted a performance of his Seventh Symphony in the Redoutensaal, in spite of his ailing health. And while his condition worsened appreciably afterward, his sense of responsibility to society outweighed any concerns for his own well-being. Even when it came to his social life (i.e., spending time in cafés and restaurants), Beethoven spared himself little. Of course, the doctors were the ones to blame for his delayed recovery. To his friend Anna Maria von Erdődy, Beethoven wrote that he had found himself a new doctor, denouncing his previous physician as a "sly Italian," who had obviously been dishonest with him and showed little understanding or vision. Beethoven also doubted the effectiveness of the prescribed treatments and medications: "I was first [...] ordered to take 6 powders and drink 6 cups of tea per day [...] now I have yet another powder, that I must also take 6 times per day, as well as a salve to be applied 3 times daily. Then I was sent here [Heiligenstadt] to avail myself of the baths, and yesterday I received a new medicine, a 'tincture,' of which I must take twelve spoonfuls daily."[19]

Beethoven was, moreover, a fussy and pessimistic patient. In the same letter to Countess Erdődy, he complained that while he hoped his trials would soon be alleviated, he also feared that—despite several signs of improvement—it would be some time before he fully recovered. The fact that his brother had died of pneumonia one year earlier must also have weighed on his mind. Another friend of his, Fanny Giannattasio, shared his grim outlook. On November 1, 1816, she wrote in her diary: "The lamentable condition of our dear Beethoven has troubled me greatly of late; he is ill, surrounded by unworthy and miserable souls, robbed of all joy in life!" Several days later she added: "Walking home [...] we encountered Beethoven. He looks none too well, and harbors grave doubts about his recovery. I was shocked."[20]

47

Post-Congress Vienna

BEETHOVEN TOOK NINE MONTHS TO RECOVER from his lung complaint, which was certainly the primary (though not the only) explanation for his marked drop in production during that time. Beethoven was "up to his ears" in problems: the rapid deterioration of his hearing, the fight for his nephew, and the deluge of day-to-day personnel and money matters were all so oppressive, he could barely concentrate on fulfilling his life's work. The impasse troubled him greatly. Occasionally he took refuge in the comforting solitude of nature; at other times he sought out the city's hustle and bustle, contacting everybody he knew who might help procure him new opportunities—preferably abroad and starting as soon as possible. Many of his diary entries profess his conviction that traveling was the only way for him to reach greater heights and to avoid slipping away into mediocrity.[1]

Beethoven's serious desire to escape Vienna was incited both by the lack of any concrete future prospects and the disappearance of his aristocratic supporters. But superseding these were two other factors, namely the new neoconservative and antidemocratic political climate (inhibiting the development of all liberal, emancipated artists), and the rising public demand for easy, nonconfrontational cultural consumption. The Vienna where Beethoven now lived was indeed nothing like the Vienna he had first encountered on his arrival twenty-five years earlier. The change was essentially the result of Metternich's fervid implementation of the agreements reached by the various European rulers in an effort to protect Europe from the scourge of a second French Revolution or a new Napoleon. He opposed those who challenged the traditional social order—liberal capitalists, academics, and artists—and cultivated the antiliberalist system that would later come to bear his name.

It should be noted that Metternich had little trouble implementing his new regime. The Viennese had a traditional loyalty to authority based on historical and conservative social undercurrents rooted in Catholic morality—Vienna had always cherished a certain nostalgic longing for an almost medieval caste system, with the nobility and the clergy as its primary driving forces. Although the Congress of Vienna (and later the Karlsbad Decrees) certainly represented major turning points, in reality these events formed part of a restoration process that was already well underway, having begun after the first Coalition War. From that moment on, the Viennese became accustomed to going about their business under the all-seeing eye of the police. Little by little, the gray-jacketed, green-collared officers—whose original mandate had been to help city life flourish through measures such as street lighting and public hygiene—began to interpret their role in a broader sense, and the term "public order" took on increasingly wider significance: drunkards, petty thieves, and illegal gamblers were arrested; there was a crackdown on trafficking and smuggling; the police intervened in public disturbances and domestic disputes; and a great deal of manpower was devoted to guarding public buildings, theaters, apartment blocks, and some of the more high-end restaurants. This rankled Beethoven immensely; he simply could not accept that petty criminals had become targets while the "big shots" themselves remained safely out of range. (He had no hesitation in calling on the police several times to assist in the conflicts with his sisters-in-law, however.)

To maintain the integrity of the "triangular" system of state, church, and morality, the *Polizeihofstelle*—sometimes also known as the "secret police"—was granted ever greater freedoms, intended to enable not only the careful monitoring of liberalist and progressive Vienna but also the identification and prompt elimination of the slightest resistance. Not only that, but the professional ranks of the police force were supplemented with reliable private spies who lived and worked among the populace, monitoring their day-to-day dealings and sending daily reports to the central intelligence service. The spy network included coachmen (the *Fiaker*, or "cabbies"), valets, waiters, and sex workers, and permitted twenty-four-hour surveillance throughout the city. The only safe refuge was the privacy of one's own home, and even then one could not always be certain.

Naturally, the regime's repressive machinery devoted particular attention to what was spoken and sung in theaters and to the texts of books, newspapers, and journals. The substance of university lectures was also carefully screened, and not even seemingly harmless items such as atlases, road maps, shop signs, and tombstone inscriptions were beyond censure. The review process served principally to delay and obstruct—undoubtedly its primary intent—and so some theaters, artists, writers, and journalists circumvented the roadblock by choosing the lesser evil of self-censorship. Some authors rose up in protest, others capitulated in resignation, while still others (such as Johann Nepomuk Nestroy) found great sport in deliberate provocation, because they knew that in the end no public official could stop performers straying from any officially sanctioned text. One final category of author remained utterly unconcerned: those who knew that arrangements could always be made, provided one knew the proper channels and was prepared to slip some money under the table. Vienna was still Vienna, after all.

There can be no doubt that the repressive climate following the congress had a major influence on the general population, and on their attitudes especially. Because of the very real possibility of secret police surveillance, citizens increasingly eschewed all forms of political involvement. By doing so, they tacitly supported the government's own agenda, which sought precisely to discourage political engagement among citizens. The landscape was complex, however. In a certain sense the general populace benefited from the new situation, and their needs aligned with those of the aristocracy. While it was a known fact that the nobility was out to repress any and all attempts at revolution, the citizenry had also had their fill of war, unrest, upheaval, and botched diplomacy. They aspired to a lifestyle that was comfortable and modest and were prepared, at least for the time being, to temper their own liberal tendencies. While most realized that new societal shifts were on the horizon and likely inevitable, it was nonetheless of the utmost importance to delay them for as long as possible.

The peaceful era between the Congress of Vienna and the revolution of 1848 has been labeled by optimistic historians as the Vormärz, or "pre-March," period. Pessimists tend to call it the "restoration period." Realists, for their part, label the era as the Biedermeier period, a reference to the fictional Swabian schoolmaster and poet Gottlieb Biedermaier (whose name translates roughly as "protector of decency, beloved by God"). Biedermeier values came to represent a mind-set of temperance and modesty and of wallowing in the typical Viennese undercurrents of melancholy and world-weariness (Weltschmerz). While certainly no fighters, the citizenry of the day were "troopers" in a sense—masters of suppressing overblown emotion, seeking compromise between dreams and reality, keeping lofty ideals at bay, and surrendering themselves to the hand of fate (an attitude often accompanied by the well-known catchphrase *Da kann man nix machen*, or "There's nothing to be done"). The Biedermeiers also avoided making important decisions, giving any clear "yes" or "no" a wide berth and blending into the scenery with chameleon-like transparency. One might say they invented the ambivalent expression "yes and no," which the Viennese merge delightfully together into a single word: *jein*.

It should therefore come as no surprise that the Biedermeiers preferred comfortable, noncommittal, subdued, and on the whole superficial forms of recreation and entertainment. A favorite pastime was the stroll through town, known in German as a *Spaziergang*. At weekends the entire family would amble from one landmark to the next via the major commercial streets and squares: from Kärtnerstrasse, Graben, and Kohlmarkt, via Am Hof and Freyung up to Bastei, and back again via Herrengasse and Michaelerplatz. Another Biedermeier staple was the coffeehouse, offering something akin to a second home where—amid a splendid decor of marble, mirrors, elegant furniture, and sparkling silverware, often with a string ensemble or improvising pianist in the background—one might enjoy a pleasant chat, read the paper, or play at billiards. The main Biedermeier events, however, were the many balls organized during the winter months, which Metternich believed were the only organized gatherings of more than three individuals at a time that constituted no threat to the state. Since the turn of the century, Vienna had been captivated by the waltz (characterized by Stefan Zweig as a bizarre hybrid of nobility and vulgarity), to which the Biedermeiers yielded utterly as a means of escaping the mundanity of existence. And of course, the requisite music shared the same enormous popularity as the dance itself. First Joseph Lanner and later Johann Strauss senior—who headed an Andy-Warhol-like composers' collective—developed a musical style that catered to the genre's specific requirements: structural clarity, melodic charm, and a strong rhythmic basis to offer some stability amid the flurry of the dance. It was music that itself, too, revolved in small circles, in the service of accessible and superficial gestures.

Beethoven and Schubert were forced to concede that the musical tastes and aspirations of the Viennese were not evolving parallel to their own. Later, too, composers of such international renown as Berlioz, Mendelssohn, and Schumann never truly found a foothold in Vienna. The same fate did not befall the Italians: Rossini's music—and to a lesser extent that of Bellini and Donizetti—unequivocally won the hearts of the Viennese. Rossini's opera *Tancredi* was first programmed in 1816 and became an overnight success. The music was all that the Viennese citizenry had been longing for: it was sprightly, elegant, effervescent, and transparent. A Rossini craze ensued, and in the years that followed no fewer than fifteen of his other operas would be programmed in the city's theaters. Metternich, too, was a Rossini enthusiast, and when the Kärntnertortheater fell into financial difficulty once again in 1821, he believed that Rossini's manager Barbaia was the only man able to keep the foundering ship afloat. First in Milan and subsequently in Naples, Barbaia had proven his keen ability to gauge public tastes, which at that time was commercially a far more valuable virtue than any rigorously conceived artistic vision.

Barbaia began work in Vienna on December 1, 1821, and earned immediate success with a guaranteed strategy: he personally accompanied Rossini and his wife—the famous operatic soprano Isabella Colbran—to the Austrian capital and programmed the Italian's works as often as possible. The first season alone saw no fewer than sixty evenings dedicated solely to Rossini. German operas cropped up now and again—such as Weber's *Der Freischütz*, and Beethoven's *Fidelio* in 1822—but remained a rare exception. One year later, during the autumn of 1823, Weber's new opera *Euryanthe* was premiered. Despite the libretto's shortcomings (Beethoven's friend Karl Holz mockingly referred to it as *L'ennuyante,* or "the bore"[2]), the first four performances were a success. Afterward, though, the management demanded several modifications, which so disfigured the work that the audience dwindled to nothing. A worse fate awaited Schubert's *Fierabras,* which was canceled even before its premiere. Rossini, it seemed, had become the standard against which all opera was measured—a phenomenon that became known as "Rossineggiare."[3]

Beethoven's response to the power and poor taste of the masses was one of both defiance and disappointment: "*Vox populi, vox Dei* they say—I have never believed so myself."[4] What *was* clear was that a world ruled by the uneducated and the self-indulgent—whom Beethoven endearingly dubbed the "Phaeacians"—had little left to offer him.[5]

48

London Plans

BEETHOVEN ONCE AGAIN SET HIS SIGHTS further afield. This time his gaze settled on England and the London Philharmonic Society, an association that was founded in 1813 by several prominent musical professionals and backed by a large number of aristocrats. The society's aims were clear, and the regulations—in true English style—were stringent: each year, from among the thirty board members and unlimited other associates, seven directors were elected to manage the eight annual spring concerts held in the Argyll Rooms. Originally, the society's founding statutes stipulated that only choral, orchestral, and chamber works be programmed; solo concertos and arias were thus excluded. The policy was amended soon enough, however, and unlike other famous concert organizations (such as the Academy of Ancient Music), the Philharmonic Society concentrated solely on contemporary works. The long list of composers who conducted their own music at the society includes such illustrious names as Weber, Mendelssohn (who wrote the *Italian* Symphony specially for the society), Berlioz, Wagner, and Tchaikovsky.

Since its very inception, the society's favorite composer had been Beethoven. The inaugural concert on March 8, 1813, included an unspecified symphony of his, and afterward hardly a performance took place where one of his works did not appear. Of the eighty concerts held during the Philharmonic Society's first decade, only six failed to include a work by Beethoven. Of course, Beethoven's prominent position was due in part to his many friends and colleagues on the board, such as Bridgetower, Clementi, Cramer, Ries, and Johann Peter Salomon from Bonn. Beethoven's principal champion, however, was an English conductor by the name of George Smart, who was unknown to him and was the default primus inter pares among the group of musician presidents. In 1814, Sir George conducted no fewer than ten performances of the

425

Mount of Olives under the society's aegis. He adored the work, programmed it for non-society concerts, and even published his own piano reduction of it. Later, in February 1815, he led the famous performances of *Wellington's Victory* in the Drury Lane Theatre, firmly establishing Beethoven's status as a cult composer. When news of these developments reached Beethoven, he had his friend Johann von Häring write a long letter asking whether Smart might assist him in finding publishers for his latest works.[1] In his eagerness to save time and without waiting for a response from Smart, Beethoven attached a list of the works in question. His letter went unanswered.

Beethoven's aspirations did not end with publishers. His greater aim was to secure commissions for new works and ultimately travel to London, where he could conduct them himself for a handsome fee. Ferdinand Ries offered the ideal contact for Beethoven's endeavor: after a European odyssey lasting several years, Beethoven's ex-pupil had settled in the English capital in 1813. There he rapidly earned admiration and a position on the Philharmonic Society's board of directors, making him the perfect target for Beethoven's entreaties. In the most thinly veiled terms, Beethoven informed Ries that he would welcome the invitation—should the society be so inclined—to compose several new works and travel to London for an *Akademie,* and asked Ferdinand to put in a good word for him. Beethoven likewise made no attempt to conceal the base materialism underlying his request; he reiterated that his London plans were due to the high cost of living in Vienna, to the drop in value of the "decree" with Kinsky, Lobkowitz, and Archduke Rudolph, and to the cost of providing for his nephew Karl, for whom he had become responsible in the meantime.[2] Beethoven had little cause to hope that his situation might improve, as he pointedly framed in a letter to Gottfried Härtel: "Eurus will remain here forever and always, in this stagnant mire!"[3]

London appealed to Beethoven not only as a temporary or permanent escape—his impression of the English capital and the opportunities it offered had, in the meantime, taken on gargantuan proportions. He told his nephew, for example, that one could earn enough in one year in England to purchase ten country estates.[4] Many of these notions were due to Haydn, whose impassioned account of London during Beethoven's early years in Vienna told of the lively concert scene and the fortunes that awaited gifted musicians in the English capital. Beethoven's enthusiasm was also partly politically inspired, especially since his Francomania had subsided. England had been a topic of particular interest at the Lichnowsky residence: the lady of the house, Christiane, had grown up in the salon of her mother, Countess Maria Thun, and been privy to the praise lavished on the English parliamentary system. She had picked up the same enthusiasm and in turn infected Beethoven, who subsequently seized every opportunity to tell English visitors how he much preferred their democratic model to the musty Hapsburg monarchy.[5]

Beethoven's interest in England was likely also fueled by the rapid and positive reception of his music there. Initial reports date from 1794, when his String Trio in E-flat (op. 3) was performed in Leicester, presumably from a score acquired in Vienna by a traveling English amateur. A profusion of London publications followed; first Robert Birchall and later Clementi ensured that the English were exposed to virtually all of the "official" opus numbers. And while the folksong arrangements commissioned by Thomson certainly served to broaden Beethoven's popularity, the hype surrounding his reputation was not truly secured until *Wellington's Victory*.

England's siren call intensified. On February 29, 1812, Beethoven wrote to Thomson saying that he would most likely be leaving Vienna; that he intended to travel first to London, and then to Edinburgh. His secretary Oliva confirmed this report three months later.[6] Though resolute, Beethoven was not entirely free of doubts. He was not an experienced traveler: since his arrival in Vienna in 1792, he had only made two concert tours, visited Lichnowsky's castle once in Troppau (Opava), and spent two summers outside Vienna—all other travel plans had come to nothing. His poor hearing was, naturally, part of the problem. In March 1815, for example, an intermediary by the name of Häring informed George Smart that while Beethoven spoke constantly of moving to London, in all likelihood his encroaching deafness would come to present an insurmountable obstacle.[7]

Communications intensified in 1815. On July 11, the general assembly of the society adopted a proposal by Smart to purchase three of Beethoven's overtures. Pianist and society member Charles Neate was tasked with visiting the master in Vienna and collecting the works; Neate had been residing in the Austrian capital since May 1815 and sought immediate contact with Beethoven through Häring. He enquired about lessons (Beethoven refused, referring him instead to Förster and limiting his own input to some compositional advice), negotiated the selection ordered by Smart, and returned to London with three overtures under his arm: the *Name-Day* overture (op. 115) and overtures to *The Ruins of Athens* (op. 113) and *King Stephan* (op. 117). The Philharmonic Society eventually performed only one overture, most likely the one for the name-day celebration. Some claim that the members were disgruntled at having to settle for secondhand works, but this cannot be the case, as Beethoven had expressly disclosed that they had already been performed earlier and "with the greatest success." Far more plausible is the proposition that during the rehearsals, Smart simply found the works disappointing. Beethoven was frank in his admission that the three overtures were not among his greatest compositional achievements, that they were first and foremost occasional pieces conceived for theatrical use, not intended for grandeur and certainly not to open a concert. He stressed that there had been a misunderstanding, laying the blame squarely on Neate, who could easily have acquired works of a more substantial nature. Beethoven thus believed that Neate's poor judgment had ruined his chances for fame in England. Neate's response—that the reputation of the overtures was so poor that he hardly dared act in Beethoven's favor again—triggered a typically Beethovenian war of correspondence. Beethoven wrote to Smart of Neate's questionable character, whereupon Neate made a desperate attempt to mitigate his prior reaction (even citing marital problems as an excuse). The incident was only resolved after a shrewd act of diplomacy by Smart; he came to Neate's defense and pacified Beethoven with the promise of a new project involving the *Moment of Glory* (op. 136).[8]

The project never came to fruition, which was of little detriment to anybody. Instead, the board of the Philharmonic Society issued a far more attractive proposal, which Ries communicated to Beethoven in a letter dated June 9, 1817. Ries was delighted with his role as an intermediary, as it provided him with a unique opportunity to express his gratitude to his former teacher and "dear old friend."[9] The offer he presented was of considerable magnitude: during the winter of 1817–18, Beethoven would travel to London to compose and conduct two "grand symphonies." The Philharmonic Society was prepared to pay 300 guineas (roughly equal to 315 pounds, or 3,000 guilders), a third of which would be paid in advance.[10] Naturally, the society demanded some degree of exclusivity (if we read between the lines, they were clearly afraid of a rival organization launching a similar project); however, it was never their intention to bind Beethoven hand and foot. In his letter to Beethoven, Ries explicitly stated that the Philharmonic Society understood the need for his time in England to be a profitable one. As a side note, Ries reminded Beethoven of Smart's earlier request for an oratorio in the style of the *Mount of Olives* but with an English text and including a major bass aria. To make the offer even more tantalizing, Ries added vague allusions to the director of the Italian opera, a "friend" of the society, who could certainly be convinced to commission an operatic work.

Such a proposal, while attractive, was hardly realistic. Nobody seemed to comprehend that it was impossible for Beethoven to compose two symphonies within the short span of eight months. Curiously, Beethoven himself offered no complaint—or might we assume that out of eagerness to leave for London, he simply chose not to divulge any personal doubts regarding the unfeasible nature of the project?

Whatever the case, Beethoven managed to delude himself and convince others—for a brief period at least—that it could be done. In the summer of 1817, he noted in his diary: "just one more symphony—then off, off, and away. And collect your pay in the meantime."[11] The import of this final remark is not to be mistaken, for Beethoven's emigration would mean backing out of the contract he had signed with Kinsky, Lobkowitz, and Archduke Rudolph. Beethoven's bold plan was thus first to collect his three-monthly stipend and then to disappear without a trace!

Beethoven wrote an extensive reply to Ries stating that he was flattered by the proposal and assured the society of his utmost dedication to giving the honorable commission the dignified execution that it deserved. He also made some practical and artistic enquiries: How large was the orchestra? How many instruments in each section? Single or double winds? What was the size of the hall, and did it have a good acoustic? In the same letter, however, he also took a gamble by raising his price, asking for a supplementary travel allowance of one hundred guineas—ostensibly to cover the costs of a travel companion to assist with his deafness—and demanding a larger advance.[12] The society would brook no haggling, and in an extraordinary meeting held on August 19, 1817, the decision was made to stand their ground.[13] Beethoven gave no immediate response, and the entire affair was forgotten.

The lines of communication were not severed entirely, however, as Smart continued to beg for his oratorio and Beethoven angled for a new invitation. It would not come until November 1822, when the Philharmonic Society placed the famous order that led directly to the composition of the Ninth Symphony. Then, too, Beethoven could not bring himself to travel to London, and Smart had no choice but to conduct the premiere of the astounding work himself—a tale that we will hear more of later.

At this juncture, a comparison with Haydn is virtually unavoidable. Haydn was eleven years older than Beethoven was when he received a similar invitation from the Philharmonic Society and made his first trip to London in

1791. It remains a curious paradox that Haydn—a provincial artist who for decades was confined to an ambit of only sixty kilometers, roughly the distance from Vienna to Eisenstadt—was daring enough to seek adventure in England, while Beethoven, who had been bowed to by emperors and kings, lived out his adventures in his living room at his piano and writing desk. Of course, he was disadvantaged by his increasing deafness and his weakened physical condition, and his sense of responsibility to his nephew undoubtedly prevented him from leaving Vienna with a clear conscience. Where Haydn was footloose, open-minded, and self-assured, Beethoven was introverted, cynical, and fearful of the unknown.

We can never know what might have become of Beethoven's career had he left Vienna and settled in London. But let us speculate anyway: it is a near certainty that the Ninth Symphony still would have reached completion (he had already started work on it), though assuredly in a very different form. Following that, and undoubtedly after some delay, he would have written a Tenth Symphony, and perhaps another oratorio and an Italian opera—the mind boggles at the possibilities. At the same time, not only would these projects have cost immense amounts of time and energy; they also would have kept Beethoven's gaze fixed on the needs and tastes of the outside world. If his circumstances and constitution had never been conducive to the genesis of the *Hammerklavier* Sonata, the *Diabelli* Variations, the *Missa solemnis,* or the late piano sonatas and string quartets, his body of work—and the course of musical history—would have been drastically altered. The question is, did Beethoven know? It is tempting to think that his reticence to travel to London was subliminally influenced by artistic considerations; that he struggled internally with the notion of subjecting himself to the commercially focused musical culture of middle-class London, secure in the knowledge that he was destined instead to tread a different path, that of the lonely, singular artist. While the road to personal happiness may have led to London, Beethoven seemed willing to renounce it for the opportunity to create his final masterpieces.

49

A Faustian Sonata and a Diabolical Contraption

FATE IS A FICKLE MISTRESS. Although Beethoven longed to travel to London and even had concrete opportunities to do so, during the winter of 1817 and 1818 he instead stayed at home, working not on a symphony that might have earned him the adoration of London audiences, but instead on one of the most outlandish, complex, tumultuous, and puzzling piano works in musical history, the Piano Sonata in B-flat Major (op. 106), more commonly known as the *Hammerklavier* Sonata. According to Czerny, Beethoven believed it to be the greatest sonata he would ever compose.[1] Its genesis spanned an uncommonly long period, even by his standards—he worked on it from November 1817 until January 1819—and all evidence points to an unprecedented and deep-seated intrinsic motivation. For although Beethoven dedicated the sonata to Archduke Rudolph, it was almost certainly—as we shall see—originally intended for himself.

Beethoven experts did not believe so for some time, however. They based their assumptions on a letter to the archduke dated March 3, 1819, in which Beethoven refers to two enclosed "pieces" for the piano that he had composed a year earlier in honor of Rudolph's name-day celebration, but which he had hitherto been prevented from sending along due to poor health. In the same letter, he announced that two additional works would follow—the second of which he described as a "grand Fugato"—thus producing a four-movement sonata. Lastly, he informed the archduke that the sonata would soon be published, offering the assurance that it had been "intended from the bottom of my heart for His Royal Highness for quite some time."[2]

A letter sent by Beethoven to Ries one year before that (on March 5, 1818) sheds an entirely different light on the matter. In it, Beethoven bemoans his suffering at what he describes as "the unfortunate relationship with this archduke, who has reduced me almost to beggary."[3] Given what we know of Beethoven's impulsiveness, we should of course take this outpouring with the usual grain of salt; nevertheless, it hardly seems likely that a mere few weeks later, on April 17 (Rudolph's name day), he would be prepared to dedicate his newest sonata to "this archduke." And even if this was his intention, why did he then change his mind? And what possessed him—after waiting an entire year—to then deliver only two movements, when the sonata was virtually already complete?

Recent investigations have cast some doubt on the sincerity of Beethoven's obsequious letter to the archduke. Some interpret his version of events as a covert attempt at manipulation,[4] rendering the archduke's name-day celebrations as a convenient alibi for a last-minute charm offensive. Beethoven certainly had reasons to employ such tactics: on January 20, 1819, the archbishop of Olmütz, Count Trauttmansdorff, passed away. This time, however, Archduke Rudolph did believe that the time was ripe for him to take office. He cannot have been indecisive, as he was swiftly and officially "elected" by the chapter on March 24 of that same year. Some time in February, after an extended period of sparse communication, the archduke sent Beethoven a messenger with the urgent request to arrange a visit. Beethoven was not at home, but found a note and assumed that Rudolph wished to discuss the *Missa solemnis* commission and possibly the associated post of Kapellmeister in Olmütz. On March 3, he composed a reply that was almost shameful in its flattery. He congratulated the archduke on the accession to his noble post, made modest mention of his artistic talents, then offered an excruciating compliment—praising the archduke as the source of both human happiness and musical inspiration—once again offered his teaching services, and reinforced his eagerness to compose a celebratory mass in honor of His Royal Highness's inauguration during the coming year. Elsewhere Beethoven alluded subtly to the frictions that had come between them in recent times, and promised to make amends by surprising Rudolph with an unexpected (but still incomplete) birthday gift. His ruse did necessitate a harmless fabrication—the antedating of his intentions by one year—and half of the gift also took the form of an I.O.U., since Beethoven could not yet part with the original manuscripts of the last two movements (he was still correcting errors in the proofs). All of this confirms the suspicion of fundamental inconsistencies regarding the timing of the dedication.

It is beyond doubt that the technical challenges of the *Hammerklavier* Sonata far exceeded the capacities of the now claw-fingered, arthritic archbishop. Czerny himself noted the sonata's difficulty, pointing out the uncommon fingerings, daring leaps, awkward hand-crossings, and unorthodox attack, and insisted that a familiarity with Beethoven's previous works was indispensable. The sonata also sorely tests the pianist's stamina, and Czerny stressed the need to play it both often and at the correct tempo to gain a true understanding.[5] Beethoven himself was fully cognizant of the immense difficulties it presented, and is said to have quipped to his publisher Carlo Artaria that the sonata would continue to frustrate pianists for the next half-century.[6]

The *Hammerklavier* Sonata is frequently characterized as "Olympian," "cyclopean," "extreme," or "diabolical." At first glance, these qualifications seem most relevant to the stupendous, ten-minute-long final fugue that beleaguers the pianist with an array of the most taxing physical and technical challenges. But the above characterizations also apply equally to the remaining movements; even the Adagio sostenuto—a seemingly endless lament, to be performed Appassionato e con molto sentimento—sets the expressive bar extraordinarily high. It was not for nothing that the pianist Hans von Bülow, a Beethoven specialist, Wagner apologist, and a pupil and son-in-law of Franz Liszt, proposed that this movement was where pianism ended, and "inspired declamation" began. According to Bülow, those incapable of such expression would do better to content themselves with simply reading the score.[7]

And yet the truly exceptional nature of the sonata lies not in its technical challenges but in its musical substance. The sheer magnitude of the various movements is legitimized by an underlying structural logic, which while barely audible is nonetheless perceptible. (An architectural analogy is appropriate here: only during the early stages of construction are the frameworks visible that hold buildings upright; later they disappear behind elaborate façades.) Many of the sonata's theoretical elements (such as the falling third that dominates both the melodic structure and the tonal progression), while essential, are more obvious to the eye than to the ear. Another salient example is that the major source of tension between the fundamental tonalities of the first movement—B-flat major and B minor—has a counterpart in the final movement. This crucial link is veiled, however, by the return of the concluding fugue's main theme,

in "retrograde" motion, that is, with all notes played in reverse order:

This stunning theoretical device is incredibly symbolic. The momentous confrontation between the theme and its own mirror image suggests a collision between two opposing worlds: that of optimism, light, and liberty on the one hand, and pessimism, darkness, and discord on the other—akin to the extremes of good and evil that endlessly plague the human psyche. Clear associations arise with Goethe's *Faust,* which had been written not ten years before.

We might continue to ruminate in this fashion for quite some time, until we reach the point where all rationality falters—a passage made up entirely of piercing trills:

The score's jagged (and really quite modern) appearance is analogous to its sound, and our ears are assaulted by pain and torment. Audiences would need to wait until the twentieth century to hear such desperation captured in music again.

By entering the realm of the inordinate, the irrational, and the inconceivable, Beethoven defied all expectations and pushed all possible limits—not least those of his listeners, who are left all but dumbfounded after a single hearing of the *Hammerklavier* Sonata. Many years of dedicated study would be necessary for audiences to penetrate the core of what is, essentially, a diabolical work. But can the same not be said of Goethe's *Faust?* The above reflections should in any case make one thing clear: Beethoven can only have composed the *Hammerklavier* Sonata for himself, and not for the archduke.

In September 1819, the *Grosse Sonate für Hammerklavier* was published in Vienna by Artaria & Co. Two months later, facilitated by Ferdinand Ries, the English edition was released by the Regent's Harmonic Institution in London, albeit without opus number or any mention of Rudolph.[8] However, amid fears that the sonata would be far too demanding for most English pianists (we need only recall Thomson's earlier concerns), the sonata was split into parts: Londoners could purchase either a three-movement sonata consisting of the Allegro, Adagio sostenuto, and Scherzo (in that order), or the final movement preceded by the introductory Largo.

While such musical dissection may seem blasphemous, the idea originated from none other than the master himself. In a long letter to Ries dated March 19, 1819—in which he fought tooth and nail to ensure a microscopic level of detail in the score and promised to send metronome markings to guard against potentially unauthorized tempi—Beethoven proposed several alternative groupings of the movements in the event that the sonata did not appeal to London tastes.[9] Beethoven was thus prepared to have his latest, greatest sonata pulled limb from limb, and all for fear of losing sales! The fact that the sonata's hard-won structural integrity was thus compromised—and with it, the purpose of the entire work—seemed of little consequence to him.[10]

The London publication was therefore what prompted Beethoven to add metronome markings to the *Hammerklavier* Sonata. Though they ought to have earned definitive authority, there is not a single pianist—not even today—who regards them as feasible in practice.[11] The measure that Beethoven had intended as protection against the whims of his interpreters thus ultimately backfired on him. The unattainability of the figures he attached to the grandest of his sonatas effectively issued a carte blanche to all skeptics of the metronome, triggering a tsunami of disbelief that would not recede for some time. Several months before his death, Beethoven made matters worse by uttering the famous words, "To hell with that infernal machinery!"[12]

Beethoven's preoccupation with tempi bordered on the obsessive. On hearing that one of his works had been performed, Beethoven's initial response was always to inquire after the tempi, Schindler claimed; all other aspects seemed to be of secondary importance.[13] The reports frequently led Beethoven to complain that far too much was left to chance and that this circumstance was in turn related to the system used to indicate the tempi, one which—according to Beethoven—had its origins in a barbaric period of musical history. Beethoven expressed his concerns as follows: "Can anything be more absurd than the term Allegro, which has only ever meant 'cheer-fully'? How frequently and far removed are we from this interpretation, so much so that the work thus described often expresses the exact opposite."[14]

In effect, the problem was twofold. Beethoven had long abandoned the notion that the four basic tempo indications—Adagio, Andante, Allegro, and Presto, or the *tempi ordinari*—were "as clear or precise as the four winds." Nor did they reveal much in the way of character. Beethoven stressed the importance of always bearing the character of a work in mind: while tempo indications formed part of a composition's external attributes, descriptions of the character revealed the work's inner spirit. In November 1817, in a letter to Ignaz Mosel, he declared his intention to renounce the *tempi ordinari* for good and to leave behind what he referred to as "absurd descriptions."[15] (He had, in part, already done so—we remember that in the opus 90 and 101 piano sonatas, the short, traditional Italian indications had already been replaced by longer descriptions in German.)

The subjective aspect of the matter was thus settled. For the objective side, Beethoven had pinned his hopes on an old friend, Johann Nepomuk Mälzel, who had returned to Vienna in November 1817 with a device in hand whose purpose was to eliminate all ambiguity concerning tempo forever: the met-ronome. Mälzel had patented the apparatus in 1815 in Paris and 1816 in London and had come to the Austrian capital to launch wholesale distribu-tion. Once again, this scheme demonstrates both his keen sensitivity to mar-ket fluctuations and—as we shall see—his utter lack of regard for considera-tions of intellectual property, or even fair play.

Attempts to quantify or "measure" musical tempi were nothing new. From as early as the seventeenth century, lists had been drawn up based on heartbeats or a comfortable walking pace; later methods involved swinging pendulums. The early nineteenth century saw a veritable race to develop more reliable techniques, as the individualization of music and wide-ranging opinions had created a pressing need for more precise timing mechanisms. Mälzel clearly understood the problem. An initial attempt in 1813 to launch a simple "Pendulum Chronometer" failed—the contraption was too cumbersome, and inaccurate besides. Although Beethoven had signed a letter of endorsement for the product (in all likelihood under duress), to others he dismissed the chronometer as "useless junk."[16] Mälzel's second attempt, however, was a success. In Amsterdam he had witnessed an invention by a certain Dietrich Nikolaus Winkel, which was propelled by a double pendulum. Without a moment's hesitation, Mälzel appropriated the concept, put a name to it, and promptly registered "his" new invention in Paris and London, proceeding to manufacture both the product and a sizeable fortune. The erroneous tempo designation "M.M."—for Mälzel's Metronome—has come to adorn virtually every published musical score since. Poor Dietrich Winkel did subsequently instigate (and win) a court case against Mälzel but saw no financial benefit whatsoever.

Beethoven, along with around forty other composers and professors of music, subsequently signed a second petition in the Viennese *Allgemeine musikalische Zeitung* urging all practitioners of music—students especially—to make rigorous use of the new invention. One year later, in February 1818, he and Salieri became the key figures in a promotional campaign run by Mälzel in the same newspaper.[17]

Unlike Beethoven's attitude to the previous chronometer in 1813, his enthusiasm for the new metronome was no longer feigned. Several months earlier, he had used it to objectively determine the metronome figures for his eight symphonies and the popular Septet (op. 20) and have them officially published.[18] Beethoven thereafter remained convinced of the metronome's value. There is a well-known account of the method he used to establish the various tempi of the Ninth Symphony: he sat at the piano and played all of the opening themes, while Karl fiddled with the metronome and noted down the corresponding values. The enterprise bore fruit, as several months before his death, in a letter to the publisher Schott, Beethoven spoke of how the success of the premiere of the Ninth Symphony in Berlin was due in no small measure to its metronomization.[19] Sadly, despite repeated promises, Beethoven's intentions to add metronome markings to the *Missa solemnis* as well as to the late piano sonatas and string quartets never came to fruition.

Despite Beethoven's assiduous use of the metronome, contentions arose almost immediately following his death regarding the proper tempi of his music. Two general trends emerged. In most geographic locations (including Vienna), interpretations of his works became gradually slower; only in Germany and some eastern European countries did the opposite occur. Mendelssohn in particular was criticized for garroting Beethoven's music with outrageous tempi, and even Wagner was initially said to have taken a rather brash approach. After some time, however—curiously enough, under the Parisian influence of François-Antoine Habeneck, who was generally regarded as the first true "Beethoven" conductor—Wagner too relaxed his tempi somewhat, thus reversing the trend in Germany.

In the debate surrounding Beethoven's tempi and the impact of his "unattainable" metronome markings, Schindler once again arrogated to himself a degree of unfounded authority. According to the following entry in the conversation notebooks dating from March 1824, he and Beethoven seem to have discussed the subject: "Yesterday, Umlauf and Schup[panzigh] were very surprised to hear how very different your tempi were compared to the rapid speeds of earlier years, and which you now seem to think are too fast [. . .] During the rehearsals in Josephstad, too, your preference for a slower Allegro was strikingly clear." Schindler went on to outline the consequences: "What a tremendous difference! And such clarity in the inner voices, which were otherwise always so inaudible or chaotic."[20]

Beethoven's response is, of course, absent. From the tone of Schindler's comments we might surmise that Beethoven agreed with his conclusions; however, musicologists have since ascertained that the above conversation actually never took place and that both remarks belong to the forgeries made by Schindler in an attempt to make history conform to his fantasy.[21]

Yet by the mid-nineteenth century, the damage had already been done, and interpretations of Beethoven's music became increasingly slower and less commensurate with the prescribed metronome markings. This practice was accompanied by countless and fundamental changes to Beethoven's scores that were necessary to make the new tempi technically feasible, including articulations, bowings, and occasionally even time signatures. In the second movement of the Fifth Piano Concerto, for example, the original alla breve was replaced by a slower 4/4 time signature—a gross injustice that was not rectified until 1996.[22]

How backward a state of affairs when the gulf between popular interpretation and Beethoven's original can only be bridged by doctoring the score!

In this context the metronome markings—which were generally considered to be too high and thus incorrect—bore the brunt of the violence. But finding a watertight justification for their alteration still proved difficult. In 1977, Vienna even hosted an entire "Beethoven Metronome Congress," where experts from a wide range of disciplines—including a professor of mechanical engineering from Berkeley and specialists from the British Horological Institute—attempted to pinpoint the shortcomings of the device used by Beethoven to set the original markings. The notion that Beethoven's metronome was defective and that the sorry old fool simply didn't notice proved as persistent as his rumored syphilis. The hypothesis can easily be rejected, however: faulty metronomes tick either too quickly—thus producing values that are too low—or with an irregular beat. The latter did indeed occur from time to time; when Beethoven was late sending in his metronome figures to Schott, he defended himself by saying that his metronome was "sick" and had been sent to a watchmaker to restore its regular pulse.[23] (This is, incidentally, also the context in which Beethoven's above-mentioned frustration with "infernal machinery" should be interpreted.) In addition, the more ardent among the antimetronomists undermined their own mechanical-defect theory by declaring some tempi as feasible and others as not—as though there are metronomes on earth whose capriciousness is selective.

The present reader will be spared the last two centuries' worth of colorful conjecture. Suffice it to say that all of the defect theories can be reduced to a single assumption, that Beethoven—the composer who agonized over every minuscule dot, accent, and slur in his scores—displayed a shocking level of indifference or incompetence when it came to determining what he himself believed to be the most important parameter of performance. Speculations of this kind have, thankfully, been laid to rest since the renewed interest in "authentic instruments." Through a combination of historically informed performance practice, a recalibration of auditory expectations, and the appurtenant gains in instrumental versatility, it has been ascertained that most of Beethoven's metronome markings are indeed attainable in practice, and that their application moreover leads to an enriched perception of Beethoven's musical language.

Some caution should still be exercised nonetheless, since tempo in music is never absolute. When adding the metronome marking to the work "So oder so" (This way or that; WoO 148), Beethoven left the following comment in the margin: "100 Mälzel, however this can only apply to the first few bars, for sensibilities also have their own meter, which at this speed (i.e. 100) cannot be fully expressed."[24] Beethoven is, indeed, known to have incorporated minor fluctuations in tempo to enrich performance rhetoric. His pupil Ries reported that despite maintaining a strict tempo throughout, Beethoven increased speed on rare occasions, while pulling back on others (during a crescendo, for example). According to Ries, the resulting effect was both striking and beautiful.[25]

There is one error of judgment to which Beethoven may have fallen prey. Composers and conductors experienced with the metronome know only too well that tempi "in the mind" are always slightly faster than tempi in performance—a common psychological pitfall with a potential margin for error of several percentage points. Any degree of freedom thus obtained is of a trivial magnitude, however.

A view traditionally expressed in Beethoven biographies is that the Allegretto from the Eighth Symphony is based on a canon composed by Beethoven several months before, called "Ta ta ta" (WoO 162), which served as both a farewell and a homage to the inventor of the metronome:

This association has given rise to the erroneous presumption that the Eighth Symphony is humorous in nature, and also fuels the deep-seated conviction that Beethoven's metronome markings were incorrect. Unlike the symphony's Allegretto scherzando, to be played at ♪ = 88, the canon's prescribed tempo is drastically slower at only ♪ = 72. If Beethoven thus allocated two fundamentally different values to the same piece of music, then they—and by extension all others—should be treated with caution. The credibility of the anecdote is undermined, however, by a number of chronological contradictions and even more so by the dubious nature of the canon's only source—Schindler—who first presented a copy of it to a publisher in 1843. It was not until ten years later, first of all in an article to the *Niederrheinische Musik-Zeitung* and later in the second reprint of Schindler's Beethoven biography from 1860, that he propagated the tale of how, in 1815, Beethoven had allowed him to transcribe a personal copy of the canon and take it home. According to Schindler, Beethoven had given together ("extemporized") this little bagatelle at a party given in 1812 to mark Mälzel's departure to London. Franz Brunsvik and Stephan Breuning were supposedly also in attendance, and as the story goes, Beethoven later used the theme as inspiration for the Allegretto scherzando.[26]

The arrant untruth of this conclusion is evident in Beethoven's own symphonic sketches, which demonstrate how laboriously he worked to sculpt just the right contours for this seemingly simplistic theme. Closer inspection reveals further leaks in the story. Schindler talks about the metronome as though the invention already existed in the spring of 1812, while we know that Mälzel only created his first version in 1813 and developed a second, completely different device between 1815 and 1817. Furthermore, Mälzel did not leave for London until 1813—after the Eighth Symphony was already complete—and there is no doubt whatsoever that Breuning was away from Vienna between 1810 and 1813. Any definitive proof was therefore to be provided by the conversation notebooks. In April 1824, Schindler apparently said (or rather, wrote) the following to Beethoven:

> I am currently playing the 2nd movement of the 8th symphony.
> ta ta ta ta, the Mälzel canon.
> It was such a jolly time, that evening when we sang the canon at the Kamehl—Mälzel sang bass,
> I still sang soprano then.
> I believe it was in late December: 1817 [*sic!*]
> A time when Your Majesty often granted me audience.[27]

It should come as no surprise that this conversation, too, is counterfeit. The canon is no more than a bastardization of the Allegretto theme, conceived by Schindler in his ardor to promote slower Beethoven tempi.

50

The Missa solemnis

A MASS FOR PEACE

IF WE ASSUME THAT IN 1809 Beethoven had already been assured the honorable duty of composing the festival Mass for the installation of Archduke Rudolph as archbishop in Olmütz, he must have had ample time to prepare. It is known that he embarked on a thorough study of the major religious works of his predecessors: Handel's *Messiah*, Haydn's *Missa Sancti Bernardi von Offida*, and the *Missa in augustiis* (the Nelson Mass), as well as Mozart's *Requiem*. But his curiosity also extended to contemporary treatments of the genre, such as those by Hummel and, especially, Cherubini, and his diaries even make mention of plans to work his way through "all the ecclesiastical chants of the monks."[1] That same year he wrote out a literal translation of the entire text of the Mass, experimented with prosodic accents in the original Latin, and left some theological commentary on the correct meaning and scope of certain words.[2]

Although contact between Beethoven and the archduke had flagged over the years, Beethoven still remained on high alert, ready to start work on the promised ceremonial music should the need arise. This also goes some way to explaining his lack of enthusiasm for other attractive vocal projects that crossed his path (including a requiem that he had promised to textile merchant Johann Wolfmayer in 1818, which might have earned him 450 guilders but that he never even started).[3] The same fate befell the oratorio that he might have written for the Friends of Music Society (Gesellschaft der Musikfreunde). In 1815 this illustrious association, of which Archduke Rudolph was the honorary chairman, had asked Beethoven to compose a major work for choir and orchestra. Beethoven's initial response was tentative, as he claimed to have "heard" that not all of the society's members were in support of the commission. After the board's emphatic denial of these rumors, the typical mercantile haggling ensued: Beethoven initially asked for 1,800 guilders but was ultimately content with 1,350—a respectable sum nonetheless. In February 1816, Beethoven informed the board not only of his agreement to the financial stipulations but also of his willingness to write for the gargantuan ensemble of seven hundred (!) performers. His only condition was that he be permitted to deviate from what he referred to as "all hitherto customary forms in the genre."[4] It was on that note that the negotiations concluded, and when the society had not received a single note in return two years later, the board sent Beethoven a reminder in May 1818. Both parties now reached agreement that a libretto should be ordered from Karl Bernard—one of the contributors to *O Moment of Glory*—based on the tale of "Der Sieg des Kreuzes" (The victory of the cross), itself a continuation of the material from the *Mount of Olives*.[5] An advance of four hundred guilders was issued one year later in June 1819. Beethoven seized it without hesitation—despite being in the midst of the *Missa solemnis* and the *Diabelli Variations*—and signed an agreement binding him to a contractual result. Now, though, Bernard was the one dragging his feet, and when he at last furnished the long-awaited text in 1823, Beethoven deemed it unusable. The society echoed his sentiments, and the project disappeared into a bureau drawer somewhere.

Beethoven thus remained unencumbered, and as soon as he heard (in February 1819) that Rudolph was finally to take up office in Olmütz, he set to work on the music for the inaugural ceremony, which was scheduled for March 1820. The *Kyrie* took shape relatively quickly, but soon afterward Beethoven's compositional engine began to stall. In more precise terms, it was running at such high intensity that the required resources—and more to the point, the available time—no longer proved adequate. To put it yet another way, although twelve months ought to have been more than enough time for an experienced composer to distill the five sections of the *ordinarium missae* into forty-five minutes of music, Beethoven's *Missa solemnis* began to assume such monolithic and monumental proportions that the deadline quickly proved unfeasible.

The roadblock sat in the *Gloria,* which—like the *Credo*—is particularly cumbersome due to the sheer volume of text to be incorporated. Its substance is also surprisingly haphazard and flits rapidly between disparate concepts (*adoramus te,* "we worship thee," and *glorificamus te,* "we glorify thee," really are two very different things), creating a dichotomy between cohesion and expression that threatens to undermine structural integrity. Beethoven resolved this dilemma in the *Gloria* by superimposing a more general musical commentary on the relationship between the heavenly/divine aspects on the one hand, and the worldly/human dimension on the other. Temporal perception forms a key conceptual parameter: the primary motif—a rising scale depicting the phrase *Gloria in excelsis Deo* (Glory to God in the highest)—recurs regularly as a kind of mantra.[6] It takes on the function of a refrain, thus providing continuity while also allowing for frequent breaks in the musical momentum. Beethoven believed that the divine embodied a timeless quality, and took every opportunity to portray as much in the music: the choir sings words such as *omnipotens* (omnipotent), *altissimus* (the Most High), and of course *Deo* (God) as long, unmetered chords forming indestructible walls of sound. Elsewhere in the text, such as the phrase *Quoniam tu solus sanctus Dominus* (For only thou art holy, thou only art the Lord), more metric complexity is employed to express the struggle of humankind to fathom the divine. The opening theme returns once more at the very last, as though suggesting that there can be no end to God's glory. A useful by-product of this stratagem was the opportunity to mitigate somewhat the final *Amen* (a Hebrew word meaning "So be it"), which Beethoven viewed as rather unpalatable and bombastic.

A further benefit of the gravity assigned to the divine was the freedom thus created to express mortality, in both an individual and a collective sense. The *Miserere* offers a telling illustration, in which Beethoven dared even to interpolate greatly impassioned, almost operatic exclamations of "ah" in the text, thus heightening the drama.

In this manner, and more so than in the *Kyrie,* the *Gloria* established the dimensions of a clear structural framework. There can be no doubt that Beethoven, who had an intuitive sixth sense for musical proportion, anticipated the consequences for the composition as a whole, especially since—as good practice dictates—he had conceptualized, noted down, and worked out his ideas for all sections of the Mass at the outset. He likely soon realized that the *Missa solemnis* would be nearly one and a half hours long, rendering it unsuitable for regular liturgical use. He was also experienced enough to know that the March 1820 deadline was all but untenable, though it was still some time before he said as much to the archduke. A letter dated December 19, 1819, commenced with the promise that the deadline would still be met—but only just. Then, following a lament to the many tribulations in his life (his ailing health, household troubles, time lost to other projects that he could not turn down, and of course the distress of the custody battle),

Beethoven wrote in a postscript, "His Royal Highness might yet wonder how I plan to complete such a work, given my present circumstances."[7]

The future archbishop had no choice but to accept Beethoven's excuses. Of course, we are not privy to the conversations prompted by this letter, as the archduke was the only person who never had any need of the conversation notebooks (the pair always met in private, so the archduke could shout into Beethoven's ear without the risk of disturbing any bystanders or divulging sensitive information). The precise moment when the archduke decided to cancel the *Missa solemnis* in favor of Hummel's Mass in B-flat Major (op. 77) and the *Te Deum* by Joseph Preindl (an organist and Albrechtsberger epigone) is unknown; likewise unknown is when Beethoven finally heard that he would no longer be offered the post of Kapellmeister in Olmütz.

This was a pivotal moment in Beethoven's life, and a particularly tragic one, since the impasse was entirely of his own creation. Allowing the *Gloria* to take on such explosive proportions triggered a chain of events in his career, the consequences of which he foresaw only too well. By failing to finish on time, not only did he forfeit the chance to put himself in the spotlight of a prestigious society event, but he also let slip a major professional advancement opportunity. Clearly, Beethoven was prepared to sacrifice these worldly ambitions in favor of higher artistic considerations. Later on, he compensated by making awkward (and at first glance, unscrupulous) attempts to generate as much income as possible from the publication of the *Missa solemnis*. In February 1820, when the road to Olmütz had been permanently closed off, he made efforts to sell the *Missa* to Simrock in Bonn. Despite knowledge to the contrary, Beethoven still pretended that the Mass would soon be performed, and the price he demanded—125 louis d'or, or 1,125 guilders—was largely based on the prestige of the event for which it had originally been intended. As soon as it became apparent that the work would no longer be performed in such an illustrious context, Simrock lowered the price to one hundred louis d'or, which Beethoven accepted without a flinch.

Beethoven continued to overplay his hand. Simrock had transferred the fee to a colleague in Frankfurt, until such time as Beethoven's good friend Franz Brentano would act as an intermediary and deliver the score there as agreed. Under the misguided apprehension that the Mass was almost complete, Brentano lent the money in advance to Beethoven, who then needed to tread very carefully to justify the subsequent delays. The completion of the *Missa solemnis* was more distant than ever; the lack of an imminent deadline now meant that Beethoven devoted more and more time to other compositional engagements, such as new piano sonatas, the *Diabelli Variations*, and sundry minor projects. None of this prevented him from continuing to peddle his "work in progress" among potential publishers, including Schlesinger in Berlin, and Peters in Leipzig. It is interesting to note the rising degree of adjectival intensity on Beethoven's part when referring to the *Missa solemnis* in these negotiations. Initially he spoke of "a great work," an epithet he had also attached to the *Hammerklavier* Sonata. Later, this became "one of my greatest works" and ultimately "the greatest work I have ever written."[8] As the superlatives rose, so too did the price—so much so that Peters swore Beethoven to secrecy regarding their financial arrangements for fear of destabilizing the market. It should also be noted that Peters was bidding high primarily to keep the Mass away from his competitor Schlesinger—a rivalry that Beethoven was only too happy to encourage, as he believed that Schlesinger had short-changed him by twelve to thirteen guilders when issuing payment for his last three piano sonatas.[9]

The web of deception spun by Beethoven among the various publishers had meanwhile become so complex that barefaced lies seemed his only way out. In a letter to Peters in November 1822, he maintained that he had actually been working on two Masses and was still uncertain as to which of the two he would furnish. The dilemma intensified in February 1823, when the original two Masses seemed to have grown to three . . . Simrock, for his part, was mollified by the promise of substitute works—which, naturally, were all but complete—and of another, otherwise unspecified Mass.

And yet the bottom line was not Beethoven's sole concern. When the *Missa solemnis* was nearing completion, and despite the fact that he had already signed three contracts and received two advance payments (which cannot have gone unnoticed in the small world of publishing), Beethoven initiated negotiations with four more interested parties: Artaria and Diabelli in Vienna, Probst in Leipzig, and Schott in Mainz. But he did not, as one might expect, play one off against the other to secure the highest fee. Despite the fact that publishers were clamoring for exclusive rights to the *Missa solemnis,* Beethoven maintained a consistent asking price, which implies that it was based on idealistic rather than practical considerations. Appearances suggest that Beethoven wished to measure the value of his masterpiece not by the fee alone but by the quantity and prestige of the potential buyers. Schott in particular knew how to strike the right chord with Beethoven, and the possibility is very real that the eventual allocation of the *Missa solemnis* (and later of the Ninth Symphony) to Schott was due in no small part to the respectful manner in which they addressed the "most eminent Royal and Imperial court Kapellmeister, Herr Beethoven."[10]

The fact that the *Missa solemnis* did not appear in print until April 1827—mere weeks after Beethoven's death—was attributable only partly to the customary difficulties of publishing a complex score. Of far greater influence were the stalling tactics set in motion by the master himself: in the spring of 1823, Beethoven revised his marketing strategy completely and devised a scheme by which he could sell the *Missa solemnis* to the royal houses of Europe and to various esteemed cultural institutes. To this end, Beethoven contacted Saxon diplomat Georg August von Griesinger, who some time before had coordinated an international sales campaign for Haydn's *Creation,* successfully attracting no fewer than four hundred subscribers. Beethoven's offering was more exclusive and would consist of an authorized, handwritten copy of the Mass—essentially a collector's item—whose value and associated price tag of fifty ducats were reliant on its status as a "limited edition." To ensure that these copies were not used for unauthorized performances or pirated editions, the initial pages of the *Gloria* were withheld and could only be obtained after payment of an additional fee. In this light, the postponement of regular printed sales—and thus also of releasing the autograph copy—was an entirely logical necessity. As an added bonus, Beethoven now at least had a legitimate excuse to escape his own self-imposed imbroglio of fully and partially made commitments.

Beethoven first petitioned the foreign embassies in Vienna. Fourteen days later, he sent a form letter to twenty-eight European dignitaries and cultural institutes, asking for expressions of interest in what he described as the most brilliant product of his spirit.[11] Responses trickled in slowly, and initially only four crowned heads took up the offer. The king of Prussia even offered payment in the form of a grand royal distinction, which Beethoven respectfully but firmly declined. Sales were also inhibited by a circulating rumor that the work was still unfinished, a rumor whose origins lay in the ailing health of Beethoven's preferred copyist, Wenzel Schlemmer. In a mild panic, Beethoven turned to Archduke Rudolph and begged him to issue a declaration that he had indeed received the full score on March 19, 1823. Whether the archduke eventually did so is unknown; what is certain is that he used his influence (again at Beethoven's request) to persuade both the grand duke of Tuscany, Ferdinand III, and Frederick Augustus I of Saxony to purchase copies of the *Missa solemnis.* Goethe, Spohr, and Cherubini also received entreaties to promote the project among their respective patrons. Beethoven ultimately succeeded in disposing of ten copies of the Mass, which after the high copyist fees (Schlemmer asked sixty guilders apiece) amounted to a tidy profit of 1,650 guilders. All customary publishers' fees paled by comparison.

Throughout the *Missa* affair Beethoven also took a rather liberal interpretation of the term "exclusivity." In April 1823, precisely when he was hawking his "unique" copies of the Mass along the gates of the European royal houses, Beethoven went in search of a publisher in London. In a rather frank letter to Ries, he admitted to harboring few scruples as far as dignitaries were concerned.[12] At the same time, he started negotiations with various major German choral societies, including the Singakademie in Berlin and the Saint Cecilia Society (Cäcilienverein) in Frankfurt. One problem with the a capella Singakademie, however, was their lack of an orchestra. Beethoven glossed over the matter, stating his conviction that it was perfectly possible to perform the work with voices alone. Singakademie director Carl Friedrich Zelter took Beethoven's enthusiasm rather literally and promptly ordered a choral arrangement of the Mass, which Beethoven just as quickly declined to produce due to a lack of time.[13] Other attempts to create a more accessible version with only organ or piano accompaniment were equally unsuccessful. In truth, this development worked in Beethoven's favor, as it allowed him to dispel rumors circulating among his—potentially hoodwinked—publishers that a piano reduction was already in circulation. Beethoven genuinely thought that by doing so, he might reestablish his own innocence in the matter.

As a bizarre and unexpected side effect of Beethoven's personal marketing strategy, the premiere of the *Missa solemnis* took place not in Vienna or London but in far-off St. Petersburg. Chance played no small part in this turn of events: in November 1822, Beethoven was offered a commission to compose several string quartets for one Nikolai Borisovich Galitzin, a young aristocrat who nurtured a particular love for music. Beethoven accepted but would tarry for two and a half more years—until the completion of the Ninth Symphony—before furnishing the first quartet. In the meantime, he asked whether Galitzin might assist him in promoting the *Missa solemnis* at the Russian court. Galitzin was only too happy to oblige and persuaded the tsar to purchase a copy (likely without much difficulty, given the affection cherished by Alexander I and his wife for Beethoven). Galitzin continued his campaign with the St. Petersburg Philharmonic Society, but it bore no fruit; afraid of dashing his idol's hopes, Galitzin simply decided to purchase the second copy himself. His efforts did not end there, as Galitzin had ambitions to hold the world premiere of the Mass at the Philharmonic Society's annual Christmas charity concert for widows and orphans. Over the course of several letters written in fine French, he successfully persuaded Beethoven to authorize the project. A pivotal argument in this process, according to Galitzin, was his commitment to safeguarding "the quality of both the voices and the ensemble" and to ensure that "this masterpiece be executed in a manner befitting its celebrated author."[14]

As usual, the allotted rehearsal time very quickly proved inadequate; Galitzin reported that the vocal parts were challenging, and much time was lost on correcting errors in the score. The premiere was therefore postponed several times, but at last, after no fewer than ten rehearsals (an eternity by the prevailing standards), Beethoven's *trésor de beauté*, as it was later described by Galitzin, resounded for the first time on April 7, 1824. The success was, by all accounts, tremendous.

And so it was that Vienna let a monumental world premiere slip through its fingers. There were reasons, of course. For one thing, the nature of the work eliminated all possibility of performance within a liturgical context, and for another, the Viennese government was under pressure from a certain Count Firmian—a local archbishop and thus a peer of Archduke Rudolph— who sought actively to repress performances of sacred works in secular settings. One major exception to this policy were the afternoon Concerts Spirituels held every second Friday of the month at Mehlgrube (at Neuer Markt square, later at Landständischer hall on Herrengasse), which in addition to popular symphonies and overtures always presented a Mass in its entirety. The initiative had received the bishop's blessing, since the concert was actually an open rehearsal for the Mass to be performed the following Sunday at St. Augustine's. Since no other rehearsals took place beforehand (the concert itself was the sole rehearsal), only well-known repertoire items were eligible for inclusion on the program—Beethoven's symphonies, the *Mass in C,* and the choral work *Calm Sea and Prosperous Voyage* made regular appearances. The performance standard can only have been lamentable; Beethoven believed the conductor, Franz Xaver Gebauer, to be arrantly incompetent (taking great pleasure in bastardizing his name as *Geh, Bauer!* or "Leave, peasant!"), and dismissed his efforts as "outhouse music."[15] That

Beethoven's *Missa solemnis* might have been premiered under such conditions was inconceivable.

Obvious alternatives were lacking. All things considered, the Friends of Music Society was really the only feasible option, for it had a large-enough following among both performers and public, adequate financial means, and enough of a foothold at court to keep any potential imperial sabotage at bay. All of this was known to Beethoven, and in January 1824 he formulated a proposition, mediated by Leopold Sonnleithner, offering the society the *Missa solemnis* in lieu of the oratorio that had already been promised and partially paid for, but never delivered. Beethoven considered the proposition highly reasonable, as the *Missa* gave more than a passing nod to oratorio style and suited the society's aims and forces extremely well.[16] Beethoven also suggested premiering his latest symphony, the Ninth, during the same concert (conveniently forgetting that the symphony had been commissioned by the London Philharmonic Society, to whom he had promised the exclusive rights for a period of eighteen months). The society board made some calculations, reached the conclusion that the costs and the risks were too great, and sent word via Sonnleithner that the project could not go ahead, thereby leaving Beethoven no choice but to go in search of other opportunities. He spoke with the management of the Hofburg Redoutensaal and of the Landständischer hall on Herrengasse and ultimately found success at the Kärntnertortheater. It was there, on May 7 and alongside the *Consecration of the House* overture (op. 124) and the Ninth Symphony, that the *Kyrie, Credo,* and *Agnus Dei* from the *Missa solemnis* were performed. The other sections were omitted due to a lack of rehearsal time.

A comprehensive account of the intricate chain of events leading up to this concert will come later; for the present, let the reader be content with a few pertinent details. Despite malevolent claims to the contrary, Vienna came in droves to this momentous musical event, filling the over 2,400-seat hall almost to capacity. This backdrop made the absence of the imperial family all the more conspicuous, the most palpable void perhaps being left by the initiator and dedicatee of the *Missa solemnis*—Archduke Rudolph himself—who was detained by important responsibilities in Olmütz. During a repeat performance fourteen days later, the *Kyrie* was all that remained of the Mass; in Beethoven's estimation the choir—whose members had complained repeatedly during rehearsals of the music's extreme difficulty—could manage no more than one chorus. Ironically, the *Credo* and *Agnus Dei* were replaced by two Italian works: the trio "Tremate, empi, tremate" (op. 116, composed by Beethoven twenty years earlier) and an aria, "Di tanti palpiti," from cult composer Rossini's *Tancredi*.

Nobody can deny that the vocal parts in the *Missa solemnis* and the Ninth Symphony place great demands on the singers, who thus often accuse Beethoven of having composed poorly for the voice. And yet this criticism is only partly justified, evidenced by the many sections in these two works that are characterized by a delicate cantabile—an *Italianità*—conveying a sense of both intense emotion and vulnerable sensibility. This duality in the required vocal technique is conceptually indispensable; rather than a sign of the composer's incompetence, the "extreme difficulties" to be overcome by the performers can instead be taken as a metaphor for the human condition and the imperfections of mankind in the face of God's omnipotence. Was it not Beethoven himself who wrote that all is dwarfed by the grandeur of the Most High?[17] A counterweight is offered by the comfort and consolation to be derived from Christ's incarnation. From the very first *Christe eleison*, stunning melodies paired symbolically in parallel thirds impart a sense of brotherhood—of comradeship, as it were—between Christ and humankind. The phrase in the *Credo* introducing Christ's incarnation—*Qui propter nos homines et propter nostram salutem descendit de caelis* (Who for all people and our salvation descended from heaven)—is a poignant and peerless example of tender musicality and sweetness.

In extremely few late-eighteenth- or early-nineteenth-century Masses is the faith in Christ professed with such stark clarity. By writing this way, Beethoven clearly went against the prevailing theological consensus (in fact, he was merely continuing the trend he had already set in the *Mount of Olives* and the Mass in C). The tonal instability at the opening of the *Credo* is a clear sign from Beethoven of the difficulty he experienced in professing the dogmas of the church, and at the ultimate confession, "I believe [...] in one holy, catholic and apostolic church," the contrapuntal fabric becomes so complex that all clarity is lost. The tenors rush headlong through the text, drowned out by loud exclamations of "*Credo!*" in the remaining voices, forming a jagged counterpoint and raising doubts as to the unity of their purported adherence to any "one church."

Beethoven broke even further with convention in the concluding *Dona nobis pacem*. Faced with the elementary conundrum of having to cap off his gargantuan work with a minuscule text, Beethoven increased the musical gravitas by augmenting the text in an ideological sense. To the complex dichotomy between the "worldly" and the "divine," a dialectical resolution is offered in the form of Beethoven's musical treatment of the term *pacem,* "peace." To underscore his intentions, Beethoven added an explanatory subscript: "Bitte um innern und äussern Frieden" (A plea for peace, both internal and external). It is essential to note that the German term *Bitte* is subject to a wide spectrum of interpretations, ranging from lowly "begging" to a more noble "prayer" or "entreaty." More mixed signals follow: his original plan was to construct the section around a simple and unpretentious melody evocative of peace, whose tonality, contours, and tempered expressiveness bore similarities with the "joy" theme from the Ninth Symphony. He ultimately abandoned this concept in favor of various motley and occasionally even unrelated motifs, as though suggesting a kind of "motivic pluralism" expressing the ecumenical nature of the message. But while diverse, the motifs are held together through a common musical undertone or ambience which embodies a clearly "pastoral" character. The 6/8 time signature, the Allegretto tempo, the undulating violins, and the overall orchestral palette of the *Dona nobis pacem* all point unmistakably to the finale of the Sixth Symphony. The message, too, is unmistakable. Given that Beethoven's love of nature was a direct extension of his understanding of the divine, it was natural for him to express his hopes for a peaceful world using the pastoral idiom.

Both inner and outer peace come at a price, however. Beethoven saw fit to interrupt the initial *Dona nobis pacem* with an outbreak of war, and again several minutes later with a highly obscure and incoherent orchestral intermezzo, offering a fitting metaphor for humankind's fear and desperation. This approach to the *Agnus Dei* was unprecedented, and Beethoven inevitably became the target of much criticism. Even the "expert" Schiller commented that Beethoven's judgment had been in error, and advised that the episode be removed.

By giving such a dramatic interpretation of the text of the Mass, Beethoven effectively imbued it with the character of an oratorio, an association he alluded to many times in his correspondence. Precisely because this dramatization of the text distances it even more from its liturgical context, Beethoven considered it more prudent than ever to emphasize the religious aspects, and so he issued the express order to perform the *Kyrie* and *Sanctus* with *Andacht,* which here means "devotion" in the sense of both "dedication" and "piety." In Beethoven's own words, it was his intention—despite the secular performance context—to elicit and excite feelings of religious fervor among the singers and the audience alike. The *Benedictus*—without doubt one of the most glorious and moving passages Beethoven ever composed—is thus preceded by what he himself dubbed a "preludium," an organ improvisation arranged for orchestra, intended to evoke (or at the very least suggest) the solemn reverence of a kneeling congregation. To further mitigate the transplantation of the Mass to the concert hall, Beethoven provided more historical context through the sporadic use of what are known as the "church modes," serving not only to push the entire Mass back in time but also to conjure up a more ecclesiastical *couleur locale*. Myriad are the instances in the score where the contrapuntal interplay creates the illusion of space and artificial reverberation, as though Beethoven wished to recreate a concert-hall equivalent of the acoustic sonorities so typical of church buildings.

Beethoven's reputation suffered greatly from the blatant opportunism with which he marketed the "divine" packaging of such an important religious and humanistic work. He personally shrugged off such accusations rather indifferently, countering that artists cannot spend every day communing with Jupiter on Mount Olympus.[18] But does this explanation suffice?

We might, without too much trouble, manufacture several rationales for the rather base spectacle staged by Beethoven when marketing his *Missa solemnis*. However, one particularly important and mitigating circumstance should not be overlooked. In May 1822 Beethoven had reconciled with his brother Johann, who had sold his pharmacy in Linz. Johann was living off his pension, resting on his laurels—both on a country estate in Gneixendorf and in a Viennese townhouse—and had adopted the lifestyle of a pseudo-aristocrat. (The Viennese were particularly averse to such behavior. They believed that Johann had pretentions to rise above his station, and mocked him as *le chevalier*, "the cavalier." According to Moritz Lichnowsky—a true aristocrat—Johann's one and only merit was bearing his famous brother's surname.[19])

Since he was still owed money by his highly respected but impecunious brother, Johann took it upon himself to restore order to Beethoven's dire financial administration. With the arrogance of a successful businessman, and in an attempt to eliminate a major financial and strategic bottleneck, he proposed several methods by which Beethoven might capitalize on the swathes of former, less-substantial works that had never found their way to a wider public. For some time, Beethoven had been inundated with requests by publishers for new work, all of which he systematically declined due to his preoccupation with more grandiose but less profitable enterprises. Such an attitude, pointing to a severe turnover problem, is beyond the understanding of any astute businessman—at a certain point Johann even dared suggest that Beethoven would do better to compose operas à la Rossini. As a compromise, they settled on issuing a long list of available compositions—military marches, second-rate lieder, and occasional chamber works—all of which are now, coincidentally, works without opus number and whose price tags were set by an ex-wholesaler in medical supplies.

It is not inconceivable that it was Johann who, on the basis of these same profitability concerns, encouraged his brother to instigate such a shameless bidding war on the *Missa solemnis,* and that the strategy of private sales to the royal houses of Europe also stemmed from his mercantile brain. Beethoven was not always so amenable to his brother's commercial strategies. When he expressed misgivings about his brother's plans to manipulate Peters, Johann's laconic reply in one of the conversation notebooks reads, "Well, that's business for you."[20]

51

The Circle Is Complete

THE LATE PIANO WORKS

BEETHOVEN LABORED OVER THE *MISSA SOLEMNIS* for four years, far longer than he worked on his only opera, *Fidelio*. Several possible causes present themselves: the sheer dimensions of the work, the disappearing deadline, and perhaps most importantly, the fact that he ceased production multiple times to work on other projects. The latter seemed to meet one of Beethoven's rather paradoxical needs, as the more massive his projects became, the more distraction was necessary for him to stay concentrated. This trait is typical of genius minds; it is as though they must work continuously to expunge the influx of new and disruptive ideas.

Beethoven had always been an avid multitasker, but during these four years of his life, he took the art to extremes. Entirely in parallel with the *Missa solemnis,* he also composed a set of variations of more than an hour in length, the *33 Veränderungen über einen Walzer von Diabelli* (op. 120, better known in English as the *Diabelli* Variations). They were begun in March 1819 and finished in April 1823, dates that correspond almost exactly to the commencement and completion of the *Missa solemnis*. Along the way, he also whipped up three piano sonatas (opp. 109, 110, and 111) and a set of bagatelles (op. 119)—a fascinating process, the more so since such compositional slaloming leads to an inevitable degree of mutual influence and cross-pollination between works. The *Diabelli* Variations offer a prime example: for no other work is a knowledge of its fitful genesis so crucial to a correct understanding of the music.

The impetus for the variations came not from Beethoven himself but from the theme's own creator. Anton Diabelli had been a close colleague of publisher Sigmund Steiner's for many years. "Diabolus Diabelli"—as Beethoven sometimes called him[1]—performed mainly revision work, made arrangements (including both two- and four-hand transcriptions of Beethoven's

Seventh Symphony), and also ran a compositional production line churning out minor piano works for the general public. In 1818, he joined forces with Pietro Cappi and launched an independent publishing business; as an initial public relations exercise, he planned the release of a set of variations based on a waltz from his own hand. The bundle was to be a unique offering, an anthology of miniatures by the most famous musicians in Vienna alongside those of many promising newcomers. No fewer than fifty composers were invited to provide one variation each, including such established names as Czerny, Hummel, Moscheles, and Schubert, as well as some striking new additions, such as Mozart's son (Franz Xaver) and a young Franz Liszt. The entire collection would be crowned by a contribution from His Highness Archduke Rudolph, who—noblesse oblige—was to furnish the concluding fugue.

Beethoven, too, graced the list of invitees. It was Schindler who incited a rather stubborn rumor that Beethoven's initial response was lukewarm, due purportedly to a skepticism toward collective projects in general (Beethoven still bore scars from a similar project in 1808, for which he produced the song "In questa tomba oscura," WoO 133), and of Diabelli's theme in particular. According to Schindler, Beethoven believed the theme to be nothing more than a "cobbler's patch," serving only to ridicule the participants in the project.[2] What Schindler neglected to explain, however, is why—after first refusing to waste any time on a single variation—Beethoven then proceeded to compose a one-hour set of no fewer than thirty-three variations on the very same "banal" material. His arguments proposing an attractive financial reward remain utterly unverifiable.

Nobody can deny that Diabelli's theme is hardly brimming with musical inspiration or charm. But let us think back to Beethoven's very first composition from 1783, when he learned that alternate standards apply when evaluating themes of this type: was it not so that themes intended for variations should be judged not on what they *are* but instead on what they might *become?* And is it so far-fetched that Beethoven, in his efforts to produce Diabelli's one variation, came to see the theme's true potential and decided to compose a full set to avoid having to sacrifice any of the gems he had unearthed along the way? Whatever the case, after only a few weeks Beethoven had already sketched the contours of twenty-three variations, including his trademark penultimate slow variation in *minore,* and a final fugue.[3] Having done so, he set the variations aside for nearly three years, redirecting his efforts to the *Missa solemnis* and his many other projects.

One such diversion was the piano method under construction by his old friend and fellow student of Albrechtsberger, Friedrich Starke, to which Beethoven had happily agreed to lend his collaboration. Starke had managed to obtain a position as horn player at the imperial opera (some say with a modicum of help from Beethoven, although these claims are contested[4]). As was common practice, he supplemented his principal duties by dabbling in a wide range of peripheral musical activities. Between 1819 and 1821, for example, he published the *Wiener Pianoforte-Schule* (Viennese pianoforte school), a collection of short piano pieces by the most eminent Viennese composers, the works being arranged in order of increasing difficulty. Beethoven's contribution was to consist of the Bagatelle in E, a four-minute "pseudo-improvisation" without any strict form but with structure nonetheless, in which rapid vivace sections in 2/4 time blend seamlessly in and out of slower adagio passages in 3/4. Unexpected, perhaps, but not entirely surprising. After the *Hammerklavier*—an Olympic, marathon achievement of epic proportions—Beethoven clearly longed for more small-scale occupations and the freedom to work within enclosed limits. For despite the spatial restrictions, removing the yoke of overarching cohesion allows greater scope for unfettered ideas, free association, and poetry. This premise is effectively the logical counterpart to that other major principle discovered by Beethoven in his student years, which states that the longer a composition lasts, the less thematic material it can support.

Fate had other plans for the Bagatelle in E, however. In that same month, April 1820, Berlin publisher Adolf Martin Schlesinger sent Beethoven a commission for three new piano sonatas. It was an attractive offer, if only because interest from a new publisher gave Beethoven an excuse to increase pressure on the others. Schlesinger's rates were also quite reasonable at a very welcome thirty ducats per sonata. In a letter from Beethoven to Brentano, he confessed the difficulty he was having keeping his head above water, necessitating "alimentary" work to cover his day-to-day expenses.[5]

And so it was that just as he was spinning the initial threads of the *Missa solemnis*—a web in which he would later become hopelessly entangled—Beethoven committed to delivering three new piano sonatas in as many months. It hardly needs mentioning that the resolution was a spectacular failure: the first sonata of the three (op. 109) was delayed by six months, and the other two (opp. 110 and 111) would not follow for another two years. Beethoven's then-incumbent secretary, Oliva, must have anticipated this complication early on and therefore suggested that Beethoven repurpose his newly composed Bagatelle in E as the opening movement for the first of Schlesinger's sonatas. The idea had merit: not only did it save time (which ultimately helped little), but it also allowed Beethoven to circumvent the almost existential crisis of conceptualizing the musical identity of his next piano sonata. The *Hammerklavier* had been the musical equivalent of a "big bang"; the Bagatelle in E forced him to return to the land of the living, as it were, and write music of less cosmic and more human proportions. The second (fast) movement of the new sonata, for example, lasts a mere three minutes. Its sinister, jagged, and short-lived phrases offer a clear contrast to the dreamlike, weightless filigree of the opening, while the concluding variations on a sarabande-like theme serve as a musical catalyst or binding agent. The wild, relentless finale to the *Hammerklavier* is all but forgotten and has been replaced by ethereal, hymn-like music, transparent and effortless. The many subtle references to Bach and especially Handel are undoubtedly no coincidence.

It is noteworthy that the new sonata was dedicated to Franz and Antonie Brentano's daughter, Maximiliane. Since we might suppose that Beethoven had long outgrown his old habit of dedicating major piano works to eighteen-year-old girls, the suspicion arises that Beethoven's generosity to Maximiliane was actually intended to mollify her father and make up for his failure to meet the obligations surrounding the *Missa solemnis*.[6]

In the meantime, Beethoven had, of course, not forgotten his promise to Starke, who was now bereft of the Bagatelle in E originally intended for his piano method. By way of compensation, Beethoven then produced no fewer than five bagatelles (op. 119, nos. 7–11). These works are the very epitome of "short and sweet," averaging twenty bars apiece and lasting around one minute each. When Beethoven tried to make a gift of them to Starke, his friend protested that he could not possibly accept such precious music without payment. Beethoven eventually packaged them up as a New Year's gift. He did receive something for them in return, but exactly what is unknown.

That is not the end of the tale, however. In February 1823, Beethoven sent a bundle of smaller compositions to Leipzig publisher Peters in an act of friendly diplomacy surrounding the *Missa solemnis* affair. These smaller works were second-rate, and many were also secondhand: we remember that Beethoven, under pressure from his brother Johann, had sifted through his piles of old, unused, and half-finished scores in an effort to salvage some saleable material. The package sent to Peters included a set of six bagatelles (the later op. 119, nos. 1–6), at least two of which dated from 1794/95 and another two from 1801/2. Peters, who had made an advance payment for some new works in good faith, was not amused and lashed out at Beethoven in a long letter. He wrote that while he himself strove for "unselfishness, stability and order" in his dealings, he failed to perceive these values in Beethoven's recent conduct. In his opinion he had been duped, and he declared the bagatelles to be not only far too short but also technically inconsistent—the level ranged from the ludicrously simple to the virtually unplayable—rendering the set unattractive to both amateurs and professionals alike. Among the various pianists that Peters had asked to play through the six bagatelles, few of them seemed willing to believe that they were by Beethoven at all. For this reason alone, Peters felt unable to publish them, fearing accusations of defrauding Beethoven's name, and stated that he would rather relinquish his investment than release the bagatelles. He did stress that his criticisms had no bearing on Beethoven as an artist, but rather as a businessman.[7]

In the meantime, Beethoven made attempts to dispose of the bagatelles elsewhere, asking Ries to try to "flog" them in London, along with the set of five Starke bagatelles.[8] This avenue brought them to Clementi, who published them in June 1823 as *Trifles for the Pianoforte*. Several months later, Schlesinger's son Maurice (who had founded a subsidiary of his father's company in the French capital) issued a pirated edition of the bagatelles in Paris. He assigned them the erroneous opus number 112, presumably under the mistaken assumption that they formed an annex to the three major piano sonatas (opp. 109–111) released by his father beforehand. Another unauthorized edition followed soon after by the small Viennese publishing house Sauer & Leidesdorf. On the European continent, Beethoven therefore earned not a single penny from the Eleven Bagatelles.

The Sonata in E Major and the Five Bagatelles were succeeded by a long compositional hiatus. Apart from one genuine bagatelle—the Allegretto (WoO 61) scribbled into the guestbook of Ferdinand Piringer, one of the directors of the Concerts Spirituels—and the odd little canon "O Tobias!" (WoO 182) composed for Steiner's other colleague, Tobias Haslinger, Beethoven produced very little for around nine months. A similar lull pervades his correspondence, as only sixteen letters to and from Beethoven remain from the same period. The conversation notebooks—those that have survived—are likewise abnormally thin.

The main culprit, as with Beethoven's previous compositional lapse in 1817, was his fragile health. His condition had so deteriorated during the spring of 1821 that an alarming notice of his illness was published in the

Allgemeine musikalische Zeitung, albeit tempered with some reports of recent improvement. But their optimism was premature, for in early March Beethoven informed Schlesinger that he had been bedridden for six weeks due to a rheumatic episode, and in the ensuing summer months he was incapacitated for a further six weeks by a bout of jaundice. The latter seemed to have been brewing for some time, suggesting not an acute case of hepatitis but rather the initial symptoms of a chronic liver condition.[9] In other words, while Beethoven was not yet at death's door, he had certainly received his first invitation.

Some years later, Beethoven explained to Gerhard Breuning that he was unable to work while ill. Still, it remains highly questionable whether his poor health was the sole explanation for his lack of productivity in the spring of 1821. It is an extreme temptation—to which some have given in—to ascribe his compositional moratorium, at least in part, to the death of Josephine Brunsvik-Deym-Stackelberg on March 31 of that same year.[10] There is not a single document, letter, or note in the conversation notebooks that could legitimize such a hypothesis, and yet the other episodes in the "immortal beloved" saga demonstrate that the complete lack of any testimony regarding Beethoven's response to Josephine's death in no way suggests the absence of any such response. On the contrary, it is scarcely imaginable that Beethoven was unmoved by Josephine's passing.

The subscribers to this theory also believe that the Sonata in A-flat (op. 110)—and to a lesser extent the Sonata in C Minor (op. 111)—composed by Beethoven during the period thereafter constitute a vivid representation of the emotional turmoil he suffered at facing Josephine's death. The A-flat sonata, they say, can thus be interpreted as a requiem for the "immortal beloved," a speculation reinforced by the sonata's lack of any dedicatee.

It is tantalizing to hear the sonata from this perspective. Beethoven's choice of tonality alone is portentous: the four flats establish a mood that is both somber and melancholic, but not despairing. Beethoven's performance notes on the first movement complete this picture, prescribing a moderato "cantabile molto espressivo," with "con amabilità (*sanft*)" added below, meaning "gently" or "tenderly." Despite the movement's robust motivic integrity, the composition seems free of all contrivance, creating the impression only of meditative song. The overall tone is one of a "lyrical minuet," which in turn conjures up inevitable associations with Josephine's favorite work, the *Andante favori.* The most fervent Josephine supporters even interpret the sonata's opening bars as one final exhortation of love from her eternal admirer, inferring the text "Liebe Josephine" (Dearest Josephine):

The central movement—of equal parts brevity and incisiveness, and with the compact character of a bagatelle—is followed by the finale, a work unparalleled in Beethoven's oeuvre due to its compelling dramatic arc and powerful underlying logic. An introductory, unmeasured recitative gives way to an Arioso dolente (in Beethoven's own German, a *Klagender Gesang,* or "lamentation"). It bears more than a passing resemblance to the aria "Es ist vollbracht" from J. S. Bach's *St. John Passion,* and invokes similar associations with sadness and suffering. The first fugue then ensues, based—hardly coincidentally—on the *Dona nobis pacem* theme from the *Missa solemnis,* which Beethoven was sketching at the time. Inner peace remains out of reach for the moment, however, when the Arioso dolente regains the upper hand, this time to be performed as a "languishing lament" and with an air of utter dejection and exhaustion: "Perdendo le forze, dolente." Ultimately, the hope giving rise to a sense of gratitude and resignation wins out, first superficially through the instruction to play "more and more energetically," but effected at a deeper musical level through the fugue's gradual transfiguration. Slowly and almost imperceptibly, the polyphony dissipates and recoalesces into hymnody, culminating in a glorious melodic proclamation with exhilarating accompaniment. This transition is more than just a steady timbral shift from one color to another: the change is fundamental, essential, comparable to a sculpture exchanging its curves for the lines of a painting. No mere transformation but a transubstantiation. No composer before Beethoven had ever attempted such a feat, and it is tempting to suppose that one might need to be deaf to even consider it.

The Sonata in A-flat Major was completed around Christmas 1821. Because Beethoven had already given much thought in the meantime to the following

Sonata in C Minor (op. 111), it was on paper relatively quickly and ready for delivery to Schlesinger in Berlin by mid-February 1822. His preparation of the score may have been somewhat overenthusiastic, as the sheer number of corrections made on the autograph copy alone had rendered it almost illegible. In May, Beethoven felt thus obliged to make a new fair copy of the second movement, but his efforts proved futile: the proofs were still so riddled with errors that Beethoven demanded not only a second but also a third round of corrections. Schlesinger refused, and understandably so. He had already roused Beethoven's distemper by subtracting the mounting additional costs from his fee, which Beethoven later welcomed as an argument to seek an alternative publisher for the *Missa solemnis.*

Both Schlesingers—senior and junior—were puzzled by the presence of only two movements in Beethoven's final piano sonata. Initially suspecting some mistake, they discreetly inquired of Beethoven whether the copyist had perhaps forgotten to send in the final Allegro. Beethoven found the suggestion so impertinent that he refused to dignify it with a response. In reply to a similar comment by Schindler, Beethoven reportedly said that he had had no time to compose a finale, and had therefore simply extended the second movement somewhat.

Two-movement "salon" works were certainly not unheard of, and some examples can even be found within Beethoven's own oeuvre: the two early sonatas (op. 49), the Sonata in F Major (op. 54), the Sonata in F-sharp Major (op. 78), and the Sonata in E Minor (op. 90). Despite these precedents, the bipartite nature of Beethoven's final piano sonata has taken on an air of mystery, particularly in light of the extended pontifications on the matter by a certain Wendell Kretschmar, the stuttering, lisping town organist from Thomas Mann's *Doktor Faustus.* When questioned as to why the Sonata in C Minor contains no final movement, Kretschmar—serving as a mouthpiece for the ideas of musicologist and philosopher Theodor W. Adorno—first laconically replies that one need only listen to the sonata to know the answer. He goes on to describe the moving dissipation of the Arietta as an end from which no return is possible, and one that bids a farewell to the sonata in the broadest sense, both as a genre and as a traditional art form.[11]

The sonata has two movements because it is a diptych. Beethoven concludes his set of three sonatas with a juxtaposition of two contrasting worlds: an Allegro in traditional sonata form, followed by a set of slow variations cast in a radical, modern mold. Myriad are the possible adjective pairs that might be associated with this antithesis: discordant vs. harmonic, turbulent vs.

transcendental, extroverted vs. introverted, real vs. mythical, chaotic vs. lucid, imperfect vs. perfect, and so on.[12] Although both movements act as mutual counterweights, the sonata's center of gravity is rooted firmly in the second movement—the Arietta—in which a sublime, hymnic theme undergoes a series of profound metamorphoses. The rhythmic complexity increases with each successive variation and ultimately disintegrates into the smallest conceivable note value—the trill—a device that in this sonata finally reaches the end of an extended emancipation process.[13] At precisely the point when the music "sublimates," dissipating into pure sound, the theme reappears in a higher, now "celestial" register. It is telling that Beethoven delayed the final manifestation of the main theme until this moment—the end of the composition process—thus capping off the cycle with a philosophical and religious statement in which the "material" gives way to the "ethereal." The *Missa solemnis,* which was nearing completion during the same period, echoes in the background.

Wendell Kretschmar's seemingly flippant remark thus carries some weight after all. Playing or listening to the ethereal conclusion of Beethoven's Sonata in C Minor inevitably evokes a profound sense of both melancholy and thankfulness, symbolizing the end of both an era and an oeuvre. In this sense, Beethoven's thirty-second piano sonata shares the fate of Mozart's forty-first symphony: although Mozart undoubtedly intended to compose more orchestral music after the mighty *Jupiter* Symphony of 1788, the temptation is almost inescapable to regard its colossal final fugue as the crowning achievement of his symphonic output.

Further work on the *Diabelli* Variations was delayed until November 1822, for various reasons. First and foremost was the urgent need to complete the *Missa solemnis.* In the spring, however, Beethoven also suffered a malady that he himself described as "gout on the chest," which incapacitated him for three and a half to five months (depending on whom one asks[14]), and for which he took a course of treatment, first in Oberdöbling and later in Baden. In the meantime, he had once again grudgingly conceded to an extended series of composition lessons with Archduke Rudolph and was plagued by worries surrounding both the marketing of the *Missa solemnis* and the spring cleaning of his old scores at his brother's insistence.

During his September sojourn in Baden, Beethoven was visited by Karl Friedrich Hensler, who offered a commission for him to compose a work for the opening of the new theater in Josefstadt. Hensler was a rather influential figure on the Viennese theater scene. He had assumed management of the Leopoldstadt theater after the death of its founder, Karl von Marinelli, and after several byways via Theater an der Wien, Pressburg, and Baden, he was issued a license to operate the Josefstadt theater in 1821. Though it was also merely a "suburban" theater, the surrounding neighborhood (the modern-day Eighth District) was far more attractive and offered greater prestige than Leopoldstadt (the Second District), which at the time was rife with violence and prostitution. In 1822, the old Theater in der Josefstadt was demolished and replaced by a brand-new building with the latest facilities.

Hensler wished to inaugurate his new "temple to the performing arts" with a celebratory revival of *The Ruins of Athens,* a work originally cobbled together by Beethoven on a libretto by Kotzebue for the opening of the new imperial theater in Pest. While the text was in need of a major overhaul—requiring less praise for the emperor, and more for the arts—the musical modifications were limited to one choral fragment and an entirely new overture, which Beethoven furnished without significant trouble or objection. He composed a "dignified" overture in the style of Handel with a slow introduction and a fugal Allegro; it was a great display of craftsmanship but lacking somewhat in inspiration. From the piano, a stone-deaf Beethoven directed both the premiere on October 3, 1822, and the three subsequent performances—exactly how he did so remains baffling. Nor do we know how much support he received from the concertmaster, as the violins were led not by an experienced player such as Schuppanzigh or Clement, but instead by Anton Schindler—a violinist who thus made his first appearance in Beethoven's life and whose musical qualities remain something of a mystery to this day.

In the weeks that ensued, Beethoven went on to compose a name-day gift for Hensler: the *Gratulationsmenuett* (Congratulatory minuet) in E-flat (WoO 3) for orchestra. He also briefly considered writing another overture based on the name B-A-C-H, but did not progress beyond some initial thematic sketches.

November 3, 1822, saw the famed reprise of *Fidelio* when, as formerly mentioned, Wilhelmine Schröder made her debut as Leonore. Only after that was Beethoven free to focus once more on the *Diabelli* Variations. Diabelli had increased pressure on Beethoven, and unlike the previous occasion there was now a concrete deal on the table. Beethoven would receive forty ducats, provided the variations were truly as substantial as Diabelli had been led to believe; if not, the sum would be lower.[15] Was the sudden crystallization of

Diabelli's offer perhaps related to rumors that Beethoven had offered his *Variations on a Waltz*—Diabelli's waltz—to a rival house?[16]

The set of twenty-three variations to which Beethoven returned after a three-year hiatus was already quite formidable. They were symmetrical, with a central moment of repose and a well-proportioned arc leading to the final climax. Beethoven had also entirely "deconstructed" the theme. Unlike his earlier works, in which the theme's contours were retained and steadily enriched, slowly aggregating new layers of meaning, each of the *Diabelli* Variations is based on a single facet of the theme, which is individually fleshed out and cast in a fitting and often divergent mold. It is no coincidence that Beethoven no longer referred to the work as "variations" (*Variationen*) but instead as "transformations" (*Veränderungen*). The whole is also liberally peppered with irony, and multiple moments of reflection are included to take stock of the project's relative absurdity—that of building a tremendous edifice on the flimsiest of foundations. This conceit reaches its hilarious climax in the eighteenth variation (which ultimately became the twenty-second) with a direct caricature of Leporello's opening phrase from Mozart's *Don Giovanni*—"Notte e giorno faticar" (Night and day, I slave away)—suggesting that Beethoven, like Leporello, considered himself a loyal but critical servant.

But despite this compositional rigor, the Beethoven of 1822—rejuvenated by the *Missa solemnis* and the last three piano sonatas—felt compelled to bring a new dimension to his work from 1819. He made several minor alterations to the beginning—the two new opening variations distance themselves yet further from the theme—and to the fifteenth variation, which in its new form serves as a caesura. Of far greater significance, however, were the eight new variations appended to the original twenty-three, which elevate the whole to new, almost philosophical heights. Beethoven's trademark penultimate variation—a slow *minore*—was expanded into a triptych; the final fugue augmented into a triple fugue; and the entire set crowned with a "minuet" setting of the theme coupled with an immense coda. Beethoven's recasting of the "modern" waltz as a "traditional" minuet in the style of Mozart is naturally of great artistic import, and the manifest references to Bach and Handel (in the fugue) imbue the set with even more historical perspective. In this sense, the *Diabelli* Variations can be heard as a reflection "in music, on music." Further extrapolation reveals, moreover, that the conclusion—a clear paraphrase of the final bars of the Arietta from opus 111—is in essence a reflection "by Beethoven, on Beethoven."

The circle was thus complete: the second movement of the Sonata in C Minor, which itself was inspired by Beethoven's previous work on the *Diabelli* Variations, now furnished the very model for the conclusion of those same variations. The similarities in the final bars are particularly striking, where after an extended passage in demisemiquavers, the texture dissipates into a mysterious pianissimo:

Unlike in the Arietta, however, Beethoven now concludes with a final, forte C-major chord. It stands out like an exclamation mark, as though punctuating the true end of an era.

But the definitive end was yet to come. One year later, and following completion of the Ninth Symphony, Beethoven added an odd postscript to his seemingly complete piano oeuvre. This time, too, his motivation was of more profane than artistic origin. The botched 1823 attempts to market the Eleven Bagatelles (op. 119) had left Beethoven with two unsettled scores, so to speak. On the one hand, his failure to sell the collection in Europe had left him without the means to repay his brother; on the other, his compositional honor had been impugned by the harsh criticism and rejection of the bagatelles by Peters in Leipzig. In March 1824, he therefore set to work on a new set of six bagatelles (op. 126), describing them in letters to various publishers as not only completely new but also of increased length and complexity. In short, they represented his best work in the genre thus far.[17]

"Bagatelles" can best be defined as "musical aphorisms." They are concise, pithy expressions of an original, highly personal, and often surprising character: profound wisdom in a nutshell. The concise format also puts more resources at the composer's disposal (remembering that a work's length should be inversely proportional to the quantity of musical material), allowing for the deployment of rhetorical devices such as antithesis, paradox, understatement, ambiguity, and irony. Beethoven was in his element and—after his work on the colossal Ninth Symphony—most likely glad of the opportunity for some lighthearted diversion on a smaller scale.

Yet despite his bagatelles' whimsical nature, and however experimental and unconventional their techniques and frameworks, these dissociations belie an underlying logic. In this sense, the opus 126 bagatelles differ markedly from their opus 119 predecessors, which seem rather disjointed by comparison. The latter bear the stamp of their haphazard origin and create the impression that they are interchangeable or that their ordering is arbitrary. The opposite is true of the six bagatelles composed in 1824. Beethoven himself described them as a "cycle,"[18] with a rhetorical structure, a robust tonal progression, and a latent, "subthematic" cohesion that, while not perceived directly or audibly, is experienced subconsciously.

The circle was now fully complete. Almost half a century after receiving his first childhood spanking for daring to improvise at the keyboard, and decades since he had electrified audiences with his wild fantasies as a pianistic demigod, Beethoven could now finally surrender to the tantalizing pleasures of scintillating ideas and vivid imagination. Trusting in his highly developed intuition for structure and proportion and free from any desire for excess or vanity, Beethoven could finally give free rein to his musical ideas—a luxury that had cost him over one hundred opus numbers and a musician's lifetime.

To complete the cycle well and truly, one final remark. The sixth bagatelle, Beethoven's very last piano work, bears the telling tempo and character indication "Andante amabile e con moto" and is based on the all too familiar motif from both the *Andante favori* and the song cycle *An die ferne Geliebte:*

Skeptics may dismiss this similarity as pure coincidence. But even so: what a beautiful one it is!

52

Estrangement

ORDINARILY, FRANZ LISZT WOULD HAVE BEEN the one to premiere Beethoven's last major work for the piano. It was he, after all, who gave the first public performance of the gargantuan *Hammerklavier* Sonata during a concert in Paris (although not until 1836). He thus had sufficient intellect, artistry, and technique to give the other enfant terrible from Beethoven's oeuvre—the *Diabelli* Variations—its first public airing. But although he certainly had the work "under his fingers," he never dared take it to the stage. His trepidation imbued the *Diabelli* Variations with an aura of unplayability, and it would be 1856 before Hans Bülow gave the work its first public performance in Berlin. The same fate befell a number of Beethoven's late string quartets, which also had difficulty finding their way to the podium. This circumstance is what was ultimately responsible for Beethoven's tragic, romanticized reputation as an outcast and a marginalized composer divorced from his audience. While certainly accurate, this is only half of the picture. There is no denying that Beethoven's late piano and chamber works constituted an interpretive minefield and that their unconventionality lent them an air that was distinctly elitist and audience-unfriendly. Beethoven's orchestral works, on the other hand, continued to enjoy immense popularity throughout the 1820s, making him by far the most-programmed composer by both the Friends of Music Society and the Concerts Spirituels. The commotion surrounding the Ninth Symphony in May 1824 merely served to affirm Beethoven's position as market leader in the symphonic segment of the Viennese music scene.

This uncommon blend of admiration and incomprehension would come to symbolize the regard afforded Beethoven during the last five years of his life in Vienna, as the personification of both a monument and an oddity.

Within the span of a few short years, the great man who had rubbed shoulders with European rulers and dignitaries and who in all likelihood had sat for more official portraits than the emperor himself was reduced to a poor, old, and slightly wretched figure, evoking in many a sense of wonder but more often feelings of pity or even outright mockery. The Viennese have always had a love-hate relationship with the extraordinary and eccentric personalities that lend the city its special allure. On the one hand, they are only too happy to provide a public forum where all manner of outlandish visionaries can vent their idiosyncrasies—from Beethoven and Freud to Hundertwasser—as though Vienna might thus vicariously be washed clean of its own eccentricities. Conversely, Vienna's deep-seated fear of change fosters in its inhabitants a well-trained ability to belittle the extraordinary through intrigue, malicious gossip, and scorn. While there is certainly no obligation to toe the line in Vienna, the alternative is to open oneself up to public ridicule.

The very least that can be said of the late Beethoven is that he was a sight to behold. The Viennese recognized him easily at a distance: he was short, heavyset, and muscular—even in his later years—and walked with a slight hunch. His flushed and pockmarked face, with its large forehead, broad nose, and thick eyebrows, was usually partly concealed by long shocks of steel-blue hair, themselves clearly strangers to both cutter and comb. His tendency to avoid the razor for days at a time was also partly responsible for the "Ossianic, demonic" impression he left on those around him, according to one journalist from the *Allgemeine musikalische Zeitung*.[1] His shabby, soiled clothing also played a part, as Beethoven went about in a dark overcoat with long, outward-flapping tails reaching to his ankles. His felt hat was worn, and always tilted slightly backward on his head, causing the rear brim to curl upward. But the hat's real deformation was in the crown, caused not only by exposure to rain but also by Beethoven's persistent habit of slamming it onto his hat stand con brio and with a theatrical flourish, an act that he replicated even when not at home.[2]

Beethoven seemed to care not a jot for his beggarly appearance. Friends of his would occasionally replace his old clothes with new ones at night and report that the following morning he had not even noticed. Curiously, these same friends also noted that he would dress smartly and fashionably whenever invited to a salon and that he did so consistently until the end of his life.

On such occasions he would wear a blue (or sometimes green) coat with shiny yellow buttons, spotless white breeches and stockings, and the proper accessories, such as a waistcoat and cravat. The only fashion he refused to follow was the wearing of a stiff wing-tip or "Gladstone" collar, which he found too suffocating. When thus dressed to the nines, Beethoven's deportment changed accordingly; he carried himself with elegance and poise, and his gestures were more courtly and refined.

His clothing aside, Beethoven's reputation as a misfit also rested on his public conduct. Children laughed at how this strange, withdrawn man would suddenly stop in the middle of the street during a walk, procure an enormous pencil, and begin scribbling hieroglyphs into his notebook while grunting or singing mysteriously to himself. Conversely, when he recognized a familiar face, Beethoven would just as easily shout out the person's name, unabashedly yelling and making wild gesticulations. Startled bystanders often stared at his lunatic behavior, to the frequent chagrin of his nephew Karl, who would turn away in embarrassment.[3] But despite the stress and strain of the preceding years, Beethoven still retained the spark of enthusiasm and exuberance that had always characterized his personality. When these came to the fore, his entire disposition and demeanor changed. His small eyes would sparkle and flicker; a broad smile took over his expression; and he would erupt into healthy, uncontrolled laughter. His eyes in particular spoke volumes, and his face could be read like an open book.

In the private sphere especially, Beethoven's kindness and generosity seemed to shine through. He chose his relationships carefully, and the trusted friends whose company he could abide were of an overwhelmingly caring and devoted nature—a loyal troupe ever ready to step in, bring order to his affairs, and lend a helping hand. They were always prepared to offer company when necessary, to lend a listening ear and offer words of encouragement or praise. These friendships were not a one-way street, however; Franz Grillparzer, for example, was of the opinion that Beethoven could be incredibly endearing and noble, with a charm that was practically irresistible. Journalist Frederich Wähner, who lived in Vienna from 1818 to 1825, described Beethoven as an engaging personality with a childlike naïveté.[4]

This was the general impression left by Beethoven on new visitors. Those unknown to him often feared the worst and were pleasantly surprised by the attentions bestowed on them by the great master. It was during his final years in particular that Beethoven appreciated receiving callers, when for a few precious hours he could forget his isolation and enjoy his guests' warm company. At such times, Beethoven would enthusiastically make the coffee himself, comprehensively demonstrating the workings of his new, state-of-the-art coffee machine. Farewells were often an emotional affair; he would embrace his guests as though he had known them for years, sometimes scribbling out a canon on a scrap of paper to mark the occasion.[5]

In true Viennese style, Beethoven spent most of his time not at home but in the city's many cafés and restaurants. In general he would select one of his regular haunts and seek refuge in a quiet corner to read the paper and enjoy a bite to eat (his favorite dishes were oysters, cold turkey, and foie gras pâté; during the week he enjoyed simple smoked herring or liverwurst on bread), accompanied by a sip of wine or beer. On more than the odd occasion he would develop a dislike for people at nearby tables, whose presence he found irritating for whatever reason, and would generally expedite their departure with his proven method of spitting obnoxiously on the floor.[6] Nobody paid any heed, nor were any eyebrows raised whenever heated discussions ensued over the settling of the bill. Miserly and mistrustful, Beethoven suspected every man and his dog of trickery—he could fly into a rage over the price of a sandwich, and the innocent waiters bore the brunt of his ire. But he generally realized his error quickly and tried to make amends by offering a large tip, which usually did the trick. The waiters knew of his occasional and scatterbrained quirks, and the times he left without paying were amply compensated for by the occasions when he asked for the bill without having ordered anything.

Beethoven was not always isolated, however, and he frequently sought out the company of friends, who shared the table with him sometimes in warm companionship, sometimes in animated discussion. A notable fact is that he sourced his new friends not from musical circles but from the ranks of opinion makers and journalists. Beethoven relished the opportunity to discuss politics and society with the senior editors of leading newspapers and journals, including Joseph Karl Bernard from the *Wiener Zeitung,* Friedrich August Kanne from the *Wiener allgemeine musikalische Zeitung,* Johann Valentin Schickh from the *Wiener Zeitschrift für Kunst, Literatur, Theater und Mode,* and Friedrich Wähner from *Janus,* a left-wing journal that was even banned for some time. Beethoven had extensive knowledge of the political landscape, and opinions to match. As the story goes, he could recite the names of all the Austrian ministers and their portfolios and was always up-to-date on developments in the British Parliament. It was during such discussions that Beethoven put his impairment to good use, chattering happily on while his interlocutors lost time committing their thoughts to paper.

Another favorite locale of Beethoven's was the music store run by Sigmund Steiner on Paternostergassl—a narrow alleyway between Graben and Kohlmarkt, which sadly no longer exists. Many well-known musicians, including Schuppanzigh, Czerny, and the young Schubert, had the habit of meeting there each morning at around eleven o'clock. Beethoven was also happy to take his "coffee break" there, enjoy some repartee, and catch up on the latest happenings in the world of music. The Beethoven literature is replete with his many antics and witticisms from the meetings at Steiner's, as well as the unavoidable gossip about those who happened not to be present.

Beethoven was not backward in coming forward. His words were succinct and to the point, and he had a tendency to exaggerate. His critical (not to mention sarcastic) nature was always a given, especially when it came to matters of government, the courts, the police, and the aristocrats' corrupt morality. He thought nothing of exhortations like "Such a rascal [of an emperor] ought to be hanged in the first tree."[7] Some of his friends warned that he should express himself more cautiously and with less volume, especially when in public or semipublic spaces, in the knowledge that the very walls in Vienna had ears. The police left him without hindrance, however; not so much out of respect but because Beethoven enjoyed considerable protections from those in the upper echelons of the ministry. In truth, people generally paid him little heed, dismissing him as merely a "fantast." One anecdote concerning an event that took place in 1821 or 1822 in Wiener Neustadt serves as an example. Beethoven had lost his way while on a stroll, had eaten nothing all day and was dressed extremely shabbily, making him look for all the world like a homeless beggar. The police, understandably, took him in, and when Beethoven tried to identify himself, the police officer is said to have replied: "Well of course, why not indeed? Scoundrel! Beethoven looks nothing like you!" Eventually the local director of music was summoned, who recognized Beethoven immediately and took him to his home, where he was given the finest guest room and some proper clothing. The next day the mayor arrived. He was most embarrassed by the incident, apologized profusely to Beethoven, and offered his private coach to return Beethoven to Baden.[8] It is with good reason that Czerny later wondered whether Beethoven might have been able to lead such an unconventional life in any other city.[9]

The tales of embarrassment began to pile up, however, until eventually it was common knowledge in Vienna that Beethoven was not merely eccentric but at the very least half mad. Beethoven knew of their attitude toward him; from as early as 1820, there is a record of Beethoven warning a visitor not to be misled by the Viennese, who thought he was insane. Beethoven knew that he could be guilty of voicing the occasional candid opinion, but other than that, he saw nothing wrong with his behavior.[10]

His closest friends, on the other hand, could not escape the realization that Beethoven's conduct was becoming more problematic by the day. His many fits of rage, uncontrollable mood swings, obsession with money, paranoid delusions, and unfounded accusations were increasing in both scope and frequency. Doctor Karl von Bursy called Beethoven's tendency to talk about himself a *"Signum diagnosticum* for hypochondria." Grillparzer believed that Beethoven found it increasingly difficult to distinguish between reality and his own version of events, and Ries even wondered whether Beethoven might be hearing voices.[11] There were many reasons for their concerns, and we will later discuss in detail how from 1821 on, the slow but steady deterioration of Beethoven's liver and pancreas, combined with excessive alcohol consumption, put his neurophysiological system under immense strain. The resulting irritability led to a vast array of interpersonal issues, the prime example being the increasingly untenable relationship with his nephew Karl. Beethoven was deeply scarred, which in turn sorely affected his health, landing him in a vicious circle. We should not forget that in the meantime, Beethoven had also become completely deaf. The only way for others to reach him was therefore via brief written messages; these were inevitably lacking in nuance and thus hardly conducive to a fluid exchange of more subtle emotions. An empathetic void was thus created, in many ways comparable to that which persists in our modern-day text-messaging culture. And so, at a time when most of his music had conquered the world, and despite his close and constant contact with patrons, publishers, and public as a musician, it was from that very same world that Beethoven, as a human being, slowly but surely drifted into estrangement.[12]

—————

53

Encounters with the Younger Generation

IN APRIL 1822, THE THIRTY-YEAR-OLD Italian composer Rossini paid a visit to the fifty-two-year-old Beethoven at his lodgings on Landstrasser Haupstrasse. Though poorly versed in Beethoven's output—having little more than a vague notion of the piano sonatas and string quartets—he was highly impressed by the *Eroica* Symphony, which he had heard not too long before. Giuseppe Carpani, a poet, librettist, and critic known to Beethoven for many years, had arranged the meeting and accompanied his guest as interpreter. In this capacity he was indispensable: Beethoven spoke a modicum of opera Italian but hardly enough to express himself with any degree of fluency, and as a self-respecting Italian, Rossini's knowledge of German was, of course, nonexistent. Add to that the familiar fuss of the conversation notebooks, and one can form an impression of the communicative shambles that ensued.

Many years later, Rossini would talk extensively of his meeting with Beethoven during a conversation with Wagner, which was in turn recorded by the Belgian musicologist Edmond Michotte. On entering Beethoven's apartment, Rossini was dumbfounded. Having occupied a royal villa in Bologna and magnificent estates in Sicily since his liaison with wealthy opera singer Isabella Colbran, it was beyond Rossini's comprehension that the most eminent composer of his day resided in what Rossini described as "a kind of shack, dirty and disorderly." He recalled large cracks in the ceiling, which being so close to the roof must have let in buckets of rain. Beethoven's own appearance was equally startling: "But what no pen could describe was the undefinable sense of sorrow that pervaded his every expression, while from underneath his dense brows, fiery eyes shone out which, though small, seemed to bore straight into one's soul."[1]

Beethoven was a charming and obliging host. But after complimenting Rossini on *The Barber of Seville*—an outstanding opera buffa that he had read with great enjoyment—he forgot himself entirely by adding the candid remark that Rossini should avoid opera seria so as not to maltreat the subject matter. When Carpani cautiously pointed out that Rossini had already written opere serie, Beethoven, without batting an eye, simply stated that he had read those too but found them unconvincing. He followed up with the crushing generalization that serious operas were simply not compatible with the Italian character, and went on to claim that the Italian understanding of music was insufficient to allow for an effective treatment of the drama. Carpani—who in a Milanese newspaper several years earlier had described *Fidelio* as highly learned but unnatural, at odds with good musical sense—could hardly believe his ears but held his tongue. Rossini, too, bit his lip and tried to salvage things by reiterating his admiration of Beethoven's genius. His ploy backfired, however, eliciting only a sigh of compassion, and the remark "O, poor unfortunate!" (*Infelice!*). The conversation plodded on, meandering through topics such as the Italian theaters, some well-known singers, and the standards of the Viennese opera troupe. On the visitors' departure, Beethoven placed his arm around Rossini's shoulder and reiterated one last time, "I wish you every success with *Zelmira*—but please, keep your *Barbers* coming!"[2]

Several hours later, Rossini attended a gala dinner at the Metternich residence. He was still reeling from his experiences earlier that afternoon, and the stark contrast between the extravagance of Metternich's opulent residence and Beethoven's paltry hovel almost had him up in arms. He voiced his objections to the First Minister, insisting that Beethoven deserved better accommodations and—more to the point—greater respect from the Viennese, and proposed launching a campaign to show solidarity and set things right. But the prevailing opinion among the well-to-do was that Beethoven had only himself to blame, and they countered Rossini's proposal with the argument that Beethoven would simply sell off any home that was given to him.

When Schumann was later told of the curious interaction between Beethoven and Rossini, he was heard to remark, "A butterfly has crossed the path of an eagle, and the eagle swerved away to avoid crushing the butterfly with the strength of its wings."[3]

More than a year later, on October 5, 1823, a meeting took place between Beethoven and the other great operatic figure of his time, Carl Maria von Weber. This time, Beethoven himself took the initiative. One week earlier at

Steiner's music store, he had met Julius Benedict, a young conductor and student of Weber's. One thing led to another, and Benedict was eventually charged with the task of inveigling Weber (who at the time was in the midst of his preparations for *Euryanthe*) to Baden so that the pair might spend an enjoyable day together. Two other fellow musicians who happened to be in the area—Tobias Haslinger and Ferdinand Piringer—were duly included in the invitation.

Alas, Beethoven made no use of the conversation notebooks that day. Instead, thoughts were exchanged via slate and stylus; the animated discussions between the two greatest figures of early German romantic opera were thus wiped away with a wet sponge. Fortunately, that evening before bed, Weber wrote extensively to his wife, Caroline, of the day's events. By his account, Beethoven gave him a touching and heartfelt welcome, embracing him six or seven times and heartily declaiming, "Ja du bist ein Teufelskerl, ein braver Kerl!" (You are a daredevil, and a fine fellow!). Beethoven proposed a walk through the magnificent Helenental valley, which was unfortunately precluded by inclement weather and problems with Weber's hip. And so it was that the entire mob ended up at Sauerhof, a newly renovated café-restaurant, where they enjoyed a sumptuous meal washed down with plenty of liquid refreshment. Weber found Beethoven most obliging and was waited on hand and foot. Of course there was animated discussion, as well as commiseration over the ungratefulness of Viennese audiences, the incompetence of the latest opera management, and the poor taste of the Italians, whereupon Weber suggested that Beethoven make a tour of Germany and England to increase not only his fame but—more importantly—his wealth. As the story goes, Beethoven responded by pretending to play the piano and shrugging, "Too late!"

At their farewell, Beethoven clasped Weber's delicate hands, embraced him several times, and promised to attend *Euryanthe* (which he never did). An emotional Weber wrote to his wife, "The wonders of this day will remain in my memory forever [. . .] I felt personally elated to be thus showered in the loving esteem of such a great genius."[4]

The warmth and friendliness of their meeting in 1823 offers a sharp contrast to Weber's occasionally harsh judgment of Beethoven during his younger years, which was more often dismissive than reverent. Although Weber's purported response to the Seventh Symphony—"Beethoven is ripe for the asylum"—smacks of Schindler's influence and is thus likely apocryphal, more reliable documents (such as a letter to Swiss publisher Nägeli from 1810) clearly reveal Weber's umbrage at being considered a "successor" to

Beethoven. In his eyes, the appellation was hardly complimentary, since he believed that his own views on music differed markedly from those of the great master. Weber disapproved particularly of Beethoven's later works, which he found to be too chaotic, tonally unstable, and contrapuntally and harmonically too complex.[5] We can safely assume that Weber was well aware of the extraordinary talent bestowed on Beethoven but not to him. When it came to technique and accessibility, however, he believed he could hold his own.

Weber's opinion softened over time, especially after having conducted *Fidelio*. In 1814 he led several performances in Prague—the first to occur outside Vienna—followed by a new season in Dresden in the spring of 1823, to great public acclaim. This latter production gave the two composers cause for correspondence, in which Weber—whose graciousness had grown, likely due to the success of *Der Freischütz* in Vienna—sang a very different tune. In a letter dated January 28, 1823, he wrote of *Fidelio* that it was a magnificent work full of German grandeur and emotional profundity, which had brought him to a fuller understanding of what constitutes the essence of Beethoven.[6] His respect seemed to be reciprocated, going by a letter from Beethoven to Dresden opera director Hans Heinrich von Könneritz, in which he respectfully refers to his "dear friend Maria Weber."[7] Here, too, extramusical factors may have lubricated relations somewhat, as Weber's success in securing Beethoven forty ducats in royalties from the Dresden production of *Fidelio* (deducted officially as "transcription fees") would certainly not have done their friendship any harm; nor would the fact that Weber persuaded the Saxon court to purchase a copy of the *Missa solemnis,* despite its refusal of Beethoven's own petition.

At the ends of their careers—Weber died one year before Beethoven—the two composers were comrades, both seated firmly in the same anti-Italian camp. On hearing at Steiner's that the premiere of *Euryanthe* had been well received, Beethoven allegedly said that the Germans would ultimately win out over the Italians. Afterward, however, when he heard how lamentable the libretto was, he offered the rejoinder: "It's always the same! The Germans cannot write good libretti."[8]

The accounts of Beethoven's meetings with Weber and Rossini come from similar sources—the composers themselves—making them potentially susceptible to romanticization. Nevertheless, they belong to the standard repertoire of Beethoven anecdotes and certainly cast a particular light on the relationships between Beethoven and his younger fellows. The same cannot be said of Franz Schubert, whose dealings with Beethoven are poorly documented.

Beethoven and Schubert must have occasionally crossed paths in Vienna. The city was relatively small, and Schubert was also known to be a regular at Steiner's on Paternostergassl. And although he left not a single entry in the conversation notebooks, they contain plenty of references to him by others. The fact that Schubert was a torchbearer at Beethoven's funeral strongly suggests a close bond with his senior colleague (Beethoven was twenty-six years older). This opinion was shared by the composer Anselm Hüttenbrenner, who accompanied Schindler and Schubert on a visit to Beethoven eight days before his death; when asked who should enter the room first, Beethoven chose Schubert. According to Hüttenbrenner, this was proof that they had known each other for some time.[9]

The time, place, and circumstances of Beethoven and Schubert's first meeting remains a mystery. Schindler puts it at 1822, when Schubert sought to dedicate his *Eight Variations on a French Song* for piano duet (D. 624) to Beethoven, and called on him personally to ask for permission to do so. Diabelli, who knew Beethoven well, is said to have accompanied him. In Schindler's account, Schubert was so in awe of Beethoven that he could barely scribble down the answers to his questions. Beethoven leafed through the score and pointed out a small harmonic error to Schubert, but immediately added that it was in no way a cardinal sin. Beethoven was "flexible" with rules, after all, having said on many occasions that there is no rule that cannot be broken for beauty's sake.[10] Still, Schubert was gravely shaken; when he left, his chief frustration was that he had given in to such intimidation. If Schindler is to be believed, Schubert never regained the courage to present himself to the master again.[11]

There is an alternative version to the above story. According to Schubert's first biographer, Heinrich Kreissle von Hellborn, who based his account on the notes by the aforementioned Hüttenbrenner, Schubert and Diabelli found Beethoven not at home, and Schubert—immensely relieved—slipped his duet under the door. Whatever the case, Beethoven seems to have held the *Eight Variations* in high esteem and played them with great enjoyment.

The timidity shown by Schubert toward Beethoven in both versions of the story is a typical and salient aspect of Schubert's image sketched by nineteenth-century musicologists. He was portrayed as a figure who basked in Beethoven's shadow and was no match for the great master. Schubert's instrumental music in particular was considered to be "devoid of rigour, too impulsive, without direction, static and lacking drama."[12] Schubert can only have been painfully aware of these deficiencies, as evinced by his alleged famous remark to Josef von Spaun: "Secretly, in my heart, I long to be able to make something of myself one day. But who can hope to do anything after Beethoven?"[13] These same historians portray Beethoven's death as a release for Schubert, claiming it was no coincidence that only afterward was Schubert able to produce his greatest works: *Winterreise*, the Piano Trios in B-flat and E-flat, the Symphony in C Major, the three final piano sonatas, and the String Quintet.

Nowadays, not a single Schubert expert credits Spaun's testimony with any veracity, and a new image of Schubert has emerged. According to Marie-Agnes Dittrich, Schubert took a "self-confident approach to Beethoven, whose influence he most likely regarded as a challenge, rather than an imposing—or worse—oppressive example."[14]

The earliest Beethoven literature makes mention of a vivid encounter that took place between Beethoven and the most talented pianist of the younger generation, Franz Liszt. Following a concert given by the eleven-year-old Liszt on April 13, 1823, in the Hofburg's smaller Redoutensaal, a captivated Beethoven was reported to have given the young boy a kiss on the forehead—a gesture interpreted by its recipient as a "blessing" and a sacred affirmation of his "holy mandate." The scene was later immortalized in the form of a lithograph made by István Halász to commemorate the fiftieth anniversary of Liszt's performing career. The gesture has since become known as the *Weihekuss*—the benedictory kiss—and has taken on a legendary significance.

Liszt's family had moved to Vienna in the spring of 1822 to allow their son to study piano with Czerny and composition with the wise old Salieri. All signs in the ten-year-old pointed to a prodigious musical talent, and on December 1, 1822, he gave his first piano recital in the Landständischer hall, where he wowed the audience with an improvisation on the Allegretto from Beethoven's Seventh Symphony. Several appearances at benefit concerts followed, and on April 13, 1823, he gave his second solo concert in the smaller Hofburg Redoutensaal, a concert that would also be his farewell to Vienna. Schindler reports that several days before the recital, Liszt had sent a request to Beethoven inviting him to provide a theme on which to base an improvisation. Beethoven apparently declined.[15]

One of the conversation notebooks casts serious doubt on whether Beethoven even attended the concert in question: why else would he have asked his brother Johann and his nephew Karl how the concert went, or about the boy's appearance? The likelihood that he gave Liszt the blessed kiss on another occasion—on hearing him play in his own apartment—is equally doubtful.

For a long time, the legend of the famous kiss was used to account for the apostolic fervor with which Liszt dedicated himself to Beethoven's music throughout his life. Liszt was indeed one of the great interpreters of Beethoven's keyboard and orchestral music. His 1836 performance of the *Hammerklavier* Sonata was received by Berlioz with rapturous admiration. He also made transcriptions not only of all Beethoven's symphonies but also of the Septet and several song cycles, and constructed a fantasy for piano and orchestra on themes from *The Ruins of Athens*. In every instance, Liszt succeeded in transferring the traditional Beethovenian orchestral color to the piano, creating works of a caliber far superseding that of a traditional piano arrangement.

Liszt also played a pivotal role in organizing the festivities in Bonn (1845) and Vienna (1880) that accompanied the unveiling of the various Beethoven monuments, as well as for the commemorative celebrations of Beethoven's one hundredth birthday in 1870. He showed especial engagement during the 1845 Bonn events, where he was of course the principal performer; he conducted the Fifth Symphony and several *Fidelio* excerpts and was the soloist in the Fifth Piano Concerto. The following day's program featured his own *Beethoven* Cantata for orchestra, choir, and soloists; he replicated this endeavor with his *Beethoven* Cantata no. 2 for the celebrations in 1870. But his efforts were not limited to the musical, as fourteen days before the opening concert was scheduled to take place in the arena of the local equestrian school, he vetoed the venue due to its poor acoustics. Instead, an enormous new wooden shed was quickly designed, erected, and decorated as a piece of "temporary festival architecture and scenery."[16] The structure was the first of three successive "Beethoven Halls," and Liszt must have poured a great deal of his own finances into the enterprise.

Despite the occasional embellishment, the common theme in the above tales is the lasting impression left by Beethoven on his younger fellows, due in no small part to the fact that for these musicians an encounter with the great master also meant a confrontation with their own selves. Another striking but logical fact is that none of them ever considered taking lessons with Beethoven or even following in his footsteps. Just as Beethoven benefited from never studying with Mozart and from spending only a short period with Haydn, the new generation of talented composers could never have blossomed fully if their growth had taken place in Beethoven's shadow. A telling example comes from a note by Schuppanzigh in the conversation notebooks about Carl Czerny, who was a true Beethoven disciple: "Yesterday we played a new trio by Czerny for the first time; I did not include any of his [Beethoven's] music on the programme, so that he [Czerny] would not be swept aside."[17] It should come as no surprise that nowadays the primary interest in the works of Ries and Czerny concerns their role in the historical documentation of Beethoven.

54

An Ode to Joy

FRIDAY, MAY 7, 1824, WAS A RED-LETTER DAY in the history of Western music. That evening in Vienna, a work was premiered whose manuscript has since become part of the UNESCO "Memory of the World": Beethoven's Ninth Symphony.[1] None of the two thousand attendees could have anticipated the symbolism that the work would come to embody, nor could they have predicted the tragedy of its future commercialization, trivialization, and relegation to the world of hackneyed popular kitsch. For let there be no mistake: while Beethoven's "Ode to Joy" might be one of the most beloved melodies of all time, it has also been bandied about with equal parts careless-ness and cavalier disregard. Debussy was right when he said that in this sense the melody shares its popular lot with the Mona Lisa, and her quizzical smile.

While the audience of 1824 had not yet been saddled with the many mod-ern preconceptions associated with the Ninth Symphony, they were not entirely free of prejudice. Expectations were high. Word of Beethoven's new symphony had spread through Vienna like wildfire and had been the subject of rumors, gossip, and intrigue for weeks. The stakes, too, were high; in February, thirty prominent figures had written an open letter to Beethoven, pleading with him to hold the premiere of the Ninth Symphony in Vienna— "his second home"—whatever the cost.[2] This petition (which was also printed two months later in the *Wiener Theaterzeitung* and the *Allgemeine musika-lische Zeitung*) was clearly more than a simple declaration of affection for a formerly marginalized Viennese musical figure; it was nothing less than a political pamphlet in defense of the "German Muse." The prevailing senti-ment was that German musical values had come under threat in recent times, and nostalgic nationalists wished to deploy Beethoven as a battering ram in their campaign to retake the fortress of opera, which had been beset by the Italians. He was summoned, as it were, to lead the charge in a sally against the perceived corruption of musical morals. The list of signatories reads as a catalogue of the Viennese cultural elite but also reveals how the times had changed. For with some notable exceptions (among them, Fries and the Lichnowskys), most aristocrats were no longer interested, and Beethoven was reliant on support from the common populace. The contrast with his opus 1 subscription campaign in 1795 could not have been any greater.

Vienna's underlying character, however, had changed very little. Hardly had the manifesto appeared than Beethoven was rumored to have staged the entire campaign himself (suspicions that were not entirely unfounded, it seems). When Beethoven "heard" the gossip, he flew into a rage and threatened to cancel the entire performance. The dust settled in early March, and the concert was rescheduled for April 8. The symphony was already complete, and no fewer than six copyists were working furiously day and night to transcribe the score and produce the necessary orchestral and choral parts, a process that was impeded somewhat by the lack of an experienced transcription coordinator. In the past, Beethoven had always enlisted Wenzel Schlemmer, a man whose experience and familiarity with Beethoven's music was so comprehensive that any handwriting issue could be resolved without needing to consult the master. Schlemmer had passed away the previous summer, and now, left without his favorite copyist, Beethoven was forced to supervise the transcription work himself. To monitor progress from close by, Beethoven insisted that the copyists come to work at his home, which for obvious reasons they refused to do. Beethoven grew increasingly aggravated and was convinced that the copyists showed a distinct lack of expertise and dedication. One year later, in preparation for a performance of the Ninth Symphony in Aachen in May 1825, Beethoven wondered whether there might not be a way to "use a stereotype technique to reproduce one's work automatically, so as to be free from these accursed copyists."[3] Beethoven's sentiments were entirely reciprocated; when his outbursts finally became too much and one of the "accursed" copyists wrote that he would no longer tolerate such tyrannical oppression, a seething Beethoven responded in enormous handwriting: "Bungling idiot! Ignorant, arrogant, supercilious ass! Go correct your own foolish mistakes before lecturing me, like a <u>sow</u> who would teach Minerva."[4]

Preparing the parts was but one of the many obstacles to be overcome. Beethoven's social impediments meant that organizing an *Akademie* in 1824 was no easier than it had been in 1808. Of course, he could avail himself of the well-intentioned help from friends, acquaintances, and his own family members Johann and Karl. But because their differing opinions could often result in vacillation between conflicting strategies and paralyzing indecision on Beethoven's part, this time Moritz Lichnowsky, Schuppanzigh, and Schindler stepped up and took control. Yet after having cunningly lured Beethoven into signing a document declaring his agreement with various practical arrangements, they received a communication from him accusing them of high treason: "I despise falsehoods—do not visit me again, there will be no Akademie."[5]

This time, the sticking points were the venue and the ensemble members. From the outset, negotiations had been underway with two hall managers: Count Pálffy from Theater an der Wien, and ex-choreographer Louis-Antoine Duport, who in the absence of general director Domenico Barbaia was serving as acting manager of the Kärntnertortheater and the Hofburg ballrooms. Theater an der Wien, where so many of Beethoven's important works had been premiered, would ordinarily have been his first choice. Pálffy had not only proposed attractive financial conditions but could also guarantee an orchestra and rehearsal facilities. There was disagreement regarding the conductor, however: not only was Beethoven bent on replacing conductor-in-residence Seyfried with Umlauf, who had led the previous year's production of *Fidelio* with gusto; he also insisted on Schuppanzigh as concertmaster instead of Clement, who was the orchestra's de facto conductor. After a seven-year absence, Schuppanzigh had returned to the Austrian capital in 1823, and because of his modern string quartet expertise, Beethoven saw him as the candidate most likely to make a success of his newest symphony. Pálffy was prepared to replace Seyfried but could not bring himself to sacrifice Clement. For one thing, he believed that Beethoven himself should be the one to deliver the bad news to his old friend, and for another, he could not guarantee that the orchestral musicians would accept Schuppanzigh's authority. One can lead a horse to water, after all. . .

The matter was of the utmost importance to Beethoven, and so he steered himself into the hands of Duport, who was prepared to make the large Redoutensaal available. Duport made no issue of Schuppanzigh's involvement, and the line-up of soloists was also freely negotiable. The potential income, on the other hand, was significantly lower, the overheads higher (including the construction of an additional stage), and the hall's availability was limited. After some rescheduling (shuffling around the dates of April 7 and 8), Beethoven's concert was briefly relocated to the smaller ballroom—an unacceptable development. Not only would the profit margin be reduced to almost nothing but Beethoven also believed that grand orchestral and choral productions simply merited a far larger audience. Partly at Karl's insistence, the enterprise was thus shifted to the Landständischer hall on Herrengasse, despite the venue's limited five-hundred-seat capacity. But Lichnowsky and Schindler used their influence to persuade him otherwise, and so it was that the final choice fell to the Kärntnertortheater after all. On April 24, Schindler finally signed a provisional contract with Duport, which included a promise by the management to do everything in its power to ensure compliance by the orchestra. Another stipulation concerned the assurance of robust forces—twenty-four violins and double winds—and of amateur reinforcements from the regular Friends of Music Society orchestra, who were only too eager to be involved.

The project was postponed for several more days until May 7, when a last-minute squabble arose regarding ticket prices. Beethoven, whose mathematical gifts, as we know, were meager, had discovered just how little he would earn from the entire enterprise, due in no small part to the mounting copyists' fees. Convinced that the theater would be full regardless, he made a final push to raise the entry fees, which Duport deflected by claiming a police restriction.

The delay was welcomed by the musicians, who thus gained more time to prepare for the performance. It was certainly no luxury: a note by Schuppanzigh in one of the conversation books after the first string rehearsal stated that "one cannot simply rush through this music."[6] Truth be told, none of the performers was equal to the task. The choir found Beethoven's writing outlandish and begged repeatedly for simplifications; Beethoven naturally refused to budge. Schindler reports that they simply left out notes as they saw fit, secure in the knowledge that Beethoven would remain oblivious, even were he to sit among the choir himself.[7] The vocal soloists, too, had fundamental objections, especially concerning the higher passages—so much so that the tenor and bass-baritone dropped out and needed to be replaced. Beethoven's consideration for the two female soloists (Henriette Sontag and Caroline Unger, two sparkling young divas who had risen to opera fame in the preceding years) was equally lacking. They had presented themselves to him of their own volition in September 1822 and instantly won his heart. Beethoven gushed to his brother of the pair's beauty, bragging that he had offered them a parting kiss on the lips.[8] Several months before the premiere of the Ninth Symphony, they visited him once more to underscore and reiterate their interest in the solo parts. Spirits were high, and Beethoven and the ladies shared many a merry glass. The next day, Caroline Unger—unaccustomed to such levels of indulgence—was particularly worse for wear, and canceled her appearance at the opera that evening. Though they likely built up some substantial credit with Beethoven that night, it was not enough to move him to make alterations to the score. In Beethoven's view, their "Italian gurgling" had led the young singers astray, and they had simply forgotten how to sing "with the proper support." Both sighed in resignation and promised to struggle on as best they could. They remained on good terms with Beethoven but continued to refer to him as the "tyrant of all singing organs."[9]

The various tensions generated by Beethoven in the months leading up to the premiere were symbolized in part by the three conductors standing on stage that evening. Umlauf, as agreed, had been appointed principal conductor. Standing amid the ensemble was Ignaz Schuppanzigh, who assisted Umlauf by leading the instrumentalists, a separate job in itself. Such conducting duos were not uncommon—especially for works requiring such considerable forces—and drew no undue attention. The announcement of Beethoven's own involvement was another matter entirely: "Herr Ludwig van Beethoven will participate in the overall direction himself."[10] The conversation notebooks reveal that there was some disagreement regarding the precise wording of the concert bills—such as whether Beethoven's recent academic endowments should be listed in their entirety[11]—but how broadly should we interpret the tight-lipped formulation that Beethoven would "participate in the overall direction"? Was his involvement intended to raise the caliber of the production? Or precisely the opposite: was it a diplomatic move to pacify him into harmless submission? All eyewitnesses agree that it was Umlauf who led the performance, with a firm but modest hand. Beethoven stood behind him to the side and gave the tempi but also enriched the musical expression with his own sweeping gestures, by all accounts "like a madman."[12] There was no confusion among the performers, however, who had all agreed to pay no heed to the master's gesticulations and to concentrate solely on Umlauf.

That evening, Beethoven experienced one of the greatest triumphs of his career. No sooner had the orchestra finished the second Scherzo movement than loud applause burst forth from the audience. Beethoven, lost in concentration and with his back to the auditorium, remained completely unaware, until Caroline Unger gently tugged at his sleeve and pulled him around to face the public. Beethoven accepted their adulation rather bashfully, and the symphony was resumed. Both the slow movement and the exceptionally long finale were also well received, although some described the double basses' recitativo passages as "gruff rumbling."[13] Performers and public alike were transported by the exhilarating final crescendo leading into the glorious apotheosis, after which the audience erupted into wild and rapturous applause, waving hats and white handkerchiefs—a gesture that must have brought immense joy to the unhearing Beethoven. According to Schindler, never before had any musician secured such a triumph. Beethoven was subjected to no fewer than five curtain calls (even members of the imperial court ordinarily settled for three) and received the public's adoration with stoic restraint.

After the concert, Beethoven, Karl, and Schindler were brought home by Joseph Hüttenbrenner—the brother of the aforementioned Anselm Hüttenbrenner, and one of the evening's choristers. When the bone-weary Beethoven read through the quittance and discovered that his share of the entire enterprise was a mere 420 guilders, he broke down in utter dejection.[14] It was the first sign of emotion he had shown all evening.

Two days later, heated words were exchanged on the subject of money during dinner at a restaurant in Prater Park, where Umlauf, Schuppanzigh, Böhm (the violinist), Schindler, and Karl were in attendance. Beethoven was in an irritable state and at one point accused Schindler and Duport of having doctored the box-office figures. Schuppanzigh and Umlauf tried to assuage his doubts by arguing that Karl himself had overseen the ticket sales and had noticed no foul play. Their efforts were in vain. Exacerbated by copious quantities of alcohol, the discussion escalated until Beethoven—who not forty-eight hours earlier had proclaimed the eternal brotherhood of man—chased all his friends away.

In a letter to Schindler later that week, Beethoven rescinded his harsh accusations from May 9. But he remained of the opinion that Schindler had caused some mishaps by acting "unwisely and of [his] own accord" and that he had once again proven himself unreliable. Then came his final, devastating remark: "As regards friendship, your case remains a difficult one. I would not under any circumstances wish to entrust you with my well-being, due to your lack of careful consideration."[15] Beethoven meanwhile had received word that the reprise of the concert had been postponed by nearly ten days, and he once again placed the blame—mistakenly but squarely—on Schindler's shoulders. (Schindler would later claim that the misunderstanding had been propagated by Beethoven's brother Johann.) The postponement was indeed disastrous, for by Sunday May 23 most of the Viennese nobility had left for the countryside or the resorts, and those who were still in town certainly had more attractive options than to attend a midday concert during such pleasant weather. The auditorium, therefore, was only half-full. Thankfully, Beethoven had bound Duport to a minimum compensation of five hundred guilders, so that he was not entirely out of pocket.

Beethoven wrote the Ninth Symphony relatively quickly, working on it from May 1823 until February 1824—nine months, to be precise. The work had been conceived long before, however, and sketchbooks from as early as 1815 and 1816 contain an embryonic form of the theme that would later grow into the symphony's Scherzo. The opening bars of the initial Allegro also have their germination in this period but were still disparate ideas without any signs of structural cohesion. And although the loss of many contemporaneous sketchbooks has distorted our understanding somewhat, Beethoven's free-form ideas seem still not to have coalesced by 1817 or 1818. The paucity of material did not preclude him, however, from entering into concrete negotiations with the London Philharmonic Society in 1817, concerning the commission of not one but two new symphonies—an undertaking that soon proved entirely too ambitious, given that he barely had enough material ready for a single symphony. It would come as no surprise if this were the real motivation behind Beethoven's rather sudden change of heart concerning the (otherwise very attractive) England project.

Despite the canceled travel plans, Beethoven's desire to compose at least one new symphony remained, and more than once he interrupted his work on the *Hammerklavier* Sonata to jot down ideas. In his characteristic fashion, Beethoven made more use of words than musical notation during this early stage of the creative process. The March 1818 sketchbooks describe an "Adagio Cantique. A symphonic song of piety in the old modes." Other scattered structural ideas date from the same period, some of which did ultimately find their way into the Ninth Symphony, namely the use of text in the final movement, the staggered entry of the voices, and a reprise of the Adagio.[16] A striking fact is that all of these ideas still remained spread across two symphonies—one of the reasons why modern musicologists debate whether the Ninth is the first symphony of an unfinished pair, or a blend of two seemingly antipodal symphonic projects. It can thus be viewed as either a minotaur or a mermaid, depending on one's perspective.[17]

Beethoven's mind was still clearly not made up in 1818, and so he put his symphony (or symphonies) away. But out of sight was never out of mind for Beethoven, and when he wrote to Ries on July 6, 1822, asking how much the Philharmonic Society was prepared to pay for a grand symphony, he must already have known what direction his new work would take. On November 15, the Philharmonic Society responded affirmatively to his proposal: the English were prepared to pay fifty pounds, subject to exclusive rights for eighteen months and a deadline in March 1823.[18] Beethoven protested the fee somewhat, demanded advance payment, and shifted the deadline again and again. He sent the *Consecration of the House* overture (op. 124) in the meantime, earning him an additional twenty-five pounds—an exorbitant fee compared to the offer on the table for the Ninth. He mentioned London travel plans to Ries more than once but maintained the scheduled premiere of the symphony for May 1824 in Vienna. Ultimately, the Philharmonic Society did not receive the score until December 1824, and the first London performance was held on March 21, 1825, two years later than originally planned. Sir George Smart conducted, but Beethoven was not present; as in 1818, the Philharmonic Society had protested his additional financial conditions. This, at least, is the official version of events.

Without waiting for a response from the Philharmonic Society, in the autumn of 1822 Beethoven pushed confidently ahead, sketching out an initial draft of the opening Allegro and noting down ideas for the second movement. Interestingly, it was during this time that Beethoven added "Finale: *Freude schöner Götterfunken*"—the opening line of the text on which the final movement is based. A mere few days later, the idea had taken on a more concrete form:

"German symphony, followed by choral entry:

Freu - de schö - ner Göt - ter - fun - ken Toch - ter aus E - ly - si - um

with or without variations. Symphony to conclude with Turkish music and a sung chorus."[19]

Although Beethoven took some time to arrive at the definitive form for the "Ode" theme, it is clear that on resuming work in October 1822, he had settled on Schiller's text as the basis for a grand choral finale and decided that the remaining movements should be conceptualized accordingly. With these structural foundations in place, he surmounted the impasse of 1818.

Much of the literature assumes that Beethoven first considered setting Schiller's "Ode to Joy" very early on, creating the impression that the Ninth is the culmination of a lifetime of creative endeavor. To set matters straight, it is true that Beethoven first became acquainted with Schiller's poem in the early 1790s and had plans to set it as a long, through-composed song. Our source for this intention is the young lawyer Bartholomeus Fischenich, whose acquaintance Beethoven had made shortly before leaving Bonn and who, in a letter to his close friend Charlotte Schiller, voiced his high expectations of Beethoven's musical setting.[20] It is unknown whether the composition was ever written—perhaps it was lost—but there is nothing to indicate any early intention on Beethoven's part to incorporate Schiller's "Ode to Joy" into a large-scale choral symphony.

Another oft-mentioned precursor is an apocryphal setting of "Ode to Joy" offered by Beethoven to his publishing friend Simrock in Bonn.[21] Whether this work actually existed is likewise unknown, though it seems improbable, given that Schiller's work had been prohibited in Vienna since 1793. Lastly, Beethoven considered writing an overture on "Ode to Joy" for choir and orchestra in 1812—a time when such an enterprise was at least feasible, as Schiller's banishment from the Viennese cultural stage was lifted in 1808 and had since been replaced by a wave of unbridled enthusiasm.[22]

It was not until 1822, when the poem's popularity had long since waned, that the "Ode to Joy" finally found a place in Beethoven's oeuvre. Not in its entirety, however: because of the specific concept he had in mind, Beethoven "cut and pasted" abridged fragments of the poem together, producing a new structure and, more importantly, new meaning. The "Ode to Joy" was originally a drinking song set to music by Christian Gottfried Körner, a friend to Schiller and a member of one of Germany's oldest Freemason lodges, The Three Swords (Zu den drei Schwerten) in Dresden. The "Ode to Joy" was thus originally intended to be sung at ritual banquets, or "Table Lodges"— lively, informal festivities which were separate from the official meetings and involved a series of toasts to the secular and Masonic authorities (often tempered by a healthy dose of irony). By the end of the eighteenth century, many musical codices had been produced containing songs suitable for such occasions. The formula was always the same: the Worshipful Master would sing the verses then invite the Brothers to join in for the chorus and perform the toast. It is generally assumed that Schiller, like Beethoven, was no Freemason but sympathized nonetheless with the society's teachings and was well informed of their traditions. Most likely he learned of the generic song format via Körner,[23] whose "Ode to Joy" was an instant success. It circulated rapidly among the German Freemasons and even found its way into general society, giving rise to abundant musical treatments. A collection of no fewer than fourteen such settings was published in 1800.

It seemed that the song's original title—"Ode to Freedom" (An die Freiheit)—was ultimately deemed too provocative. In 1803, even Schiller saw fit to rein in the unbridled spirit of his prerevolutionary version from 1785. That which in the now-familiar version is "sternly divided by custom" (*Was die Mode streng geteilt*) was originally "divided by custom's sword" (*Was der Mode Schwerdt geteilt*), and the typical Freemason proclamation "Beggars and Lords will become brothers" (*Bettler werden Fürsten Brüder*) was diluted to the more politically correct "All humankind will become brothers" (*Alle Menschen werden Brüder*).

These two exceptions aside, Beethoven opted for Schiller's grittier original from 1785. But retaining the original structure—with its nine verses and as many refrains—was impossible, and so the material was condensed and reorganized. Only the first three verses were used, and a contrasting middle section features the fourth, first, and third refrains in that order. The final section repeats several fragments from the above, while inserting repetitions of individual words and additional accents, creating the illusion of a large-scale "textual crescendo." Beethoven's creative dramaturgy thus produced a version that is rhetorically far more compact, and which, for good reason, has become better known than the longer and weaker original.

The formal modifications in turn drastically altered the poem's message. Not only did Beethoven remove all references to drinking; he also eliminated the verses whose import was purely political. The original toasting song was thus ideologically upgraded into a prophetic hymn with utopian overtones, in which the magic of joy herself, the "daughter from Elysium," brings people "together in brotherhood" as well as in harmony with the Creator ("Brethren, beyond the starry sky, there must a loving father live"). The drinking song thus metamorphosed into an exalted symphonic proclamation, a transformation with which Beethoven—since his work on the *Diabelli* Variations—was only too familiar.

But how to embody "joy" in music? Beethoven had made several previous attempts, in the finale of *Leonore/Fidelio,* the *Choral Fantasy,* and the closing movements of the Third and Fifth symphonies. For the Ninth, he elected not to evoke a sense of joy through the character of the theme itself but instead via a prolonged crescendo culminating in ecstatic heights. Beethoven's "Ode" theme is characterized by an unprecedented degree of musical economy and self-restraint. The rhythm consists almost entirely of a single note value (the crotchet), and with the exception of one low tone the melody dwells within the very limited range of a fifth. Beethoven uses every means at his disposal to build the momentum toward an exhilarating climax: the music rises gradually out from the depths, accelerating slowly but surely (interrupted by occasional and suspenseful moments of repose) and gaining in volume (achieved in part through the use of "Turkish" instruments, underscoring the message of inclusiveness), until finally a trancelike state is achieved through rapid textual and musical repetition. The conclusion takes on the character of a solemn cry, a rallying call for all humanity to unite as one. One hears the ardent masses surging, their fragmented and staccato declamation of "Diesen Kuss der ganzen Welt" (This kiss is giv'n to all the world) generating warm feelings of brotherhood and earthly bliss, free from the chains of fear, oppression, and demagogy. It was thus that a tormented old man—who had experienced precious little in the way of joy—placed an exclamation mark after a musical and philosophical essay on the triumph over loneliness and solitude. It is deeply tragic that the success of his efforts remained largely unknown to him.

The Ninth Symphony invariably leaves audiences in rapturous intoxication. So it was on May 7, 1824, and so it has remained ever since. The euphoria is due at least in part to the dramatic arc crafted so expertly by Beethoven, a crucial and highly irregular component of which is the intrusive opening to the finale—Wagner dubbed it the *Schreckensfanfare,* or a "fanfare of terror." The orchestra erupts in a diabolical fortissimo, an infernal shambles of dissonant winds and chaotic syncopation. Nowadays we might label such an outburst as a "cacophony," a term that was unfamiliar to early-nineteenth-century music lovers due to the absence of any expectation that such a phenomenon might appear. This fact notwithstanding, to modern audiences, whose eyes and ears have since been brutally desensitized by all manner of influences, the opening still gives the sense that the world is falling apart.

The overwhelming impact of the finale's opening chords is brought into starker relief by the character of the preceding material, that is, nearly forty minutes of seemingly innocent entertainment in the form of three perfectly ordinary symphonic movements, all atypical of Beethoven's late style. They are not overly original, having a clear structure and some degree of predictability— at first glance, they could even be labeled as slightly simplistic. Electrifying anticipation is created, however, by the waiting soloists and the ocean of choristers, whose silent presence creates an unnerving and monumental backdrop. The tension is broken at last by the apocalyptic intrusion, followed by several wordless recitatives by the cellos and double basses, interspersed with brief reminiscences of the first three movements. Beethoven elucidated the underlying significance of this passage in his sketchbooks by providing an accompanying text that, while not sung, nonetheless indicates the precise meaning of the instrumental recitatives and provides the keys to a proper understanding. In his own words, Beethoven explains how the preceding three movements represent three possible resolutions to the terrors of the world: first exalted majesty, followed in turn by Dionysian exuberance and then dreamlike melancholy.[24] Each movement is given brief consideration at the outset of the finale, only to be rejected as a final solution by the entry of the instrumental recitative once more. Beethoven's comment on the first fragment reads, "No, this won't do—I require something more pleasing." The Scherzo citation also meets with disapproval: "Nor this—it is no better, merely livelier." Even the reprise of the idyllic Adagio cannot satisfy him: "No, again, it is too tender and sweet. I need something brighter, more cheerful . . . I shall proceed to sing something of my own [. . .] I ask that you join in with me." This is the moment when listeners are first introduced to the opening bars of the "Ode" theme—still unaware of the notion of freedom it connotes—after which Beethoven rejoices: "Ha, this is it! The joy I seek—I have found it."[25]

The stream of joy that subsequently courses through the orchestra does not culminate in an ecstatic climax just yet; instead, it is deconstructed using the same techniques employed by Beethoven in his late piano sonatas. The piercing "fanfare of terror" dispels all illusions one last time, until the first soloist finally takes the floor, with a text penned by Beethoven himself: "O friends, such sounds begone! Let us instead strike up strains more pleasing and joyful!" According to Schindler, Beethoven struggled at length with the problem of how to integrate the Schiller text into the Ninth Symphony. By Schindler's account, his initial thoughts were along the lines of, "Let us sing the song of the immortal Schiller!"[26] But this fragment was clearly too blunt and weak, and it was only after an extended incubation period that he hit upon "O friends . . . ," which successfully galvanized the overall concept.

This solution at first gives an awkward impression, as the text hovers in a no-man's-land between spoken declamation and song. Yet herein lies precisely its strength and originality: it is via this unsingable recitative that Beethoven bids an emotional farewell to the music of the past—and, thereby, to the past in general—allowing him to throw open the gates irrevocably to a Utopia where all are welcome.

In an effort to spread his message far and wide, Beethoven wished to dedicate the Ninth Symphony to one of the most powerful rulers of the day. Though his first thought was Alexander I of Russia, the monarch's death on December 1, 1825, forced Beethoven to seek out an alternative. His second choice was Frederick William III of Prussia, who had previously extended a gesture of respect by purchasing a copy of the *Missa solemnis*. After some diplomatic preliminaries involving the Prussian ambassador in Vienna, on September 27, 1826, Beethoven sent a specially prepared, calligraphic, and ornately bound manuscript of the symphony to Berlin. Two months later, he received a brief but respectful letter of gratitude from the Prussian king, inviting Beethoven to collect his requital—a diamond ring—from the embassy. Beethoven was extremely put out, and when the imperial jeweler made the shocking discovery that the stone was not in fact a diamond but an ordinary red stone, Beethoven even contemplated returning it. In the end he decided to cut his losses and sell the so-called diamond ring, earning him a grand total of three hundred guilders for a manuscript that today is considered part of the "Memory of the World."

Despite Beethoven's scant recompense overall, the Ninth Symphony was an overwhelming success, much to the joy of the influential Viennese opinion makers who had lobbied to ensure the premiere was held in Vienna. The *Allgemeine musikalische Zeitung* sang the praises of the symphony in a piece spanning three successive issues, the longest critique ever published in the journal's history. And to please the adoring fans, the *Zeitung* even had a new portrait of the master engraved and included as a free supplement—a tribute still paid today by newspapers and magazines to the modern idols of popular music and sport.

55

Decline

UNLIKE THE LATE PIANO SONATAS and, as we shall see, the late string quartets, the originality of the Ninth Symphony lay not in the finer details of its harmonic grammar or vocabulary but rather in its broader overall concept. As a symphony aimed first and foremost at the general public, this more accessible approach was both necessary and unavoidable. Beethoven's greatest struggle was with the final movement—a thorny and perennial conundrum throughout the history of music—but as soon as the proverbial Gordian knot had been cut, the symphony was on paper relatively quickly.

The achievement becomes even more impressive in light of the many distractions that plagued Beethoven at the time: not only his exploits with the *Missa solemnis*, but also his deteriorating health. While Beethoven's correspondence and the conversation notebooks contain reports of the usual digestive troubles, in April 1823 we read for the first time of an eye condition that was so serious, Beethoven's doctor Karl Smetana urged him to read and write sparingly or else his composing days would be numbered.[1] Smetana sincerely believed that Beethoven was at risk of going blind, and the symptoms persisted until March 1824. Until that time, Beethoven could only work sporadically. He was averse to sunlight, suffered pain in his eyes, and was constantly warned against rubbing them when they itched. The symptoms seem to have abated somewhat in 1825, only to resurface again in January 1826. After this date, the source materials make no further mention of the condition.[2]

The fact that the author of the Ninth Symphony was not only deaf but also half-blind is little known. Beethoven's visual impairment was understandably overshadowed by both the real and perceived scope of his hearing problem— it was his progressive deafness, after all, that had so shaped his life and work, and had thus become inextricably linked to his identity and image. But

Beethoven's ocular problems were far from trivial. He discovered quite early that he was myopic and needed a pair of thick glasses (dubbed his "double lorgnette" by Gerhard Breuning) to see long distances.[3] Beethoven later also used reading glasses, and the conversation books even make mention of regular visits to opticians and eye specialists.

Beethoven's first genuine "eye condition" did not present until 1823. Looking at the symptoms—photophobia, pain, and cloudy vision—specialists now agree that Beethoven most likely suffered from uveitis, the most extensive variety of internal optical inflammation. For a long time, the medical profession had classified uveitis as idiopathic, or a stand-alone condition unrelated to any other known ailment or cause. Medical specialists have since uncovered a direct link between uveitis and diabetes, proving that in some cases untreated diabetes can cause damage to the internal tissues of the eye, resulting in inflammation of the uveal tract.[4]

This fact sheds new light on what is known of Beethoven's medical history. Heavy drinking, for example, is known to severely tax not only the liver but also the pancreas, ultimately causing a marked drop in insulin production. Such cases are classified as "type-2 diabetes," and the suspicion that Beethoven suffered this kind of diabetes is supported by the report of the autopsy performed on his body the day after he died. After the founding of the Federal Pathologic-Anatomical Museum by Emperor Francis II in 1796, it had become fashionable to request an autopsy after one's death, the results of which were then recorded and stored in a centralized database. Beethoven had followed the trend, requesting an investigation into the underlying cause of his deafness and other complaints. The autopsy report—drawn up in impeccable medical Latin by the young doctor Johann Wagner and by Beethoven's personal physician Andreas Wawruch—provides answers to many questions.[5] Beethoven's liver had indeed shriveled to half the normal size and was as tough as leather; his pancreas, too, was swollen and had hardened somewhat. Particularly revealing is the observation that his renal papillae were in an advanced state of necrosis, which played a crucial role in the final stages of Beethoven's decline. Renal papillary necrosis is a rare condition, and risk groups seem to include both alcoholics and diabetics.

Beethoven's ocular troubles were only some of the many symptoms pointing to pancreatic deterioration. A range of earlier and later complaints is also commensurate with the same diagnosis: the frequent recurrence of gout, the poor healing of abdominal punctures made during his final weeks, his unsettling weight loss in 1825 (without any associated loss of appetite or thirst), and even certain lower-back problems. Nineteenth-century medicine had not yet identified these clinical patterns, and the additional devastating effects of excessive alcohol consumption were likewise unknown. Only sporadically did doctors attempt to persuade Beethoven to exercise some moderation in this respect. In the summer of 1807, his doctor Johann Schmidt prescribed regular walks, little work, lots of sleep, a proper diet, and "a moderate intake of spirits."[6] The most drastic intervention, made by Dr. Anton Braunhofer, dates from 1825. Braunhofer practiced a Viennese school of medicine that would nowadays be classified under "naturopathy," and focused on unburdening the body as much as possible to allow healing processes to take their natural course. Braunhofer prescribed a strict diet that eliminated any intake of coffee, tea, wine, or strong spices. Beethoven was permitted a cup of hot chocolate in the morning; otherwise, his diet was limited to unseasoned soup, soft-boiled eggs (without pepper), and a few glasses of almond milk.[7] Beethoven protested, saying he had heard of an English doctor, Brown, who claimed that some ailments were in fact *caused* by a lack of stimuli and were better treated by means that would provoke a strong response. But Braunhofer gave no quarter—despite Beethoven's insistent threats to find another doctor—and even rejected the compromise of diluting white wine to make a "spritzer." Braunhofer's perseverance ultimately won out, and after several weeks of abstinence Beethoven's condition had improved so markedly that he was able to return to work and resume his previous lifestyle. In gratitude for his recovery, he inscribed the following remark above the (recently completed) Molto adagio from the String Quartet in A Minor (op. 132): "Hymn of thanks from a convalescent to the deity, in the lydian mode." The possibility cannot be excluded that Beethoven's euphoric proclamation was to a large extent attributable to the end of his imposed and torturous dietary abstinence.

There can be no doubt that Beethoven's predilection for alcohol had a devastating effect on his health, yet many attempts were made after his death to trivialize his alcohol consumption. One voice claims that he seldom drank more than one bottle of wine with a meal, while another anecdote in which he lost a drinking contest to George Smart (hardly a surprising outcome, given the Englishman's reputation) supposedly offers evidence of his limited tolerance for alcohol. The most outspoken denialist was, of course, Schindler, who issued a harsh denouncement of Dr. Wawruch and his detailed autopsy report outlining Beethoven's various terminal conditions and the treatments prescribed. The report was not published until after Wawruch's death in 1842 (in the *Wiener Zeitschrift für Kunst, Literatur, Theater und Mode*). It discreetly suggests that one of Wawruch's key palliative measures during Beethoven's final months was the copious administration of alcoholic beverages varying in both quality and origin. Schindler claims that he pressed Wawruch to make no mention of it, fearing the backlash if Wawruch were to cite alcoholism as one of the primary causes of Beethoven's death. Wawruch refused to omit anything, and so Schindler set about undermining his credibility by trivializing his relationship with Beethoven in the subsequent editions of his biography. According to Schindler, Wawruch hardly knew Beethoven and was consulted only as a last resort when no other doctor was available. Lastly, to banish all conjecture on the subject, Schindler attested that Beethoven's favorite drink was "fresh spring water."[8]

56

Karl's Emancipation

IT IS CLEAR THAT BY 1821 Beethoven had become physically and mentally trapped in a vicious circle. His excess consumption of alcohol over an extended period had taken its physical toll and undermined his mental stability, which in turn fueled his desire for more alcohol. Though eventually his body would collapse, mentally he remained functional for several years, most likely because during this period—despite his work on the *Missa solemnis*, the *Diabelli* Variations, and the Ninth Symphony—he was spared any debilitating conflicts with those closest to him, and most notably with his young nephew Karl.

Relations with his nephew had stabilized in the summer of 1820. Karl had found his feet at school and improved his grades, much to the satisfaction of his proud uncle, who eagerly showed the reports to all and sundry. The development came as a respite, and the meetings between the fifteen- and fifty-year-old were usually convivial. The conversation notebooks provide evidence of the open and relaxed atmosphere in which the open-hearted Karl could "converse" with Beethoven on a wide range of topics. The relative serenity of their tenuous camaraderie was enough to convince Beethoven that he no longer needed to live in close proximity to the Blöchlinger institute. In March 1821 he left his apartment, only a few doors down from the boarding school on Kaiserstrasse, and moved to Ungarngasse in Landstrasse on the other side of the city.

Matters had been greatly simplified by the distance kept in the meantime by Karl's mother, Johanna. She was busy with her newborn daughter and no longer intruded as a hindrance or a source of conflict. Beethoven even made several conciliatory gestures: in the autumn of 1820 he seemed prepared to shoulder a portion of Johanna's debts to Steiner, and when he heard of her escalating medical bills in the spring of 1823, he considered waiving the three-monthly maintenance payment. Interestingly, the conversation books suggest that it was Karl who advised against doing so, fearing that Beethoven's generosity might encourage his mother's profligate lifestyle.[1]

That same year also saw an end to the ten-year conflict between Beethoven and his only surviving brother. Beethoven had taken lodgings near Johann's winter address in Vienna and sought his brother's advice in important financial, material, and legal matters. As already discussed, Johann even lent Beethoven considerable sums of money in exchange for the rights to several new compositions.

The ceasefire with Johann would last but a short while, however, as a series of minor incidents and aggravations put their relationship under increasing strain. The last will and testament that Beethoven had drawn up on March 6, 1823—which left everything to his nephew Karl and explicitly excluded his brother Johann—certainly did little to improve relations. The last straw came several months later, when Beethoven caught wind of his sister-in-law's affair with a military officer while her husband lay bedridden. As he had done in 1812, Beethoven set out to sabotage Johann's marriage by lodging a complaint with the police. To make matters worse, it was at roughly this time when Beethoven learned of the will drawn up by Johann himself, which strongly favored his wife. Beethoven was especially galled that everything would thus be siphoned away to Therese's daughter instead of his nephew Karl, whom Beethoven still regarded as Johann's sole legal heir.[2] He wrote and sent several letters on the subject, characterizing Amalie as a "bastard," Therese as a "fat slob" and a "current and former whore," and the pair as "riff-raff." Beethoven then put actions to words, declaring his unwillingness to "degrade" himself further by "spending any more time in such ignoble company,"[3] and moved house once again, first to Baden and later returning to Landstrasse.

In late August 1823, Karl graduated from the Blöchlinger institute with excellent grades in most subjects (including religious studies). It bolstered his spirits, and friends who had not seen him for some time barely recognized him; the seventeen-year-old had matured both physically and mentally and was now a strapping young lad brimming with confidence. Meanwhile he had also decided to attend the university and study philology, an immensely popular discipline at the time. Although Beethoven did not wholeheartedly approve, he raised no objections, content in the knowledge that he would be able to spend more time in the company of his foster child. And indeed, they spent the summer months together in Baden in relative harmony. Karl performed some secretarial work for his uncle and was even treated to freshly composed fragments from the Ninth Symphony that Beethoven was working on—a rare privilege. Minor incidents were unavoidable, of course, but were generally limited to quibbles regarding Karl's leisure activities, dismissive comments about a dubious friend, and sporadic accusations of clandestine trysts with his mother.

In October, both returned to Vienna. Beethoven continued work on the Ninth Symphony and Karl took to student life like a duck to water, gleefully reporting to his uncle, "We study, we sleep, we drink, we laugh—what more could one want?"[4] In short, they were on excellent terms, and when Beethoven was overburdened with preparations for his new *Akademie* (which was to feature the premiere of his new symphony and excerpts from the *Missa solemnis*), he could rely not only on Karl's logistical assistance (including help with ticket sales and monitoring of cash flow) but also on his emotional support. Beethoven was stretched to his limits and at loggerheads with practically everybody—except his nephew, who was always beyond reproach. A single heated public altercation was reported after the reprise of the concert on May 23, but it was resolved just as quickly.

Karl's eagerness to help his uncle served to cover up some problems that had arisen in connection with his studies. In April, Karl had already showed signs of an ever-increasing fear of failure, but Beethoven, whose own plate was full at the time, did not pursue the matter. Karl then postponed a major exam in June. The appointment of a private tutor helped little, and by July the problem could no longer be ignored. Things came to a head: in response to an enquiry from Beethoven about how his nephew saw his future, Karl wrote in the conversation book that he was seriously considering a soldier's life. Karl had indulged in romantic tales of the army before—attracted by the rugged camaraderie and the fact that one could smoke all day—to which Beethoven had never paid much heed. His sudden confrontation with the harsh reality left him gobsmacked, and after several minutes of stunned silence he responded with a terse "not on your life," and Karl was summarily ordered to repeat his first year at the university.

From that moment on, all trust was lost. While uncle and nephew continued to share a residence—an apartment on Johannesgasse in the center of town—the tensions between them must have been palpable. Beethoven's suspicious nature was largely to blame. He assumed that Karl's poor results were due to a lack of dedication—a Beethoven could never be lacking in talent, after all—and he was constantly badgering Karl (and several secret informants) about his progress, schedule, and private lessons. Karl, under-standably, was frustrated. It should come as no surprise that during the nego-tiations with the London Philharmonic Society in December 1824, when Beethoven began haggling about travel expenses, Karl's stern advice was to pursue an alternative strategy; he clearly feared that the agreement might otherwise fall through and was eager to escape his uncle's watchful eye.

Relations became increasingly unstable in 1825, when Karl suddenly decided to quit his philology degree and begin commercial studies. Although Beethoven could not argue the fact that a bookkeeper would earn more than a professor,[5] and—hailing from middle-class roots himself—was certainly not averse to a life in business, he nonetheless saw the move as a backward step. At the same time, he had no choice but to grit his teeth and support Karl in his decision, as the threat of a military career was not yet off the table. Despite being in the middle of the academic year, Karl was still permitted to enroll in the Polytechnic Institute at Karlsplatz. Beethoven did his utmost to bring this seemingly doomed enterprise to a successful end; vice dean Franz Michael Reisser was found willing to act as cocustodian, reassuring Beethoven that Karl would be properly supervised. A private tutor was hired at the cost of two thousand guilders, or twice the earnings from the Viennese performances of the Ninth Symphony. During the summer months, when Beethoven traditionally retreated to Baden, Karl was sent to live with Mathias Schlemmer, a public servant who lived not far from the institute. Karl continued to travel to Baden every weekend, where he helped his uncle with his administration and ran errands—a very time-consuming distraction from his studies. Far more detrimental, however, were the many letters Beethoven sent from Baden to Vienna. Slipping into an ever-deeper depres-sion, Beethoven bombarded his nephew with admonitions and well-meant advice as well as personal confessions and frustrations of such a type that would nowadays be reserved for the psychologist's office.

A prime example of Beethoven's stranglehold on Karl was the ruthlessness with which he crushed a very promising career opportunity in September 1825. Publisher Maurice Schlesinger had traveled to Vienna to negotiate Beethoven's latest string quartets. Both he and Karl were present at the pre-view of the String Quartet in A Minor (op. 132), held at the hotel-restaurant Zum wilden Mann on Kärntnerstrasse. They engaged in conversation, and Schlesinger suggested—most likely in a misguided attempt to curry Beethoven's favor—that the future businessman Karl might assist him in establishing an art dealership in London. To this end, he proposed taking

Karl with him to Paris, where he could learn the tricks of the trade. Karl's illustrious surname would undoubtedly have opened many promising doors—doors which his uncle, alas, slammed shut at the very outset. Although Beethoven raised ideological objections (claiming that art dealers become rich on the backs of artists), a simple inability to sever the umbilical cord with his adoptive son is a far more likely explanation. In any case, not another word was spoken on the matter.

Shortly thereafter, in October 1825, Beethoven moved to a spacious apartment in the Alte Schwarzspanierhaus in Alservorstadt, his last official address. Karl helped him to haul his possessions, arrange furnishings, and find a housekeeper. Tensions were high, however; eventually Karl reached a tipping point, and uncle and nephew came to blows. Beethoven's fear of losing Karl began to take on obsessive proportions, as did the uncontrollable urge to monitor his every move. Beethoven even went so far as to instruct his close friend and violinist Karl Holz to schedule regular billiard sessions with Karl, so that he might analyze their final scores and attribute any improvement on Karl's part to illicit hours spent away from his studies in bars and cafés. Beethoven also continued to insist on the embarrassing practice of collecting his—now adult—nephew from the gates of the institute, whereupon, arm in arm, they would both return home. Not to mention the ludicrous proposition by Beethoven to chaperone Karl to a carnival ball ... It took all of Karl Holz's powers of persuasion to convince Beethoven of the laughable impression he would make: a deaf old man, in disguise but still clearly recognizable, clumsily leaping and jerking about on the dance floor—and all merely to catch a glimpse of whatever young lady his young nephew might be flirting with!

As one might expect, Karl grew weary of the constant need to justify his behavior. The conversation notebooks are rich with comments such as "I'm no child, you know" and "You know when I am at home. Surely you cannot expect me to tell you where I am every hour of the day? Just as I have no idea where you are if I do not find you at home."[6] In fairness, it should be added that Karl was, in a manner of speaking, running with the hare and hunting with the hounds. He was already old enough and self-assured to extricate himself from his paranoid uncle's grip had he wished to do so, but the material advantages of his dependency on Beethoven were not to be sneezed at. Beethoven's status was useful to him in all manner of ways, and occasionally Karl touted his ability to manipulate his uncle. According to Schindler, Karl even bragged that he could do whatever he liked with Beethoven and that a few friendly, flattering words were enough to placate him afterward.[7] Karl was therefore not entirely blameless in prolonging the conflict.

Meanwhile, Karl's studies had taken a turn for the worse. His chosen field was quite heavy in arithmetic, which had once more proven beyond him. He returned to playing truant and postponing exams, and (according to Schindler) he even squandered or gambled away the money he had received for private tutelage. In the summer of 1826, the world closed in on Karl: Beethoven's doctor had advised him to break his custom of spending the summer months in Baden and instead to remain in the city. Beethoven gladly seized the opportunity, as it also allowed him to retain a tighter grip on his nephew. Karl thus lost all hope of respite, and on August 6, 1826, in a fit of desperation, he shot himself in the head.

Karl's suicide attempt came as a surprise, but only somewhat. The previous day Karl had mentioned to his landlord Schlemmer that he had so many mounting debts, he wished he were dead. Schlemmer and his wife wasted no time: a search through his cupboards revealed two loaded pistols, which they confiscated on the spot. Beethoven, alarmed, mobilized his entire network to bring Karl to him, but was unsuccessful. Karl instead went into town, pawned his watch, and used the money to purchase two new weapons. He wrote two farewell letters (which, alas, are lost), chose a sinister backdrop—the Rauhenstein castle ruins in the Helenental valley near Baden, one of Beethoven's favorite spots—and pulled the trigger. The first bullet flew into empty space, while the second bounced off his temple. Karl had—perhaps intentionally—aimed poorly. Hours later a coachman came upon the seriously but not fatally wounded Karl, and at the boy's express request took him to his mother's house on Adlergasse. The dramatic impact of this decision cannot be overestimated, not least because Beethoven was forced to confront the harsh reality of his own part in the tragedy. It was there, lying in bed at his mother's house, that Karl made the heart-wrenching plea to his *Ersatzvater:* "Do not torment me any longer with grievances and accusations. It is over."[8]

Most pages from the conversation notebooks pertaining to these events have been torn out, making a factual reconstruction problematic. While Schindler is the most obvious suspect, on this occasion we cannot exclude the possibility that Beethoven himself destroyed important pieces of evidence, fearing a shameful confrontation with the police and the law.

For a gentleman in the early nineteenth century, nothing could be worse than a bungled suicide attempt owing to one's own ineptitude. The physical suffering was the least of Karl's worries, as the day after committing his desperate act he was removed from his mother on police orders and transferred to a secure ward of the Vienna General Hospital—walking distance from Beethoven's home on Schwarzspanierstrasse—where he received surgery and spent six weeks recovering. As additional treatment he was assigned a pastor, ironically from the Congregation of the Most Holy Redeemer, a group known as the "Redemptorists," or "liberators," whose job it was to administer fanatical religious preachings and steer Karl back onto the path of righteousness. Lastly, he was subjected to a traumatic interrogation, which served only to demonstrate just how poorly such matters were understood in the early nineteenth century. Karl was withdrawn and offered little cooperation, but ultimately yielded and made an astonishing confession: "I became a worse person through my uncle's attempts to make me a better one."[9] Karl was discharged from the hospital on September 25 and spent only one day in a "normal" jail before being set free—most likely thanks to his famous uncle's reputation.

Beethoven was deeply affected, not only by the dramatic events themselves but also by the subsequent deluge of gossip and mockery that flowed through the city. He, too, was subjected to humiliating interrogations, as though an apology were necessary for his failure to raise Karl, an endeavor to which he had been only too dedicated. Karl also felt it was better for them not to see each other for some time. Beethoven honored his wish and was thus initially denied any opportunity to make amends or come to terms with the past. Beethoven was desolate, and Schindler described the languidness of his movements, as though he had suddenly become a man of seventy, devoid of energy or expression, utterly deflated and extremely frail. He was a broken man.[10]

Several weeks passed before Beethoven saw his nephew again, when their conversation turned mainly to Karl's future. Since Vienna offered no prospects whatsoever for an ex-suicide victim, the military really was the only feasible remaining option. Breuning, who still held a senior post in the Ministry of Defense and therefore knew the terrain, could but agree. The army, he believed, was ideal for those in need of limitations, and the best place to learn to live a frugal life.[11] Beethoven had no counterargument to this rather sobering observation and so did the only thing he could: he rallied all of his contacts to find a respectable post in the military for his nephew. And he succeeded. Karl was assigned to the Eighth Infantry Regiment, stationed in Iglau (Jihlava, 150 kilometers northwest of Vienna) and led by Archduke Ludwig, Archduke Rudolph's elder brother.

Still, Beethoven's expectations for Karl had not been tempered entirely, and he hoped that Karl might soon rise up through the ranks. On the basis of a distorted understanding of advancement protocols he had garnered from the aristocrats, he tried to help by dedicating one of his final quartets, the String Quartet in C-sharp Minor (op. 131) to Joseph von Stutterheim, the direct head of Karl's regiment and friend to Breuning. There is no record of the field marshal–lieutenant's reaction when he found a copy of Beethoven's quartet—the greatest he had ever written, according to the composer—among his correspondence.[12] One can only imagine.

Pragmatic steps were taken to aid Karl in his transition to the military. On the advice of several good friends, Beethoven transferred custody of Karl to Breuning, which amounted to an implicit admission of guilt. Uncle and nephew then traveled to Johann's estate in Gneixendorf, ostensibly to recover from the commotion of the previous months. In reality, Karl was waiting for his hair to grow back, to conceal the physical stigma on his head before braving the harsh judgment of the barracks.

Beethoven's decision to accompany Karl to Gneixendorf was highly irregular, as he had received a similar invitation from Johann less than a month before and rejected it in a curious fashion:

I am not coming –

Your brother??????!!!![13]

While Beethoven's reticence to travel to Gneixendorf was certainly due in part to his disdain for his sister-in-law Therese, it is entirely probable that he was also jealous of the wealth amassed by his younger brother in so uninspiring a fashion. Perhaps more importantly, he may have been afraid of a potential alliance against him between Karl, Johann, and Therese. Under pressure from Breuning, Beethoven ultimately set his own interests aside in favor of his nephew's, and on September 29, 1826, the two arrived in Gneixendorf. Their accommodations were in a separate wing of the castle. Beethoven was allocated a spacious apartment with plenty of sunlight, painted walls, an open fireplace, and a private bathroom—for which his dear brother charged him four guilders per day.

Despite his luxurious surroundings, Beethoven felt ill at ease. He was withdrawn, reserved, took solitary walks, barely responded when asked what he wanted to eat, and was silent at the dinner table. He did manage to complete some work: with Karl's assistance he determined the metronome markings for the Ninth Symphony and put the finishing touches on both the String Quartet in F Major (op. 135) and the new final movement of the String Quartet in B-flat (op. 130). It is not an uncommon opinion among experts that this music sounds "as though the composer himself is no longer present."[14]

The Beethoven brothers engaged in many a conflict: Karl was a recurring theme, of course, as was money and the matter of Johann's estate, which had left a bad taste in Beethoven's mouth. On the morning of November 27, Beethoven made the abrupt decision to take Karl back to Vienna. The cause of their hasty departure is still the subject of some debate. Schindler's account mentions poor weather, as well as Beethoven's frustration at the inappropriate degree of intimacy shown by Therese in nursing young Karl back to health;[15] more puritan speculations stop at an escalated financial disagreement. In any case, Johann refused to grant Beethoven the use of his closed carriage for the journey, thus subjecting Beethoven and Karl to two full days of wind and rain. On their return, Beethoven was ill—gravely ill, as it would turn out—and in a subsequent chapter we will discuss in detail how precious time was lost in the search for a competent doctor. A stubborn rumor spread by Schindler holds Karl partly responsible for the delay.[16] Beethoven had reportedly instructed him to summon a doctor, a task that Karl apparently delegated to a coffeehouse waiter (while playing billiards, if the most slanderous version is to be believed), who in turn tarried a full day before taking any action.

Karl could not leave for Iglau to take his military oath until January 1827. But because he still needed to pass muster, order a uniform, and negotiate his wage (which Beethoven had insisted not be too low, so as to ease the transition between his old and new circumstances), he was forced to spend another four weeks in the company of his languishing uncle. His final entries in the conversation notebooks—his last words to Beethoven—bear witness to the difficulties of their life together: "I wish you joy for the new year, and I can only apologise for causing you displeasure since the very first night."[17] Nevertheless, on January 3, the day before he would bid a final farewell to the young man who for over ten years had constituted his greatest source of misery and preoccupation, Beethoven ordered his lawyer Johann Baptist Bach to authenticate his will and testament from 1823, expressly designating Karl, his "dear nephew," as the sole beneficiary.

Beethoven died around ten weeks later. The notice of his passing sent to Karl was delayed by several days. While an estimated twenty thousand people accompanied Beethoven to his final resting place, the absence of his "dear nephew" was by far the most conspicuous.

Karl served in the military for five years and had risen to the rank of sublieutenant by the time he was "honorably" discharged in the spring of 1832. He later wed Karoline Naske, the mother of his then eight-month-old daughter. Another three daughters would follow and then a son, who was given the portentous name of Ludwig and would eventually seek his fortune in America in the 1870s. Perhaps he understood the difficulties faced by a van Beethoven—especially one named Ludwig—when building a life in Austria. His father, Karl, led a life of serial professional disillusionment: an agricultural venture in Moravia went to seed after two years, and all attempts thereafter to secure a position in Vienna—despite endorsements from the emperor himself—were thwarted by his sullied reputation. The stigma of his suicide attempt undoubtedly played a role; however, the harsh judgment that fell on him during the formation of the very first Beethoven myths immediately after the composer's death cannot be underestimated. The words of Gerhard Breuning, the son of Karl's ex-guardian Stephan, will serve as an example: "I loathe to speak of Beethoven's immeasurable suffering at the hands of his scatterbrained and desultory nephew Karl, who never recognised the boundless love of an uncle concerned only for his future, and whose heinous ingratitude instead paved the way to Beethoven's final illness."[18]

In the end, the only option available to Karl was to live off the interest on the assets bequeathed to him by Beethoven. Given the additional and considerable inheritance he received in 1848 from his other uncle, Johann, he managed without any trouble. Karl van Beethoven died on April 13, 1858, at the age of fifty-two. The cause of death was liver cancer.

57

Money Matters

TWICE IN HIS LIFE, BEETHOVEN SIGNED a will and testament designating Karl as his sole heir. He became so preoccupied with the notion that
his nephew might be at the mercy of the world without a penny to his name,
that his obsession with wealth eventually took on pathological proportions.
The financial circumstances surrounding the Ninth Symphony and the *Missa
solemnis* are enough to show that Beethoven was virtually paranoid when it
came to money, which helped to bring about his reputation as something of
a mercenary.

This same reputation was reinforced by the fact that on his deathbed,
Beethoven succeeded in wheedling a further hundred pounds (roughly one
thousand guilders) out of the London Philharmonic Society. Officially the
sum was an advance on an *Akademie* to be organized at a later date, but for
which no firm plans had yet crystallized. Three rather maudlin letters by
Beethoven give the impression that the hundred pounds were intended as an
almsgiving, to relieve him of his most pressing debts.[1] Beethoven was well
prepared for a rainy day, however; soon after his death, certificates for seven
bank shares were found hidden carefully away in a small wooden box, each to
the value of one thousand guilders. In this light, Beethoven's desperate plea
for financial support from England takes on an air of deliberate deception.

Schindler's role in the interpretation of this "share affair" was a nefarious
one. Immediately upon the master's death, Schindler wrote to Ignaz
Moscheles, stating that the Viennese were up in arms because Beethoven had
dared to enlist financial support from a foreign nation (England). He spoke
in Beethoven's defense, arguing that once Beethoven was no longer able to
compose in his old age (which Schindler had believed might easily reach
seventy), he would have no choice but to sell off his shares one by one, leaving

him in serious financial difficulty.[2] In his biography published fifteen years later, however, Schindler sang an entirely different tune, declaring that the public outcry following Beethoven's death—accusing the German people of allowing one of their greatest figures to wither away and die—was unfounded. Schindler endorsed the view that Beethoven had clearly been the architect of his own suffering, thus setting the tone for future assessments.[3]

Beethoven's preference for begging over selling his assets was, of course, closely related to the deep-seated fear of poverty instilled in him as a boy—a complex that the prevailing economic conditions and overwhelming spirit of pessimism did little to alleviate. Granted, Beethoven had earned relatively large sums from the *Missa solemnis* and the Ninth Symphony (2,500 and 1,150 guilders, respectively—both substantial amounts relative to his prior earnings), but when the uncontrolled inflation and escalated costs of living are taken into account, Beethoven's purchasing power was actually lower than ever. As an independent artist he also lacked the safety net of any social insurance, making the six-monthly bank dividends his only source of income during times of illness (which, Beethoven realized, were becoming ever more frequent). Against this backdrop, it is understandable that Beethoven continued to apply for permanent posts at various courts. In 1819 he had assumed that Archduke Rudolph would appoint him in Olmütz, and in 1822 he appealed to his aristocratic friends Dietrichstein and Moritz Lichnowsky in the hope of replacing the recently departed court composer Anton Teyber. A year later, he enquired of the Esterházys whether they might consider reinstating Haydn's previous post of Kapellmeister.[4] All attempts were in vain. Times had changed since the middle classes had ejected the aristocracy from the cockpit of society. The need for grand ceremonial gestures and appurtenant staff among the nobility had diminished, while the middle classes provided no viable alternative; the fact that they worked for their income made them less inclined to divert their hard-won earnings into cultural and musical undertakings. For Beethoven, though, the main obstacles were still his own character and the increasing obscurity of his music. In February 1823, although it was already clear that no replacement would be sought for Teyber, Beethoven briefly entertained the possibility of composing a new Mass to earn some goodwill with the emperor. On hearing the suggestion, Count Dietrichstein advised Beethoven to take inspiration from the work of former Kapellmeister Georg Reutter, who had died in 1772 (!) and whose music the emperor greatly admired. Of course Beethoven's "own great genius" would have free rein, but the Mass should not be too long or complicated, with simple instrumentation and devoid of virtuosic vocal parts. It was also to be predominantly homophonic—with perhaps the occasional *brief* fughetta—while the *Hosanna, Sanctus,* and *Dona nobis pacem* demanded the utmost compositional restraint.[5] Unsurprisingly, Beethoven did not give the enterprise a second thought.

Beethoven thus had good reason to tread carefully with his savings, which explains why he opted time and again to take out new loans and fiercely negotiate new contracts rather than sacrifice his precious shares. The idea to invest as an insurance policy against unpredictable economic fluctuations came from publisher Sigmund Steiner in July 1816. Despite a large outstanding debt that he held with Steiner at the time, Beethoven somehow managed to provide Steiner with four thousand guilders in cash as an investment in his business in 1816. The exact source of these funds is unknown; one possibility is payment in arrears for work completed in 1814. Three years later, Beethoven recalled his investment and used it to purchase eight shares in the recently established National Bank. This transaction would ultimately ruin his relationship with Steiner, who was so generous as to repay the loaned four thousand guilders in full despite Beethoven's outstanding debt with him of half that sum. When Steiner insisted on a prompt resolution in 1820, Beethoven contested the calculation of the interest. Although he had demanded an 8 percent return on his investment with Steiner, he found 6 percent preposterously high for his own loans, some of which had been running for five years or more. Steiner was at a loss to comprehend Beethoven's lack of consideration or gratitude, and it was a blow from which their friendship would never recover. Beethoven thus lost a major source of financial support, forcing him to sell one of his bank shares in 1821.

It is noteworthy that several months after purchasing his shares, on July 13, 1819, Beethoven made concrete plans to purchase a country residence in Mödling. For a time it indeed seemed likely that he might succeed in acquiring the Christhof, an old presbytery in the town center, but his bid was too low. Exactly how Beethoven intended to fund the venture is unclear, especially since he was in desperate need of ready funds only a few weeks later. Could it be that Beethoven's judgment was clouded by the splendid Gneixendorf estate his brother Johann had acquired on August 2?

During the last five years of his life, Beethoven maintained a precarious balance between money, debts, and shares. Like a veteran broker, he followed developments in the share market with a keen eye; one moment he would buy shares, only to sell them again a few months later, and before he knew it he became trapped in the revolving door of financial speculation. On more than one occasion Beethoven used his shares as collateral to take out additional loans, sometimes in order to repay existing debts—or worse, the mounting interest. His traditional sources of income were not inexhaustible. Publishers would only go so far with advances for new projects or vague guarantees of exclusivity. Beethoven did try to appease them with older works now and again, such as his failed attempt in 1822 to offer Artaria & Co. a set of 1797 variations on "Là ci darem la mano" for two oboes and English horn (WoO 28) as compensation for the overdue repayment of a loan from 1820. Nineteenth-century banks proved just as uncharitable as they are today, for despite his position as a shareholder, Beethoven was repeatedly confronted with his inability to present sufficient collateral to secure new loans. He had no choice but to generate credit at lower levels, by withholding what he owed to his tailor (Lind) and wine merchant (Seelig). Ultimately, it was his brother and seasoned businessman Johann who advised Beethoven on his financial transactions and who kept the wolves at bay more than once (although there is some evidence of heated discussions on the matter).

We can only imagine Beethoven's anxiety at teetering so deliberately on the brink of financial ruin. Still, after 1821 Beethoven had no further cause to dip into his assets, and the will and testament dated January 3, 1827 (designating Karl as sole heir and the beneficiary of all his worldly goods) makes specific mention of "7 bank shares, and whatever cash remains."[6] After deductions—funeral expenses, medical bills, and outstanding rent and debts—Beethoven bequeathed his nephew a total of nearly ten thousand guilders, hardly a meager sum, and for a musician especially. Comparative studies of other composers' incomes reveal that Beethoven had earned and saved relatively well. The salaries of opera singers were of course far higher; among composers and Kapellmeisters, only the estates left by Haydn and Salieri were significantly larger. Not only did both live far longer than Beethoven, but they also had the luxury of combining a sizeable government pension with appreciable and ongoing private sources of income. Mozart, on the other hand, died much younger, and a comparison with Beethoven tips the scales in the opposite direction, as Mozart's estate yielded capital worth 592 guilders, and 1,473 guilders in debt. Mozart was known for his more decadent lifestyle; his wardrobe and furniture were worth double and six times those of Beethoven, respectively, and even included an ornate aristocratic billiard table.[7]

One final aspect should not be overlooked: Beethoven's estate also included two pianos and the set of quartet instruments gifted to him by

Lichnowsky during his early years in Vienna. True, the value of "original" instruments has grown exponentially over the intervening centuries (when Beethoven died, the quartet of instruments was appraised at a paltry seventy-eight guilders). But even despite the lack of an Amati or Guarneri, it is still tempting to imagine how wealthy the modern owner might be, not only of such a splendid consort of instruments but also of an original Broadwood and a Graf *Hammerklavier*.

58

The Discovery of Heaven

THE LATE STRING QUARTETS

A TRIPTYCH FOR ST. PETERSBURG

After finishing the Ninth Symphony, Beethoven immediately set to work on the String Quartet in E-flat Major (op. 127), the first in a set of three that he had promised some time before to the young Russian aristocrat Nikolai Borisovich Galitzin. On November 9, 1822, Galitzin had sent a letter addressed to "Monsieur Louis van Bethoven a Viennes" (even coming from far-distant St. Petersburg, no further details were necessary to ensure that the letter would reach him), asking him to compose "one, two or three new quartets."[1] Galitzin had close ties to Vienna: a distant uncle of his had served there as Russian ambassador for decades, and Nikolai himself had lived in the capital between the ages of eight and eleven, which is when he developed his fondness for music. In the same letter to Beethoven, he described himself as an ardent music lover, an excellent cellist, and above all, a fervent admirer of the great master's works. As an amateur composer himself, he had even arranged several of Beethoven's piano sonatas for string quartet.[2] He would later write that the general preponderance of poor taste in society offended him and that he was immensely frustrated by what he called "Italian charlatanism," which he saw as a fleeting trend in comparison to Beethoven's great masterworks.[3] Because money was also no object to Galitzin, he seemed to be a man after Beethoven's own heart.

To ensure that he would receive at least one quartet, Galitzin had formulated the commission in vague terms—requesting "one, two or three quartets"—and left the price to the master's discretion. Beethoven needed no further encouragement, and on January 25, 1823, he promised—in his best French—to deliver the first quartet before the end of February 1824, or by mid-March at the very latest. Given that his livelihood was dependent on the "products of his spirit," he took the liberty of setting the rather exorbitant rate of fifty ducats apiece.[4] Galitzin balked neither at the fee nor at Beethoven's insistence to retain the publication rights, and promptly transferred the first fifty ducats to Vienna.

Beethoven's confidence in committing to such a short deadline was partly due to the existing ideas for a new string quartet that he had been sketching since the spring of 1822, before the commission had even arrived from St. Petersburg. But despite the ready availability of fertile material, his desire to complete other major works—combined with unforeseen barriers to the development of a new and adequate quartet idiom—made the timely fulfillment of his promise to Galitzin impossible. Galitzin was most distressed; at one point he suspected that the score had even been lost in transit, and mobilized the Russian embassy in Vienna to courier a new copy to St. Petersburg via diplomatic post. In the end, he was kept waiting an additional year: Beethoven completed the first quartet in February 1825, and after a run-through on March 6 followed by several corrections, the score was ready to be dispatched on March 20. The next two quartets, the String Quartet in A Minor (op. 132) and the String Quartet in B-flat Major (op. 130), presented far less trouble and were completed respectively in July and December of 1825.[5]

Now, however, it was Galitzin's turn to break his promise. There was some initial confusion when Galitzin received his copy of the *Missa solemnis* before the first of the string quartets—despite having ordered the Mass afterward—thus casting doubt on the purpose of the original outlay of fifty ducats, which Beethoven mistakenly believed was for the *Missa*. The miscommunication was not cleared up until a second payment of fifty ducats was transferred to Beethoven (less ten guilders in bank fees, much to the composer's immense frustration). Galitzin then tarried with the payment of the hundred ducats for the next two quartets and the twenty-five ducats for the *Consecration of the House* overture (op. 124), which Beethoven had dedicated to him in the meantime. Galitzin asked for Beethoven's understanding in November 1826, citing recent severe financial difficulties. But despite these problems—and the fact that he had been drafted to fight in the Russian army against the Persians—Galitzin promised to meet his financial obligations as soon as possible.[6] He never did, and the last letter that Beethoven wrote from his deathbed, on March 21, 1827, was an arrears notice to Galitzin's banker in St. Petersburg.

The matter dragged on for quite some time. It would be eight years, in 1835, before Beethoven's nephew Karl received a first installment of fifty ducats, but not until 1852—after denouncements by Schindler in his first two biographies—was the debt finally settled in full. Never was there any mention of interest, although Galitzin's son, the conductor and composer Yuri Nikolayevich Galitzin, did transfer a sum of 125 ducats to Ludwig van Beethoven junior in 1858, to "demonstrate the appreciation of Russian musicians" for his great-uncle's music.[7]

Galitzin's subservient role in his dealings with Beethoven was made abundantly clear when under the apprehension of having paid for the first quartet, he powerlessly looked on as it was premiered in Vienna before he had seen or heard a single note. Beethoven was oblivious to any wrongdoing on his part; for twenty-five years it had been his custom to test out his quartets in Schuppanzigh's laboratory, to assure himself of results commensurate with his high standards. Under these conditions, the fate of the String Quartet in E-flat Major (op. 127) was thus placed in Schuppanzigh's hands. Schuppanzigh was genuinely convinced that the quartet could be learned in ten days and scheduled the premiere for March 6, 1825. He was gravely mistaken. Aside from some internal frictions among the players (Linke, the cellist, was put out because Beethoven had promised him the quartet for a benefit concert), the group lost vast amounts of time trying to find their feet within Beethoven's latest idiom. The allotted rehearsals were inadequate, and much of the music fell apart during the premiere. The second violinist, Karl Holz, described the performance as "half-baked."[8]

Beethoven was spared the live experience of this debacle. He was not in the audience—never again would he attend public performances of his own music—and was only informed afterward by his nephew Karl and brother Johann of the poor ensemble playing and the overall lack of cohesion. In one of the conversation books, Johann—who was as much a musician as Beethoven was a pharmacist—imputed the fault to Schuppanzigh: "His belly is getting so big, he will soon be unable to hold the violin!"[9] The first violinist was thus held accountable, and since his technique was obviously not to blame (Beethoven had toned down the virtuosity somewhat), the failure was ascribed to a lack of musical intelligence. A typical musicians' intrigue followed, and a reluctant Beethoven was pressured into stabbing the leader of his quartet—and good friend—in the back. Schuppanzigh was replaced by the brightest rising star in the glittering firmament of Viennese violinists, Joseph Böhm. He led the violin seminar at the Viennese conservatorium, mentored such violinists as Georg Hellmesberger and Joseph Joachim, and had built up a solid reputation as a quartet player during Schuppanzigh's extended absence. Intensive rehearsals were held with the composer present, who offered pertinent remarks on the interpretation based entirely on visual cues. One anecdote from Böhm tells how, shortly before the dress rehearsal, Böhm and his colleagues had secretly agreed not to observe a new tempo change added by Beethoven to the conclusion of the work. Beethoven watched the rehearsal from a corner of the room, and when it was over he called out that the finale now "sounded" far better, and the Meno vivace was officially dropped. The subsequent performances on March 18 and 23 (the latter seeing two complete renditions) and April 7 were now a success, not only because three of the four quartet members had played the work before under Schuppanzigh but also because the audience became increasingly at ease with each successive hearing, allowing for more nuanced judgment. The sensational press naturally gravitated toward the controversy surrounding Schuppanzigh and Böhm, though not all criticism was aimed at the former. The *Allgemeine Theaterzeitung,* for example, argued that any impartial observer would be forced to admit that given the time at his disposal, Schuppanzigh had done all he could, and that the premiere simply ought to have been postponed.[10] The conclusion was true, in any case: in his eagerness to dazzle audiences with Beethoven's newest quartet, Schuppanzigh had certainly been overambitious.

The work's reputation was unscathed by the public debate, however. Quite the opposite: that same April, Joseph Mayseder—a former second violinist from the original Schuppanzigh quartet and a player with a wealth of Beethoven experience—led a performance that easily held its own alongside Böhm's acclaimed interpretation. It seemed that professional string players in Vienna unofficially began vying to deliver the most well-received performance of Beethoven's first Galitzin quartet. Over the ensuing years, according to Holz, many of Vienna's amateur quartets would learn the E-flat major quartet with "diabolical fervor." The occasional need for a "fifth quartet member"—who was to give the beat during the nebulous slow movement—is at once a telling and trivial detail.[11] What these many initiatives do show is that Beethoven's late string quartets were far less removed from early-nineteenth-century chamber music practice than is generally supposed.

The entire Schuppanzigh affair gave rise to another historical presupposition, one of far greater consequence: that performers and listeners of Beethoven's late string quartets require a highly developed capacity for musical perception and analysis. Granted, Schuppanzigh was hardly a paragon of musical intellect, a fact that many commentators were happy to affirm: "While he certainly has something that others cannot learn, he himself has learned nothing else" (Karl Holz). Or, "he could not so much as tell a seventh chord from a triad" (Schindler).[12] His discussions with Beethoven also reveal little in the way of erudite scholarship, literary knowledge, artistic ideology, or philosophical interest. Yet despite what might be considered "shortcomings," Schuppanzigh's innate musicianship proved valuable to Beethoven time and again, and cannot have been what sabotaged the performance of the String Quartet in E-flat. Schuppanzigh also denied the presence of any insurmountable "technical difficulties," instead attributing the ensemble's struggles to an "originality [. . .] that is, at first, incomprehensible."[13]

What exactly did Schuppanzigh mean by incomprehensible originality? An important clue lies in his own discourse regarding the perilous ensemble writing,[14] in which he essentially confesses an inability to gain any rational or structural purchase on the work as a whole. The slow second movement, the foundation around which the entire composition is built, doubtless presented particular difficulties. A modern-day perusal of the score clearly reveals that the movement is a theme and variations, but this fact—especially on a first hearing—escapes the listener almost entirely. While the theme itself appears uncomplicated, natural, and free, at the same time it eschews the traditional trappings of a "theme." It displays hardly any momentum, direction, or progression of any kind, as though the musical "impetus" is no longer of any relevance. Nor is there is any cause to suspect that the material could form the basis of a set of variations lasting over fifteen minutes, since the "theme" is essentially an extended variation in itself. The mold of gentle spontaneity in which the theme is cast belies the fact that Beethoven worked on it for an exceptionally long time. Once completed, he then applied the full range of variation techniques he had developed during the late piano works, in the process becoming so detached from the original material that all notion of space and time is lost—for composer, performer, and listener alike. This "diffuse" sense is reinforced by the independence of the four instrumental parts, exhibiting a disparity that at times threatens to unravel the musical fabric. It is no coincidence that—contrary to his ordinary practice of sketching in one voice only, even when composing symphonies—Beethoven's sketches of the late quartets include full four-part textures, as the coordination (or lack thereof) among the parts, the equalization of the contrapuntal hierarchy, and the game of attraction and repulsion had become integral to his conceptualization of the idiom. This latter aspect was the cause of Schuppanzigh's woe. Left without any clearly accented beats to serve as signposts, his only recourse was to seek out his own auditory waypoints—an undertaking thwarted by the lack of a full score to provide a comprehensive visual overview. The ability to acquire such an overview, incidentally, is entirely unrelated to one's musical intelligence or powers of analysis; the lack of a score can only be compensated for by copious rehearsals and frequent opportunities to play through the work as a whole, both of which were in short supply.

Beethoven was well aware of this problem and therefore urged the publishers of the late quartets to issue not only the instrumental parts but also the full scores. Like many of Beethoven's innovations, this step was unconventional but necessary.

Having thus refamiliarized himself with the genre, less than six months later, in July 1825, Beethoven completed the String Quartet in A Minor (op. 132), the second of the three he had promised to Galitzin. We should also remember that for a four-week period in April and May, Beethoven was debilitated by serious gastrointestinal problems that prevented him from putting pen to paper. As already mentioned, Beethoven's doctor Anton Braunhofer had decided on a slow and steady approach, prescribing a strict diet that sorely tested Beethoven's patience and willpower. It was not until mid-May, when he was already in Baden with hopes of expediting his recovery, that Beethoven was able to resume his work. So relieved was he to see the end of his dietary asceticism that he composed an extended "Hymn of thanks from a convalescent to the deity, in the lydian mode," to serve as the centerpiece for his newest string quartet. The "hymn" comprises three chorale-like fragments in the old organ style, alternating with two animated, "more modern" interludes, which—according to Beethoven's notes in the score—express "a newfound strength." Beethoven's explicit decision to employ the Lydian mode was no mere flight of fancy: his extensive research on the old church modes had taught him that in earlier times the Lydian mode had been associated with feelings of comfort and consolation. The otherworldly ambience thus evoked is rich with sacred contemplation; in the conversation notebooks, both Karls (Holz and the nephew) report that Johann Wolfmayer—a wealthy clothing merchant and longtime, discreet supporter of Beethoven's—wept like a child on hearing the movement for the first time. Several pages later, nephew Karl also remarks that many listeners were astonished at Beethoven's ability to conjure up such variety using only the few notes of the Lydian mode.[15]

Despite also being dominated by its second movement, like its E-flat predecessor, the second Galitzin quartet shows the early signs of a stylistic evolution, one whose full scope would not become apparent until the completion of the later quartets, but whose beginnings are already discernible. The Quartet in A Minor consists no longer of the traditional four movements but of six (although depending on one's view of the final three movements, the figure could be reduced to five, or perhaps even four[16]). The work is a succession of what Beethoven himself termed "fragments," whose length and substance are no longer dictated by the preservation of internal mutual proportions but are instead allowed to develop freely in the facilitation of a narrative drama. The extreme discontinuity, stark contrasts, and many interruptions in the first movement are an early sign that Beethoven is exploring uncharted aesthetic waters. Tempi change without warning, and the music meanders freely between utter abstraction and rich, almost Schubertian lyricism.

Beethoven announced his completion of the String Quartet in A Minor on July 6, 1825, but Galitzin would not receive his copy until after New Year's Day 1826. While the intermittent postal connections between Vienna and St. Petersburg were partly to blame, a far more problematic factor was the convoluted procedure employed to ready the final manuscript for performance and delivery. The cellist, Linke, had been charged with the transcription of the instrumental parts on the presumption that his familiarity with Beethoven's music would enable him to decipher the master's all-but-illegible handwriting. Then, on the basis of Linke's fair copies, professional copyist Wenzel Rampl—the late Wenzel Schlemmer's successor—was to prepare two full scores: one for Galitzin, the other for the publisher. The waters were further muddied, of course, by the flashes of inspiration that always came to Beethoven while reviewing the proofs.

Karl Holz was to courier the only precious copy of the autograph manuscript from Baden to Vienna and back. Panic briefly ensued when he suddenly fell silent, prompting fears in Beethoven that he had somehow made off with the score. Nephew Karl was dispatched to make enquiries; he discovered that Linke had ceased work due to the headache of deciphering Beethoven's inscrutable handwriting, and that Holz—with the best of intentions—had taken over. His lack of transcription experience is what had caused the understandable delays and troubling lack of communication.

To ensure that the music contained no errors, both Karls advised Beethoven to arrange a private hearing to play the quartet through informally. There was an added bonus: the publisher Schlesinger junior had come to Vienna to negotiate Beethoven's latest quartet and would thus have an opportunity to hear the new work firsthand. Beethoven agreed to the session on the condition that it be held in the utmost secrecy, without any casual observers. Schlesinger's own room at Zum wilden Mann on Kärntnerstrasse was ultimately chosen as the venue, as the double-glazed windows offered additional sound insulation. And so, wedged between the table and the bed, a reinstated Schuppanzigh and his quartet gave two complete renditions of the work on two separate occasions, on September 9 and 11 (four times in total). Schlesinger was impressed, and he had Beethoven sign a contract then and there for the rights to both the Quartet in A Minor and the incipient Quartet in B-flat Major, laying half of the agreed fee (eighty ducats) on the table. The audience at the second session was slightly larger, and afterward (encouraged by the beautiful weather) the whole entourage went out to share a meal together. Beethoven was beside himself with joy, and after many a well-filled glass he sank down at the piano to charm the assembly with an improvisation—a rare treat that had not been heard in many years.

The official premiere was held on November 6, 1825. Because Schuppanzigh was not in Vienna at that time, Holz played the first violin part. By all accounts, the response was overwhelmingly positive.

The third of the Galitzin quartets, the String Quartet in B-flat Major (op. 130), took far longer to reach players and public, not least because of Beethoven's decision to break with all tradition and compose a gargantuan fugue as the quartet's final movement. Despite having started the work in May 1825 (while still preoccupied with the String Quartet in A Minor), he felt confident and made good progress, and the new quartet was ready before Christmas. By then it had grown into a six-part monstrosity, whose focus—unlike the previous two quartets—now lay in its fast-paced and complex outer movements. The four central sections they enclosed were pleasing and palatable to the ear: two brief, folklorish dances, a charming Andante (with the additional note by Beethoven, Poco scherzando), and a stunningly beautiful Cavatina. The two dances were well received, garnered immediate applause, and were played again; when Beethoven heard as much (after having waited out the performance in a neighboring café), he is reported to have sneered: "Of course, always the tasty delights. Why not the fugue?" Some sources claim that he followed up with: "Uncultured swine! Asses!"[17] Beethoven himself considered the Cavatina to be the work's crowning glory. Holz said that he had composed it in a mood of "plaintive melancholy," that never before had Beethoven's own music affected him so deeply, and that the very thought of the work brought tears to his eyes.[18]

The public's enthusiasm for the four central movements was thus easy to fathom and contrasted sharply with their incredulity at the surrounding material. The first movement indeed seems to make little sense, and for the first time the scholarly vocabulary commonly employed to discuss Beethoven's music falls short. This first movement alone is brimming with contrasts, and if the first repeat is included, counts no fewer than twenty tempo and mood changes. Although similar juxtapositions can certainly be found in earlier quartets, these are more easily associated with readily identifiable feelings: humor, cheerfulness, melancholy, or anguish. Opus 130, on the other hand, presents the listener with music of an anonymous, faceless, abstract, and occasionally even purely mechanical nature.

The same is even truer of the final movement, a colossal fugue whose architecture and duration—over fifteen minutes—trumps even the finale of the *Hammerklavier*. Though Schindler's assessment of the work warrants little consideration (he dubbed it "the monster of all quartet music"[19]), the opinion of Igor Stravinsky is far more interesting: "this absolutely contemporary piece of music that will be contemporary forever [. . .] It is pure interval music, this fugue, and I love it beyond any other."[20] Its modernity is largely attributable not only to its rhythmic complexity and extreme dissonance— the profound tonal dissociation of some sections presages developments in the twentieth century—but also to its structural ambiguity, which has prompted a decades-long musicological debate regarding the work's formal classification. Beethoven himself provided a hint by inscribing on the title page, "tantôt libre, tantôt recherchée" (partly free, partly studied). This appellation probably comes closest to describing the reality, for what Beethoven titled a "grande fugue" is in fact only 40 percent fugue; the rest is a virtuosic blend of sonata and variation form. It is nothing short of a masterpiece—an intellectual and emotive tour de force—in which Beethoven strives to transcend both the chaos of the opening movement and the beauty of the four central movements. What is more, the final fugue can easily be considered the exhilarating climax to the three Galitzin quartets as a set and perhaps even to Beethoven's entire compositional career.

Nineteenth-century audiences listened with different ears, of course. The *Allgemeine musikalische Zeitung* published a review of the Quartet in B-flat Major, in which the first five movements met with a mixture of appreciation ("the great composer, who, particularly in his earlier years, struggled to find moderation and direction, expresses himself here with brevity and succinctness") and criticism ("some sections are bizarre, jagged and capricious").[21] When reviewing the final movement, however, the critic mercilessly describes it as "utterly inscrutable, like Chinese." He follows up with a tirade of creative effrontery, launching such salvos as "Babylonian," "the chaotic tuning of an orchestra," and "music in which only Moroccans might revel." The criticism was tempered somewhat by the reviewer's final note: "the time may yet come when that which at first seemed shrouded in mists and confusion will reveal itself in forms both clear and pleasing."[22] The critic's ambiguity looks forward to the now widely accepted opinion that was initially put forward by music critic Theodor Helm, framing the *Grande Fugue* as a prime example of *Augenmusik,* or "music for the eyes": music that is meant to be studied and understood but not heard—let alone enjoyed.[23]

Publisher Mathias Artaria shared this opinion and feared that the bizarre finale might imperil sales of the Quartet in B-flat.[24] He found a valuable ally in Karl Holz, who had successfully won Beethoven's trust and was therefore the perfect person to try to talk Beethoven into composing an alternative final movement. Holz himself was already sympathetic to the cause, recalling only too well how the players had struggled to learn the *Grande Fugue.* (When Holz fell asleep in a restaurant after rehearsal one day, Schuppanzigh remarked to Beethoven, "The final movement has done him in." When Beethoven later enquired of Holz as to which part was so difficult, he replied, "All of it."[25])

Holz succeeded, and he recounted many years later how he brought Beethoven around with a wily combination of practical considerations and clever argumentation. The essence of his case, however, was simple: he believed that the *Grande Fugue* had so dwarfed Beethoven's extraordinary achievements in quartet writing up to that time that it deserved a life of its own, with a dedicated opus number.[26] Beethoven was receptive to the idea, and six months after the premiere of the Quartet in B-flat Major, having already completed the Quartet in F Major (op. 135) and—more importantly—while recovering in Gneixendorf from the tribulations of Karl's attempted suicide, Beethoven reconceptualized the finale and wrote an entirely new closing movement.

We will never know precisely what moved Beethoven to abandon his original idea. Some believe he capitulated for the money;[27] but the very thought that Beethoven could be brought to an intervention of such magnitude by a measly twelve ducats is highly doubtful. Equally unlikely is the theory that Beethoven, especially in the wake of his nephew's suicide drama, suddenly developed a sensitivity to public opinion, contradicting his long-held, firm belief that "they will appreciate it one day."[28] From what we know of Beethoven, there can only be one explanation: he came to the realization himself that his original concept—the fugal finale as a transcendental synthesis—simply did not work in practice. It is entirely possible that Beethoven became so carried away with the fugue's energy and thematic potential that he lost all sense of scale within the quartet as a whole, like an artist who, mid-painting, suddenly switches to thicker brushes and an altered perspective. Nor can it have escaped him that the sumptuous central movements, the Cavatina in particular, invariably lulled audiences into a state of tender fragility, which was all too easily shattered by the unrelenting, cataclysmic power of the final fugue. Such a harsh impact can surely never have been Beethoven's intention.

The alternative finale is clearly less about making an impact. The music maintains a greater compositional distance and carries undertones of reflection, catharsis, emotional detachment, and tender consolation. The influence on Beethoven of his work on the Quartet in F Major (op. 135) is readily apparent, although one might just as easily interpret the movement as a musical manifestation of Beethoven's mental state during troubled times. Despite its retrospective leanings, the new closing Allegro is by no means regressive—on the contrary, its outward simplicity belies a complex, barely audible yet rigorous structure and multilayered textures characteristic of Mahler. Occasionally, the movement even looks ahead to the brilliant, high-romantic sound of some Dvořák quartets. In this sense, the new finale—the last full movement that Beethoven would ever compose—was progressive in its own way.

Meanwhile the *Grande Fugue*—or the *Grosse Fuge,* as it is now more commonly known—was left to fend for itself and establish a reputation on its own merits. It was a slow process: the first public performance of it as a separate work took place in 1852, and records show that until 1875 it received only four performances throughout Europe.

KARL HOLZ, BEETHOVEN'S LAST CONFIDANT

Artaria's appointment of Karl Holz as mediator in the matter of the *Grosse Fuge* was a carefully considered strategic choice. As an archetypal second violinist (only on very rare occasions would Holz replace Schuppanzigh as leader), he was accustomed to being flexible and was well versed in the art of diplomacy and compromise. His loyalty was unquestioned—we need only remember how he leapt to Schuppanzigh's defense following the E-flat quartet debacle. He quickly earned Beethoven's trust and would scarcely leave his side during the composer's final years.

Holz had joined the Böhm quartet in 1821, and it was then that he and Beethoven first met. They developed closer ties when Holz became second violinist under Schuppanzigh in 1823, and their bond was further strengthened by the trauma of the String Quartet in E-flat two years later. It is also known that he paid a visit to Beethoven on April 2, 1825, to check tempi for the Fourth Symphony, which he was to conduct several days later for the Concerts Spirituels. After helping to prepare the score and parts for the Quartet in A Minor the following summer, he became Beethoven's go-to for the usual panoply of minor tasks and chores. And so it was that Holz took the place of Schindler, who had been unceremoniously shown the door one year earlier. Schindler never forgave Holz and took ample opportunity in his Beethoven biography to settle the score.

Beethoven treated Holz, unlike Schindler, as a true friend. He referred to him openly as such and regularly took him out to eat, once prompting nephew Karl to quip: "Holz is invited to lunch 365 days a year. And even when he is not invited, he invites himself."[29] Their closeness was facilitated to a large extent by Holz's broad intellectual and cultural interests—he could recite Schiller for hours—plus the fact that he shared Beethoven's sense of humor, which verged on the sarcastic. Remarks such as, "This city has bureaucracy, military, money and religion in spades, but not enough good sense," would always score well with Beethoven.[30] Holz was also a master wordsmith and the author of many ironic neologisms; his vocabulary included inventions such as "tonemasonry" (meaning "music"), "competitive musicianship" (for a "concert"), and "screechmetalworkers" (for "trumpet players"). Beethoven found his gems hilarious and insisted that their use be adopted and maintained by future generations.[31]

Holz's fondness for wine certainly did his friendship with Beethoven little harm. Of prime importance, however, was his competence as a musician and the fact that Beethoven could discuss compositional matters with him freely and openly. The conversation books are rich with detailed questions and observations on the interpretation of Beethoven's string quartets. Holz once remarked, for example, that the *Grosse Fuge* would be perfectly feasible if played at a slower tempo. A lively exchange sprang up regarding the String Quartet in C-sharp Minor (op. 131) on the issue of whether its seven movements should be played through without pause. Beethoven clearly answered in the affirmative, to which Holz responded, "But how shall we repeat movements during the concert?" and, "When can we retune?" He relaxed his position somewhat over the course of the discussion, eventually promising to order higher-quality strings and conceding that "the audience's chatter between movements is never that edifying anyway."[32] Although Beethoven remained adamant, the fact that he even considered an exchange of ideas provides a context for the weighty discussion surrounding the replacement of the *Grosse Fuge* and the role played therein by Holz.

It is interesting to note that Holz—a man whose technique and musicianship were sufficient not only to premiere the late string quartets (viewed by most experts as the nigh-unconquerable summit of Beethoven's entire oeuvre) but also to debate their merits with the composer himself—was not a professional musician. He earned his living as a public servant and practiced music alongside his work, or more accurately, "during" his work. He would often gloat that his official duties were so few, they could be completed within the hour; the remaining time was his to employ as he saw fit. Provided that he was physically present and kept himself adequately occupied, there was no problem.[33] Holz did add the justification that he was poorly paid and could not live from his salary alone, thus leaving him no choice but to give violin lessons. The practice was common enough at the time, and nobody thought anything of it.

Holz's social position was a clear sign that the fabric of society was changing. The young Beethoven had composed mainly for aristocrats, people who had not the slightest notion of what "work" entailed and who could dedicate vast quantities of their time to musical pursuits (in essence, all of their time was "free time"). By contrast, toward the end of his life Beethoven composed for members of the working populace who had enough spare time to practice music to a high standard. (Holz once expressed a fear that a potential marriage might present a greater obstacle than his job to "continuing to serve music as a worthy acolyte."[34])

Whatever the case, Holz took maximum advantage of his social status to be of service to Beethoven. He was the last in a long line of kind souls who—sometimes officially, occasionally unsolicited, but usually with the best of intentions—helped Beethoven to cope with the tedious practicalities of life as a composer: Beethoven's brother Kaspar Karl, then Ferdinand Ries, Nikolaus Zmeskall, Ignaz Gleichenstein, Franz Oliva, Nannette Streicher, the other brother Johann, nephew Karl, and Anton Schindler. This cavalcade of assistants is symbolic of Beethoven's restlessness in his ongoing search for security. The other lists—of love interests, doctors, publishers, and addresses—further reinforce this impression of vulnerability and mental instability.

"MUST IT BE? IT MUST BE!"

Long before the final notes of the String Quartet in B-flat (op. 130) were on paper and the Galitzin commission was complete, Beethoven had already resolved to write at least one more string quartet—a surprising development in light of his existing plans to compose several other major works, including a tenth symphony, an oratorio, and perhaps even an opera. His extended sojourn in the quartet genre was attributable in part to a set of banal material circumstances and publishing deals. In September 1825, Beethoven had promised the Schlesingers two quartets: the first, the Quartet in A Minor, had been delivered as agreed, but the second, the Quartet in B-flat Major, had been sold to Mathias Artaria to keep the Viennese pot boiling. Beethoven was thus obliged to produce another quartet, which was to be the Quartet in C-sharp Minor (op. 131). On its completion, however, Beethoven could not resist the temptation to sell it to Schott in Mainz, as gratitude for the publisher's efforts surrounding the *Missa solemnis* and the Ninth Symphony. In so doing, Beethoven thus committed himself to writing at least one more quartet, the String Quartet in F Major (op. 135).

Other considerations were certainly at play. In the preceding years, an enormous demand for new chamber music had arisen thanks to the growing league of semiprofessional musicians such as Holz; Schlesinger believed that Beethoven could earn far more by focusing on chamber music rather than large symphonic works. At one time, Schlesinger had expressed a wish to publish three quartets and as many quintets by Beethoven, to serve as a vehicle for a complete edition of his chamber music. Other publishers, too, came knocking at Beethoven's door. This popularity challenges somewhat the traditional view that Beethoven, following the overwhelming success of the Ninth Symphony, retired from public view to concentrate solely on cerebral works for his own enjoyment.

Holz presents yet another potentially significant artistic argument for why, after the quartets in E-flat major (op. 127), A minor (op. 132), and B-flat major (op. 130), Beethoven felt the need to compose two more works in the genre. While Beethoven was working on the three Galitzin quartets, Holz tells of how he was inundated by a ceaseless stream of wonderful but unusable ideas, which called for an alternative outlet. Beethoven would interject: "Good fellow, inspiration has struck again! [...] But it will need to wait until the next quartet—the current one already has too many movements."[35] Seen in this light, the compulsion that Beethoven felt to compose two more string quartets after finishing the three for Galitzin seems analogous to the genesis of the Sixth and Eighth symphonies, which served as repositories for the overflow of ideas from the Fifth and the Seventh.

The Quartet in C-sharp Minor does indeed differ markedly from its previous siblings, particularly in its treatment of continuity and discontinuity. Although there are officially seven movements, all sources suggest that the numbering—which was not present in the original manuscript but added later by Beethoven—was motivated by practical rather than artistic considerations. The quartet is essentially a concatenated stream of fragments of varying lengths, whose transitions are so seamless that they no longer audibly parse as separate movements. The form's hierarchical elements blend into one another, making the contrasts *between* the movements barely distinguishable from those *within* the movements. The result is an ingenious series of overlapping longer and shorter episodes, whose interplay seems simultaneously both deliberate and desultory. The quartet thus comes across as a forty-minute-long improvisation, but one without a trace of the arbitrary. As with the late piano sonatas, Beethoven's ultimate freedom of expression was born from a complete mastery of the idiom. He made no fewer than six hundred pages' worth of sketches for the Quartet in C-sharp Minor, testifying to a deliberate attempt to establish all of the motivic and underlying interrelationships from the very outset.[36] It was precisely this degree of rational control that allowed for Beethoven's now seemingly unbridled surrender to the power of his imagination, and which may very well account for his appraisal of the Quartet in C-sharp Minor as the greatest he ever wrote.

A hearing of the String Quartet in F Major (op. 135) is enough to remind us that it was composed, for the most part, in the dramatic wake of Karl's attempted suicide. It was a time when Beethoven was forced to bid an emotional and rational farewell to the long-cherished relationship with his adoptive son, an ordeal that also released him from his pathological obsession with that very same relationship. Today the quartet's reputation is dominated by its place as both the final work in a set of five and Beethoven's last major composition (it is succeeded only by the alternative finale to the Quartet in B-flat Major and the aptly titled canon "Wir irren allesamt" (We all make mistakes; WoO 198). These observations, too, color our impressions of the F-major quartet. But despite the near certainty that Beethoven would have gone on to compose other works if his health had not deteriorated (such as the string quartet he had already started for Schlesinger), the impression that he succumbed to a profound exhaustion—even resignation—is difficult to shake. In a letter to Schlesinger dated October 30, 1826, he confessed that his final quartet, and the last movement especially, had been an arduous undertaking. But he ultimately succeeded, spurred along by several reminders from Schlesinger and his own financial need. The letter continues with an extended lament on the lack of any experienced copyists in Gneixendorf, obliging him to complete the laborious and time-consuming transcription work himself.[37] When he was finished, Beethoven added the telling superscript to the final movement: "The Difficult Decision—Must it be?—It must be!"

Both the above-mentioned letter and the inscription might be read as an apology for the limited scope of the final quartet and possibly even for a seeming lack of inspiration. At a little over twenty minutes, the Quartet in F Major is barely half the length of the previous three—and it would have been even shorter had Schlesinger not talked Beethoven out of his plan to compose only three movements instead of four.[38] The dimensions of the F-major quartet are therefore closer to those of Beethoven's initial explorations in the genre, and closer still to those of Haydn and Mozart. The latter association in particular has prompted some commentators to place it in the neoclassical basket as a kind of "homage," eliciting immediate connotations of a "return," a "retrospective," and of "reconciliation with the past." In one fell swoop, the quartet cycle is thus deemed complete.

These commentators forget, however, that the F-major quartet is brimming with exuberant devices that were foreign to music of the eighteenth century, such as sudden interruptions, forceful tremolos, and frenzied repetitions. Yet more radical are Beethoven's explorations at the opposite end of the expressive spectrum where he pares down the melody and harmony in a typically romantic fashion, not to mention his flouting of formal classical conventions. His decision to leave the final repeat up to the players' discretion, with the express instruction "si repete la seconda parte al suo piacere" (second part to be repeated ad libitum), demonstrates an unprecedented level of structural relativism.

But is "relativism" not the very essence of this final movement? How else should we interpret Beethoven's preface to it, expressed in the form of two musical motifs?[39]

The Difficult Decision

There is a simple explanation. From the semantic relationship between the two motifs—the rising question and falling answer—it would seem obvious to resolve the dispute in the affirmative. In reality, nothing could be further from the truth: after a sonata-form movement (and a rather terse one by Beethoven's standards), a coda presents the "answer" motif as a series of tentative fermatas, lending it an unstable, searching quality. These musings are followed by a quirky pizzicato passage in all the parts, invoking a distinctly ironic character. Beethoven thus answers his own profound, almost existential question, with what seems like a musical wink.

The F-major quartet marks the end of a two-and-a-half-year compositional undertaking in which Beethoven, beset by grueling circumstances, devoted himself exclusively to this most highly demanding genre of chamber music. While the five quartets are all certainly independent works, it is very tempting to seek an underlying logic between them. One common approach is to view the three Galitzin quartets—crowned by the *Grosse Fuge*—as the foundation of the set, and the other two as commentaries of varying scope. This classification is consistent with the quartets' chronology and history but enters shaky territory once the *Grosse Fuge* is discounted and replaced by the alternative finale, which was composed later. For this reason, some musicologists instead group the quartets into pairs based on their structure: E-flat Major is coupled with A Minor (owing to their similarly weighty slow movements), and B-flat Major with C-sharp Minor (due to their numerous sections and more elaborate outer movements). Under this model, the Quartet in F Major becomes a counterbalancing "macrocoda."[40] Still others see the quartets in A Minor, B-flat Major, and C-sharp Minor as the heart of the entire cycle,[41] an arrangement supported by Beethoven's use of the same four-note motif in each:

(op. 132)

(op. 130)

(op. 131)

This theory puts the climax of the set in the fourth quartet (in C-sharp), recasting the first and last quartets as prelude and epilogue, respectively.

Such intellectual musings are worthwhile, as they show us that answers can be simultaneously right and wrong, and that there are many overlapping gray areas. It is precisely the music's inherently ambiguous nature that gives rise to such disparate opinions among musicologists regarding their form. But does it even matter? The logic governing the musical material exists, after all, on a subplane so far removed from auditory experience—at the level of the subconscious and unconscious—that it loses virtually all relevance to any aesthetic judgment. Listeners to Beethoven's late string quartets are forced, even more so than by the late piano sonatas, to abandon all notion of space, time, and hence of form, and to surrender to the purely emotive qualities of the music. At the end of a journey spanning almost fifty years, in which he first struggled to channel and control his imagination before setting it free once more, Beethoven finally brought audiences to the point of dissociation between musical thought and feeling, between materialism and spirituality. It is here at this existential brink that all rationality, argument, and reason fail.

_____

59

Comoedia finita est

THE RETURN JOURNEY FROM GNEIXENDORF left Beethoven extremely ill. His fragile constitution was sorely tested by the dreadful weather, the discomfort of the open carriage, and the virtually medieval conditions in which he spent the night. Valuable time was subsequently lost on the search for a competent doctor, for which (as mentioned previously) Schindler held Karl responsible. In reality, it was an unfortunate series of events that led to Beethoven's treatment being delayed until December 5, three days after his return to Vienna. Doctors Braunhofer and Von Staudenheim were both approached but made paltry excuses; the former in particular, it was later said, did everything in his power to avoid any and all association with the imminent death of his world-famous patient. Another doctor, Dominik von Vivenot, was himself ill, and so the choice fell to Professor Wawruch, who lived only a few streets away. Having never met Wawruch, Beethoven was initially wary, and it took all of Karl Holz's powers of persuasion to bring Beethoven around. It was to mark this occasion that Beethoven produced the final piece of music he would ever write: a canon on the fitting text, "Wir irren allesamt" (We all make mistakes).

Wawruch was a lover of music and a passionate cellist. On his first visit to the terminally ill Beethoven, he wrote piously in the conversation notebook, "A great admirer of your name shall do his utmost to bring rapid relief."[1] Wawruch was shocked at the pitiful condition in which he found his idol. The report on Beethoven's final days, published by Wawruch in 1842, stated that Beethoven had a fever, was coughing up blood, showed signs of asphyxiation, and could lie only on his back due to the pain in his left side. But while Wawruch's principal diagnosis mentioned only severe pneumonia, his questions to Beethoven confirm underlying suspicions that there was more at play. The prescribed anti-inflammatory treatment was effective, however, and after several days Beethoven could sit up again and even work a little. Alas, his rejuvenation was short-lived, and one week later Wawruch returned to find his patient in a worrying state. He was jaundiced, with a wraithlike appearance due to extreme vomiting, and complained of pain in his liver and lower abdomen. Wawruch suspected that the condition had been triggered by a fit of uncontrolled emotion, most likely anger (in Wawruch's own words, "frustration due to ingratitude and unjust recriminations"). It is tempting to speculate about potential emotional incidents around that time, concerning Karl in particular. Yet the real answer may not call for such far-flung theories; although Beethoven had bested the pneumonia, his bruised and battered body had paid a high price, which is perhaps what allowed his chronic but dormant liver condition to suddenly become acute. The result, in any case, was "ascites," or an abnormal buildup of fluid in the abdomen and feet.[2]

The underlying cause of the ascites could not be combated, and so treatment focused on improving Beethoven's overall well-being and quality of life. In practice this boiled down to performing a regular "paracentesis," a grisly procedure whereby the abdomen is punctured with a needle and a drain inserted to allow large quantities of fluid to escape. This "dirty work" was, of course, not performed by doctors themselves but instead by so-called *Wundärzte,* or "wound doctors": the surgeons of their day, but in reality of a lesser order than the doctors they served. In Beethoven's case, a certain Dr. (!) Seibert was summoned, who was head of the nursing staff at the Vienna General Hospital and had some experience with paracenteses. It was also he who visited Beethoven daily to clean his wounds and change the dressings.

The first abdominal puncture was made on December 20, 1826. Beethoven was extremely apprehensive, but once he heard that the procedure had also been recommended by Dr. Staudenheim, he was reassured and gave his consent. Just as Seibert was about to make the incision, Beethoven reportedly cried out, "Herr Professor, you remind me of Moses with his staff, poised to extract the water from the rocks!"[3]

An assembly had gathered to observe the procedure: Beethoven's brother Johann (who had hastened to Vienna from Gneixendorf), nephew Karl, and ... Anton Schindler. In the preceding weeks, Schindler had managed to worm his way back into Beethoven's circle by making use of the partial vacuum created by Karl Holz's recent marriage. (While Holz's availability had become limited, he still remained Beethoven's right-hand man, particularly when it came to money matters.)

It should be said that Beethoven suffered no lack of support or comfort during this difficult period. In addition to those named above, Stephan Breuning also made frequent visits. When his own health prevented him from coming (he would die only several months after Beethoven), he sent his son Gerard, who would bring tasty treats and cheer the patient up with the latest news from the city.[4] Johann Pasqualati was another frequent contributor; Beethoven's final few months of correspondence mention how Pasqualati brought him many delicacies, including champagne and peach or cherry compote.

Once word had reached town of Beethoven's deteriorating condition, many of those from outside Beethoven's intimate circle also felt the need to visit: officially to wish the master a speedy recovery but in reality to say their final farewells. The conversation books list the names of Karl Bernard, Franz Clement, Anton Diabelli, Ignaz Gleichenstein, Tobias Haslinger, Moritz Lichnowsky, Ferdinand Piringer, Ignaz Schuppanzigh, and Andreas Streicher, as well as fellow composers Schubert and Hummel. The latter, it seems, visited Beethoven at least three times, once in the company of his young wife, to the old master's great delight.

When the Friends of Music Society eventually heard that Beethoven's days were numbered, the institution sent him a certificate of honorary membership on March 7, 1827. This gesture galls somewhat on the realization that the decision to do so was taken over a year before, on January 31, 1826, and that the signed certificate had been lying around since October 26. It is also doubtful whether Beethoven particularly valued the all-but-posthumous honor.

One gift that did give him comfort and solace, however, arrived from London on January 5, 1827: a large package containing an edition of the complete works of Handel. Two and a half years earlier, Beethoven had made the acquaintance of Johann Andreas Stumpff, a German harp maker living in England. Stumpff was particularly struck by Beethoven's great admiration for Handel, and when he heard that Beethoven had not the financial means to acquire a copy of the opera omnia himself, Stumpff offered to do what he could. By all accounts, Beethoven was overjoyed with the gift, and Gerhard Breuning later described Beethoven's childlike giddiness when showing off the complete edition's forty volumes to him. According to Breuning, Beethoven had long yearned for a copy, since he revered Handel above all other composers as a source of endless inspiration and learning. After asking Gerhard to lay the scores on his bed, he proceeded to leaf through them one by one, pausing here and there to admire certain passages. Even days later, the pile of scores was never beyond arm's reach. Beethoven seems to have been quite effusive regarding the edition, as on January 27 an article appeared in the *Wiener Zeitschrift für Kunst, Literatur, Theater und Mode* titled "Complete works of Händel delivered to Beethoven as a gift."[5]

As expected, the operation on December 20 brought only temporary relief, and a reprise was necessary on January 8, 1827. Almost equally predictable was Beethoven's dissatisfaction with his new doctor. Spurred on by Schindler (who for reasons unknown simply could not get along with Wawruch), Beethoven insisted on a replacement. A crisis meeting was held on January 11, 1827, with the goal of instating Dr. Malfatti; the doctor's response was rather muted, however. Although his official argument was an unwillingness to undermine the treatment already administered by his colleague ("Tell Beethoven that as a master of harmony, he will realise that I must also live in harmony with my colleagues"[6]), the real reason for keeping his distance were his prior unpleasant experiences with Beethoven as a patient from over ten years before. He now limited his assistance to occasional advice and sporadic visits.

Nevertheless, Wawruch and Malfatti did consult together and jointly decided to switch to a palliative strategy. According to Wawruch, it was Malfatti's idea, "given Beethoven's predilection for alcohol," to serve him regular glasses of ice-cold punch.[7] Beethoven offered no protest. One other "medicine" in particular earned his approval: to prevent dehydration, Beethoven was advised to observe a low-sodium diet and to drink plenty of diuretics (substances that promote urination). These included floral teas, almond milk, soup made from parsley or celery, and—to Beethoven's great joy—white wine from the Rhineland and Austria. From that moment on, all correspondence between the greatest composer of his day and the publisher of his finest works (the Schott brothers in Mainz) was dedicated to the sourcing of white wine from the Rhineland and Moselle regions.[8] From other letters and the conversation notebooks, we can glean that Beethoven made do with Austrian wine in the meantime, although opinions concerning its medicinal qualities were divided. While some placed their faith in an aged Gumpoldskirchner, others recommended Grinzinger, while Johann swore by a good Gneixendorfer. And any guests who brought wines of various other origins or quality (such as Hungarian or Swabian wines) were, of course, never turned away. Lastly, Beethoven wrote that he also enjoyed a crisp pint now and again, a Hornerbier from Lower Austria. The end clearly justified any available means.

The medicinal effect was, in any case, immediate. Wawruch reported that Beethoven slept better and his spirits lifted; he returned to making his witty remarks and cherished notions of returning to work soon. But several days later, Wawruch was forced to concede that the beneficial effects of the "treatment" were fading, for in his boundless enthusiasm, Beethoven had far exceeded the prescribed "dosage" and the negative side effects became pronounced. Alcohol increases blood flow to the brain, and Beethoven became prone to drowsiness, drunken snoring, and incoherent speech. Sometimes his throat became so inflamed that his voice turned hoarse or abandoned him altogether. Wawruch's notes say that Beethoven became unmanageable, and once colic and diarrhea had joined the list of symptoms, another intervention was planned.

Any attempts to persuade Beethoven to moderate his intake were abandoned after the fourth operation on February 27, when it became obvious—not least to Beethoven himself—that the situation was dire and that the only remaining option was to alleviate Beethoven's suffering as much as possible.

The final puncture must have been a gruesome sight indeed. Reports say that on insertion of the drain, a foul substance spurted forth, reaching the middle of the room and so drenching the bedsheets that an oilcloth was spread over the mattress. The amount of pus seeping from the wound between punctures had increased, making it difficult to keep the dressings dry. The wound itself was also ulcerating, despite the presumed application of lead poultices.[9]

Beethoven's condition deteriorated rapidly thereafter. The young composer and conductor Ferdinand Hiller later told of how he and his teacher, Hummel, visited Beethoven one last time on March 23. Hiller describes a pitiful sight, how Beethoven lay devoid of strength, silent and motionless, emitting only the occasional grunt or groan. The sweat beaded on his forehead, and Hiller said that he would never forget Beethoven's grateful expression when Mrs. Hummel gently dabbed his face with her fine batiste handkerchief.[10]

Now that everybody was expecting the worst, Wawruch felt that it was time for his terminal patient to "fulfil his final duties as a citizen and a Christian."[11] Beethoven's loved ones—led by his brother Johann, Schindler, and the Breunings senior and junior—first had Beethoven sign a codicil to his former will and testament from January 3. The preceding months had seen several heated discussions regarding the precise construction via which Karl should receive his inheritance, prompted by fears that Karl—should he receive the entire amount as a lump sum—would immediately either squander everything or divert some of it to his mother. The various parties settled on a compromise: the capital would be frozen and only made accessible to the "next generation," while Karl's portion would be limited to a monthly interest payment.[12] A lucid Beethoven—who knew his family only too well—ultimately insisted on a sufficiently broad definition of the term "next generation"; while the codicil initially stipulated that the liquid assets go to Karl's "lawful heirs," in the final version this phrase was replaced expressly with "natural or testamentary heirs."[13]

It is nonetheless very symbolic that Beethoven's very last signature was placed on a document that, while intended to support his nephew, simultaneously hamstrung him financially. By all indications, Beethoven had great difficulty gripping the quill, and when writing his name, he forgot the second *e* and the *h*.

On the following day, the twenty-fourth of March, a second critical matter was resolved: a priest was summoned to Beethoven's bedside to administer his last rites. In a letter to Schott several weeks later, Schindler wrote, "Our last remaining wish was to reconcile Beethoven with heaven, and in so doing, to show the world that he ended his life as a true Christian."[14] Beethoven, who for his whole life had known God but not religion and had generally always looked on the church and its representatives with some disdain, is said to have agreed to the ceremony. Once the priest had left the room, Beethoven uttered the now famous phrase *"Plaudite amici, comoedia finita est!* [Applaud, friends, the comedy is over!] Did I not always say it would end like this?"[15]

Beethoven's utterance was a paraphrase of the final words of Emperor Octavius Augustus. The witnesses to this piece of "theater"—so vividly recounted by Schindler—were not quite sure how to take it. Gerhard Breuning, one of those present, attributed the quip to Beethoven's "beloved, sarcastic sense of humour."[16] Precisely which "comedy" he was referring to is still the subject of some debate. To be on the safe side, Gerhard Breuning also asserted that Beethoven was far from the mocker of the church that he was often made out to be.[17]

Several hours later, a servant entered the room bearing a crate of the finest Rüdesheimer wine (from 1806—an excellent vintage) that had just arrived from Mainz. When Schindler placed two bottles on the bedside table, Beethoven turned to them and uttered his final words: "Pity!—pity!—too late!"[18] A spoon was used to help him sample some of the ambrosial fluid, but those few drops were all he managed to consume, as he fell into a coma that same evening.[19]

Vienna, Monday, March 26, 1827. Beethoven has now been unconscious for two days. He survived a perilous night, much to the surprise of his doctor, Professor Wawruch. Over the course of the day, his breathing has grown ever shallower and more unstable, and it seems unlikely that he will last until nightfall. For the past few days, his closest friends have taken turns to keep a strict vigil at his bedside. Now, however, they are all gathered around him: his brother Johann, the Breunings senior and junior, and Schindler. There is also a woman present whose identity cannot be ascertained; some believe it was Johann's wife, Therese, while others propose that it was Karl's mother, Johanna. Because both hypotheses raise some embarrassing questions, many simply assume that it was Beethoven's housekeeper, Sali. In any case, we might consider it highly symbolic that the only woman present at Beethoven's bedside during his final moments remains faceless.

Some time later, another musician arrives, Anselm Hüttenbrenner. He has made a special trip from Graz and is accompanied by the young artist Joseph Teltscher, who proceeds to make several extremely unflattering sketches of the dying master. Stephan Breuning finds his morbid preoccupation unbearable and begs him to stop. Meanwhile, Johann begins rifling through Beethoven's possessions in search of bank certificates, and what remains of the payments from the London Philharmonic Society. The others are outraged and throw him out.

Stephan Breuning and Schindler are the next to depart; they head to Währing cemetery to select a plot for Beethoven's final resting place. Shortly after five o'clock, the young Gerhard Breuning also leaves to keep an appointment at school. The only two remaining are Hüttenbrenner and the unknown woman. By now, masses of dark clouds have gathered and cast their ominous shadows onto the city below. An unexpected storm breaks: snow and hail gush down, a crash of thunder is heard, and a bolt of lightning throws the chamber into stark relief. Beethoven's eyelids suddenly fly open. He lifts himself up, raises his clenched right fist in a display of rage and defiance—and then collapses. His eyes seem to glaze over. Hüttenbrenner offers support with his right arm and tries to assist Beethoven's breathing with his left—but to no avail. The breath is gone from the master's lips, and his heart has stopped. Hüttenbrenner closes Beethoven's eyelids, and kisses his forehead, eyes, mouth, and hands. Then he looks at his watch: it is a quarter to six.[20]

ACKNOWLEDGMENTS

A biography will always remain a work in progress, as advances in scholarship, feedback from readers, and the author's own increasing understanding all contribute to an ongoing need to update and refine the existing narrative. The Beethoven anniversary celebrations in 2020—ten years after this book first appeared in print—offer the ideal opportunity to produce a revised edition of this biography of Beethoven. But the book's first loyal readers should have no fear: they will be pleased to know that the structure, content, and style of the original have all been preserved.

I remain thankful nonetheless to the great many people who, each in their own way, helped me to produce the first edition of this book over ten years ago: Beethoven scholars Dr. Hans-Werner Küthen, Dr. Anja Mühlenweg, and in particular Dr. Rita Steblin, who generously shared with me her (then unpublished) findings surrounding the riddle of the "immortal beloved." I am also indebted to Professor Herman Van der Wee, Professor Jan Roegiers, and Dr. Sus Herbosch for their respective and indispensable contributions in the fields of economics, history, and medicine. I have very fond memories of the expertise, dedication, and exemplary judgment shown by Leonoor Broeder, my coach and editor from the very beginning, as well as the many conversations with Dutch Beethoven specialist Jos van der Zanden, who thoroughly studied the manuscript and shared his scholarly insights in the spirit of unconditional collegiality.

Special gratitude must go to the entire team at the Beethoven-Haus in Bonn for their warmth and generosity in welcoming me into their fold. First, I wish to thank the institute's director, Malte Boecker, whose substantial efforts opened the doors not only to the Beethoven world, but also to the world at large. I am indebted to the director of the musicology department, Professor Christiane Siegert, for her profound and critical scrutiny of the book's every detail, as well as to Dr. Julia Ronge and Dr. Beate Angelika Kraus for generously sharing their vast Beethoven expertise on many occasions. I would be remiss if I did not acknowledge the many other helpful colleagues from the Beethoven-Haus, who are too numerous to name here.

My gratefulness also extends to the German and English translators of the book, Andreas Ecke and Brent Annable, for their critical approach to the text and many valuable suggestions.

I remain obliged to the many performers in whose company I have forged a path through the great master's oeuvre over the previous decades, and whose insights and experiences have aided in the formation of my own artistic vision. This list of musical comrades is long; still, I would like to make special mention of Kristian Bezuidenhout, Frank Braley, Till Fellner, Johannes Leertouwer, Alexander Melnikow, Christian Zacharias, and Thomas Zehetmair.

Regarding the English edition, my sincere thanks go to Alexandra von Schroeter (née Wegeler) and Felix Wegeler for the generous manner in which they made this translation possible, and to Dr. Barbara von Bechtolsheim, whose enthusiasm for my book paved the way to America. I also wish to thank Raina Polivka and the entire team at University of California Press for their dedication and expertise in facilitating the production of this edition, along with Flanders Literature for their crucial assistance in making the translation a reality.

As in the first edition of my Beethoven biography, my final acknowledgment is reserved for all those who have shown me invaluable support in myriad ways over the previous years. I cannot possibly name them all here, but those I am talking about know only too well how much their devoted friendship means to me. Lastly, my greatest thanks go to my wife, Inez, and my sons, Vincent and Leonard, for their acceptance of how Beethoven dominates not only my existence but also theirs, and for the life we lead together as a team.

NOTES

AmZ   *Allgemeine musikalische Zeitung,* Leipzig, 1798/99–1865.

BBr   *Ludwig van Beethoven: Briefwechsel* [correspondence], Gesamtausgabe [complete edition], ed. Sieghard Brandenburg, 7 vols., Munich, 1996–98.

BBS   *Bonner Beethoven-Studien,* Veröffentlichungen [publications] des Beethoven-Hauses, series 5, Bonn, 1999–.

BF   *Beethoven Forum,* Urbana, IL, and Lincoln, NE, 1992–.

BJ   *The Beethoven Journal,* San José, CA, 1995–. (Previously *The Beethoven Newsletter,* 1986–1994).

BKh   *Ludwig van Beethovens Konversationshefte* [conversation books], ed. Karl-Heinz Köhler, Grita Herre, Dagmar Beck, and Günter Brosche, 11 vols., Leipzig, 1968–2001.

BLex   *Das Beethoven-Lexikon,* ed. Heinz von Loesch and Claus Raab, Laaber, 2008.

BLuW   *Ludwig van Beethoven: Leben und Werk in Zeugnissen* [testimonies] *der Zeit,* ed. Robbins H. C. Landon, Zurich, 1994 (1970).

BSZ   *Beethoven aus der Sicht seiner Zeitgenossen in Tagebüchern, Briefen, Gedichten und Erinnerungen,* ed. Klaus Martin Kopitz and Rainer Cadenbach, 2 vols., Munich, 2009.

BTb   *Beethovens Tagebuch 1812–1818,* ed. Maynard Solomon, Bonn, 1990/2005.

TDR   Alexander Wheelock Thayer, *Ludwig van Beethovens Leben,* ed. Hermann Deiters (1901) and Hugo Riemann, 2 vols., Leipzig, 1917.

TF   Alexander Wheelock Thayer, *Thayer's Life of Beethoven,* 1866, ed. Elliot Forbes, Princeton, NJ, 1967.

WR   Franz Gerhard Wegeler and Ferdinand Ries, *Biographische Notizen über Ludwig van Beethoven,* Coblenz, 1838.

PROLOGUE

1. *BLuW,* 236–37.
2. Ibid., 234.
3. Egon Friedell, *Kulturgeschichte der Neuzeit,* Munich, 1976 (1927–31), 29.
4. In a rather unflattering portrait of Schindler that appeared in the Augsburger *Allgemeine Zeitung* on April 29, 1841, Heinrich Heine claimed that Schindler distributed name cards bearing the text "Ami de Beethoven" (cited in Peter Clive, *Beethoven and His World: A Biographical Dictionary,* Oxford, 2001, 314).
5. For a more detailed account of these events, see Alan Tyson, "Ferdinand Ries (1784–1838): The History of His Contribution to Beethoven Biography," in *19th-Century Music* 7, no. 3 (1984): 209–21.
6. Anton Schindler, "Für Beethovens Verehrer," in *Kölnische Zeitung,* no. 280. (Dagmar Beck and Grita Herre, "Anton Schindlers fingierte Eintragungen in de Konversationsheften," in *Zu Beethoven: Aufsätze und Annotationen,* ed. Harry Goldschmidt, Berlin, 1979, 13.)
7. *BKh,* 6: 125.

1. LOUIS VAN BEETHOVEN

1. Jansenism was a seventeenth- and eighteenth-century religious and political movement that arose primarily in France in response to certain developments in the Catholic Church and the absolutism of the ruling classes.
2. Cf. Max Braubach, Kurköln, *Gestalten und Ereignisse aus zwei Jahrhunderten rheinischer Geschichte,* Münster, 1949, 296.
3. Cf. Claus Canisius, *Beethoven: "Sehnsucht und Unruhe in der Musik." Aspekte zu Leben und Werk,* Munich, 1992, 25.
4. Cf. TDR, 1: 25.
5. Cf. Maynard Solomon, "Economic Circumstances of the Beethoven Household in Bonn," *Journal of the American Musicological Society* 50 (1997): 331–51.

2. JEAN VAN BEETHOVEN

1. German Beethoven biographers have universally Germanized the name "Jean Van Beethoven" into "Johann van Beethoven." But because he went by "Jean" his entire life and since it was the name used on all official documents, this book will refer to Beethoven's father by the original name given to him in Mechelen.
2. Cf. Canisius, *Beethoven,* 28.
3. Jean van Beethoven's alcoholism must be viewed within the proper context. Wine consumption was extremely high in eighteenth-century Rhineland since wine was a far healthier alternative to beer and safer than drinking the polluted water.

Many of Jean van Beethoven's colleagues also seem to have teetered on the brink of controlled wine consumption. A report on the Kapelle from 1784 includes negative remarks on nearly half of the members—the voices of four of the eleven singers were described as "poor" and "worn out."

4. Cited by Klaus Kropfinger, "Beethoven," in *Die Musik in Geschichte und Gegenwart, Personenteil,* 2, Kassel, 2001, column 693.

5. Canisius, *Beethoven,* 30–32.

6. Cf. ibid., 129–36.

7. *BBr,* no. 2236.

3. THE EARLY YEARS

1. Beethoven biographer Maynard Solomon offers an extensive psychoanalytical commentary on the fact that Jean van Beethoven's first child, who was born in April 1769 but died a week later, was also named Ludwig, and on the pressures suffered by a young boy going through life bearing the name of a previously deceased sibling. According to Solomon, Beethoven felt an overwhelming guilt at having "appropriated" his elder brother's identity, and had internalized the obligation to posthumously fulfill the ruined expectations of his former brother's life, of which Beethoven himself had constructed an idealized view. Solomon uses the term "imaginary companion" (Maynard Solomon, "The Posthumous Life of Ludwig Maria van Beethoven," in *Beethoven Essays,* Cambridge, MA, 1988, 77–92). Solomon's hypothesis is, however, a twentieth-century interpretation that is by no means applicable within the context of an eighteenth-century family.

2. Beethoven himself was never completely sure of his own birth date. In the Rhineland area, as in Austria and other states of Germany, birthdays were celebrated not on one's date of birth but on one's religious name day.

3. Contemporary Bonn's Bonngasse 20, where the Beethoven-Haus museum stands today.

4. Cited by Margot Wetzstein, ed., *Familie Beethoven im Kurfürstlichen Bonn,* Bonn, 77–92.

5. According to the testimony of Bonn cellist Bernhard Mäurer: "Aside from music, he [Beethoven] understood nothing of social life. He was thus often ill-tempered when in company, did not know how to converse properly, and withdrew into himself. He sometimes seemed a misanthrope" (cited by Frederik Kerst, ed., *Die Erinnerungen an Beethoven,* Stuttgart, 1913, 1: 10–11).

6. Cited by Wetzstein, *Familie Beethoven im kurfürstlichen Bonn,* 41.

7. Ibid., 99.

8. Beethoven's opportunity to practice on a clavichord was extremely important for his musical development. In the late eighteenth century it was generally accepted that playing on a harpsichord, while beneficial to dexterity, was bad for musicality. The clavichord offered a broader range of nuance, which encouraged more expressive

and imaginative playing. At the time, the Beethovens were in no financial position to obtain a more modern pianoforte (Tilman Skowroneck, "The Keyboard Instruments of the Young Beethoven," in *Beethoven and His World*, ed. Scott Burnham and Michael P. Steinberg, Princeton, NJ, 2000, 155).

9. Maynard Solomon, *Beethoven*, Frankfurt am Main, 1987, 22.

10. Thomas Mann, *Die Entstehung des Doktor Faustus*, Frankfurt am Main, 1949, 189.

11. *BBr*, no. 59.

12. Ludwig Schiedermair, *Der junge Beethoven*, Hildesheim–New York, 1978 (1925), 130; and *BLuW*, 26.

13. Cited in Wetzstein, *Familie Beethoven im kurfürstlichen Bonn*, 118.

14. Max Braubach, "Die Mitglieder der Hofmusik unter den vier letzten Kurfürsten von Köln," in *Colloquium Amicorum, Joseph Schmidt-Görg zum 70. Geburtstag*, ed. Siegfried Kross and Hans Schmidt, Bonn, 1967, 48.

4. CHRISTIAN GOTTLOB NEEFE

1. For a more comprehensive treatment of the term *Originalgenie* in relation to Carl Philipp Emanuel Bach and Beethoven, see Peter Rummenhöller, "Carl Philip Emanuel Bach und Ludwig van Beethoven—zwei "Originalgenies,"" in *Die 9 Symphonien Beethovens: Entstehung, Deutung, Wirkung*, published by Renate Ulm, Kassel, 1994, 68–76. C. P. E. Bach's influence on Beethoven was also of a technical nature; a large part of the *Essay* concerns piano fingering and how it can be improved to benefit expressiveness. Beethoven would continue to experiment with ingenious fingerings his entire life to help realize his musical intentions.

2. Carl Czerny, *Erinnerungen aus meinem Leben*, ed. Walter Kolneder, Baden-Baden, 1968, 15.

3. Cited by *BLuW*, 27.

4. Neefe was Beethoven's main teacher during this period, but not the only one. For a long while Beethoven also took violin lessons from Franz Ries, a family friend who at one time was also concertmaster of the Kapelle.

5. Hans-Josef Irmen, *Beethoven in seiner Zeit*, Zülpich, 1998, 32. The following passages on the Illuminati are also chiefly informed by Irmen's book.

6. Ibid., 64.

5. THE YOUNG PROFESSIONAL

1. Cf. TDR, I: 149.

2. Cf. WR, 14.

3. Schiedermair, *Der junge Beethoven*, 46.

4. Cf. Wetzstein, *Familie Beethoven im kurfürstlichen Bonn*, 41.

5. In the Beethoven literature, this trip to the Netherlands is generally dated at 1781. However, several newly discovered sources reveal that it took place in 1783 (Luc van Hasselt, "Beethoven in Holland," *Die Musikforschung* 18 [1965]: 181–83; Jos van der Zanden, "Beethoven in Nederland," in *Beethoven: Nieuwe onthullingen*, Haarlem, 1993, 19–27; ibid., "Een schetsblad in Den Haag," 110).

6. Cited by Wetzstein, *Familie Beethoven im kurfürstlichen Bonn*, 110.

6. BONN TURNS TO VIENNA

1. On Belderbusch's death in 1784, it was revealed that he had received bribes—in the form of gifts—from Beethoven's father in return for assurances of a promotion. Belderbusch never kept his word, and Jean van Beethoven submitted a damages claim to the court. His claim was, of course, rejected.

2. "Let others wage war. Thou, happy Austria, marry."

3. Although it is exceedingly difficult to make a precise conversion, as a rule of thumb one guilder can be considered to have been worth around thirty euros. This is an extrapolation to 2009 of estimates made in the year 2000 (Roman Sandgruber, "Geld und Geldwert: Vom Wiener Pfennig zum Euro," in *Vom Pfennig zum Euro: Geld aus Wien*, exhibition catalogue from the Vienna Museum, 2002, 62–79).

4. Cf. Max Braubach, *Maria Theresias jüngster Sohn Max Franz, letzter Kurfürst von Köln und Fürstbischof von Münster*, Munich, 1961, 93.

5. Ibid., 169.

6. Comment by Neefe in Reichard's "Theaterkalender auf das Jahr 1791," cited in John D. Wilson, *Operatic Life in Bonn during Beethoven's Youth: Special Exhibition in the Beethoven-Haus, Bonn, 22nd October 2015–2nd March 2016*, 2015, 10–11.

7. Cited in Schiedermair, *Der junge Beethoven*, 57.

8. Cf. Mozart, letter from January 23, 1782: "On this matter, I can attest that […] if he were already Elector of Cologne, I would already be his Kapellmeister" (Wolfgang Amadeus Mozart, *Briefe und Aufzeichnungen*, ed. Wilhelm A. Bauer, Otto Erich Deutsch, and Joseph Heinz Eibl, Kassel, 1962–75, 3: 194). Cf. also TDR, 1: 186; and Lewis Lockwood, *Beethoven: The Music and the Life*, New York, 2003, 40.

7. BEETHOVEN'S FIRST CRISIS

1. Solomon, on whose writings much of this passage is based, refers to a "compositional hiatus" (Maynard Solomon, *Beethoven*, 36; and "Beethoven's Productivity at Bonn," *Music and Letters* 53 [1972]: 165–72). However, some commentators believe that several works composed between 1785 and 1790 have been lost, creating the mere appearance of a hiatus.

2. Cf. Solomon, *Beethoven*, 26.

3. *BBr*, no. 6.

4. Cited in Solomon, "Beethoven's Productivity at Bonn," 169.

5. Maynard Solomon divides Beethoven's time in Bonn into three periods: 1782–85, 1785–90, and 1790–92 (ibid., 165–72). He believes that because there are so few extant sources pointing to any kind of compositional activity whatsoever, there is a case to be made for a "Bonn moratorium." Lewis Lockwood and Douglas Porter Johnson contest this position, stating that the absence of source materials does not automatically imply a lack of activity (cf. Lewis Lockwood, "Review of *Beethoven*, by Maynard Solomon," *Nineteenth-Century Music* 3 [1979]: 76–82; and Douglas Porter Johnson, *Beethoven's Early Sketches in the "Fischhof Miscellany" Berlin Autograph 28*, Ann Arbor, MI, 1980, 1: 219–25).

6. Cf. Barry Cooper, *Beethoven*, Oxford, 2000, 22; and Lewis Lockwood, *Beethoven*, 47.

7. Anton Schindler, *Biographie von Ludwig van Beethoven*, 4th ed., Münster, 1871 (1840), 1: 15.

8. Cf. Dieter Haberl, "Beethovens erste Reise nach Wien," *Neues musikwissenschaftliches Jahrbuch* 14 (2006): 215–55. Haberl reaches this conclusion following an in-depth study of the "Regensburg Diarium," a journal published between 1760 and 1810 containing lists of incoming and outgoing visitors to the city, which included the movements of various musicians. His analysis differs fundamentally from the prevailing view up until that time, which put Beethoven's departure from Bonn in late March 1787 and his arrival in Vienna on Easter Saturday (April 7), and supposes that he left the Austrian capital again only two weeks later. This hypothesis was formulated by Eduard Panzerbieter in 1927, based on the established fact that Beethoven spent the night in Munich on both April 1 and April 25. Panzerbieter believed these dates were indications of the journey to and from Vienna, and on the basis of the customary travel times from Bonn to Munich, and Munich to Vienna, he reconstructed Beethoven's trip entirely around them (Eduard Panzerbieter, "Beethovens erste Reise nach Wien im Jahre 1787," *Zeitschrift für Musikwissenschaft* 10 [1927/28]: 153–61). Haberl's well-founded theory posits that Beethoven spent both of these nights in Munich on the return trip home. If true, it means that rather than spending only two weeks in the capital, Beethoven instead spent two months there, putting his journey into a completely new perspective.

9. Cf. Schindler, *Biographie*, 1: 5; and O. Jahn, *Wolfgang Amadeus Mozart*, Leipzig, 1856–59, 2: 40.

10. Czerny, *Erinnerungen aus meinem Leben*, 11.

11. Ibid.

12. Beethoven's playing differed fundamentally from that of the Bohemian prodigy Johann Nepomuk Hummel. Mozart taught Hummel for free and helped organize his first concerts in Vienna. Hummel was not only younger (and thus more pliable) than Beethoven, but his playing was described as "pearly and light," putting it far closer to Mozart's end of the pianistic spectrum. The Viennese public eventually became divided into two camps: Hummel (Mozart's pupil) vs. Czerny (Beethoven's pupil). A similar divide later emerged between Chopin and Liszt.

13. Cf. Solomon, *Beethoven*, 40; and Klaus Kropfinger, *Beethoven*, Kassel, 2001, 86.

14. *BBr*, no. 3.

15. Cited by TDR, 1: 219.

8. A SECOND HOME, AND NEW HORIZONS

1. WR, 20.

2. Cf. Anton Schindler, *Biographie,* 1: 17–18.

3. Cf. WR, 37. *Raptus* (Lat.): plundering, abduction. The implication was that during a *raptus* Beethoven was "robbed" of his senses.

4. Hans-Josef Irmen sought to explain this behavior through Beethoven's self-awareness as a free artist, which drove him to sabotage any access to the opposite sex at the first sign of any official relationship that might potentially pose a threat to his artistic calling (Irmen, *Beethoven in seiner Zeit,* 85).

5. In a letter to Eleonore dated November 2, 1793 (one year after his move to Vienna), Beethoven writes of a "disastrous fight" and confesses bitter regret: "I realised how dreadful my behaviour had been, but there was no turning back time; what I wouldn't give to erase those deeds from my life, my conduct that was both dishonourable and a poor reflection of my true character!" (*BBr,* no. 11).

6. These dedications are the Rondo for Piano and Violin (WoO 41), the Allegro for Orphica (WoO 51), and—probably—the Variations on a Theme by Dittersdorf (WoO 66). The Allegro for Orphica was long thought to be an (incomplete) sonata for piano. Klaus Martin Kopitz, however, recently unearthed the work's true identity (Klaus Martin Kopitz, "Beethoven as a Composer for the Orphica: A New Source for WoO 51" *BJ* 22, no. 1 [2007]: 25–29). The orphica was a small and portable keyboard instrument with a limited range, used mostly for outdoor performances.

7. *BBr,* nos. 439, 2236, and 2255.

8. WR, 58.

9. *BBr,* no. 65. Belderbusch's relationship with Babette Koch was a scandal that rocked Bonn for many years. After his wife had left him for Baron von Liechtenstein, Belderbusch engaged Babette Koch as a private tutor for his children. After many years of more or less secret concubinage, followed by divorce proceedings before the French court, the couple married in 1802. Babette Koch thus made an enormous leap up the social ladder—Napoleon's wife Josephine was even godmother to one of her children. Babette Koch died very young while giving birth to her fourth child in 1807.

10. Schiedermair, *Der junge Beethoven,* 195–96.

11. Beethoven carried Plutarch's *Parallel Lives* with him his entire life (in a German translation by Gottlob Benedict von Schirach). After his death, an extremely well-thumbed copy was found among his belongings.

12. After Beethoven died, many of Shakespeare's plays were found on his bookshelf, in translations by both Eschenburg (1787, 1806) and Schlegel/Tieck (1825). According to Schindler, Beethoven preferred the Eschenburg translation, finding Schlegel's clumsy, contrived, and too free in places. In 1810, Beethoven nonetheless

recommended the Schlegel translation to Therese Malfatti, the object of his affections at the time (*BBr*, no. 442).

9. RENEWED VIGOR AND THE FIRST MAJOR WORKS

1. Nowadays Martín y Soler's fame rests chiefly on the explicit reference to his opera *Una cosa rara* (A strange thing) in Mozart's *Don Giovanni*.

2. It is of note that these singers were registered as *Schauspieler* (actors). In those times, a far narrower distinction was drawn between "actors who could sing" and "singers who could act."

3. WR, 17.

4. Cf. letter dated November 26, 1777 (Mozart, *Briefe und Aufzeichnungen*, 2: 147).

5. WR, 17.

6. Kerst, *Die Erinnerungen an Beethoven*, 1: 17–19. Cf. also *BLuW*, 33.

7. *BBr*, no. 1917.

8. TDR, 1: 268–73.

9. Cf. Solomon, *Beethoven*, 69.

10. Ernst Herttrich, "Kantaten," in Beethoven, *Werke: Gesamtausgabe,* ed. Sieghard Brandenburg, Klaus Kropfinger, Hans-Werner Küthen, Emil Platen, et al., 56 vols., Munich, 1961–, series 10, 1: 320.

11. When Johann Sebastian Bach journeyed to Lübeck in 1705, he attended two concerts featuring Buxtehude's *Trauermusik* (funeral music) for the death of Emperor Leopold I, and a polychoral cantata in honor of his successor, Joseph I.

12. Cited by Solomon, *Beethoven*, 69.

13. For example, the second *Fidelio* finale drew directly from the soprano aria and chorus "Da stiegen die Menschen ans Licht" (And the people rose into the light).

14. Cited by Solomon, *Beethoven*, 69.

15. An oboe concerto (Hess 12) was sadly lost. There was also an unfinished violin concerto (WoO 5), and during this period Beethoven also worked on a piano concerto (which would later become the Second Piano Concerto in B-flat).

16. Cf. Jürgen Uhde, *Beethovens Klaviermusik I: Klavierstücke und Variationen,* Stuttgart, 1968, 235–57.

10. FAREWELL TO BONN

1. Beethoven retained fond memories of Salomon. On his death in November 1815, he wrote to Ferdinand Ries, "Salomon's death pains me greatly; he was a noble man" (*BBr*, no. 908).

2. Cf. TDR, 1: 307.

3. *Die Stammbücher Beethovens und der Babette Koch* (facsimile), ed. Max Braubach, Bonn, 1995, 19.

4. It was E. T. A. Hoffmann in 1812 who first discussed the musicohistorical significance of Haydn, Mozart, and Beethoven as a Viennese triumvirate. Strangely enough, he referred to them even then as "romantic composers" (Charles Rosen, *The Classical Style: Haydn, Mozart, Beethoven*, 2nd ed., London, 1976, 19).

5. The second page of the logbook in which Beethoven meticulously recorded all of his travel expenses contains the following entry: "A one-Thaler [...] tip, as the fellow risked life and limb to take us straight through the middle of the Hessian army, and drove like the blazes" (Dagmar von Busch-Weise, "Beethovens Jugend Tagebuch," *Studien zur Musikwissenschaft* 25 [1962]: 70–71).

11. VIENNA IN 1792

1. Cf. Frances Trollope, *Vienna and the Austrians*, Stuttgart, 1966, 113 (A.&W. Galignani & Company, 1838, 215).

2. Cf. Jean-Paul Bled, *Wien, Residenz, Metropole, Hauptstadt*, Vienna, 2002 (1989), 140.

3. It is striking that most aristocrats with ties to Beethoven were part of the "Bohemian collective," a separate and powerful clique within the larger group of the nobility that maintained a clear separation from their Austrian and Hungarian fellows.

4. Anne Louise Germaine de Staël-Holstein, *De l'Allemagne*, Paris, 1968 (1813), 89–91.

5. Cf. Helga Peham, *Leopold II: Herrscher mit weiser Hand*, Graz, 1987, 300–301.

6. Cf. Irmen, *Beethoven in seiner Zeit*, 121.

7. Johann Pezzl, *Neue Skizze von Wien*, Vienna, 1805, 1: 161 (cf. also Alice M. Hanson, "Incomes and Outgoings in the Vienna of Beethoven and Schubert," *Music and Letters* 64 [1983]: 178).

8. Cf. Buch-Weise, *Beethovens Jugend-Tagebuch*, 68–88.

9. This is the result of a deep-seated Viennese belief in the need to dress according to one's station, itself a response to an imperial decree of 1671 outlining the dress code for court personnel and public servants. Due to the power of the bureaucratic hierarchy, fine apparel became the ideal way to cultivate an image in society.

10. The lessons were unsuccessful. According to his pupil Ries, Beethoven was unable to dance in time (cf. WR, 120).

12. BEETHOVEN'S FIRST PATRON

1. Lichnowsky also joined lodges in Vienna, Prague, and Regensburg. It was in the latter city where he met Joseph Schaden in 1786, the man who would assist Beethoven with his first trip to Vienna one year later. It is therefore entirely possible that Lichnowsky first heard Beethoven's name at a lodge in Regensburg.

2. Cf. Irmen, *Beethoven in seiner Zeit,* 164.

3. Razumovsky's uncle, of humble origins, quickly managed to work his way to the top of the hierarchy at court and into the bed of Tsarina Elisabeth. It is thought that he may even have married her in secret and succeeded in amassing an enormous fortune.

4. A stubborn rumor once circulated in Vienna that the princess successfully disguised herself as a prostitute with the intention of catching her husband in fla-grante delicto, in true *Marriage of Figaro* style. Christiane Lichnowsky also seems to have been deeply scarred by a double mastectomy, which was performed to treat a cancer-like illness.

5. Lulu von Thürheim, *Mein Leben,* ed. René van Rhyn, Munich, 1923, 2: 18ff (cf. also *BLuW,* 48–49).

6. Cf. Walter Brauneis, "'wegen schuldigen 1435 f 32 xr'.—Neuer Archivfund zur Finanzmisere Mozarts im November 1791," *Mitteilungen der Internationalen Stif- tung Mozarteum* 39 (1991): 159–64.

7. Cf. *Mozartbriefe,* 3: 186 (letter dated December 22–25, 1782).

8. Carl Czerny, *Erinnerungen aus meinem Leben,* ed. Walter Kolneder, Baden-Baden, 1968, 9.

9. This was the theme from the third movement, a theme and variations based on Weigl's *L'amor marinaro.* Incidentally, this is the only variation movement in Beethoven's official oeuvre that is based on a theme by another composer—one reason why Beethoven briefly considered replacing it.

10. Cf. WR, 81–82; and TDR, 2: 175.

11. Cf. TDR, 2: 461.

12. Cf. TDR, 2: 68.

13. Ignaz von Seyfried, *Ludwig van Beethoven's Studien im Generalbasse, Con- trapuncte und in der Compositions-Lehre,* Vienna, 1832 (cf. Kerst, *Die Erinnerungen an Beethoven,* 1: 37ff).

14. Cf. Carl Czerny, "Anekdoten und Notizen über Beethoven," in Czerny, *Über den richtigen Vortrag der sämtlichen Beethoven'schen Klavierwerke* (Vienna, 1842), ed. Paul Badura-Skoda, Vienna, 1963, 21.

15. Cf. WR, 33.

16. Cf. WR, 34.

17. These four marvelous instruments are currently part of the collection in the Bonn Beethoven-Haus. Each of them bears Beethoven's "LVB" stamp below the neck and an engraved "B" on the back. The instruments had previously been attrib-uted to famous makers: the violins to Giuseppe Guarneri and Nicola Amati, the viola to Vincenzo Ruger (1690), and the cello to Andrea Guarneri (1712). These attributions are no longer considered to be accurate, however.

18. Schindler, *Biographie,* 1: 22.

19. Lichnowsky had a castle in Grätz close to Troppau (modern-day Opava, around sixty kilometers west of Ostrava on the Czech-Polish border).

20. Cf. *BBr,* no. 258. Cited from a report by Dr. Anton Weiser, Lichnowsky's doctor, in Theodor von Frimmel, *Ludwig van Beethoven,* 4th ed. Berlin, 1912, 44. It

remains uncertain whether this remark was written or verbal. There are certain parallels between this story and another nineteenth-century anecdote about Mozart. When Emperor Joseph II was asked why he tolerated Mozart's indecorous behavior, he is said to have replied, "I can meet a new general every day, but never another Mozart" (cf. Jürgen May, "Beethoven and Prince Lichnowsky," in *BF* 3 [1994]: 36).

21. Cited by Martin Geck and Peter Schleuning, *"Geschrieben auf Bonaparte"*: *Beethovens "Eroica": Revolution, Reaktion, Rezeption,* Reinbek bei Hamburg, 1989, 26.

13. HAYDN AND ALBRECHTSBERGER

1. Cf. James Webster, "The Falling-Out between Haydn and Beethoven: The Evidence of the Sources," in *Beethoven Essays: Studies in Honor of Elliot Forbes,* ed. Lewis Lockwood and Phyllis Benjamin, Cambridge, 1984, 3–45.

2. Cf. Claus Canisius, *Beethoven: "Sehnsucht und Unruhe in der Musik." Aspekte zu Leben und Werk,* Munich, 1992, 103–4; and *BBr,* no. 13.

3. *BBr,* no. 14.

4. WR, 86.

5. Cf. Barry Cooper, *The Beethoven Compendium: A Guide to Beethoven's Life and Music,* London, 1991, 154.

6. TDR, 2: 141.

7. Cf. Gerd Indorf, *Beethovens Streichquartette: Kulturgeschichtliche Aspekte und Werkinterpretationen,* Freiburg im Breisgau, 2004, 139.

8. Cited by Ludwig Finscher, *Joseph Haydn und seine Zeit,* Laaber, 2000, 424.

9. Cf. note by Stoll in TDR, 3: 60.

10. Gerhard von Breuning, *Aus dem Schwarzspanierhause: Erinnerungen an L. v. Beethoven aus meiner Jugendzeit,* Vienna, 1874, 98.

11. Cf. letter from Albrechtsberger to Breitkopf (August 17, 1798), cited by Martin Staehelin, "A Veiled Judgment of Beethoven by Albrechtsberger?" in *Beethoven Essays: Studies in Honor of Elliot Forbes,* 48.

12. Cited by Irmen, *Beethoven in seiner Zeit,* 134.

13. Cited by Peter Clive, *Beethoven and His World: A Biographical Dictionary,* Oxford, 2001, 4.

14. *BKh,* 7: 296.

15. Cited by Irmen, *Beethoven in seiner Zeit,* 134.

16. *BBr,* no. 65.

17. Cf. *BBr,* nos. 2100, 2101, and 2255.

14. CAREER PLANS

1. TDR, 1: 404.

2. *BBr,* no. 18.

3. This is the work now known as the Second Piano Concerto, since it was published after—although written before—the first.

4. *Wiener Zeitung,* April 1, 1795, cited in *BLuW,* 44.

5. The announcement that Beethoven was to play a "completely new work" has led many Beethoven commentators to believe that this was the premiere of the First Piano Concerto (op. 15). Based on rigorous analysis of the sketches and other materials, Leon Plantinga argues convincingly that this cannot be the case. The use of the phrase "completely new" is, moreover, a common nineteenth-century marketing ploy and should never be taken too literally (cf. Leon Plantinga, *Beethoven's Concertos: History, Style, Performance,* London, 1998, 64, 327).

6. The original final movement would eventually lead an independent life as the Rondo in B-flat (WoO 6).

7. Sketches exist of all of the versions cited here, but no full piano parts. The Second Piano Concerto was also published in great haste. In 1801 Beethoven was scarcely motivated to conduct a thorough revision of the solo and orchestral parts (the concerto was, in his opinion, not his best work). The score used for modern performances, and the piano part especially, is therefore most probably incomplete and in many respects inferior to the renditions given by Beethoven himself.

8. Cited by Irmen, *Beethoven in seiner Zeit,* 150.

9. He would later write out these cadenzas for his pupil Ferdinand Ries (WoO 59).

10. WR, 36.

11. Schindler, *Biographie,* 2: 68.

12. A similar circumstance occurred in 1812 when Beethoven rehearsed the Horn Sonata (op. 17) with Friedrich Starke. The piano was a semitone flat, and so Beethoven transposed the entire work up into F-sharp major. According to Starke, Beethoven played beautifully and the music flowed effortlessly from his fingers, giving not the slightest impression that he was transposing.

13. *BBr,* no. 11.

14. *BBr,* no. 15.

15. Ibid.

16. Cf. Carl Czerny, "Anekdoten und Notizen über Beethoven," 21.

17. For a comprehensive treatment of this subject matter, see Michael Broyles, *The Emergence and Evolution of Beethoven's Heroic Style,* New York, 1987, 9–94.

18. The better-known Twelve Contredanses (WoO 14) composed later are, interestingly, far less compact. Rather than being conceptualized as a set, this collection was in fact a collage of earlier dances that were composed separately and assembled in 1801/1802.

19. Cited by *BLuW,* 50.

20. Beethoven sent a letter from Prague to his brother Nikolaus, telling of his happiness: "Let me say first of all that I am well, very well, my art has won me friends and esteem, what more could I ask? [...] Some money will also come my way this time" (*BBr,* no. 20).

21. Cited in *Beethoven und Böhmen: Beiträge zu Biographie und Wirkungsgeschichte Beethovens,* ed. Sieghard Brandenburg and Martella Gutiérrez-Denhoff, Bonn, 1988, 434–35.

22. The opus number of this concert aria is abnormally high for a work dating from this period. Because Beethoven always strove to number his most important works chronologically, it is usually possible to make a reasonable guess at when a work was written from its opus number. Beethoven often negotiated with several publishers simultaneously, however, which occasionally led to errors in the allocation of opus numbers. Some were used twice (such as op. 29 for the String Quintet and the Piano Sonatas in G Major, D Minor, and E-flat Major, the later op. 31), while others were not used at all. The gaps were filled in later—both during his lifetime and posthumously—with vocal and other works, thus introducing some anachronisms. The most salient instances are "Adelaide" (op. 46), the *Gellert* Lieder (op. 48), the Two Rondos for Piano (op. 51), and the Octet for Winds (op. 103).

In 1955, Georg Kinsky catalogued most of the unassigned works as *Werke ohne Opuszahl* (works without opus number), abbreviated as WoO. His list was supplemented in 1957 by Willy Hess (whose additions are abbreviated as "Hess"). It is interesting to note that music—unlike painting or literature—is the only art form to use the system of opus numbers.

23. The Variations on "See the Conq'ring Hero Comes" (WoO 45) for cello and piano also date from this period. It is likely that Beethoven became acquainted with this theme at the Berlin Choral Society (Singakademie), where Handel's oratorio *Judas Maccabeus* regularly featured in the repertoire.

24. Letter from C. Czerny in *Cocks's London Musical Miscellany* (August 2, 1852), cited in TDR, 2: 14.

25. WR, 109.

26. In 1809, Beethoven became a corresponding member of the Royal Netherlands Academy of Arts and Sciences in Amsterdam. He also became a member of the Ljubljana Philharmonic Society in 1819, an honorary member of the Stiermarken Music Association in 1822, a member of the Royal Swedish Academy of Music in Stockholm in 1826, and an honorary member of the Vienna Friends of Music Society (Musikfreunde) in 1826. The city of Vienna made him an honorary citizen in 1815.

27. WR, 109–10.

28. This entire passage on Louis Ferdinand is based on Walter Brauneis, "composta per festeggiare il sovvenire di un grand uomo. Beethovens Eroica als Hommage des Fürsten Franz Joseph Maximilian von Lobkowitz für Ferdinand von Preussen," *Österreichische Musikzeitschrift* 53, no. 12 (1998): 4–24.

29. The "Fischhof Miscellany" is a copy of a set of documents from various sources collected for biographical purposes (cf. Clemens Brennis, "Das Fischhof-Manuskript in der Deutschen Staatsbibliothek," in *Zu Beethoven: Aufsätze und Dokumente,* ed. Harry Goldschmidt, Berlin, 1984, 2: 47).

30. Aloys Weissenbach, *Meine Reise zum Kongress in Wien: Wahrheit und Dichtung,* Vienna, 1816 (cf. Peter J. Davies, *Beethoven in Person: His Deafness, Illnesses, and Death,* Westport, CT, 2001, 141).

15. FAMILY, FRIENDS, AND LOVES IN VIENNA

1. Johann Ferdinand von Schönfeld, *Jahrbuch der Tonkunst von Wien und Prag,* Vienna, 1796, 7.

2. Very few of Kaspar Karl's compositions are known to us. The Twelve Minuets are often played and have even been recorded on LP and CD. They were long presumed to be by his elder brother Ludwig and were catalogued as WoO 12.

3. Evidence for Wegeler's Freemason membership is found in his 1797 arrangement of Beethoven's song "Der freie Mann" (The free man, WoO 117) based on a Masonic text, which he subsequently published as "Maurerfragen" (Masons' questions). This version of the song became very popular and formed the basis for the later "Opferlied" (Song of sacrifice, op. 121b).

4. *BBr,* no. 2101.

5. WR, 47.

6. WR, xiii.

7. Breuning, *Aus dem Schwarzspanierhause,* 18.

8. *BBr,* no. 185.

9. *BBr,* no. 197.

10. *BBr,* no. 67.

11. *BBr,* no. 51.

12. *BBr,* no. 67.

13. *BBr,* no. 66.

14. Cf. Solomon, *Beethoven,* 109.

15. *BBr,* no. 67.

16. *BBr,* no. 111.

17. *BBr,* nos. 2236 and 35. "Muck-hauler" is one possible translation of *Zmeškall* in Czech! Beethoven enjoyed elaborate wordplay and produced endless comical and other variations on this theme. It should be noted, however, that Beethoven's final letter to Zmeskall (on February 1, 1827) commenced with the salutation "Mein Sehr werther Freund!" (My highly valued friend!). He signed off with "Herzlich ihr alter Theilnehmender Freund" (Affectionately, your devoted old friend) *BBr,* no. 2258.

18. Letter dated November 23, 1791, to Bossler's *Musikalische Korrespondenz* (cf. Schiedermair, *Der junge Beethoven,* 85).

19. Cf. Clive, *Beethoven and His World,* 398–99.

20. Cf. TDR, 2: 132.

21. WR, 42.

22. *BBr,* no. 2255; and WR, 42.

23. WR, 43.

24. WR, 117.

25. Cf. Carl Czerny, *Über den richtigen Vortrag der sämtlichen Beethoven'schen Klavierwerke* (Vienna, 1842), ed. Paul Badura-Skoda, Vienna, 1963, 40.

26. Cf. Solomon, *Beethoven,* 179; and Barry Cooper, *Beethoven,* Oxford, 2000, 110.

27. Cf. Solomon, *Beethoven,* 35, 39.

28. Cf. Irmen, *Beethoven in seiner Zeit,* 64.

29. Cf. Kerst, *Die Erinnerungen an Beethoven,* 2: 186.

30. *BBr,* no. 20.

31. *BBr,* no. 1731.

16. IN ANTICIPATION OF GREATER THINGS

1. Beethoven virtually bombarded the Brownes with dedications. In addition to these variations, the Three String Trios (op. 9), the Piano Sonata (op. 22), the *Gellert* Lieder (op. 48), and the Variations on a Theme from *The Magic Flute* (WoO 46) were dedicated to the count, and the Piano Sonatas (op. 10) and the Variations on a Theme by Süssmayr (WoO 76) to the countess. The stream of dedications stopped on the event of the countess's death in 1803. As mentioned in an earlier chapter, Count Browne himself eventually died in an asylum.

2. "Subthematicism" is the term given by musicologists to categorize thematic musical connections that exist at a deeper, usually less readily identifiable level. This principle will gain in importance in Beethoven's later works.

3. For a long time it was assumed that "Adelaide" was first performed at the Hofburg in Vienna during the birthday celebrations of Elisabeth Alexeievna, the empress of Russia, on January 25, 1815, with Beethoven at the piano and Franz Wild as tenor. This performance also acquired iconic status as Beethoven's final public appearance as a pianist. On hearing Wild's interpretation, Beethoven is said to have been so moved that he promised Wild an orchestrated version of "Adelaide," which he never produced (cf. TDR, 3: 488). Recent research by Rita Steblin has rendered these theories untenable (cf. Rita Steblin, "Beethoven in Unpublished Viennese Court Documents from 1814," in *Beethoven und der Wiener Kongress [1814/15]: Bericht über die vierte New Beethoven Research Conference Bonn, 10. bis 12. September 2014,* ed. Bernhard R. Appel, Joanna Cobb Biermann, William Kinderman, and Julia Ronge, Bonn, 2016, 121–38).

4. In the appendixes to the 1811 edition of his poems. Cited in *BBr,* no. 47, footnote 3.

5. Approximately eight thousand pages' worth have now been catalogued, spread out across four hundred or so sources. An illustrative example is provided by the fate of the so-called Sauer sketchbook, which contained the sketches made by Beethoven between April and December 1801. Sauer, a Viennese music publisher, purchased it at auction in 1827, tore it apart, and sold it off page by page to souvenir hunters. Of its original ninety-six pages, only twenty-two have been identified in various collections around the world, leaving a significant gap in our knowledge of this crucial half year in Beethoven's career.

6. Ignaz von Seyfried, *Ludwig von Beethovens Studien,* appendix (TDR, 2: 568ff).

7. "Une Visite à Beethoven," *Le Mercure Musical (La Revue Musicale S.I.M.)* 2, no. 1 (May 1906): 8. Publié par [published by] Jean Chantavoine.

17. LOBKOWITZ'S "CENTER OF EXCELLENCE"

1. This concert hall (which can still be visited today) was not very large: only fifteen meters long and eight meters wide.

2. Johann Friedrich Reichardt, *Vertraute Briefe geschrieben auf einer Reise nach Wien und den Österreichischen Staaten zu Ende des Jahres 1808 und zu Anfang 1809,* Munich, 1915, 2: 38ff. (cf. Jaroslav Macek, "Franz Joseph Maximilian Lobkowitz: Musikfreund und Kunstmäzen," in *Beethoven und Böhmen: Beiträge zu Biographie und Wirkungsgeschichte Beethovens,* ed. Sieghard Brandenburg and Martella Gutiér-rez-Denhof, Bonn, 1988, 166).

3. Beethoven wrote the Quartet in D Major first (the later op. 18, no. 3); those in F major and G major were completed afterward. When the quartets were published in 1801, the publisher chose the current order (F, G, D) on Schuppanzigh's recom-mendation. The same occurred with the second set of three: the Quartet in A Major (op. 18, no. 5), despite having been composed first, was placed after its younger sib-ling, the Quartet in C Minor (op. 18, no. 4).

4. *BBr,* no. 67.

5. This first version exists as a complete set of four quartet parts transcribed by a copyist, which have been preserved at the Beethoven-Haus in Bonn since 1913.

6. For a comprehensive analysis of these two versions of the first movement of the String Quartet in F Major (op. 18, no. 1), see Janet M. Levy, *Beethoven's Compo-sitional Choices: The Two Versions of Opus 18, No. 1, First Movement,* Philadelphia, 1982.

18. THE IMMORTAL BELOVED: EPISODE ONE

1. Anna von Brunsvik was—*in tempore non suspecto*—one of the many aristo-cratic subscribers to Beethoven's Piano Trios (op. 1).

2. Cf. *Die Memoiren der Gräfin Therese Brunsvik,* cited in La Mara, *Beethovens unsterbliche Geliebte: Das Geheimnis der Gräfin Brunsvik und ihre Memoiren,* Leip-zig, 1909, 63–64. The content of this chapter is largely based on Marie-Elisabeth Tellenbach, *Beethoven und seine "Unsterbliche Geliebte" Josephine Brunswick,* Zurich, 1983.

3. Harry Goldschmidt, *Um die Unsterbliche Geliebte,* Leipzig, 1977, 173. Accord-ing to Goldschmidt, Therese had a predilection for "self-flagellation." She also suf-fered abnormal curvature of the spine and took regular treatments at Bohemian spa

towns (cf. George R. Marek, *Ludwig van Beethoven: Das Leben eines Genies,* Munich, 1970, 232).

4. Personal correspondence from Canadian-Austrian researcher Dr. Rita Steblin. See also Rita Steblin, *"Auf diese Art mit A geht alles zu Grunde"*: A New Look at Beethoven's Diary Entry and the 'Immortal Beloved,'" in *BBS* 6 (2007): 155.

5. The Violin Sonata in A Major (op. 47) was premiered by Beethoven and Bridgetower on May 24, 1803, at a concert in the *Augarten* hall. While Beethoven had originally intended to dedicate the sonata to Bridgetower, an altercation between them (supposedly over a competing love interest) caused Beethoven to change his mind. He dedicated it instead to the French violinist Rodolphe Kreutzer, whence the sonata derives its current name.

6. Cf. Ernst Pichler, *Beethoven: Mythos und Wirklichkeit,* Vienna, 1994, 162ff.

7. Beethoven had met Marie Bigot at the Razumovsky residence, where her husband was the librarian. She was an excellent pianist—rumor has it that she played the *Appassionata* flawlessly *a prima vista*—and Beethoven was happy to take her on as a pupil. In March 1807, Beethoven pushed the bounds of intimacy a little too far and asked Marie (who was sixteen years his junior) out on a private walk. In a fit of jealousy, her husband, already irked by Beethoven's excessive familiarity when greeting his pupil, wrote an angry letter. Beethoven wrote an apology in reply, professing the strength of his ethical principles in his dealings with married women (*BBr,* nos. 272 and 273).

8. *BBr,* no. 216.

9. *BBr,* no. 70.

10. *BKh,* 2: 365–67.

11. Cf. Ludwig Rellstab, "Theodor: Eine musikalische Skizze," *Berliner allgemeine musikalische Zeitung* 32 (August 11, 1824): 274; and Wilhelm von Lenz, *Beethoven: Eine Kunst-Studie,* Hamburg, 1860, 3 (series 2/2): 78. The nineteenth century is rich with alternative and apocryphal theories on the origins of the *Moonlight* Sonata. Perhaps the most striking is that of the "blind girl." When Beethoven played for her and noticed moonbeams shining on the keyboard, he purportedly raced home in order to capture the magical moment in music (cf. Michael Ladenburger and Friederike Grigat, *Beethovens "Mondscheinsonate": Original und romantische Verklärung,* Bonn, 2003 [*Begleitpublikationen zu Ausstellungen des Beethoven-Hauses,* vol. 14]).

12. Czerny, "Anekdoten und Notizen über Beethoven," 13.

19. THE ROAD TO A BROADER PUBLIC

1. Reichardt, *Vertraute Briefe,* 2: 133.

2. *BBr,* no. 85.

3. For purposes of historical clarity, she will be referred to as "Maria Theresa of Naples and Sicily" in order to avoid confusion with her grandmother Maria Theresa,

empress from 1740 to 1780 (cf. John A. Rice, *Empress Marie Therese and the Music at the Viennese Court,* Cambridge, 2003, 1).

4. Cf. TDR, 2: 173.

5. Beethoven's later disdain for the Septet is rather puzzling; in 1802–3 he made his own arrangement of the work for piano, clarinet (or violin), and cello for his doctor, Johann Schmidt. It was published in 1805 and even received its own opus number (op. 38).

6. A series of minor misunderstandings and historical fabrications was responsible for the long-held and mistaken belief that she commissioned Haydn's *Theresienmesse.*

7. Cited in *BBr,* 1: 51 (facsimile).

8. Cited in TDR, 2: 172.

9. *AmZ,* 1800, column 49. Cited in Stefan Kunze, *Ludwig van Beethoven: Die Werke im Spiegel seiner Zeit. Gesammelte Konzertberichte und Rezensionen bis 1830,* Laaber, 1987, 22.

10. Ibid.

11. Cited in Constantin Floros, *Beethovens Eroica und Prometheus-Musik,* Wilhelmshaven, 1978, 38.

12. Cited in Egon Voss, "Schwierigkeiten im Umgang mit dem Ballett 'Die Geschöpfe des Prometheus' von Salvatore Viganò und Ludwig van Beethoven," *Archiv für Musikwissenschaft* 53 (1966): 22.

13. *BBr,* no. 60.

14. Constantin Floros made a reconstruction based on a scenario published by Viganò biographer Carlo Ritorni in 1838. Because Ritorni's sources are unclear and his proposed scenario contains numerous anomalies, Floros's hypothesis is of little practical value (cf. Floros, *Beethovens Eroica und Prometheus-Musik,* 35–72; and Voss, "Schwierigkeiten im Umgang mit dem Ballett 'Die Geschöpfe des Prometheus,'" 21–40).

15. This also explains why the final sections in Beethoven's score are designated by the dancers' names rather than dramatically inspired titles: "Solo di Gioia," "Solo della Signora Cassentini," "Coro e Solo di Viganò," etc.

20. A WORD FROM THE CRITICS

1. *AmZ,* 1799, column 541–42, cited in Kunze, *Ludwig van Beethoven,* 16–17.

2. *AmZ,* 1799, column 541–42, cited in Kunze, *Ludwig van Beethoven,* 18. Emphasis in original.

3. *AmZ,* 1799, column 570–71, cited in Kunze, *Ludwig van Beethoven,* 18.

4. *AmZ,* 1798, column 25–27, cited in Kunze, *Ludwig van Beethoven,* 16–17.

5. *AmZ,* 1799, column 366–68, cited in Kunze, *Ludwig van Beethoven,* 91.

6. *AmZ,* 1798, column 25–27, cited in Kunze, *Ludwig van Beethoven,* 16.

7. *AmZ,* 1800, column 373–74, cited in Kunze, *Ludwig van Beethoven,* 19.

8. *AmZ,* 1799, column 570–71, cited in Kunze, *Ludwig van Beethoven,* 18.

9. *BBr,* no. 54.

10. *BBr*, no. 59.

11. Mozart, *Briefe und Aufzeichnungen,* 2: 102, 134.

12. *AmZ,* 1807, column 94–96, cited in Kunze, *Ludwig van Beethoven,* 600.

13. *AmZ,* 1802, column 569–70, cited in Kunze, *Ludwig van Beethoven,* 24. Emphasis in original.

14. *BBr,* no. 158.

15. *AmZ,* 1805, column 321, 501/502, cited in Kunze, *Ludwig van Beethoven,* 50. Emphasis in original.

16. *BBr,* no. 254.

17. Cf. *BBr,* no. 176.

18. Cited in Kerst, *Die Erinnerungen an Beethoven,* 1: 287. Maynard Solomon contests that Rochlitz fabricated these meetings, as his account contains several inaccuracies (cf. Solomon, "Beethoven's Creative Process: A Two-Part Invention," in *Beethoven Essays,* 135–37). Not all Beethoven experts agree with this harsh assessment, however.

21. THE DISCIPLES

1. Cf. Czerny, *Erinnerungen,* 14.

2. The son of Beethoven's colleague Aloys Förster, who was a piano student of Beethoven's for a time, later told of how his teacher forced him to restrict his movements by placing knitting needles on the backs of his hands. If the needles fell to the floor, Beethoven would pick them up and use them to rap his pupil across the knuckles (cf. Kerst, *Die Erinnerungen an Beethoven,* 1: 71).

3. Czerny, *Erinnerungen,* 23.

4. The notion of codifying and distilling piano technique into separate exercises was nothing new. In 1804, the German-English pianist and composer Johann Baptist Cramer had published a *Studio per il pianoforte:* a collection of forty-two etudes (which was later expanded to one hundred), each addressing one aspect of piano technique. Beethoven set great store by these exercises and viewed their study as a necessary preparation for the performance of his own music. He later gifted a copy, including his own personal annotations, to his nephew Karl. These comments might speak volumes today about Beethoven's approach to piano technique, were it not for the fact that some of them were fabricated by Schindler.

5. Czerny's notes on Beethoven interpretation were used as a reference by none other than Johannes Brahms. In a letter to Clara Schumann, he wrote, "I am firmly convinced of the benefits of studying Czerny's great volume, particularly regarding his vision on the interpretation of Beethoven [. . .] his fingerings in particular are fascinating" (cf. *Clara Schumann—Johannes Brahms: Briefe aus den Jahren 1853—1896,* published by Berthold Litzmann, Leipzig, 1927, vol. 2).

6. Beethoven took Ries on as a pupil, despite insisting that it would be better for him to go to Paris: "Vienna is bursting at the seams, making it hard even for those with talent to get by" (*BBr,* no. 65).

7. WR, 75.

8. *BBr,* no. 136; and WR, 94.

9. WR, 92, 94, 100.

10. Czerny, *Erinnerungen,* 20.

11. *BBr,* no. 87.

12. WR, 112–13.

13. Cf. WR, app. 22–23: "I [Gerhard von Breuning] had Pleyel's *Klavierschule,* with which Beethoven—as with all others—was not satisfied. He once said to me, as I sat at his bedside: 'Had I not lacked the time, I would very much have liked to write my own piano method ... but I would have written something totally different.'"

22. THE HEILIGENSTADT TESTAMENT

1. Personal communication with Dr. Sus Herbosch. For a general overview of Beethoven's illnesses, see Peter J. Davies, *Beethoven in Person: His Deafness, Illnesses, and Death,* Westport, CT, 2001.

2. *BBr,* nos. 70 and 65.

3. *BBr,* no. 65.

4. Ibid.

5. *BBr,* no. 70.

6. Cf. Solomon, *Beethoven,* 148.

7. See chapter 16, note 3, concerning the date of Beethoven's final public appearance as a pianist.

8. TDR, 3: 418.

9. For a general overview of the hypotheses, see Davies, *Beethoven in Person,* 137ff.

10. Around the turn of the nineteenth century, medical treatments occasionally did more damage than the disease itself, and Beethoven's condition was exacerbated by the way his typhus was treated. A standard nineteenth-century remedy was to administer quinine, for example, until the American doctor Cook discovered in 1869 that quinine is a potent neurotoxin, particularly when taken in large doses (which in Beethoven's case cannot be excluded, given his propensity for excess). Quinine thus often had the opposite of the intended effect: its neurotoxic side effects aggravated infections, resulting in deafness and, potentially, blindness. This being the case, there is a definite possibility that Beethoven was a victim of quinine poisoning (personal communication with Dr. Sus Herbosch).

11. This is not the case with conductive hearing loss, which affects the outer and middle ear. These people still hear their own voices very well and speak more softly as a result.

12. Recent laboratory tests conducted at the Health Research Institute and Treatment Center in Naperville, Illinois, on several samples of Beethoven's hair revealed that he had not ingested abnormally high doses of mercury. Had he suffered

from syphilis, the reverse would have been true, since mercury was part of the standard treatment for syphilis at the time (cf. Christian Reiter, "The Causes of Beethoven's Death and His Locks of Hair: A Forensic-Toxicological Investigation," *BJ* 22, no. 1 [2007]: 2–5.

13. *BBr*, no. 67.

14. Ibid.

15. *BBr*, no. 70.

16. Beethoven never finished this work, which is not to be confused with the Triple Concerto in C (op. 56).

17. *BBr*, no. 86.

18. This letter was found in a secret drawer shortly after his death, along with the "Letter to the immortal beloved" from 1812 and two female portraits. Schindler sent a copy to Rochlitz, who immediately published the Heiligenstadt Testament in the *Allgemeine musikalische Zeitung*. In the late nineteenth century, after many trials and tribulations, the letter found its way into the Hamburg State and University Library.

19. *BBr*, no. 106.

20. Cf. Claus Canisius, *Beethoven: "Sehnsucht und Unruhe in der Musik."* *Aspekte zu Leben und Werk*, Munich, 1992, 155–64.

21. Cf. Owen Jander, "The Rhetorical Structure of Beethoven's Heiligenstadt Testament," *BJ* 22, no. 1 (2007): 17–21.

22. TF, 400; and *BTb*, no. 88, p. 72.

23. For a comprehensive analysis of this interpretation of the Heiligenstadt Testament, see Canisius, *Beethoven*, 155–64; and Hans-Werner Küthen, "Das 'Heiligenstädter Testament' im Licht der Freimaurerei: Beethovens 'letzter Wille' als ein Beweis für Seine Zugehörigkeit zur Logenbruderschaft?" *Hudební veda* 38 (2001): 376–96.

23. A "NEW WAY" FORWARD

1. *BBr*, no. 113.

2. Cited in Czerny, *Erinnerungen*, 43.

3. *BBr*, no. 108.

4. Schindler was responsible for this nickname and bases his claim on a reported conversation with Beethoven on the sonata's deeper significance. Beethoven supposedly answered that a reading of Shakespeare's *The Tempest* would provide sufficient explanation, although Schindler added that he never knew which passage Beethoven specifically alluded to (Schindler, *Biographie*, 2: 221). Since then, Beethoven specialists have sought in vain for a connection between the sonata and the play by Shakespeare.

5. Beethoven made a special point of this in a letter to Breitkopf & Härtel: "Because these v[ariations] differ so greatly from my earlier sets, rather than simply assigning them an ordinary number (such as 1, 2, 3, etc.) as with my previous works,

I have included them among the number of my <u>truly great musical compositions</u>, the more so because the themes are of my own invention" (*BBr*, no. 123).

6. *AmZ*, 25 May 1803.

7. *BBr*, no. 60.

8. *BBr*, no. 97. Beethoven himself proposed his own transcription of the Piano Sonata in E Major (op. 14, no. 1) for string quartet, several passages of which were completely new. In a letter to Breitkopf & Härtel, he wrote of how proud he was of the result: "I know for certain that very few would be capable of the same."

9. *BBr*, no. 200, footnote 5.

10. *BBr*, no. 136.

24. THE *LABORATORIUM ARTIFICIOSUM*

1. Schindler, *Biographie*, 2: 192.

2. *BBr*, no. 48.

3. *BBr*, no. 707.

4. Cf. Barry Cooper, *Beethoven and the Creative Process*, Oxford, 1990, 125.

5. Cf. Claus Raab, "Sforzato," *BLex*, column 679a.

6. Cited in TDR, 4: 420.

7. Cf. Kurt Westphal, *Vom Einfall zur Symphonie: Einblick in Beethovens Schaffensweise*, Berlin, 1965, 18–19. A comprehensive overview of Beethoven's compositional methods can be found in Cooper, *Beethoven and the Creative Process*.

25. PUBLISHING PAINS AND THE "WAREHOUSE OF THE ARTS"

1. *BBr*, no. 110.

2. Ibid.

3. *BBr*, no. 119.

4. *BBr*, no. 127, footnote 4.

5. Beethoven commonly used two copyists: Wenzel Schlemmer, who ran a copyists' studio in Vienna (he himself had stopped copying long before, but he oversaw the work of his many staff and made interpretive decisions in the event of poor legibility), and his former assistant Wenzel Rampl. It was Schlemmer in particular who had developed a "sixth sense" for deciphering Beethoven's hieroglyphics.

6. A good example is provided by the drastic changes introduced for the second editions of the Fifth and Sixth symphonies, which were separated from the initial print run by a period of sixteen months. During this intervening period, the works were rehearsed and performed for the first time, and Beethoven made significant changes to the scores as a result. In a letter to Breitkopf & Härtel, he asked for the publisher's understanding: "When I sent them [the symphonies] to you, I had not

yet heard either one—and one must not consider oneself or one's creations so godly that they are immune to improvements here and there" (*BBr,* no. 359).

7. Cf. Cooper, *Beethoven,* 127ff.

8. The lack of legal security that persisted for some time is comparable to the current lack of regulation for the online distribution of recorded music.

9. *BBr,* no. 54.

10. *BBr,* no. 465.

11. *BBr,* nos. 1920, 1873, and 1783.

12. Cf. report in the *Wiener Zeitung,* October 22, 1803, cited in TDR, 2: 405–6.

13. *BBr,* no. 464.

26. COMPOSER IN RESIDENCE

1. In a letter to Hoffmeister in 1802, Beethoven wrote that "both the imperial city and the imperial court are teeming with clods." And one year later: "Consider for a moment that every man and his dog has a permanent post and can be certain of his livelihood; but dear Lord, wherever shall a *parvum talentum com* [*sic*] *ego* [a meager talent as mine] find employment?" (*BBr,* nos. 84 and 157).

2. It is no coincidence that the new theater's curtain portrayed a scene from *The Magic Flute.*

3. Report from Ignaz von Seyfried, cited in Kerst, *Die Erinnerungen an Beethoven,* 1: 77.

4. *BBr,* no. 176.

5. Various sources suggest that Beethoven was introduced to the material by his fellow composer and ex-musical director of the Kärntnertortheater, the Italian Ferdinando Paër. Paër was himself working on a *Leonore*-themed opera at the time and may have fanned Beethoven's enthusiasm for the story. German Beethoven commentator Klaus Martin Kopitz recently formulated the hypothesis that Therese von Zandt—a pianist, singer, and music critic from Düsseldorf—introduced Beethoven to Bouilly's *Léonore.* Kopitz also suggests that Beethoven had a love affair with Therese during this period, despite the lack of any mention of her throughout the Beethoven biographical source materials (cf. Klaus Martin Kopitz, "'Sieben volle Monate': Beethoven und Therese von Zandt," *Musica* 49 [1995]: 325–32).

6. Cf. *BBr,* no. 127.

7. Originally the Terzetto "Tremate, empi, tremate" for soprano, tenor, bass, and orchestra (op. 116) was also included on the program but was removed at the last minute for fear that the program was too long.

8. WR, 76.

9. Cited in Kunze, *Ludwig van Beethoven,* 233.

10. TF, 329–30.

11. TF, 371.

12. Cited in Kunze, *Ludwig van Beethoven,* 232–34.

13. TDR, 2: 387ff.

14. Cited in Kunze, *Ludwig van Beethoven*, 233.

15. TDR, 2: 387.

16. *BBr*, no. 158, footnote 10.

17. Cited in Kunze, *Ludwig van Beethoven*, 36; and Jean and Brigitte Massin, *Ludwig van Beethoven*, Paris, 1967, 629.

18. Hector Berlioz, *Beethoven: Étude critique des symphonies de Beethoven*, Paris, 1844, 30; Alexandr Ulybyshev, *Beethoven, ses critiques et ses glossateurs*, Paris, 1857, 144; Adolf Bernhard Marx, *Ludwig van Beethoven, Leben und Schaffen*, Berlin, 1884, 222.

19. George Grove, *Beethoven and His Nine Symphonies*, London, 1998, 28.

20. Reprises were held in Vienna in 1803 on July 21 and August 4, and also on March 27, 1804 (in an altered form).

21. *BBr*, no. 523.

22. Cf. *BBr*, no. 519.

23. Ibid.

24. *BBr*, no. 545. It was in this adulterated form that the *Mount of Olives* was performed for nearly two hundred years.

27. SALIERI'S OPERA LESSONS

1. For a long time it was thought that Beethoven commenced lessons with Salieri in 1792; however, recent research has convincingly demonstrated that the correct date is 1801 (cf. Julia Ronge, *Beethovens Lehrzeit: Kompositionsstudien bei Joseph Haydn, Johann Georg Albrechtsberger und Antonio Salieri*, Bonn, 2011, 141).

2. "U, I, O sono vocali ingrati, dove evita di fare molte note o colorature." Cited in Gustav Nottebohm, *Beethoven's Studien: Beethoven's Unterricht bei J. Haydn, Albrechtsberger und Salieri*, Leipzig, 1873, 210.

3. *BBr*, no. 350.

4. Cf. Clive, *Beethoven and His world*, 303; and Ronge, *Beethovens Lehrzeit*, 69, footnote 435.

5. Cf. TDR, 1: 365.

28. THE MYSTERY OF THE *EROICA*

1. Cf. *BBr*, nos. 152, 165, and 173.

2. Cf. Martin Geck and Peter Schleuning, *"Geschrieben auf Bonaparte"*: *Beethovens "Eroica,"* Reinbek bei Hamburg, 1989, 139.

3. Beethoven met Kreutzer in the spring of 1798 as a member of a French delegation led by Ambassador Jean-Baptiste Bernadotte. Their acquaintance was brief, as a diplomatic blunder forced Bernadotte and his entourage to leave Vienna in haste.

Many Beethoven biographers believe that Bernadotte suggested the idea of a Bonaparte symphony to Beethoven in 1798; however, this theory stems directly from Schindler. There are plenty of reasons to doubt it, not least of which were the troubled relations between Bonaparte and Bernadotte at the time. Some years after Bernadotte had been crowned King Charles XIV John of Sweden and Norway, Beethoven wrote two letters to him in which he recalled their pleasant meeting from 1798, neither of which made any mention of a Bonaparte symphony.

4. Hector Berlioz, *Voyage musical en Allemagne et en Italie*, Paris, 1844, 1: 264.

5. *BBr*, no. 84. Italics from translator.

6. Sources show that the Triple Concerto in C Major (op. 56) was also tried out during these sessions.

7. Tomislav Volek and Jaroslav Macek, "Beethoven's Rehearsals at the Lobkowitz's," *Musical Times* 127 (1986): 75–80.

8. WR, 79.

9. Cf. *BBr*, no. 212.

10. This fact explains several interesting instructions written by Beethoven on the title page; for example, advising the first horn player to sit in between the two others.

11. WR, 78.

12. *BBr*, nos. 165 and 188. Emphasis by author.

13. Published in *Der Freimüthige*, April 26, 1805. Cited in Irmen, *Beethoven in seiner Zeit*, 247.

14. Ibid.

15. Cited in Geck and Schleuning, *"Geschrieben auf Bonaparte,"* 136.

16. *BBr*, nos. 205 and 210.

17. *BBr*, no. 212.

18. Frederik Slezak, *Beethovens Wiener Originalverleger*, Vienna, 1987, 58.

19. Cited in Walter Brauneis, "'. . . *composta per festeggiare il souvenire di un grand Uomo*': Beethovens 'Eroica' als Hommage des Fürsten Franz Joseph Maximilian von Lobkowitz für Ferdinand von Preussen," *Österreichische Musikzeitschrift* 53, no. 12 (1998): 4–24. The remaining commentary in this chapter is also based largely on the above article. Incidentally, Brauneis does not exclude the possibility that the original manuscript of the *Eroica*—which must have been in Lobkowitz's possession, but which is now lost—was at one time also owned by the family of Louis Ferdinand.

20. TDR, 2: 519. Here Beethoven was paraphrasing Cherubini, who directed the following, far more subtle recrimination at the young Bonaparte: *"On peut être habile sur le champ de bataille et ne point se connaître en harmonie"* (One can be a master on the battlefield but not know the first thing about harmony). It seems that Cherubini relayed as much to Beethoven (Geck and Schleuning, *"Geschrieben auf Bonaparte,"* 62).

21. Cited in Jacques-Gabriel Prod'homme, "The Baron de Trémont: Souvenirs of Beethoven and Other Contemporaries," *Musical Quarterly* 6 (1920): 378.

22. Czerny, "Anekdoten und Notizen über Beethoven," 14.

23. *BKh*, 1: 209.

24. TDR, 3: 505.

25. Cooper, *Beethoven and the Creative Process*, 43.

26. Floros, *Beethovens Eroica*, 73–104; Geck and Schleuning, *"Geschrieben auf Bonaparte,"* 108–29.

27. Cf. A. B. Marx, *Ludwig van Beethoven*, 180–95; and Ulybyshev, *Beethoven, ses critiques, ses glossatiers*, 173–80. Due to the possible anomalies present in this interpretation, in 1925 the German musicologist Paul Bekker proposed performing the funeral march *after* the scherzo.

28. For a comprehensive treatment of this subject, see Scott Burnham, "On the Programmatic Reception of Beethoven's Eroica Symphony," *BF* (1992): 1–24.

29. *BBr*, no. 218.

30. Cf. Kurt Dorfmüller, Norbert Gertsch, Julia Ronge, Gertraut Haberkamp, and Georg Kinsky, *Ludwig van Beethoven: Thematisch-bibliographisches Werkverzeichnis*, Beethoven-Haus, Bonn, 1: 301.

29. THE IMMORTAL BELOVED: EPISODE TWO

1. The wholesaler Johann Baptist Pasqualati von Osterberg was a passionate music lover with some talent at the piano, and he even seems to have composed several waltzes and polonaises. He helped Beethoven in many ways, by organizing the ticket sales for some of his concerts and providing legal advice during the dispute with the Kinsky family from 1812 on. He remained a good friend to Beethoven until the end of his life. Two weeks before he died, Beethoven thanked Pasqualati for all that he had done for him, saying, "Heaven bless you for everything, but for your loving kindness to me in particular" (*BBr*, no. 2275).

2. Cited in Marie-Elisabeth Tellenbach, *Beethoven und seine "Unsterbliche Geliebte" Josephine Brunswick*, Zurich, 1983, 64.

3. Ibid., 65.

4. *BBr*, no. 216.

5. *BBr*, nos. 219, 202, and 203.

6. *BBr*, no. 216.

7. For a long time—based on a letter to her mother from March 1805—it was believed that Josephine was given this song as a New Year's gift. However, studies of Beethoven's sketchbooks reveal that he commenced work on it in June 1804, immediately after starting to see Josephine again.

8. Stendhal believed that there were seven stages to true love: (1) Admiration; (2) Sensual thoughts; (3) Hope; (4) Love is born; (5) The first crystallization begins; (6) Doubt is born; and (7) The second crystallization begins (cf. Marie Henri Beyle-Stendhal, *On Love*, Plymouth, 1920, 22ff.).

9. Cited in Tellenbach, *Beethoven und seine "Unsterbliche Geliebte,"* 65. Emphasis by Charlotte Brunsvik. The succeeding quotations come from this same book.

10. Cited in Rita Steblin, "Josephine Gräfin Brunsvick-Deyms Geheimnis enthüllt," *Österreichische Musikzeitschrift* 57, no. 6 (2002): 29.

11. In 1830, according to Alice M. Hanson, 40 percent of children were born out of wedlock (Alice M. Hanson, *Musical Life in Biedermeier Vienna*, Cambridge, 1985, 11). Jean-Paul Bled even places this figure at around 50 percent in 1860, easily the highest in Europe (Bled, *Wien*, 252).

12. *BBr*, no. 215.

13. *BBr*, no. 250. Emphasis by Josephine. (Of this letter, only a draft survives.)

14. *BBr*, no. 294.

15. *BBr*, no. 295.

16. Tellenbach, *Beethoven und seine "Unsterbliche Geliebte,"* 91.

17. Cf. Steblin, "Josephine Gräfin Brunsvick-Deyms Geheimnis enthüllt," 23–31; and "Auf diese Art mit A," *BBS* 6 (2007): 147–80.

18. Steblin, "Auf diese Art mit A," 155. See also Dagmar Skwara and Rita Steblin, "Ein Brief Christoph Freiherr von Stackelbergs an Josephine Brunsvik-Deym-Stackelberg," *BBS* 6 (2007): 181–87. This theory is confirmed by a police inspector's report from 1815, stating that "the moral reputation of the countess is hardly in her favour" (Tellenbach, *Beethoven und seine "Unsterbliche Geliebte,"* 140).

19. Tellenbach, *Beethoven und seine "Unsterbliche Geliebte,"* 106–9.

20. *BBr*, no. 367.

21. Cf. *BBr*, no. 442.

22. See Cooper, *Beethoven and the Creative Process*, 226. In 1867, Ludwig Nohl reported having come across this "charming little piano piece" among the belongings of a certain Mrs. Bredl in Munich (Ludwig Nohl, *Neue Briefe Beethovens*, Stuttgart, 1867, 28). Since it was only a transcription, in the absence of the original manuscript Breitkopf & Härtel did not include it in the *Complete Beethoven Edition* compiled between 1862 and 1865. In 1925, Max Unger hypothesized that Nohl's reading of the scribbled "Elise" was perhaps a misinterpretation of "Therese" and that the Bagatelle in A Minor had been composed for Therese Malfatti (Ludwig Nohl, "Beethoven und Therese Malfatti," *Musical Quarterly* 11 [1925]: 70). Michael Lorenz has reconstructed the provenance of *Für Elise*, offering a potential explanation for how it arrived in the hands of Babette Bredl. In her will, Therese Malfatti bequeathed all of her musical possessions (including a number of Beethoven autographs) to her regular duet partner and family friend, Rudolf Schachner. We can therefore reasonably assume that the manuscript of *Für Elise* went first to Schachner and later passed to his mother, Babette Bredl (Michael Lorenz, "Die 'Enttarnte Elise': Elisabeth Röckels kurze Karriere als Beethovens 'Elise,'" *BBS* 9 [2011]: 169–90).

In 2009, Klaus Martin Kopitz made world headlines with his controversial theory that *Für Elise* was written for Elisabeth Röckel, the younger sister of opera singer Joseph Röckel (Florestan from the second season of *Leonore*) and wife of fellow composer Johann Nepomuk Hummel. Beethoven and Mrs. Röckel seemingly had a more than passing acquaintance. Kopitz subsequently expounded his theory in *Beethoven, Elisabeth Röckel und das Albumblatt "Für Elise,"* Cologne, 2010. The theory was quickly debunked by Michael Lorenz, however (cf. Kopitz, *op. cit.*).

23. Cf. Renate Moering, "Bettine von Arnims literarische Umsetzung ihres Beethoven-Erlebnisses," in *Der "männliche" und der "weibliche" Beethoven: Bericht über den Internationalen musikwissenschaftlichen Kongress vom 31. Oktober bis 4. November 2001 an der Universität der Künste Berlin,* published by C. Bartsch, B. Borchard, and R. Cadenbach, Bonn, 2003, 251–77.

24. In 1839, Bettina Brentano published three of Beethoven's letters to her in the journal *Athenaeum für Wissenschaft, Kunst und Leben.* Beethoven specialists are now in agreement that only the letter dated February 10, 1811 (*BBr,* no. 485) is authentic (cf. Klaus Martin Kopitz, "Antonie Brentano in Wien (1809–1812): Neue Quellen zur Problematik 'Unsterbliche Geliebte,'" *BBS* 2 [2001]: 115–44; and Moering, "Bettine von Arnims literarische Umsetzung ihres Beethoven-Erlebnisses," 251–77).

25. Various dates have been put forward for the origin of the *Appassionata.* There is a growing consensus, however, that Beethoven worked on it from the summer of 1804 until the autumn of 1805; that the autograph dates from 1806; and that the first edition appeared in February 1807 (cf. Martha Frohlich, *Beethoven's "Appassionata" Sonata,* Oxford, 1991, 41–49).

26. While "four hands" arrangements of great masterworks were common in the nineteenth century (and a highly lucrative business), the accessibility of these types of arrangements had a rather perverse side effect on the character of the *Appassionata.* Since its unforgiving technical demands are an essential component of the idiom and also serve as a metaphor for the desperation expressed in the music, the ease and facility of the piano duet version actually served to undermine the very essence of the sonata.

27. Czerny later pointed out that proper Beethoven interpretation demands not only a classical legato touch for melodic themes (in which case he said that more vitality was required in the fingers), but also a special breed of legato for parallel chords. Czerny testified that Beethoven was a master at playing chords in smooth succession without the aid of the pedal (Rosenblum, *Performance Practices,* 423).

28. WR, 99.

29. For many years the Brunsviks incorrectly claimed that Beethoven composed the *Appassionata* during a visit to Martonvásár. Franz Liszt was prompted by this story to visit the Brunsvik residence between giving two concerts in Pest, to perform the sonata at its "sacred place" of birth. Therese was a captive listener.

30. *BBr,* no. 220.

31. WR, 102.

30. IN SEARCH OF THE PERFECT PIANO

1. The full title is as follows: *Kurze Bemerkungen über das Spielen, Stimmen und Erhalten der Pianoforte, welche von Nannette Streicher, geborne Stein, in Wien verfertigt werden: Ausschliessend nur für die Besitzer dieser Instrumente aufgesetzt* (Brief

remarks on the playing, tuning, and care of fortepianos: made in Vienna by Nannette Streicher née Stein, drawn up exclusively for the owners of these instruments), Vienna, 1801.

2. *BBr*, no. 22.

3. *BBr*, no. 23.

4. The Walter grand's more powerful action even necessitated a "backcheck," a mechanism that prevented the hammer from rebounding back into the string after the initial strike.

5. The effect was relative, however. Pianist and composer Johann Nepomuk Hummel attested that from a distance Viennese pianos sounded better than their English counterparts due to their transparency of sound, and could cut through the orchestra with greater facility (cf. Christo Lelie, *Van Piano tot Forte: De geschiedenis en ontwikkeling van de vroege piano*, Kampen, 1995, 153).

6. Despite his desire for a more robust sound, Beethoven was interested first and foremost in more delicate playing. The dynamic indications in his piano sonatas pertaining to subtle shades of softness (from *mp* to *ppp*) outnumber those for degrees of loudness (*mf* to *fff*) almost two to one (cf. Rosenblum, *Performance Practices*, 58). His playing, too, was extremely sensitive, and his scores were covered in articulation and fingering marks. The primary aim of Beethoven's fingerings was to prioritize expressiveness over ease of execution, making them frequently very unorthodox and occasionally uncomfortable.

7. Beethoven received the "Erard no. 133." Two years earlier, Haydn had been gifted the "Erard no. 28" for the same reason. The occasionally unexpected twists and turns of such promotional strategies are exemplified by the fact that the "Erard no. 30" was given to Napoleon's wife, Josephine.

8. And so this instrument ended up in Linz, where it can still be viewed today in the State Museum of Upper Austria (Oberösterreichisches Landesmuseum).

9. Cf. Reichardt, *Vertraute Briefe*, 2: 385ff.

10. The surviving body of Beethoven correspondence (*BBr*) includes over sixty letters dating from 1817–18 written both to and from Nannette on problems of this nature.

11. *BBr*, no. 1137.

12. Rather than a workshop or studio, the Broadwoods' business was a bona fide factory where the instruments were assembled on a "production line" by individuals specializing in a range of disciplines: cabinetmakers, piano technicians, string tensioners, etc.

13. The value of this gift increased even further when it was signed by multiple great piano virtuosos: Friedrich Kalkbrenner, Ferdinand Ries, Giacomo Gotifredo Ferrari, Johann Baptist Cramer, and Charles Knyvett.

14. *BBr*, no. 1242. "My dearest friend Broadwood! Never have I experienced greater joy than that upon reading the note in which you promise me the honour of one of your pianos. I shall regard it as a sacred altar upon which to offer up to Apollo the most beautiful products of my spirit. As soon as I have your glorious instrument, my dearest B[roadwood], I promise to send to you as a keepsake the

fruits of inspiration that come to me during the very first moments I spend at it. I can only hope that they are worthy of your instrument."

15. After Beethoven's death, the Broadwood made its way via a Viennese music trader into the hands of Franz Liszt, who treated it with all the reverence of a holy relic. In 1874 he bequeathed it to the Hungarian National Museum in Pest, where it still stands today.

16. This piano is currently on display in the Beethoven-Haus in Bonn.

17. Cf. Kerst, *Die Erinnerungen an Beethoven,* 1: 309.

31. *LEONORE*

1. Kinsky and Halm, *Das Werk Beethovens,* 174.

2. At the premiere, *Léonore* was introduced as a work "based on events in France from several years before." We now know that this was an exaggeration: Bouilly, who had a reputation as a *cachotier* (slyboots), fused various events together into an amalgam, adding a good deal of his own imagination in the process (cf. David Galliver, "Léonore, ou L'amour conjugal: A Celebrated Offspring of the Revolution," in *Music and the French Revolution,* ed. Malcolm Boyd, Cambridge, 1992, 164, 168).

3. This aria is the literal centerpiece, not only of the second act but of the entire opera.

4. Cf. *BBr,* no. 237.

5. Cf. *BBr,* no. 239.

6. Like his colleagues, Beethoven always left the overture until last; since only the orchestra was required, its rehearsal could be postponed until the very end. It was long believed that an initial overture to the opera—now known as *Leonore I*—was scrapped following a private performance at the Lichnowskys because it was considered too light in character. Beethoven then supposedly (and hastily) composed a new overture, *Leonore II,* which was subsequently reworked into *Leonore III* for the reprise in 1806. Gustav Nottebohm had pointed out as early as 1870 that the Lichnowsky tale was completely unfounded and that the so-called *Leonore I* was actually composed later for a production in Prague in 1807. Since this production never took place, the overture was never used. After Beethoven's death in 1827, it was rediscovered and sold for a pittance to a publisher, Haslinger. It received opus number 138 and was performed for the first time on February 7, 1828, during a concert given in Vienna by the cellist Bernhard Romberg. It was Felix Mendelssohn who first thought of programming all of the *Leonore* and *Fidelio* overtures during a single concert (on January 9, 1840) in their numerical (but anachronistic) order. Nottebohm's strong arguments were further substantiated by Scottish Beethoven expert Tyson in 1975 (see Alan Tyson, "The Problem of Beethoven's 'First' Leonore Overture," *Journal of the American Musicological Society* 28 [1975]: 292–34). Despite the historical evidence to the contrary, the reputation of *Leonore I* as an inadequate first draft stubbornly persists to this day.

A fundamental respect in which *Leonore I* differs from its two predecessors is in the more restrained use of material from the rest of the opera. Beethoven believed—and rightly so—that it was dramatically counterproductive to give away certain key elements at the outset, such as the liberating trumpet signal in the opera's climax.

7. Cf. Schindler, *Biographie*, 1: 133.

8. TF, 384.

9. *BBr*, no. 236.

10. Beethoven was appeased somewhat during the second set of performances in March 1806: *Fidelio* still appeared on the posters, but *Leonore* was used for the libretto. For the third season in 1814, only *Fidelio* was used, with Beethoven's full approval. The Beethoven literature generally draws a distinction between the 1805/1806 versions, which are both titled *Leonore,* and the 1814 version, which is called *Fidelio.*

11. Bouilly's original also only comprised two acts. Beethoven and Sonnleithner had decided on a three-act structure for the first production, meaning that Beethoven quickly needed to compose an introduction to the second act, which was ready only just in time. This new structure did result in a marvelous symmetry: each act now included six numbers, and the first and last acts mirrored one another by gradually increasing the number of protagonists from one to four. The downside to the tripartite form was that by the first intermission, the audience had still seen none of the actual drama.

12. The critics, too, believed the opera to be far shorter. The *Allgemeine musikalische Zeitung* printed this: "Beethoven has brought his opera, *Fidelio,* back to the stage in a reworked and abridged form. It is now a full act shorter, but is the better for it and was much more well-received" (*AmZ,* 1806).

13. *BBr*, no. 245.

14. Cited in TF, 397–98.

15. *BBr*, no. 248.

16. Cf. Ibid.

17. Cf. TF, 509ff.

18. *Journal des Luxus und der Moden* 21 (1806): 287. Cited in Kunze, *Ludwig van Beethoven,* Vienna, 1991, 46.

19. Cited in Günther Tolar, *So ein Theater! Die Geschichte des Theaters an der Wien,* Vienna, 1991, 46.

20. WR, 92. Ries does not mention the count's full name, abbreviating it only to "P . . ."

21. *BBr*, no. 302.

32. THE GOLDEN YEARS

1. Cf. Clive, *Beethoven and His World,* 14.

2. Cf. J. F. Ritter von Schönfeld, *Jahrbuch der Tonkunst von Wien und Prag,* Vienna, 1796, 75, 92. Cited in Indorf, *Beethovens Streichquartette,* 99.

3. Cf. TDR, 2: 125; and Indorf, *Beethovens Streichquartette,* 101–2.

4. *AmZ*, February 27, 1807, column 400. Cited by Kunze, *Ludwig van Beethoven*, 72.

5. Cited in Joseph Kerman, "Beethoven Quartet Audiences: Actual, Potential, Ideal," in *The Beethoven Quartet Companion*, ed. Robert Winter and Robert Martin, Berkeley, 1994, 16.

6. This did not stop Beethoven from later dedicating the Violin Concerto to his friend Stephan Breuning.

7. The final movement, according to Czerny, was not finished until two days before the premiere, leaving just enough time for copyists to produce the orchestral parts. The fact that Beethoven did not start on the Violin Concerto until late November is confirmed by a letter sent to Breitkopf & Härtel that offered several new works—some of which were still in progress—but made no mention of the Violin Concerto (*BBr*, no. 260).

8. The concerto's technical bias and specific difficulties explain why it is rarely performed at eisteddfods or other competitions.

9. Cf. Shin A. Kojima, "Die Solovioline-Fassungen und Varianten von Beethovens Violinkonzert op. 61: Ihre Entstehung und Bedeutung," *Beethoven Jahrbuch* 8 (1975): 97–145; and Alan Tyson, "The Textual Problems of Beethoven's Violin Concerto," *Musical Quarterly* 53/54 (1967): 482–502.

10. The rather bland left-hand part of this arrangement has led some commentators to believe that the piano version was prepared by a student or assistant and that Beethoven merely checked, corrected, and approved it. Even if this is true, the possibility cannot be discounted that even such limited involvement is what prompted Beethoven to alter the violin part.

11. Cf. TDR, 3: 10.

12. *BBr*, nos. 325 and 340.

13. *AmZ*, 1812, column 381. Cited by Kunze, *Ludwig van Beethoven*, 84.

14. Cited in Martin Geck, *Von Beethoven bis Mahler: Die Musik des deutschen Idealismus*, Stuttgart, 1993, 35.

15. Despite Richard Wagner's 1852 essay on the *Coriolan* Overture, it is folly to take Shakespeare's play as the basis for its interpretation. Both Beethoven and Collin only knew the Coriolan legend from Plutarch's *Parallel Lives*—Shakespeare's version was not translated into German until 1830.

16. Cf. *BBr*, no. 10, footnote 2.

17. Cf. Clive, *Beethoven and His World*, 74; and *BBr*, no. 2201.

18. Cf. WR, 101.

19. *BBr*, 291.

20. *BBr*, 292.

21. Haydn struggled with the same deadlines and lack of rehearsal time. (It is no coincidence that the *Nelson* Mass was nicknamed the *Missa in angustiis*, or "Mass for troubled times.") Likewise, the *Creation* Mass was not ready until after the princess's name day; luckily, the next available Sunday for the performance was not until five days later. In Haydn's case, however, the limited timeframe was never a problem, since his style was already very familiar to the performers.

22. *BBr,* no. 293.

23. Schindler, *Biographie,* 1: 189. Given that Schindler is the only source for this incident and his account contains several inaccuracies (it is known, for example, that Beethoven remained in the vicinity for another three days), the veracity of the anecdote has been called into question. The fact remains, however, that after the premiere of the *Missa* and Esterházy's veiled rejection, Beethoven's relationship with him deteriorated. When writing to Schindler in 1823, asking him to inquire as to the prince's response to the *Missa solemnis* invitation, Beethoven remarked, "I hold no hopes for success, as I suspect that I can count on no generosity from him, given what has happened in the past" (*BBr,* no. 1662).

24. "La messe de Beethoven est insupportablement ridicule et detestable [...] J'en suis colerè *[sic]* et honteux." Cited in *BBr,* no. 292, footnote 2.

25. *BBr,* nos. 1486 and 1266.

26. Beethoven participated in at least three concerts: on April 11 and 13, and on November 15.

27. For some time it was believed that the Fourth Piano Concerto premiered during a pair of concerts at the Lobkowitz residence in March 1807. Leon Plantinga has convincingly demonstrated that this cannot be the case (cf. Plantinga, *Beethoven's Concertos,* 210–13).

28. Cited in Marianne Pandi and Fritz Schmidt, "Musik zur Zeit Haydns und Beethovens in der Pressburger Zeitung," *Haydn Yearbook* 8 (1971): 225; and David Wyn Jones, *The Symphony in Beethoven's Vienna,* Cambridge, 2006, 124.

29. The final section of "Seufzer eines Ungeliebten—Gegenliebe" (Sighs of one unloved—requited love; WoO 118).

30. The deterioration in Beethoven's playing had many causes. He had not considered himself a pianist for some time and barely practiced anymore. He may also have been suffering the aftereffects of a serious finger infection (known as "whitlow" or "felon") from earlier in the spring. It is unknown how Beethoven contracted the infection, only that it became so serious that amputating all or part of the finger was presented as an option. Although the treatment he received was clearly adequate (and included mustard-based herbal poultices), it is altogether possible that Beethoven continued to suffer from stiffness in the digits.

31. The common practice of labeling the opening of the Fifth Symphony as the "knocking motif" owes its origins to Schindler, who claimed to have heard Beethoven say, "Here is fate knocking at the door" (Schindler, *Biographie,* 1: 159). The "Fate" nickname for the symphony as a whole can also be traced back to this—probably apocryphal—quotation.

32. Cited in *Beethoven: Interpretationen seiner Werke,* published by Albrecht Riethmüller, Carl Dahlhaus, and Alexandre L. Ringer, Laaber, 1996, 1: 501.

33. *BBr,* no. 325.

34. The *Pastoral* sketches reveal that Beethoven considered closing this symphony with a choral movement, as he eventually would in the Ninth Symphony.

35. Cited in *Ludwig van Beethoven: Thematisch-bibliograpisches Werkverzeichnis,* published by Kurt Dorfmüller, Norbert Gertsch, and Julia Ronge, Munich, 2014, 1: 373.

1. *AmZ,* May 3, 1809 (cited in *BBr,* no. 375, footnote 6).

2. *BBr,* no. 350.

3. Beethoven made the following piece of wordplay in a letter to Countess Erdődy: "Brauchle wird sich vom <u>Brauchen</u> wohl nicht entfernen, und [S]ie werden wie immer Tag und Nacht von ihm Gebrauch machen" (*BBr,* no. 934). Translated literally: "Brauchle will no doubt stay true to his <u>needs</u>, and you shall be able to make use of him day and night."

4. Opinion on what sparked this dispute is divided. It is generally assumed that Beethoven was angry at the countess for having paid his servant extra to work for her as well; Solomon, however, makes claims that the countess paid the servant for sexual favors (cf. Solomon, *Beethoven,* 201).

5. Their suspicions were entirely justified: King Jérôme of Westphalia was forced to secede on October 26, 1813.

6. *BBr,* no. 776.

7. Cited in Martella Gutiérrez-Denhoff, "'O Unseeliges Dekret': Beethovens Rente von Fürst Lobkowitz, Fürst Kinsky und Erzhertog Rudolph," in *"Alle Noten bringen mich nicht aus den Nöthen!!": Begleitpublikationen zu Ausstellungen des Beethoven-Hauses,* ed. Nicole Kämpken and Michael Ladenburger, Bonn, 2005, 49.

8. Ibid.

9. Cf. Johann Friedrich Reichardt, *Vertraute Briefe* (March 27, 1809), cited in Sven Hiemke, *Ludwig van Beethoven: Missa solemnis,* Kassel, 2003, 34.

10. Cf. Ingrid Fuchs, "'Ohne Geld, keine Musik': Zu den Preisen von Noten und Musikinstrumenten in der Beethoven-Zeit," in *"Alle Noten bringen michnicht aus den Nöthen!!"* 94.

11. *BBr,* no. 665.

12. Frederik Weissensteiner, *Die Österreichischen Kaiser: Franz I—Ferdinand I—Franz Joseph I—Karl I,* Vienna, 2003, 38.

13. The Austrian government had also had little experience with the paper currency introduced in 1780 and believed the problem could be solved simply by printing mountains of additional banknotes. Between 1805 and 1811, the number of notes in circulation tripled.

14. Cf. Marek, *Ludwig van Beethoven,* 413. Unlike the revised edition of Thayer's biography (TDR, 3: 298), the original (highly edited) version from 1866 to 1879 contains no details on the circumstances of Kinsky's death.

15. Cf. Jaroslav Macek, "Beethoven und Ferdinand Fürst Kinsky," in *Beethoven im Herzen Europas,* published by Hans-Werner Küthen and Oldrich Pulkert, Prague, 2000, 230.

16. *BBr,* nos. 644 and 661.

17. *BBr,* nos. 553, 661, and 615.

34. NEW PROSPECTS

1. *BBr*, no. 392.

2. Johann Joseph Fux, *Gradus ad Parnassum oder Anführung zur Regelmässigen Musicalischen Composition*, Leipzig, 1742, "Des Verfassers Vorrede an den Leser."

3. Cf. Clemens Brenneis, *Ludwig van Beethoven: Ein Skizzenbuch aus dem Jahre 1809* [Landsberg 5], Bonn, 1993, 1: 75.

4. *BBr*, nos. 392 and 408.

5. Cited in Ludwig Nohl, *Beethoven nach den Schilderungen seiner Zeitgenossen*, Stuttgart, 1877, 116.

6. Cited in TF, 473–74.

7. Cf. Carl Dahlhaus, *Ludwig van Beethoven: Approaches to His Music*, Oxford, 1991, 202–18.

35. AN IMPERIAL PUPIL

1. Cf. *BBr*, no. 636.

2. Cf. Hiemke, *Ludwig van Beethoven*, 34.

3. Literally in German: "[...] dass dem gnädigsten Hern auf einmal alles Pfaffthum und Pfaffthun verschwunden ist, und also die ganze Sache nichts seyn wird" (*BBr*, no. 523).

4. It is difficult to properly estimate the scope and content of the archduke's library, as sections of the catalogues have been scattered or lost. However, some sources indicate the presence of at least 2,500 scores (including many Beethoven manuscripts) and 500 books (cf. Sieghard Brandenburg, "Die Beethovenhandschriften in der Musikaliensammlung des Erzhertogs Rudolph," *Zu Beethoven* 3 [1988]: 141–76).

5. While it is true that Beethoven began the Triple Concerto in 1804, Schindler's claim that Archduke Rudolph premiered the work in collaboration with professionals Carl August Seidler and Anton Kraft is false. If such were the case, Beethoven would almost certainly have dedicated the work to Rudolph and not to Lobkowitz—who organized the first private performance at his own home a full year before the official premiere. The rehearsals (with Seidler and Kraft) were held at the home of Paul Bigot de Morogues, suggesting that his wife, the gifted pianist Marie Bigot, played the piano part. Later speculations attributing the modest technical demands of the Triple Concerto to the archduke's limited capacity at the piano are therefore unfounded.

6. It seems that the archduke never considered taking piano lessons, explained in part perhaps by his struggles with chronic rheumatoid arthritis and gout. These conditions often prevented him from playing for long periods, and in 1814 he was forced to give up the piano entirely.

7. Beethoven was unhappy with the French translations of the title and subtitles added by Breitkopf & Härtel to make the sonata more commercially appealing. (Piano works with titles such as *Les Adieux de Paris* or *Les Adieux de Londres*—"Farewell to Paris" or "Farewell to London"—were very much in vogue.) To Beethoven, *Das Lebewohl* had an entirely different, more personal, and emotionally profound connotation than *Les Adieux*, which was more commonly used for "large groups or cities" (cf. *BBr*, no. 523).

8. This "theory course" was published in 1832 by the conductor Ignaz von Seyfried, as *Ludwig van Beethoven's Studien im Generalbasse, Contrapuncte und in der Compositions-Lehre* (Ludwig van Beethoven's studies in thorough-bass, counterpoint and theory of composition), falsely suggesting that Beethoven had written an original composition treatise.

9. Kinsky and Halm, *Das Werk Beethovens*, 701.

10. For a detailed discussion of this subject matter, see Tibor Szász, "Figured Bass in Beethoven's 'Emperor' Concerto," *Early Keyboard Journal* 6–7 (1988–89): 5–71; and "Beethoven's basso continuo: Notation and performance," in *Performing Beethoven*, ed. Robin Stowel, Cambridge, 1994, 1–22.

11. Cited in TF, 599.

36. BEETHOVEN AND GOETHE

1. *BBr*, no. 408.

2. Cf. Frederik Schiller, "Über Egmont, Trauerspiel von Goethe," in *Werke*, Frankfurt am Main, 1966, 4: 371–80.

3. Cf. TDR, 3: 202ff.

4. Ibid., 203.

5. In 1821, German poet Friedrich Mosengeil wrote "narrative interludes" to replace the original stage dialogue in concert performances of the *Egmont* music. A host of other writers and directors—from Franz Grillparzer to Peter Stein—have since followed his example.

6. *BBr*, no. 545.

7. Beethoven's willingness to work with Kotzebue may come as somewhat of a surprise, given the former harsh criticism of Beethoven's music he had published in his own cultural magazine, *Der Freimüthige*. Kotzebue's political ideologies also lay in the conservative-reactionary camp that Beethoven had always so reviled.

8. On this occasion, the original overture (among other things) was replaced with a new work, *The Consecration of the House* (op. 124), and a writer of popular theater, Karl Meisl, also cobbled together a new text.

9. Cf. TDR, 3: 283ff.

10. *BBr*, no. 591.

11. Ibid., footnote 4.

12. Cf. Karl Otto Conrady, *Goethe: Leben und Werk*, Munich, 1994, 852.

13. Letter from Zelter to Goethe dated September 14, 1812. (*Briefwechsel zwischen Goethe und Zelter in den Jahren 1799 bis 1832,* ed. Edith Zehm and Sabine Schäfer, Munich, 1998, 1: 286.)

14. *BBr,* no. 493. Franz Seraficus Oliva would perform secretarial duties for Beethoven until their inevitable falling out in the summer of 1811, after which they parted ways. Ties were not reestablished until 1819, when Oliva once again did some temporary work for Beethoven.

15. *BBr,* no. 509.

16. *BBr,* no. 586.

17. *BBr,* no. 1562.

18. Goethe, *Werke,* Weimarer Ausgabe, IV (Briefe), 23, no. 6348.

19. *Briefwechsel Goethe-Zelter,* ed. Werner Pfister, Zurich, 1987, 95.

20. *BBr,* no. 591.

37. THE IMMORTAL BELOVED: EPISODE THREE

1. Cf. Clive, *Beethoven and His World,* 379.

2. *BBr,* no. 579.

3. *BBr,* no. 583.

4. *BBr,* no. 582.

5. Cf. Tellenbach, *Beethoven und seine "Unsterbliche Geliebte."* Tellenbach bases her research on the pioneering work of Siegmund Kaznelson in *Beethovens Ferne und Unsterbliche Geliebte,* Zurich, 1954; and Jean and Brigitte Massin, *Recherche de Beethoven,* Paris, 1970.

6. Solomon cites three documents that may help reconstruct Josephine's whereabouts in the summer of 1812 (Maynard Solomon, "Recherche de Josephine Deym," in *Beethoven Essays,* Cambridge, MA, 1988, 157–204). This evidence does not rule out the possibility that Josephine stayed in Prague in early July 1812.

7. Cf. Steblin, "Auf diese Art mit A," 180.

8. Ibid., 169–71.

9. *BBr,* no. 582.

10. Cf. Steblin, "Auf diese Art mit A," 173.

11. *BTb,* no. 1, 30; and Steblin, "Auf diese Art mit A," 151–55.

12. Cf. Goldschmidt, *Um die unsterbliche Geliebte,* 83–166; W. Thomas-San-Galli, *Die "unsterbliche Geliebte" Beethovens: Amalie Sebald. Lösung eines vielumstrittenen Problems,* Halle an der Saale, n.d.; and Oldrich Pulkert, "Beethovens 'Unsterbliche Geliebte,'" in *Ludwig van Beethoven im Herzen Europas,* published by Hans-Werner Küthen and Oldrich Pulkert, Prague, 2000, 383–407.

13. The original diary is lost. Anton Gräffer made a copy shortly after Beethoven's death, which for a long time was also presumed lost. Thankfully, there was also a transcription of the transcription—known as the Fischhof Miscellany—on which musicologists based their research for many years. The Gräffer transcription has

since resurfaced and has been republished (cf. TF, 5–18; and Brenneis, "Das Fischhof-Manuskript in der Deutschen Staatsbibliothek," 27–31).

14. Steblin, "Auf diese Art mit A," 175.

15. *BBr*, no. 933.

16. Tellenbach, *Beethoven und seine "Unsterbliche Geliebte,"* 146.

17. *BBr*, no. 696.

18. Cited in Goldschmidt, *Um die Unsterbliche Geliebte*, 183.

19. Ibid., 199.

38. *SE NON È VERO . . .*

1. Cited in Tellenbach, *Beethoven und seine "Unsterbliche Geliebte,"* 15–16.

2. Cf. Beethoven, *Dreizehn unbekannte Briefe an Josephine Gräfin Deym geb. v. Brunsvik*, ed. Joseph Schmidt-Görg, Bonn, 1957.

3. A new candidate was recently nominated: the Paris-born resident of Vienna, Almerie Esterházy, who we know spent the summer of 1812 in Karlsbad. Czech Beethoven researcher Oldrich Pulkert considers this sole fact sufficient evidence on which to base his Almerie hypothesis (cf. Oldrich Pulkert, "Beethovens 'Unsterbliche Geliebte,'" 383–407). For a recent list of all candidates and their proponents, see Yayoi Aoki, *Beethoven: Die Entschlüsselung des Rätsels um die "Unsterbliche Geliebte,"* Munich, 2008; and John E. Klapproth, *Beethoven's Only Beloved: Josephine!* Charleston, SC, 2011, 319–41.

4. Cf. Maynard Solomon, "Recherche de Josephine Deym," in *Beethoven Essays*, 157; "Antonie Brentano and Beethoven," in *Beethoven Essays*, 165–89; and *Beethoven*, 231.

5. Ernst Pichler, *Beethoven: Mythos und Wirklichkeit*, Vienna, 1994, 273.

6. Cf. Solomon, *Beethoven*, 239.

7. Of significant weight in Solomon's argumentation for Beethoven's considerable affection for Antonie Brentano, and thus for her candidacy as his "immortal beloved," is the dedication to her of the *Diabelli* Variations (op. 120) and the English edition of the Piano Sonata in C Minor (op. 111); and to her daughter Maximiliane of the Piano Sonata in E Major (op. 109) and the Piano Trio in B-flat (WoO 39) (Solomon, "Antonie Brentano and Beethoven," 181–82). John E. Klapproth counters this argument by demonstrating that all of the above dedications (excepting the Piano Trio, whose provenance we now better understand) were made more than ten years after the "unforgettable" summer of 1812. Klapproth believes that Beethoven intended the dedications as compensation for his outstanding loans with the Brentanos (Klapproth, *Beethoven's Only Beloved*, 240).

8. *BBr*, nos. 625 and 1008.

9. *BTb*, no. 122, 87.

10. *BKh*, 1: 254.

11. Cf. Solomon, *Beethoven*, 339–40; and "Beethoven's Tagebuch of 1812–1818," in *Beethoven Studies* 3 (1982): 273.

12. *BKh*, 1: 55.

13. Tellenbach, *Beethoven und seine "Unsterbliche Geliebte,"* 285.

39. THE END OF THE CLASSICAL SYMPHONY

1. Gneixendorf is very close to Krems. The property was four hectares in size, and in addition to a small castle—which can still be visited today—it contained several stables, barns, and a mansion.

2. *BBr,* no. 585.

3. *BBr,* no. 665.

4. *BTb,* nos. 19, 38, 46, and 92.

5. Cf., among others, Maynard Solomon, "Pastoral, Rhetoric, Structure: The Violin Sonata in G, op. 96," in *Late Beethoven: Music, Thought, Imagination,* Berkeley, CA, 2003, 71–91.

6. *BBr,* no. 983.

7. "Symphony in A-Dur, op. 92: Analyse und Essay," in *Die 9 Symphonien Beethovens,* ed. Renate Ulm, Kassel, 1999 (1994), 211.

8. Cf. Leopold Schmidt, *Beethoven: Werke und Leben,* Berlin, 1924, 215.

9. For a long time, Beethoven was known as the "musical Jean Paul." This rather unfortunate association (Beethoven's music was far too well structured and rational to warrant a comparison with the lawless fantasy of the cult poet) disappeared around the mid-nineteenth century, when Jean Paul's own star began to fade.

10. Cf. memorandum dated August 10, 1809, cited by Desmond Seward, *Metternich: Der erste Europäer. Eine Biographie,* Zurich, 1993, 70.

40. MUSIC FOR THE MASSES

1. The risky nature of Beethoven's conducting style is illustrated by an account from Spohr, who tells of an incident that took place during a rehearsal of the Seventh Symphony. Beethoven neglected to observe a fermata in the first movement, making his choreographic conducting hilariously incongruent with the orchestra's playing over the course of the ensuing twelve bars. Spohr also noted that Beethoven tended to hunch behind the stand for piano passages and leap into the air during the fortes. Occasionally he did the opposite, which can only have added to the confusion (cf. *BLuW,* 175–76).

2. *AmZ,* 1814, column 70–71, cited in Kunze, *Ludwig van Beethoven,* 270.

3. Beethoven, *Werke: Gesamtausgabe,* II, 1, ed. Hans-Werner Küthen, 124.

4. Irmen, cited by *Beethoven in seiner Zeit,* 363.

5. Cf. *AmZ,* March 23, 1814, column 201ff.

6. Mälzel's chess automaton once beat a flabbergasted Napoleon. It later transpired that the "automaton" was in fact being manipulated by an experienced chess player hidden behind a curtain.

7. Cf. Matthias Wendt, "Die Zeit der großen äußeren Erfolge: Die Auseinandersetzung um Beethovens Opus 91, 'Wellingtons Sieg oder die Schlacht bei Vittoria,'" in *Beethoven, Mensch seiner Zeit,* ed. Siegfried Kross, Bonn, 1980, 73.

8. Cf. *BBr,* no. 728.

9. Cf. TDR, 3: 397.

10. Cf. *BBr,* no. 728.

11. Cf. *BBr,* no. 742, footnote 2.

12. *BTb,* no. 16: 37; and *BKh,* 1: 326.

13. For a more detailed evaluation of *Wellington's Victory,* see Hans-Werner Küthen, "'Wellingtons Sieg oder die Schlacht bei Vittoria': Beethoven und das Epochenproblem Napoleon," in *Beethoven zwischen Revolution und Restauration,* ed. Helga Lühning and Sieghard Brandenburg, Bonn, 1989, 259–74.

14. Heinrich Heine, "Reisebilder, Vierter Teil, Englische Fragmente," in *Werke und Briefe,* ed. Hans Kaufmann, Berlin, 1972, 3: 479.

41. A LUCRATIVE SIDELINE

1. Cf. *BBr,* no. 679, footnote 6.

2. *BBr,* no. 259. "Je m'éfforcerai de rendre les compositions faciles et agréables autant que je pourrai, et autant que cela peut s'accorder avec cette Elévation et cette originalité du Style, qui selon votre propre aveu caracterisent mes ouvrages asses [*sic*] avantageusement, et dont je ne m'abaisserai jamais."

3. *BBr,* no. 457.

4. His commitment to these arrangements is demonstrated by his express request that the violin and cello parts—which Thomson had specified should be optional—not be left out (cf. *BBr,* no. 556).

5. Cf. *BBr,* nos. 457, 515, and 556.

6. Cf. *BBr,* no. 590.

7. *BBr,* no. 623. "Je suis bien faché de ne pas y pouvoir vous complaire. Je ne suis pas accoutumé de retoucher mes compositions; Je ne l'ai jamais fait, penetré de la verité que tout changement partielle altere le Caractere de la composition. Il me fait de la peine que Vous y perdes mais Vous ne sauries m'en imputer la faute, puisque c'etant a Vous de me faire mieux connoitre le gout de Votre pays & le peu de facilité de vos executeurs."

8. *BBr,* no. 556.

9. Cf. Marc Vignal, *Joseph Haydn,* Paris, 1988, 1399–1400; and Ludwig Finscher, *Joseph Haydn und seine Zeit,* Laaber, 2000, 526.

10. *BBr,* no. 1303. "l'honneur ne permit pas, de dire a quelqu'un, ce qu'on en gagne."

11. Ibid. "vous ecrivés [*sic*] toujours facile très facile—je m'accomode tout mon possible, mais—mais—mais—l'honorare pourroit pourtant être plus difficile ou plutôt pesant!!!!! [. . .] si vous cries [*sic*] facile—je crieroi difficile pour facile!!!!!"

12. Cited in Barry Cooper, *The Beethoven Compendium: A Guide to Beethoven's Life and Music,* London, 1991, 268.

1. Cf. *BBr*, no. 707, footnote 4.
2. *BBr*, no. 504.
3. Breuning, *Aus dem Schwarzspanierhause*, 96.
4. Cf. TF, 602.
5. *BBr*, no. 588.
6. It is a widely held belief, based on an entry in the conversation notebooks from April 1823, that Beethoven clung to this hope for quite some time. The entry was made by Schindler, however, and should be interpreted with the greatest caution.
7. *BBr*, no. 332.
8. *BBr*, no. 707.
9. Ibid.
10. *BBr*, no. 705.
11. Cf. TF, 572–73.
12. The composer and conductor Otto Nicolai attempted to solve this problem by interposing the *Leonore III* overture at this point, a makeshift solution that was later adopted by Gustav Mahler. The practice has been part of the opera's performance tradition ever since.
13. Friedrich Treitschke, "Fidelio," in *Orpheus: Musikalisches Taschenbuch für das Jahr 1841*, cited in *BKh*, 2: 1001.
14. Cf. TDR, 3: 425 ff.
15. Cited in TDR, 3: 429.
16. *BBr*, no. 727.
17. In his correspondence with other opera houses, it is striking that Beethoven consistently included Rocco's aria but strongly recommended against performing it due to its stagnating effect on the drama. Beethoven was less prescriptive when it came to the new version of Leonore's aria: although he warned that it had been written with a particular singer in mind, he left its inclusion up to the artistic directors.
18. Cited in Alfred von Wolzogen, *Wilhelmine Schröder-Devrient: Ein Beitrag zur Geschichte des musikalischen Dramas*, Leipzig, 1863 (cf. *Fidelio: Texte, Materialien, Kommentare*, published by Attila Csampai and Dietmar Holland, Reinbeck bei Hamburg, 1981, 153).
19. Cf. TDR, 4: 317.
20. Although the publication of operatic scores was not yet common practice, Beethoven considered publishing *Fidelio* nonetheless, in hopes of combating the spread of illegal copies. The project most likely stalled due to financial concerns. The full score of *Fidelio* was not published until 1826, unlike the piano version, which was released by Artaria & Co. only three months after the revised opera's premiere, in August 1814. It was prepared by Ignaz Moscheles and supervised by Beethoven, who added many corrections. Because of time pressures, Johann Nepomuk Hummel was asked to complete work on the finale. Beethoven thought the result sounded too much like Hummel and not enough like Beethoven, ultimately consigning his piano reduction to the dustbin.

21. *BBr*, no. 828.

22. *BBr*, no. 875.

23. *BBr*, no. 707.

24. Cited in Hermann Keckeis, "Revolution und Idealismus: Auf dem Weg vom deutschen Singspiel zur deutschen Oper," in *Fidelio/Leonore: Annäherungen an ein zentrales Werk des Musiktheaters. Vorträge und Materialien des Salzburger Symposions 1996*, ed. Peter Csobáldi et al., Anif, 1998, 73. For more detailed discussions on the evolution from *Leonore* to *Fidelio*, see *Von der Leonore zum Fidelio: Vorträge und Referate des Bonner Symposions 1997*, ed. Helga Lühning and Wolfram Steinbeck, Frankfurt am Main, 2000.

43. FROM COFFEE AND CAKE TO CONGRESS AND KITSCH

1. Cited in Michael Ladenburger, "Der Wiener Kongress im Spiegel der Musik," in *Beethoven zwischen Revolution und Restauration*, 276.

2. Beethoven would not complete this overture until the following year; it was first performed during a benefit concert in the Redoutensaal on December 25, 1815.

3. Cf. TDR, 3: 460–62.

4. The first mention of this anecdote is from Schindler's 1840 biography; an exaggerated version appears in the third edition (1860). Maria Rössner-Richarz raises serious doubts as to Schindler's credibility, however (cf. Maria Rössner-Richarz, "Beethoven und der Wiener Kongress aus der Perspektive von Beethovens Briefen und Dokumenten," in *Beethoven und der Wiener Kongress [1814/15]: Bericht über die vierte New Beethoven Research Conference Bonn, 10. bis 12. September 2014*, published by Bernhard R. Appel, Joanna Cobb Biermann, William Kinderman and Julia Ronge, Bonn, 2016, 79 and 107).

5. Cf. Birgit Lodes, "'Le congrès danse': Set Form and Improvisation in Beethoven's Polonaise for Piano, Op. 89," *Musical Quarterly* 93 (2010): 414–49.

6. Cited in Pichler, *Beethoven: Mythos und Wirklichkeit*, 303.

7. Ibid., 304.

8. *BBr*, no. 802.

44. THE FIGHT FOR A CHILD

1. Cf. Clive, *Beethoven and His World*, 14.

2. Cf. *BBr*, no. 852.

3. *BBr*, no. 866.

4. Section 5 of the testament originally read, "Alongside my wife, I appoint my brother Ludwig van Beethoven as co-custodian." Both the beginning of the sentence ("alongside my wife") and the "co-" were struck out (cf. *BBr*, no. 865, footnote 4).

5. Cited in Stefan Wolf, *Beethovens Neffenkonflikt,* Munich, 1995, 78. This chapter is largely based on the information in that book.

6. *BTb,* no. 80.

7. Cf. Kerst, *Die Erinnerungen an Beethoven,* 1: 200.

8. Cf. *BBr,* no. 1152.

9. Cited in Kerst, *Die Erinnerungen an Beethoven,* 1: 46.

10. *BBr,* no. 904.

11. Until April 1817, Beethoven lived in the Lambertisches Haus on Seilerstätte. He then moved to the Gasthof Zum römischen Kaiser on Renngasse; Zum grünen Kranz on Landstrasser Hauptstrasse; Zum grünen Baum on Gärtnerstrasse; the Gasthof Zum alten Blumenstock on Ballgasse; Zur goldenen Birne on Schwibbogengasse; and lastly Zu den zwei Wachsstöcken on Kaiserstrasse.

12. Cf. TDR, 4: 97.

13. *BTb,* no. 158, 100–101. The house was sold on July 2, 1818, for 16,000 guilders. After subtracting 7,000 guilders in debts and 2,000 guilders for Karl's inheritance, Johanna was left with 7,000 guilders for herself.

14. *BTb,* no. 171.

15. *BBr,* no. 1311, footnote 4.

16. Cf. *BKh,* 1: 188.

17. Cf. Clive, *Beethoven and His World,* 261.

18. The rich "royal and imperial" bell-founder Johann Caspar Hofbauer continued to support Johanna for the rest of his life. Among the Beethovens it was rumored that Hofbauer never knew that Ludovika's real father was a medical student from Hungary named Samuel Raicz de Nagy, who rented a room from the Van Beethovens even while Kaspar Karl was still alive.

19. Cf. *BBr,* no. 1286.

20. Cf. Wolf, *Beethovens Neffenkonflikt,* 149–55.

21. Ibid., 174.

22. Cf. Solomon, *Beethoven,* 288.

23. Cf. Wolf, *Beethovens Neffenkonflikt,* 173–76.

45. FROM THE "IMMORTAL BELOVED" TO A "DISTANT BELOVED"

1. Cf. Steblin, "Auf diese Art mit A," 174.

2. Ibid., 178, footnote 106.

3. While the Quintet (op. 16) was originally composed for piano and winds, string parts were also included with the first edition. We also know for certain that horn player Punto took part in the concert on February 11, 1816, and so it is conceivable that the work was then performed with a mixture of strings and winds.

4. *BBr,* no. 902. See also Czerny, *Erinnerungen,* 34.

5. *BKh,* 6: 325.

6. *BBr,* no. 933.

7. Note the difference between the text of the original title, "A song cycle [. . .] with accompaniment for the pianoforte," and that of the second edition, "A song cycle [. . .] for voice and pianoforte."

8. Cited in Tellenbach, *Beethoven und seine "Unsterbliche Geliebte,"* 162.

9. Cf. Tellenbach, *Beethoven und seine "Unsterbliche Geliebte,"* 134.

10. *BBr,* no. 1421.

46. LONGING FOR GREATER THINGS

1. The Belgian musicologist François-Joseph Fétis was the first to apply the triptych model to Beethoven in 1835. The Russian theoretician on French music Wilhelm von Lenz built on Fétis's work in 1852, after which the scheme became galvanized (cf. Maynard Solomon, "The Creative Periods of Beethoven," in *Beethoven Essays,* 116–25).

2. Cf. Letter from Carl Czerny in *Cocks's London Musical Miscellany* (1852), cited in Carl Czerny, *Erinnerungen aus meinem Leben,* ed. Walter Kolneder, Baden-Baden, 1968, 52ff.

3. Cf. Maynard Solomon, "The Creative Periods of Beethoven," in *The Music Review* 34 (1973): 30–38 (four stages); William S. Newman, *A History of the Sonata Idea,* Chapel Hill, NC, 1963, 505–37 (five stages); and Joseph Kerman and Alan Tyson, *Beethoven,* Stuttgart, 1992, 88–130 (eight stages). James Webster provides a detailed overview in "The Concept of Beethoven's 'Early Period,'" *BF* 3 (1994): 19–23.

4. Cf. TDR, 3: 195. Beethoven obtained these quotes from Schiller (from *Die Sendung Moses*), who in turn had them from Voltaire (*Des Rites Egyptiens*). These volumes were relatively well known in intellectual circles and had also found their way into certain Masonic rituals (cf. Cooper, *Beethoven Compendium,* 146).

5. *BKh,* 1: 211, 235.

6. The parallels between the turning points in 1802 and 1816 are striking. In both years, Beethoven's life was thrown into turmoil by an event that brought serious and far-reaching psychological and practical consequences. The full existential implications of these events are documented in two song cycles, the *Gellert* Songs and *An die ferne Geliebte.* Music was what allowed Beethoven to survive both crises, resulting each time in a new compositional direction. In both instances, he first concentrated on piano music, the genre where he felt most at home and where he always went in search of freer forms of expression. Next he composed major choral works with religious inspiration (the *Mount of Olives* and the *Missa solemnis*). Emboldened by these efforts, he went on to produce newly conceptualized, large-scale symphonic works (the *Eroica* and the Ninth Symphony). Lastly, his new experiences were crystallized into sets of string quartets (the *Razumovsky* Quartets and the late string quartets). If only he had written a counterpart to *Leonore* and completed the *Faust* project in 1822/23, the symmetries would be perfect.

7. Cf. Carl Czerny, *Anekdoten und Notizen über Beethoven,* ed. Paul Badura-Skoda, Vienna, 1963, 15.

8. *BBr*, no. 1061. This witticism was repeated by Beethoven in several letters and is a reference to a review in the Vienna *Allgemeine musikalische Zeitung* describing his Seventh Symphony as "difficult to execute" (*schwer zu exequiren*).

9. Ibid.

10. Cf. Czerny, *Anekdoten und Notizen über Beethoven*, 15.

11. Beethoven prescribed a rather odd 4–3 fingering here, which leaves the second note hardly touched. The result is one of an additional vibration (*Bebung*, meaning "quivering" or "trembling") reminiscent of a similar effect used by string or wind instruments. Czerny described precisely how this effect can be achieved on the piano (Czerny, *Über den richtigen Vortrag*, 82). On the instruments of the day, a gradual transition from *una corda* to *tutte le corde/tre corde* and back not only effected a crescendo and diminuendo but also significantly modified the instrumental timbre.

12. Cf. Dietrich Kämper, "Klaviersonate B-Dur 'Hammerklaviersonate,' op. 106," in *Beethoven: Interpretationen seiner Werke,* ed. Albrecht Riethmüller, Carl Dahlhaus, and Alexandre L. Ringer, Laaber, 1996, 2: 149.

13. The individuality of Beethoven's fugues can actually be more readily compared to the more theatrical approach taken by Handel—whom Beethoven hailed as "the greatest composer who ever lived"—than to those of the more cerebral Bach, "the immortal god of harmony" (TF, 871; and *BBr*, no. 59).

14. Beethoven had already experimented in this area while composing the Cello Sonatas in C Major and D Minor (op. 102) in 1815. The first sonata in particular displays many structural parallels with the Piano Sonata in A Major. It is noteworthy that Beethoven reversed the order of these works, as though to emphasize that the Piano Sonata in A Major was his first work in the new style, rather than the earlier-composed cello sonatas.

15. Cited in Clive, *Beethoven and His World,* 103.

16. Cf. *BBr*, nos. 1065, and 1093.

17. *BBr*, nos. 1065, 1069, and 1071. Beethoven could not resist exploiting the similarity between the German words *geleert* (emptied) and *gelehrt* (erudite): "Will aber auch noch ebenfalls einen Geleerten wollte ich sagen einen Gelehrten heute darüber befragen" ("In any case, I still intend to ask a vacuous—whoops, I mean a venerable—scholar about that today") (*BBr*, no. 1069).

18. Cited in Kinsky and Halm, *Das Werk Beethovens,* 287; and Alan Tyson, "The Authors of the op. 104 String Quintet," in *Beethoven Studies* 1 (1973): 159.

19. *BBr*, no. 1132.

20. Cited in Tellenbach, *Beethoven und seine "Unsterbliche Geliebte,"* 152.

47. POST-CONGRESS VIENNA

1. Cf. *BTb*, nos. 50 and 116.

2. *BKh*, 8; 117.

3. Quote from Giuseppe Carpani, cited in Clive, *Beethoven and His World,* 67.

4. Cited in TF, 1046.

5. BBr, no. 725. The Phaeacians were a seafaring folk in Greek mythology, who had a reputation for good hospitality and for leading a carefree and happy life. In Homer's *Odyssey,* Odysseus is brought by Nausikaa, the daughter of the Phaeacian king Alkinos, to her father's court where he introduces himself during the guest dinner. The Austrians used the term "Phaeacians" to characterize people leading a superficial, pleasure-loving, and hedonistic lifestyle, and this is the sense invoked here by Beethoven.

48. LONDON PLANS

1. Cf. *BBr,* no. 790. Johann von Häring was a textiles merchant who played the violin relatively well—he led the second violins in the orchestra of the Friends of Music Society and also served as concertmaster for the Liebhaber concerts in 1807 (until Beethoven replaced him with Franz Clement). He also maintained many ties with England through his business dealings; he lived in London for some time, spoke excellent English, and acted as an interpreter for Beethoven.

2. Cf. *BBr,* no. 933.

3. *BBr,* no. 950. In Greek mythology, Eurus (son of the dawn goddess Eos and the dawn god Astraios) represented the east or southeast wind and was known for his crippling and destructive influence.

4. *BKh,* 4: 196.

5. Cf. Cooper, *Das Beethoven-Kompendium,* 173.

6. Cf. *BBr,* nos. 556 and 578.

7. Cf. *BBr,* no. 790.

8. *BBr,* nos. 983, 987, and 988.

9. Cf. *BBr,* no. 1129.

10. Ibid. The Philharmonic Society's proposal was made in guineas, the alternative currency circulating in England that was used primarily for larger transactions. In 1717, one guinea was worth twenty-one shillings, while a pound was only worth twenty shillings. Until the decimal system was introduced in 1971, the English continued to express the value of more "aristocratic" goods in guineas, such as doctors' and lawyers' fees and the price of real estate, horses, and artworks.

11. *BTb,* no. 119.

12. Cf. *BBr,* no. 1140.

13. Cf. Pamela J. Willetts, *Beethoven and England: An Account of Sources in the British Museum,* London, 1970, 44.

49. A FAUSTIAN SONATA AND A
DIABOLICAL CONTRAPTION

1. Czerny, *Anekdoten,* 16.

2. *BBr,* no. 1292.

3. *BBr*, no. 1247.

4. Cf. Norbert Gertsch, "Ludwig van Beethovens 'Hammerklavier'-Sonate op. 106: Bemerkungen zur Datierung und Bewertung der Quellen," *BBS* 2 (2001): 63–93. This passage in the book is largely based on this article.

5. Cf. Czerny, *Über den richtigen Vortrag*, 65.

6. Cited in Wilhelm von Lenz, *Beethoven: Eine Kunst-Studie (serie)*, Hamburg, 1860, 5: 32.

7. Kämper, "Klaviersonate B-Dur 'Hammerklaviersonate' op. 106," 144.

8. A subsequent London edition (published by Cramer in 1821) was dedicated to Maximiliane Brentano, the daughter of Franz and Antonie Brentano.

9. *BBr*, no. 1295.

10. Additional perspective is offered by Beethoven's last-minute decision to add an extra bar to the opening of the slow movement, precisely to improve the cohesion between the sections (including the final fugue) (cf. *BBr*, no. 1309).

11. One of the few pianists who ever dared to observe Beethoven's metronome markings strictly and consistently when recording the *Hammerklavier* Sonata was Arthur Schnabel. His 1935 recording remains utterly unconvincing, however, due to a total lack of transparency and the mediocre playing overall. Schnabel later qualified the recording as "the product of youthful idolatry" (cf. William S. Newman, *Beethoven on Beethoven: Playing His Piano Music His Way*, New York, 1988, 87).

12. *BBr*, no. 2187.

13. Cf. Schindler, *Biographie*, 2: 247, footnote 2.

14. *BBr*, no. 1196.

15. Ibid.

16. Cited in TF, 687.

17. *AmZ*, December 17, 1817.

18. Cf. *BBr*, no. 1196, footnotes 2 and 7.

19. Cf. *BBr*, no. 2244.

20. *BKh*, 5: 217ff.

21. Cf. Dagmar Beck and Grita Herre, "Anton Schindlers fingierte Eintragungen in den Konversationsheften," in *Zu Beethoven: Aufsätze und Annotationen*, ed. Harry Goldschmidt, Berlin, 1979, 13.

22. Cited in Hans-Werner Küthen, *Beethoven Werke, III, 3 (Klavierkonzerte II) Kritischer Bericht*, Munich, 1996, 51.

23. *BBr*, no. 1950.

24. Cited in Hans-Werner Küthen, *Beethoven Werke, X, 1 (Lieder und Gesänge mit Klavierbegleitung), Kritischer Bericht*, Munich, 1990, 74.

25. WR, 106.

26. Schindler, *Biographie*, 1: 195–97.

27. Cf. *BKh*, 5: 232ff. Schindler further undermines his own report by giving two separate dates for the party in question: 1812 in his biography, and 1817 in the conversation notebooks.

1. Solomon, "Beethoven's Tagebuch," in *Beethoven Essays*, 294.

2. Cf. Birgit Lones, *Das Gloria in Beethovens Missa solemnis,* Tutzing, 1997, 19ff.; and Sven Hiemke, *Ludwig van Beethoven: Missa solemnis,* Kassel, 2003, 56.

3. Johann Nepomuk Wolfmayer is among the more picturesque peripheral figures in Beethoven's life who generally receive little biographical attention. His main appearance is usually in a footnote telling of the one letter he wrote to Beethoven to confirm their verbal agreement for a requiem. But he was also a Beethoven supporter from the very beginning, and there is a very touching story of how he visited Beethoven regularly, always wearing a brand-new jacket, which he would secretly switch with one of Beethoven's threadbare garments. Wolfmayer stayed true to Beethoven until the end; he was a torchbearer at his funeral, and the String Quartet in F Major (op. 135) is dedicated to him.

4. *BBr,* no. 898.

5. The story goes that on the eve of battle, the emperor had a vision that was a deciding factor in his own conversion to Christianity and the spread of the religion throughout the Roman Empire.

6. The truth compels us to note that Beethoven borrowed this technique from Cherubini, who had used a similar approach in his *Mass for St. Cecilia in F Major* (1810).

7. *BBr,* no. 1361.

8. *BBr,* nos. 1365, 1446, and 1468.

9. Cf. *BBr,* nos. 1465, 1469, and 1473.

10. *BBr,* no. 1852.

11. *BBr,* no. 1550.

12. *BBr,* no. 1641.

13. Cf. *BBr,* nos. 1563, 1577, and 1621.

14. *BBr,* nos. 1752 and 1763.

15. *BBr,* no. 1380.

16. *BBr,* no. 1773.

17. Cf. *BBr,* no. 803.

18. *BBr,* no. 1468.

19. Cf. *BLuW,* 222.

20. *BKh,* 2: 263.

51. THE CIRCLE IS COMPLETE

1. Cf. *BBr,* no. 808.

2. Cf. Schindler, *Biographie,* 2: 35. Schindler described it as a *Rosalie,* a cobbler's term used by eighteenth-century composers to describe the excessive and banal repetition of motifs one step higher or lower—in essence, it was a derogatory term for "sequences." *Rosalien,* or "shoe roses," were rose-shaped patches sewn on to shoes

to give the impression of covering the smell of "stinking, foul-toed feet" (Jacob and Wilhelm Grimm, *Deutsches Wörterbuch,* Munich, 1899–1984, 9, column 1864).

3. To be clear, Beethoven himself made mention of only twenty-two variations; one of them was unnumbered.

4. Cf. Clive, *Beethoven and His World,* 348; and *BLex,* 719.

5. *BBr,* no. 1445.

6. In June 1812, Beethoven had gifted an Allegretto in B-flat (WoO 39) to the nine-year-old Maximiliane, with a touching dedication: "For my little friend Maxe Brentano, to encourage her at the piano."

7. Cf. *BBr,* no. 1604.

8. Cf. *BBr,* no. 1580. An interesting side note: while in that same letter Beethoven suggested publishing both sets of bagatelles together, he insisted that a distinction be maintained between them. Clementi, and after him Schlesinger and Sauer & Leidesdorf, ignored his wishes. The Eleven Bagatelles have remained inseparable ever since, despite the fact that—unlike the later Six Bagatelles (op. 126 from 1824)—they were not conceived as a set but are instead an arbitrary collage of unconnected pieces.

9. According to Dr. Andreas Wawruch, who treated Beethoven during his final months and whose detailed medical report on his patient was published in 1842, Beethoven had suffered from hemorrhoids since the age of thirty (Andreas Ignaz Wawruch, "Ärztlicher Rückblick auf L. van Beethoven's letzte Lebensepoche," *Wiener Zeitschrift für Kunst, Literatur un Mode* 27 [April 30, 1842], 86: 681–85, published by Michael Lorenz; Andreas Ignaz Wawruch, "Medical Review on the Final Stage of L. van Beethoven's Life," *BJ* 22, no. 2 [2007]: 88). This, too, was a sign of early liver problems (verbal communication from Dr. Sus Herbosch).

10. Cf. Tellenbach, *Beethoven und seine "Unsterbliche Geliebte,"* 199; and Barry Cooper, *Beethoven,* Oxford, 2000, 285.

11. Thomas Mann, *Doktor Faustus,* Frankfurt am Main, 1987 (1947), 57–58.

12. The imperfect/perfect juxtaposition becomes more apparent when looking at the time signatures from an early-music perspective, as the first movement is in quadruple time, or *tempus imperfectum,* while the second is in triple time, or *tempus perfectum.*

13. This progressive diminution of note values necessitated the development of a new notation system. The Western system is based on the binary subdivision of note values (a semibreve can be divided into two minims, four crotchets, eight quavers, etc.); only triple or compound time signatures (such as 3/4 or 6/8) offer a nonbinary subdivision. For the Arietta, Beethoven uses uncommon time signatures that allow for more ternary ratios: 6/16 is subdivided into 3:2:3; 12/32 into 3:2:2:3; and 9/16—which is actually a veiled 27/32—into 3:3:3. For somebody of supposedly limited mathematical ability, this is quite a feat!

14. Cf. *BBr,* no. 1466.

15. *BBr,* no. 1507.

16. Beethoven had offered his *Diabelli* Variations to Peters for thirty ducats on June 5, 1822.

17. Cf. *BBr*, no. 1901. See also *BBr*, no. 1783.

18. Cited in TDR, 4: 478.

52. ESTRANGEMENT

1. Ibid., 105.

2. Cf. Breuning, *Aus dem Schwarzspanierhause*, 96.

3. Ibid.

4. Cf. Solomon, *Beethoven*, 294; Kerst, *Die Erinnerungen an Beethoven*, 2: 97–98.

5. Cf. the accounts of Karl Holz, Ludwig Rellstab, Louis Schlösser, and George Smart (cited in *BSZ*, 459, 698–99, 816, and 921). The words of Marie Pachler-Koschack are particularly moving: "Only my side of the conversation was in writing; not until our parting did he pen me a musical farewell, which—as you might imagine—I cherish as though it were a relic" (*BSZ*, 545).

Beethoven composed over forty canons in total for a wide variety of occasions: New Year's Day, birthdays, greetings, farewells, and so on. It is striking that most were written after 1819, as though these musical mementos were what allowed Beethoven to circumvent his communicative disability and express his emotions to the people he cared for.

6. Cf. Kerst, *Die Erinnerungen an Beethoven*, 1: 267.

7. Cf. TF, 647.

8. Cf. TF, 4: 224ff.

9. Czerny, *Anekdoten und Notizen über Beethoven*, 14.

10. Cf. Ludwig Nohl, *Beethoven nach den Schilderungen*, Stuttgart, 1877, 141.

11. Cf. *BLuW*, 181; Solomon, *Beethoven*, 334; and WR, 107.

12. It is a telling fact that nearly two hundred letters to and from Beethoven remain from 1825, and nearly a hundred and fifty from 1826—far exceeding the average taken across his final years in general.

53. ENCOUNTERS WITH THE YOUNGER GENERATION

1. Cited in Kerst, *Die Erinnerungen an Beethoven*, 1: 292.

2. Cited in Richard Osborne, *Rossini: Leben und Werk*, Munich, 1988, 73.

3. Robert Schumann, *Gesammelte Schriften über Musik und Musiker*, ed. Martin Kreisig, Leipzig, 1914, 1: 128.

4. Cf. TDR, 4: 462ff.

5. Cf. John Warrack, *Carl Maria von Weber*, Cambridge, 1976, 100–103.

6. *BBr*, no. 1541.

7. Cf. *BBr*, no. 1704. The strong nineteenth-century tendency to lace Beethoven's opinions on Carl Maria von Weber with bitterness is based on conversation-book

entries by various visitors (nephew Karl, Frederik Kanne, and Karl Holz), suggesting that Weber's success was due to the *Fidelio*-like character of several sections in *Der Freischütz*. It is assumed that Beethoven concurred with these views, despite the lack of any supporting evidence.

8. Cited in TDR, 4: 465.

9. Cf. Hans J. Fröhlich, *Schubert*, Munich, 1978, 307.

10. Cf. *BBr*, no. 2003, footnote 9.

11. Cf. Schindler, *Biographie*, 2: 176.

12. Marie-Agnes Dittrich, "Schubert," in *BLex*, column 665a.

13. Ibid.

14. *BLex*, column 665a.

15. Cf. Schindler, *Biographie*, 2: 178.

16. Jörg Rüter, "Die Bonner Beethovenhalle," *Bonner Geschichtsblätter* 39 (1989): 427.

17. *BKh*, 11: 249.

54. AN ODE TO JOY

1. Strangely, only the physical manuscript was designated a piece of world heritage—not the music itself.

2. Cf. *BBr*, no. 1784.

3. *BBr*, no. 1950.

4. *BBr*, no. 1953.

5. *BBr*, nos. 1801, 1802, and 1803.

6. Cf. *BKh*, 6: 117.

7. Cf. Schindler, *Biographie*, 2: 77.

8. Cf. *BBr*, no. 1493.

9. *BLuW*, 211; and Schindler, *Biographie*, 2: 76.

10. *BKh*, 6: 96.

11. Schindler maintained that Beethoven's membership to the Royal Academies of Amsterdam and Stockholm warranted mention. Schuppanzigh protested, saying that Beethoven's status made him "the dictator and president of all the world's academies" regardless and that "intelligent people would regard such a postscript as pure vanity" (*BKh*, 6: 134 ff.).

12. TDR, 5: 93.

13. *AmZ*, April 6, 1864 (Cf. *BLuW*, 212). The recitativo passages were controversial from the outset, since they far exceeded the technical capabilities of most of the performers. Beethoven had clearly drawn inspiration from the double-bass virtuoso Domenico Dragonetti, with whom he had collaborated on a memorable performance of his Cello Sonata (op. 5, no. 2) in 1799. Dragonetti had been the principal bass soloist of the London Philharmonic Society in the 1820s, and Beethoven clearly had his abilities in mind when composing the recitatives.

Despite resistance from some players, for the Viennese premiere Beethoven insisted that the basses maintain the faster tempo, while playing both in time and non-legato. Subsequent performances quickly saw a reduction in the speed, as well as the inclusion of all kinds of clever articulation tricks. The more experienced players who had performed under Beethoven himself were against these modifications, however.

14. Cf. *BLuW*, 213.

15. *BBr*, no. 1833.

16. TF, 888.

17. The notion that Beethoven had already conceived of a Tenth Symphony to follow the Ninth is supported by a comment from violinist Karl Holz, who worked closely with Beethoven during his final years: "Beethoven played through the entire *Tenth symphony* at the piano. There were also sketches of all the movements, although they were inscrutable to all but him" (Sieghard Brandenburg, "Die Skizzen zur Neunten Symphonie," *Zu Beethoven* 2 [1984]: 113). Recent research has revealed that around four hundred bars from the late sketchbooks pertain to this symphony. On the basis of these findings, English musicologist Barry Cooper made a recon-struction of Beethoven's Tenth Symphony in 1988.

18. *BBr*, no. 1510.

19. TF, 889.

20. Clive, *Beethoven and His World*, 111.

21. Cf. Dieter Hildebrandt, *Die Neunte: Schiller, Beethoven und die Geschichte eines musikalischen Welterfolgs,* Munich, 2005, 112.

22. Although Beethoven eventually abandoned this idea, the thematic material that he had already produced was reused in 1814/15 for the *Name-Day* overture (op. 115).

23. Cf. Hildebrandt, *Die Neunte*, 67.

24. Beethoven's decision to put the Scherzo before the Adagio is striking and essential to the overall dramaturgical concept, in which the second movement's escape into Dionysian intoxication precedes the retreat into melancholic introspec-tion in the third movement.

25. Cf. Gustav Nottebohm, *Zweite Beethoveniana: Nachgelassene Aufsätze,* Leipzig, 1887, 190ff.

26. Schindler, *Biographie*, 2: 55.

55. DECLINE

1. Cited in *BBr*, no. 1650.

2. Cf. TDR, 5: 5; and Davies, *Beethoven in Person*, 200–202.

3. Cf. *BLuW*, 198. A pair of very strong glasses has been preserved in the Beethoven-Haus, with a diopter of minus 4.

4. Verbal communication from Dr. Sus Herbosch.

5. Cf. Wawruch, "Medical Review on the Final Stage of L. van Beethoven's Life," 87–91; and Michael Lorenz, "Commentary on Wawruch's Report: Biographies of Andreas Wawruch and Johann Seibert, Schindler's Responses to Wawruch's Report, and Beethoven's Medical Condition and Alcohol Consumption," *BJ* 22, no. 2 (2007): 92–100.

6. *BBr*, no. 286.

7. Cf. *BKh*, 7: 224ff. (cited in Margot Wetzstein, *Aus Beethovens letzten Jahre: "Ich bin in Todesangst wegen dem quartett,"* Bonn, 2001, 8).

8. Schindler, *Biographie*, 2: 194.

56. KARL'S EMANCIPATION

1. Cf. *BKh*, 2: 327.

2. Beethoven's suspicions were only partly justified. When Therese died in 1828, Johann was only obliged to transfer half of the family assets to his step-daughter. When she, in turn, died in 1831, her fortune went to her husband, Karl Stölzle, whom she had married the year before. There are those who believe that Johann never recovered from this financial blow; however, these claims are contradicted by the sizeable inheritance that Karl received on Johann's death in 1848.

3. *BBr*, no. 1731.

4. Cf. *BKh*, 4: 275.

5. *BKh*, 7: 290.

6. *BKh*, 9: 287 and 323.

7. TF, 994.

8. *BKh*, 10: 87; cf. Wolf, *Beethovens Neffenkonflikt*, 126.

9. *BKh*, 10: 169.

10. Schindler, *Biographie*, 2: 127.

11. Cf. TDR, 5: 360.

12. Cf. Lenz, *Beethoven: Eine Kunst-Studie*, 5: 217.

13. *BBr*, no. 2189.

14. Cited in Erwin Ratz, "Die Originalfassung des Streichquartettes Op. 130 von Beethoven" (1957), in *Gesammelte Aufsätze*, Vienna, 1975, 74.

15. Cf. Schindler, 2: 131.

16. Ibid., 2: 132.

17. *BKh*, 11: 68.

18. Rudolf Klein, "Gerhard von Breuning über Beethovens Beziehungen zu seinen Verwandten: Ein unbekannter Entwurf zu einem Artikel," *Österreichische Musikzeitschrift* 29 (1974): 71.

Stefan Wolf rightly noted that Karl's overwhelmingly negative reputation must have been the main reason why not one of the original Beethoven biographers took the trouble to ask him personally for his version of events (Wolf, *Beethovens Neffenkonflikt*, 245).

57. MONEY MATTERS

1. Cf. *BBr*, nos. 2256 and 2260.

2. Cf. Albert Leitzmann, ed., *Ludwig van Beethoven: Berichte der Zeitgenossen, Briefe und persönliche Aufzeichnungen, gesammelt und erläutert*, Leipzig, 1921, 1: 370–71.

3. Schindler, *Biographie*, 2: 96.

4. Cf. *BBr*, no. 1685, footnote 6.

5. *BBr*, no. 1578.

6. *BBr*, no. 2246.

7. Cf. Nicole Kämpken, "'In allen Geschäftssachen ein schwerer Kopf': Beethovens Vermögensverhältnisse," in *"Alle Noten bringen mich nicht aus den Nöthen!!" Beethoven und das Geld: Begleitbuch zu einer Gesellschaft der Musikfreunde in Wien*, ed. Nicole Kämpken and Michael Ladenburger, Bonn, 2005, 105–13; Alice M. Hanson, "Incomes and Outgoings in the Vienna of Beethoven and Schubert," *Music & Letters* 64, nos. 3/4 (1983): 173–82; and Julia Moore, "Beethoven and Inflation," *BF* 1 (1992): 191–223.

58. THE DISCOVERY OF HEAVEN

1. *BBr*, no. 1508.

2. A string quartet by Galitzin was published in St. Petersburg, based on the outer movements of the Piano Sonata in C Major (op. 53) and the slow movements of the Cello Sonata in A Major (op. 69) and the Piano Sonata in E-flat Major (op. 7). Some historians theorize that Schuppanzigh, who lived in the Russian capital from 1816 to 1823, greatly influenced Galitzin's adoration of Beethoven.

3. Cf. *BBr*, no. 1752.

4. *BBr*, no. 1535. Beethoven made one more curious promise: "I am aware that you play the cello yourself, and I shall endeavour to satisfy you in this respect." It is indeed noteworthy that in the three Galitzin quartets (opp. 127, 132, and 130), several prominent opening phrases are given to the cello.

5. The String Quartet in A Minor (op. 132) is chronologically the second in the set. Due to the vicissitudes of numbering when dealing with several publishers at once, it received a later opus number than both the third Quartet in B-flat Major (op. 130) and the fourth Quartet in C-sharp Minor (op. 131), despite having been composed earlier.

6. Cf. *BBr*, no. 2230. The last of the Russo-Persian wars (1826–28) in the Caucasus had begun several months earlier.

7. Cited in Clive, *Beethoven and His World*, 136.

8. *BKh*, 7: 208.

9. Ibid., 101.

10. *Allgemeine Theaterzeitung*, April 28, 1825, 212 (cf. Indorf, *Beethovens Streichquartette*, 108).

596 · NOTES TO PAGES 509–517

11. *BKh,* 10: 25 and 104.

12. *BKh,* 10: 139; and Czerny, *Anekdoten,* 21.

13. *BKh,* 7: 198.

14. Ibid., 201.

15. Cf. *BKh,* 8: 109, 160, and 182.

16. Current practice (for use on CD tracks, in program notes, etc.) generally divides the Quartet in A Minor into five movements. Beethoven himself consistently referred to six, seeing the Marsch and the following Recitativo as the fourth and fifth movements, respectively. He briefly considered inserting a second dance movement (titled Alla danza tedesca) to replace the current fourth movement but ultimately settled on the shorter Marsch, saving the Alla danza tedesca for the next quartet.

17. Cited in Lenz, *Beethoven: Eine Kunst-Studie,* 5: 218; and Solomon, *Beethoven,* 421.

18. Cited in Kerst, *Die Erinnerungen an Beethoven,* 2: 187.

19. Schindler, *Biographie,* 2: 114.

20. Cited in Joseph Kerman, *Les quatuors de Beethoven,* Paris, 1974 (1966), 233.

21. *AmZ,* 1826. Cf. Kunze, *Ludwig van Beethoven,* 559.

22. Ibid., 559ff.

23. Cf. Theodor Helm, *Beethovens Streichquartette: Versuch einer technischen Analyse dieser Werke im Zusammenhang mit ihrem geistigen Gehalt,* Leipzig, 1885, 171.

24. Mathias Artaria was the nephew of Domenico Artaria who ran the parent company in Vienna. Mathias moved from Mannheim (where his father had a music publishing business) to Vienna in 1818, where he started his own company.

25. *BKh,* 8: 246–47.

26. Holz and Artaria first convinced Beethoven to publish a piano duet version of the *Grosse Fuge,* for which they believed there was greater market demand. The transcription of the work was entrusted to a pianist by the name of Halm, a Brunsvik protégé for whom Beethoven held little regard (Beethoven once said of him, *"Nicht jeder Halm gibt Ähren." Halm* means "stalk" in German, and a free translation of this wordplay might read, "Not every [corn]stalk has good ears") (cf. Clive, *Beethoven and His World,* 147). When Halm presented his work to Beethoven, the master was very displeased. He felt that Halm had sacrificed the thematic integrity for the comfort of the players and immediately made a new version himself.

27. Cf. Erwin Ratz, "Die Originalfassung des Streichquartettes Op 130 von Beethoven," in *Gesammelte Aufsätze,* Vienna, 1975, 69; and Klaus Kropfinger, "Von der Werkstatt zur Aufführung: Was bedeuten Beethovens Skizzen für die Werkinterpretation?" in *Über Musik im Bilde,* ed. B. Bischoff et al., 1, Köln-Rheinkassel, 1995, 310.

28. Cited in TDR, 5: 1044.

29. *BKh,* 9: 275.

30. *BKh,* 8: 32.

31. The original puns in German: *Tonwerkerei, Tonstreitwerkversammlung,* and *Schmettermessingwerker* (cf. Gerd Indorf, *Beethovens Streichquartette:*

Kulturgeschichtliche Aspekte und Werkinterpretationen, Freiburg im Breisgau, 2004, 127; and *BBr*, no. 2043).

32. Cf. *BKh*, 10: 63ff.

33. *BKh*, 8: 47.

34. Ibid., 276.

35. Cited in Kerst, *Die Erinnerungen an Beethoven,* 2: 187; and Lenz, *Beethoven: Eine Kunst-Studie,* 5: 216.

36. For a detailed discussion of these sketches, see Robert Winter, *Compositional Origins of Beethoven's Opus 131,* Ann Arbor, MI, 1982.

37. *BBr*, no. 2224, footnote 2.

38. Although it is unclear which movement Beethoven composed last, given the tonal scheme it seems logical that the slow movement (in the contrasting tonality of D-flat major) formed part of the original concept.

39. The motto attached to this movement has a long history. Ignaz Dembscher, a wealthy music lover, did not attend the premiere of the Quartet in B-flat by the Schuppanzigh quartet, on the strong conviction that he could organize a better performance at his own home led by Mayseder, and that obtaining the necessary instrumental parts from Beethoven would present little trouble. But given that Schuppanzigh had prepared them himself by hand, Beethoven wanted fifty guilders to hire the parts. When Dembscher was informed, his alleged response was, "Muss es sein?" (Must it be?). Beethoven's reply came in the form of a canon, titled "Es muss sein" (It must be; *BBr*, no. 2174, footnote 1). Schindler's alternative account—concerning salary payments to staff—is far more banal and almost certainly apocryphal (Schindler, *Biographie,* 2: 157).

40. Cf., Kerman, *Les quatuors de Beethoven,* 275.

41. Cf. Paul Bekker, *Beethoven,* Berlin, 1912, 532; and Carl Dahlhaus, *Ludwig van Beethoven und seine Zeit,* Laaber, 1987, 272–75.

59. COMOEDIA FINITA EST

1. *BKh*, 10: 298.

2. Cf. Wawruch, "Medical Review on the Final Stage of L. van Beethoven's Life," 87–91; and Lorenz, "Commentary on Wawruch's Report: Biographies of Andreas Wawruch and Johann Seibert," 92–100.

3. Cited in TF, 1023.

4. Gerhard Breuning would later document his memories of this period (Gerhard Breuning, *Aus dem Schwarzspanierhause: Erinnerungen an L. v. Beethoven aus meiner Jugendzeit,* Vienna, 1874). This "memoir" is the primary source of information on Beethoven's final years.

5. *BBr*, no. 2256, footnote 1. The collection referred to here is the complete Handel edition by Samuel Arnold.

6. Cited in TF, 1031.

7. Wawruch, "Medical Review on the Final Stage of L. van Beethoven's Life," 90.

8. Cf. *BBr*, nos. 2262, 2266, and 2278.

9. This point has been debated in medical circles of late. Recent research at the University of Vienna on Beethoven's hair has revealed abnormally high levels of lead in his blood in the days following his abdominal punctures, potentially caused by dressings containing lead salts. Other academics believe that Dr. Seibert treated Beethoven's erysipelas (also known as "rose" or "St. Anthony's fire") simply by keeping the wound dry; in which case the abnormally high lead concentrations are most probably attributable to lead-based sweeteners added to Beethoven's Moselle wine (cf. Reiter, "Causes of Beethoven's Death and His Locks of Hair," 2–5).

10. Cf. TDR, 5: 483ff.; and *BLuW*, 230.

11. Wawruch, "Medical Review on the Final Stage of L. van Beethoven's Life," 90.

12. Cf. Schindler, *Biographie*, 2: 146; and TDR, 5: 484ff. After signing the testament on January 3, Beethoven received a letter from Stephan Breuning (one of Karl's guardians) with the following recommendation: "Karl has proven himself very irresponsible until now, and we do not know how his character will continue to develop. Therefore, in his own best interests and for the sake of his future, I believe it would be better to deny him direct access to the capital either for the duration of his life, or for a few years at least, until he comes of age at 24. The annual interest will be enough for him to live from initially, in any case [...] I fear that temporary means will not be sufficient to prohibit Karl from accruing debts that will later need to be settled with the inheritance" (*BBr*, no. 2247).

13. Cf. TF, 1047.

14. *BBr*, no. 2291.

15. Ibid. According to Gerhard von Breuning, Beethoven spoke these words not after the visit by the priest but one day earlier, following a visit from his doctor (cf. Breuning, *Aus dem Schwarzspanierhause*, 104ff.; and BBr, no. 2291, footnote 5). In a letter to Ignaz Moscheles, Schindler also wrote: "yesterday [March 23] he said to me and to [Herr von] Breeuning: *plaudite, comoedia finita est*" (*BBr*, no. 2286).

16. TDR, 5: 485.

17. Cf. Breuning, *Aus dem Schwarzspanierhause*, 105.

18. *BBr*, no. 2291.

19. Ibid.

20. Cf. Kerst, *Die Erinnerungen an Beethoven*, 2: 232ff.

BIBLIOGRAPHY

This bibliography contains the principal works consulted in the writing of this book. As a rule, journal articles are not included; for these, the reader is referred to the endnotes.

The lists are by no means exhaustive and are intended only as a guide to further reading. For a more comprehensive Beethoven bibliography, please see Klaus Kropfinger, "Beethoven," in *Die Musik in Geschichte und Gegenwart,* ed. Frederik Blume and Ludwig Finscher, Kassel, 1994–2008, Personenteil, 2, col. 667–915. The "Selected Bibliography" in Maynard Solomon, *Beethoven,* 2nd ed., New York, 1998 (1978) is also highly recommended and is accompanied by a practical commentary.

PRIMARY SOURCES: WRITINGS OF BEETHOVEN, AND COMMENTARIES

Beethoven, Ludwig van. *Briefwechsel: Gesamtausgabe.* Edited by Sieghard Brandenburg. 7 vols. Munich, 1996–98.
———. *Konversationshefte.* Edited by Karl-Heinz Köhler, Grita Herre, Dagmar Beck, and Günter Brosche. 11 vols. Leipzig, 1972–2001.
———. *Symphonien.* Edited by Jonathan Del Mar. Kassel, 1996–99.
———. *Werke: Gesamtausgabe.* Edited by Sieghard Brandenburg, Klaus Kropfinger, Hans-Werner Küthen, Emil Platen, et al. 56 vols. Munich, 1961– .
Braubach, Max, ed. *Die Stammbücher Beethovens und der Babette Koch* (facsimile). Bonn, 1995.
Busch-Weise, Dagmar von. "Beethovens Jugend Tagebuch." *Studien zur Musikwissenschaft* 25 (1962): 68–88.
Johnson, Douglas, Alan Tyson, and Robert Winter, eds. *The Beethoven Sketchbooks: History, Reconstruction, Inventory.* Oxford, 1985.

Nottebohm, Gustav. *Beethoveniana: Aufsätze und Mitteilungen*. Leipzig, 1880.
———. *Zweite Beethoveniana: Nachgelassene Aufsätze*. Leipzig, 1887.
Solomon, Maynard, ed. *Beethovens Tagebuch 1812–1818*. Bonn, 1990–2005.

REFERENCE WORKS

Clive, Peter. *Beethoven and His World: A Biographical Dictionary*. Oxford, 2001.
Cooper, Barry, ed. *The Beethoven Compendium: A Guide to Beethoven's Life and Music*. London, 1991.
Das Beethoven-Handbuch. Published by Albrecht Riethmüller. 6 vols. Laaber, 2008–19.
Das Beethoven Handbuch. Published by Sven Hiemke. Kassel, 2009.
Digitales Archiv, Beethoven-Haus Bonn. www.beethoven-haus-bonn.de
Dorfmüller, Kurt, ed. *Beiträge zur Beethoven: Bibliographie, Studien und Materialen zum Werkverzeichnis von Kinsky-Halm*. Munich, 1978.
Green, James F. *The New Hess Catalog of Beethoven's Works*. West Newbury, VT, 2003.
Kerman, Joseph, and Alan Tyson. s.v. "Beethoven." In *The New Grove Dictionary of Music and Musicians*. 2nd ed. London, 2001.
Kinsky, Georg, and Hans Halm. *Das Werk Beethovens: Thematisch-bibliographisches Verzeichnis seiner sämtlichen vollendeten Kompositionen*. Munich, 1983 (1955).
Klein, Rudolf. *Beethovenstätten in Österreich*. Vienna, 1970.
Kropfinger, Klaus. s.v. "Beethoven." In *Die Musik in Geschichte und Gegenwart*. 2nd ed. Edited by Frederik Blume and Ludwig Finscher, 2, col. 667–915. Kassel, 2001.
Loesch, Heinz von, and Claus Raab, eds. *Das Beethoven-Lexikon* (*Das Beethoven-Handbuch,* vol. 6). Laaber, 2008.
Ludwig van Beethoven: Thematisch-bibliograpisches Werkverzeichnis. Published by Kurt Dorfmüller, Norbert Gertsch, and Julia Ronge in collaboration with Gertraut Haberkamp and Beethoven-Haus Bonn. 2 vols. Munich, 2014.
Smolle, Kurt. *Wohnstätten Ludwig van Beethovens von 1792 bis zu seinem Tod*. Munich, 1970.

WORKS BY AND ABOUT CONTEMPORARIES
OF BEETHOVEN

Breuning, Gerhard von. *Aus dem Schwarzspanierhaus: Erinnerungen an Ludwig van Beethoven*. Vienna, 1874.
Czerny, Carl. "Anekdoten und Notizen über Beethoven." In *Über den richtigen Vortrag der sämtlichen Beethoven'schen Klavierwerke*. Edited by Paul Badura-Skoda. Vienna, 1963.
———. *Erinnerungen aus meinem Leben*. Edited by Walter Kolneder. Baden-Baden, 1968.

Kopitz, Klaus Martin, and Rainer Cadenbach, eds. *Beethoven aus der Sicht seiner Zeitgenossen in Tagebüchern, Briefen, Gedichten und Erinnerungen.* 2 vols. Munich, 2009.

Kunze, Stefan. *Ludwig van Beethoven: Die Werke im Spiegel seiner Zeit. Gesammelte Konzertberichte und Rezensionen bis 1830.* Laaber, 1987.

Robbins Landon, H. C., ed. *Ludwig van Beethoven: Leben und Werk in Zeugnissen der Zeit.* Zurich, 1994 (1970).

Schindler, Anton. *Biographie von Ludwig van Beethoven.* 4th ed. Munster, 1871 (1840).

Schlosser, Johann Aloys. *Ludwig van Beethoven: Eine Biographie.* Prague, 1828.

Schmidt-Görg, Joseph, ed. *Des Bonner Bäckermeisters Gottfried Fischer: Aufzeichnungen über Beethovens Jugend.* Munich, 1971.

Seyfried, Ignaz von, ed. *Ludwig von Beethovens Studien im Generalbasse, Contrapunkte und in der Compositionslehre.* Vienna, 1832.

Spohr, Louis. *Selbstbiographie.* Kassel, 1860/61.

Wegeler, Franz Gerhard, and Ferdinand Ries. *Biographische Notizen über Ludwig van Beethoven.* Koblenz, 1838.

———. *Nachtrag zu den biographischen Notizen über Ludwig van Beethoven.* Koblenz, 1845.

Wetzstein, Margot, ed. *Familie Beethoven im kurfürstlichen Bonn.* Bonn, 2006.

BIOGRAPHIES OF BEETHOVEN

Brisson, Elisabeth. *Ludwig van Beethoven.* Paris, 2004.

Canisius, Claus. *Beethoven: "Sehnsucht und Unruhe in der Musik." Aspekte zu Leben und Werk.* Munich, 1992.

Cooper, Barry. *Beethoven.* Oxford, 2000.

Geck, Martin. *Beethoven: Der Schöpfer und sein Universum.* Munich, 2017

———. *Ludwig van Beethoven.* Reinbek bei Hamburg, 2001 (1996).

Irmen, Hans-Josef. *Beethoven in seiner Zeit.* Zülpich, 1998.

Jones, David Wyn. *The Life of Beethoven.* Cambridge, 1998.

Lockwood, Lewis. *Beethoven: The Music and Life.* New York, 2003.

Marek, George R. *Ludwig van Beethoven: Das Leben eines Genies.* Munich, 1970.

Massin, Jean, and Brigitte Massin. *Ludwig van Beethoven.* Paris, 1997.

Morris, Edmund. *Beethoven: The Universal Composer.* London, 2007.

Pichler, Ernst. *Beethoven: Mythos und Wirklichkeit.* Vienna, 1994.

Rexroth, Dieter. *Beethoven: Monographie.* Mainz, 1982.

Solomon, Maynard. *Beethoven.* 2nd ed. New York, 1998 (1978).

Thayer, Alexander Wheelock. *Ludwig van Beethovens Leben* (1866). Edited by Hermann Deiters (1901), revised by Hugo Riemann (1917). Leipzig, 1917.

———. *Thayer's Life of Beethoven* (1866). Edited by Elliot Forbes. Princeton, 1967.

Aoli, Yayoi. *Beethoven: Die Entschlüsselung des Rätsels um die "Unsterbliche Geliebte."* Munich, 2008.

Bartsch, Cornelia, ed. *Der "männliche" und der "weibliche" Beethoven: Bericht über den Internationalen musikwissenschaftlichen Kongress vom 31. Oktober bis 4. November 2001 an der Universität der Künste.* Bonn, 2003.

Baur, Eva Gesine. *Emanuel Schikaneder: Der Mann für Mozart.* Munich, 2012.

Bettermann, Silke. *Beethoven im Bild: Die Darstellung des Komponisten in der bildenden Kunst vom 18. bis zum 21. Jahrhundert.* Bonn, 2012.

Brandenburg, Sieghard, and Martella Gutiérrez-Denhoff, eds. *Beethoven und Böhmen: Beiträge zu Biographie und Wirkungsgeschichte Beethovens.* Bonn, 1988.

Brisson, Elisabeth. *Le sacre du musicien: La référence à l'antiquité chez Beethoven.* Paris, 2000. Broyles, Michael. *Beethoven in America.* Bloomington, 2011.

Cooper, Martin. *Beethoven: The Last Decade 1817–1827.* Oxford, 1985 (1970).

Davies, Peter J. *Beethoven in Person: His Deafness, Illnesses, and Death.* Westport, CT, 2001.

De Nora, Tia. *Beethoven and the Construction of Genius: Musical Politics in Vienna 1792–1803.* Berkeley, 1995.

Goldschmidt, Harry. *Die Erscheinung Beethoven.* Leipzig, 1974.

——. *Um die Unsterbliche Geliebte.* Leipzig, 1977.

Hermand, Jost. *Beethoven: Werk und Wirkung.* Cologne, 2003.

Kagan, Susan. *Archduke Rudolph, Beethoven's Patron, Pupil, and Friend: His Life and Music.* Stuyvesant, 1988.

Klapproth, John E. *Beethoven's Only Beloved: Josephine! A Biography of the Only Woman Beethoven Ever Loved.* Charleston, SC, 2011.

Kopitz, Klaus Martin. *Beethoven, Elisabeth Röckel und das Albumblatt "Für Elise."* Cologne, 2010.

Küthen, Hans-Werner, and Oldrich Pulkert, eds. *Ludwig van Beethoven im Herzen Europas.* Prague, 2000.

Loos, Helmut, ed. *Beethoven und die Nachwelt: Materialien zur Wirkungsgeschichte Beethovens.* Bonn, 1986.

Lühning, Helga, and Sieghard Brandenburg, eds. *Beethoven zwischen Revolution und Restauration.* Bonn, 1989.

Mathew, Nicholas. *Political Beethoven.* Cambridge, 2013.

May, Jürgen, ed. *Beiträge zu Biographie und Schaffensprozess bei Beethoven: Rainer Cadenbach zum Gedenken.* Bonn, 2011.

Nottebohm, Gustav. *Beethoven's Studien. Beethoven's Unterricht bei J. Haydn, Albrechtsberger und Salieri.* Leipzig, 1873.

Prössler, Berthold. *Franz Gerhard Wegeler: Ein rheinischer Arzt, Universitätsprofessor, Medizinalbeamter und Freund Beethovens.* Bonn, 2000.

Ronge, Julia. *Beethovens Lehrzeit: Kompositionsstudien bei Joseph Haydn, Johann Georg Albrechtsberger und Antonio Salieri.* Bonn, 2011.

Rumph, Stephen. *Beethoven after Napoleon: Political Romanticism in the Late Works*. Berkeley, 2004.

Schiedermair, Ludwig. *Der junge Beethoven*. Hildesheim, 1978 (1925).

Schmidt-Görg, Joseph. *Beethoven: Die Geschichte seiner Familie*. Bonn, 1964.

Schmitt, Ulrich. *Revolution im Konzertsaal: Zur Beethoven-Rezeption im 19. Jahrhundert*. Mainz, 1990.

Smezak, Frederik. *Beethovens Wiener Originalverleger*. Vienna, 1987.

Solomon, Maynard. *Beethoven Essays*. Cambridge, MA, 1988.

Stricker, Rémy. *Le dernier Beethoven*. Paris, 2001.

Tellenbach, Marie-Elisabeth. *Beethoven und seine "Unsterbliche Geliebte" Josephine Brunswick*. Zurich, 1983.

Verleyen, Frans. *De laatste uren van Ludwig: Herinneringen aan Beethoven*. Groot-Bijgaarden, 1995.

Walden, Edward. *Beethoven's Immortal Beloved: Solving the Mystery*. Lanham, MD, 2011.

Wetzstein, Margot, ed. *Das Haus in der Rheingasse: Beethovens Wohnhaus im Kontext der Bonner Geschichte (1660–1860). Gottfried Fischers Materialsammlung*. Bonn, 2010.

———, ed. *Familie Beethoven im kurfürstlichen Bonn: Neuauflage nach den Aufzeichnungen des Bonner Bäckermeisters Gottfried Fischer*. Bonn, 2006.

Willets, Pamela J. *Beethoven and England: An Account of Sources in the British Museum*. London, 1970.

Wolf, Stefan. *Beethovens Neffenkonflikt*. Munich, 1995.

Zanden, Jos van der. *Beethoven: Nieuwe onthullingen*. Haarlem, 1993.

MUSIC: GENERAL

Brisson, Elisabeth. *Guide de la musique de Beethoven*. Paris, 2005.

Dahlhaus, Carl. *Ludwig van Beethoven und Seine Zeit*. Laaber, 1987.

Hiemke, Sven, ed. *Beethoven Handbuch*. Kassel, 2009.

Kinderman, William. *Beethoven*. Oxford, 1995.

Küster, Konrad. *Beethoven*. Stuttgart, 1994.

Riethmüller, Albrecht, ed. *Das Beethoven-Handbuch*. Laaber, 2012– .

———, Carl Dahlhaus, and Alexandre L. Ringer, eds. *Beethoven: Interpretationen seiner Werke*. 2 vols. Laaber, 1996.

Rolland, Romain. *Beethoven: Les grandes époques créatrices (1928–1957)*. Edited by Marie Romain Rolland. Paris, 1980 (1966).

Rosen, Charles. *The Classical Style: Haydn, Mozart, Beethoven*. London, 1976 (1971).

Stanley, Glenn, ed. *The Cambridge Companion to Beethoven*. Cambridge, 2000.

Tovey, Donald F. *Essays in Musical Analysis*. London, 1935–44.

Badura-Skoda, Paul, and Jörg Demus. *Die Klaviersonaten von Ludwig van Beethoven.* Wiesbaden, 1970.

Bergé, Pieter, Jeroen D'hoe, and William E. Caplin, eds. *Beethoven's Tempest Sonata: Perspectives of Analysis and Performance.* Leuven, 2009.

Bertagnolli, Paul. *Prometheus in Music: Representations of the Myth in the Romantic Era.* Hampshire, 2007.

Boucourechliev, André. *Essai sur Beethoven.* Arles, 1991.

Brown, Clive. *Die Neubewertung der Quellen von Beethovens Fünfter Symphonie.* Wiesbaden, 1996.

Broyles, Michael. *The Emergence and Evolution of Beethoven's Heroic Style.* New York, 1987.

Buch, Esteban. *La Neuvième de Beethoven: Une histoire politique.* Paris, 1999.

Buchbinder, Rudolf. *Mein Beethoven: Leben mit dem Meister.* St. Pölten, 2014.

Burnham, Scott. *Beethoven Hero.* Princeton, NJ, 1995.

———, and Michael P. Steinberg, eds. *Beethoven and His World.* Princeton, 2000.

Cook, Nicholas. *Beethoven: Symphony No. 9.* Cambridge, 1996 (1993).

Cooper, Barry. *Beethoven and the Creative Process.* Oxford, 1990.

Csobáldi, Peter, et al., eds. *Fidelio/Leonore: Annäherungen an ein zentrales Werk des Musiktheaters. Vorträge und Materialien des Salzburger Symposions 1996.* Anif, 1998.

Damschroder, David. *Harmony in Beethoven.* Cambridge, 2016.

Drabkin, William. *Beethoven: Missa solemnis.* Cambridge, 1991.

Drake, Kenneth. *The Beethoven Sonatas and the Creative Experience.* Bloomington, 1994.

Eichhorn, Andreas. *Beethovens Neunte Symphonie: Die Geschichte ihrer Aufführung und Rezeption.* Kassel, 1993.

Floros, Constantin. *Beethovens Eroica und Prometheus-Musik.* Wilhelmshaven, 1978.

Friesenhagen, Andreas. *Die Messen Ludwig van Beethovens.* Cologne, 1996.

Frohlich, Martha. *Beethoven's "Appassionata" Sonata.* Oxford, 1991.

Geck, Martin. *Die Sinfonien Beethovens.* Hildesheim, 2015.

———. *Von Beethoven bis Mahler: Die Musik des deutschen Idealismus.* Stuttgart, 1993.

———, and Peter Schleuning. *"Geschrieben auf Bonaparte." Beethovens "Eroica": Revolution, Reaktion, Rezeption.* Reinbek bei Hamburg, 1989.

Gleich, Clemens-Christoph von. *Beethovens Prometheus-Variationen in neuer Sicht.* Salzburg, 1996.

Goebl-Streicher, Uta, Jutta Streicher, and Michael Ladenburger, eds. *Beethoven und die Wiener Klavierbauer Nannette und Andreas Streicher,* exhibition catalogue, Beethoven-Haus Bonn. Bonn, 1999.

Goldschmidt, Harry. *Das Wort in Beethovens Instrumentalbegleitung.* Keulen, 1999.

Gülke, Peter. *". . . immer das Ganze vor Augen": Studien zu Beethoven.* Stuttgart, 2000.

———. *Zur Neuausgabe der Sinfonie Nr. 5 von Ludwig van Beethoven: Werk und Edition.* Leipzig, 1978.

Hein, Hartmut. *Beethovens Klavierkonzerte: Gattungsnorm und individuelle Konzeption.* Stuttgart, 2001.

Hess, Willy. *Beethovens Oper Fidelio und ihre drei Fassungen.* Zurich, 1953.

Hiemke, Sven. *Ludwig van Beethoven: Missa solemnis.* Kassel, 2003.

Hildebrandt, Dieter. *Die Neunte: Schiller, Beethoven und die Geschichte eines musikalischen Welterfolgs.* Munich, 2005.

Hinrichsen, Hans-Joachim. *Beethoven: Die Klaviersonaten.* Kassel, 2013.

Huizing, Jan Marisse. *Ludwig van Beethoven: Die Klaviersonaten. Interpretation und Aufführungspraxis.* Mainz, 2012.

Indorf, Gerd. *Beethovens Streichquartette: Kulturgeschichtliche Aspekte und Werkinterpretation.* Freiburg im Breisgau, 2004.

Jones, David Wyn. *Beethoven: Pastoral Symphony.* Cambridge, 1995.

———. *The Symphony in Beethoven's Vienna.* Cambridge, 2006.

Jones, Timothy. *Beethoven: The "Moonlight" and Other Sonatas, Op. 27 and Op. 31.* Cambridge, 1999.

Kerman, Joseph. *The Beethoven Quartets.* New York, 1966.

Kinderman, William. *Beethoven's Diabelli Variations.* Oxford, 1987.

———, ed. *The String Quartets of Beethoven.* Urbana, 2006.

Lelie, Christo. *Van Piano tot Forte: Geschiedenis and ontwikkeling van de vroege piano ca. 1450–1867.* Kampen, 1995.

Levy, Janet M. *Beethoven's Compositional Choices: The Two Versions of Opus 18, No. 1, First Movement.* Philadelphia, 1982.

Lindley, Mark, Conny Restle, and Klaus-Jürgen Sachs. *Beethovens Klaviervariationen op. 34: Entstehung, Gestalt, Darbietung.* Mainz, 2007.

Lockwood, Lewis. *Beethoven's Symphonies: An Artistic Vision.* New York, 2015.

———, and Mark Kroll, eds. *The Beethoven Violin Sonatas: History, Criticism, Performance.* Urbana, 2004.

Lühning, Helga. *Leonore: Oper in zwei Aufzügen von Ludwig van Beethoven. Das Libretto der Aufführung von 1806.* Bonn, 1996.

———, and Wolfram Steinbeck, eds. *Von der Leonore zum Fidelio: Vorträge und Referate des Bonner Symposions 1997.* Frankfurt am Main, 2000.

Mauser, Siegfried. *Beethovens Klaviersonaten.* Munich, 2001.

Mühlenweg, Anja. "Ludwig van Beethoven 'Christus am Ölberge' op. 85: Studien zur Entstehungs- und Überlieferungsgeschichte." Dissertation, University of Würzburg. Munich, 2004.

Münster, Arnold. *Studien zu Beethovens Diabelli-Variationen.* Munich, 1982.

Philippot, Michel P. *Diabolus in musica: Les variations de Beethoven sur un theme de Diabelli.* Paris, 2001.

Plantinga, Leon. *Beethoven's Concertos: History, Style, Performance.* New York, 1998.

Reid, Paul. *The Beethoven Song Companion.* Manchester, 2007.

Rexroth, Dieter. *Beethovens Symphonien: Ein musikalischer Werkführer.* Munich, 2005.

Sachs, Harvey. *The Ninth: Beethoven and the World of 1824.* New York, 2010.

Schenker, Heinrich. *Beethoven: Fünfte Sinfonie.* Vienna, 1925.

———. *Beethovens Neunte Sinfonie.* Vienna, 1969 (1912).

Schmenner, Roland. *Die Pastorale: Beethoven, das Gewitter und der Blitzableiter.* Kassel, 1998.

Sipe, Thomas. *Beethoven: Eroica Symphony.* Cambridge, 1998.

Solomon, Maynard. *Late Beethoven: Music, Thought, Imagination.* Berkeley, 2003.

Stowel, Robin. *Beethoven: Violin Concerto.* Cambridge, 1998.

Uhde, Jürgen. *Beethovens Klaviermusik.* 3 vols. Stuttgart, 1980 (1968).

Ulm, Renate, ed. *Die 9 Symphonien Beethovens.* Kassel, 1999 (1994).

Watson, Angus. *Beethoven's Chamber Music in Context.* Woodbridge, 2010.

Westphal, Kurt. *Vom Einfall zur Symphonie: Einblick in Beethovens Schaffensweise.* Berlin, 1965.

Wiese, Walter. *Beethovens Kammermusik.* Winterthur, 2010.

Will, Richard. *The Characteristic Symphony in the Age of Haydn and Beethoven.* Cambridge, 2002.

Winter, Robert, and Robert Martin, eds. *The Beethoven Quartet Companion.* Berkeley, 1994.

Wu, Kuei-Mei. *Die Bagatellen Ludwig van Beethovens.* Cologne, 1999.

Zickenheiner, Otto. *Untersuchungen zur Credo-Fuge der Missa Solemnis von Ludwig van Beethoven.* Munich, 1984.

PERFORMANCE PRACTICE

Barth, Georg. *The Pianist as Orator: Beethoven and the Transformation of Keyboard Style.* Ithaca, 1992.

Brown, Clive. *Classical and Romantic Performing Practice 1750–1900.* Oxford, 1999.

Huizing, Jan Marisse. *Ludwig van Beethoven: Die Klaviersonaten. Interpretation und Aufführungspraxis.* Mainz, 2012.

Lockwood, Lewis, and the Juilliard String Quartet. *Inside Beethoven's Quartets: History, Performance, Interpretation.* Cambridge, MA, 2008.

Newman, William S. *Beethoven on Beethoven: Playing His Piano Music His Way.* New York, 1988.

Rosen, Charles. *Beethoven's Piano Sonatas: A Short Companion.* New Haven, CT, 2002.

Rosenblum, Sandra P. *Performance Practices in Classic Piano Music: Their Principles and Applications.* Bloomington, 1988.

Schiff, András. *Beethovens Klaviersonaten und ihre Deutung "Für jeden Ton die Sprache finden . . . ": András Schiff im Gespräch mit Martin Meyer.* Bonn, 2007.

Stowel, Robin, ed. *Performing Beethoven.* Cambridge, 1994.

———. *Violin Technique and Performance Practice in the Late Eighteenth and Early Nineteenth Centuries.* Cambridge, 1985.

Taub, Robert. *Playing the Beethoven Piano Sonatas.* Pompton Plains, 2002.

Weinzierl, Stefan. *Beethovens Konzerträume: Raumakustik und symphonische Aufführungspraxis an der Schwelle zum modernen Konzertwesen.* Frankfurt am Main, 2002.

HISTORY

Braubach, Max. *Kurköln: Gestalten und Ereignisse aus zwei Jahrhunderten rheinischer Geschichte.* Munich, 1949.

———. *Maria Theresias jüngster Sohn Max Franz.* Vienna, 1961.

Conrady, Karl Otto. *Goethe: Leben und Werk.* Munich, 1994.

Friedell, Egon. *Kulturgeschichte der Neuzeit.* 2 vols. Munich, 1976 (1927–31).

Goethe, Wolfgang von. *Aus meinem Leben: Dichtung und Wahrheit.* Frankfurt am Main, 2007.

Hörold, Dietrich, and Manfred van Rey, eds. *Geschichte der Stadt Bonn.* 4 vols. Bonn, 1989.

Kennedy, Paul. *Aufstieg und Fall der grossen Mächte: Ökonomischer Wandel und militärischer Konflikt von 1500 bis 2000.* Frankfurt am Main, 1989.

Kissinger, Henry A. *Das Gleichgewicht der Grossmächte: Metternich, Castlereagh und die Neuordnung Europas 1812–1822.* Zurich, 1986 (1962).

Möller, Horst. *Fürstenstaat oder Bürgernation: Deutschland 1763–1815.* Munich, 1998 (1994).

Porter, Lindsay. *Who Are the Illuminati?* Essex, 2005.

Presser, Jacques. *Napoleon: Historie en legende.* Amsterdam, 1989 (1946).

Zehnder, Frank Günter, and Werner Schäfke, eds. *Der Riss im Himmel: Clemens August und Seine Epoche.* 7 vols. Cologne, 2000.

VIENNA

Bled, Jean-Paul. *Wien: Residenz, Metropole, Hauptstadt.* Vienna, 2002 (1998).

Bruckmüller, Ernst. *Sozialgeschichte Österreichs.* Munich, 2001.

Hanson, Alice M. *Musical Life in Biedermeier Vienna.* Cambridge, 1985.

Helczmanovski, Heimold. *Beiträge zur Bevölkerungs- und Sozialgeschichte Österreichs.* Vienna, 1973.

Jahn, Michael. *Die Wiener Hofoper von 1794 bis 1810: Musik und Tanz im Burg- und Kärnthnerthortheater.* Vienna, 2012.

Kann, Robert A. *A History of the Habsburg Empire 1526–1918.* Berkeley, 1977.

Kramar, Konrad, and Petra Stuiber. *Die schrulligen Habsburger: Marotten und Allüren eines Kaiserhauses.* Vienna, 1999.

Kreszowiak, Tadeusz. *Freihaustheater in Wien, 1797–1801: Wirkungsstätte von W.A. Mozart und E. Schikaneder.* Vienna, 2009.

Leidinger, Hannes, Verena Moritz, and Berndt Schippler. *Das Schwarzbuch der Habsburger: Die unrühmliche Geschichte eines Herrschergeschlechtes.* Vienna, 2003.

Morrow, Mary Sue. *Concert Life in Haydn's Vienna: Aspects of a Developing Musical and Social Institution.* Stuyvesant, NY, 1988.

Peham, Helga. *Leopold II.* Vienna, 1987.

Rice, John A. *Empress Marie Therese and the Music at the Viennese Court, 1792–1807.* Cambridge, 2003.

Rumpler, Helmut. *Eine Chance für Mitteleuropa: Bürgerliche Emanzipation und Staatsverfall in der Habsburgermonarchie. 1804–1914. (Österreichische Geschichte,* ed. Herwig Wolframn, vol. 8). Vienna, 2001.

Seward, Desmond. *Metternich, der erste Europäer: Eine Biographie.* Zurich, 1993 (1991).

Siegert, Heinz, ed. *Adel in Österreich.* Vienna, 1971.

Tolar, Günter. *So ein Theater! Die Geschichte des Theaters an der Wien.* Vienna, 1991.

Vocelka, Karl. *Glanz und Untergang der höfischen Welt: Respräsentation, Reform und Reaktion im Habsburgischen Vielvölkerstaat. 1699–1815. (Österreichische Geschichte,* ed. Herwig Wolfram, vol. 7.) Vienna, 2001.

Waissenberger, Robert, ed. *Wien 1815–1848: Bürgersinn und Aufbegehren. Die Zeit des Biedermeier und Vormärz.* Vienna, 1986.

Weissensteiner, Frederik. *Die Österreichischen Kaiser.* Vienna, 2003.

———. *Die Söhne Maria Theresias.* Vienna, 2004.

Zweig, Stephan. *Die Welt von gestern: Erinnerungen eines Europäers.* Hamburg, 1970 (1944).

SERIES AND JOURNALS

Beethoven Forum. Urbana, IL, and Lincoln, NE, 1992–2007.

Beethoven-Jahrbuch. Veröffentlichungen des Beethoven-Hauses Bonn. Series 2. Bonn, 1953–83.

The Beethoven Journal. Published by Ira F. Brilliant Center for Beethoven Studies and the American Beethoven Society. San José, CA, 1995– . (Previously, *The Beethoven Newsletter,* 1986–94.)

Beethoven Studies. Edited by Alan Tyson. 3 vols. Cambridge, 1973–82.

Begleitpublikationen zu Ausstellungen. Veröffentlichungen des Beethoven-Hauses. Bonn, 1992– .

Bonner Beethoven-Studien. Veröffentlichungen des Beethoven-Hauses. Series 5. Bonn, 1999– .

Schriften zur Beethoven-Forschung. Veröffentlichungen des Beethoven-Hauses. Series 4. Bonn, 1964– .

Zu Beethoven: Aufsätze und Annotationen. Edited by Harry Goldschmidt. 3 vols. Berlin, 1979–88.

ILLUSTRATION CREDITS

All illustrations were generously provided by the Beethoven-Haus in Bonn.

Following page 22

Christian Horneman, *Ludwig van Beethoven,* ivory miniature, 1802
(H. C. Bodmer Collection, HCB Bi 1)

Inigo Shury, *Mechelen Town Center,* engraving, mid-nineteenth century
(B 2076)

Lorenz Janscha, *The Electoral Palace in Bonn*, etching by Johann Ziegler after a
watercolor (B 962)

François Rousseau, *Coadjutor Maximilian Francis's Visit to Bonn,* oil painting,
1780 (B 2242)

Lorenz Janscha, *View of the Rhein and Siebengebirge Mountains,* Bonn, ca. 1790,
photograph of an engraving by Johann Ziegler (NE 81, vol. I, no. 149)

Reiner Beissel, *Garden View of Beethoven's Birthplace in Bonn,* drawing
(B 670)

Joseph Neesen, *Beethoven at Age Fifteen,* reproduction of a lithograph by the
Becker brothers (B 322)

Gerhard von Kügelgen, *Group Silhouette of the von Breuning Family,* 1782,
reproduction of a silhouette presumed to be by Gerhard von Kügelgen
(B 2369)

Amelius Radoux, *Ludwig van Beethoven* (senior), copy by Toni Bücher of a
painting (B 983)

Gerhard von Kügelgen, *Helene von Breuning,* oil painting (B 2387)

Johann Georg Schallenberg, *Franz Anton Ries,* oil painting (B 2052)

Johann Heinrich Richter, *Franz Gerhard Wegeler,* painting (B 2050)

Lorenz Janscha, *Promenade at the Vienna City Limits,* reproduction of a watercolor (B 2391/133)

Carl Schütz, *Kohlmarkt Square, Vienna,* reproduction of an engraving by Carl Schütz after an original drawing (B 2391/93)

Ludwig van Beethoven, letter to Franz Gerhard Wegeler in Bonn, June 29, 1801 (Wegeler Collection, W17)

Johann Raulino, *View of Heiligenstadt in Vienna,* early nineteenth century, photograph of a lithograph (Ley, vol. 2, no. 333)

Following page 214

Willebrord Joseph Mähler, *Ludwig van Beethoven,* oil painting, 1815 (B 2388)

Vincens Reim, *St. Augustin's and the Palais Lobkowitz in Vienna,* ca. 1825, photograph by Atelier Sachsse of an etching (B 1558)

Carl Schütz, *St. Michael's Square and Riding School in Vienna,* 1789, engraving (B 2174)

Anonymous, *Kärntnertortheater in Vienna,* ca. 1840, sketched reproduction of an anonymous nineteenth-century engraving (Ley, vol. 6, no. 1033)

Theater an der Wien, ca. 1830, engraving by Johann Wenzel Fuchs after a drawing by Eduard Gurk (B 2121)

Carl Schütz, *University Square in Vienna,* 1790, reproduction of an engraving (B 2391/116)

Anonymous, *Razumovsky Palace in Landstrasse, Vienna,* ca. 1825, engraving (B 2086)

Johann Baptist Lampi, *Countess Josephine Deym von Stritetz, née von Brunsvik,* painting (B 2149)

Anonymous, *Palace of Count Joseph Deym in Vienna,* watercolor, ca. 1800 (Ley, vol. 2, no. 301)

Nikolaus Lauer, *Antonie Brentano with Her Children Georg and Fanny,* pastel (B 1945)

Anonymous, miniature portrait from Beethoven's estate of an unknown woman, presumed to be Countess Giulietta (Julie) Guicciardi (H. C. Bodmer Collection, HCB V 9 d)

Anonymous, *Therese Malfatti,* photograph of an anonymous pastel (Ley, vol. 3, No. 521)

Jan Rustem, *Christine von Frank, née Gerhardi,* photograph of a painting [NE 81, vol. II, no. 243]

R., *The Teplitz Bathhouse,* ca. 1840, etching signed with the monogram "R." (B 2330)

Anonymous, *Inside the Main Bathhouse in Karlsbad,* ca. 1845, lithograph by C. Hering after an anonymous drawing (B 2258)

Beethoven, sketch of the Eighth Symphony (op. 93) autograph (H. C. Bodmer Collection, HCB Mh 86)

Beethoven, sketch of *King Stephan* (op. 117), autograph (NE 129)

Following page 406

Ferdinand Georg Waldmüller, *Ludwig van Beethoven,* 1823, reproduction of a painting destroyed in the Second World War (B 362)

Lorenz Janscha, *People Promenading by the Coffee Houses in Prater Park,* ca. 1810, etching by Johann Ziegler after a drawing (B 2340)

Johann Nepomuk Hoechle, *The Main Redoutensaal Ballroom in Vienna,* ca. 1815, photograph of a watercolor drawing (Ley, vol. 4, no. 658)

Johann Baptist Lampi, *Rudolph, Archduke of Austria,* ca. 1819, anonymous oil painting, perhaps by Johann Baptist Lampi senior (BHB, no catalogue no.)

Beethoven's "Wittgenstein" sketchbook, autograph (H. C. Bodmer Collection, HCB BSk 1/49)

Ferdinand Wolanek, letter to Ludwig van Beethoven, between March 23 and 26, 1825, including notes and a draft response from Beethoven, autograph (BH 31)

Joseph Daniel Böhm, *Beethoven on His Walk,* ca. 1820, rubbing by Fr. Trau from two engraved silver plates (B 2317)

Beethoven's calling card (R 19 a)

Small wax seal with Beethoven's initials (R 18)

Page from a conversation notebook, September 9, 1825 (H. C. Bodmer Collection, no number)

Ear trumpets ordered by Beethoven from Johann Nepomuk Mälzel in 1813 (no archive number; from Ernst Herttrich, *Eine Biographie in Bildern,* p. 78)

Johann Nepomuk Hoechle, *Beethoven's Final Home in Vienna,* 1827, photograph of a wash drawing (Ley, vol. 7, no. 1275)

Joseph Teltscher, *Beethoven on His Deathbed,* March 1827, reproduction of a sketch (B 68)

Franz Xaver Stöber, *Beethoven's Funeral Procession before the House of the Black-Robed Spaniards,* 1827, watercolor (BHB, B 209)

INDEX OF WORKS

INDEX OF PEOPLE

Breuning family, 12, 48–49, 51, 64–66, 114, 116, 118, 122, 392

Bridgetower, George Augustus Polgreen, 141, 218, 425, 559n5

Broadwood, James, 252, 571n12

Broadwood, John, 252, 571n12, 571n14

Broadwood, Thomas, 252, 571n12

Browne, Countess Anna Margaretha von, 125, 557n1

Browne, Count Johann Georg von, 74, 125, 165, 266, 557n1

Brunsvik, Countess Anna von, 138, 139, 140, 141, 146, 142, 146, 558n1 (ch 18)

Brunsvik, Countess Charlotte von, 568n9

Brunsvik, Countess Josephine von. See Deym, Countess Josephine von

Brunsvik, Franz von, 244, 336, 346, 441

Brunsvik, Therese von, 138, 140, 236–38, 244, 261, 331–32, 336–37, 402, 403, 407, 408, 570n29

Brunsvik de Korompa, Anton von, 138, 139, 141

Brunsvik family, 142, 234–35, 402, 408, 337, 402, 408

Bülow, Hans von, 433, 468

Bursy, Dr. Karl von, 473

Buxtehude, Dieterich, 90, 550n11

Byron, Lord George Gordon, 364

Cappi, Pietro, 456

Carpani, Giuseppe, 474–75

Casanova, Giacomo, 63–64

Castelli, Ignaz Franz, xviii

Castlereagh, Robert Stewart, 352

Catherine II (empress of Russia), 81

Charles XIV John (king of Sweden), xix, 566–67n3 (ch 28)

Charles Alexander of Lorraine, 34

Charles Theodore (elector of Bavaria), 4

Cherubini, Luigi, 171, 201, 202, 255, 262, 272, 308, 442, 447, 567n20, 590n6

Chopin, Frederic, 548n12

Choron, Alexandre-Étienne, 13

Clary, Countess Josephine von, 106, 122

Clemens August of Bavaria (archbishop-elector of Cologne), 4, 5, 6, 7, 34, 35, 36

Clement, Franz, 93, 223, 263, 272–75, 464, 484, 534, 588n1 (ch 48)

Clementi, Muzio, 83, 183, 195, 197, 243, 249, 275, 281, 315, 363, 416, 425, 427, 459, 591n8

Cobenzl, Ludwig von, 221

Colbran, Isabella, 424, 474

Colfs, Antoine, xvi, 3

Colfs, Louis, 3

Collin, Heinrich Joseph von, 263, 278, 307, 371

Colloredo, Anton Theodor von, 312

Conti, Giacomo, 149, 191

Cooper, Barry, 122, 594n17

Cramer, Johann Baptist, 25, 32, 183, 425, 561n4, 571n13, 589n8

Czerny, Carl, xvii, 25, 44, 61, 85, 103, 108, 122, 146, 161–67, 170, 181, 196, 214, 227–28, 315, 393–94, 403, 411, 413–14, 431, 433, 456, 472, 479, 481, 570n27, 574n7, 587n11

Dalayrac, Nicolas-Marie, 201

Da Ponte, Lorenzo, 40, 213

Debussy, Claude, 482

Dembscher, Ignaz, 598n39

Demmer, Friedrich, 261

Demmer, Thekla, 376

Deym, Carl, 236

Deym, Countess Josephine von (née Brunsvik), 87, 138–43, 173, 232, 233–40, 238–39, 242, 244, 254, 257, 261, 267–68, 286, 331, 332, 333–36, 337–39, 341, 390, 401–4, 407–8, 460, 568n7, 569n18, 579n6

Deym, Fritz, 236, 334, 402

Deym, Vicky, 239, 408

Deym von Stritetz, Count Joseph, 139, 140, 141–42, 146, 232, 332, 334, 408

Deym-Goltz family, 332

Diabelli, Anton, 93, 195, 446, 455–56, 464–65, 478, 534

Dickens, Charles, 129

Diebitsch, Johann Karl von, 351

Dietrichstein, Count Moritz Joseph von, 288, 378, 379, 510

Dittersdorf, Karl Ditters von, 52, 58, 60, 104, 549n6

Dittrich, Marie-Agnes, 479

Donizetti, Gaetano, 424

Dragonetti, Domenico, 593n13 (ch 54)

Dressler, Ernst Christoph, 31, 43
Duport, Jean-Louis, 108
Duport, Jean-Pierre, 108
Duport, Louis-Antoine, 484–85, 487–88
Duschek, Josepha, 106
Dussek, Johann Ladislaus, 183, 226, 247, 249, 354, 357

Elisabeth Alexeievna (empress of Russia), 385, 557n3
Emilie M., 402
Enghien, Louis Antoine, Duke of, 221
Eppinger, Heinrich, 157
Erard, Sébastien, 218, 249–52, 571n7
Erdődy, Countess Anna Maria von, 74, 298, 299, 300, 301, 311, 346, 418, 419, 576n3
Ertmann, Dorothea von, 416
Eschenburg, Johann Joachim, 549n12
Esterházy, Countess Almerie, 335, 580n3
Esterházy, Countess Maria Theresia, 382
Esterházy, Prince Nikolaus Joseph (Nikolaus I), 282
Esterházy, Prince Nikolaus (Nikolaus II), 74, 93, 147, 231, 265, 282–84, 286, 510, 575n23
Esterházy, Prince Paul Anton (Anton I), 282
Esterházy, Princess Maria Josepha Hermenegild (née Liechtenstein), 74
Eybler, Joseph von, 104

Fasch, Carl Friedrich, 137
Fayolle, François, 13
Ferdinand III (grand duke of Tuscany), 447
Ferrari, Giacomo Gotifredo, 571n13
Fétis, François-Joseph, 586n1
Filippi, Anton, 214
Firmian, Count Leopold von, 449
Fischenich, Bartholomeus, 52, 53, 490
Fischer, Cecilia, 16, 17
Fischer, Gottfried, 16
Floros, Constantin, 229, 560n14
Forkel, Johann Nikolaus, 43, 157
Förster, Emanuel Aloys, 269, 427, 561
Forti, Anton, 376
Francis I (emperor of Austria). See Francis II
Francis II (Holy Roman emperor, and emperor of Austria as Francis I), 76, 94, 146, 221, 222, 258, 284, 312, 496

Frank, Christine von (née Gerhardi), 151, 122
Frank, Dr. Johann Peter, 169
Frederick II (Frederick the Great, king of Prussia), 107, 109
Frederick Augustus I (king of Saxony, and elector of Saxony as Frederick Augustus III), xix, 106, 107, 447
Frederick Augustus III. See Frederick Augustus I
Frederick William II (king of Prussia), xix, 107, 108
Frederick William III (king of Prussia), xix, 166, 494
Freud, Sigmund, 182, 371, 469
Freund, Philip, 157
Friedell, Egon, vii, xxi
Fries, Count Moritz von, 74, 83, 93, 173, 191, 193, 483
Frimmel, Theodor von, 552n20
Fröhlich, Johann Baptist, 395
Fuchs, vice Kapellmeister, 283
Fux, Johann Joseph, 89, 90, 308, 313, 577

Galitzin, Nikolai Borisovich, 448–49, 514–522, 527–28, 530, 596nn1,4 (ch 58)
Galitzin, Yuri Nikolayevich, 516
Gallenberg, Count Wenzel Robert von, 142
Gassmann, Florian, 213–14
Gaveaux, Pierre, 254, 257
Gebauer, Franz Xaver, 449
Geck, Martin, 229
Gelinek, Abbé Joseph, 83
George IV, King of England, 406
Gerhardi, Christine. See Frank, Christine von (née Gerhardi)
Giannattasio del Rio, Anna (Nanni), 392–95, 399
Giannattasio del Rio, Franziska (Fanny), 392–95, 399, 419
Giovane, Dutchess Julie von, 141, 146
Gleichenstein, Ignaz von, 239, 240, 280–82, 298–99, 300, 301, 311, 526, 534
Gluck, Christoph Willibald von, 43, 84, 130
Goethe, Johann Wolfgang von, 27, 140, 152, 176, 240–41, 292, 318–19, 326–29, 330, 335, 370, 381, 388, 434–35, 447, 579n13 (ch 36), 609, 619

Goldoni, Carlo, 52
Goldschmidt, Harry, 558n3 (ch 18)
Gossec, François-Joseph, 217
Graaf, Christian Ernst, 33
Graf, Conrad, 253
Gräffer, Anton, 579n13 (ch 37)
Graun, Carl Heinrich, 7
Grétry, André Modeste, 201, 217, 255
Griesinger, Georg August von, xx, 159,
    192–93, 224, 379, 447
Grillparzer, Franz, xviii, 378–79, 470, 473,
    579n5
Grossmann, Gustav Friedrich, 26, 29, 52
Grove, George, 209
Guicciardi, Giulietta (Julie), 142, 173, 337
Gyrowetz, Adalbert, 52, 319, 381

Habeneck, François-Antoine, 438
Halász, István, 479
Halm, Anton, 189, 597n26
Handel, George Frideric, xvii, 95, 98, 183,
    209, 272, 371, 415–416, 442, 458, 464–
    65, 534, 555n23, 587n13
Hanson, Alice M., 569n11
Häring, Johann von, 426–27, 588n1 (ch 48)
Haslinger, Tobias, 459, 476, 534, 572n6
Hasse, Johann Adolph, 7
Haydn, Joseph, xvii, xx, 27, 58, 60, 62–63,
    65–67, 89, 90–98, 100, 103, 104, 108, 111,
    119, 131, 134, 144, 146, 147–49, 159,
    186–87, 189, 190, 192, 195, 197, 205, 208,
    209, 212, 215, 224, 225, 230, 268–69,
    282–85, 288–89, 308, 350, 364–65, 367,
    385, 426, 429, 430, 442, 447, 481, 510,
    512, 529, 551n4 (ch 10), 560n6 (ch 19),
    571n7, 574n21
Heine, Heinrich, 362, 544n4 (prologue)
Hellborn, Heinrich Kreissle von, 478
Heller, Ferdinand, 30
Helm, Theodor, 523
Hellmesberger, Georg, 517
Hensler, Karl Friedrich, 463, 464
Herbosch, Dr. Sus, 541, 562n1, 591n9,
    594n4
Herder, Johann Gottfried von, 27, 66, 412
Hess, Willy, 415, 550n15, 555n22
Hiller, Ferdinand, 536
Hiller, Johann Adam, 23, 26

Himmel, Friedrich Heinrich, 109
Hirsch, Carl Friedrich, 95
Hofbauer, Johann Caspar, 585n18
Hofbauer, Ludovika, 398, 585n18
Hoffmann, E. T. A., 321, 379, 551n4 (ch 10)
Hoffmeister, Franz Anton, 100, 195–96,
    565n1
Holz, Karl, 415, 424, 503, 516–19, 520–28,
    593n7 (ch 53), 594n17
Homer, 412, 588n5 (ch 47)
Honrath, Jeanette d', 122
Horneman, Christian, 117
Huber, Franz Xaver, 209
Hugo, Victor, 411
Hummel, Elisabeth (Elise; née Röckel),
    536, 569n22
Hummel, Johann Nepomuk, xix, 103, 111,
    196, 214, 283–84, 355, 364–65, 381, 442,
    445, 456, 534, 536, 548n12, 569n22,
    571n5, 583n20
Hundertwasser, Friedensreich, 469
Hüttenbrenner, Anselm, 478, 487, 538, 539
Hüttenbrenner, Joseph, 487

Irmen, Hans-Josef, 28, 546n5, 549n4

Jean Paul (Johann Paul Richter), 351
Jeitteles, Aloïs Isidor, 405
Joachim, Joseph, 275, 517
Joseph II (Holy Roman emperor), 29, 34,
    37, 57, 72, 73, 76, 83, 99, 200, 204, 213,
    219, 258, 284, 339, 552–53n20
Junker, Carl Ludwig, 56, 57

Kalkbrenner, Friedrich, 571n13
Kanka, Johann Nepomuk, 386
Kanne, Friedrich August, 381, 471, 592–
    93n7 (ch 53)
Kant, Immanuel, 39, 52, 412–13
Karl Ludwig (archduke of Austria), 221, 222
Kaufmann, Joseph, 417, 418
Kaunitz, Wenzel Anton von, 27
Keglevics, Barbara von. *See* Odescalchi,
    Princess Barbara
Kielmansegge, Countess Auguste Char-
    lotte von, 218
Kinsky, Carolina Maria von, Kinsky, Ferdi-
    nand Johann Nepomuk von, 73, 284,

Marx, Adolf Bernard, 208, 229
Marx, Karl, 197
Matthisson, Friedrich von, 126
Mattioli, Cajetan, 12, 31, 40
Mäurer, Bernhard, 545n5 (ch 3)
Maximilian Francis (archbishop-elector of
    Cologne), 34, 36, 37, 38, 40, 54, 55, 66,
    95–96, 97, 113
Maximilian Friedrich von Königsegg-
    Rothenfels (archbishop-elector of
    Cologne), 7, 29, 31, 35–37, 42
Mayer, Sebastian, 260, 261
Mayseder, Joseph, 315, 517, 598n39
Méhul, Etienne-Nicolas, 202, 217, 255, 272
Meisl, Karl, 578n8 (ch 36)
Mendelssohn, Felix, 107, 209, 275, 279,
    424–25, 438, 572
Metastasio, Pietro, 214
Metternich, Klemens von, 77, 302, 352, 382,
    420–21, 423–24, 475
Meyerbeer, Giacomo, 214, 355
Michotte, Edmond, 474
Milder-Hauptmann, Anna, 374, 375, 378
Molière, 52
Mollo & Co. (music publisher), 135, 193
Monsigny, Pierre-Alexandre, 202
Montagu, Lady Mary Wortley (née Pierre-
    pont), 72
Monteverdi, Claudio, 261
Moscheles, Ignaz, 103, 214, 216, 355, 456,
    506, 583, 599
Mosengeil, Friedrich, 578n5
Mozart, Franz Xaver, 456
Mozart, Leopold, 162, 273
Mozart, Wolfgang Amadeus, xvii, 4,
    20–21, 26, 31–32, 40–41, 43–45, 56, 58,
    60, 62–63, 66, 80–83, 90–91, 97–98,
    100, 104–8, 111, 118–19, 121, 134–35, 139,
    147–49, 156–57, 159, 161–62, 181, 187,
    190, 197, 200, 203, 207–8, 212, 214–16,
    229, 230, 256, 260, 264, 268–69, 272–73,
    289, 308, 317, 370, 377, 442, 456, 463,
    465, 481, 512, 529, 548n12, 550n1 (ch 9),
    551n4 (ch 10), 552–53n20
Müller, Joseph. See Deym, Count Joseph

Nägeli, Hans Georg, 183, 194, 476
Nagy, Samuel Raicz de, 585n18

Napoleon Bonaparte, 15, 76, 154, 162, 217–
    19, 221–23, 226–29, 282, 297, 299, 302,
    306, 351–52, 354–56, 358, 362, 381–82,
    420, 549n9, 571n7, 581n6 (ch 40)
Neate, Charles, 228, 427–28
Neefe, Christian Gottlob, 23–29, 30–32,
    38–39, 42–43, 46, 54, 57, 94–95, 98, 126,
    161, 415, 547n6 (ch 6)
Nestroy, Johann Nepomuk, 422
Neukomm, Sigismund, 367
Nicolai, Otto, 583n12
Nohl, Ludwig, 569n22
Nottebohm, Gustav, 572n6
Noverre, Jean-Georges, 151
Nussböck, Leopold, 397

Obermayer, Amalie, 500
Obermayer, Therese. See Beethoven,
    Therese van
Odescalchi, Princess Barbara (Babette; née
    Countess Keglevics), 122, 125
Oeser, Adam Friedrich, 24
Oliva, Franz Seraficus, 327, 427, 457, 526,
    579n14
Oppersdorff, Count Franz Joachim Wenzel
    von, 276, 277, 298
Ovid, 412

Paderewski, Ignaz, 164
Paër, Ferdinando, 259, 260, 377, 565n5
Paisiello, Giovanni, 58
Palestrina, Giovanni Pierluigi da, 284
Pálffy, Count Ferdinand von, 133, 265–66,
    370, 383, 384, 484
Pasqualati von Osterberg, Johann Baptist,
    389, 568n1
Pereira, Henriette, 307
Pestalozzi, Johann Heinrich, 236–37, 397
Peters, Carl Friedrich, 446, 454, 458–59, 466
Peters, Karl, 343, 397–98
Pezzl, Johann, 77
Pfeiffer, Tobias Friedrich, 17, 21, 31
Pichler, Caroline, 307
Pichler, Ernst, 141, 341
Piringer, Ferdinand, 459, 476, 534
Plantinga, Leon, 554n5, 575n27
Pleyel, Ignaz Joseph, 52, 84, 195, 281, 354,
    357, 364–65, 562n13

Pliny, 412
Plutarch, 51, 173, 412, 549n11, 574n15
Polledro, Giovanni Battista, 326
Potter, Cipriani, 95
Preindl, Joseph, 445
Probst, Heinrich, 446
Proudhon, Pierre-Joseph, 197
Pulkert, Oldrich, 576
Punto, Giovanni (Johann Wenzel Stich),
    150, 585n3

Quantz, Johann Joachim, 107

Radicchi, Giulio, 376
Rampl, Wenzel, 520, 564n5 (ch 25)
Razumovsky, Count Andrey, 73, 80, 119,
    176, 221, 268–69, 270–71, 277, 281, 291,
    382, 386, 403, 552n3, 559n7, 586n6
Razumovsky, Countess Maria Elisabeth
    (née Thun), 73, 80, 81
Recke, Elisabeth von der, 325
Reicha, Antonin, 38, 54
Reicha, Joseph, 40, 54, 57–58
Reichardt, Johann Friedrich, 132, 146, 251,
    298, 318, 371
Reiss, Johanna. See Beethoven, Johanna van
Reisser, Franz Michael, 502
Rellstab, Ludwig, 143
Reutter, Georg Edler von, 510
Ries, Anna, 48
Ries, Ferdinand, xxii, 95, 108, 115–16, 122,
    165–66, 193, 196, 205, 217, 219, 220, 222,
    231, 243, 245, 266, 287, 298, 336, 354,
    425–26, 428–29, 432, 435, 440, 448,
    459, 473, 481, 489, 526, 550n1 (ch 10),
    551n10, 571n13, 573n20
Ries, Franz Anton, 27, 38, 48, 56, 58, 78, 92,
    95 164, 546n4 (ch 4)
Ries, Johann, 48
Righini, Vincenzo, 60
Ritorni, Carlo, 560n14
Roche, Maximiliane de la, 241
Rochlitz, Friedrich, xxii, 159, 160, 318,
    561n18, 573n18
Röckel, Elisabeth (Elise). See Hummel,
    Elisabeth
Röckel, Joseph, 263–64, 569n22
Rode, Pierre, 313, 345, 347–48

Romberg, Andreas Jakob, 54, 56–57, 124
Romberg, Bernhard Heinrich, 54, 57–58,
    124, 572
Rossini, Gioachino, xviii, xix, 379, 424, 451,
    454, 474–75, 477
Rovantini, Franz Georg, 21, 31
Rudolph (archduke of Austria), 74, 95, 166,
    247, 299, 300, 303, 304, 306–8, 311–17,
    318, 322, 328, 340, 345, 375, 384, 397,
    426, 429, 431–32, 435, 442, 443, 447,
    449–50, 456, 463, 506, 577n5
Rust, Wilhelm Karl, 170

Saal, Ignaz, 148, 369
Saal, Thérèse, 148
Sailer, Johann Michael, 397
Salieri, Antonio, 43, 58, 92–93, 99, 111, 122,
    213–16, 266, 290, 355, 437, 479, 512,
    566n1 (ch 27)
Salm-Reifferscheid, Count Sigismund von,
    39
Salomon, Johann Peter, 63, 425, 550n1 (ch 10)
Salomon, Philipp, 63
Satzenhofen, Caroline von, 35
Sauer & Leidesdorf (music publisher), 459,
    557n4, 591n8
Saurau, Countess Gabriele (née Hunyady),
    382
Schaden, Joseph Freiherr von, 45, 46, 551n1
    (ch 12)
Schenk, Johann Baptist, 90
Schickh, Johann Valentin, 471
Schikaneder, Emanuel, 199, 200–204
Schiller, Charlotte, 490
Schiller, Johann Christoph Friedrich von,
    52–53, 66, 247, 319, 320, 329, 370–71,
    383, 412, 452, 490–91, 493, 525, 586n4
Schindler, Anton Felix, xxii–xxiv, 43–44,
    49, 101, 115, 142, 160, 186, 216, 283, 299,
    313, 337, 436, 438, 441, 456, 462, 464,
    476, 478–79, 484–85, 487, 493, 497–
    98, 503–505, 507, 509, 510, 516, 518, 522,
    525, 527, 532–33, 535–538, 544n4 (pro-
    logue), 549n12, 561n4, 563n18, 563n4,
    566–67n3, 575n23, 583n6, 584n4,
    589n27, 590n2 (ch 51), 593n11 (ch 54),
    595n5 (ch 55), 598n39, 599n15
Schirach, Gottlob Benedict von, 549

Schlechta, Franz von, xviii
Schlegel, August Wilhelm von, 240, 549–50n12 (ch 8)
Schlemmer, Mathias, 502, 504
Schlemmer, Wenzel, 417, 447–48, 483, 520, 564n5 (ch 25)
Schlesinger, Adolf Martin, 446, 457–59, 460, 462, 527, 529
Schlesinger, Maurice, 459, 462, 502, 521, 527
Schleuning, Peter, 229
Schmerling, Joseph von, 403
Schmidt, Dr. Johann Adam, 169, 174, 283, 497, 560n5 (ch 19)
Schnabel, Arthur, 164, 589n11
Schneider, Eulogius, 57, 87
Schneider, Friedrich, 315
Schönfeld, Johann Ferdinand von, 111
Schott's Sons (music publisher), 198, 437, 439, 446, 527, 535, 537
Schreiber, Christian, 211, 286
Schröder-Devrient, Wilhelmine (née Schröder), 375–78, 464
Schubert, Franz, xvii, 126, 214, 243, 323, 375, 387, 406, 423–24, 456, 472, 478–79, 520, 534
Schumann, Clara (née Wieck), 350, 561n5
Schumann, Robert, 275, 278–79, 424, 475
Schuppanzigh, Ignaz, xvii, 119, 123, 124, 141, 148, 161, 247, 268, 269, 270–71, 273–74, 354, 403, 464, 472, 481, 484–85, 486, 487, 516–519, 521, 523, 525, 534, 558n3 (ch 17), 593n11 (ch 54), 596n2 (ch 58), 598n39
Schwarzenberg, Eleonore, 307
Schwarzenberg, Maria Karolina von. See Lobkowitz, Maria Karolina von
Schwarzenberg, Prince Joseph Johann Nepomuk von, 74, 131, 133–34, 265
Scott, Sir Walter, 364, 368
Sebald, Amalie, 326, 335, 500
Seelig (wine merchant), 512
Seibert, Dr. Johann, 533, 599n9
Seidler, Carl August, 577
Seyfried, Ignaz von, 128, 202, 205, 206, 264, 484
Shakespeare, William, 52, 240, 370, 412, 563n4, 574n15

Simrock, Heinrich, 254
Simrock, Nikolaus, 27, 38, 56, 58, 96, 102, 194–95, 198, 217–19, 222, 224, 281, 445–46, 490
Smart, Sir George, 349, 425, 426, 427, 428–429, 489, 497, 592n5 (ch 52)
Smetana, Dr. Karl von, 495
Socrates, 413
Solomon, Maynard, 18, 119, 122–23, 339, 341, 343, 545n1, 547n1 (ch 7), 548n5, 561n18, 576n4
Sonnenfels, Joseph von, 339
Sonnleithner, Joseph von, 191, 204, 217, 225–26, 254, 257–59, 262, 371, 573n11
Sontag, Henriette, 485
Spaun, Josef von, 479
Spohr, Louis, 159, 196, 243, 309, 350, 355, 447, 581n1 (ch 40)
Spontini, Gasparo, 196
Stackelberg, Christoph von, 237–38, 333–35, 338, 401–3, 407, 408
Stackelberg, Josephine von. See Deym, Countess Josephine von
Stackelberg, Laura von, 238
Stackelberg, Minona von, 331–32, 334, 338, 401, 408
Stackelberg, Theophile von, 238, 402
Stadion-Warthausen, Johann Philipp von, 307
Staël, Madame de (Germaine), 75, 307
Starke, Friedrich, 457–59, 554n12
Staudenheim, Dr. Jakob von, 532, 533
Steblin, Rita, 237–38, 332, 334–35, 338, 402, 541, 557n3, 559n4
Steibelt, Daniel, 83, 85, 183–84
Stein, Anna Maria (Nannette). See Streicher, Nannette
Stein, Friedrich, 287
Stein, Johann Andreas, 45, 246
Stein, Matthäus Andreas, 246, 253
Steiner, Sigmund, 358, 363, 387, 416, 455, 459, 472, 476–78, 499, 511
Stendhal (Henri-Marie Beyle), 152, 568n8
Sterkel, Abbé Johann, 55, 56, 62
Stich, Johann Wenzel. See Punto, Giovanni
Stieler, Joseph Karl, 342
Stölzle, Karl, 595n2
Stoupy, Jean-François, 3